Dominican Republic & Haiti

Scott Doggett
Leah Gordon

LONELY PLANET PUBLICATIONS
Melbourne • Oakland • London • Paris

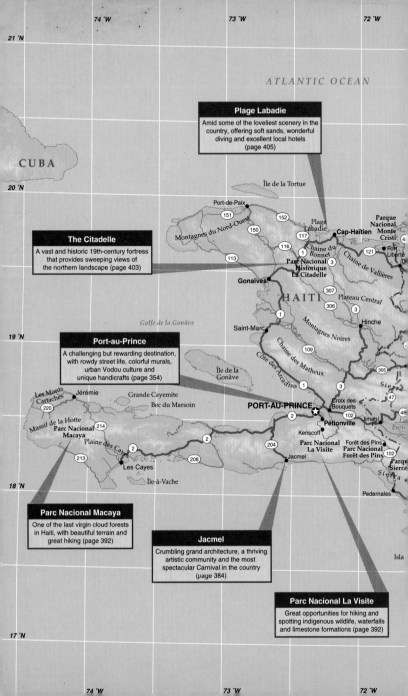

ATLANTIC OCEAN

Plage Labadie

Amid some of the loveliest scenery in the country, offering soft sands, wonderful diving and excellent local hotels (page 405)

CUBA

Île de la Tortue

Port-de-Paix

151

152

Plage Labadie

Cap-Haïtien

Parque Nacional Monte Cristi

The Citadelle

A vast and historic 19th-century fortress that provides sweeping views of the northern landscape (page 403)

Montagnes du Nord-Ouest

150

117

116

Chaîne du Bonnet

121

Fort Liberté

113

Parc Nacional Historique La Citadelle

3

Chaîne de Vallières

Gonaïves

HAITI

307

Plateau Central

306

Hinche

Golfe de la Gonâve

Saint-Marc

1

Montagnes Noires

Port-au-Prince

A challenging but rewarding destination, with rowdy street life, colorful murals, urban Vodou culture and unique handicrafts (page 354)

109

Chaîne des Mateheux

305

Côte des Arcadins

Île de la Gonâve

Les Monts Cartaches

Jérémie

220

Grande Cayemite

Bec du Marsoin

1

3

Sierra

47

48

Croix des Bouquets

PORT-AU-PRINCE ★

102

Jimani

Massif de la Hotte

Parc Nacional Macaya

214

2

Plaine des Cayes

Kenscoff

Pétionville

213

2

208

204

Parc Nacional La Visite

Forêt des Pins

Parc Nacional Forêt des Pins

Parc Sierra

Les Cayes

Jacmel

Île-à-Vache

Parc Nacional Macaya

One of the last virgin cloud forests in Haiti, with beautiful terrain and great hiking (page 392)

Pedernales

Isla

Jacmel

Crumbling grand architecture, a thriving artistic community and the most spectacular Carnival in the country (page 384)

Parc Nacional La Visite

Great opportunities for hiking and spotting indigenous wildlife, waterfalls and limestone formations (page 392)

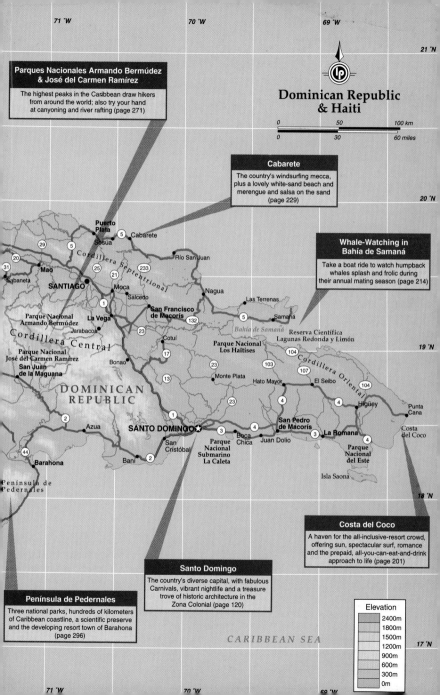

Dominican Republic & Haiti

Parques Nacionales Armando Bermúdez & José del Carmen Ramírez

The highest peaks in the Caribbean draw hikers from around the world; also try your hand at canyoning and river rafting (page 271)

Cabarete

The country's windsurfing mecca, plus a lovely white-sand beach and merengue and salsa on the sand (page 229)

Whale-Watching in Bahía de Samaná

Take a boat ride to watch humpback whales splash and frolic during their annual mating season (page 214)

Costa del Coco

A haven for the all-inclusive-resort crowd, offering sun, spectacular surf, romance and the prepaid, all-you-can-eat-and-drink approach to life (page 201)

Santo Domingo

The country's diverse capital, with fabulous Carnivals, vibrant nightlife and a treasure trove of historic architecture in the Zona Colonial (page 120)

Península de Pedernales

Three national parks, hundreds of kilometers of Caribbean coastline, a scientific preserve and the developing resort town of Barahona (page 296)

0   50   100 km
0   30   60 miles

21 °N

20 °N

19 °N

18 °N

17 °N

71 °W   70 °W   69 °W

Puerto Plata
Sosúa
Cabarete
Río San Juan
SANTIAGO
Mao
Sabaneta
Cordillera Septentrional
Moca
Salcedo
San Francisco de Macorís
Nagua
Las Terrenas
Samaná
La Vega
Jarabacoa
Cotuí
Bahía de Samaná
Reserva Científica Lagunas Redonda y Limón
Parque Nacional Armando Bermúdez
Cordillera Central
Parque Nacional José del Carmen Ramírez
San Juan de la Maguana
Bonao
DOMINICAN REPUBLIC
Parque Nacional Los Haïtises
Monte Plata
Cordillera Oriental
El Seibo
Hato Mayor
Higüey
Punta Cana
SANTO DOMINGO
Azua
San Cristóbal
Baní
Boca Chica
Juan Dolio
San Pedro de Macorís
La Romana
Costa del Coco
Parque Nacional Submarino La Caleta
Parque Nacional del Este
Isla Saona
Barahona
Península de Pedernales

Elevation
2400m
1800m
1500m
1200m
900m
600m
300m
0m

CARIBBEAN SEA

Dominican Republic & Haiti
1st edition – July 1999

Published by
Lonely Planet Publications Pty Ltd A.C.N. 005 607 983
192 Burwood Rd, Hawthorn, Victoria 3122, Australia

Lonely Planet Offices
Australia PO Box 617, Hawthorn, Victoria 3122
USA 150 Linden St, Oakland, CA 94607
UK 10a Spring Place, London NW5 3BH
France 1 rue du Dahomey, 75011 Paris

Photographs
Scott Doggett, Paul Gerace, Leah Gordon, Gianfranco Lanzetti

Some of the images in this guide are available for licensing from
Lonely Planet Images.
email: lpi@lonelyplanet.com.au

Front cover photograph
Painting by Eliesel Mercedes (photo by Paul Gerace)

ISBN 0 86442 647 X

text & maps © Lonely Planet 1999
photos © photographers as indicated 1999

Printed by Colorcraft Ltd, Hong Kong

Contents – Text

GETTING THERE & AWAY 114

GETTING AROUND THE DOMINICAN REPUBLIC 116

SANTO DOMINGO 120

AROUND SANTO DOMINGO 160

SOUTHEASTERN DOMINICAN REPUBLIC 182

NORTHEASTERN DOMINICAN REPUBLIC 210

NORTHWESTERN DOMINICAN REPUBLIC 245

CENTRAL HIGHLANDS 271

SOUTHWESTERN DOMINICAN REPUBLIC 290

HAITI 307

FACTS ABOUT HAITI 309

FACTS FOR THE VISITOR 333

GETTING THERE & AWAY 350

GETTING AROUND HAITI 351

PORT-AU-PRINCE 354

Contents

Contents – Maps

The Authors

Scott Doggett

Scott's interest in Latin America became personal when, in 1983, as a recent graduate of the University of California at Berkeley, he moved to El Salvador to work as a photojournalist. His initial career was followed by postgraduate study at Stanford University; reporting assignments for United Press International in Los Angeles, Pakistan and Afghanistan; and, most recently, seven years as a staff editor for the *Los Angeles Times*. Scott is the author of Lonely Planet's *Panama* guide, coauthor of Lonely Planet's *Mexico* guide and an author and coeditor of *Travelers' Tales: Brazil*. At the time this book went to press, he was finishing work on Lonely Planet's first guide to Las Vegas and preparing to start work on LP's first Yucatán guide. Scott's work has also appeared in the travel sections of America's leading newspapers, and in *Escape* and *Outside* magazines.

If you have just returned from the Dominican Republic and would like to apprise him of an attraction or service that he may be unaware of, Scott would like to hear from you. His email address is sdoggett@aol.com.

Leah Gordon

Leah Gordon is a London-based photojournalist and film-maker. She left the Polytechnic of Central London with a degree in film and photographic arts, and went on to take a postgraduate diploma in photojournalism at the London College of Printing. Her photographs have appeared in many national newspapers and journals, including the *Independent*, *Daily Telegraph*, *Guardian*, *London Times Magazine*, *Vogue* and the *Face*.

She made her first trip to Haiti in 1991, and has returned over a dozen times to cover coups and Carnivals. She has photographed projects in Haiti for Christian Aid, Amnesty International and Save the Children Fund. She co-curated 'Haiti: Photos, Paintings and Ironworks' at the October Gallery, London, and has exhibited her photographs of Haiti at the National Portrait Gallery, London. Leah also codirected and produced *A Pig's Tale*, a documentary set in Haiti, for Channel 4 TV UK.

FROM THE AUTHORS

Scott Doggett This book is dedicated to my wife, Annette, an incredible catch, and to my parents, who have always been there for me.

Quite a number of people at Lonely Planet's US office assisted me with this labor of love. To you all, a heartfelt thank you. Special thanks to Maia Hansen, chief editor of this book, and to editors Jeff Campbell and Ben Greensfelder; if this book has any polish on it, they deserve all the credit. My hat also goes off to senior editor Brigitte Barta, who oversaw production of the book, and Laura Harger and Susan Charles, who stepped in at layout, as well as to Eric Kettunen, who does a superlative job of managing Lonely Planet's editorial and business operations for the Americas. I am also extremely grateful to production manager Scott Summers; cartographers Patrick Huerta, Andy Rebold, Monica Lepe and Mary Hagemann; illustrator Hayden Foell; and designers Henia Miedzinski and Margaret Livingston – the talented people who created, selected and/or shaped everything in this book except the text. Thanks also to Joslyn Leve and Erica Pelino, who answered the phones at LP US, and who had every right to tell me to stop calling so much, but instead were friendly every time – thank you, thank you and thank you. Of course, none of us would be doing what we're doing if our books weren't reaching our esteemed readers; I raise my margarita glass in salute to everyone in publicity, marketing and sales.

Leah Gordon I would like to thank Charles Arthur, who gave me much help, support and feedback during the writing of the Haiti section of this book. Thanks also to Barbara and Octavio Zuniga, who lost a TV lounge each time I stayed in Haiti; Milfort Bruno, without whom I would never have survived my first trip; Richard Fleming, twitcher extraordinaire, for supplying input to the bird-watching section; Linette Frewins, to whom I say only this – *Quand Même*; Ian Murray, Rachel Boyes and little Josh, for supplying my northern writing retreat; Marg Duston, for her vine-clad words; Jacques Bartoli, for always having a spare apartment in Pacot; Stephanie Armand and Alex LaFond, at the Haitian Secretary of State for Tourism; Chantal Regnault and Jergen Leth, for wonderful company on the verandah of the Peabody House, and tireless research of the best restaurants in Pétionville; Laurie Richardson, for her friendship, help and translation; Gwo Zagou and his community, for all the kombit songs; Carlos Jara, for his knowledge of Haitian art; Edgar Jean Louis and the Société Achadé, for the many Vodou ceremonies; Aboudja, the president of Soukri; Kathy Klarreich and Jean Raymond, for their wonderful club and music; Jean Yves Urfié, for his knowledge of Haitian literature; Mick and Claire, for lending me the all-important CD player; Anne Parisio, for her diving expertise; Michelle Karshan, Bobby Duval and Jane Regan; John Engle, Paul Paretsky, Bob Corbett and Corbettland; and Walter Bussenius, Brian D Oates, Greg Chamberlaine and Linda Polman. Thanks also to the Vodou Collective – Kathy Grey, Michel Degraff, Patrick Bellegard-Smith, Leslie Desmangles, Guy Antoine, Emmanuel Evedrine and Jean Saint-Vil; Cinders Forshaw, Kay Hart and Annabel Edwards, for their friendship; and Ron and Dorothy Gordon, for their support.

This Book

Scott Doggett was the coordinating author for this 1st edition of *Dominican Republic & Haiti*. Scott researched and wrote the introductory chapters and the Dominican Republic chapters, and Leah Gordon researched and wrote the chapters on Haiti.

FROM THE PUBLISHER

This 1st edition of *Dominican Republic & Haiti* is a product of Lonely Planet's US office. Many people contributed their time, energy and patience to this book. The book was edited by Maia Hansen with much help from Jeff Campbell. Brigitte Barta, Ben Greensfelder, Sue Peters, Andrew Nystrom and Julie Connery also assisted with editing. Patrick Huerta, Andy Rebold and Monica Lepe drew and corrected the maps with guidance from Alex Guilbert, and Henia Miedzinski designed the book with guidance from Margaret Livingston and Scott Summers. Paige Penland, Robert Reid, Andrew Nystrom and Julie Connery proofread the chapters, Joslyn Leve assisted with map proofing and Laura Harger indexed the chapters. Sandra Greensfelder helped out with some last-minute changes and Susan Charles helped with layout review. Hayden Foell, Lara Sox-Harrison, Jim Swanson, John Fadeff and Mark Butler drew the illustrations. Hayden drew the chapter ends and also drew the border for the boxed text and country title pages, which was created from an ancient Taíno Indian design. Rini Keagy created the cover.

Many thanks go to Brigitte Barta for her guidance and supervision, and later to Laura Harger for so thoroughly and competently taking over in her absence.

Foreword

ABOUT LONELY PLANET GUIDEBOOKS

The story begins with a classic travel adventure: Tony and Maureen Wheeler's 1972 journey across Europe and Asia to Australia. Useful information about the overland trail did not exist at that time, so Tony and Maureen published the first Lonely Planet guidebook to meet a growing need.

From a kitchen table, then from a tiny office in Melbourne (Australia), Lonely Planet has become the largest independent travel publisher in the world, an international company with offices in Melbourne, Oakland (USA), London (UK) and Paris (France).

Today Lonely Planet guidebooks cover the globe. There is an ever-growing list of books, and there's information in a variety of forms and media. Some things haven't changed. The main aim is still to help make it possible for adventurous travelers to get out there – to explore and better understand the world.

At Lonely Planet we believe travelers can make a positive contribution to the countries they visit – if they respect their host communities and spend their money wisely. Since 1986 a percentage of the income from each book has been donated to aid projects and human-rights campaigns.

Updates Lonely Planet thoroughly updates each guidebook as often as possible. This usually means there are around two years between editions, although for more unusual or more stable destinations the gap can be longer. Check the imprint page (following the color map at the beginning of the book) for publication dates.

Between editions, up-to-date information is available in two free newsletters – the paper *Planet Talk* and email *Comet* (to subscribe, contact any Lonely Planet office) – and on our website at www.lonelyplanet.com. The *Upgrades* section of the website covers a number of important and volatile destinations and is regularly updated by Lonely Planet authors. *Scoop* covers news and current affairs relevant to travelers. And, lastly, the *Thorn Tree* bulletin board and *Postcards* section of the site carry unverified, but fascinating, reports from travelers.

Correspondence The process of creating new editions begins with the letters, postcards and emails received from travelers. This correspondence often includes suggestions, criticisms and comments about the current editions. Interesting excerpts are immediately passed on via newsletters and the website, and everything goes to our authors to be verified when they're researching on the road. We're keen to get more feedback from organizations or individuals who represent communities visited by travelers.

Lonely Planet gathers information for everyone who's curious about the planet – and especially for those who explore it firsthand. Through guidebooks, phrasebooks, activity guides, maps, literature, newsletters, image library, TV series and website, we act as an information exchange for a worldwide community of travelers.

Research Authors aim to gather sufficient practical information to enable travelers to make informed choices and to make the mechanics of a journey run smoothly. They also research historical and cultural background to help enrich the travel experience and allow travelers to understand and respond appropriately to cultural and environmental issues.

Authors don't stay in every hotel because that would mean spending a couple of months in each medium-size city and, no, they don't eat at every restaurant because that would mean stretching belts beyond capacity. They do visit hotels and restaurants to check standards and prices, but feedback based on readers' direct experiences can be very helpful.

Many of our authors work undercover; others aren't so secretive. None of them accept freebies in exchange for positive write-ups. And none of our guidebooks contain any advertising.

Production Authors submit their raw manuscripts and maps to offices in Australia, the USA, the UK or France. Editors and cartographers – all experienced travelers themselves – then begin the process of assembling the pieces. When the book finally hits the shops, some things are already out of date, we start getting feedback from readers and the process begins again....

WARNING & REQUEST

Things change – prices go up, schedules change, good places go bad and bad places go bankrupt – nothing stays the same. So, if you find things better or worse, recently opened or long since closed, please tell us and help make the next edition even more accurate and useful. We genuinely value all the feedback we receive. Julie Young coordinates a well-traveled team that reads and acknowledges every letter, postcard and email and ensures that every morsel of information finds its way to the appropriate authors, editors and cartographers for verification.

Everyone who writes to us will find their name in the next edition of the appropriate guidebook. They will also receive the latest issue of *Planet Talk*, our quarterly printed newsletter, or *Comet*, our monthly email newsletter. Subscriptions to both newsletters are free. The very best contributions will be rewarded with a free guidebook.

Excerpts from your correspondence may appear in new editions of Lonely Planet guidebooks, the Lonely Planet website, *Planet Talk* or *Comet*, so please let us know if you *don't* want your letter published or your name acknowledged.

Send all correspondence to the Lonely Planet office closest to you:

Australia: PO Box 617, Hawthorn, Victoria 3122
USA: 150 Linden St, Oakland, CA 94607
UK: 10A Spring Place, London NW5 3BH
France: 1 rue du Dahomey, 75011 Paris

Or email us at: talk2us@lonelyplanet.com.au

For news, views and updates, see our website: www.lonelyplanet.com

HOW TO USE A LONELY PLANET GUIDEBOOK

The best way to use a Lonely Planet guidebook is any way you choose. At Lonely Planet, we believe the most memorable travel experiences are often those that are unexpected, and the finest discoveries are those you make yourself. Guidebooks are not intended to be used as if they provided a detailed set of infallible instructions!

Contents All Lonely Planet guidebooks follow the same format. The Facts about the Country chapters or sections give background information ranging from history to weather. Facts for the Visitor gives practical information on issues like visas and health. Getting There & Away gives a brief starting point for researching travel to and from the destination. Getting Around gives an overview of the transport options available when you arrive.

The peculiar demands of each destination determine how subsequent chapters are broken up, but some things remain constant. We always start with background, then proceed to sights, places to stay, places to eat, entertainment, getting there and away, and getting around information – in that order.

Heading Hierarchy Lonely Planet headings are used in a strict hierarchical structure that can be visualized as a set of Russian dolls. Each heading (and its following text) is encompassed by any preceding heading that is higher on the hierarchical ladder.

Entry Points We do not assume guidebooks will be read from beginning to end, but that people will dip into them. The traditional entry points are the list of contents and the index. In addition, however, some books have a complete list of maps and an index map illustrating map coverage.

There may also be a color map that shows highlights. These highlights are dealt with in greater detail later in the book, along with planning questions and suggested itineraries. Each chapter covering a geographical region usually begins with a locator map and another list of highlights. Once you find something of interest in a list of highlights, turn to the index.

Maps Maps play a crucial role in Lonely Planet guidebooks and include a huge amount of information. A legend is printed on the back page. We seek to have complete consistency between maps and text, and to have every important place in the text captured on a map. Map key numbers usually start in the top left corner.

Although inclusion in a guidebook usually implies a recommendation, we cannot list every good place. Exclusion does not necessarily imply criticism. In fact, there are a number of reasons why we might exclude a place – sometimes it is simply inappropriate to encourage an influx of travelers.

Introduction

With merengue-filled nights and sugary beaches, Hispaniola has the intoxicating feel of other Caribbean islands like Jamaica, Tortola and Martinique, but in many intriguing ways it is incomparable. For starters, it is home to two countries, with two very different peoples. The Haitians speak mostly Creole, seek salvation through Vodou, and have yet to find a way to rid themselves of corrupt and compassionless leaders whose greed has made Haiti the poorest country in the West. The Dominicans speak Spanish, have shed their African religions for Christianity, and have recently managed to free themselves from decades of dictatorial rule.

Hispaniola boasts Santo Domingo, the first city built by Europeans in the New World, replete with the first paved road, the first hospital and the first university in the Western Hemisphere. The island's residents range from millions of illiterate farmers who scrape just enough nutrients out of their dirt plots to get by, to world-famous musicians, artists and athletes. Its landscape consists of many hundreds of kilometers of white-sand beaches, fertile valleys that grow the tobacco used in the world's finest cigars and tumbling rivers that careen from the tallest mountains in the Caribbean.

In the Dominican Republic, maintaining close family ties and cultivating friendships are top priorities, and music is a part of everyday life. Merengue, the quintessential Dominican beat, is more than just music; it is a tool to foster those relationships. That is why you hear it everywhere – at the beach, on the bus and in the street. Dominicans need little excuse for a party, and Santo Domingo, Puerto Plata and several other Dominican towns all host merengue festivals. Each year, Santo Domingo is also the site of not one but two Carnivals that feature elaborate floats, lots of merengue and dancing in the streets.

But every culture has its shadow side, and the DR, as Dominicans commonly call their homeland, is no exception. Beneath the Carnival masks are some sinister faces. The police can be as venal and corrupt, the rich as cynical and selfish, as any on the planet. If

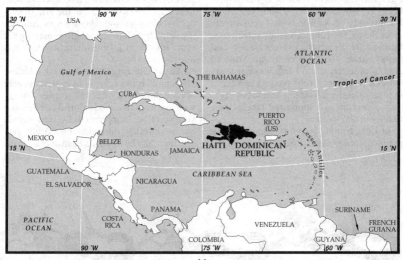

you commit a crime and know the right people, you walk; if you don't, you could face years in jail.

The country's apparent racial fluidity, one eventually realizes, is only skin deep. Deep prejudices exist despite the racial mixing that has taken place on the island over the years with the arrival of Spanish, African, French, German, Puerto Rican, Cuban, Jewish, Japanese, Arab and other immigrants. The upper class tends to be white, the middle class mulatto, and the poor are virtually all black. The lighter a person's skin color, the more desirable that person is considered as a mate and the more intelligence that person is assumed to have. As strange as it might seem, those attitudes are shared by Hispaniolans of all color. It explains why the fairer-skinned Dominicans generally look down upon Haitians – and why so many Dominicans apply color-lightening cosmetics, a custom followed even by former dictator Rafael Leonidas Trujillo.

For most Haitians, however, cosmetic concerns are unimportant in the face of the relentless hardship. Not long ago in Haiti, it was a religious taboo to cut down a cottonwood tree. This was where a father would bury the umbilical cord of a new child, believing it held the baby's soul. Nowadays, it's not only cottonwoods that consistently meet the ax; the country's many subsistence farmers are also cutting down mango and papaya trees to make charcoal. Most of Haiti's precious topsoil has washed away without these trees' root systems to keep it in place, and the mountains and valleys that only a century ago supported jungles now barely sustain weeds.

In 1996, Haitian peasants began building massive stone walls in ravines to prevent the loss of topsoil due to heavy rain. They had completed more than a thousand walls at the time Hurricane Georges struck in September 1998. The hurricane destroyed most of the country's crops and caused an estimated US$1.2 billion in damage. Sadly, most of the handmade walls were reduced to debris along with many other structures.

At times, religion is the only thing that sustains the people of Haiti. Like most Caribbean residents, the majority of Haitians consider themselves Catholics but they have, in fact, combined elements of Roman Catholicism and tribal religions of western Africa to create another religion, Vodou. Vodou rituals are unforgettable to behold, and while not unique to Haiti, they are surely best observed there due to the rich and colorful traditions of the people.

If you delve into the island's culture, explore its personalities as well as its natural attractions, you'll find in Haiti a people who maintain an admirable sense of humor and hope in the face of upheaval and hardship. Their love of life abounds in their perspectives, their paintings and their music. Before you know it, you'll discover that Haiti has captured your spirit, despite its pervasive poverty. In the DR, you'll find a people who have managed to overcome the grip of successive dictators and who are now embracing democracy like never before, making yet more history in a land where so much has already been made.

As you'll discover in the pages that follow, Hispaniola is more than just a pretty beach. Although if that's what you're after – along with glorious water and colorful coral reefs – you won't be disappointed. But few islands are as culturally intriguing, historically rich and naturally beautiful as Hispaniola.

Facts about Hispaniola

HISTORY
Early Peoples

Several millennia prior to the arrival of Christopher Columbus in 1492, several groups of people reached Hispaniola from South America in three distinct migratory waves. Archaeological evidence indicates that all three groups migrated from eastern Venezuela or thereabouts, although at least one historian, citing cultural similarities between the migrants and Peru's mountain people, contends that the last group may have begun its journey in the Peruvian Andes.

The earliest-known inhabitants of Hispaniola reached the island about 2600 BC, using huge dugout canoes that allowed them to island hop, over a period of many years, from the southern tip of the Lesser Antilles north and west into the Greater Antilles. However, most of the islands are within sight of each other and currents favor travel from south to north – two factors that greatly facilitated the Indians' movement from island to island. What prompted these people to leave the lush forests of South America for unknown islands remains a mystery.

The first migrants were nomadic people who moved about Hispaniola, living in caves or beneath overhangs on the banks of rivers. They confined their fishing to rivers and collected the remainder of their food. They didn't farm or hunt, and they weren't pottery makers. Like the early Neolithic societies of ancient Europe, these people used stone tools and they were culturally unsophisticated. Their ancestors have yet to be determined, although most archaeologists suspect these migrants are descendants of Indians who lived in Amazonia around 3500 BC.

The second group of migrants, often referred to as Saladoids, are related to the ancient Arawaks who mostly lived in the Guianas and on Trinidad. But historians disagree over whether the Saladoids, who reached Hispaniola about 250 BC, were a splinter group of Arawakan-talking Indians of the Guianas and Trinidad or instead were neighbors with their own language and customs who descended from Arawak stock many generations earlier. These migrants were named Saladoids by scientists who believe that the group originated from Saladero, Venezuela.

Unlike their predecessors, the Saladoids were excellent ceramists. And by tracing Saladoid pottery, archaeologists have been able to determine that these people spread throughout most of the Greater Antilles (which include Hispaniola, Cuba, Jamaica and Puerto Rico) and the Lesser Antilles (which include the Virgin, Leeward and Windward Island chains), displacing or absorbing the first group of migrants.

The third migratory wave began just prior to the Christian era and lasted approximately one millennium. Historians disagree on exactly where these people came from. Some contend that these migrants spread from the Peruvian Andes to the Caribbean coast and from there gradually spread through the Windwards, then the Leewards and eventually reached Puerto Rico, Hispaniola and Cuba.

Others contend that the third migrant group originally lived along the banks of the Orinoco River in the Venezuelan section of Amazonia. At an undetermined time, for an unknown reason, these Indians are thought to have canoed down the Orinoco to the Atlantic Ocean, where over a period of many years they repeatedly returned to the northbound equatorial current and rode it from one island to another all the way to Hispaniola and Cuba.

In time this third group of arrivals spread out across most of the West Indies and absorbed or eliminated most members of the two earlier migratory groups. By 700 AD these migrants had a distinct culture and occupied the Bahamas and all of the Greater Antilles except for western Cuba, where another ethnic group, the Guanahatabeys, resided. It was this relatively sophisticated third group – who called themselves Taínos, or 'friendly people' in their tongue – that occupied Hispaniola when an Italian navigator known as Cristoforo Colombo in Italian and Cristóbal Colón in Spanish set foot on the jungle-draped island.

The Taínos

The estimated 400,000 Taínos on Hispaniola at the time of Columbus' arrival lived in permanent villages, each of which was governed by a chief. The villages typically contained between 1000 and 2000 people, who resided in wood-and-thatch houses and slept in hammocks. The houses were irregularly arranged around a main plaza. Several related families often lived in a single house, none of which was partitioned for privacy.

The villages were loosely organized into district chiefdoms, each ruled by one of the village chiefs in the district. The district chiefdoms were, in turn, grouped into regional chiefdoms, each headed by the most prominent district chief. The regional chiefs represented the pinnacle of Taíno nobility, which the Taínos referred to as the *nitaíno* class; a second class, composed of commoners and called the *naboria*, also existed. There was no third class in Taíno society; the Taínos' sense of justice did not permit slavery.

The men wore only loincloths, if anything at all. Unmarried women wore headbands, while married women wore short skirts. Taíno women also wore necklaces and colorful belts to make themselves more attractive. They wore little if anything else. Both Taíno men and women painted themselves before ceremonies. Red was a favorite color, and it is widely held that it was the Taínos' use of red paint that gave rise to the European misconception that American Indians have red skins.

The Taínos were environmentalists long before the word entered anyone's vocabulary. Instead of simply slashing and burning the forest to make a clearing for crops and then moving on once the soil became depleted of nutrients – as is the prevalent practice in the tropics today – the Taínos heaped mounds of

Woodpeckers & Women

Taíno mythology is rich – and often somewhat bizarre. The story of woman's creation is a case in point.

According to Taíno elders, in the beginning the human race lived in two caves that couldn't be left on sunny days lest the people be turned into stone by the sun's rays. Angered by the sun, an Indian named Guaguyona decided to leave the caves, and he convinced all of the women to join him. As days passed the remainder of the men grew upset that they had no women. They went out to find some on rainy days, but to no avail.

Then one day the men came upon several persons who were neither male nor female. The men tried to catch them but the genderless creatures slipped through their grasps like eels. A chief then sent for some people whose hands had turned rough from a disease, and with their roughened hands the diseased people were able to catch the slippery, sexless creatures.

The men held the genderless persons against the ground, bound their hands and feet, and covered their bodies with woodpeckers. The birds pecked at the place where the female sex organs usually are. And this, according to Taíno mythology, is how men came to enjoy the company of women.

Conveniently, the sun's rays stopped turning people into stones from that day forward, and people were able to go about freely during daylight hours.

earth in more permanent fields to cultivate root crops such as cassava and sweet potato in the soft alluvial soil. The mounded fields, called *conuco*, retarded erosion and facilitated weeding and harvesting.

The Taínos were skilled at fishing as well, and they reduced their waste through conservation measures. Spanish chroniclers wrote that the Taínos caught fish using nets, spears, traps, hooks attached to lines, even a mild poison that slowed the reflexes of river fish and made them easy to grab. To prevent waste, the Taínos kept fish and sea turtles in pens until needed. They also decoyed wild parrots with tame ones, and augmented their diets with manatees and iguanas.

The Taínos believed in two supreme deities: Yúcahu, the lord of the cassava and the sea, and his mother, Atabey, goddess of fresh water and human fertility. They also believed in a plethora of lesser spirits, such as those of their ancestors as well as spirits who lived in trees and other features of the landscape.

Yúcahu, Atabey and the lesser spirits were called *zemis*. The Taínos paid tribute to many of them by idolizing natural objects believed to be inhabited by powerful spirits. Each Taíno possessed many such idols, which typically consisted of a rock, a shell or a piece of wood carved in a human likeness. The idols were prized for the power they were believed to confer to their owners. People viewed their idols as being the best, and they passed them on through inheritance and trade.

The number of children in each nuclear family typically varied from three to five. Boys were instructed in farming, fishing and hunting, girls in household chores and the making of ceramic and woven goods.

In their free time, men traded spare homemade goods at fairs held in the main plaza. Because the Taínos had no currency, the actual value of items traded wasn't always equal. But, Spanish chroniclers noted, the Taínos rarely quarreled. Their sense of tribal unity generally overcame personal differences. They avoided fights within the clan and with other clans and tribes. To prevent bloodshed, the Taínos were careful not to hunt or fish in territories belonging to the Guanahatabeys on Cuba and the cannibalistic Caribs in the Windward Islands.

Had the Taínos survived their encounter with the Spaniards, it's likely they would have contributed much to the world. As it was, slave traders carried the Taínos' principal crop, cassava, as well as the Taínos' techniques for cultivating and processing the nutritious plant, to sub-Saharan Africa, where it was widely adopted. Cassava eventually reached India and Southeast Asia, where it has become a staple food in areas unsuitable for rice cultivation.

The Taínos also introduced Europe to the sweet potato, bean, squash and peanut, and to fruits such as the guava, mamey and pineapple. The Taínos on Cuba and Hispaniola also introduced the rest of the world to tobacco, which they smoked as cigars (indeed, the Taíno word for tobacco was *tabaco*). Today, some of the world's finest cigars continue to originate from land once worked by these extinct people.

Although the Spaniards would have encountered the canoe (*canoa*) and the hammock (*hamaca*) soon enough – native peoples in soon-to-be-conquered Panama were using them as well – they first saw these objects on Hispaniola and added them to their culture. Among other English words that originated with the Taínos are 'barbecue,' 'hurricane' and 'savanna.'

The Taínos are known for something else as well: Before Spanish abuses and diseases wiped them out, the Indians are thought to have given the invaders syphilis. Taíno myths describe the symptoms of the deadly venereal disease in exact detail, and lesions found on Taíno skeletons could have been syphilis induced. What's more, an epidemic of the disease broke out in the Mediterranean Basin immediately after Columbus returned from his first voyage.

Whether the Taínos introduced syphilis to the Old World or only contributed a more virulent form of the disease is one of the many questions about them that will probably never be answered.

Columbus Spies 'Japan'

Had the Taínos been warlike, like the Caribs of the Windward Islands, their culture might have survived the Spanish Conquest. But the Taínos were a peaceful lot, and the Spaniards who arrived on Hispaniola were well armed, mean and greedy. The Spaniards needed people to work the gold mines they found on the island, and it wasn't going to be them. They enslaved the Taínos and gradually killed them off with Old World diseases and abysmal treatment. Fewer than a thousand Taínos were still alive 30 years after the arrival of the Spaniards.

But it's hard to believe that anyone aboard the *Pinta*, the *Niña* or the *Santa María* could have envisioned the holocaust their voyage would spark in a world they didn't even know existed when they left Spain on August 3, 1492, in search of Asia. Yes, Asia. Due to miscalculations of the earth's circumference and of the size of Asia and Europe, the flotilla's leader – the Great Explorer himself – expected to reach eastern Asia by sailing 3860km to the west. Indeed, when Columbus reached the New World, he mistook Cuba for Japan.

Columbus' first of four expeditions set sail from Palos, Spain, carrying about 90 men. Other mariners were struggling to round the tip of Africa so they could sail east to the Indies, that is, to India with its spices and to Japan, where rumors had it that there were scores of pagodas roofed with the purest gold. But the 90-odd souls aboard the *Pinta*, *Niña* and *Santa María* were bent on getting there the short way – by sailing west to meet the East.

Three days out, the mast of the *Pinta* was damaged by strong winds, forcing the flotilla to make a brief stop at the Canary Islands, just off the coast of Morocco. There, the ships took on provisions and made final repairs. On September 6 the three vessels again unfurled their sails and set a course due west – straight for Japan, or so Columbus figured.

Land was sighted just before dawn on October 12, and later that day the expedition dropped anchor near the small Bahamian island of Guanahaní under the gaze of many bedazzled Indians who paddled out to greet the strange winged ships. Certain he had reached some part of Japan, Columbus gave thanks to God for guiding him to the Indies. In God's honor he named the island San Salvador (Holy Savior) and called the welcoming people *los Indios*.

Columbus then made plans to enslave them and rob them of their valuables. But finding no gold or spices on the island, the little fleet moved on, leaving the 'Indians' of San Salvador alone for the time being.

In the following weeks the ships made additional landings, including one at Cuba. Surely *this* island was part of the Grand Khan's domain, Columbus thought, but again he found no treasure there, only native people breathing smoke through tight rolls of leaves.

So the Spaniards and their Italian navigator moved on, and eventually a mountainous landscape appeared before them, reminding Columbus of the mountains of Spain. He named the island La Isla Española, 'the Spanish Island,' later corrupted to Hispaniola, which the people of the Dominican Republic and Haiti share today. As night was falling, Columbus ordered his ships to drop anchor. They'd investigate the large island the following day. Or so they thought.

It was December 23, and those aboard the creaking wooden ships likely would have been content to spend the night anchored off the coast of Haiti had the chief of a nearby village not come aboard and, using mostly hand signals, told the Spaniards of gold in a place called Cibao, located on the island farther east. So anxious was Columbus to get his hands on gold that he immediately set sail – in darkness, in uncharted water with lots of protruding rocks and many coral reefs. The next day passed uneventfully with contrary winds permitting little movement, but that night – on Christmas Eve – disaster struck: the *Santa María* crashed into a coral reef and was doomed.

The next day scores of Taínos, seeing the wooden ship breaking up on the reef, paddled out to help the conquistadors. Their chief, a man named Guacanagarí, told his braves to salvage everything that could be useful to the white men. Among the salvaged goods were the frames and planking of the *Santa María*, with which Columbus ordered a fort to be built. He named the fort La Villa de Navidad – the Village of the Nativity – because, Columbus reckoned, the loss of the ship and the founding of the settlement must be God's will. It *was* Christmas Day, after all. The fort was erected near the present site of Cap-Haïtien, Haiti.

The Conquest

With his two good ships, the *Pinta* and the *Niña*, Columbus returned to the Old World with excellent news: He had found a shortcut to the West Indies, and (based on the report of the village chief who spoke of the Cibao Valley) there was much gold to be had there. Columbus had even left behind 39 men and lots of provisions at a fort they'd built, so that they could amass fortunes during his absence. The admiral fully expected to find La Navidad stocked high with gold upon his return.

In Spain, Columbus was embraced as a hero. Everywhere he went people came out to greet him. The ambitious son of an ordinary Italian couple suddenly had fine clothes, a retinue of servants and the attention of a nation. He was even received as a dignitary by King Ferdinand and Queen Isabella, who bestowed upon him impressive titles, including 'admiral of the ocean sea' and 'Viceroy and Governor of the Indies.' Most important, the royal couple gave him 17 ships with which to return to the West Indies and bring back treasure.

The scene Columbus encountered upon his return to La Navidad in November 1493 was hardly what he expected: the fort had been burned to the ground, and scattered about were the bodies of the 39 men he'd left behind. The men had taken to kidnapping and raping Taíno women, and a Taíno chief ordered the white men hunted down and killed. Undeterred, Columbus established another settlement approximately 110km east of the first and named it La Isabela, in honor of the queen of Spain. He also sent prospectors inland to search for gold.

La Isabela didn't fare well. The town was repeatedly struck by epidemics, a fire leveled two-thirds of its buildings, and a hurricane destroyed several ships at anchor – all within the first 18 months. Before leaving for Spain in March 1496, the admiral named his brother Bartholomew governor of the island and ordered the capital of the New World moved in his absence. The construction of Santo Domingo, which still stands as one of the supreme monuments of Spain's colonial adventure, was begun that year.

But if things weren't going as smoothly as expected for the Europeans, life had taken a terrible turn for the Taínos. Since the start of 1494, the Spanish lust for gold had made life unbearable for the Indians. The 17 ships that comprised Columbus' second flotilla had brought 1200 men, mostly soldiers whose mission was to haul in all of the island's gold for the Crown as well as for themselves. And they enslaved the Taínos to assist them in their endeavor.

Columbus: Man of Many Faces

What did Christopher Columbus look like? No one really knows. If a portrait of the admiral was painted during his lifetime, it doesn't appear to have survived. Instead, the images of the great Italian explorer that appear in schoolbooks around the world are merely artists' renditions of the man, all of which may be far from accurate. A couple of renditions appear here.

Over the next 25 years the Taínos were forced to work in mines, where hunger and disease killed most of them. Many Taínos became so desperate that they committed suicide, usually by drinking poison. Spanish chronicles note that Taíno women killed their own newborns to keep them out of slavery. A 1508 census revealed that only 60,000 of the island's original Taíno population of 400,000 remained. By early 1519, the native population had fallen to less than 3000. By the end of that year, the gold mines were spent and the last of the 'friendly people,' about 500 of them, joined a rebel chief named Enriquillo and fled into the mountains.

The depletion of the gold mines and the virtual extinction of the Taíno population led to a socioeconomic transformation on the island. Gold mining was replaced by cattle raising and sugar production. Hides and sugar were exported to Spain in return for merchandise and manufactured goods. Due to the absence of Taínos, who'd done the manual labor the Spaniards so detested, the owners of cattle ranches and sugarcane plantations turned to African slaves. The first several hundred arrived in 1520; by 1568 the number of black slaves had risen to about 20,000.

The French

During most of the 16th century Spain was at war with France and England, and both countries offered support to pirates who hindered Spanish trade in the West Indies. As a result, French and English pirates seized Spanish ships operating in the Caribbean and the Atlantic and even raided Hispaniola on occasion, generally setting fire to plantations and terrorizing the island's residents. Out of fear of such attacks, colonial authorities ordered that a wall be built around the capital city of Santo Domingo.

Also because of the pirate attacks, fewer ships attempted to reach Hispaniola from Spain. As a result – and to the great dismay of the Spanish king – many of the island's cattlemen and plantation owners began selling their hides and sugar to French, English, Portuguese and Dutch smugglers

who had settled in the West Indies. By the end of the century this trade, illegal as far as the Spanish Crown was concerned, actually drove the economies of northern and western Hispaniola.

At the start of the 17th century, the Spanish king was so fed up with the trade between the colonists and Spain's enemies that he ordered the abandonment of the smuggling centers of Puerto Plata, Monte Cristi and Bayajá in the north and La Yaguana in the west. The residents of these towns resisted the depopulation of the areas, and as a result much bloodshed followed.

An unforeseen effect of the depopulations was that they allowed Spain's enemies, particularly French and English adventurers, to move into northern and western Hispaniola. Their encroachment encouraged other settlers – and even other governments – to attempt to claim a piece of the second-largest island in the West Indies. In fact, by 1655 England wanted control of all of Hispaniola, and it sent 34 warships and 13,000 men to capture the island. On Sunday, April 25, the English attacked Santo Domingo but were repelled by the city's defenders.

Despite their victory over the English invaders, the Spaniards continued to have trouble with English and French settlers on Hispaniola. The French were increasingly expanding into Spanish territories in the Caribbean, and by 1677 there were 11 French villages on Hispaniola totaling more than 4000 settlers, most of whom were tobacco growers. During that same year the French attacked and took control of Santiago, 140km northwest of Santo Domingo, near the center of the present-day Dominican Republic.

In addition to their trouble with the French, the Spanish colony bore the brunt of a hurricane that ripped through the island in 1668, wiping out buildings, forests and crops. The economy, already sputtering due to the lack of trade with Spain on account of pirates, went into a nosedive. When a ship arrived in Santo Domingo in early 1669 carrying 400 slaves – the first such shipment to reach the island in years – money was so scarce the colonists could afford to buy only

140 of the slaves. Adding to the colonists' woes, later that year a smallpox epidemic killed about 1500 island inhabitants.

The war between France and Spain ended in 1679, and within a year Paris made the first of its many requests that a boundary be established recognizing Saint-Domingue – the French colony that now existed on the western half of the island ('Santo Domingo' then referred to both the capital city and the Spanish colony in general). Specifically, Paris wanted a border drawn at San Cristóbol, only 28km to the west of the city of Santo Domingo, with the western half of the island

ceded to France. The Spanish denied every request, but the French colony continued to grow anyway. By 1716 it contained 30,000 free residents and 100,000 slaves, compared to only 18,400 total inhabitants in the Spanish colony.

To offset this disparity and to solve the problem of poverty on the Canary Islands, also in Spain's possession, the king ordered that Canarios be shipped to Hispaniola. Despite the effort to boost the number of its colonists on Hispaniola, Spain felt compelled to establish a border in 1731. That border, conveniently established along the

The Slave Trade

The story of the slaves brought to Hispaniola is one of great cruelty and heartache, as most of us today are well aware. It involved a horrendous trip across the Atlantic during which approximately a fifth of the slaves died, mostly from malnutrition and disease. In the end, around half a million Africans were brought to the island in chains.

By the time the Portuguese reached the West African coast in 1450, an organized intercontinental slave trade – which had transported millions of Africans north and east to slaveholding Islamic states – had already been established, beginning in the seventh century. A northern route carried as many as 10 million slaves across the Sahara to North Africa and to Egypt. An eastern network took another 5 million slaves north to Egypt and the Middle East, or across the Red Sea to Saudi Arabia.

After the Europeans arrived, Africans continued to control the supply of slaves, adding a transatlantic trade route to their established network. Because they had no immunity to malaria or yellow fever, the Europeans did not try to set up their own networks but instead established forts along the coast and purchased slaves from African dealers.

Due to demand from North Africa, the Middle East, Saudi Arabia and finally the New World, the slave business from the 16th century through the 18th century was a seller's market, and the Europeans usually agreed to whatever the African sellers offered.

European traders named slaves after the port where they had been purchased, since the Europeans generally didn't know where their bondmen had been captured. Today, the precise places of origin of Caribbean blacks are unknown.

The notorious 'middle passage' between Africa and the New World was hell on earth. Slave ships were surprisingly small, and into their cargo holds the captains would pack 300 terrified men, women and children. The men were shackled together in pairs at the wrist and leg and provided half the space given a convict. The far smaller number of women and children had it only slightly better.

Outbreaks of measles, smallpox and other communicable diseases ravaged the slaves and crews aboard these insidious ships. But by far the biggest killers during the middle passage were scurvy (food on the ships consisted mainly of dried beans, corn and palm oil) and amebic dysentery. It's been estimated that in order to bring 500,000 slaves to Hispaniola more than 100,000 slaves died – mostly victims of these two diseases who never finished the three- to six-month journey from West Africa to the New World.

lines of two rivers, was amended and finalized in 1777 following 13 years of negotiations with the French.

Haiti's Independence

Dissension arose in Saint-Domingue about the same time the line was drawn between the two colonies.

Mulattos, the offspring of white masters and female slaves in the French colony, were free people who could acquire full citizenship. Toward the end of the 18th century, the mulatto class owned one-third of the colony's property but they were treated as second-class citizens by the white population. The mulattos demanded equality, and their demands for equality sparked the colony's black slaves (who comprised the majority of the population) to revolt. Their bloody uprising pitted them against all of the colony's landowners – the mulattos as well as the whites.

The Spanish colonists on the eastern half of the island immediately supported the slaves' call for independence in a move intended to weaken France's grip on western Hispaniola and perhaps afford Spain a chance to retake the entire island. At the time of the revolt, there were about 500,000 slaves in Saint-Domingue, compared to 60,000 in Santo Domingo. Saint-Domingue's whites sided with Britain, which had colonies in the West Indies and hoped to add the French colony to its empire. The mulattos aligned themselves with the French government, which decided to recognize the equality of mulattos and whites without anticipating British involvement.

When war again broke out between France and Spain a year later (in March 1793), the slave leaders Jean François, Jean Biassou and François-Dominique Toussaint L'Ouverture joined the Spanish frontier commanders in a fight against the French. But the alliance between the slaves and the Spaniards lasted less than a year, ending in September 1793 when France abolished slavery. With abolition, Toussaint and his men decided to switch allegiances, taking up arms with French soldiers waging war against the Spaniards.

Fighting continued on Hispaniola until October 1795, when news reached the island that Spain had signed a treaty with France ceding all parts of the island under Spanish control to the French Republic. It was agreed that the inhabitants of Santo Domingo would have one year to relocate. Within weeks, many of the Spanish colonists emigrated to Cuba, where they quickly realized that all of the arable land had been claimed. In addition, the cost of living was so high that only the wealthiest colonists could afford to live comfortably there.

When news from the émigrés reached Santo Domingo, the colony's residents were outraged. Adding to their dismay were reports that English pirates were attacking colonists as they attempted to leave Hispaniola. In the meantime, Britain launched repeated attacks against the French in a bid to take control of the island. Topping things off, many of the Spanish colonists still owned slaves, but the French had no white troops to take control of Santo Domingo and they did not dare send in Toussaint's troops because of the fear that the former slaves instilled in the Spanish residents.

As time passed Toussaint became increasingly restless. The date by which the Spanish colonists were supposed to be gone (July 22, 1796) came and went, with most of the residents refusing to budge without assurances from the Crown that they would be compensated for their losses. Several years passed, with French and Spanish authorities wavering on what to do. Finally, Toussaint could wait no more. In January 1801 he marched his troops into Santo Domingo and immediately abolished slavery in the colony.

Toussaint's control of Santo Domingo lasted less than a year. French army commander Napoleon Bonaparte, who regarded Saint-Domingue as key to potential French exploitation of the Louisiana Territory, dispatched 20,000 troops to Hispaniola. These troops, joined by white colonists and mulatto forces, wore down the black army. Recognizing that he couldn't defeat his numerically superior enemy, Toussaint agreed to meet with French General Charles Victor Emmanuel Leclerc to discuss a possible treaty.

Instead, he was seized at gunpoint and shipped to France, where he died of neglect in a dungeon a year later, in April 1803.

With the betrayal of Toussaint, the fighting between Saint-Domingue's former slaves and French troops, led by General Donatien Rochambeau, resumed. But to Rochambeau's dismay Bonaparte signed a treaty that allowed the purchase of Louisiana by the USA. With the treaty, the French essentially abandoned most of their ambitions for the Western Hemisphere. When reinforcements Bonaparte had promised to deliver failed to arrive, Rochambeau fled to Jamaica rather than face the retribution of former-slaves-turned-rebels.

With Rochambeau's flight, the era of French colonial rule on Hispaniola ended. On January 1, 1804, Haiti proclaimed its independence and thus became the first black republic in the New World. A year after that, Jean-Jacques Dessalines, who had been one of Toussaint's chief lieutenants, crowned himself emperor of the Republic of Haiti. Dessalines would be the first of many dictators the Haitian people would endure.

Dominican Independence

For the people of Santo Domingo, establishment of their independent state was still a long time coming. A small French presence remained in the city of Santo Domingo, which Dessalines intended to defeat during his first year as emperor in an effort to unify the island under the Haitian flag. But he abandoned those plans upon hearing that a French naval squadron was in the vicinity of the capital. The Spanish colonists would have their way for a while longer.

By 1808, many of the émigré Spanish landowners had returned to Santo Domingo and taken steps to ensure that they would never live under French rule. They convinced the Haitians to provide them weapons with which to defend themselves against possible French aggression, and they encouraged British adventurers on the Peninsula de Samaná to prevent French ships from reaching Santo Domingo. Their steps worked; within a year all French representatives on the island had fled, and authorities in Seville had accepted the reincorporation of the former colony into Spain.

The period from 1809 to 1821 is often referred to by historians as España Boba (Foolish Spain). During that period Spain's inept management of the colony allowed its economy to severely deteriorate. Finally, on November 30, 1821, Spanish lieutenant governor José Núñez de Cáceres announced the colony's independence from Spain. He named the new country Spanish Haiti and requested admission to the Republic of Gran Colombia (a country that included present-day Ecuador, Colombia, Panama and Venezuela). Before a reply came forth, Haitian leader Jean-Pierre Boyer invaded Santo Domingo and united the country under a single flag.

For the next 22 years (from 1821 to 1843) things grew increasingly worse for the Dominican people. Under Haitian rule, Haitian soldiers commandeered what they needed from the Dominicans to feed themselves. The Dominicans viewed the Haitians' behavior as criminal. Moreover, the Dominicans tended to view the dark-skinned Haitians as inferiors and resented their authority. For their part, the Haitians disliked the fairer-skinned Dominicans, whom they tended to associate with former slave owners.

The mutual dislike grew as the years passed until by 1843 it had reached a boiling point. All that was needed to spark a popular insurrection in the former Spanish colony was a revolutionary figure who could channel the Dominicans' anger, and such a person came along in Juan Pablo Duarte, an idealist who had gone to Europe as a student and was shocked by the economic conditions that prevailed in Santo Domingo upon his return.

Duarte, who today is hailed as the father of the Dominican Republic, established a resistance movement that turned the anti-Haitian sentiment into action. On February 27, 1844 – a day forever celebrated as Dominican Independence Day – the separatist movement headed by Duarte executed a bloodless coup in Santo Domingo city. During the next 16 days all of the eastern

GIANFRANCO LANZETTI

Portrait of Juan Pablo Duarte in the Museo
Casa de Juan Pablo Duarte, Santo Domingo

towns announced their decision to separate from Haiti, and thus the Dominican Republic was born.

From then until 1864, two men dominated the political scene in the new republic: General Pedro Santana Familias, military chief of the Dominican army, and Buenaventura Báez Méndez, a rich landowner and mahogany exporter. During the twenty years from 1844 to 1864, these selfish, power-hungry men alternately led the Dominican Republic by means of force and, some would say, treason: In 1861, Santana agreed to the republic's annexation by Spain just so that he could retain power. He also sent into exile the principals in the republic's creation – Duarte, Ramón Mella and Francisco del Rosario Sánchez. The annexation agreement gave Spain a mortgage on customs receipts and a reduction of import duties on Spanish ships entering the country.

Despite Santana's behavior, the Dominican people weren't about to become a colony of Spain again. In what became know as the Restoration War, thousands of poorly armed Dominicans declared war on the Spanish soldiers that had been sent to the island. The Dominicans put up such a fight that on March 3, 1865, the queen of Spain signed a decree annulling the annexation and withdrew her soldiers from the island. From that day forward, the Dominican Republic has been a fully independent country.

Modern Nations

For the modern histories of Haiti and the Dominican Republic, see the beginning of each country's section in this guide.

GEOGRAPHY

Hispaniola is near the center of the West Indies, a series of islands that form a 2400km arc extending from near the southeastern tip of the USA to within 10km of Venezuela. Or, put another way, the West Indies run from the Straits of Florida all the way to Trinidad, the wondrous island atop South America where the calypso and the limbo were born.

Hispaniola is about 960km southeast of Florida and about half that distance north of South America. To the north of the island is the Atlantic Ocean, to the south the Caribbean Sea, to the west Cuba and to the east Puerto Rico.

Hispaniola is shared by the Dominican Republic and Haiti, with the DR occupying roughly two-thirds of the island (48,734 sq km) and Haiti occupying roughly one-third (27,750 sq km).

Eight mountain ranges divide Hispaniola. The main range is the Cordillera Central, which extends from Santo Domingo northwest into Haiti, where it becomes the Massif du Nord. The range makes up approximately one-third of Hispaniola's landmass.

The island's longest river is the Río Yaque del Norte, and its largest lake is Lago Enriquillo. Both are in the Dominican Republic, as is the Caribbean's tallest mountain, Pico Duarte, which rises to 3175m and is blanketed by pine forest at its uppermost elevations.

GEOLOGY

Until about 200 million years ago, the earth's surface consisted of a single ocean and one great landmass. Then the giant continent began to break apart under the strain of molten rock welling up from deep within the earth. The planet's crust separated into thick 'plates' that have been moving apart and colliding at a snail's pace ever since.

Hispaniola and other islands of the West Indies were first pushed up from the seabed by a great volcanic welling about 140 million years ago. For about the next 20 million years an enormous mountain range known as the Caribbean Andes formed to the east of present-day Central America.

Beginning about 65 million years ago, the Caribbean Plate separated from the giant Pacific Plate and the former plate was forced downward and under the much larger plate. During this time, the Caribbean Sea formed in a depression created by the movement of several plates, and most of the Caribbean Andes disappeared under the new sea.

Today, the Caribbean Plate is moving very slowly to the southwest and is being overtaken by both the North and South American Plates at a rate of about 2cm each year. At that rate, Pico Duarte, which is a fairly arduous hike these days, should be an easy 'hop' in another several million years.

The movement of the Caribbean Plate is cause for mild concern for travelers to Hispaniola, as the island is susceptible to earthquakes. Earthquakes don't pose nearly the threat to the island that hurricanes do, but if you happen to be at the beach and feel a powerful earthquake, run – don't walk – away from the beach. Large temblors at sea often create tidal waves called *tsunamis*. Such waves can travel several kilometers inland before dissipating. The danger that these waves pose in the seconds and minutes following a big off-shore quake should not be underestimated.

Volcanoes are also a product of plate movement, and some of the islands to the east and to the south of Hispaniola are prone to volcanic activity. However, there are no active volcanoes on Hispaniola today and there haven't been for many years.

CLIMATE

Hispaniola is in the tropics, and the tropics – at least at sea level – are synonymous with humidity. So while the island's high temperatures don't approach those of most deserts, the heat can at times be just as oppressive.

The average annual temperature on the island is 26°C, the highs and lows varying with altitude rather than with season. In fact, there really is only one season on Hispaniola: summer. But at sea level throughout the island, expect the high to reach 30°C, whereas if you're in the mountains you can expect a high of 24°C. Likewise, lows along the coast typically hover around 20°C, while in the mountains single-digit temperatures are common.

Depending on whether there's a breeze or not, the humidity at the lower elevations will be tolerable, perhaps even ideal if you suffer from dry skin; or it will be such that you can expect to start sweating the moment you leave your air-conditioned hotel room.

Unlike the temperatures, which fluctuate little during the year, there are distinct rainy seasons on Hispaniola, and they vary from one location to another. Along the northern coast, the rainy season generally lasts from October through May. Along the southern coast, it generally lasts from May through October. Northern and eastern towns tend to receive more rain than southern towns.

But certain cities tend to receive much more rain than others, regardless of the overall north-south rainfall patterns. For example, Puerto Plata averages 176cm of rain annually, while Monte Cristi – also on the northern coast – averages only 67cm. Santo Domingo usually receives 138cm of rain each year, while Baní – only 40 minutes' drive to the west – generally receives a full one-third less rainfall.

Hurricanes

Hispaniola's four-month-long hurricane season is described in a popular rhyme: 'June – too soon; July – stand by; August – a must; September – remember.' Well, hurricanes aren't really a 'must' in August (this is a rhyme, for goodness' sake), but when they strike they are usually deadly. One that struck the island in 1979 killed more than a thousand people, and Hurricane Georges in 1998 killed several thousand people.

If a hurricane is forecast when you're here, you'd be wise to leave the island. At the very least, head for the mountains – far from the dangerous sea swell that usually accompanies hurricanes. Under no circumstances do you want to be within a kilometer of the beach due to the very real risk of being swept out to sea.

If you find yourself confronting a hurricane, try to keep your wits about you. This is not the time to get drunk and show your friends how 'brave' you are by running to the end of the pier or otherwise acting stupid. Avoid the urge to stand near windows, as hurricanes have a habit of shattering them and spraying glass fragments and other debris like bombs.

If time permits, stock up on enough items to meet your needs for at least one week. These items include packaged food, bottled water, flashlights and plenty of flashlight batteries. Remember: After a hurricane it could be several weeks before tap water, electricity, phone service, natural gas and gasoline are available, and food can be in extremely short supply as well. After Hurricane Georges,

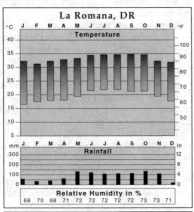

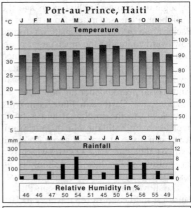

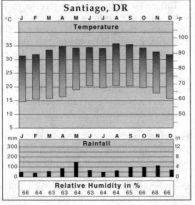

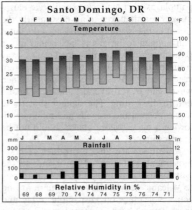

High-Velocity Winds

Caribbean hurricanes originate off the coast of Africa, forming as winds rush toward a low-pressure area and swirl around it due to the rotational forces of the earth's spin. The storms move counterclockwise across the Atlantic, fed by warm winds and moisture, building up force in their 3000km run toward Central and North America.

On the islands, the first stage of a hurricane's approach is called a tropical disturbance. The next stage is a tropical depression. When winds exceed 64km/h, the system is upgraded to a tropical storm and is usually accompanied by heavy rains. The system is called a hurricane if wind speed exceeds 120km/h and intensifies around a low-pressure center, the so-called eye of the storm.

Hurricane systems can range from 80km in diameter to devastating giants more than 1600km across. Their energy is prodigious – far more than the mightiest thermonuclear explosions ever unleashed on earth. The area affected by winds of great destructive force may exceed 240km in diameter. Gale-force winds can prevail over an area twice as great.

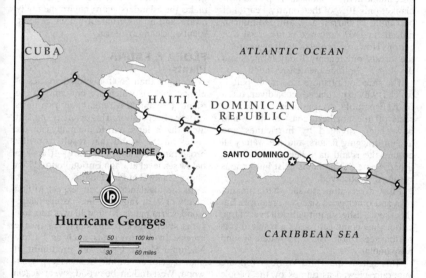

The strength of a hurricane is rated from one to five. The mildest, a Category 1 hurricane, has winds of at least 120km/h. The strongest and rarest hurricanes, the Category 5 monsters, pack winds that exceed 250km/h; Hurricane Mitch, which killed more than 10,000 people in Central America in late 1998, was a rare Category 5 hurricane. Hurricanes travel at varying speeds, from as little as 10km/h to more than 50km/h.

For current tropical-storm information, go to the *Miami Herald*'s website (www.herald.com) and scan the top menu for hurricane and storm information. Another excellent place to find current tropical-storm information is the website maintained by the US National Oceanic and Atmospheric Administration (www.esdim.noaa.gov/weather_page.html).

some parts of the island were without electricity for two months.

ECOLOGY & ENVIRONMENT

Hispaniola's environmental record is a particularly depressing one. In Haiti, hardly a hill stands that hasn't been denuded. Most of the country's trees have been felled for firewood and construction – a tragic but understandable occurrence given the grinding poverty in which most Haitians live. Without trees to hold dirt in place, much of the land's topsoil has been washed away, leaving hillsides that support only weeds.

Pine, hardwood and other tree cover, once ample in the Dominican Republic, now blanket only 10% of the country. Fearful of becoming as barren as Haiti, Dominican officials in 1967 outlawed commercial tree cutting. However, professional loggers aren't the forests' only enemy. Today, farmers and developers continue the deforestation.

The situation offshore isn't much better, which is why experienced scuba divers often find Hispaniola disappointing. The coral reefs off the northern coast of the island have been ravaged by hurricanes and anchor-dragging fishers, and the waters all around the island have been grossly overfished. Some fishing limits exist but none is enforced or observed.

Most divers hope to see sharks, manta rays and other good-size sea creatures, but the island's fishers habitually kill every large critter they come across. As a result, divers seldom see sizable fish in the waters around Hispaniola.

Throughout the Third World, rivers are generally viewed as dumps by the people who live near them. Such is the case on Hispaniola. Few rivers on the island aren't lined with refuse. One stretch of the Río Yaque del Norte in the Dominican Republic is litter free because employees of a local rafting company routinely sweep it for trash. Elsewhere the river is blanketed with garbage.

Likewise, the beaches in front of the island's many all-inclusive resorts are litter free only because resort workers sweep them. Maintained this way, they are as gorgeous as any in the world. But beaches elsewhere on Hispaniola are strewn with plastic waste, most of it the result of illegal dumping and thoughtless beach-goers.

Garbage is a problem even in urban tourist areas, such as the Zona Colonial of Santo Domingo. Many of the sidewalks in the area have so much garbage on them that people prefer to walk in the streets. Although there's regular trash pickup there, cans are not required. As a result, residents simply place their bagged garbage on sidewalks, where dogs scatter it about.

Government officials agree that Hispaniola's litter and pollution problems are severe, and most agree that they are likely to get worse. Few efforts are being made to make the islanders more environmentally aware, and no government money is being spent on clean-up efforts.

FLORA & FAUNA
Plants

With more than 5600 identified species of plants, 36% of which are endemic to the island, Hispaniola is remarkably rich in its variety of vegetation. This diversity of plant life is due in large part to the many climatic zones on the island that result from the broad range of elevations there – from 40m below sea level at Lago Enriquillo to 3175m above sea level at Pico Duarte.

In the highlands one can expect to find plenty of West Indian cedar, pasture fiddlewood, sierra palms, Krug wild avocado, tree ferns, even thick bamboo groves beside creeks. In dry lowlands, such as Parque Nacional Monte Cristi, the predominant plant species are Monte Cristi sage, poisonwood, West Indian boxwood, sweet acacia and wild frangipani. Healthy mangrove forests can be found along some parts of the coast.

Birds

In general, Hispaniola is not a mecca for bird watchers. Although no bird count has ever been conducted on the island, it certainly hasn't much to offer the birder when compared to such regional birding hot spots as Panama, Venezuela and Costa Rica. Island birding generally doesn't compare well to mainland birding. However, there are a handful of endemic birds on Hispaniola. Birders will want to keep an eye out for the Hispaniolan trogon, the Hispaniolan parrot and the Hispaniolan woodpecker.

Other birds of interest are the ruddy duck, which is easily identified by its bright blue beak and a white streak across its otherwise black head; the flamingo, which can stand more than a meter tall and is pink-white except for its black-tipped beak and orange-red underwing (visible only during flight); and the stygian owl, a large brown-and-white bird with two protruding clusters of feathers above its eyes that resemble bushy eyebrows.

Until very recently, the book of choice for this area – indeed the only major field guide that included Haiti – was James Bond's *Birds of the West Indies*, the book that inspired spy novelist Ian Fleming to create the famous 007 while staying in his Jamaican getaway cottage. Bond has finally been improved upon by the 1998 *A Guide to the Birds of the West Indies*, by Herbert Raffaele et al. This is a fabulously illustrated book

Ten Tips for Environmentally Conscious Travelers

1. **Don't litter.** Remember: Take only photographs, leave only footprints. If you see litter, pick it up. Support recycling programs.

2. **Respect nature and history.** Never take 'souvenirs' such as shells, plants or artifacts from historical sites or natural areas. Treat shells, sea urchins, coral and other marine life as sacred.

3. **Don't buy products made from endangered species.** Many species of plants and animals are killed to make trinkets for tourists. By buying products made of tortoise shell, coral, bird feathers or similar materials, you are contributing to the decimation of wildlife. Shop with a conscience.

4. **Keep to the footpaths.** When you're hiking, always follow designated trails. Natural habitats are often quickly eroded and animals and plants disturbed by walkers who stray off the beaten path.

5. **Don't touch or stand on coral.** Coral is extremely sensitive and is easily killed by snorkelers and divers who fail to honor this law of nature: Human contact is deadly. Boaters should never anchor on coral – use mooring buoys. It's the law!

6. **Choose environmentally conscious businesses.** Try to patronize hotels, tour companies and merchants that act in an environmentally sound manner. When deciding with whom to do business, consider each company's impact on waste generation, noise levels and other pollution, energy consumption and the local culture.

7. **Help local communities gain a share of tourism revenues.** Many local communities are hard-pressed to survive, and they derive little benefit from tourism profits. Educate yourself on community tourism and ways you can participate. Use local guides whenever possible.

8. **Respect others' privacy.** Don't intrude into people's lives or privacy. Ask permission before taking photographs of individuals and before entering private property.

9. **Respect the community.** Learn about the customs of the regions you visit and support local efforts to preserve the environment and traditional culture.

10. **Educate others.** Politely intervene when other travelers act in an environmentally or socially detrimental manner. Educate them about the potential negative effects of their behavior.

that covers all the birds from Grand Cayman to Barbados in great detail, but unlike Bond's more travel-friendly volume, it definitely won't fit into your hip pocket.

Land Animals

There never were any big cats on Hispaniola – no jaguars, no ocelots, no pumas. And compared to nearby Central America, parts of which absolutely teem with large exotic creatures, Hispaniola is a bit of a dud.

But that's not to say the island has nothing to offer in the way of land-based wild things. Hundreds of American crocodiles make their home on Hispaniola and can be easily viewed by boat at Lago Enriquillo in the Dominican Republic and Etang Saumâtre in Haiti. Also at Lago Enriquillo are members of an endemic species of rhinoceros iguanas. Some of these iguanas are more than a meter long and have disturbing red eyes set in spiky black faces.

The forests contain lots of tarantulas, but their bite doesn't produce the kind of wild-eyed, foam-at-the-mouth reaction followed by uncontrollable spasms and certain death Hollywood would lead you to believe. However, the bites can be excruciating. There are no poisonous snakes on Hispaniola, although desert campers should turn their boots over and give them a hefty shake each morning before putting them on; scorpions – whose bites can be fatal – *love* to sleep in boots, and the little buggers abound in Hispaniola's dry lowlands.

Sea Creatures

The largest animal in the vicinity of Hispaniola is the humpback whale, which returns to the West Indies from the North Atlantic every January. From then through March, the second rarest of all whales circulates between several breeding areas, including Bahía de Samaná on the northeast side of the island and Banco de la Plata, a large reef system about 100km north of Puerto Plata. Upwards of 10,000 humpback whales reach Dominican waters annually.

There are two species of manatee found in the Caribbean Sea to the south and east of the island: the Caribbean manatee and the Antillean manatee. Also known as sea cows, these walrus-resembling critters are docile, playful and very curious – when they see snorkelers or divers they tend to swim toward them to give the humans a closer look.

There are eight species of sea turtle in the world, and four can be found in the waters around Hispaniola: the loggerhead, green, hawksbill and leatherback. Although not a common sight, these wonderful marine turtles can occasionally be seen in the Atlantic as well as in the Caribbean.

Cruelty to Animals

Second only to baseball, cockfights are the most popular sport on Hispaniola. The owners and trainers of gamecocks often regard their birds with profound affection and respect. They truly do not want their animals to die. But no one can effectively argue that lashing spurs to an animal and teaching it to use them to slice another animal to death *isn't* an act of cruelty. (In Haiti, as opposed to the Dominican Republic, gamecocks do not usually fight to the death.)

The issue of cruelty is murkier when an animal is sacrificed in the name of a god – especially when the sacrifice is conducted ostensibly to produce rain, which would benefit animals as well as people. On Hispaniola, cocks, goats, pigs and bulls are occasionally sacrificed during Vodou ceremonies. In most instances, death occurs quickly and the animal is eaten – not simply left to rot untouched like the animals that are unwitting performers in Mexican bullfights.

Far more prevalent is the merciless use of bird cages. All over Hispaniola people keep big birds in little cages as pets. Many of the birds, barely able to endure their captivity, scrape their heads against the bars. Others, particularly parrots, yank out their own feathers in acts of pure frustration.

Endangered Species

All of the island's large animals, and many of its small ones, are headed toward extinction.

The following creatures appear on the World Conservation Monitoring Center's list of endangered species for Hispaniola: humpback whale, Pacific pilot whale, Caribbean monk seal, Atlantic spotted dolphin, Caribbean manatee, Antillean manatee, American crocodile, rhinoceros iguana, Hispaniola ground iguana, loggerhead turtle, green turtle, leatherback turtle, hawksbill turtle, three species of freshwater turtle and dozens of bird species. The list goes on and on.

A half dozen environmental groups have published pamphlets describing the slaughter and habitat destruction taking place on or near Hispaniola. Haiti and the Dominican Republic have outlawed certain species-endangering practices, but they aren't enforcing the laws. Except for the creation of national parks, next to nothing is being done to protect the animals listed above and many others too numerous to mention here. Sadly, even in the national parks animals are not safe because no one is protecting the parks against poachers or encroachment.

National Parks

Hispaniola has many national parks that are well worth visiting. Even Haiti, which has chopped down more than 98% of its original tree cover, boasts two mountain parks: Parc La Visite, with a mixture of pine and montane cloud forest, and Parc Macaya, which contains the country's only remaining cloud forest. Another site worth visiting is Etang Saumâtre, where a boat ride on the crocodile-lined lake makes for exciting memories.

The Dominican Republic has 10 national parks, every one of which offers the visitor something intriguing. Parque Nacional Submarino La Caleta is a marine park near Santo Domingo that contains some lovely coral and a scuttled salvage boat that's popular with divers. Two highland parks make for fine trekking and contain many huts for campers' use.

Parque Nacional Los Haïtises, at the western end of Bahía de Samaná and best visited by boat, contains numerous mangrove forests and thousands of stubby hills

that lend themselves well to exploring. Parque Nacional Jaragua features a lake that's a haven to flamingos; the park is also home to gorgeous and seldom-visited white-sand beaches.

For more detailed park information, see the National Parks section on each country.

GOVERNMENT & POLITICS

Both of Hispaniola's countries are trying to overcome pasts ruled by dictators and upheaval. The Dominican Republic is doing a good job of it. In electing President Leonel Fernández to a four-year term in August 1996, the Dominicans ushered in their youngest and most progressive president and put behind them the kind of authoritarian rule typified by his predecessor, former President Joaquín Balaguer.

Within weeks of taking office, Fernández shocked his nation by forcibly retiring two dozen generals and then firing his defense minister for insubordination after the official refused to submit to questioning by the civilian attorney general. The then-42-year-old president showed the world that the military no longer determines the fate of the Dominican Republic, and ever since then he has been seeking political and economic reform for his country.

Meanwhile, Haiti's once-promising future appears uncertain. In the late 1990s, after US and United Nations intervention to restore democracy following years of dictatorships, Haiti remains mired in a dizzying array of political, economic and social crises that are undermining US and UN efforts to help restore even the most basic institutions and human rights: justice and the rule of law.

At the time this was penned, in late 1998, Haiti didn't even have a government. The last one had fallen a year earlier when the prime minister resigned, and political infighting was preventing the appointment of his successor. As a result, hundreds of millions of dollars in international aid, earmarked for a country that is the poorest and least developed in the Americas, remained frozen.

Making matters worse, the corruption and violence that led to the US/UN bailout efforts continue to rule Haiti's political scene, according to diplomats, politicians, economists and average Haitians. Press reports in 1998 cited scores of instances in which police were directly involved in crimes or failed to investigate them, and allegations that judges, magistrates and prosecutors were selling justice were widespread in the country.

What's more, a combination of underpolicing, judicial corruption and political paralysis had made Haiti a drug trafficker's paradise. In 1998 a top US antidrug official called Haiti the 'drug trafficking crossroads of the Caribbean,' and seizures by US agencies that police Haitian waters indicate that tons of Colombian cocaine go through Haiti en route to the USA each year.

ECONOMY

Until recently, one word described the economy of the island: farming. In the Dominican Republic, sugar revenue led that country's economy until the early 1980s, when sugar prices hit a 40-year low and the USA – its chief market – reduced its imports of sugar in response to lobbying efforts by domestic producers.

In the meantime the Dominican Republic began to diversify its economy to include mining, manufacturing and tourism. By the end of the 1980s exports of gold, silver, ferronickel and bauxite constituted 38% of the country's gross domestic product, and the number of hotels on the island had quadrupled. During the late 1990s, tourism became the country's top revenue leader and hotels seemed to be under construction almost everywhere.

The story is considerably different across the border. Haiti's economy remains peasant based, with an average farm size of less than 1 1/2 hectares. Seventy-five percent of the country's people fall below the World Bank's absolute poverty level, and the unemployment rate hangs around 70%. Industry and commerce are limited, and political upheaval continues to thwart much-needed foreign investment.

During the late 1990s, inflation – created by the sudden appearance of Colombian drug money – was soaring while per-capita income remained frozen at 1994 levels of about US$300 a year. Tens of millions of dollars were flowing through the Haitian economy, but much of it was the proceeds of drug traffickers, currency speculators and corrupt politicians, which created few jobs and little development.

The fastest-growing industries in Haiti in late 1998 were private security firms and the daily lottery.

POPULATION & PEOPLE

Hispaniola's indigenous inhabitants were the Taíno Indians, all but a fraction of whom were wiped out within 30 years of their initial contact with Europeans. With the Taínos' extinction, the Spanish colonists (and later the French colonists as well) imported hundreds of thousands of African slaves during a period lasting more than 200 years.

Almost from the start, there was much mingling of the races. Today there are approximately 15 million people on the island, the vast majority of whom are black or mulatto. As a result of the amount of 'mixed blood' on the island, you don't find nearly the degree of racial tension here that you find elsewhere in the Caribbean.

However, there *is* quite a bit of tension between the Haitians and the Dominicans. Many Haitians, citing events that took place more than a hundred years ago, feel their neighbors *stole* territory that rightfully belongs to Haiti. They look at their own barren mountains and then at the pine-covered peaks and fertile valleys of the Dominican Republic with anger.

For their part, some Dominicans look upon the Haitians as inferiors who live in grinding poverty because that's all they're capable of. Most of the lowly work done in the Dominican Republic, such as cutting sugarcane during harvest, is done by Haitians. Dominicans, for the most part, feel that manual labor is beneath them.

SOCIETY & CONDUCT
Traditional Cultures
With the elimination of the Taíno Indians nearly 500 years ago, little remains of the indigenous culture that flourished on the island prior to 1492. And although most of Hispaniola's people are descendants of Africans with rich cultures, those Africans were slaves whose cultures were taken from them.

Today the 'traditional' cultures that exist on the island are post-Columbian, which doesn't make them any less respectable. On the contrary, the primitive art of Haiti and the music of the Dominican Republic are known worldwide, as are the spiritual beliefs held mostly by Haitians living in both countries and known as Vodou.

Popular Attitudes
With a few exceptions, the people you encounter throughout Hispaniola will be friendly, good-humored and willing to help. In rural areas, if you have white skin and speak a foreign language, expect to be viewed as a curiosity. Indeed, where white people aren't prevalent it's common for local children to either fear you as a freak of nature or approach you with amusement such as they would a zoo animal.

Increasingly, children and adults, in rural areas as well as urban areas, look at white people as money-dispensing machines. With

annoying but understandable frequency, whites are approached by people saying, 'Give me a dollar,' and by tour guides offering their services. In both instances, a polite 'No, thank you' will usually turn the solicitor away without any hard feelings.

In general, tourists are well received in Haiti and the Dominican Republic, as local people see them bringing badly needed revenue into their countries. And despite US military intervention in Haitian and Dominican affairs in times past, Americans in particular tend to be looked upon with envy and respect (thanks mostly to Hollywood). They are also viewed as good tippers, which makes them popular with people in the service industry.

In Haiti, if you are white, get used to hearing '*blan, blan*' shouted at you. This is a generic term for 'foreigner' rather than a jibe at your color and should not be taken as any kind of insult. Likewise, you may hear '*gringo*' or '*gringa*' called out to you in the Dominican Republic. Most of the time it's intended as a greeting, and a smile is a welcome reply.

Throughout the island people tend to be very polite and friendly, offering greetings even to total strangers. On a quiet street in Haiti and throughout the Haitian countryside, saying '*Ça va?*' (how goes it?) or '*Salut*' (hello) to those you see is important. The traditional Creole greeting is '*Ki jan ou ye*' (how are you?), to which the standard reply is '*M pa pi mal*' (not too bad).

The same friendliness applies on the eastern two-thirds of the island, although of course the salutations are in Spanish – not French or Creole. Typical greetings are '*Buenos días*' (good morning), '*Buenas tardes*' (good afternoon) and '*Buenas noches*' (good evening/night). The standard reply is to repeat the same.

Dos & Don'ts
Haitians and Dominicans generally are wonderfully welcoming to strangers, even though it would be understandable for most of them to look upon the usually much-wealthier foreigners with resentment. Also, Hispaniolans won't think badly of you if you

attempt to speak one of their languages and butcher it in the process.

However, most Haitians and Dominicans dress conservatively, and they are offended by certain clothing practices. Beachwear, for example, should never be worn away from the beach or poolside. Dress can be casual but it should never be sloppy (always tuck your shirt in, never walk around in an undershirt, leave your frayed cutoffs at home). Skirts above the knee are considered risqué. Men should wear a shirt, except at the beach or poolside.

No matter where you go, photography can be a problem, and Hispaniola is no exception. While most people on the island are pleased to have their photograph taken, don't assume that everyone will be. In general, ask before you shoot. If you don't speak the local language, pointing at your camera then at the subject will usually convey your request. Please abide by the response.

RELIGION

More than 90% of the people on Hispaniola are professed Roman Catholics, and Roman Catholicism is the official religion of Haiti and the Dominican Republic. In fact, most Dominicans don't attend Mass regularly; their popular religious practices are far removed from Roman Catholic orthodoxy. They generally ignore the advice of clergy on matters that are not strictly religious on the assumption that priests have little understanding of secular affairs.

In Haiti, most people consider themselves Roman Catholics, but the majority actually believe in and practice at least some aspects of Vodou. The belief system of Vodou revolves around family spirits called *lwa* who are inherited through maternal and paternal lines. These spirits are thought to protect the children. In return, families 'feed' the lwa through periodic rituals in which food, drink and other gifts are offered.

The rituals of Vodou are often led by a priest or a priestess. During the ritual the worshipers invoke the lwa by drumming, dancing, singing and feasting, and the lwa

Vodou or voodoo?

In editing this book, there was much debate about whether to use the spelling 'voodoo' or 'Vodou' for the religion practiced in Haiti. *Webster's Collegiate Dictionary* uses 'voodoo,' the most commonly known spelling for the word. However, *The Chicago Manual of Style* shows that the names of all other religions – including smaller religious sects and branches – always appear capitalized. Additionally, those who practice the religion in Haiti consistently use the spelling 'Vodou,' and actually differentiate their spiritual practice from the more Americanized belief, 'voodoo.' In recognition of the religion and out of respect to its followers, we have chosen to use the spelling 'Vodou' throughout this book.

Recommended books about Vodou include *Divine Horsemen: The Living Gods of Haiti*, by Maya Deren, and *Spirits of the Night: The Vaudun Gods of Haiti*, by Selden Rodman and Carol Cleaver.

For more information on Vodou, check the Vodou Page at: members.aol.com/racine125/index.html.

take possession of the dancers. Each dancer then behaves in a manner characteristic of the possessing spirit and while in an ecstatic trance performs cures and gives advice.

The third-largest religious group on the island is Protestant, comprised mostly of Baptists but including Pentecostals, Adventists and others as well. A very small percentage of the people on the island practice Judaism or follow Islam.

LANGUAGE

English, the 'universal' language, isn't widely spoken on the island outside of all-inclusive resorts and the better hotels. German is spoken by the staffs of some North Coast resorts.

Spanish is the official language of the Dominican Republic, and it's spoken by

99% of that country's inhabitants (the 1% who don't speak Spanish represent newcomers who haven't learned the language). Perhaps 5% of the Dominican population speaks English.

French is the official language of Haiti, but only 10% of the populace – mainly the ruling class – speaks it. The rest of the people

speak Creole, the origins of which are still debated (most scholars believe it arose from a pidgin that developed between French colonists and African slaves). Only one in every 20 Haitians is fluent in both languages. Few Haitians speak English.

See the Language chapter at the end of the book for useful words and phrases.

Regional Facts for the Visitor

HIGHLIGHTS

What makes Hispaniola truly special is its rich history, so much of which is marked by superlatives, and the condition of many of its colonial buildings. Of the various places on the island where colonial structures can be found, Santo Domingo's Zona Colonial is by far the most impressive. Among the dozens of colonial buildings that are fully or partially intact are the oldest church in the New World and the New World's first hospital. There are a number of museums in the district, even a big old fort.

Humpbacks, considered by *Moby Dick* author Herman Melville to be the 'most light-hearted and gamesome of all the whales,' put on quite a show every January, February and March off the Dominican Republic's north coast – in Bahía de Samaná and out at Banco de la Plata, a vast reef system 100km north of Puerto Plata. The whales arrive to mate and calve, and the male humpbacks leap out of the water in displays of strength for the females. Such displays are unforgettable, and tourists can witness them from shore or boat.

Less spectacular than the colonial structures and the leaping whales but still worthy of inclusion in a Hispaniola highlights reel are dozens of the island's beaches. Not all are postcard perfect, but lovely stretches of sand can be found all around the island. Perhaps the best ones are on Cayo Levantado in Bahía Samaná and just east of Bayahibe in the Dominican Republic, and at Raymond-les-Bains and Plage Labadie in Haiti.

Although most of the island's national parks are fairly unimpressive when compared to the national parks of Central and South America, they aren't without their moments. In the Dominican Republic, Parque Nacional Isla Cabritos is famous for its crocodiles, iguanas and flamingos, and the Parque Nacional Los Haïtises resembles prehistoric swampland – its thousands of small, partly submerged, jungly hills make

for excellent exploration by boat. Other parks contain some fine hiking trails. The best hiking trail in Haiti is in the south, in Parc La Visite.

However, most of the island's visitors head for an all-inclusive resort in the Dominican Republic, and this winds up being virtually all of Hispaniola they see. These visitors are whisked directly to their accommodations from small international airports and devote themselves exclusively to sun worship and pleasures of the heart and gastrointestinal tract. It's fair to say that the all-inclusive resort is the highlight for many visitors to Hispaniola.

SUGGESTED ITINERARIES

The vast majority of tourists visiting the island only spend time in the Dominican Republic, and most of those travelers arrive at Las Américas International Airport, outside of Santo Domingo. See the introductory Getting There & Away chapter for more arrival information.

Below are suggested itineraries for people considering visiting both Haiti and the Dominican Republic during a single trip. They are designed for travelers who want to take in as many sights as possible in the time specified; they are not designed for people seeking rest and relaxation.

If you want to lie on a beach every day and party hearty every night, you'd be wise to stay at one or two all-inclusive resorts your entire trip. All-inclusives are situated on the island's best beaches and they are designed for fun, with no shortage of sand, pools, cocktails, dance clubs and water sports.

Anyone planning on seeing much of Haiti by car should be advised that such travel is very time-consuming due to the poor condition of its roads.

Top Sights in a Week

Spend your first night in Santo Domingo's Zona Colonial, changing money and touring the historic district the next day. Spend your second night in the Zona Colonial and get off to an early start the next day, destined for Sosúa by express bus or by plane via the Puerto Plata airport. Spend the next day at Playa Sosúa and strolling the lively town. Early the next morning, take a bus to the junction of Hwy 1 near Bisono, and from there catch a bus to Monte Cristi; from there catch a bus to Dajabon, where you'll cross the border into Haiti. From there, take a bus or a taxi to Cap-Haïtien, wrapping up a full day of traveling.

The next day, travel to the mountain-top fortress of La Citadelle, 25km outside Cap-Haïtien at the village of Milot. While in Milot, also see the ruins of Sans Souci before returning to Cap-Haïtien for the night. The next morning, head back to the border, crossing into Dajabon, and from there catch an express bus to Santo Domingo and the Zona Colonial. With the time remaining, catch your breath and take in the rest of Santo Domingo (see its chapter for details).

Two Weeks

Like the one-week itinerary, this one is intended for heavy-duty sightseers, and it can also be done by bus. Bus travel lets visitors see more of the island and gives them a better feel for daily life, and short of walking, it's the least expensive way to get around. That said, some portions of this itinerary can be done by plane.

Making reservations is always a good idea, especially if you're traveling on a tight schedule such as the one suggested here. Consult the appropriate chapters of this guide, choose accommodations and tours according to taste and budget, and book rooms and tours *before* leaving home. In this way you can reduce the risk of unpleasant surprises.

Day 1 – Arrive in Santo Domingo and stay in the Zona Colonial or along the *malecón*, as those are the city's most scenic neighborhoods.

Day 2 – Spend the day touring the Zona Colonial, stay a second night, and possibly take in some nightlife.

Day 3 – Head to the mountain town of Jarabacoa and overnight there.

Day 4 – Run the Río Yaque del Norte the next morning and visit Jarabacoa's waterfalls or do some hiking near La Cienaga in the afternoon.

Day 5 – Head to Samaná and overnight.

Day 6 – If you're in Samaná between December and March, go on a whale-watching excursion. Any time of year, tour Parque Nacional Los Haïtises. Both can be done in one fun day.

Day 7 – Head to mellow, beachside Las Terrenas and overnight, or if you're looking for a more active scene, head to Cabarete, one of the world's top windsurfing sites.

Day 8 – In Las Terrenas, consider exploring the coast on Jet Ski. If in Cabarete, consider taking a guided bicycle tour to a scenic inland area.

Day 9 – For more of the coast at a different locale, head to Sosúa. If you're more historically inclined, visit Parque Nacional La Isabela instead.

Day 10 – Head to Cap-Haïtien. Take a bus to the junction of Hwy 1 at Bisono, catch another one to Monte Cristi, and from there catch a bus to Dajabón. Arrive early enough at Dajabón to cross the border before it closes (4 pm). Catch a bus to Cap-Haïtien and overnight there.

Day 11 – Travel to the mountain-top fortress of La Citadelle, 25km outside Cap-Haïtien at the village of Milot. While in Milot, also see the ruins of Sans Souci before returning to Cap-Haïtien for the night.

Day 12 – Head to Labadie, a village along a beautiful strip of coast, in the morning. Explore the coast by boat during the day, and spend the night near Plage Labadie.

Day 13 – Leave Labadie early for the border, but before reaching it, stop off at Fort Liberté to visit Fort Dauphin. Cross the border and catch a bus for Santo Domingo.

Day 14 – Before catching your flight home, if time permits, take in more Santo Domingo sights, such as the Jardín Botánico Nacional and the Mercado Modelo.

Three Weeks

An itinerary for three weeks would pick up where the two-week itinerary left off, with the night of the 14th being spent in Santo Domingo. The fourth week follows:

Day 15 – Head to Barahona early the next morning, check into a hotel, then do some prearranged snorkeling or diving in the area in the afternoon.

Day 16 – Check out of the hotel and leave for Parque Nacional Isla Cabritos no later than 9 am. After touring the crocodile-ringed lake and visiting the iguana-spotted island, cross into Haiti at the border at Jimani and continue on to Port-au-Prince. Overnight there.

Day 17 – Spend the day and night at Port-au-Prince, visiting the Cathedral of St Trinité, the Iron Market and the national cemetery.

Day 18 – Travel to the port town of Jacmel, hitting the road early to allow time to stroll one of Haiti's prettiest towns. Overnight in Jacmel.

Day 19 – Visit either the natural pools and waterfalls at Bassins Bleu or the lovely beach at Raymond-les-Bains. Overnight in Port-au-Prince.

Day 20 – Make your way back to Santo Domingo, either by bus or by plane, and spend the night in the capital city. Return home the next day.

Four Weeks

The three itineraries suggested above involve a lot of time on the road, lots of packing and unpacking, and many early morning departures. They are, as previously mentioned, designed for heavy-duty sightseers – people really trying to pack in a lot of sights. For those travelers who enjoy such itineraries but are in need of oxygen after week three, an additional week on the island might best be spent peacefully cooling your feet at one of the resorts on the east coast of the Dominican Republic (in the vicinity of Playa Punta Cana or Playa Bávaro).

The more adventure- and budget-minded traveler might consider taking a bus to Higüey and from there to Miches, relaxing at one of the remote Swiss-run *pensiónes* out toward Punta El Rey. Or, better yet, take a bus to Boca Chica and rent a motorcycle, then cruise up to Cabañas Playa Tortuga, on

the northeast coast near El Cedro. Stay there for several days and then depart for one of the intimate and rustic Swiss-run hotels (see the Southeastern Dominican Republic chapter for more details).

Visiting these two areas gives you a chance to bodysurf, to explore nearby lagoons best reached by foot, boat or motorbike, and to stop and smell the blooming *broughtonia domingensis* without missing a do-or-die bus connection.

To extend your stay in Haiti instead, consider spending another night in Jacmel and visiting the beaches west of town. The next day return to Port-au-Prince and from there visit the Barbancourt Rum Distillery near Pétionville for touring and tasting.

If hiking suits you, make your next stop Kenscoff, a highlands resort town that many of the country's elite retire to in July and August to escape the heat. The air up at Kenscoff is refreshingly cool and there are many hiking trails in the area. See the Around Port-au-Prince chapter for additional ideas.

PLANNING
When to Go

The best time to visit Hispaniola is a matter of personal taste. Although the island's average temperatures vary little from month to month, Hispaniola has distinct, localized dry and rainy seasons that vary around the island. If the purpose of your trip is primarily to relax on a beach and soak up sun, make sure to check when the local dry season is for the area you will be visiting. See each country's Facts for the Visitor chapter for particulars.

Bear in mind that it can be very difficult to find a hotel room in some cities during certain times of the year. The busy tourist season in the Dominican Republic is from early December through Easter Sunday; in Haiti, it's especially busy around Carnival in February.

Maps

International Travel Maps (☎ 604-879-3621, fax 604-879-4521, www.nas.com/~travelmaps), a division of ITMB Publishing Ltd, 345 West Broadway, Vancouver, BC, Canada V5Y 1P8, publishes an excellent map of the Dominican Republic (1:500,000). Hildebrand's Travel Map, a division of Karto+Grafik, Verlagsgesellschaft mbH, Schonberger Weg 15, Frankfurt/Main, Germany, 60488, publishes a very good map of Hispaniola (1:816,000) that includes inset maps of Santo Domingo, Port-au-Prince and Cap-Haïtien.

Neither of these maps is available on the island, and the country maps that are available tend to be of very poor quality; see the Haiti section for a couple of possible recent exceptions. If you intend to travel about the island, don't count on being able to obtain good country maps upon arrival.

Also be advised that maps for Hispaniola's cities and towns are difficult to come by. Most of the city and town maps found in this guide were created by Lonely Planet cartographers using base maps drawn by the author or maps that were obtained with great difficulty.

What to Bring

Clothing Be prepared to dress conservatively while visiting Hispaniola; it's better to be overdressed despite the heat than to offend local sensibilities by strolling through town in swimming trunks or halter tops. In general, the Dominican Republic is somewhat more conservative than Haiti: in the DR, men tend to wear dress shirts and trousers, and women prefer dresses or skirts to pants; in Haiti, men tend to wear T-shirts and jeans (except on Sundays, when they wear dress shirts), and women wear second-hand dresses from the USA or T-shirts and skirts.

> ## Floss It
>
> For the cost of a crummy cigar, you can buy a vacation-saving item called dental floss. It's cheap, it's light, it's strong and it's outrageously useful. Got a fishhook but no line? Try green waxed dental floss. Need to secure a mosquito net? Reach for the floss. Forgot to pack a clothesline? String up a line of floss instead. Got a tear in your jeans or a rip in your pack? A little dental floss and a sewing needle and life goes on.
>
> Dental floss comes in 50m and 100m lengths and is sold in nifty little cases complete with built-in cutters. Some say it can even remove decay-causing material from between teeth and under gums! Now in cinnamon, mint and grape flavors.
>
>

Short dresses and short pants are items that identify the tourist; in fact, short pants are not permitted in government buildings and they're frowned upon in churches. Haitians and Dominicans never wear beachwear away from the beach or the swimming pool, and you should follow that custom; bring light cotton wraps and T-shirts that can be put on over swimsuits.

The tropical sun is incredibly deceiving, especially to snorkelers and body surfers who can't feel its heat. Just 15 minutes of direct, unprotected exposure to the tropical sun can result in a trip-ruining burn. If you burn easily, consider wearing light cotton shirts with long sleeves and donning light cotton pants.

In the highlands you will need warmer clothing – bring heavier pants such as jeans and a cold-weather jacket, possibly even a sweater. A waterproof, loose-fitting poncho can be your best friend as it tends to rain a lot in the mountains on Hispaniola. Hiking boots are recommended, although sturdy walking shoes will do for shorter excursions.

Other Items Due to the ferocity of the tropical sun, a hat, sunglasses and sunblock are essential items. Most toiletries are readily available on Hispaniola, but some can be very expensive. Shampoo, soap, toothpaste, toilet paper, razors and shaving cream are easy to buy anywhere but in the smallest villages. To save money and for convenience, bring your own contact lens solution, feminine napkins, tampons, contraceptives and deodorant.

Don't forget the all-important insect repellent containing deet (see the Health section for details), which may be easier to find at home. Besides, if you buy it before you leave home, you'll have it when you need it.

Other useful items include a flashlight (with spare batteries) for nighttime strolls and for when the electricity fails at your budget hotel; a pocket knife; diving and/or snorkeling equipment; fishing equipment; a small sewing kit; a money belt or pouch; lip balm; and a pocket-size Spanish-English, French-English or Creole-English dictionary.

VISAS & DOCUMENTS

See the individual countries' Facts for the Visitor chapters for information on passports, visas, driver's licenses and other documents.

EMBASSIES & CONSULATES

An embassy is a mission from one government to another. A consulate is a mission in a foreign country that promotes the home country's business interests and protects its citizens. If you need help from your home government while in a foreign country, call upon your nearest consulate or the consular section of your embassy.

If you're in trouble while abroad, most consulates can help you by contacting relatives or friends, by suggesting reliable doctors or clinics, by providing a list of lawyers and so on. Consulates do not usually provide emergency funds or airline tickets home, and they rarely get deeply involved in legal matters.

For lists of embassies and consulates, see each country's Facts for the Visitor chapter.

CUSTOMS

Customs officers only get excited about a few things: drugs, weapons, explosives and unde-

clared currency. If you try to bring illegal drugs, explosives or any sort of firearm onto the island and are caught, you will be sent to prison. If you try to smuggle money onto the island and are caught, you will be imprisoned and your money will be confiscated.

Additionally, customs officers don't like it when someone tries to avoid paying import taxes. Import taxes are levied on property brought to the island for sale. If a customs officer checks your luggage and discovers that you've arrived with 25 brand-new Nikon cameras, you will be asked to pay import taxes.

In general, articles classified as 'personal luggage' – luggage that's for personal use – will not pose a problem in clearing customs. There are certain limits: You are not permitted to bring in more than 1 liter of alcohol or 200 cigarettes, and gift articles cannot have a total value exceeding US$100 without incurring import taxes.

MONEY
Currency & Exchange Rates

For details on the currencies of Haiti and the Dominican Republic and the current exchange rates, see Money in each country's Facts for the Visitor chapter.

Exchanging Money

It's safest to change money at a bank or an exchange office, although in Haiti that may mean having to wait in line for an hour. There is a black market in Haiti, and it consists of moneychangers who generally give better rates than the banks. They can be really handy if you are far from a bank, want to avoid the wait or if it's after banking hours. Be sure to count your money carefully.

There are moneychangers on the streets of the Dominican Republic as well, but here it's best to avoid them. They don't generally offer better rates than do the banks or exchange offices, and the wait to change money at these institutions is not as bad as in Haiti. Some of the finer hotels will also change money, though usually at an unfavorable rate.

Most banks exchange common foreign currencies (especially the US dollar, the

German mark and the French franc) and there are exchange offices in most cities. The exchange rates offered by the banks and the exchange offices generally don't differ much.

Traveler's Checks US-dollar traveler's checks are the most readily accepted on Hispaniola. Other types can be a problem, and getting any kind of traveler's checks cashed in villages and in the countryside can be a nightmare.

Also, be forewarned that it's often difficult or impossible to exchange traveler's checks on weekends. Always make sure to change money on a Friday, so that you'll be supplied with cash for the weekend.

ATMs Automated teller machines can now be found in many cities on Hispaniola. They often provide instructions in English and issue local currency debited against your home cash-card account or credit card. However, machines do break down. Don't depend on ATMs to supply all your local-cash needs. Have traveler's checks and/or a credit card for backup.

Costs

See each country's Facts for the Visitor chapter for details on costs. In general, Haiti is less expensive to visit than the Dominican Republic, but neither country is particularly inexpensive unless you take advantage of an airfare/accommodations package deal before leaving home.

Tipping

In general, residents of Hispaniola are poor tippers, and foreigners are generally regarded as good tippers. A tip of 5% is acceptable, a tip of 10% is considered generous and a tip of 15% is usually seen as excessive. Tips are rarely left in small eateries, although they're greatly appreciated. Beware that tips are often included in checks as a 'service fee.' See Tipping in the Facts for the Visitor chapter of each country for further details.

Bargaining

Bargaining is a common practice for many things in Hispaniola, and it's the rule for

handicrafts and items at open-air markets. Bear in mind that Haitians and Dominicans view most tourists as rich, and they jack up their prices accordingly. If you pay the first price quoted, you may pay many times the going rate. By haggling, you're simply trying to obtain the price a local would pay. See 'How to Bargain' in the Dominican Republic's Facts for the Visitor chapter for advice.

The price of a hotel room is usually set and fairly firm, but if you arrive during a quiet time of year or if the hotel doesn't appear to have many guests, it might be worth your while to haggle.

One good way of doing this is to ask for the room rate, pause when you hear the reply, and then ask if the hotel has any less-expensive rooms. If the answer is no, mention that the quoted rate exceeds your budget. Then, picking up your bags and moving toward the door, ask if the hotel might consider offering you a discount – say, 50% off the rack rate.

It never hurts to be bold, and while you may not get a room for half price, often you may get one for 20% or more below the going rate. If you say at the outset that you'd be staying several days or more, the desk clerk might be more inclined to reduce the standard rate.

POST & COMMUNICATIONS
Sending & Receiving Mail

Almost every city and town on the island has a post office where you can buy postage stamps and send or receive mail. However, the service is generally terrible, and in most cases you will arrive back in your home country *long* before your mail reaches its destination – if it ever does.

See each country's Post & Communications section for more details.

Telephone

Local calls are reasonably priced on the island, unless you're calling from a luxury hotel (which will likely charge a beefy service fee). International calls are generally very expensive, regardless of where the call originates. See each country's Telephone section for more details.

To call establishments listed in this guide from your home, follow the international calling procedures for your home telephone company, which will include dialing an access code for international service, then the country code, the area or city code and then the local number.

Fax

Many mid-range and most top-end hotels have fax machines, as do airlines, car rental companies, tourist offices and other businesses. When making reservations or asking for information, a fax is often the cheapest and most efficient way of going about it. The recipient will get written instructions, which makes translations easier and minimizes the chance for errors. Also, faxes usually take less time than voice calls, saving you money on telephone tolls.

Email & Internet Access

Haiti and the Dominican Republic are several years behind the USA, Canada and Europe in terms of email access and addresses. Due to the poor quality of telecommunications links between the island and the outside world, you can't count on being able to sign on even if you're traveling with a laptop and using international access numbers such as those provided by America Online and CompuServe.

As of late 1998, Internet cafés were beginning to make an appearance, using special telephone lines rarely found on the island. Also, the Dominican Republic's major telephone company was in the process of installing public Internet-access computers at many of its offices, some of which can now be used on a per-hour basis. By the time you visit, most of the island's cities and its tourist-popular towns should have Internet access.

INTERNET RESOURCES

The World Wide Web is a rich resource for travelers. You can research your trip, hunt down bargain airfares, book hotels, check on weather conditions or chat with locals and other travelers about the best places to visit (or avoid!).

There's no better place to start your Web explorations than the Lonely Planet website (www.lonelyplanet.com). Here you'll find succinct summaries on traveling to most places on earth, postcards from other travelers and the ThornTree bulletin board, where you can ask questions before you go or dispense advice when you get back. You can also find travel news and updates to many of our most popular guidebooks, and the sub-WWWay section links you to the most useful travel resources elsewhere on the Web. See also each country's Internet Resources section in this book for other specific websites.

The following are some additional websites that you might find useful in planning a trip to Hispaniola.

CIA World Factbook
www.odci.gov/cia/publications/pubs.html
This site offers a comprehensive view of each country in the world through facts and statistics on such topics as population, economy and government.

Library of Congress Catalogs
www.lcweb.loc.gov/catalog/online.html£word
Wondering what books have been published on Haiti and/or the Dominican Republic? This site can tell you.

US Department of Health,
Centers for Disease Control & Prevention
www.cdc.gov/travel/index.htm
This is the site for current health information for international travel. News of recent disease outbreaks and prevailing vaccine recommendations appear here.

US Department of State
www.state.gov/
This site addresses topics of importance to the international traveler, including the level of crime and the quality of health care in every country.

BOOKS

Information about bookstores throughout Hispaniola can be found in the regional chapters. Many of the books mentioned here are more easily found in developed countries than in either Haiti or the Dominican Republic. Also note that few books sold on the island are published in English.

The following books provide worthwhile background reading on Hispaniola and the Caribbean. For specific books about Haiti and the Dominican Republic, see Books in the Facts for the Visitor chapter of each country.

Guidebooks

If your stay on Hispaniola is part of an island-hopping adventure through the entire Caribbean, consider purchasing *The Caribbean & The Bahamas* by James Henderson, *Caribbean Islands Handbook* by Sarah Cameron or *Adventuring in the Caribbean* by Carol Fleming.

For information on the most satisfying diving and snorkeling sites in the region, see *Best Caribbean Diving* by Susanne and Stuart Cummings. In the same vein, *Best Dives of the Caribbean* by Joyce and Jon Huber is helpful.

Divers and snorkelers should check out Lonely Planet's *Pisces Guide to Caribbean Reef Ecology* by William Alevizon, *Field Guide to Coral Reefs: Caribbean and Florida* by Susan and Eugene Kaplan and *Coral Reef Fishes: Caribbean, Indian Ocean, and Pacific Ocean* by Ewald Lieske and Robert Myers.

Are you cruising to the Caribbean islands? Consider picking up a copy of *Caribbean by Cruise Ship* by Anne Vipond. The book is written specifically for the shipboard passenger, painting a vivid portrait of each island and its people, history and attractions.

If you're planning on walking across many of the islands, you'll be glad to know that Tim O'Keefe already has. His *Caribbean Afoot: A Hiking and Walking Guide to Twenty-Nine of the Caribbean's Best Islands* is as delightful to read as it is informative.

History & Politics

There are scores of books on the history and politics of the Caribbean. Those titles mentioned here are but a fraction of the whole. They are listed in chronological order, the most recent titles appearing first.

Americas: The Changing Face of Latin America and the Caribbean by Peter Winn (1995) discusses the region's economic and political systems, racial and ethnic identities, the influence of the Catholic Church and a whole lot more.

The title of Jan Rogozinski's 1992 book, *A Brief History of the Caribbean: From the Arawak and the Carib to the Present,* says it all, although 'brief' is a slight misnomer: it's a well-referenced, well-written 324 pages.

The Modern Caribbean is a 1989 collection of 13 original essays by experts in Caribbean studies. Edited by Franklin Knight and Colin Palmer, the essays examine the region's complexities of race, politics, language and environment.

The Spanish Caribbean: From Columbus to Castro by LL Cripps, published in 1979, presents a concise history of the Spanish Caribbean from the perspective of a Marxist historian.

Caribbean Patterns by Sir Harold Mitchell, published in 1972, remains one of the best reference guides for gaining an understanding of the history and current political status of nearly every island group in the Caribbean.

Piracy

There are many books written about the pirates of the Caribbean. Among the better ones are *The Early Spanish Main* by Carl Sauer, *A General History of the Pyrates* by Daniel Defoe and *The Loss of the El Dorado* and *The Overcrowded Barracoon*, both by VS Naipaul.

The Buccaneers of America by AO Exquemelin recounts some of the most remarkable assaults committed by French and English pirates against the Spaniards, and it's written by one of the 17th-century buccaneers who witnessed them.

The Quicksilver Galleons is a fascinating read by Pedro Borrell about the salvaging of the Spanish galleons *Nuestra Señora de Guadalupe* and *El Conde de Tolosa*. It contains a treasure trove of photos of the riches recovered from the two historic wrecks.

Last but not least, Barry Burg addresses a little-known facet of pirate life in his 1995 release, *Sodomy and the Pirate Tradition:*

English Sea Rovers in the Seventeenth-Century Caribbean.

Literature

A diverse legacy of literature has come out of the Caribbean, and these titles will serve as an introduction for the new Caribbean reader.

If I Could Write This in Fire: An Anthology of Literature from the Caribbean, edited by Pamela Maria Smorkaloff, contains 15 selections that focus on the underlying themes of the region's literature: the plantation, colonial education, rural and urban life, exile and the diaspora.

Caribbean (Traveller's Literary Companion), edited by James Ferguson and Jason Wilson, offers excerpts from novels, short stories, poems, and travel writing. Among the authors whose work is sampled are Graham Greene, Ernest Hemingway and VS Naipaul.

Caribbean Women Writers, edited by Harold Bloom, contains essays by women of African, European and mixed ancestry who write of their motherlands, of exile, of folk traditions and of formal English schooling. Not a book for light thinkers.

The Farming of Bones by Edwidge Dantcat is a sobering novel by a Haitian-American woman. It's set in Hispaniola in 1937 during a bloody eruption of the endless hostility between Haiti and the Dominican Republic.

Cooking

The Caribbean is a culinary melting pot, in which influences from Africa, Europe and East Asia are mixed in a rich array of native produce and seafood. Not surprisingly, many books have been written on the food of the region.

Caribbean Cooking: The Best Dishes of the Islands, from Soup to Bread to Dessert, by John Demers, is perhaps the best of the bunch. It contains more than 200 fabulous recipes, from drinks to appetizers to entrées and desserts. Each recipe is accompanied by easy-to-follow instructions.

Dorinda's Taste of the Caribbean: African-Influenced Recipes from the Islands by Dorinda Hafner is another top-notch work. A product of her PBS-TV cooking show, *A Taste of the Caribbean,* the book includes more than a hundred recipes for delicious traditional Caribbean dishes.

Other praiseworthy Caribbean cookbooks include *Cook, Eat, Cha Cha Cha: Festive New World Recipes* by Philip Bellber and Ian Reeves, *The Complete Book of Caribbean Cooking* by Elizabeth Lambert Ortiz and *Caribbean and African Cooking* by Rosamund Grant and Maya Angelou.

FILMS

Many films, ranging from the lowly *Porno Holocaust* to the widely acclaimed *The Godfather: Part II,* have been shot in full or in part on Hispaniola. The following is a partial list of those films.

1492: Conquest of Paradise: Released in 1992 to celebrate the 500th anniversary of Columbus' discovery of the New World, this big-budget film shows some of the disastrous effects the Europeans had on the Taíno Indians.

The Serpent and the Rainbow: In this 1988 thriller, a chemist visits Haiti searching for a rumored drug that renders the recipient totally paralyzed but conscious. His investigation exposes him to the social chaos that is Haiti during the revolution that ousted dictator Papa Doc.

Azucar Amarga (Bitter Sugar): This Spanish-language film, released in 1996 and set around a love story, attempts to open the viewer's eyes to Fidel Castro's failed socialist utopia and shows how the most loyal of his followers are inevitably turned into exiles in their own homeland.

Sorcerer: Based on the French film *Wages of Fear,* this 1977 thriller follows the trials of a handful of desperate men who are given the chance to escape from a remote site deep in the Amazon in return for transporting crates of unstable dynamite through miles of jungle in ancient trucks.

NEWSPAPERS & MAGAZINES

Some international newspapers, such as the *International Herald Tribune, The Times* (of London) and *USA Today,* plus leading magazines such as *Newsweek, Time* and *The*

Economist can be found at pharmacies in the island's largest cities. However, they usually cost about three times what you'd pay for them at home.

There are several magazines about the Caribbean that can get you acquainted with the region before you arrive. *Caribbean Travel & Life* is a glossy, bi-monthly magazine that covers travel throughout the Caribbean. *Caribbean World* is a similar magazine, published quarterly and with an up-market focus. *Caribbean Week* is a high-quality, bi-weekly news magazine that covers travel, politics, fashion, economics and trends throughout the region.

For periodicals published in Haiti and the Dominican Republic, see Newspapers & Magazines in the Facts for the Visitor chapter of each country.

RADIO & TV

There are nearly 200 radio stations and 20 commercial TV stations on the island. Satellite TV, once available only in the most expensive hotels on the island, is increasingly standard fare among mid-range hotels as well. Due to the island's proximity to the USA, even TV sets that aren't hooked up to satellite dishes often receive American channels.

PHOTOGRAPHY & VIDEO
Film & Equipment

Common print film manufactured by Kodak and Fuji is readily available in areas frequented by tourists, but it usually costs twice what you'd pay in North America. Slide film is considerably rarer, usually limited to Kodak's Ektachrome and Agfachrome.

More important, film is heat sensitive, but it seems many Hispaniolans are unaware of this fact. Often a store's entire stock of film will be on display in the front window – directly exposed to the intense tropical sun. Film that's been 'stored' this way usually produces washed-out images.

Remember: Film remains heat sensitive inside your camera. Never leave your camera sitting in the sun, and before and after you've used a roll of film, try to keep it in a cool place. Many people make the mistake of leaving film in glove compartments, which can get very hot.

Camera equipment is available on the island, but like film it tends to be pricey and limited in selection. If taking photographs is important to you, bring everything you think you'll need with you. Same goes with batteries. Because batteries lose power when heated, those found on shelves in the tropics often have lost half their life before they're purchased.

Photography

The greatest potential disappointment when you get processed photographs of your trip is a washed-out look. This is most often due to overexposure. The bright tropical light can fool even the most sophisticated light-metering systems.

To avoid this problem, consider purchasing a polarizing filter. A polarizing filter is primarily used to darken a pale blue sky and to remove reflections from glass and water surfaces. No serious photographer would visit an island without one.

The filter mounts on your lens and is rotated within the filter ring. Its position determines the effectiveness of the polarizer. At a right angle to the sun the effect is greatest, heightening the contrasts so that the subject is clearly visible – removing, for example, the glare off the ocean and bringing the sailboat you're aiming at into sharp focus.

If you intend to take most of your photos outside during daylight hours, consider purchasing a 'slow' film, which will provide the best color rendition. Fujichrome Velvia is the pro's choice among slide films, followed closely by Kodachrome 25 and 64. For print film, avoid film with an ISO higher than 100.

A common mistake photographers make is failing to compensate for the contrast between dark faces and bright backgrounds. This failure generally produces a featureless black head against a correctly exposed background. Most new cameras these days have a fill-in flash that, if the subject is close enough, can eliminate this problem. If you aren't already familiar with this feature on your camera, now's the time to learn how to use it.

Video

Video cameras and tapes are widely available in photo supply stores in the island's largest cities and in towns that receive many foreign visitors. Prices are significantly higher than in North America or Europe. VHS is standard.

Restrictions

It is illegal to take pictures in the island's airports and of police stations and penal institutions. Also, many police officers do not like having their pictures taken, and they have the authority to arrest you for photographing them without authorization. Additionally, you can expect to have your film confiscated and many questions asked if you take any photos inside a bank or government building.

Photographing People

In general, Hispaniolans enjoy having their pictures taken and will be happy to pose for your camera. However, just as you might not enjoy having someone photograph you without asking, you should ask permission first. This is especially true of people who are working: women selling in the markets very often disapprove because they dislike being photographed in their dirty work clothes. Men carrying large loads on hand-pulled carts can also resent having a camera poked at them while they toil.

Increasingly, you will be asked to pay for the photo. This is especially true in areas that see heavy tourist traffic. Many locals have grown tired of being treated like objects of art or even zoo animals, and have taken the attitude that they deserve compensation for being 'framed.'

If you intend to take lots of photos of Hispaniolans, consider bringing a Polaroid camera in addition to your 35mm camera. By presenting a stranger with a photo of him- or herself, you can usually eliminate whatever tension may have initially existed between you and your subject and can now capture a warm and welcome expression.

If local people make any sign of being offended by your desire to photograph them, you should put your camera away and apologize immediately, both out of decency and for your own safety.

Airport Security

It's a good idea to avoid sending your film through airport X-ray machines. While most won't damage your film, there's no point in taking the chance. Most security personnel will hand-inspect your film if you ask them to, removing the necessity of having it X-rayed. Don't forget to have your camera hand-inspected if it has film inside.

Some people – particularly sales personnel at camera stores – swear by lead-lined film pouches, which, incidentally, you can buy at most camera stores. Be advised the pouches are heavy and expensive, and nine times out of 10 when X-ray machine operators see one on the screen, they do two things: First, they crank up the X-rays to penetrate the lead, and second, they nearly always instruct a security officer to hand-inspect the pouch.

TIME

Hispaniola is four hours behind Greenwich Mean Time. In autumn and winter, this means it's one hour ahead of New York, Miami and Toronto. However, the island does not adjust for daylight-saving time as do the USA and Canada; hence it's in the same time zone as New York, Miami and Toronto from the first Sunday in April to the last Sunday in October.

Here's the time in some other cities when it's noon on Hispaniola:

City	Summer	Winter
Paris, Rome	6 pm	5 pm
London	5 pm	4 pm
GMT/UTC	4 pm	4 pm
New York, Toronto	noon	11 am
Chicago, New Orleans	11 am	10 am
San Francisco, LA	9 am	8 am
Perth, Hong Kong	1 am*	midnight*
Sydney, Melbourne	3 am*	2 am*
Auckland	4 am*	2 am*

*next day

ELECTRICITY

Hispaniola uses the same electrical system as the USA and Canada: electrical current is 115 to 125 volts AC, 60 Hz, with two- and three-pin, flat-pronged plugs. Transformers and adapters are necessary to run electrical appliances brought from Europe; these can be bought at most major airports.

WEIGHTS & MEASURES

Haiti and the Dominican Republic use the metric system. For conversion information, see the inside back cover of this book. Because of the great commercial influence of the USA, you may find that ounces, pounds, feet, miles and US gallons are used informally, at village markets for instance. Officially, however, everything's metric.

LAUNDRY

The largest cities have laundries and dry-cleaning shops where you can leave your clothes to be cleaned; the most convenient ones are mentioned in this book. Often you can have your laundry back in a day; dry cleaning usually takes at least overnight. Outside the large cities, your best bet is to ask about laundry service through your hotel.

TOILETS

In a hot climate, where your body loses lots of moisture through perspiration, you have less frequent need of toilets. This is good, as public toilets are virtually nonexistent. Use the ones in cafés, restaurants and your hotel.

Some of the luxury buses are equipped with toilets. The first one to use it gets a clean toilet, and it goes downhill after that. Bus station toilets can be indecent.

HEALTH
Predeparture Preparations

Ideally, you should make sure you're as healthy as possible before you start traveling. If you're going for more than a couple of weeks, make sure your teeth are OK; there are lots of dentists on the island you would not want working on you. If you wear glasses, take a spare pair and your prescription.

Health Insurance A travel insurance policy to cover theft, loss and medical problems is a wise idea. Travel agencies sell them; STA Travel and other student travel organizations usually offer good value.

Some policies specifically exclude 'dangerous activities,' which can include scuba diving, motorcycling and even trekking. If such activities are on your agenda, be sure to read the fine print carefully.

Medical Kit If you're planning on being very active during your stay on Hispaniola, it's prudent to take a small first-aid kit with adhesive bandages, a sterilized gauze bandage, an antiseptic agent, a fever thermometer, tweezers and scissors.

If you're planning long hikes, consider also taking Caladryl (which is good for sunburn, minor burns and itchy bites); aspirin, ibuprofen or acetaminophen for pain or fever; insect repellent containing deet; and an antihistamine such as Benadryl for colds and allergies.

Don't forget a full supply of any medication you're already taking; the prescription might be difficult to match on the island.

Illness Prevention Specific immunizations are not normally required for travel to Hispaniola. All the same, it's a good idea to be up to date on your tetanus, polio and typhoid-paratyphoid immunizations. If you plan to stay for more than a few weeks in the region and you're adventurous in your eating, an immune globulin shot and/or Havrix are also recommended for protection against infectious hepatitis. You only need a yellow fever certificate to enter the country if, within the last six months, you have been to a country where yellow fever is present.

If you're staying for more than a couple of weeks, you also might consider taking chloroquine to prevent malaria. No other antimalarial drugs are needed. Be aware that chloroquine requires a prescription and that it must be taken at least one week before entering a malarial area to be effective. See Malaria, below, for further discussion.

Food spoils easily in the tropics, mosquitoes roam freely and sanitation is not always the best, so you must take special care to protect yourself from illness. The most important steps you can take are to be careful about what you eat and drink, to stay away from mosquitoes (or at least make them stay away from you) and to practice safe sex.

If you come down with a serious illness, be very careful to find a competent doctor and don't be afraid to get a second opinion. You may want to telephone your doctor at home for consultation as well. In some cases it may be best to end your trip and fly home for treatment, difficult as this may be.

Basic Rules

Food & Water Food can be contaminated by bacteria, viruses and/or parasites at any point when it is harvested, shipped, handled, washed (if the water is contaminated) or prepared. Cooking, peeling and/or washing food in pure water is the way to get rid of the germs. To avoid gastrointestinal diseases, avoid salads, uncooked vegetables and unpasteurized milk or milk products (including cheese). Make sure the food you eat has been freshly cooked and is still hot. Do not eat raw or rare meat, fish or shellfish. Peel fruit yourself with clean hands and a clean knife.

Tap water in Haiti and the Dominican Republic is extremely unhealthy. Bottled water is widely available and reasonably priced. Use it for drinking, washing food, brushing your teeth and making ice. Tea, coffee and other hot beverages should be made with bottled water. Ice served at most restaurants is safe. At roadside stands and other cheap eateries, ask for no ice.

Canned or bottled beverages are safe, including soda, beer, wine and liquor.

Protection Against Mosquitoes Many serious tropical diseases are spread by infected mosquitoes. In the entire Caribbean, malaria is present throughout the year only in Haiti and the Dominican Republic. If you protect yourself against mosquito bites, your travels will be both safer and more enjoyable.

Insect Repellent

The most effective ingredient in insect repellent is deet. You can buy repellent with 15% to 90% of this ingredient. Lotions are best for direct contact with the skin, while pump sprays are best for applying repellent to clothing.

If you find that deet irritates your skin, consider using a lower strength; most people find repellent containing 30% deet to be effective and user friendly. Everyone should avoid getting deet in their eyes, on their lips and on other sensitive parts. Because deet can dissolve plastic, try not to get it on camera equipment, plastic eyewear and so on.

Deet can be toxic to children and shouldn't be used on their skin. Instead, try Avon's Skin So Soft, which has insect-repellent properties and isn't toxic. Camping stores often sell insect repellents such as Green Ban that don't contain any toxins, but some people find them to be less effective than deet-based repellents. You might want to try both.

You can also use mosquito coils. They burn like incense but release a smoke that insects hate. Be sure to follow instructions that come with the coils, as the smoke can be harmful when coils are used without adequate ventilation.

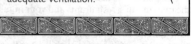

Some mosquitoes feed during the day, others at night. In general, they're most bothersome when the weather is not too hot – especially in the evening and early morning, and on overcast days. There are many more mosquitoes in lowland and coastal regions and in the countryside than there are in cities and in highland areas.

Mosquitoes seem to be attracted more to dark colors than to light, so in mosquito-infested areas wear light-colored long trousers, socks, a long-sleeved shirt and a hat. Mosquitoes also seem to be attracted by scents such as those in perfume, cologne, lotions, hair spray and so on, so avoid using these products if possible.

Sleep in screened rooms or beneath mosquito netting, making sure to dispose of the little suckers who somehow get in there with you. Check to make sure screens are intact, and that all openings to the outside are either screened or blocked.

Use insect repellent that has at least a 20% but no more than a 30% concentration of deet on clothing and exposed skin. Repellents with higher concentrations of deet work longer, but are also more likely to cause allergic reactions.

Medical Problems & Treatment

Traveler's Diarrhea The food in a different country has different bacteria from what your digestive system is used to – germs that your immune system may not be prepared to combat. If you plunge right into the local culture and eat lots of food with high concentrations of these different bacteria, your body's natural defenses will be overwhelmed and you may get sick.

Travelers to many less-developed countries suffer from traveler's diarrhea (TD), a condition defined as having twice as many (or more) unformed bowel movements as normal; typically one has four or five watery stools per day.

Symptoms In addition to frequent watery stools, other possible symptoms include abdominal cramps, nausea, fever, malaise, a bloated feeling and urgency of bowel movements. The disease usually hits within the first week of travel, but it may hit at any time and may hit more than once during a trip. A bout of TD typically lasts three or four days, but may be shorter or longer.

Prevention Epidemiologists recommend that you *do not* take medicines for TD prophylaxis; that is, don't take any medicine just in the hope that it will prevent a case of the disease. Taking prophylactic medicines such as antibiotics, Pepto-Bismol or Lomotil can actually make it *easier* for you to get the disease later on by killing off the benign digestive bacteria that help to protect you from the 'foreign' bacteria.

Instead, observe the rules of safe eating and drinking, and don't overdo it early in your trip. For the first week after arrival, be extremely careful and conservative in your eating habits, avoid overeating or eating heavy or spicy food, don't get overtired and don't drink lots of alcoholic beverages or coffee.

Treatment If you come down with a case of TD, take it easy, with no physical exertion; stay in bed if you can. Be especially careful to replace fluids and electrolytes (potassium, sodium, etc) by drinking caffeine-free soft drinks or glasses of fruit juice (high in potassium) with honey and a pinch of salt added, plus a glass of pure water with a quarter teaspoon of sodium bicarbonate (baking soda) added; weak tea, preferably unsweetened and without milk, is all right.

Avoid dairy products. Eat only salted crackers or dry toast for a day or so. After that, eat easily digested foods that are not fatty or overly acidic. Yogurt with live cultures is particularly good as it helps to repopulate the bowel with benign digestive organisms. When you feel better, be particularly careful about what you eat and drink from then on.

As for medications, it's best if you cure yourself without them. If you must have some chemical help, go to a doctor, who may recommend one of the following treatments as described in the US Public Health Service's book, *Health Information for International Travel*. Treatments and dosages should be determined by a competent medical doctor who can tell you about side effects and contraindications; those noted here are the regular ones for otherwise healthy adults (*not* children) and are for information only.

- Bismuth subsalicylate (Pepto-Bismol) – One ounce of liquid or the equivalent in tablets every half hour for four hours. This treatment is not recommended if symptoms last more than 48 hours, or if you have high fever, blood in the stool, kidney problems or are allergic to salicylates. Children under the age of two should not be given this medicine. Your tongue may turn black after taking Pepto-Bismol. This is a harmless side effect.

- Diphenoxylate and loperamide (Lomotil, Imodium) – These are antimotility agents made from synthetic opiate derivatives. They temporarily slow down the diarrhea but do not cure it, they increase the risk of getting TD again, and they can make you sluggish or sleepy. They should not be used if you have a high fever or blood in the stool, or if you are driving a motor vehicle or operating machinery (your alertness is impaired). In any case, don't use them for longer than two full days.

- Doxycycline (100mg twice daily); or trimethoprim (200mg twice daily); or trimethoprim (160mg)/sulfamethoxazole (800mg once daily) – These are antibiotics that may be required if there are three or more loose stools in an eight-hour period, especially with nausea, vomiting, abdominal cramps and fever.

Heatstroke Only slightly less common than traveler's diarrhea are the illnesses caused by excessive heat and dehydration. These are more dangerous because they display fewer symptoms.

Symptoms If you exercise excessively in heat you're not accustomed to, or if you fail to replace lost fluids and electrolytes (salt, potassium, etc), you can suffer from dizziness, weakness, headaches, nausea and greater susceptibility to other illnesses, such as traveler's diarrhea. This is heat exhaustion, heat prostration or, in severe cases, heatstroke. In this last case, exposure to intense heat can cause convulsions and coma.

Prevention Protect yourself against heat-related diseases by taking special care to drink lots of fluids. If you urinate infrequently and in small amounts, you're not drinking enough fluids. If you feel tired and have a headache, you're not drinking enough fluids. Don't just drink when you're thirsty; make it a habit to drink frequently, whether you're thirsty or not.

Alcohol, coffee and tea are diuretics – they make you urinate and lose fluids. They are not a cure for dehydration; rather, they're part of the problem. Drink pure water, fruit juices and soft drinks instead; go easy on the beer. Salty food is good to eat in hot climates as the salt helps your body retain fluids.

Other measures to take against the heat: Don't overdo it. Don't overexert yourself. Wear light cotton clothing that breathes and cools you; wear a hat and sunglasses. Allow yourself frequent rest breaks in the shade and give your body a chance to balance itself. Use sunblock to prevent bad sunburn. Be doubly cautious if you spend time near or on the water, as the sun's glare from sand and water can double your exposure.

Treatment Treating heatstroke requires lowering the body temperature immediately. Put the victim in the shade and remove any excess clothing. Soak the heatstroke victim with cold water – immersing the person in a tub of cold water is even better, if possible. If cold water is not available, fan the victim. Seek medical attention as soon as possible.

Fungal Infections Hot-weather fungal infections are most likely to occur on the scalp, between the toes or fingers (athlete's foot), in the groin (jock itch or crotch rot) and on the body (ringworm). You get ringworm – which is a fungal infection, not an actual worm – from infected animals or by walking on damp areas such as showers and bathroom floors. Medicine is required to treat a fungal infection. An antifungal powder or cream, such as those generally available without a prescription, will usually do the job.

Other Illnesses

Though you're unlikely to contract anything more than an unpleasant bout of traveler's diarrhea, you should be informed about the symptoms and treatments of these other diseases just in case. Those listed here exist on Hispaniola throughout the year.

Dengue Fever Symptoms include the fast onset of high fever, severe frontal headache and pain in muscles and joints; there may be nausea and vomiting, and a skin rash may develop about three to five days after the first symptoms, spreading from the torso to arms, legs and face. It is possible to have subclinical dengue (that is, a 'mild' case of it) and also to contract dengue hemorrhagic fever, a very serious and potentially fatal disease.

Dengue is spread by mosquitoes. Risk of contraction, though low for the average traveler, is highest during periods of heavy rain, several hours after daybreak and before dusk, and on overcast days. There are four different dengue viruses, but no medicines to combat them.

There is no effective treatment for dengue. The disease is usually self-limiting, which means that the body cures itself. If you are generally healthy and have a healthy immune system, the disease may be unpleasant but it is rarely serious. To prevent against getting dengue, see the section Protection Against Mosquitoes, above.

Dysentery There are two types of dysentery, both of which are characterized by diarrhea containing blood and/or mucus. A stool test is necessary to determine which type you have.

Bacillary dysentery – the most common variety – is short, sharp and nasty but rarely persistent. It hits suddenly and lays you out with fever, nausea, cramps and diarrhea, but it is self-limiting. Treatment is the same as for traveler's diarrhea; as it's caused by bacteria, the disease responds well to antibiotics if needed.

Amebic dysentery is caused by amebic parasites and is more dangerous. It builds up slowly, cannot be starved out, gets worse if untreated and can permanently damage your intestines. Do not have anyone other than a doctor diagnose your symptoms and administer treatment.

Giardiasis This is caused by a parasite named *Giardia lamblia*, and it's contracted by eating fecally contaminated food or beverages or by contact with a surface that has been similarly contaminated. Symptoms usually last for more than five days (perhaps months!), may be mild or serious, and may include diarrhea, abdominal cramps, fatigue, weight loss, flatulence, loss of appetite and/or nausea. If you have gastrointestinal gripes for a length of time, talk to a doctor and have a stool sample analyzed for giardia.

Hepatitis Hepatitis A (formerly called infectious hepatitis) is the most common travel-acquired illness that can be prevented by vaccination. Protection can be provided in two ways, either with the antibody immune globulin or with a vaccine called Havrix.

Havrix provides long-term immunity (possibly more than 10 years) after an initial course of two injections and a booster at one year. It may be more expensive than immune globulin (also called gammaglobulin), but it certainly has many advantages, including length of protection and ease of administration. Finish your shots at least three weeks before your trip if you want full protection when you arrive.

Immune globulin is not a vaccination but a ready-made antibody that has proven very successful in reducing the chances of hepatitis infection. Because it may interfere with the development of immunity, it should not be given until at least 10 days after administration of the last vaccine needed; it should also be given as close as possible to departure because it is at its most effective in the first few weeks after administration and the effectiveness tapers off gradually between three and six months.

Hepatitis is spread by contaminated food. The symptoms are fever, chills, headache, fatigue, feelings of weakness and aches and pains, followed by loss of appetite, nausea, vomiting, abdominal pain, dark urine, light-colored feces and jaundiced skin. The whites of the eyes may also turn yellow. In some cases victims may feel unwell, tired, have no appetite, experience aches and pains and be jaundiced. You should seek medical advice, but in general there is not much you can do apart from rest, drink lots of fluids, eat lightly and avoid fatty foods.

Hepatitis B, which used to be called serum hepatitis, is spread through contact with infected blood, blood products or bodily fluids, for example through sexual contact, unsterilized needles and blood transfusions. Other risk situations include having a shave or tattoo in a local shop, or having your ears pierced. The symptoms of type B are much the same as type A except that they are more severe and may lead to irreparable liver damage or even liver cancer.

Although there is no treatment for hepatitis B, an effective prophylactic vaccine is readily available in most countries. The immunization schedule requires two injections at least a month apart followed by a third dose five months after the second. Persons who should receive a hepatitis B vaccination include anyone who anticipates contact with blood or other bodily secretions, either as a health care worker or through sexual contact with the local population, particularly those who intend to stay in the region for a long period of time.

Hepatitis Non-A Non-B is a blanket term formerly used for several different strains of hepatitis, which have now been separately identified. Hepatitis C is similar to B but is less common. Hepatitis D (the 'delta particle') is also similar to B and always occurs in concert with it; its occurrence is currently limited to IV-drug users. Hepatitis E, however, is similar to hepatitis A and is spread in the same manner, through water or food contamination.

Tests are available for these strands, but are very expensive. Travelers shouldn't be too paranoid about this apparent proliferation of hepatitis strains; they are fairly rare (so far) and following the same precautions as for A and B should be all that's necessary to avoid them.

Sexually Transmitted Diseases Sexual contact with an infected sexual partner spreads these diseases. While abstinence is the only 100% preventative, using condoms and otherwise observing safe-sex procedures is usually effective.

Gonorrhea and syphilis are the most common of these diseases: sores, blisters or rashes around the genitals, discharges or pain when urinating are common symptoms. Symptoms may be less marked or not observed at all in women.

Syphilis symptoms eventually disappear completely, but the disease continues and can cause severe problems in later years. The treatment of gonorrhea and syphilis is by antibiotics.

There are numerous other sexually transmitted diseases, for most of which effective treatment is available. However, there is no cure for herpes and there is also no cure for HIV/AIDS. Abstinence is the only effective preventative; using condoms is next best.

HIV/AIDS can be spread through infected blood transfusions, and most developing countries cannot afford to screen blood for transfusions properly. HIV/AIDS can also be spread by dirty needles – vaccinations, acupuncture and tattooing are potentially as dangerous as intravenous drug use if the equipment is not clean.

Malaria This is the one disease that everyone fears and the one about which you must make an important decision. Symptoms may include jaundice (a yellow cast to the skin and/or eyes), general malaise, headaches, fever and chills, bed sweats and anemia. Symptoms of the disease may appear as early as eight days after infection, or as late as several months after you return from your trip. You can contract malaria even if you've taken medicines to protect yourself.

Malaria is spread by mosquitoes, which bite mostly between dusk and dawn. Risk of infection is low in the major resort areas and in the highlands, and it's lower during dry periods than during periods of heavy rain. But it is fair to say that somewhere on the island you will encounter mosquitoes. They may or may not carry infectious diseases.

The best way to protect yourself against malaria is to protect yourself against mosquito bites (see that section above). You can also take medicines to protect against malarial infection, usually chloroquine phosphate (Aralen) or hydroxychloroquine sulfate (Plaquenil), though other medicines may be indicated for specific individuals. You must consult a doctor on the use of these medicines, and get a prescription to buy them.

Begin taking the medicine *one or two weeks before you arrive* in a malarial area, continue taking it while you're there, and also for a month after you leave the area, according to your doctor's instructions. Taking medicine does not absolutely guarantee that you will not contract malaria, however.

Talk to your doctor about whether or not it's worthwhile for you to take an antimalarial. Most malaria medicine increases a person's susceptibility to sunburn; there are other risks as well, especially for pregnant women. Call a hospital or clinic that specializes in tropical diseases for further details. If you think you've contracted malaria, seek medical aid.

In the USA, call the Centers for Disease Control's toll-free telephone information system (☎ 800-526-6367) or the CDC Malaria Hotline (☎ 404-332-4555); in the UK, the Medical Advisory Service for Travellers Abroad (MASTA) of the London School of Hygeine and Tropical Medicine (☎ 0891-224100); in Australia, the Traveller's Medicine and Vaccination Centre in Sydney (☎ 02-9221-7133). Check out the very good information and guidance on the CDC's useful website at www.cdc.gov/travel/index.htm. Whether or not you take medicine, do be careful to protect yourself against mosquito bites.

Rabies The rabies virus is spread through bites by infected animals, or (rarely) through broken skin (from scratches or licks) or through the mucous membranes (as from breathing rabid-bat-contaminated air in a cave, for instance). Typical signs of a rabid animal are mad or uncontrolled behavior, inability to eat, biting at anything and everything and frothing at the mouth.

If any animal (but especially a dog) bites you, assume you have been exposed to rabies until you are certain this is not the case – there are no second chances. First, immediately wash the wound with lots of soap and water – this is very important! If it is possible and safe to do so, try to capture the animal alive, and give it to local health officials who can determine whether or not it's rabid.

Begin rabies immunization shots as soon as possible; if you are taking antimalarial medicine, be sure to mention this to the doctor because antimalarial medicines can interfere with the effectiveness of rabies vaccine. Rabies is a potentially fatal disease, but it can be cured by prompt and proper treatment.

Schistosomiasis This parasitic worm makes its way into the bodies of certain tiny freshwater snails and then into humans swimming, wading or otherwise touching the infected water in pools and ponds. Two or three weeks after your dip, you may experience fever, weakness, headache, loss of appetite, loss of weight, pain in the gut and/or pain in the joints and muscles. You may have nausea and/or coughing. Six to eight weeks after infection, evidence of the worm can be found in the stools.

After this very unpleasant month or two, diagnosis can correctly identify schistosomiasis as the culprit, and you can get rid of it quickly and effectively by taking an inexpensive medicine. To guard against the illness, don't swim in fresh water that may be infected by sewage or other pollution. If you do expose your skin to water that is infected with schistosomiasis, rub the skin vigorously with a towel and/or rub alcohol on it.

Typhoid Fever This serious disease is spread by contaminated food and beverages and has symptoms similar to those of traveler's diarrhea. If you get it, you should have close supervision by a competent doctor for a while and perhaps spend a short time in the hospital. Inoculation can give you some protection but is not 100% effective. If diagnosed and treated early, typhoid can be cured effectively.

Hospitals & Clinics

Almost every town and city on the island has either a hospital or medical clinic. They are generally inexpensive for typical ailments (diarrhea, dysentery) and minor surgery or injury (stitches, sprains).

If you must use these services, try to ascertain the competence of the staff that's treating you. Compare their diagnoses and prescriptions to the information in this section. If you have questions, call your embassy and get a referral for a doctor, or call home and have your doctor advise you.

Women's Health

Gynecological problems, poor diet, lowered resistance due to the use of antibiotics for stomach upsets and even contraceptive pills can lead to vaginal infections when traveling in hot climates. Wearing skirts or loose-fitting trousers and cotton underwear will help to prevent infections.

Yeast infections, characterized by a rash, itch and discharge, can be treated with a vinegar or even lemon-juice douche or with yogurt. Nystatin suppositories are the usual medical prescription. Trichomonas is a more serious infection; symptoms are a discharge and a burning sensation when urinating. Male sexual partners must also be treated, and if a vinegar-water douche is not effective, medical attention should be sought. Flagyl is the prescribed drug.

Pregnant women should avoid all unnecessary medication, but vaccinations and antimalarial prophylactics should still be taken where possible. Additional care should be taken to prevent illness, and particular attention should be paid to diet and nutrition. Most miscarriages occur during the first three months of pregnancy, so this is the most risky time to travel. The last three months should also be spent within reasonable distance of good medical care, as quite serious problems can develop at this time.

WOMEN TRAVELERS

Women traveling in Hispaniola should not encounter any particular problems, especially if they dress conservatively and learn to ignore the catcalls and whistles they will encounter from men in some parts of the island. In fact, when it comes to unwanted attention from men, Haiti presents fewer problems than other countries in the region.

Modest dress is important and highly regarded, especially in the Dominican Republic. For the most part on Hispaniola, only prostitutes wear shorts, miniskirts and skimpy or form-fitting tops, and foreign women who dress the same are often treated with less respect. Make sure to cover up beachwear when you walk into town or public buildings, and some women even put on T-shirts over their suits when they swim. If you have any doubts about what's appropriate, follow the lead of the local women.

It is not difficult for women to travel alone on Hispaniola, but they may receive numerous attempts by men to chat them up. While meeting and getting to know the locals can be a great experience, make sure you don't put yourself in a compromising situation. Avoid being alone with one or more strange men at a remote site, on an empty city street or on a secluded stretch of beach. If you feel at all uneasy about the direction in which an encounter is headed, follow your instincts and immediately end the conversation politely but firmly.

Be aware that in the Dominican Republic there is a tacit understanding that if a man treats a lady to a night on the town, the night won't end with just a good-bye kiss at her doorstep. If you accept an offer for dinner from a local man, be very clear about your intentions and what his expectations should be. In addition, there are many subtle gestures a Hispaniolan man uses to indicate that the woman he is walking with is 'taken.' A casual arm around the waist may indicate to all who see that you are now dating exclusively, with all that that implies. Unless this is the impression you want to give, make sure to end all such small gestures immediately.

In short, when dealing with local men, make sure to let them know in no uncertain terms where your relationship stands at all times.

Finally, use common sense when traveling alone: avoid secluded areas, don't hitchhike or camp alone and don't walk city streets at night unaccompanied. A single woman should also avoid taking a taxi, especially after sunset.

GAY & LESBIAN TRAVELERS

There is a very large gay and lesbian community on Hispaniola, as well as a lot of people who go both ways, particularly in the Dominican Republic. However, while the Dominican Republic has a number of gay nightclubs, in Haiti few people are openly gay, and there are no longer any overtly gay bars.

In general, public displays of affection by homosexuals are frowned upon. Private affection is the best policy, except in any of the bars that cater to gays and lesbians. There, almost anything goes.

For more information and advice, contact the International Gay & Lesbian Travelers Association (☎ 800-448-8550, www.spectrav .com/_29073.html), Box 4974, Key West, FL 33041, USA, a network of travel industry professionals dedicated to encouraging, promoting and selling gay and lesbian travel. If you're looking for a travel agent familiar with gay and gay-friendly tours and lodgings, try these folks.

Out & About (www.outandabout.com), a gay and lesbian travel newsletter available only through the Web, addresses subjects such as top vacation spots for gays and lesbians and which car rental companies won't penalize you for being gay. It provides lists of websites where you can find virtually anything related to gay travel. Issues of *Out & About* typically cost US$5.

DISABLED TRAVELERS

People who are confined to a wheelchair will find Hispaniola a difficult place to travel around. Few hotels (not even all-inclusive resorts) are designed with wheelchairs in mind, and years will pass before either Haiti or the Dominican Republic spend the money to re-do curbs at intersections so wheelchair users can enter and exit sidewalks with ease. There isn't a bus on the island with a lift for wheelchair-bound riders, and negotiating the streets anywhere but in the largest cities can become a nightmare.

SENIOR TRAVELERS

Many airlines and travel companies court seniors with discounts, but Hispaniola is virtually devoid of seniors' discounts.

The American Association of Retired Persons (☎ 800-441-7575), 1909 K St NW, Washington, DC 20049, offers discounts on hotels, car rentals, etc, through its Purchase

Privilege Program. It also arranges travel for members through AARP Travel Experience. Annual membership costs US$8.

Senior travelers should pay particular heed to the medical advice given above on the dangers of dehydration and exposure to excessive heat and sun.

TRAVEL WITH CHILDREN

Children are highly regarded throughout the Caribbean and can often break down the barriers and open the doors to local hospitality. For a wealth of good ideas, pick up a copy of Lonely Planet's *Travel with Children* by Maureen Wheeler.

If you are traveling with a small baby, make sure to protect it from mosquitoes at night with a net over its cot.

DANGERS & ANNOYANCES
Safety

Haiti and to a far lesser extent the Dominican Republic demand caution. Tens of thousands of foreign visitors enjoy the beauties of the island and the friendliness of its people every year, the huge majority without untoward incidents of any kind. But dangerous undertows can be found off the coasts of both countries, and failure to appreciate the risks posed by an advancing hurricane catches many people in the Caribbean by surprise every year. Also, Hispaniola contains some of the poorest areas in the Western Hemisphere, and robbery is common. Travelers should follow all of the basic guidelines outlined below.

Up-to-date travel advisories are available from the US Department of State's website (see Internet Resources, earlier in the chapter). If you do not have Internet access, US citizens can telephone the Department of State's Citizens Emergency Center (☎ 202-647-5225); British subjects can contact the UK Foreign Office's Travel Advisory Service (☎ 020-7270-3000).

Your best defenses against trouble are up-to-date information and reasonable caution. You should take the time to contact your government, inquire about current conditions and trouble spots, and follow the advice offered.

Reduce your odds of being a victim of crime by following these precautions:

- Unless you have immediate need of them, leave most of your cash, traveler's checks, passport, jewelry, airline tickets, credit cards, etc, in a sealed, signed envelope in your hotel's safe; obtain a receipt for the envelope. Virtually all hotels except the very cheapest provide safe-keeping for guests' valuables. You may have to provide the envelope (bring some so you won't have to waste time shopping for them).

- Leave any other valuable items you don't immediately need in a locked suitcase in your hotel room. This is often safer than carrying them with you, particularly if you are roaming about late at night.

- Have a money belt or a pouch on a string around your neck, place your remaining valuables in it and wear it *underneath your clothing*. Only carry a small amount of ready money, around US$20 or so, in a pocket or an otherwise empty wallet or bag, which you could easily hand over in case of a robbery.

- Beware that any purse or bag in plain sight may be slashed or grabbed. Often two thieves work together, one cutting the strap, the other grabbing the bag. At ticket counters in airports and bus stations, keep your bag snug between your feet, particularly when you're busy talking to a ticket agent.

- Do not wander alone in empty city streets or isolated areas, particularly at night.

- Do not leave any valuables visible in your vehicle when you park it in a city, unless it is in a guarded parking lot.

- Finally, leave your Rolex, expensive jewelry and fancy camera at home. For one thing, sand and sea spray are two of the worst enemies of fine machinery. For another, these items tempt robbers and are easy to steal.

Reporting a Robbery or Theft

There's little point in going to the police after a robbery unless your loss is insured, in which case you'll need a statement from the police to present to your insurance company. You'll probably have to communicate with them in Spanish or French, so if your own is poor, take a more fluent speaker along. With luck you should get the required piece of paper without too much trouble. You may have to write it up yourself, then present it for official stamp and signature.

LEGAL MATTERS

Police officers in Haiti and the Dominican Republic are sometimes (if not often) part of the problem rather than the solution. Police in both countries can detain people without just cause, and the criminal justice systems in Haiti and the Dominican Republic are such that redress for wrongs experienced at the hands of police officers and/or soldiers is all but impossible. You can expect no help from your embassy, and complaining to a higher-ranking officer generally won't help matters and could substantially harm them. Sadly, the corrupt cop who stops you and presses you for a bribe is a common figure on Hispaniola. The less you have to do with the law, the better.

Whatever you do, *don't* get involved in any way with illegal drugs: don't buy or sell, use or carry, or associate with people who do – even if the locals seem to do so freely. As a foreigner, you are at a distinct disadvantage, and you may be set up by others.

BUSINESS HOURS

Most businesses in the DR open weekdays at 9 am, close for *siesta* from 12:30 until 2:20 pm, and then reopen until 6 or 7 pm. In Haiti, most businesses open weekdays at 7 am and close at 4 pm but many close earlier on Friday. Haitian government offices close for an hour at midday, and many banks are only open until 1 pm. The majority of businesses on the island, including many banks in the DR, are open on Saturday as well, although usually for fewer hours.

Sunday on Hispaniola is indeed a day of rest. Local people put on their best clothes, go to church, then spend the afternoon relaxing in the parks or strolling along the streets. Most businesses are closed, though some towns and villages have Sunday markets. Bus service is curtailed in some areas.

PUBLIC HOLIDAYS

The big national holidays are dictated by the Roman Catholic Church calendar. Christmas and Holy Week (Semana Santa), leading up to Easter, are the most important. Hotels and buses are packed during

Holy Week, especially in the towns along the coast.

A partial list of island holidays appears below. See Public Holidays & Special Events in each country's Facts for the Visitor chapter for a complete list.

January

January 1 – *New Year's Day* is a legal holiday in Haiti and the Dominican Republic.

January 6 – *Día de los Reyes Magos* or 'Day of the Three Wise Men' in the Dominican Republic.

February

Week of February 27 – *Carnival*, the island's biggest festival, is celebrated with parades, dancing and drinking.

April

During *Holy Week*, the week preceding Easter Sunday, things are especially busy. Since the holiday is celebrated with much drinking, stay off the highways if you can avoid them.

December

December 25 – *Christmas Day* is an official holiday on the island; most Hispaniolans take December 24 off as well.

ACTIVITIES
Windsurfing

The bay beside Cabarete on the northeastern shore of the Dominican Republic is one of the top windsurfing sites in the world. And the best time to be there is May through July, when average wind speed exceeds 25km/h (15mph) and wind in excess of 40km/h (25mph) is common.

As unlikely as it might seem, the bay is also used by beginners, since a reef near the mouth of the bay prevents heavy chop from reaching the shore. So all levels of windsurfers will find this a great spot. All the equipment needed to windsurf is available for rent on the beach.

Surfing

Most of the winds reaching Hispaniola are coming from the northeast, which means that the best surfing on the island can be found along the northern and eastern coasts. And the site where the best breaks can be found is just west of Sosúa in the Dominican

Republic, where waves with 3m faces are not uncommon from August into October.

There are lots of good breaks south of Bahía Samaná down to about El Macao, and on the opposite coast there are some decent waves south of Barahona, although the waves in the Caribbean never get as big as the waves in the Atlantic.

Long boards are available for rent in Cabarete, and that's about it. If you plan to surf Hispaniola, bring your own board.

Diving & Snorkeling

There are two kinds of diving and snorkeling available off Hispaniola: Caribbean and Atlantic. Caribbean diving is noticeably warmer and considerably less choppy than the Atlantic, and it contains smaller though more colorful fish. Also, because hurricanes strike the Atlantic coast, the coral reefs north and east of the island are in much worse shape than those to the south and west.

As such, most snorkelers avoid the colder, rougher Atlantic and keep to the south and west coasts. Indeed, from June through at least September the waters off the north and east coasts are so rough and murky that few divers or snorkelers enter the ocean then.

In general, the diving and snorkeling along Hispaniola's northern coast isn't spectacular, although there are some shipwrecks to explore. It's not much better off the east coast, mainly due to overfishing but also due to reef damage. Diving and snorkeling is better off the south coast. The best dive spots are near Barahona, which is served by a dive operator, and Cabo Rojo, near Pedernales, which is not served by a dive operator.

There are also some good spots along the Côte des Arcadins in Haiti, the west coast of the island. Near St Marc is the Zombie Hole, a 200m drop where the world's largest sea sponge resides.

Hiking

Because of its many mountains, Hispaniola offers the hiker lots of possibilities. In the Dominican Republic, the most popular trek is to the top of Pico Duarte, which at 3175m is the highest point in the Caribbean. There are numerous trails to the summit, all of which are flanked by pine forest. The cool mountain air is a welcome change from the heat and humidity of the lowlands.

One of the most frequently used trails to Pico Duarte is reached from the town of Jarabacoa, near the center of the Dominican Republic, which also has several fun, shorter walks to waterfalls with swimming holes. In Haiti, the Macaya and La Visite National Parks have a couple of interesting hikes.

Bicycling

See the Bicycle section in the introductory Getting Around chapter for details on bicycling on Hispaniola.

Canyoning

Rappelling, also known as canyoning, is practiced at only one spot on Hispaniola, near the town of Jarabacoa in the Dominican Republic. Two companies offer canyoning adventures on the area's cliffs; the scenery is quite attractive, with two nearby waterfalls. However, unless you've done some rappelling and have some experience already, you'd be wise to pass on the opportunity here. The instruction given by the companies is fleeting, and the risk of serious injury if you panic or slip is great.

LANGUAGE COURSES

Spanish-language courses are available in the Dominican Republic and French lessons are sometimes available in Haiti. For details, see the Language Courses section in the Dominican Republic's Facts for the Visitor chapter.

WORK

By law you must have a work permit to work in Haiti or the Dominican Republic, and due to high unemployment rates in both countries their governments make it quite costly to obtain one; the costs often amount to three months' wages or more, making it impractical for any foreigner hoping to work on the island for one or two seasons. Obtaining residency status – another hurdle – usually requires the aid of a lawyer and can be quite expensive. If you still want to work

in the DR or in Haiti, contact your embassy to obtain the name of a reputable lawyer.

The Amigos de las Américas (☎ 713-782-5290, 800-231-7796, fax 713-782-9267, www .amigoslink.org), 5618 Star Lane, Houston, TX 77057, USA, is a nonprofit voluntary service organization that works on public health projects in the Caribbean, including the Dominican Republic. Volunteers spend from four to eight weeks in a village, usually living with local families. The program is open to anyone over 16.

ACCOMMODATIONS

Accommodations on Hispaniola run the gamut: from rat-infested cabins in national parks and budget hotels that may or may not have running water and electricity, to colonial-era, mid-range hotels and all-inclusive resorts with world-class beaches and golf courses.

Reservations

Hotel reservations are a must the last two weeks of December, the first two weeks of January and the week preceding Easter. They are an extremely good idea from mid-January through March, when vacancies can be a problem. Also, by booking a room at a certain price ahead of time, you can avoid having to pay for a more expensive room because all of the standard rooms are occupied.

Be advised that rates at the better hotels and at the all-inclusive resorts are considerably lower when rooms are booked through a travel agent in your home country. That's because there is tremendous competition between the better hotels and resorts, and to compete effectively, these businesses present travel agents with enticing package deals to offer prospective travelers.

Camping

By law you can camp on the beaches on Hispaniola, but in reality most of the island's pretty beaches have resorts on them, and resort staff will throw you off those beaches faster than you can say 'tent' if you try to erect one. There are few organized campsites on the island, with most of those being in Parque Nacional Armando Bermúdez and Parque Nacional José del Carmen Ramírez in the Dominican Republic. Generally speaking, camping outside a national park is not a safe thing to do on Hispaniola.

Hotels

While there are some inexpensive-yet-decent places to stay on the island, for the most part you won't find the kind of low rates so common in Guatemala, Mexico and other parts of Latin America. That's because the cost of living on the island is surprisingly high, due to the fact that so many of the goods are imported and so many local businesses are guilty of price gouging (even the weak local beers cost US$1.25!).

Budget lodgings – those costing US$10 to US$25 a double – typically come without air conditioning and do not have generators to provide electricity during power outages. The lack of a generator is a big deal because power outages are common on the island, and when they occur, the ceiling fans in budget hotels stop turning and the guests start sweating – heavily. Hostels and guest houses, which save people money elsewhere, are unheard of on Hispaniola.

The middle range (US$25 to US$80) consists mostly of air-conditioned hotels and motels, some with appealing colonial ambiance, others quite modern with green lawns, tropical flowers and swimming pools shaded by palm trees; still others are urban multilevel structures with many services and amenities, including satellite TV.

All-inclusive resorts are in the Dominican Republic only, and there are *lots* of them. Generally speaking, each is situated beside a lovely beach that is swept daily, and each has at least one swimming pool, restaurant and bar – and some have several of each. They also offer daily sightseeing excursions at an additional cost. When booked overseas as part of a package, which usually includes airfare, double room rates range from about US$60 per night up to more than US$250. Rack rates – the rate a person wandering in off the street pays – can be as much as 50% higher.

FOOD

Dishes from all over the globe are available on the island, including many of the Indian, German and Thai standbys. But as you might expect, Haiti and the Dominican Republic have two very distinct and different culinary traditions. Haitian restaurants typically serve either French or Creole cuisine, and sometimes a mixture of both, while restaurants in the Dominican Republic offer Spanish-influenced dishes similar to those found in Puerto Rico and Cuba – food that's tasty and satisfying if a bit greasy.

Haiti's Creole specialties include jerked beef, conch and deep-fried pork, and its French specialties include *escargot* and frogs' legs smothered in garlic. Dominicans tend to prefer their *sancocho* – a stew consisting mostly of vegetables and seven types of meat. Goat stew and tripe stew are also very popular in the Dominican Republic. Throughout the island fresh fish is readily available, as is grilled range chicken.

For more on Hispaniolan cuisine, see Food in the Facts for the Visitor chapter for each country.

DRINKS

Because of the hot climate in many parts of the island, you will find yourself drinking lots of fluids. Indeed, it's a good idea to drink plenty of bottled water or soft drinks even if you don't feel particularly thirsty to prevent dehydration and heat exhaustion. Drinking bottled beverages is especially important because the tap water is not safe to drink (see the Health section in this chapter).

Nonalcoholic Drinks

Bottled or purified water is widely available in hotels and shops. You can also order safe-to-drink fizzy mineral water by saying 'soda.'

Besides the easily recognizable, internationally known soft drink brands such as Coca-Cola, Pepsi, Sprite and 7-Up, you will find sugary red (strawberry), purple (grape) and yellow (apple) sodas. Extracto de Malta, a sweet and heavy bottled drink made from malt extract, is quite popular in the Dominican Republic.

Fresh fruit and vegetable juices are also popular drinks on Hispaniola. Almost every town has a stand serving one or more of these. Typical offerings include papaya, pineapple and passionfruit juices. Also available from street vendors are cups of shaved ice topped with guava or tamarind syrup. Beware the shaved ice: it isn't likely to be purified water, although the vendors insist it is.

Another delicious but somewhat dangerous treat are the local milkshakes made with various kinds of fruit. While the ingredients may be safe to consume, the containers the drinks are blended in are usually washed in tap water and re-used before they've had time to dry. Many a tourist has found him- or herself scrambling for a bathroom only an hour after consuming a local shake.

Alcoholic Drinks

Beer is by far the most popular beverage on the island. In Haiti, the top local brew is Prestige, while Presidente is the beer of choice in the Dominican Republic. In both countries it's not uncommon for a tourist to be approached and asked for money for beer. Even traffic cops won't hesitate to stop you and ask for beer money. In the heat of the tropics, nothing satisfies quite like an ice-cold beer.

Wine, on the other hand, is infrequently ordered. Most of it is imported from Chile, France and the USA, and despite their high prices the available brands usually represent some of the lowest-quality wines produced in those countries. This is especially true in the Dominican Republic, where red wine is often served chilled.

Much more popular than wine are the local and inexpensive rums, which are usually served with Coke or fruit punch. Rum is a white or straw-colored spirit varying in strength from 40% to 75% alcohol. Dark rums are made by adding a small amount of caramel or by aging in special wooden casks. Which variety or brand of rum is best is a matter of personal choice.

ENTERTAINMENT

There is no shortage of bars and dance clubs, even venues for live music, in the Dominican Republic, but Haiti has never had much in the way of a bar scene. Most are expensive hotel bars catering to businesspersons and tourists.

In those Dominican cities favored by tourists – Sosúa, Cabarete, Las Terrenas, Puerto Plata and Santo Domingo in particular – a new dance hall featuring merengue and American rock 'n' roll seems to open every month (and almost as quickly, last year's hot spot closes its doors for good). Most of these places don't get hopping till well past midnight. In Haiti, a small selection of nightclubs, most in Port-au-Prince, Pétionville and Kenscoff, primarily showcase two Haitian musical styles, *compas* and *racines*.

Cinemas are, for the most part, limited to the capital cities. First-run Hollywood creations in English with French or Spanish subtitles are the norm.

Baseball is the primary spectator sport on the island, and you may chance upon a game on any afternoon. Cockfights are usually held on Sunday, in an arena usually near the edge of town. Eightball and billiards are also popular, and most cities have at least one pool hall.

SHOPPING

Haitian art is widely regarded as the best in the Caribbean. The country is famous for its primitivist paintings, which emphasize brilliant colors and simple scenes of rural life. Some of Haiti's hundreds of painters have moved from primitive art toward impressionism and cubism. Whether you're in the art market or not, a stroll through any of Haiti's art galleries is time well spent.

Less popular than the paintings but quite lovely and uniquely Haitian are knee-high wooden statues depicting ordinary Haitians in their typical attire. The statues, once carved only from fine mahogany, are still made from handsome jungle hardwoods. Beware: When moved from the humidity of the tropics to a more arid climate, the statues occasionally split open as the wood dries.

Other exotic souvenirs from the island include *rada* drums played at Vodou ceremonies, tooled-leather scabbards for your machete and woven straw shoulder bags.

Some of the finest amber in the world is found in the Dominican Republic, and many tourists looking for a lovely gift opt for amber jewelry. Perhaps the best stores for Dominican amber are in Santo Domingo and Puerto Plata.

Also found on Hispaniola – and found nowhere else – is larimar, a semiprecious gemstone that closely resembles turquoise. Due to the level of competition among jewelers on the island, amber and larimar bargains abound. If you like to shop for exotic and eye-catching objects, you're going to enjoy shopping on Hispaniola.

Getting There & Away

The easiest way to get to Hispaniola is by air. More than a dozen major airlines provide service to the Dominican Republic and an even larger number of charter airlines make regular flights to and from the country. Far fewer airlines fly to Haiti, but among the ones that do are the major carriers Air Canada and American Airlines.

Of course, it's also possible to reach the island by sea. Cruise ships, yachts and sailboats call at the Dominican Republic. Cruise ships have discontinued service to Haiti. The island's seaports of entry are located at Port-au-Prince and Cap-Haïtien in Haiti, and at Luperón, Samaná, Puerto Plata and Santo Domingo in the Dominican Republic.

AIR
Airports & Airlines
The island's primary international airports are located near Santo Domingo and Port-au-Prince, with charters also arriving at Cap-Haïtien, Puerto Plata, Punta Cana and elsewhere.

Miami, Florida, is the main hub for flights going to Hispaniola. The flight takes 1³/₄ hours. If your flight doesn't make a stopover in Miami, chances are you may change airlines there. There are also flights to Santo Domingo from the following cities:

Origin	Duration
Madrid, Spain	8¹/₂ hours
Paris, France	9 hours
Frankfurt, Germany	10 hours
Caracas, Venezuela	2 hours
Panama City, Panama	2¹/₄ hours
Bogotá, Columbia	2¹/₂ hours
Havana, Cuba	2 hours
San Juan, Puerto Rico	30 min

Flights from Toronto, Ontario, and New York City also go to Puerto Plata, DR (4 hours and 3¹/₂ hours, respectively). American Airlines is the major carrier serving the island from North America. There are numerous charter flights from many destinations, and several airlines also offer inter-Caribbean service.

Buying Tickets
There are dozens of airfares that apply to any given route. They vary with each company, class of service, season of the year, length of stay, dates of travel, and date of purchase. Your ticket may cost more or less depending upon the flexibility you are allowed in changing your plans. The price of the ticket is even affected by how and from whom you buy it.

Travel agents are the first people to consult about fares and routes. Once you've learned the basics about routes and fares from the major airlines, you can consult ticket consolidators and/or charter airlines to see if their fares are lower.

Besides excursion fares, there are many tour packages to the Dominican Republic that typically provide a roundtrip airfare, transfers, and accommodations. Tour packages are by far the most economical way to visit the Dominican Republic. Some even allow you to extend your stay in order to tour the island on your own.

Tour packages change in price and features as the seasons change. Packages are advertised in the travel sections of major newspapers, and travel agents who sell them generally have something to offer someone considering a trip to the Dominican Republic. At the time of writing, tour packages were not being offered for Haiti.

Ticket consolidators (called bucket shops in the UK) are organizations that buy thousands of tickets from airlines at considerable discounts and then resell them to the public with a slight markup, often through travel agents but mostly through newspaper ads. Consolidator ads typically include tables of destinations, accompanying fares and a toll-free number to call.

Travelers with Special Needs

If you have special needs of any sort – you have a broken leg, you're vegetarian, traveling in a wheelchair, taking a baby or terrified of flying – you should let the airline know as soon as possible so that they can make arrangements accordingly. You should remind them when you reconfirm your booking (at least 72 hours before departure) and again when you check in at the airport.

Airports and airlines can be surprisingly helpful, but they do need advance warning. Most international airports will provide escorts from check-in desk to plane when needed, and there should be ramps, lifts and reachable phones. Aircraft toilets, on the other hand, are likely to present a problem for wheelchair-bound travelers; discuss this with the airline at an early stage.

Deaf travelers can ask that airport and in-flight announcements be written down for them.

Children younger than two travel for 10% of the standard fare (free on some airlines), as long as they don't occupy a seat. They don't get a luggage allowance either. 'Skycots' should be provided by the airline if they're requested in advance; these will hold a child weighing up to about 10kg (22lb). Children between two and 12 can usually occupy a seat for one-half to two-thirds of the full fare and do get a luggage allowance. Strollers can often be taken as carry-on luggage.

The USA & Canada

There are direct flights to the Dominican Republic from the following North American cities: Boston, Dallas, Minneapolis, Detroit, Atlanta, Miami, Newark, New York, Ottawa, Toronto, Montreal, Quebec City and Halifax.

Five major airlines serve the Dominican Republic from North America, with American Airlines offering the greatest number of daily flights. Other major carriers are Continental, Air Atlantic, Northwest and TWA. Of these carriers, American also offers the lowest roundtrip fares; at the time of writing, fares to Santo Domingo were US$251 from Miami and US$477 from Toronto.

American offers daily service to Haiti and Air Canada offers a twice-weekly flight. A low-season roundtrip ticket from Toronto (via Montreal) to Port-au-Prince on Air Canada costs about US$450, and from Miami to Port-au-Prince on American it's US$233 roundtrip. Expect to pay more around Christmas and New Year's Day.

Be forewarned that charter airlines tend to come and go with much greater frequency than the major carriers. At the time of writing, more than 60 charter airlines were providing service to the island. Among them were Air Castle, Allegro, America Trans Air, Aviacsa, Champion Air, Express One, Falcon Air, Florida Jet, Hop-a-Jet, Laker Airways, Miami Air, National Air, North American, Pacific Island, Ryan International, Sky Trek, Sun Country, Teltord Aviation and Trans Meridian.

The UK

For cheap (bucket shop) tickets from London, pick up a copy of *Time Out*, *TNT* or any of the other magazines that advertise discount flights. The magazine *Business Traveller* also has a great deal of good advice on airfare bargains. Most bucket shops are trustworthy and reliable, but the occasional sharp operator appears – *Time Out* and *Business Traveller* give some useful advice on precautions to take.

Agents offering cheap fares to Hispaniola include Journey Latin America (☎ 0181-747-3108, www.journeylatinamerica.co.uk/index.html) at 16 Devonshire Rd, Chiswick, London W4 2HD, and STA Travel (☎ 0171-937-9962, www.sta-travel.com/index.html), with its office at 86 Old Brompton Rd, London SW7 3LQ.

Air Travel Glossary

Baggage Allowance This will be written on your ticket and usually includes one 20kg item to go in the hold, plus one item of carry-on luggage.

Bucket Shops These are unbonded travel agencies specializing in discounted airline tickets.

Bumped Just because you have a confirmed seat doesn't mean you're going to get on the plane (see Overbooking).

Cancellation Penalties If you have to cancel or change a discounted ticket, there are often heavy penalties involved; insurance can sometimes be taken out against these penalties. Some airlines impose penalties on regular tickets as well, particularly against 'no-show' passengers.

Check In Airlines ask you to check in a certain time ahead of the flight departure (usually one to two hours on international flights). If you fail to check in on time and the flight is over-booked, the airline can cancel your booking and give your seat to somebody else.

Confirmation Having a ticket with the flight and date you want doesn't mean you have a seat until the agent has checked with the airline that your status is 'OK' or confirmed. Meanwhile you could be just 'on request.'

Courier Fares Businesses often need to send urgent documents or freight securely and quickly. Courier companies hire people to accompany the package through customs and, in return, offer a discount ticket that is sometimes a phenomenal bargain. In effect, what the companies do is ship their freight as your luggage on regular commercial flights. This is a legitimate operation, but there are two shortcomings – the short turnaround time of the ticket (usually not longer than a month) and the limitation on your luggage allowance. You may have to surrender all your allowance and take only carry-on luggage.

ITX An ITX, or 'independent inclusive tour excursion,' is often available on tickets to popular holiday destinations. Officially it's a package deal combined with hotel accommodations, but many agents will sell you one of these for the flight only and give you phony hotel vouchers in the unlikely event that you're challenged at the airport.

Lost Tickets If you lose your airline ticket, an airline will usually treat it like a traveler's check and, after inquiries, issue you another one. Legally, however, an airline is entitled to treat it like cash – if you lose it, it's gone forever. Take good care of your tickets.

MCO An MCO, or 'miscellaneous charge order,' is a voucher that looks like an airline ticket but carries no destination or date. It can be exchanged through any International Association of Travel Agents (IATA) airline for a ticket on a specific flight. It's a useful alternative to an onward ticket in those countries that demand one, and is more flexible than an ordinary ticket if you're unsure of your route.

No Shows No shows are passengers who fail to show up for their flight, whether due to

Air Travel Glossary

unexpected delays, disasters, forgetfulness or, sometimes, because they made more than one booking and didn't bother to cancel the one they didn't want. Full-fare passengers who fail to turn up are sometimes entitled to travel on a later flight. The rest of us are penalized (see Cancellation Penalties).

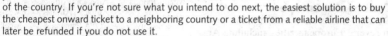

On Request This is an unconfirmed booking for a flight.

Onward Tickets An entry requirement for many countries is that you have an onward or return ticket; in other words, a ticket out of the country. If you're not sure what you intend to do next, the easiest solution is to buy the cheapest onward ticket to a neighboring country or a ticket from a reliable airline that can later be refunded if you do not use it.

Open-Jaw Tickets A return ticket on which you fly to one place but return from another. If available, this can save you backtracking to your arrival point.

Overbooking Airlines hate to fly with empty seats, and since every flight has some passengers who fail to show up (see No Shows), airlines often book more passengers than they have seats available. Usually the excess passengers balance those who fail to show up, but occasionally somebody gets 'bumped.' If this happens, guess who it is most likely to be? The passengers who check in late.

Point-to-Point Tickets These are discount tickets that can be bought on some routes in return for passengers waiving their rights to a stopover.

Reconfirmation At least 72 hours prior to departure time, you must contact the airline and 'reconfirm' that you intend to be on the flight. If you don't do this, the airline can delete your name from the passenger list and you could lose your seat. You don't have to reconfirm the first flight on your itinerary or if your stopover is less than 72 hours. It doesn't hurt to reconfirm more than once.

Restrictions Discounted tickets often have various restrictions on them – advance purchase is the most common. Others are restrictions on the minimum and maximum period you must be away, such as a minimum of 14 days or a maximum of one year. See Cancellation Penalties.

Round-the-World Tickets RTW tickets give you a limited period (usually a year) in which to circumnavigate the globe. You can go anywhere the carrying airlines go, as long as you don't backtrack. The number of stopovers or total number of separate flights is decided before you set off, and they usually cost a bit more than a basic return flight.

Standby This is a discounted ticket on which you only fly if there is a seat free at the last moment. Standby fares are usually available only on domestic routes.

Travel Periods Ticket prices vary with the time of year. There is a low (off-peak) season and a high (peak) season, and often a low-shoulder season and a high-shoulder season as well. Usually the fare depends on your outward flight – if you depart in the high season and return in the low season, you pay the high-season fare.

Remember, Before You Fly...

- Always reconfirm airline reservations, even for short flights.
- Arrive at the airport an hour before departure for domestic flights.
- Arrive at the airport two hours before departure for international flights.

Continental Europe

Discount tickets are available at low prices in several European cities, including Amsterdam, Paris and Frankfurt. Check the travel sections of major newspapers in these cities for advertisements offering the lowest airfares to Hispaniola.

There are direct scheduled or charter flights from Europe to the Dominican Republic departing from airports in Madrid, Rome, Milan, Lisbon, Paris, Amsterdam, Frankfurt, Bonn, Berlin, Hamburg, Dusseldorf, Munich, Stuttgart, Helsinki, Brussels, London and Glasgow, among others.

The cheapest fares from Europe to the Dominican Republic are on charter flights, such as those operated by Air Europa from Spain and LTU from Germany. Both Air Europa and LTU also have regularly scheduled flights to and from the Dominican Republic, as does Air France, Air Portugal, Alitalia, Iberia, Condor, Hapag-Lloyd, Iberia and Martinair.

Air France flies weekly to Port-au-Prince, via Pointe-à-Pitre, Guadeloupe. There are no other direct flights from Europe to Haiti.

The Caribbean

Airlines providing intra-Caribbean service to and from Hispaniola include Aeropostal, Air France, Air Guadeloupe, Air Santo Domingo, ALM, American Airlines, American Eagle, COPA, Cubana de Aviación, Dominair, Iberia, Lynx Air and Sky King.

Airlines link the Dominican Republic with the following Caribbean sites: San Juan and Mayagüez (Puerto Rico), Havana, Providenciales (Turks and Caicos Islands), Bonaire, Aruba, Curaçao, Antigua, St Martin, Pointe-à-Pitre (Guadeloupe) and Port-au-Prince.

The following is a list of cities in the Caribbean with direct flights to and from Haiti's Port-au-Prince International Airport, the airlines that serve them and the frequency of flights.

Origin	Airline	Frequency
Havana, Cuba	Aerocaribbean	weekly
Kingston, Jamaica	Tropical Airlines	2 weekly
Miami, Florida	American Airlines	2 daily
	Antillean Airlines	5 weekly
Panama City	COPA Panama	weekly
Pointe-à-Pitre	Air Guadeloupe	weekly
San Juan	Air Guadeloupe	weekly
Santo Domingo	Air Guadeloupe	weekly
	Caribintair	daily
		(except Sun)

Four times a week, Lynx Air International runs a flight from Fort Lauderdale, Florida, to Cap-Haïtien (on Wednesdays the flight goes in and out of Miami instead). Contact the Lynx Air offices in Pétionville (☎ 57-9986), 8 Rue Chavannes, or at Cap-Haïtien airport (☎ 62-1386).

Check with a local travel agent for details on Turks and Caicos National Airlines, which runs daily flights to Providenciales in the Turks and Caicos Islands.

Latin America

Airlines, including ACE, Aerolíneas Argentinas, AeroPerú, Aeropostal, Aserca, Iberia and LanChile, link the DR directly with the following Latin American cities: Bogotá, Caracas, Panama City, Santiago, La Paz and Cancún.

At the time of writing only two airlines were providing regular service between Hispaniola and Central America: COPA, the Panamanian airline, and LACSA, the Costa Rican carrier.

Australia & New Zealand

There are no direct flights from Australia or New Zealand to Hispaniola. The cheapest and most common way of getting there is via the USA. Check the travel sections of major newspapers for bargain airfares, and consult a travel agent for package tours.

SEA

At the time of writing, three cruise ships paid regular visits to the Dominican Republic and one called upon Haiti. Generally, cruise ships are a poor way to see anything because they usually allow their guests to spend only part of a day exploring a single town or neighborhood and then they're en route to another quick stop somewhere else. All the same, cruise ships pay brief visits to Santo Domingo's Zona Colonial and one makes a brief stop at a lovely beach near Cap-Haïtien.

The Holland America Line offers an 11-day trip from Fort Lauderdale, Florida, that calls upon Nassau, Santo Domingo, San Juan, St John, St Kitts, St Thomas and Out Island before returning to Ft Lauderdale. The per-person price ranges from US$1295 to US$5438. Carnival Cruise Lines sets sail from San Juan, Puerto Rico, on a seven-day roundtrip that includes stops at St Thomas, Guadeloupe, Grenada, St Lucia and Santo Domingo. The per-person price for the seven-day roundtrip ranges from US$1109 to US$2209.

Also making a seven-day roundtrip that originates in San Juan is Norwegian Cruise Line. The line's *Norwegian Sea* cruises to Santo Domingo, Aruba, Curaçao, St Croix and St Thomas before returning to San Juan. Prices ranges from US$1807 to US$3087.

WARNING

The information in this chapter is particularly vulnerable to change: Prices for international travel are volatile, routes are introduced and canceled, schedules change, special deals come and go, and rules and visa requirements are amended.

Airlines and governments seem to take a perverse pleasure in making price structures and regulations as complicated as possible. You should check directly with the airline or a travel agent to make sure you understand how a fare (and any ticket you may buy) works. In addition, the travel industry is highly competitive and there are many hidden costs and benefits.

The upshot of this is that you should get opinions, quotes and advice from as many airlines and travel agents as possible before you part with your hard-earned cash. The details given in this chapter should be regarded as pointers and are not a substitute for your own careful, up-to-date research.

Getting Around Hispaniola

Bus travel is an easy and inexpensive way to get around Hispaniola. Air travel saves time, so if you're short of it and aren't particularly interested in brushing shoulders with locals, flying may be your best option. Renting a car on Hispaniola can be an expensive and somewhat risky undertaking. A cheaper alternative for getting around the Dominican Republic is renting a motorcycle – this is recommended for experienced riders only. There are no motorcycle rental companies in Haiti.

AIR

There is daily air service between Santo Domingo and most of the Dominican Republic's other tourist areas, and limited air service between Port-au-Prince and most of Haiti's other tourist areas. There are also flights available between the two capital cities.

You can avoid some fairly long and probably crowded bus trips by taking a plane between these points (fares are one way):

Santo Domingo – Puerto Plata	US$54
Santo Domingo – Port-au-Prince	US$75
Puerto Plata – Punta Cana	US$59
Puerto Plata – La Romana	US$59
Port-au-Prince – Cap-Haïtien	US$45

Be advised that these puddle-jumping flights, all offered by Air Santo Domingo, are aboard aircraft unlike the large, confidence-bestowing jetliner you likely flew in on. These planes have more in common with the turboprops of ages past: They are reliable to a fault but they rattle like old East German cars, and when there's a rain cloud in the sky they can bounce around like beach balls.

If you're at all afraid of flying and can barely muster the willpower to board a Boeing 747, leave these short-run flights to others and, as they say in the USA, go Greyhound (take the bus).

BUS

Buses are an excellent way to get around the Dominican Republic and Haiti.

There are two bus companies in the Dominican Republic: Metro Buses and Caribe Tours. Both operate fleets of large, air-conditioned buses with on-board bathrooms, and both serve the country's major towns and cities. For a fraction of what you'd pay in taxi or air fare, you can usually get close to anywhere you want to be via Metro Buses and Caribe Tours. Fares and schedules are located in the Getting Around the Dominican Republic chapter.

One can also elect to flag down the smaller local buses, or gua-guas, that continuously run up and down major highways, and the públicos, privately owned minivans and pickup trucks that pick up passengers on major city streets.

Although Haitian buses are somewhat dilapidated, they provide the cheapest means of getting around. The bus network is extensive and can get you to some pretty out-of-the-way places. Bus travel in Haiti is also a great way to meet the locals. Haitian buses, taptaps, also run in smaller minivan versions. For more information on bus travel in Haiti, see the Getting Around Haiti chapter.

TAXI

There are three kinds of taxi on the island. In addition to the small and midsize cars with 'taxi' markers on their roofs, in Haiti there are publiques (shared taxis) and in the DR there are scores of motoconchos (motorcycle taxis) driven by youngsters. Many taxis can be hired to go longer distances as well.

If you want to get anywhere efficiently in Haiti you pretty much have to travel by car, and if you don't have a rental, taxis are the way to go. Not only are taxis faster than buses, they are also safer. Be aware, however, that most taxis in Haiti do not operate after dark.

CAR

Getting around Hispaniola by car is great, so long as you're not doing the driving. If you are, be aware that in Haiti and the Dominican Republic the overriding attitude toward foreign tourists is that they're rich and therefore ought to pay all accident-related costs regardless of fault. Moreover, police and judges in both countries share this sentiment.

Lonely Planet does not condone breaking the law, but be aware that many foreigners on the island advise not stopping or even slowing down if you have an accident. This is outrageous advice (especially if someone is hurt), but the universal feeling is that your life could be ruined if you allow either of the island's criminal court systems to decide your fate. You can expect to languish in prison for months, even years, before your case is heard.

Additionally, it doesn't matter whose fault an accident is; as far as others are concerned, you – as a foreigner – can afford to pay (and therefore *should* pay) for any damages incurred.

If you decide to rent a car, you should realize the deck is stacked against you should something dreadful happen. Be forewarned that while you will be required to purchase motor vehicle insurance, only rarely is it comprehensive and even then there's usually a high deductible.

Due to a high percentage of accidents and auto burglaries involving rental cars, auto rental companies on Hispaniola charge premium rates. You can expect to pay at least US$50 a day plus insurance for an economy car.

MOTORCYCLE

It is not possible to rent motorcycles in Haiti, but it is possible to do so in the Dominican Republic. If you are an experienced and defensive motorcyclist, getting around the Dominican Republic on a bike is a great way to see the country.

Be aware that just as it is not possible to take a rental car from the Dominican Republic into Haiti and vice versa, taking a rental motorcycle across the border is also prohibited.

BICYCLE

If you are the type of person who gets upset each time a motorist passes you with hardly an arm's length to spare, you won't want to ride on Hispaniola. Even on wide streets with no oncoming traffic, Hispaniola motorists rarely think of giving a bicyclist some breathing room. Time and again cars whiz past cyclists with very little space separating them.

Bicycles are available for rent in the Dominican Republic, and whether they're a good idea or bad depends more or less on you. The Dominican Republic is a large country, and if it's your intention to get around it on a bicycle, you've got to be in superb condition; most people underestimate the draining effect the tropical heat has on a person. Likewise, they underestimate the number of hills on the island. Even the coastal highways are terribly hilly.

Due to the condition of the roads in Haiti, bicycling there is not recommended unless you've brought with you a sturdy mountain bike with very rugged tires; even then, be prepared for flat tires. And never let the bike out of your sight. At night, bring it into your hotel room. Rental bicycles are not available in Haiti, which means you've got to bring your own.

Many airlines will allow you to transport a well-boxed bicycle as regular baggage instead of charging a special-handling fee. If you do bring your bike with you, be sure to bring a good lock as well.

HITCHHIKING

Hitchhiking is never entirely safe in any country in the world, and we don't recommend it on Hispaniola. Travelers who decide to hitch should understand that they are taking a small but potentially serious risk. People who do choose to hitch will be safer if they travel in pairs and let someone know where they are planning to go.

At the time of writing, Haiti was plagued with crime and many of its people were desperate. A foreign tourist willing to accept a ride from whomever pulls over and opens the door is just asking for trouble. While the situation isn't so bleak in the Dominican

Republic, it too has its share of people who are just scraping to get by.

If you decide to ignore this warning and thumb it anyway, be advised that hitchhiking on the island is not necessarily free transport. In most cases, if you are picked up by a truck, you will be expected to pay a fare similar to that charged on the bus (if there is one working the area). In some areas, pickups and flatbed stake trucks *are* the 'buses' of the region, and every rider pays. On Hispaniola, few people ride for free.

BOAT

Boats are widely used on Hispaniola. A ferry transports people and cargo between Samaná and Sabana de la Mar in the Dominican Republic, and boats are used to take tourists from Hispaniola to small nearby islands and up some of the larger rivers.

Are the boats safe? Sort of. While this book was being written, a typical Dominican boat with a skipper and two German tourists aboard capsized as the three were on their way to Isla Saona, near the southeast corner of the island. One of the tourists died and the other barely got out alive. The buzz around the island in the days following the tragedy was that local skippers take too many chances. The one involved in the death of the German tourist was seen showing off by crashing into oncoming waves shortly before his boat flipped.

ORGANIZED TOURS

There is no shortage of tour operators on the island, and in the tourist areas and at the resorts you'll always see advertisements for one tour or another. The tours are always activity oriented – 'spend a day rafting on the Río Yaque del Norte,' 'look for that special gift at the Amber Museum,' and so on – and usually they're a good value.

Generally speaking, the best tour operators are the ones working with all-inclusive resorts. That's because the resorts are careful in selecting the tour operators they are willing to recommend to their clients; a tour operator that performs poorly and leaves tourists feeling cheated reflects badly on the resort served by the tour operator.

For specific information regarding the tours that are available in Haiti and the Dominican Republic, see Organized Tours in the Getting Around chapter for each country.

Dominican
Republic

PAUL GERACE

Facts about the Dominican Republic

The Dominican Republic is one of those rare countries that enjoys a full year of spring-summer weather. It is topped with several mountain ranges sprinkled with lush valleys and gorgeous waterfalls. But totally unique to the country is its place in history – home to the first European city in the New World, Santo Domingo. Many of the structures from that bygone era of great discovery and great tragedy still stand and make for excellent viewing.

The country also features scores of superb white-sand beaches lined with thousands of swaying coconut palms that face inviting blue water. Along certain stretches of coast are thick mangrove forests looking much the way they have for thousands of years. Home to countless gnarled trees, and one of the world's few remaining habitats for manatees, their eerie black rivers make for great exploring by small boat.

Among the country's other natural attractions are Bahía de Samaná, where humpback whales return from the frigid North Atlantic each year to breed and to bear their young in a cycle that's millions of years old; Lago Enriquillo, a large saltwater lake where crocodiles abound and flamingos, scorpions and iguanas roam the shore; and Parque Nacional Los Haïtises, a vast area of bird-filled swamps and low-lying hills blanketed in dense vegetation that lend themselves well to adventure.

Despite its many historic and natural attractions, many visitors are drawn to the country by its people, who embrace life with great passion and frequently celebrate it with wild parties disguised as festivals. In fact, Santo Domingo has not one but two Carnivals, complete with parades, elaborate floats, lots of live music and plenty of dancing in the streets. A pre-Lent Carnival is celebrated in Santiago, Cabral, Monte Cristi and La Vega as well.

But that's not all. There are two major merengue festivals each year, both of which are only slightly less raucous than Carnival.

There's an annual three-day Latin Music Festival in Santo Domingo that attracts the biggest names in Latin jazz, salsa, merengue and *bachata* (Dominican 'country' music). Puerto Plata holds a weeklong Cultural Festival that is part music concert, part harvest festival and part arts-and-crafts fair. Cabarete goes nuts the entire month of February, hosting numerous events including the Encuentro Classic, the Dominican national surfing and windsurfing championships. Sosúa prefers to do its wild partying during Holy Week.

Whether you're looking to party, relax, explore and/or roam the first European city in the Americas, the Dominican Republic has a lot to offer.

HISTORY
A Nation Divided

The history of the Dominican Republic since independence in 1865 has been plagued by recurring domestic conflict and foreign intervention. The Restoration War of 1864, which returned control of the country to the Dominicans, left the cities of Puerto Plata, Santiago and Monte Cristi in ruins and the economy in shambles.

Moreover, the national unity that existed during the war against Spain collapsed the moment the Spanish troops left Hispaniola. For all practical purposes the postwar republic consisted of more than a dozen territories, each ruled by one of the guerrilla leaders who, allied in battle, had ousted the Spaniards the previous year. But with the Spaniards gone the alliance disintegrated and the military men struggled among themselves for control of the nation.

Out of this chaos came a junta of generals that in 1868 brought Buenaventura Báez, a wealthy mahogany exporter, to power. By the time he was pressured to resign as president in 1874, his corrupt administration had assassinated or imprisoned hundreds of opponents, looted the public treasury and leased Bahía de Samaná and the adjacent

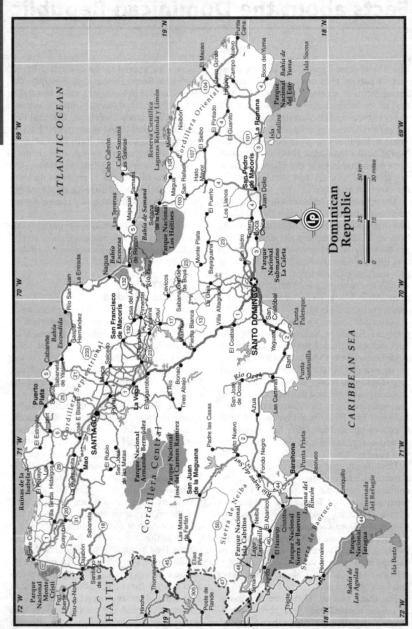

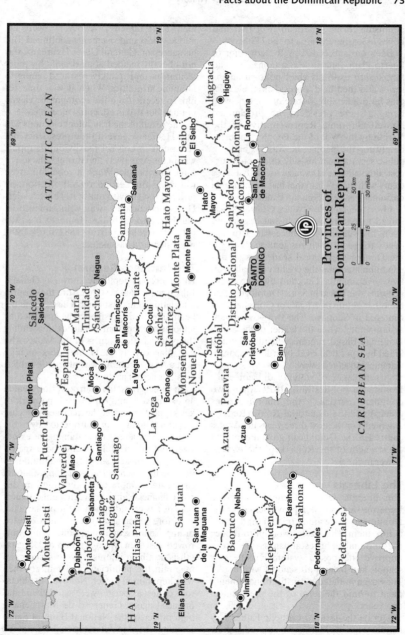

Provinces of
the Dominican Republic

peninsula to an American firm that had hopes of leasing the area to the US Navy.

Báez was succeeded by the governor of Puerto Plata, Ignacio María González, who forced into exile his chief political adversaries and then held a presidential election that he predictably won. Not content with being a mere president, he proclaimed himself 'Supreme Representative of the Nation by the Will of the People.' Unfortunately for the people, he was no better a public servant than his silly title would suggest, although he did manage to nullify Báez's treaty with the US firm that had leased Bahía de Samaná and the Samaná Peninsula.

Over the next few years González was forced to resign, as was his successor and even his successor's successor. Corrupt deeds triggered each resignation. By 1878 the Dominican political scene was so discombobulated that the country actually had two governments: One, led by a group of generals, was based in Santo Domingo, while the other, set up by friends of González, was centered in Santiago. The two-government system ended when the leader of the Santo Domingo-based regime, fearful of being killed by a political rival, boarded a Spanish warship and sailed away.

A semblance of stability did not enter Dominican politics until 1879, when two dominant parties – the liberal Azules (Blues) and the dictatorial Rojos (Reds) – emerged. For the next three years the Azules controlled the Dominican government, but the strength of the Rojos kept the Azules' power in check.

The Liberals

The liberals, led by General Gregorio Luperón, were a vast improvement over the Dominican governments that had come before them. The Azules worked to reduce the national debt, establish a free press, improve the postal system, create new schools and furnish all schools with books. They even initiated a constitutional amendment to limit the term of the president to two years.

During the term of Catholic Father Fernando Arturo de Meriño, who served as pres-

ident after Luperón's two years were up, public-works improvements continued. But his successor, General Ulises Heureaux, was not liberally minded at all despite his party affiliation and quickly restored chaos to Dominican politics. When it was time for him to recede from the spotlight, he rigged not one but two presidential elections.

The result of the fraudulent elections was that Heureaux gave up the presidency but remained in control by dividing support within the Azul party and through the use of force and payola. When a rebellion arose following the second rigged election, he ordered the army to quash it. Those leaders Heureaux couldn't sway with violence he humbled through bribes. Heureaux basically ruled the country from 1882 until 1899, when he was assassinated.

The Ruthless General

Heureaux was popularly known as General Lilís, a name that resulted from the mispronunciation of his first name, Ulises. From the beginning of his presidency, he governed by appointing men from all parties, thus ending the political effectiveness of the Azules, who had placed only party members in high posts. As a result, he was able to establish loyalties across party lines.

In his eagerness to retain power, he created an extensive – and expensive – network of key supporters. Indeed, he managed to secure a national loan from Europe to cover the enormous expense of maintaining his extensive political clientele. Today, more than a century later, key support for Dominican presidential, senatorial and congressional candidates is more often generated by discreet financial gifts between public figures than by any consideration of the public good.

Before he was assassinated, Lilís executed or imprisoned scores of opponents and borrowed vast sums from a group of US capitalists at a high interest rate to sustain and maintain the politicians and military men who kept him in power. Not even the dictator's closest associates were safe. When Lilís' financial agent, Generoso de Marchena, a high officer of the National Bank of Santo Domingo, tried to put a stop to the dictator's irresponsible spending, even he was imprisoned for one year and then executed.

Toward a US Protectorate

Shortly before Lilís was slain on July 26, 1899, he closed the National Bank and replaced it with the US-owned-and-operated San Domingo Improvement Company. Not only did he leave the treasury drained, but he placed control of the country's monetary system – even its key sugar industry – in the hands of Americans. As the 19th century ended, the government was so unpopular with Dominicans that the mastermind behind Lilís' assassination, Horacio Vásquez, initially led the new government.

With Lilís' death, it soon became clear that the Dominican government was economically ruined. Its only source of revenue was the money being collected at the customs offices in Monte Cristi, Puerto Plata, Samaná and Sánchez, but most of that was being pocketed by corrupt officials. As a result, the DR could not repay the debts it acquired from American and European capitalists during Lilís' administration.

The Americans called on the US government to intervene, and it did by taking control of the customs houses in 1905 and guaranteeing repayment of all loans. However, the US Senate stopped short of ratifying a plan proposed by President Theodore Roosevelt that would have established a protectorate over the Dominican Republic. The decision to seize control of the customs offices and administer them marked the first of many times the USA would intervene in Dominican politics.

A Benevolent Leader

The first few years of the 20th century were tumultuous ones for the Dominican Republic, as military men and politicians maneuvered to fill the leadership void created by Lilís' death. During this time two brief civil wars came and went; the country adopted a new constitution and held a presidential election that very oddly attracted only one candidate, Ramón Cáceres. On July 1, 1905, Cáceres was sworn in as president for the next six years.

Cáceres was one of the first leaders of the Dominican Republic who wasn't hell-bent on using the office of the presidency primarily for his own financial gain. During his 3½ years in office, Cáceres linked the cities of Moca, Santiago and Puerto Plata by railway; improved the postal service and installed new telegraph lines; rebuilt the nation's most important docks; erected lighthouses; funded new schools; and even constructed several highways. He was a benevolent leader.

But even benevolent leaders make mistakes, and Cáceres made a fatal one when he increased export taxes on Dominican sugar to pay for public improvements. The taxes angered wealthy plantation owners, whose interest in community good was exceedingly shallow. On November 19, 1911, the benevolent president was shot to death while enjoying his weekly Sunday drive in the country. With his death, a power vacuum once again enveloped the DR, and a destructive struggle to fill it ensued.

The USA Takes Control

The various bloody rebellions that took place between 1911 and 1914 resulted in Senator José Bordas Valdez's ascension to the presidency without any elections. Once again, a power-hungry individual in a struggling democracy had occupied the office of the president through undemocratic means. And once again, intense fighting took place throughout the country as others sought to control the government.

But this time things were different. The US government, concerned that revolutions in the Caribbean posed a threat to America's national security, took the position that only by managing the political and financial affairs of the region's countries could the continual political instability in the area be suppressed. In line with that conviction, US President Woodrow Wilson threatened to send in marines if free and fair elections weren't held. As a result, free and fair elections were held on October 25, 1914, and Juan Isidro Jimenes was elected president.

Wilson made further demands. He insisted that the country's armed forces be placed under US control and that an American financial expert be assigned to administer the receipts of the customs offices. He believed that political stability in the Dominican Republic and repayment of the loans could only be achieved if the country's cash cow remained out of local hands.

Jimenes refused to agree to these demands. At the same time, a powerful general and his followers decided to remove Jimenes by impeaching him before Congress – an act the local US representative viewed as a probable coup d'état. The USA offered Jimenes troops from US warships in the area, and though he only requested weapons, the marines were sent in. In short time they occupied every significant town in the republic.

Between 1916 and 1924, the Dominican Republic was under US control. The USA, while respectful of most civil liberties, prohibited Dominicans from owning weapons. It also banned the publication or broadcast of anything anti-American. And, most important, it controlled the Dominican budget. Wilson had placed control of the country in the hands of the US Navy; its mission was to stabilize the political and economic conditions of the country, which it succeeded in doing.

But by 1924, the American situation had changed considerably, and these changes affected US policy overseas. Wilson was no longer president, WWI was over and the USA, which had previously feared German attacks on the Panama Canal without American troop presence in the DR, was considerably less concerned with the republic's strategic importance. After fighting a war in Europe, the USA was looking inward. It was time to bring the troops home – from Europe and elsewhere. And it did.

The Rise of Trujillo
The years from 1924 to 1930 were good ones for most Dominicans. President Horacio Vásquez was in power when the Americans left, and he was a progressive and altruistic individual. During his administration, major roads were built, creating access to the countryside. The government built many schools during these years and initiated irrigation programs and sanitation services.

By 1927, jobs and money were abundant. Peace allowed commerce, agriculture and industry to flourish. In Santo Domingo and other cities, houses built of palm slats and thatch gave way to concrete structures. In many ways, the modernization of the Dominican Republic – accelerated greatly by the US military occupation – had begun, placing much importance on public-works projects.

Despite these improvements in the country, party politics continued to be viewed as the road to power and satisfaction of personal ambitions. Pacts remained based more on personal interests than on public good. Despite the model presidency Vásquez provided to his successors, most viewed the office as a means to attain wealth rather than a means to enrich the lives of the people.

Among them was Rafael Leonidas Trujillo, chief of the former Dominican National Police, which changed its name to the National Army in May 1928. Trujillo became rich stealing from the army's budget, and he increased his political position by placing friends in high military posts. In February

Rafael Leonidas Trujillo

1930, Trujillo forced Vásquez and his vice president to resign.

With Vásquez out of the picture, and after using the army to assassinate or imprison all rivals, Trujillo held an election in which he – the sole candidate for president – was elected to the highest office in the land. Within weeks of the election, Trujillo formed a terrorist band, La 42, which roamed the country, killing everyone who posed any threat to him. After a half-dozen years of political freedom, tyranny had returned to the DR.

The Trujillo Era

Gun advocates like to say that if firearms are outlawed, only outlaws will have firearms. In a very real way, when the Americans banned private possession of guns in the DR a dozen years earlier, they left the nation at the mercy of whoever *did* have guns. This was fine when the only people who had guns in the DR were US Marines. But after they left, the only people with guns were members of the National Army. And in 1930, its chief chose to become an outlaw.

Tossing aside democratic values and his country's constitution, Trujillo ruled the Dominican Republic with an iron fist from 1930 to 1947 and indirectly thereafter until his assassination in 1961. During these years, Trujillo used his government to amass a personal fortune by establishing monopolies that he and his wife controlled. In a short time he had his hand in every significant business in the DR, including prostitution. By 1934 Trujillo was the richest man on the island.

Because his own personal wealth was directly linked to the wealth of his country, Trujillo carried out the most grandiose program of public works and construction ever realized in the DR. Seemingly everywhere there was a bridge, highway or irrigation canal being built, with peasant families settling on uncultivated lands donated by the state. Agricultural production soared. Trujillo also pressed for industrial progress, and during his rule scores of factories were opened. The economy flourished.

But Trujillo's repressive ways outweighed the economic improvements. Anyone who criticized the dictator or his government,

directly or indirectly, faced imprisonment or worse. The torture and killing of political prisoners was a daily event in Trujillo's DR. And his brutality wasn't confined to his enemies. Upset by the number of Haitians who had settled in the Dominican Republic, in 1937 he ordered his troops to shoot them on sight. They obeyed, killing approximately 20,000 of them. The Dominican government later paid the Haitian government US$525,000 in reparations.

Democratization & War

At the time of Trujillo's assassination on May 30, 1961, puppet President Joaquín Balaguer was in office. As he was merely a figurehead used by Trujillo, Balaguer had neither a power base nor a popular following. A groundswell of unrest soon forced him to share power with a seven-member Council of State that included two of the men who'd taken part in the roadside ambush that left Trujillo fatally wounded. The council guided the country until elections could be organized.

On December 20, 1962, the scholar and poet Juan Bosch Gaviño was elected president in the first free elections the Dominican Republic had seen in many years. His liberal government enacted land reform and created a new constitution that separated church and state, guaranteed civil and individual rights, and endorsed civilian control of the military.

The changes annoyed wealthy landowners and military leaders alike, and on September 25, 1963, Bosch was toppled in a military coup. After more than 30 years of Trujillo, the Dominican people were allowed to enjoy democracy for less than a year before authoritarian rule was again imposed upon them.

But this time the military found itself with a fight on its hands. Bosch and a group of supporters who called themselves the Constitutionalists took to the streets and seized the National Palace. The military responded with tank assaults and bombing runs, but the Constitutionalists fought on – until the USA intervened in the civil war. A US force totaling 20,000 men occupied the Dominican Republic until elections were organized.

Puppet President No More

The election of July 1, 1966, pitted Bosch the benevolent reformer against Balaguer, a throwback to the Trujillo era. Unfortunately for Bosch, most of the voters feared his victory would rekindle the civil war. Balaguer won handily, garnering 57% of the vote. He would go on to serve as president for the next 12 years.

Realizing that the military posed a threat to the presidency, Balaguer headed off opposition from the armed forces by rewarding officers loyal to him, purging those he suspected of being disloyal and frequently reassigning officers. He used the National Police to curtail nonmilitary opposition, and his reelections in 1970 and 1974 were mostly accomplished through intimidation.

In Balaguer's defense, the economy expanded at a record rate, fueled by favorable world prices for sugar. Foreign investment, foreign aid and an upturn in tourism also contributed to high levels of growth. But by the late 1970s plunging sugar prices and rising oil costs had brought the Dominican economy to a standstill. In elections that Balaguer initially tried to fix (he backed off when the USA threatened him), a wealthy cattle rancher named Silvestre Antonio Guzmán came out on top.

Another Crooked Leader

With Guzmán's election, the Dominican people announced they had had enough of Trujillo-style politics. Guzmán promised fundamental social reforms, and the people turned out in great numbers to vote for him. Unfortunately, he proved no more benevolent than Balaguer, no different than all of the other Dominican presidents who had assumed office primarily to enrich themselves.

Guzmán's government was scandal-ridden almost from the start. He appointed his own children, his children's friends, his brothers and many other relatives to high government positions. Guzmán's administration was rife with corruption. In his first year in office, Guzmán added no fewer than 8000 people to the government payroll in an undisguised attempt to win their loyalty.

How bad was his administration? Its expenses quickly accounted for 85% of the national budget, bringing public-works programs to a grinding halt. Guzmán's government began borrowing heavily from abroad, throwing the nation into debt. Despite all the payoffs his people passed around, Guzmán's popularity diminished rapidly. Well before his four years were up, Guzmán's political party had chosen Salvador Jorge Blanco as its presidential candidate for 1982.

Blanco projected an image of irreproachable integrity. It was the right image for the time; he defeated Balaguer, who sought to regain his former office. Guzmán and his family were disgraced. On the night of July 3, 1982, following foreign press reports that exposed some of Guzmán's corrupt practices, Guzmán committed suicide by shooting himself in the head.

A Valiant Effort

When Blanco took the reins in 1982, he had one major objective: undoing the economic damage his predecessor had done. The Dominican Republic had little money in the bank and many budget problems. Additionally, due to widespread state subsidies the internal price structure was too low when compared to that of the USA, the DR's main trading partner.

Blanco's plan was to borrow money from foreign lenders for a short time while he initiated legislation geared to put the economy into overdrive. Sadly for him and the Dominican people, just as Blanco took office Mexico declared a moratorium on its foreign debt and stopped paying its creditors. From then on, foreign banks refused to extend credit to the DR unless it came to an agreement with the International Monetary Fund (IMF).

In its negotiations with the IMF, Blanco's regime agreed to a plan of fiscal austerity that included a reduction in governmental salaries, a rise in prices and new restrictions on imports. But because they publicly denounced the unpopular austerity measures as IMF initiatives (which in fact they were not), Blanco administration officials had a difficult time convincing the public to view the measures as a necessary remedy for past mistakes.

Despite widespread anger at the austerity measures, Blanco adhered to them and slowly the economy picked up and inflation was brought under control. Blanco's fiscal policy worked.

Unfortunately, in his efforts to prevent the military from posing a threat to him, he fired far too many officers – more than 4000 at a time when the armed forces had less than 22,000 members. Without the support of the military, and under attack for alleged (though eventually unsubstantiated) improprieties, Blanco disappeared from the political scene on May 16, 1986, as Balaguer was elected to his fifth term.

Balaguer's Return

Although he was 80, blind with glaucoma and in poor health, Balaguer was able to return to power by carefully measuring public opinion and telling the people what they wanted to hear. It also didn't help Blanco that there was tremendous internal strife within his administration regarding the austerity measures, although their benefits were becoming apparent toward the end of Blanco's term in office.

From 1986 until the presidential election of 1994, Balaguer ran his government like a dictatorship. First, he accused most of his political rivals of crimes and imprisoned them or forced them into exile. He then set about reversing everything that had been accomplished by the IMF/Blanco adjustment program. His efforts had the effect of devaluating the Dominican peso fivefold and causing the annual inflation rate to soar to 60%.

In response to the worsening economic crisis, street protests occurred with increasing frequency as people saw their real income plunging. Such protests generally ended in violence, with police and soldiers opening fire on the demonstrators. By 1990, the Dominican people had been so rapidly impoverished by inflation and devaluation that many had fled their homeland. By the end of that year, 900,000 Dominicans – or

12% of the Dominican population – had moved to New York.

Despite the insidious effects his economic policies were having on his people, Balaguer rigged the 1990 election so that he could remain in power for at least another four years. He did the same thing again in 1994, but this time the military threatened to intervene, and the international outcry in response to his fraud-marred reelection was so great that Balaguer agreed to cut his last term short and hold elections 18 months later. And good to his word, the then-90-year-old strongman hosted the cleanest presidential election in Dominican history.

The Dominican Republic Today

On June 31, 1996, Leonel Fernández, a lawyer who grew up in New York City, edged out three-time candidate José Francisco Peña Gómez in a runoff election for president. Fernández achieved a come-from-behind victory with the support of Balaguer, who had never made a secret of his dislike of Peña Gómez. But even Peña Gómez, the popular former mayor of Santo Domingo, acknowledged that Fernández had defeated him fair and square.

In the first months of his presidency, the then-42-year-old Fernández shocked his nation by forcibly retiring two dozen generals, encouraging his defense minister to submit to questioning by the civilian attorney general and then firing the defense minister for insubordination – all in a single week. Dominicans braced for a military reaction. Nothing happened.

The Dominican Republic needed to change, Fernández stated, and he was going to usher in those changes. He had a plan to fight corruption, which included the creation of a presidential commission and new powers for the attorney general. He spoke of his plans to overcome the severe economic problems that plagued the country. And he urged the DR's three major parties to work together to improve law enforcement, to improve health care and education, and to end the electric power failures that are a daily occurrence in many Dominican cities.

But no sooner had Fernández begun his mission than Peña Gómez died of a lung edema, and a week later Fernández was served a crushing defeat spurred by the death of the popular ex-mayor. The Dominican Revolutionary Party (PRD), which was led by Peña Gómez, won 24 of 30 senate seats and 80 of 149 seats in the lower house. The leftist PRD and the conservative Social Christian Reformist Party of Balaguer consolidated their power, making it easier for them to override presidential vetoes and stymie Fernández's initiatives.

At the time this was being penned, in late 1998, Fernández's centrist Dominican Liberation Party was failing in all of its efforts at reform. And Fernández, who had high hopes for his presidency, was little more than a figurehead. For the millionth time in Dominican history, the greed of a few was thwarting the betterment of the masses. As the end of the millennium approached, the DR was still a country without social security, adequate schools or hospitals, with an ailing and undernourished population and a political system that largely didn't care about any of these things.

GEOGRAPHY

The Dominican Republic is located on the island of Hispaniola, which it shares with Haiti to the west. The DR occupies roughly two-thirds of the island (48,734 sq km) and Haiti the other third (27,750 sq km). The two countries share a 388km border that was established in a series of treaties, the most recent of which was signed in 1936.

The mountains and valleys of the Dominican Republic divide the country into northern, central and southwestern regions. The northern region borders the Atlantic Ocean and consists of the Atlantic coastal plain, the Cordillera Septentrional (Northern Mountain Range), the Valle del Cibao (Cibao Valley) and the Península de Samaná (Samaná Peninsula).

The central region is dominated by the Cordillera Central (Central Range), which runs eastward from the Haitian border and turns southward at the Valle de Constanza to end at the Caribbean Sea. The Cordillera

Central reaches a height of 3175m at Pico Duarte, the highest point in the Caribbean. Another significant feature of the central region is the Caribbean coastal plain, which consists of a series of limestone terraces that gradually rise to a height of about 100m.

The southwestern region lies south of the Valle de San Juan and encompasses the Sierra de Neiba, which extends 100km from the Haitian border to the Río Yaque del Sur. Much of the southwestern region is covered in desert, and it is here that Lago Enriquillo, a saltwater lake, is located below sea level. At its center is Isla Cabritos, which is famous for its huge iguanas. The lake is home to more than 500 crocodiles.

The most significant river in the country is the Río Yaque del Norte, which is 296km long and has a drainage basin area of 7044 sq km. The river starts near Pico Duarte at an altitude of 2580m and empties into the Bahía de Monte Cristi on the northwest coast. It is quite popular with rafting companies operating out of the mountain town of Jarabacoa.

CLIMATE

The Dominican Republic has a primarily tropical climate, with more local variations in temperature than seasonal ones. In general, August is the hottest month and January and February are the coolest ones.

Rain does vary significantly with season. As previously mentioned (see Climate in the Facts about Hispaniola chapter), the northern coast is wettest from October through May, while the rainy season for the southern coast is May through October. The north usually receives much more rainfall than the south.

Dominican rain isn't of the just-long-enough-to-cool variety found in much of Central America, the Hawaiian Islands and elsewhere. A June shower in Santo Domingo can seem like the floodgates of heaven have opened and might last half a day, pause for several hours, and then resume. There's no mistaking that you're in the tropics during such times.

The Dominican Republic is in a hurricane channel. Hurricanes are extremely dangerous and should be avoided, even if that means cutting a long-awaited vacation short or spending what remains of it elsewhere.

Anyone who has lived through a hurricane – which may produce winds topping 200 km/hr and rainfall greater than 500mm in a 24-hour period – will tell you there's absolutely nothing fun about them.

ECOLOGY & ENVIRONMENT

The ecological and environmental problems confronting the Dominican Republic are numerous and severe. They include deforestation, erosion, overfishing, urban encroachment and water pollution, and although the Dominican people need only look to neighboring Haiti to see the threat these problems pose, next to nothing is being done to combat them.

Virtually all of the DR's ecological and environmental obstacles stem from *the* crisis-causing problem of our times: overpopulation. Although most Dominican families struggle to feed themselves, the typical Dominican woman continues to bring into the world more than three children on average. In Haiti the typical woman bears more than five children on average, and because many Haitians settle in the DR, their high birth rate poses yet another problem for the Dominican government.

A poor country cannot hope to make inroads against major environmental problems when its population is soaring, and the DR has yet to find a solution for its high growth rate. Birth control in the republic has encountered strong resistance from both sexes, especially in the countryside and the smaller cities. Many Dominican men believe birth control threatens their masculinity, and many Dominican women refuse to use contraception because some methods produce nausea and other unpleasant side effects.

Additionally, most of the Dominicans are Catholic, and the Roman Catholic Church does not condone the use of contraceptives. Abortion is banned except for the strictest medical reasons.

As the population increases in this agriculture-based society, trees are felled for building material and to create cropland and development tracts. Because two-thirds of the country is mountainous, the removal of trees means a loss of roots to hold topsoil in place, and erosion comes with the next rain. A growing population also means more space is needed for housing, which leads to urban encroachment on wilderness areas. The encroachment upsets natural balances, leading to further environmental damage.

Sealife

Another problem in the DR is that Dominican fishers kill most anything they come across. If you visit the Acuario Nacional in Santo Domingo, you'll see a manatee in one of the pens. There's a story behind the playful creature: In 1993, a man came across it and its mother while he was fishing near Barahona. Although it is illegal to kill the highly endangered manatee, the man hacked the mother to death with a machete. He boasted about killing it, and when a local newspaper got wind of what he'd done and reported it, he was required to pay a small fine. The baby, unable to fend for itself, was found on the brink of starvation and was brought to the Acuario Nacional.

Environmentalists thought the man got off lightly, but the official reaction didn't surprise them. Wildlife regulations are rarely enforced in the Dominican Republic, and as a result, violations are common. It is, for example, against the law to kill sea turtles. Yet, sea-turtle meat and sea-turtle soup appear on the menus at many Dominican restaurants.

Sometimes violators aren't punished even when they admit breaking the law. A case in point: In 1995, a German dive operator noticed several lobster traps in Parque Nacional Submarino La Caleta and broke them up. The man who set the traps notified police and the dive operator was arrested. When brought before a judge, he admitted to smashing four of the wooden traps.

The fisherman, however, claimed that he had placed 25 lobster traps in the national park and that the German had destroyed them all. With that, the judge sentenced the dive operator to several months in jail, levied a US$5000 fine against him, and ordered him to pay the fisherman US$2500 – US$100 for every trap the fisherman accused him of smashing.

In spite of admitting that he'd set traps in a national park, the fisherman faced no punishment whatsoever.

Electricity

In an effort to curb costs, the government frequently shuts off electrical power to entire cities. These outages, which happen without warning, day and night, often last for hours at a time and occur nearly every day. In recent years people have taken to the streets to protest, and general strikes have been held. During one such protest, the army was called in to break it up and soldiers opened fire, killing a young man and wounding others.

Due to the frequency of the power outages, which can turn an air-conditioned room into a stifling sauna in 30 minutes, many hotels have equipped themselves with generators. However, it never hurts to ask if the hotel has a generator before you check in. In the Dominican Republic, the common expression for 'Do you have a generator?' is '¿Tiene usted una planta?'

FLORA & FAUNA

In prehistoric times, most of present-day Dominican Republic was blanketed with dense tropical forests inhabited by a tremendous diversity of flora and a varied fauna of birds, reptiles, spiders and insects. The country's complex landscape, which is composed of multiple valleys and hills, swamps and savannas, lakes and ponds, contained many ecological niches that were eventually settled by the Taínos and their ancestors.

Today most of the forests and animals are gone, many of the swamps have been drained or filled in to make way for development, and the vast savannas are being used for cattle production or to grow sugarcane, bananas, tobacco and corn. But the Dominican Republic continues to offer the nature enthusiast world-class whale watching, lovely mangrove forests to explore by boat, fine opportunities for hiking and plenty of endemic plants and birds to look out for.

Plants

The exact number of plant species in the Dominican Republic has yet to be determined, but well over 5000 have been documented, with more than a third of them appearing on Hispaniola and nowhere else. These are very impressive numbers for a Caribbean island, and they are due mostly to the variety of vegetation zones that appear across the country, which range from desert to subtropical forest to montane forests. There are 20 such zones in all.

Of these vegetation zones, by far the most prevalent is the subtropical forest, which blankets the slopes of many of the country's valleys and is found throughout the Península de Samaná. Subtropical forest is easily identified by the presence of royal palms, which tend to be shorter than most and have thick trunks and large, curving fronds. Mahogany, cashew, jaguar palm, ground oak and yellowwood trees are also common to the subtropical forest.

Thorn and succulent forests, which abound in the southwest corner of the Dominican Republic, are known for their cacti, agaves and thorn trees. Parque Nacional Jaragua, the country's largest protected area, consists primarily of thorn forests and receives less than 700mm of rain a year. The park is notable for its constant high temperatures and despite being in the tropics is a true desert by anyone's reckoning.

The montane forests of the Dominican Republic generally appear around 2000m in elevation and are characterized by ferns, bromeliads, heliconias, orchids, and palm and pine trees. Much of the original pine forest has been felled for timber and to make room for cattle pastures and coffee plantations, but some large tracts still exist. The majority of the land in Parque Nacional Armando Bermúdez and Parque Nacional José del Carmen Ramírez is forested with pine trees, for example.

The country boasts two varieties of mangrove forests: the red and the white. The more luxuriant of the two, the red, is also the more common. It's found along many sections of the Dominican coast, and is profuse around Bahía de Samaná. The white variety is found there as well and is somewhat profuse near Lago de Oviedo in the south-western part of the country.

Mangrove is best explored by boat, and entering it is always a 'heart-of-darkness' experience. The forest's roots resemble long, black bony fingers, and they disappear into slow-moving water that's unusually foreboding. Explorers often report feeling that they are being watched when they are in mangrove. Tourists tend to keep one eye on the

ominous water and one eye on the branches overhead, as if expecting a snake to strike from either place. You'll be pleased to know that the mangroves in the Dominican Republic contain neither poisonous snakes nor crocodiles nor swamp monsters – at least none that anyone's lived to tell about.

Birds
When compared to Panama, Colombia and Venezuela – where some national parks

Those Colorful Trees

The Dominican Republic is home to some gorgeous blooming trees. Listed below are a few you may encounter on your travels.

Flamboyant blooms April through August. This large, spreading, colorful tree is easily identified by its five-petal red flowers and brown machete-like pods. The tree is native to Madagascar and is found in parks and gardens in the DR. It is known locally as *flamboyán*.

Elephant's ear blooms October through November. This tree, known in Costa Rica as the *guanacaste*, reaches 25m and is found in public places. It takes its name from its fruit, which is brown and resembles an ear. The flowers are small, white and spherical. The local name is *oreja*.

Mango blooms November through April. A native of India, this spreading tree is famous for its sweet fruit, which is eaten raw or made into jam, candy, sodas and ice cream. The flowers are tiny, white and edible, although the sap can cause itching.

Mammee-apple blooms May through September. This native of the Antilles bears delicious fruit that is served raw and in jam. The round, green-brown fruit is the size of a baseball. The flowers have four white petals. The tree can grow to 30m and is taller than it is wide. Its local name is *mamey*.

Jacaranda blooms March through June. The variety of jacaranda found on Hispaniola is found nowhere else. Growing up to 10m, the tree's flowers are trumpet-shaped and mostly white with some purple. The species originates in Brazil.

Sandbox blooms May through August, and in November and December. This native of the American tropics reaches 30m, is shaped like an oak and bears red berries, tiny brown flowers and pods that look like little pumpkins. The fruit is poisonous. The local name is *jabilla*.

Cashew blooms April through August. This American tropics native, which is wider than it is tall, is famous for its delicious nut. The nut is attached to a yellow, meaty growth that looks like a piece of fruit – but it isn't; in fact, it's quite poisonous. The flowers are red and white. The local name is *cajul*.

Star-apple blooms May through October. This popular cultivation tree produces sweet green apples that are said to have many health-giving properties. The tree, which can reach 25m, takes its name from star-shaped seeds. The flowers are tiny and yellow. The local name is *caimito*.

contain more than 400 species of bird – the Dominican Republic's country total of 218 is no big deal. However, the DR does have a good number of endemic birds, and many of the species that aren't endemic to the country are still a treat to behold.

Some of the birds any naturalist would want to look out for are discussed in the Flora & Fauna section of the Facts about Hispaniola chapter, near the beginning of this book. Also see the boxed text below.

Land Animals

There are 33 species of mammal living in the Dominican Republic, the most notable being the Hispaniolan solenodon (a small night creature that lives in caves and looks like a rat) and the Hispaniolan hutia (another cave-dwelling, ratlike rodent that hunts at night), both of which are endemic to Hispaniola, on the verge of extinction and rarely seen. Also in country are several dozen reptilian species.

Sharing the country and looking much the way they did millions of years ago are American crocodiles, Ricord iguanas, rhinoceros iguanas, Hispaniolan boas and Hispaniolan geckos. In some lagoons, don't be surprised if you see turtles. Because of their large size, these Hispaniolan freshwater slider turtles are occasionally mistaken for sea turtles. They are mostly found in Lago del Rincón, near Barahona.

Birds of a Dominican Feather

The Dominican Republic is home to some notable winged creatures, including the following:

Hispaniolan Lizard Cuckoo There's no mistaking this endemic and endangered bird when you see it. Its eyes are bright red and its body as well as its long beak are bluish gray. A dash of light-brown feathers is usually visible about the throat. The bird's sloped head gives it an intense appearance. It appears in greatest numbers in Parque Nacional José del Carmen Ramírez.

Burrowing Owl Most commonly found in Parque Nacional Jaragua, this owl is brown with whitish spots and has a blackish band across its chest and captivating yellow eyes. It's active by day as well as night, and it tends to bob up and down on long legs when nervous. Burrowing owls are generally seen perched on the ground or on low vantage points such as thorn trees.

Narrow-Billed Tody This pint-size endangered bird is easily identified by its bright-green head and back, its white underside and a dash of red under its short brown beak. It can best be found in Parque Nacional Sierra de Baoruco in the southwest corner of the Dominican Republic, where it hops from branch to branch looking for tasty bugs. It's known locally as *chi-cuí*.

American Kestrel This medium-size hawk, with its notable black mustache stripe and bluish-gray wings, is generally seen perched atop telephone poles or on wires or exposed branches in the vicinity of Puerto Plata. During migration between North and South America, the flight of thousands of these falcons often produces a faint black streak in the sky.

Hudsonian Godwit This endangered bird stands approximately 35cm tall and has a finger-length, slightly upturned bill that's blackish toward the tip and pinkish to orange near the face. Its nonbreeding plumage is a uniform brownish gray above and on the breast, with whitish feathers elsewhere. Its legs are grayish to black. You'll find these exotic-looking birds near mudflats.

More than likely, there were many more species living in the Dominican Republic at the time Columbus arrived, but habitat destruction since then and the introduction of the mongoose to the country by Europeans hoping to contain the rat population have taken their toll on native species. Today, the number of goats, dogs and horses in the DR – all brought over from the Old World – dwarfs the number of native mammals there.

Sea Creatures

Humpback whales migrate from the chilly North Atlantic to the West Indies every year. Of all the places they could choose to mate and to bear young, 80% of the species visit just two sites, both off the Dominican coast: Bahía de Samaná on the east side of the country, and Banco de la Plata, a sea bank about 100km north of Puerto Plata. The much smaller and less-showy Pacific pilot whale (it's not apt to breach as often as the humpback) also plies the ocean to the east and north of the Dominican Republic.

Also found in the Bahía de Samaná, as well as the Bahía de Neiba near Barahona, are Caribbean manatees and Antillean manatees – two of the four species (the others are the South American manatee and the African manatee). Popularly known as sea cows, manatees graze on water plants, rarely stray far from home and can weigh up to 600kg. They're odd-looking animals with fleshy bodies shaped like cigars; the head is at the fat end and a horizontally flattened, rounded tail is at the tapered end. Its forelimbs are flippers set close to the head; it has no hind limbs at all. Manatees usually live peacefully in small family groups. They are also very curious animals. If you're lucky enough to find yourself in the water with one, don't be frightened if one approaches you. It isn't attacking. Most likely it just wants a closer look.

Four of the world's eight sea turtle species can be found in the water lapping at the shores of the DR: the leatherback, the green, the loggerhead and the hawksbill. The leatherback, which has a leathery hide instead of a shell, is the largest of the bunch

Four of the world's eight species of sea turtle call the Dominican Republic home.

and can weigh up to 600kg. The green, which is named for the color of its fat, is the fastest of the eight species, reaching speeds up to 32km/hr. The hawksbill, named after its hooked upper jaw that resembles a hawk's beak, faces probable extinction for its gorgeous shell, which is black or dark brown and richly splashed with yellow. The loggerhead is the second-largest of the sea turtles, with a head that resembles a parrot's yet is the size of a man's.

Cruelty to Animals

The popularity of cockfights in the Dominican Republic is a less-appealing part of the country's culture. 'Sadism' is the word many people would associate with the act of watching an animal die for enjoyment. The issues of cockfights, caged birds and animal sacrifices have been discussed at some length in the Cruelty to Animals section of the Facts about Hispaniola chapter.

Sadly, there's also no shortage of stray dogs or cats, sick and underfed, on the streets and in the countryside of the DR. But in a country where so many people are improperly cared for and simply can't afford to get their pets spayed or neutered, it's inhumane not to be sympathetic toward the owners as well as their pets.

Endangered Species

As mentioned in Facts about Hispaniola, all of the island's large animals and many of its smaller ones are headed toward extinction. Unfortunately, next to nothing is being done to prevent their loss. A half-dozen environmental groups have published pamphlets describing the poaching and habitat destruction taking place in the DR, but none has done more than that.

The Dominican Republic has outlawed certain species-endangering practices such as killing sea turtles for their meat, but the government is not enforcing its wildlife-protection laws; for example, *carey*, the local word for sea turtle, actually appears on menus throughout the country. The government has created 10 national parks, but the animals in them continue to die because no money is being spent on anti-poaching and anti-encroachment operations.

Likewise, there are quotas on fishing and there are fishing seasons for some species, but because the regulations are not being enforced nobody is respecting them. The sea around the Dominican Republic used to be filled with lobsters. Today, many Dominican restaurants offer 'petite lobsters.' In fact, there is no species of small lobster in the area; there are only baby lobsters. In their haste to make money, fishers are catching and restaurateurs are serving lobsters before they've had time to mature and reproduce.

Sadly, the closer one looks at the conservation scene in the Dominican Republic, the more disappointed, hopeless and jaded one becomes. When Columbus first saw the northwestern corner of Haiti in 1492, he declared the vista of verdant forests *maravilloso*. When French ecologist Jacques-Yves Cousteau visited the area nearly 500 years later, he described it as 'beyond salvation.' The DR has managed to slow its environmental destruction, but it is clearly headed down the same path Haiti traveled unless substantial action is taken – and soon.

NATIONAL PARKS

The republic's 10 national parks include most of its climatic and vegetation zones and offer outdoor enthusiasts many excellent options for adventure. Below is a brief description of each park. Further details may be found in the appropriate regional chapters.

Parque Nacional Armando Bermúdez

The landscape in this 766-sq-km park is the result of volcanic activity about 60 million years ago. It now consists mostly of subtropical mountainous rain forest and subtropical mountainous humid forest. Most of the park is blanketed in pine trees, tree ferns and palm trees, and it is here among cool mists that you can occasionally find the hawklike Hispaniolan trogon, which is quite captivating with its white beak, sapphire-blue head, breast and wings, and ruby-red lower feathers. Wild boars are also present in the park.

Parque Nacional del Este

This 430-sq-km park consists mainly of dry forest and subtropical humid forest on a remote peninsula, but it also includes a 110-sq-km island with lovely white-sand beaches. The territory is generally flat and well covered with trees, many of which are endemic to Hispaniola. The West Indian manatee and the bottlenose dolphin inhabit the ocean bordering the park, and the park contains several caves bearing Taíno artwork. The highly endangered Hispaniolan hutia and Hispaniolan solenodon are found here as well.

Parque Nacional Los Haïtises

This 208-sq-km park at the throat of Bahía de Samaná contains scores of lush hills that jut out of the ocean and make for excellent exploration by boat. It's believed that the knolls are made up mostly of coral and that they were submerged until about 40 million years ago, when earth movements pushed the mounds above sea level. The area receives a tremendous amount of rainfall, which permits subtropical humid forest plants such as bamboo, ferns and bromeliads to thrive. The Hispaniolan parakeet resides here.

Parque Nacional La Isabela

This park was established in the mid-1990s to protect the site where Columbus founded the second European settlement in the New World (the first was at La Navidad in present-day Haiti). Today all that remains of the settlement are some barely discernible ruins and a barely discernible cemetery (some of the original settlers are buried here), but a museum has been constructed at the site and it contains many objects that were used by the earliest European settlers, including such personal effects as jewelry and buckles.

Parque Nacional Isla Cabritos

This 24-sq-km park is quite unusual and memorable. It consists solely of a bone-dry island that's a refuge for iguanas, scorpions, flamingos, crows and cacti. The island is in a 200-sq-km saltwater lake that varies from 4m to 40m below sea level, the depth fluctuating with the amount of water in the lake. To get to the island and inspect the huge lizards that dwell there, you must get a ride from a park ranger – which is easy to do. On the way, he will take you to a river's mouth that teems with crocodiles. Swim at your own risk.

Parque Nacional Jaragua

This park, the country's largest at 1400 sq km, includes an arid expanse of thorn forest, an extensive marine area and the remote islands of Beata and Alto Velo. Although hot and dry, the park hosts an impressive variety of birds such as the American frigate bird, the roseate spoonbill, the little green heron and the black-crowned palm tanager. The park's beaches are nesting grounds for hawksbill turtles, and a lagoon inside the park is famous for its flamingos that migrate to the Dominican Republic from Florida each winter.

Parque Nacional José del Carmen Ramírez

This 764-sq-km park is home to the Caribbean's tallest peak – Pico Duarte – and the headwaters of three of the DR's most important rivers, the Yaque del Sur, the San Juan and the Mijo. Although frost occasionally visits parts of the park, the vegetation zone is clearly subtropical humid mountain forest – which is another way of saying that it's jungly yet cool, a fine combination. Here you can expect to see bamboo, ferns and juniper at the warmer lower elevations, and a preponderance of Creole pines higher up.

Parque Nacional Monte Cristi

This 530-sq-km park consists of subtropical dry forest, coastal lagoons and seven islets. Although quite dry for the tropics, receiving less than 600mm of rain each year, Monte Cristi park is home to many seabirds, including great egrets, brown pelicans and yellow-crowned night herons. American crocodiles are said to inhabit the park's lagoons as well. At night the narrow road that skirts much of the park and connects the town of Monte Cristi with the border town of Dajabon is said to be frequented by Vodou zombies.

Parque Nacional Sierra de Baoruco

This 800-sq-km park consists mostly of crystallized limestone and rises from dry plains just above sea level to large tracts of pine forest above 2000m. The vegetation varies wildly from cacti and thorn trees to forests of broadleaf trees to pine forests at its highest elevations. More than 150 species of orchid have been identified in this park, as have 49 bird species, including the white-necked crow (which can only be found on Hispaniola). The rare Hispaniolan parrot also makes its home here.

Parque Nacional Submarino La Caleta

Although the smallest of the DR's national parks at only 10 sq km, La Caleta is one of the country's most popular. It is 22km east of Santo Domingo and mainly attracts divers and snorkelers, although the park includes a stretch of shoreline as well. The marine park has a maximum depth of 180m, but the depth generally ranges from 10m to 50m. There are several coral reefs here, with a fair number of colorful fish, octopi and eels. And there's a good-size boat that was purposely scuttled in 1984, the year the park was created. Because the boat is in shallow, calm water, it's a fine site for beginning divers.

GOVERNMENT & POLITICS

The country is governed as a wholly independent republic and has been since 1865. Over the years it has had numerous constitutions; today it adheres to the one adopted in 1966.

The executive power is exercised by the president, who is elected (together with a vice president) by direct vote for a four-year term. There is a National Congress, consisting of a senate and a Chamber of Deputies; their members are also elected to four-year terms. The judicial system is headed by a Supreme Court, which consists of at least nine judges elected by the senate. All three branches of government participate in the legislative process. Bills for consideration by the legislature may be introduced by members of either house, by the president or by Supreme Court justices.

In late 1998, there were more than a dozen political parties in the Dominican Republic. New ones are established every couple of years and others fade from the political radar just as rapidly. However, there are only three major parties: the Partido de la Liberación Dominicana (Dominican Liberation Party, or PLD); the Partido Reformista Social Cristiano (Social

Christian Reformist Party, or PRSC); and the Partido Revolucionario Dominicano (Dominican Revolutionary Party, or PRD).

The leader of the PLD, Leonel Fernández, is also the country's current president; his term is scheduled to end in the summer of 2000. A reform-minded leader hoping to bring change to his largely impoverished nation, Fernández has been encountering stiff legislative opposition from both chambers of Congress, which are controlled by the PRSC and the PRD. Both the PRSC and the PRD represent the country's wealthy elite, whose chief objective is to maintain the status quo.

A survey financed partly by the US government and conducted by an independent research institute in the Dominican Republic in mid-1998 found that most Dominicans felt left out of the political process. Another poll, published a week later in the staid national daily *El Listín Diario* and headlined 'Fernández Good, The Government Bad,' showed that most respondents feel they have little real choice in who is elected to serve them.

ECONOMY

The economy of the Dominican Republic is primarily agricultural, with the leading cash crops being coffee, cocoa, tobacco and sugar. Manufacturing is largely oriented toward agricultural processing. A surge in tourism has given rise to an increasingly active service sector, but most of these jobs pay less than US$10 per day. In fact, most jobs in the DR offer lousy pay, and there aren't enough of them to go around. Unemployment hovers around 50%, with many people having to work three or four jobs to make ends meet. A full 60% of Dominicans live in extreme poverty.

The Dominican Republic is a country where very few people achieve what residents in developed countries would widely regard as humble dreams: getting an education, getting a decent job, owning a car one day. Life for the average Dominican is hard. So hard, in fact, that on a per capita basis more people try to get to the USA from the Dominican Republic to start a new life than

from any other country. Or put another way, the 1 million Dominicans in the USA constitute the largest migrant community in proportion to its homeland's population; the Dominican Republic has 8.2 million people.

The most-traveled illegal route into the USA is across the once-mighty Río Grande, which separates the USA from Mexico. The second-most-traveled back route into the USA is from the US commonwealth of Puerto Rico by plane; immigration papers are not usually checked when boarding or disembarking such flights. Most Dominicans who reach Puerto Rico to catch their dreamed-of freedom flight, however, reach the commonwealth on flimsy boats that carry them there via the 100km-wide Mona Passage.

This clandestine route, little known outside the Caribbean, is littered with the bones of many thousands of Dominicans whose boats capsized in the passage, where 3m swells are the norm. These boats, known locally as *yolas*, are usually provided by smugglers who charge about US$750 per head for the one-way trip. In 1998 the number of people making the journey was growing, mostly because they felt the Dominican economy only enriched a wealthy few and left the nation's middle class and poor far behind.

Sadly, more than ever young Dominicans – women as well as men – have turned to trafficking and/or selling drugs as a means to escape their financial holes. While there are no hard statistics on the illegal trade, US law enforcement officials in late 1998 estimated that Dominican drug traffickers were transporting as much as one-third of the approximately 300 metric tons of cocaine that enter the USA each year.

POPULATION & PEOPLE

In the Dominican Republic's population of 8.2 million, about 70% are of mixed ancestry, both mestizo and mulatto, with small minorities (about 15% each) of pure Caucasian (Spanish) and African origin.

In terms of economic class, fewer than 5% of Dominicans are members of the wealthy elite, about 35% belong to the middle sector and more than 60% are poverty-stricken people without regular employment or prospects of a better life.

Color plays a strong role in the republic's socioeconomic picture, with the wealthy elite consisting mostly of light-skinned people and the poor sector consisting almost exclusively of dark-skinned people.

Race plays a strong role even within each sector. In the middle class, for example, those near the top end of this economic sector tend to be light skinned, and the skin color generally darkens as one proceeds down the income scale. Likewise, the more rural an area, the lower the incomes that are found there.

EDUCATION

By law every Dominican is supposed to attend school through grade six. However, only 17% of rural schools offer all six grades, and less than half of the Dominican population ever enrolls in secondary school. All but the poorest students are required to buy their own books, which is reason enough for many parents not to send their children to school. The country's literacy rate for adults ranges from 74% to 82% depending on the agency contacted.

There are 28 institutions of higher learning in the Dominican Republic. All but one – the Universidad Autónoma de Santo Domingo (Autonomous University of Santo Domingo), which traces its lineage directly to the Universitas Santi Dominici, established in 1538 – are private colleges or universities. Most are operated by the Roman Catholic Church. Total enrollment for all of the universities and colleges in late 1998 topped 100,000 students.

ARTS
Music

Merengue is by far the most popular music in the Dominican Republic. From the minute you arrive in the DR until the minute you leave the country, merengue will be coming at you at full volume, regardless of your fondness for it. At a restaurant, in public buses or taxis – it's there. At the beach or walking down the street – yet more merengue. It is the opiate of the Dominican

masses. With merengue blaring away, only the deaf can think about their troubles.

Merengue is the dance music of the Dominican Republic, and if you attend a dance club there and take a shine to the music, you may want to pick up some cassettes or CDs before leaving the country. There are many merengue bands in the DR; the nation's favorites include Los Hermanos Rosario, Coco Band, Milly y Los Vecinos, Fernando Villalona, Rubby Perez, Miriam Cruz and perhaps the biggest name of all, Juan Luis Guerra.

Whereas merengue might be viewed as urban music, bachata is definitely the country's country music. This is the music of breaking up, of broken hearts, of one man's love for a woman or one woman's love for a man, about life in the country. Among the big names of bachata are the late Rafaelito Engarnaciom, Raulín Rodríguez, Antony Santos, Joe Veras, Luis Vargas, Quico Rodríguez and Leo Valdez.

Salsa, like bachata, is heard on many Caribbean islands, and it's very popular in the DR. If you like the music, it may interest you to know that the following individuals and groups enjoy particularly favorable reputations in the DR: Tito Puente, Tito Rojas, Jerry Rivera, Tito Gómez, Grupo Niche, Gilberto Santa Rosa, Mimi Ibara, Marc Anthony and Leonardo Paniagua.

Painting

The Dominican art scene today is quite healthy, thanks in no small part to dictator Rafael Trujillo. Although his 31 years of authoritarian rule in many ways negated the essence of creative freedom, Trujillo had a warm place in his heart for paintings, and in 1942 he established the Escuela Nacional de Bellas Artes (National School of Fine Arts). Fine Dominican artwork predates the school, but it really wasn't until the institution's doors opened that Dominican art underwent its definitive development.

If much of the work looks distinctly Spanish, it's because the influence is undeniable. During the Spanish Civil War (1936-39), many artists fled the fascist regime of General Francisco Franco Bahamonde and started new lives for themselves in the Dominican Republic. Among those artists, who would eventually influence thousands of Dominican artists, were Manolo Pascual, José Gausachs, José Vela-Zanetti, Eugenio Fernández Granell, and José Fernández Corredor.

The republic's finest painters are too numerous to name here, but if you happen to visit any of the many galleries in Santo Domingo and elsewhere, you might want to keep an eye out for paintings by Adriana Billini Gautreau, who is famous for portraits that are rich in expressionist touches; Jaime Colson, whose cubist forms tended to emphasize the social crises of his day; Luis Desangles, who is considered the forerunner of folklorism in Dominican painting; Mariano Eckert, whose works represent the realism of everyday life; Juan Bautista Gómez, whose paintings depict the sensuality of the landscape with suggestive images; and Guillo Pérez, whose paintings of oxen, carts and cane fields convey a poetic vision of life at the sugar mill.

Well represented in the Dominican Republic by Dominican and Haitian artists is what's commonly called 'primitive art,' which at its best conveys rural Caribbean life with simple and colorful figures and landscapes. Little importance is placed on detail, but rather everyday scenes and activities are presented in a childlike, coloring-book manner. Also well represented is Dominican modern art, which generally ranges from disturbing to very disturbing and in the minds of many begs the question, 'Is this art or is this doodling being presented as art?' The best place to judge for yourself is the Museo de Arte Moderno in Santo Domingo.

Literature

The Dominican Republic's literary history dates to the Spanish colonial period. It was then that Bartolomé de Las Casas, a Spanish friar, pleaded for fair treatment of the Taínos and recorded the early history of the Caribbean in his beautifully written *Historia de las Indias* (History of the Indies), selections of which are translated into

English, such as *In Defense of the Indians*. During this same era, Gabriel Téllez, a priest who helped to reorganize the convent of Our Lady of Mercy in Santo Domingo, wrote his impressive *Historia general de la Orden de la Mercéd* (General History of the Order of Mercy).

During the Haitian occupation of Santo Domingo (1822-44), French literary style became prominent and many Dominican writers who emigrated to other Spanish-speaking countries made names for themselves there. With the first proclamation of independence (in 1844), Félix María del Monte created the country's principal poetic form – a short patriotic poem based on local events of the day.

During the late 19th century and early 20th century, three literary movements occurred in the Dominican Republic: *indigenismo*, *criollismo* and *postumismo*. Indigenismo exposed the brutalities the Taínos experienced at the hands of the Spaniards. Criollismo concerned the local regions of the country and the people who lived there. Postumismo was a new style of prose and poetry that broke from traditional literary restraints. Trujillo's dictatorship gave rise to this underground literary movement that dealt with repression. Some writers, such as Manuel and Lupo Fernández Rueda, used clever metaphors to protest the regime. Juan Bosch, writing from exile, penned numerous stories that openly attacked Trujillo.

Most of the popular writing being done by Dominicans today is coming from the expatriate community living in New York City. Their work tends to focus on the hardships of life in the DR today, the frustration of the people, their dreams. In her 1991 book *How the Garcia Girls Lost Their Accents*, novelist Julia Alvarez describes an emigrant Dominican family in New York. Other well-known contemporary Dominican writers include José Goudy Pratt, Jeannette Miller and Ivan Garcia Guerra.

Architecture

The quality and variety of architecture found in the Dominican Republic has no equal in the Caribbean. In Santo Domingo and in Santiago, you can see examples of Cuban Victorian, Caribbean gingerbread and art deco. The buildings in Puerto Plata vary between the vernacular Antillean and the pure Victorian, sometimes English, sometimes North American. And, of course, the late Gothic style that was dominant in Europe during the early Middle Ages abounds in the Zona Colonial of Santo Domingo and elsewhere.

San Pedro de Macorís, distinguished for producing more major league baseball players than any other city in the Dominican Republic, was also the first city to use reinforced concrete in its construction – an event that accompanied a heavy demand for housing following the installation of its first sugar factory in 1876. Huge buildings of an eclectic or late Victorian style were created with the improved concrete.

Even the homes of simple farmers, far from a town in places rarely seen by outsiders, have a look that's all their own: single story, porchless, with plank siding inside and out, but more colorful than a handful of jelly beans. Though these houses are usually square and otherwise boring as a cube, one wall might be painted firetruck red, another mango-flesh orange, a third wall as pale blue as a bird's egg, the fourth wall as yellow as a lemon. The window frames might be white, the front door shocking pink. Such homes are as pleasing to the eye as their occupants usually are to the soul.

SOCIETY & CONDUCT
Traditional Culture
The Spaniards wiped out this country's indigenous people as well as their culture. The slaves they brought from Africa to work in the sugarcane fields came from many tribes with rich traditions, but the Spaniards refused to let them speak their native tongues and prohibited African ceremonies.

Today the culture found in the republic is mostly passed down from Spain. As mentioned above, Dominican art has been heavily influenced by Spanish painters. But much more important, the religion of the people – Roman Catholicism – was imported from Spain. With this religion the people adopted a European sense of ethics, of good and evil, right and wrong. From nursery rhymes to educational methods, the Dominicans have learned quite a lot from the Spaniards.

Of course, the ancestors of today's Dominicans were not treated as equals by the Spaniards. They were slaves. And in this horrible role they developed a toughness that still endures. No matter how deep their frustrations, no matter how distant their prospects for a comfortable life, Dominicans rarely show their pain, and they walk with their heads held high. About the easiest way to look like a fool in the eyes of a typical Dominican is to lose your temper, to whine, to feel sorry for yourself.

And because Dominicans are used to rolling with the punches, complaining usually doesn't change anything. So, good advice for anyone traveling to the DR is: Don't worry, be happy – because worrying, being sad and complaining here isn't likely to change a thing. Service throughout the country is terrible. If good service is important to you, don't come here. Food here is generally overcooked to kill bacteria and possible parasites; if you really must have your steak medium-rare, request it blood red. In short, you'll be much happier with your Dominican stay if you adhere to the old adage, 'When in Rome, do as the Romans do.'

Dos & Don'ts
Politeness is a very important aspect of social interaction in the Dominican Republic. When beginning to talk to someone, even in such routine situations as in a store or on the bus, it's polite to preface your conversation with a greeting to the other person – a simple '*Buenos días*' or '*Buenas tardes*' and a smile, answered by a similar greeting on the other person's part, gets a conversation off to a positive start.

When you enter a room, even a public place such as a restaurant or waiting room, it's polite to make a general greeting to everyone in the room – again, a simple 'Buenos días' or 'Buenas tardes' will do. Handshakes are another friendly gesture and are used frequently.

Pay attention to your appearance when in the DR. Dominicans on the whole are very conscious of appearance, grooming and dress; it's difficult for them to understand why a foreign traveler, who is naturally assumed to be rich, would go around looking scruffy when even poor Dominicans do their best to look neat. Try to present as clean an appearance as possible, especially if you're dealing with officialdom (police, immigration officers, etc); in such cases it's a good idea to look not only clean, but also as conservative and respectable as possible.

Dress modestly when entering churches, as this shows respect for local people and their culture. Short pants are not allowed in government buildings. Some churches in heavily touristed areas will post signs at the door asking that shorts and tank tops not be worn in church, but in most places such knowledge is assumed.

Also think about safety in connection with your appearance. Particularly in the capital, locals will warn you against wearing even cheap imitation jewelry: you could be mugged for it. If you have any wealth, take care not to flaunt it.

RELIGION

Ninety-eight percent of the Dominican population professes to be Roman Catholic. For most of the populace, however, religious practice is limited and formalistic. Few actually attend Mass regularly. Most Haitian immigrants and their descendants also profess to be Catholic, but in fact adhere to Vodou and practice it in secret because the government and the general population regard the folk religion as pagan.

LANGUAGE

The country's official language is Spanish, and it is the language every Dominican speaks. Some English and German are also spoken by individuals in the tourist business – hotel clerks, tour operators, etc. Any tourist who doesn't already speak some Spanish and is intending to do some independent travel in the Dominican Republic, outside Santo Domingo or Puerto Plata, would be well advised to learn a little Spanish and carry a Spanish dictionary.

See the Language chapter at the back of the book for some useful words and helpful phrases.

Facts for the Visitor

HIGHLIGHTS

Most people who visit the Dominican Republic stay at an all-inclusive resort, where they soak up the sun on a white-sand beach during the day and dine, drink, dance and *dormir* at night. Some guests spice up their stays with excursions provided by the resorts at additional cost. Most, however, are content to enjoy the facilities at their respective resorts and leave exploration to others. The highlights offered here are intended for adventurous spirits, which doesn't necessarily exclude the resort crowd. Some of the all-inclusives are situated such that their guests can stay in a gated community *and* take advantage of some of the best sights that the country has to offer.

Zona Colonial

The colonial district of Santo Domingo is one of the finest in the world. The first colonial European city in the western hemisphere contains some superlative historic buildings as well as dozens of excellent examples of late Gothic architecture.

Whale Watching

According to the World Wildlife Fund, Bahía de Samaná on the northeast coast is one of the top spots in the world for observing whales in the wild – and you don't even have to step onto a boat to see them (although that is the most exciting way). The best time for whale watching is January and February.

Croc Encounters

There are some 500 American crocodiles in Lago Enriquillo, and a boat ride on the lake to one of their favorite beaches – followed by a visit to Isla Cabritos, home to some huge, rare and rather outgoing iguanas – is a very memorable way to spend a morning.

Take a Hike

Nature lovers won't be disappointed with the waterfalls Jarabacoa has to offer, the loveliest of which is rarely visited due to the walk involved. While in the area, consider ascending Pico Duarte, the Caribbean's tallest mountain.

Be a Beach Bum

The bay at Cabarete is world famous among windsurfers, but even if you don't try it (windsurfing lessons and rentals *are* available), just hanging out at the beach, sipping cold ones and watching the hard-body types bounce off waves, is a kick. At night everyone parties hearty, especially during the Encuentro Classic races in June.

PLANNING
When to Go

The busy tourist season in the Dominican Republic is from early December through Easter Sunday, especially during the week preceding Easter and around Christmas and New Year's Day. Around Easter, many Dominicans head to the North Coast towns of Sosúa, Cabarete and Puerto Plata, making hotel rooms scarce. Likewise, the northern beach resorts are packed with German, French and Italian tourists from Christmas to New Year's, while the resorts along the eastern and southern coasts tend to attract a lot of Canadians and Americans around the holidays.

If you can pick any time of the year to visit, the beginning or end of the dry season is best for most people. For the northern coast, the dry season runs June through September. For the southern coast, it's November through April.

If you're only interested in seeing the colonial district of Santo Domingo, don't mind lots of rain and prefer to visit when few other foreigners do, consider visiting toward the end of the capital city's rainy season (which lasts from May to October). The city receives an average of 168mm of rain each month at this time, and not surprisingly, there are fewer tourists and the district is at its cleanest. See the Climate section in the Facts about the Dominican

Republic chapter for information about the country's weather.

Maps

Generally speaking, the maps available in the Dominican Republic are usually out of date, of poor quality and hard to come by. The maps found in this guide are far superior to maps available in country. Possibly the best map of the Dominican Republic is produced by International Travel Maps (☎ 604-879-3621, fax 604-879-4521, www.nas .com/~travelmaps), 345 West Broadway, Vancouver, BC, Canada V5Y 1P8.

TOURIST OFFICES
Local Tourist Offices

There are only four government-run tourist offices in the Dominican Republic, two of which are located in Santo Domingo. The main office is the Secretaría de Estado de Turismo (☎ 809-221-4660, fax 682-3806), at Oficinas Gubernmentales, Bloque D, Av México, at Av 30 de Marzo. A branch office is located in the heart of the Zona Colonial, on Calle Isabel La Catolica beside Parque Colón. Both offices are open weekdays during normal business hours. The branch office is also open Saturday. The staff at both offices speaks English and Spanish. Maps and brochures are rarely available.

A third government-run tourist office is located in Samaná, and a fourth is located in Río San Juan. In addition, there is a private tour agency in Las Terranas that dispenses helpful information free of charge. See the Northeastern Dominican Republic chapter for further details regarding offices mentioned here.

There are also information counters at Los Américas International Airport and at Aeropuerto Gregorio Luperón near Puerto Plata. In addition to speaking Spanish and English, the staff attending these counters speaks some German.

Tourist Offices Abroad

The following Dominican tourist offices are staffed by people who speak Spanish and the primary language of the country in which they are situated.

Argentina
 (☎ 54-11-4813-7704, fax 54-11-4814-0824)
 Arenales 1942 1B, Buenos Aires

Belgium
 (☎ 32-2-350-0840, fax 32-2-640-9561)
 Ave Louise 160 A, Louizalaan, Brussels 1050

Canada
 Ontario
 (☎ 416-361-2126, fax 416-361-2130)
 35 Church St, Unit 50 Market Square,
 Toronto M5E 1T3

 Quebec
 (☎ 514-499-1918, fax 514-449-1393)
 2980 Rue Crescent, Montreal H3G 2B8

Chile
 (☎/fax 56-2-227-5187)
 Aguas Claras 1571 B, Oficina 101, La Reina,
 Santiago de Chile

Colombia
 (☎ 57-1-629-1459, fax 57-1-213-8645)
 Transv 29N 120-59, Barrio Santa Bárbara,
 Santa FT, Bogotá

France
 (☎ 33-1-4312-9191, fax 33-1-4312-9193)
 11 Rue Boudreau, Paris 75009

Germany
 (☎ 49-69-9139-7878, fax 49-69-283430)
 Consulate General of the Dominican
 Republic, Hochstrasse 17-2, D-60313, Frankfurt

Italy
 (☎ 39-2-805-7781, fax 39-2-865-861)
 Piazza Castello 25, 20121 Milano

Puerto Rico
 (☎ 787-722-0881, fax 787-724-7293)
 Ave Ashford 1452, Edificio Ada Ligia,
 suite 307, San Juan 00907

UK
 (☎ 44-20-7495-4322, fax 44-20-7491-8689)
 1 Hay Hill, Berkeley Square,
 London WLX 7LF, England

USA
 Florida
 (☎ 305-444-4592, fax 305-444-4845)
 2355 Salzedo St, suite 307, Coral Gables,
 Miami 33134

 Illinois
 (☎ 773-529-1336, fax 773-529-1338)
 561 W Diversey Pkwy, suite 214,
 Chicago 60614-1643

 New York
 (☎ 212-575-4966, fax 212-575-5448)
 1501 Broadway, suite 410,
 New York 10036

VISAS & TOURIST CARDS

Entry requirements are prone to change, so visitors should reconfirm the information provided here with the nearest Dominican embassy or consulate at least six weeks prior to departure to allow time to obtain a visa if required.

At the time this book was written, visitors from Argentina, Ecuador, Israel, Japan, Liechtenstein, Peru, South Korea, the UK and Uruguay needed nothing more than their valid passports to enter the Dominican Republic. Tourist cards, available upon arrival for US$10, and a valid passport were required for all citizens of the following countries: Albania, Antigua, Aruba, Australia, Austria, Bahamas, Barbados, Belgium, Brazil, Bulgaria, Canada, Chile, Croatia, Curaçao, Czech Republic, Denmark, Dominica, Finland, France, Germany, Greece, Hungary, Ireland, Italy, Jamaica, Luxembourg, Mexico, Monaco, Netherlands, Paraguay, Poland, Portugal, Romania, Russia, San Marino, St Lucia, St Vincent, Slovenia, Spain, Sweden, Switzerland, Surinam, Trinidad & Tobago, Tunisia, Turks & Caicos Islands, USA, Venezuela and Yugoslavia.

Citizens of all other countries were required to obtain a visa from a Dominican embassy or consulate prior to departure. The amount of time the visa remains valid and the requirements for extension vary from country to country. Citizens of countries that are not mentioned here should check with Dominican officials for the current entry regulations pertaining to them.

Tourist Card Extensions

A tourist card is good for 90 days from the date of issue. If you want to stay more than 90 days, you must apply for another tourist card at least two weeks before your original expires. This can only be accomplished at the Secretaría de Estado de Relaciones Exteriores (Ministry of Foreign Affairs), on Av Independencia in Santo Domingo; see the Santo Domingo chapter and map for the exact location. The ministry is open weekdays during normal business hours.

The time-consuming routine for purchasing a tourist card at the ministry is as follows.

First, looking from the roadside gate, go to the small two-story building located in the far-right corner of the compound. There, request Form 509, which costs US$10. It asks numerous questions, such as, 'In which other countries have you been?', all of which are in Spanish only. When you've completed the form, go to the main building, to the office with a small 'Consular' sign posted on the lawn out front. Here you will find a small room full of people looking as if they've been there all day, and they probably have.

Walk past these people and enter the first room on the right, the director's office. Present your completed Form 509, your passport, one photocopy of each page of your passport and two passport-size photos of yourself. Your passport and new tourist card will be ready for pickup at the same office two weeks later. Whatever you do, don't just take a seat in the front room and expect to be waited on; it won't happen.

If this all sounds like a big hassle, that's because it is. If you want to avoid it, you can ignore the extension requirements (ie, buying a new tourist card) and simply pay a fine at the time you leave the country. The fine is rarely more than US$10. But beware that the amount of the fine varies from immigration officer to immigration officer, and a particularly greedy one could demand US$20 or more.

The other risk you run is that you place yourself at the mercy of any police officer who asks to see your tourist card. This can pose a serious problem if you're pulled over by a traffic officer, because most of them levy 'fines' regardless of whether you've broken a law or not – and they tend to exact sizable fines if they catch tourists driving without a license or traveling without valid documents.

A traffic officer who notices that your tourist card has expired might decide to fine you US$50, US$100 or even more. Be aware that all such fines are negotiable. To keep them under control, never keep more than US$50 in your wallet; keep the rest of your cash in a pouch secured out of sight. Whatever you do, keep your cool. Traffic officers in the DR have the authority to arrest you without reason.

EMBASSIES & CONSULATES
Dominican Embassies

All of the republic's diplomatic missions are listed here. If you live in a country where a Dominican embassy or consulate does not exist and you need to obtain a visa, the government asks that you contact the nearest Dominican diplomatic mission.

Argentina
(☎ 54-1-811-4669)
Av Santa Fe 1206, Segundo Piso 'C,'
Buenos Aires

Belgium
(☎ 32-2-646-0840)
Av Louise 160 A, 2C, Brussels 1050

Brazil
(☎ 55-61-248-1144)
Shis 01-17 Conjunto 03, Casa 13,
Brasilia

Canada
(☎ 514-499-1918)
2080 Rue Crescent, Montreal,
Quebec H36 2B8

Chile
(☎ 562-245-1287)
Av Diagonal Oriente 1796,
Santiago de Chile

China
(☎ 886-2-707-9006)
Chung Cheng Rd 10, Tulip Building,
Taipei, Taiwan

Colombia
(☎ 57-1-621-1925)
Carrera 16-4 No. 86 A-33, Apdo 301,
Bogotá

Costa Rica
(☎ 506-283-8103)
Lomas de Ayarco Curridaban,
San José

Ecuador
(☎ 593-2-244-927)
Av Patría 850 y Av 10 de Agosto,
Apdo de Correos 2-67-A-622, Quito

France
(☎ 01 40 50 84 97)
17 Rue La Fontaine, Paris 75016

Germany
(☎ 49-228-364-956)
Burgstrasse 87, Bonn

Guatemala
(☎ 502-2-369-3580)
18 Av 1-50, Zona 15 Villa Hermosa,
Ciudad de Guatemala

Haiti
(☎ 509-57-3697)
121 Pétionville, Apdo 56, Puerto Principe

Honduras
(☎ 504-390-130)
Colonia Miramonte, Calle Principal No 2116,
Tegucigalpa

Israel
(☎ 9723-6957580)
Sderot Shaul Hamelech 4, Apdo 81,
Tel Aviv

Italy
(☎ 39-6-807-4665)
Via Domenico Cheline 10, Rome 00197

Japan
(☎ 81-3-499-6020)
Kowa 38 Building, Minato-Ku,
Tokyo

Mexico
(☎ 52-5-533-0215)
Av Insurgentes Sur 216, Despacho 302,
Apdo 505, Roma Sur, CP 06170,
Mexico DF

Panama
(☎ 507-223-6431)
Apdo Postal 6250, Zone 5,
Panamá

Peru
(☎ 511-440-3378)
Av 26 de Julio 779, Piso F,
Lima

Puerto Rico
(☎ 809-725-9550)
1612 Ponce de León Av, San Juan 00909

Spain
(☎ 34-1-431-5321)
Paseo de la Castellana 30, Primera Derecha,
Madrid

USA
(☎ 202-332-6280)
1715 22nd St NW, Washington, DC 20008

Embassies & Consulates in the Dominican Republic

There are dozens of diplomatic missions in the republic, all of which are located in Santo Domingo and are listed in the local telephone directory. A partial list appears here. To mail an item to any of these missions, simply write in 'Santo Domingo, República Dominicana' following the street address.

Brazil
(☎ 809-532-0868)
32 Av Winston Churchill

Canada
(☎ 809-685-1136)
30 Av Máximo Gómez

Denmark
(☎ 809-549-5100)
504 Av Abraham Lincoln

Finland
(☎ 809-565-8816)
38 Av César Nicolás Penson

France
(☎ 809-221-8408)
353 Av George Washington

Germany
(☎ 809-565-8811)
73 Calle Juan Tomás Mejía

Great Britain
(☎ 809-472-7111)
Av 27 de Febrero

Haiti
(☎ 809-686-5778)
33 Calle Juan Sánchez Ramírez

Israel
(☎ 809-542-1653)
80 Calle Pedro Henríquez Ureña

Italy
(☎ 809-689-3684)
4 Calle Rodríguez Objío

Japan
(☎ 809-567-3365)
Av Torre BHD

Sweden
(☎ 809-685-2131)
31 Av Máximo Gómez

Switzerland
(☎ 809-533-3781)
2 Calle Recodo, Edificio Monte Mirador

USA
(☎ 809-221-2171)
Av César Nicolás Penson

CUSTOMS

You are permitted to bring in up to one liter of alcohol, 200 cigarettes and gift articles not exceeding US$100 without incurring import taxes. See the Customs section in the introductory Facts for the Visitor chapter for further details. If you still have questions, contact the nearest Dominican diplomatic mission.

MONEY
Currency

The Dominican monetary unit is the peso. Its symbol is RD$, and it is divided into 100 centavos. It comes in coins of one, five, 10, 25 and 50 centavos, as well as one-peso coins. Paper money is available in denominations of five, 10, 20, 50, 100, 500 and 1000 pesos.

Exchange Rates

Generally it is possible to exchange US and Canadian dollars and German marks in areas frequented by tourists without any trouble. It is also possible to exchange Japanese, Swiss, Italian and Spanish money, although fewer banks are willing to do it. Do not expect to be able to change money from anywhere else. Currency exchange rates at the time of writing were:

Country	Unit		Pesos
Australia	A$1	=	9
Canada	C$1	=	10
euro	€1	=	17
Germany	DM1	=	9
Haiti	Gourdes 10	=	9
Japan	¥100	=	13
New Zealand	NZ$1	=	8
Spain	Ptas100	=	10
UK	UK£1	=	25
USA	US$1	=	15

Exchanging Money

Generally you will receive a slightly better exchange rate at a bank than you will at an exchange office. Also, by law Dominican banks are required to place a slate in public view stating the various exchange rates for the day. This is not the case with exchange offices, which means that you're more likely to be taken advantage of there.

The most widely accepted currency for exchange is the US dollar. Some stores and restaurants will even accept it in lieu of Dominican pesos. If you plan on doing much travel within the DR, you'd be wise to consider arriving with US dollars. Also, credit cards and traveler's checks are not widely accepted outside of Santo Domingo.

DOMINICAN REPUBLIC

American Express traveler's checks are the most often accepted.

While the thought of carrying around lots of cash in the DR may make you a little nervous, you might like to know that many establishments will add a 5% fee to credit card transactions. Also, conversion mistakes are not uncommon. If you're from the USA and use a credit card to buy something totaling 1500 Dominican pesos (the equivalent of US$100), there's a fair chance your bill will arrive in the amount of US$1500. These errors (or are they?) happen more often than they should.

Black Market The black market consists of young men who approach you on the street offering to exchange their Dominican pesos for your US dollars, German marks or whatever, for *less* than you'd get at a bank or exchange market. The only reason to do business with these people is if you're in need of Dominican pesos and the banks and exchange offices aren't open and won't re-open in time to satisfy your needs.

In general, it's a bad idea to use black marketeers here. Not only are their rates unfavorable, but there's a good chance they run faster and fight better than you do. If you hand over US$500 to a black marketeer on a public street and he shortchanges you, chances are he'll be walking away when you discover that you've been cheated and he'll start running if you go after him. If you're able to catch him, expect a fight and expect to be hurt.

Another reason to avoid these guys is that you're letting a total stranger know not only how much money you're carrying, but also where you carry it. That's just the kind of information muggers love to have, and there are bound to be some black marketeers in the DR who conspire with muggers.

Costs

The Dominican Republic is widely regarded among travel agents as the least-expensive destination in the Caribbean – but there's a catch. Those travel agents consider only the costs of package tours, which generally include chartered flights to and from the DR and all-inclusive resort accommodations.

Generally speaking, the Dominican Republic *is* an excellent bargain for its all-inclusive resorts. At an all-inclusive resort you pay one sum in advance for your accommodations and meals. Generally there are several plans from which to choose. For example, one plan may give you the option of paying for accommodations and dinners only. Another plan might include so many days of golf. At the time of writing, it was possible to buy 10-day packages from England, Germany and Canada for as little as US$1000.

The cost of independent travel in the DR, however, is no bargain. If, for example, you show up at an all-inclusive resort without a reservation, you can expect to pay at least US$100 per night including meals. And during the high tourist season, you could have trouble finding a room at an all-inclusive resort even if you were willing to pay two or three times that amount.

Of course, not every hotel is an all-inclusive. Unlike countries such as Mexico and Guatemala, where you can find a decent place to stay for US$10 or less each night, that's not the case in the Dominican Republic. Here, the nightly rate at a decent budget hotel is closer to US$25 (by 'decent' we mean one that's secure, clean and comfortable).

Likewise, the cost of food is reasonable only if you've bought an all-inclusive package or are willing to eat poor-quality food meal after meal. This is because much of the food in the DR is imported from the US or Europe; because overfishing has led to a decrease in supply and an increase in price of seafood on the island; and because of monopolistic practices within certain industries.

The best bargains on the island are transit costs (both bus and domestic airfare prices are very reasonable), cigars (if you avoid stores that cater to tourists) and rum (it's cheap and of top quality). But who wants to spend their vacation on a bus, drinking rum and smoking cigars? Besides, smoking isn't permitted on Dominican buses.

Taxes & Tipping

The government imposes an enormous 23% tax on hotel rooms. This tax generally is not included in the quoted nightly rate; if you're calling to make a reservation, always ask if the quoted rate includes all taxes. This hotel tax is a rude surprise to many visitors.

The government also imposes an 8% sales tax on food and drink. In addition, it imposes a 10% gratuity on restaurant bills that is supposed to be split by kitchen staff. 'Kitchen staff' does not include your server. If you are happy with the service, a tip of 5% to 10% of the total food cost is appreciated. Likewise, taxi drivers and hotel porters don't argue when they're tipped.

Bargaining

There is no blanket rule concerning bargaining in the DR; in some places it's done, and in some places it isn't. It's never done in restaurants or supermarkets, but it's often done in stores and public markets. As a general rule, if you see an item you want,

assume that its posted price is negotiable and offer to buy it for half of the posted price. Almost always, the seller will say that half off is 'impossible,' but he or she may respond by offering a 10% discount. If that's the case, you are now bargaining.

POST & COMMUNICATIONS

Post

There are post offices in every town but the hours of service vary, and the service itself is terrible and should be avoided. Although the rates are low – it costs well under US$1 to send a letter from the DR to anywhere else – the likelihood of your mail ever reaching its intended destination is about 50%. Nobody trusts the post office to deliver anything international. Even more remote is the likelihood of a letter or parcel reaching its intended destination in the DR.

If you absolutely need to send or receive a letter or parcel, use one of the reliable international courier services such as UPS, DHL or Federal Express. These couriers

How to Bargain

Bargaining is a skill. Some people are good at it, others are not. The seller usually knows exactly what he or she is willing to accept in return for parting with the object of your desire. However, a good bargainer can convince the seller that the object really isn't worth what the seller thinks it's worth. Entire books have been written on the art of negotiating. If the subject fascinates you, consider buying one of these books, but expect to pay too much for it!

As a general rule, know what you're looking at before you begin bargaining. For example, if you're considering buying an amber necklace, visit at least several stores so you know: 1) if you're looking at a common style, 2) if it's competitively priced, and 3) if you're looking at real amber or plastic (you'll know the difference after visiting a few stores). If the style is common, hint that you can find it elsewhere for less. If it's competitively priced, try to get it for 20% below the posted price; a greater discount is not realistic.

One mistake novice bargainers commonly make is showing too much interest in an object. If you really want that amber necklace, decide what it's worth to you. If that price is 50% below the posted price and the seller is only willing to drop the price by 10%, then know that it's time to walk. However, if you and the seller are close on a price, as a final tactic simply state what you're willing to pay and begin moving toward the door. If you get halfway down the street and the seller hasn't called out to you, at least you know the seller's true 'final offer' – something maybe worth reconsidering.

service most Dominican cities, and their phone numbers and addresses are provided in local telephone directories.

Telephone

Two telephone companies serve the Dominican Republic: Codetel and Tricom. Of the two, Codetel is by far the more popular as it offers clearer connections, lower prices and Internet access from its public-service offices. The maps included in this guidebook identify most of the public-service office locations for both companies. Pay phones that accept Dominican coins (but not major credit cards) are also commonplace.

The per-minute rate from the Dominican Republic varies substantially depending on where you're calling from. When calling from a hotel, in addition to the regular long-distance fee, you can be assessed a service charge by the hotel that's nearly as much. Therefore, it's generally a bad idea to call home from your hotel.

Calls placed from Codetel or Tricom pay phones during normal weekday business hours are billed at the following per-minute direct-dial rates: US$0.15 to Canada or the USA, US$0.30 to Europe and US$0.40 to Japan or Australia. Rates to these areas are significantly lower after 6 pm and on weekends. The per-minute rate for domestic calls is a flat US$0.08 a minute.

Codetel offices throughout the country are open 8 am to 10 pm daily. Tricom hours vary from office to office but generally are from 9 am to 5 pm Monday through Saturday, closed Sunday.

Telephone Cards A nifty product available at all Codetel offices is the Comuni card, which sell for 25, 45, 95 and 145 Dominican pesos (ie, US$1.67, US$3, US$6.34 and US$9.67). These cards can be used at all Codetel offices and pay phones, which you'll find in most communities in the DR.

To use the Comuni card, first scratch off the thin film of block-out material on the back to expose the card's secret code. Then, dial 611 if you want to hear dialing instructions in English, or 311 if you want them in Spanish.

Either way, you'll first be told to dial in the secret code, then the number of the party you wish to reach. If your party is in the USA, Canada or the Caribbean, dial 1 followed by the area code and telephone number. For all other countries, dial 011, then the country code, city code and the telephone number.

Once you begin speaking with your party, the credit remaining on your card winds down. You may use the same card for more than one call, until the credit is exhausted. When the credit is low, a voice message will interrupt your conversation and notify you that you have one minute remaining. Comuni cards can be used for domestic as well as international calls.

Fax

Many hotels will send faxes at their guests' request, but the service can be quite expensive and the fax may not be sent as promptly as you'd like (hotels, after all, aren't in the telecommunications business).

The best option is to send faxes from Codetel as the company does not charge for transmission errors; if it takes 10 tries before your one-page fax goes through, you will be charged the same reasonable fee had the fax gone through on the first attempt. You can also receive faxes at Codetel offices.

It's also possible to send and receive faxes at Tricom offices, but Tricom charges for every attempt made to send the fax. If it takes 10 attempts to send your one-page fax, you will be billed for the equivalent of 10 short phone calls.

Email & Internet Access

In mid-1998 Codetel began installing computers in all of its offices. Today anyone can access the Internet and send and receive email from most Codetel offices in the country. However, the staff at many of the offices do not know how the computers work and, therefore, cannot answer even the most basic connection questions. If getting online will be important to you during your stay in the DR and you aren't familiar with email or the Internet, become familiar with them before your departure.

At the time of writing, Codetel computers offered three startup icons: one for Internet connection, one for sending email and one for the MIRC chat group. The computers also have games, a word-processing program and printers. Be aware that the machines will not accept floppy disks due to attempts by some users to infect them with computer viruses.

Rates for computer use, including Internet access, are about US$2.50 an hour. There's an additional charge of US$0.50 per printed page. Laptop users will be glad to know that most of the public phones at Codetel offices allow you to plug into modem jacks.

INTERNET RESOURCES

Dominican Republic One
www.dr1.com/index.shtml
This site is maintained by the Dominican government's tourism department and contains some helpful tourist information on the DR.

PoliSci.com, the Political Reference Desk
www.polisci.com/world/nation/DR.htm
This site includes a veritable 'who's who' of Dominican politicians, from the current president to the names of every member of his cabinet.

Amnesty International
www.amnesty.org
Here you'll find annual reports on worldwide human rights violations; check this website to learn the latest news concerning systematic human rights abuses in the DR.

Governments on the WWW: Dominican Republic
www.gksoft.com/govt/en/do.html
This site provides a host of links to agencies and departments of the Dominican government, including the Office of the President and the Office for the Promotion of Foreign Investment.

International Law Office of Manuel G Espinosa & Associates
law.home.mindspring.com
Find information about the one-day divorces that are available in the Dominican Republic.

Worldwide Business Briefings
www.worldbiz.com/dominican.html
This site offers advice on how to do business in the Dominican Republic and how to develop relationships with Dominican business partners.

Debbie's Dominican Republic Travel Page
www.computan.on.ca/~pdowney/links.html
Debbie's travel page contains links to scores of DR-related websites, from where to stay to where to buy Dominican cigars.

While there are dozens of other potentially useful Dominican websites, be aware that many such sites were created and are maintained by people whose vested interests prevent them from providing entirely accurate information.

See the Internet Resources section in the introductory Facts for the Visitor chapter for more general websites.

BOOKS

The Books section in the previous Facts for the Visitor chapter provides information on titles that focus on the Caribbean region and Hispaniola. The titles mentioned here are more focused, concerning subjects specific to the Dominican Republic.

The Dominican Republic: A National History by Frank Moya Pons describes the history of the Dominican Republic from its aboriginal population to the arrival of the Spaniards and the nation's history from then through 1990. It's widely regarded as the best book on the subject.

Two other books that give readers good insight into why the country is the way it is today are *The Struggle for Democratic Politics in the Dominican Republic* by Jonathan Hartlyn, and *Dominican Republic and Haiti: Country Studies* by Richard Haggarty et al.

Baseball fans will appreciate the following books, each of which offers an insightful look into the country's national pastime: *El Béisbol* by John Krich, *Sugarball: The American Game, the Dominican Dream* by Alan M Klein and *The Tropic of Baseball: Baseball in the Dominican Republic* by Rob Ruck.

Merengue and bachata are the music of the Dominican Republic, and two fine books discuss their origins and social significance: *Bachata: A Social History of Dominican Popular Music* by Deborah Pacini Hernandez, and *Merengue: Dominican Music and Dominican Identity* by Paul Austerlitz.

Many other titles shine a spotlight on Dominican culture. Two of particular social value are *The Dominican Diaspora: From the Dominican Republic to New York City – Villagers in Transition* by Glenn Hendricks, and *Peasant Politics: Struggle in a Dominican Village* by Kenneth Evan Sharpe.

NEWSPAPERS & MAGAZINES

Although it was not the case for most of the last century, freedom of the press is respected in the Dominican Republic today. The nation's most-read newspapers are *El Listín Diario*, *Hoy*, *Ultima Hora*, *El Siglo* and *El Nacional*. There are no local English-language newspapers. However, the *International Herald Tribune*, *The New York Times* and *The Miami Herald* are available at bookstores and some newsstands in Santo Domingo and elsewhere.

Many of the popular magazines you would find in bookstores in the USA are available in the DR, and quite a number of Spanish-language magazines published primarily in South America are available as well.

RADIO & TV

There are more than 140 radio stations in the Dominican Republic, most of which feature merengue, bachata and baseball. There are seven local TV networks, and most of Miami's local stations are well received. About half of the country's TV sets tap into cable or satellite programming as well. Baseball, American movies and soap operas are the local favorites.

LAUNDRY

Laundromats are surprisingly difficult to find in the Dominican Republic. Your best bet is to ask a hotel receptionist if he or she knows of a nearby laundry. In many instances a member of the hotel's cleaning staff will wash, dry and fold your clothes for around US$4 per load if you inquire at the front desk.

HEALTH

Tap water in the Dominican Republic is not safe to drink, so you must either purify water yourself or drink the widely available and reasonably priced bottled water, as most locals do.

Malaria is present, especially in lowland rural areas, but there is no risk in the highlands. Chloroquine is the recommended antimalarial. Dengue fever is also present, as are dysentery, giardiasis, hepatitis and typhoid fever. See the Health section in the introductory Facts for the Visitor chapter for more about protecting your health while traveling.

WOMEN TRAVELERS

All of the advice in the Women Travelers section of the introductory Facts for the Visitor chapter applies to the Dominican Republic. The only thing to stress is that modest dress is highly regarded, and wearing conservative clothing translates into being treated with more respect.

Specifically, shorts should be worn only at the beach, not in town and never in a church or government building. Skirts should be at or below the knee. Be sure to wear a bra, as not doing so is regarded as provocative. Many local women swim with T-shirts over their swimsuits; in places where they do this, you may want to do the same to avoid stares and unwanted come-ons.

Beyond that, simply follow basic common-sense precautions when traveling alone: avoid isolated streets and places, especially at night, and don't hitchhike or camp alone.

GAY & LESBIAN TRAVELERS

There is a large gay and lesbian community in Santo Domingo, and quite a number of nightclubs cater to homosexuals (see the Entertainment section of the Santo Domingo chapter for details). Additionally, lots of Dominican men are bisexual. However, public displays of affection are not welcome and carry a certain degree of risk.

The overriding local attitude toward men kissing men and women kissing women is that whatever you do behind closed doors is OK, but keep it behind closed doors. Of course, that's not the overriding attitude toward displays of affection at gay and lesbian clubs, where scenes can get steamy at times.

BUSINESS HOURS

Banks are generally open 8:30 am to 3:30 pm weekdays and closed weekends; however, quite a number of them have ATMs that are always in operation. Most other businesses are open 8:30 am to 12:30 pm and 2:30 to 6:30 pm weekdays; those serving the tourist industry are usually open on Saturday as well. Government office hours are officially

7:30 am to 2:30 pm weekdays, although only secretaries are actually in much before 9 am.

PUBLIC HOLIDAYS & SPECIAL EVENTS

The following dates are public holidays:

January 1 – *New Year's Day*

January 6 – *Epiphany/Día de los Reyes Magos* (Day of the Three Wise Men)

January 21 – *Our Lady of Altagracia*

January 26 – *Duarte Day*

February 27 – *Independence Day, Carnival*

March/April – *Holy Thursday, Holy Friday* and *Easter Sunday*

April 14 – *Pan-American Day*

May 1 – *Labor Day*

July 16 – *Foundation of Sociedad la Trinitaria*

August 16 – *Restoration Day*

September 24 – *Our Lady of Mercedes*

October 12 – *Columbus Day*

October 24 – *United Nations Day*

November 1 – *All Saints' Day*

December 25 – *Christmas Day*

A number of special events throughout the year are worth attending. The best of the bunch are presented below.

Carnivals

That's right – Carnivals, with an *s*. The fun-loving Dominicans celebrate Carnival (*Carnaval*, in Spanish) twice a year in Santo Domingo. The first one, which is the climax of the pre-Lent celebration all throughout the country, always begins two or three days prior to February 27 – to coincide with the anniversary of Dominican independence from Haiti – and ends two or three days later.

The second Carnival, which is timed to coincide with the anniversary of the republic's declaration of war against Spain in 1863, begins the day before August 16 and ends the day after. Although the Carnival celebrated in February is by far the more boisterous of the two, both celebrations feature spectacular floats, wildly costumed performers, lots of dancing and rum, rum and more rum.

Carnival dates back to colonial times, when on the eve of Lent the inhabitants of Santo Domingo would don costumes and walk the streets of town. The masks they wore symbolized good and evil, and they held theatrical performances in the vicinity of churches. Most of the plays were forgotten over time and replaced with games, dancing and drinking.

Today, most Dominicans freely admit to not knowing anything about the origins of Carnival, but they celebrate it with profound gusto all the same. And not just in Santo Domingo; every major city in the country has its own version of Carnival, with different festivities but the same goal – fun. The largest and most traditional Carnivals outside of Santo Domingo, all of which are held in February or March, are celebrated in Santiago, Cabral, Monte Cristi and La Vega. See the respective city sections for further details.

Merengue Festivals

There are two major merengue festivals each year, both of which are only slightly less raucous than Carnival. The wilder of the two is held the last week of July and the first week of August on the marvelous malecón in Santo Domingo. Along the strip, in hotel ballrooms and on terraces, on patches of green and in makeshift bars under glistening

Merengue dancers

stars, the world's top merengue bands play for the world's best merengue dancers.

The event has become so big that, in 1998, so-called extensions of the Santo Domingo merengue festival reached out to Boca Chica and Juan Dolio, both just a bus ride away down Hwy 4. Major merengue parties broke out on beaches and lasted all night – night after night.

The country's other merengue festival is held in Puerto Plata during the first week of October. The entire length of Puerto Plata's malecón is closed to vehicular traffic during the festival. Food stalls are set up on both sides of the broad seaside street and a huge stage is erected upon which many famous merengue singers perform. This Carnival is different from the one in Santo Domingo in that it also includes a harvest festival and an arts-and-crafts fair: Visitors can watch how traditional dishes are prepared using just-harvested crops, and they can observe how many traditional crafts are made.

Latin Music Festival

This huge, annual three-day event – held at the Olympic Stadium in Santo Domingo every June – attracts the top names in Latin music, including jazz, salsa, merengue and bachata players. Among the dozens of featured artists that regularly attend are Enrique Iglesia, salsa king Tito Rojas and merengue living legend Fernando Villalona. The exact dates of this event vary; if you're interested, contact the nearest Dominican tourism office for specifics.

Cultural Festival

Similar in many ways to Carnival, Puerto Plata's weeklong Cultural Festival brings merengue, blues, jazz and folk concerts every June to the Fuerte San Felipe, at one end of the lovely malecón. Troupes from Santo Domingo perform traditional songs and dances, including African spirituals and famous salsa steps. Also held during the third week of June in Puerto Plata, a few blocks away near the Parque Central, is an arts-and-crafts fair where local artisans exhibit their wares.

Cabarete Alegría

Alegría means 'gaiety,' and being gay – as in happy – is the objective in Cabarete during the entire month of February. Cabarete is a hopping place every month, but it's particularly festive during February, when each weekend features a special event.

Events vary yearly, but they generally include activities such as mountain bike races, kite-flying contests and sand-castle-building competitions. The fourth weekend of the month always plays host to the Dominican national surfing and windsurfing championships, held at nearby Playa Encuentro.

Encuentro Classic

Cabarete is one of the top windsurfing sites in the world, and the best time of the year there for the sport is the beginning of summer, when the region's winds – and hurricanes! – are at their mightiest.

Every year during the third week of June, the Encuentro Classic (EC) features course races for various skill classes. On the water, but competing in different events, are world-class year-round windsurfers, very good seasonal windsurfers and a lot of people (the majority) who are out just to have a great time – and that's what matters most at the EC. In case any participants forget that, every night of the week there are concerts and parties on the beach.

Holy Week, Sosúa Style

OK, there isn't really a festival named 'Holy Week, Sosúa Style.' But there might as well be, because the week preceding Easter Sunday – especially the four days leading up to the holiday – are packed with crowds seeking and having fun.

Dominicans from all over the country flock to this restaurant- and bar-packed town beside the big bay to enter volleyball contests, drink themselves silly, soak up sun on the sweeping beach and dance the night away at one of the town's very hip clubs (not necessarily in that order). During the Holy Week, Sosúa entertains Dominicans at their most gregarious.

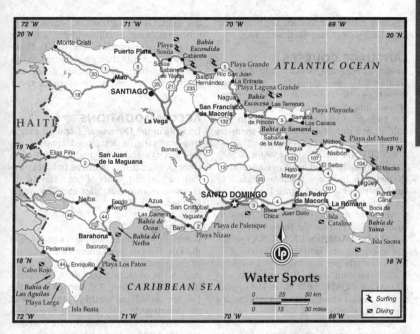

Water Sports

0 25 50 km	
0 15 30 miles	

🏄 Surfing
◪ Diving

ACTIVITIES

All the activities mentioned here are discussed in detail in the regional chapters that follow. There are many possibilities for hiking in the Dominican Republic, especially in the Central Highlands. Not only do most of the DR's national parks lend themselves well to wilderness treks, but the country's many kilometers of unprotected beaches – such as those along the Coconut Coast, from Punta Cana north to Playa del Muerto – also make for popular exploring. If you think walking on sand isn't rigorous enough for someone as rugged as yourself, consider that American football players often head to beaches for cardiovascular workouts during their off-season.

There are some excellent spots for surfing in the Dominican Republic, especially along the north and east coasts. Some of the best breaks occur just west of Sosúa, yet there is also good surfing south of Bahía Samaná.

Diving is another popular sport in the DR, and many of the all-inclusive hotels offer lessons and certification. While there are some areas to dive and explore shipwrecks along the north coast, the southern coast is preferred by most as the water is warmer and the reefs somewhat more protected. The waters off Barahona and Cabo Rojo, near Pedernales, are two of the best spots.

Another healthy activity that takes in some of the splendor the country is bicycling. If you're into the sport, chances are you've already got a bike and should consider bringing it with you. Some airlines treat bicycles as standard baggage, ie, without special fees or requirements (just make sure your bike is properly boxed, so it doesn't get hung up on conveyor belts or damage anyone's luggage). Check with your airline beforehand.

Under the Highlights section earlier in this chapter, you'll find information about whale watching in Bahía de Samaná and boating on Lago Enriquillo, a lake filled with crocs.

LANGUAGE COURSES

Unlike Cuernavaca, Mexico, and Antigua, Guatemala – two cities that are known throughout the Americas for their many Spanish-language schools – there are but a few such programs in the Dominican Republic, and only two worthy of mention here. Both are in Santo Domingo.

ENTRENA (☎ 809-567-8990, fax 566-3492, entrena@codetel.net.do), Calle Rafael Bonnelly 26, has been teaching Spanish to English-speaking people since 1982. Its long list of clients ranges from Peace Corps employees and members of the US Army to baseball players from the Toronto Blue Jays and Oakland Athletics. ENTRENA specializes in one-on-one instruction involving six hours of study per day, five days a week, at US$375 for four weeks. Instruction is also offered on a US$10/hour basis. The organization can also arrange for you to stay with a Dominican family.

AmeriSpan (fax 215-751-1986, www .amerispan.com/au_about.html), PO Box 4000, Philadelphia, PA 19106, USA, a reputable American program founded in 1993, offers 20 hours of one-on-one instruction per week, a private room with a host family, three meals daily, airport pickup and travel insurance for US$1250 for four weeks. Also included in the cost are some afternoon activities such as field trips, history lectures and popular movies.

WORK

The Dominican government really frowns upon foreigners working in the DR, unless they're working for free. There's an assumption here that most any foreigner working in the republic is earning money that a resident Dominican could and should be earning. As a result of this logic, the government makes it very costly for a foreigner to work here by requiring that you obtain an expensive work permit.

In addition, any foreigner who doesn't have residency status must leave the country every six months for a period of no less than one week. Obtaining residency status is very time-consuming, usually requires a lawyer and can cost upwards of US$10,000. However, a lawyer with the right connections can sometimes bring the expense down and shorten the process, which averages about one year.

ACCOMMODATIONS

Lodging in the Dominican Republic ranges from camping in designated areas of national parks and quiet nights at intimate (though often rustic) pensions, to hotel stays with air con and plenty of hot water, to all-inclusive resorts that offer excellent value for the money.

Camping

Generally speaking, camping is a bad idea in the DR. For one thing, there's a real dearth of campgrounds; secondly, campers are a rare and mostly unwelcome sight. The notion of wealthy foreigners (all foreigners in the DR are considered wealthy) moving about the countryside with tents like nomads is upsetting to most Dominicans. They tend to take the attitude that such behavior is just plain improper – not the kind of thing people of means ought to be doing. People with money stay in hotels, not on the beach or in the bush like the homeless.

But that's not to say there's no place for camping in the DR. In fact, there are many designated camping areas in Parque Nacional Armando Bermúdez and Parque Nacional José del Carmen Ramírez. However, few campsites have a ready source of water and the few with toilets – well, let's just say that after closer inspection most people prefer to head into the woods with a shovel and a handful of toilet paper.

Also found within these national parks are free cabins, which have rather healthy rat populations but are otherwise OK (they're dry, they keep the rain off, they're warmer than outside and they offer some degree of security from weirdos). A number of people who use the cabins choose to erect tents inside them and zipper up at night to prevent roaming rats from getting too close. Tents also keep bugs off you while you snooze.

Pensions

Small and intimate, pensions are appearing in the Dominican Republic with increasing frequency. A rather high percentage of them are owned and run by Europeans who dreamed of having their own lovely pension in the American tropics and made their dream a reality. Such places are generally located near a lovely beach and are relished a great deal more by people who'd rather lie in a hammock and listen to waves break on a mostly empty beach than by people whose idea of a perfect afternoon is slamming back sweet drinks at a crowded poolside bar.

Pensions are to the Dominican Republic what B&Bs are to Europe. At a pension, expect to be greeted by the owner when you arrive and to converse at length with that person during your stay, most likely at the dinner table and again at breakfast. Personal service is emphasized; at the large resorts, where 200 people might sit down to dinner simultaneously and the 'owner' is a faceless corporation, it's hard not to feel like a number. At pensions, many guests develop a rapport with the owner and initiate an annual pilgrimage. Many return to the tranquillity and friendship they know awaits them at the same pension year after year.

Hotels

Hotels in the Dominican Republic fall into three general categories: the budget hotel, which is usually uncomfortably warm and short on creature comforts; the modern hotel, which is considerably pricier than the budget hotel but has air con, maid service and cable or satellite TV; and the executive hotel, which typically contains hundreds of amenities-packed rooms, several restaurants, at least two bars, conference rooms and swimming pools.

Resorts

By far the most popular lodging option in the republic is the all-inclusive resort. Before setting foot on Hispaniola, you hand over a fixed amount of money to a travel agent or tour operator who has arranged for your flight to and from the DR; you're met at the airport and whisked away to a sprawl-ing beachside hotel where you'll spend your time variously at the beach, in your room, in one of several restaurants, bars and swimming pools, and possibly in a dance club or participating in a sport such as snorkeling or playing golf.

Dominican all-inclusives are among the least expensive found anywhere in Latin America. The better resorts have Jacuzzis and steam rooms, and offer massage and aerobics. They're an excellent value even if the food usually isn't all that good and the number of guests leaves you feeling a bit like one cow in a large herd.

FOOD
Snacks

Dominicans love snacks, and many of the things they snack on can't be found outside the Caribbean. By far the most common snack in the DR – one served at every celebration – is the *pastelito* (meat-filled turnover). Pastelitos are a tradition enjoyed by generations of Dominicans, and they are widely available. If you see a street vendor removing crescent-shaped pastries from boiling oil, chances are he's just cooked up some pastelitos.

Although they are sometimes filled with white or orange cheese, most of the time they contain beef or chicken. Before being tucked into a circle of dough and cooked, the meat is stewed with onions, olives, tomatoes and a variety of seasonings and is chopped and mixed with peas, nuts and raisins.

Other traditional Dominican snacks include *empanaditas de catibía* (yucca-flour turnovers), *quipes* (cracked-wheat and ground-beef fritters), *frituras de batata* (sweet-potato fritters), *fritos maduros* (ripe plantain fritters), *rollitos de plátano maduro con queso* (ripe plantain and cheese fritters), *tostoncitos* or *platanitos* (green plantain chips), *yaniqueques* (Johnny cakes) and *rosqueticos* (cornmeal rings).

Main Dishes

The most typical Dominican meal is known as *la bandera* (the flag); it consists of white rice, red beans, stewed meat, salad and fried green plantains. It's usually consumed with a juice. Most people find the meal a bit bland, but it's balanced nutritionally, it's economical and it doesn't take a long time to prepare.

Fortunately, most Dominican dishes are quite tasty. Columbus didn't find the Spice Islands, but he did find islands with spice. The Taínos used pepper and other local spices to jazz up their meals. Today, though the native peoples are gone, their influence on Dominican cuisine remains.

Likewise, slave ships brought to the DR not only Africans who had their own ways of cooking, but also some of the spices acquired in Africa. And the Spaniards brought to the New World the spices they knew and loved from Europe, such as allspice, cinnamon,

cloves and nutmeg. As a result of their culinary blending, many Dominican dishes are flavorful, rich and spicy.

One of the dishes that is most dear to Dominican hearts is *sancocho de siete carnes* (seven-meat soup), which features sausage, chicken, beef, goat, salt pork, smoked pork chops and fresh pork chops. These seven meats are combined with many vegetables to prepare the favorite and most representative of Dominican soups. It's generally served at family reunions, all kinds of parties and other celebrations.

Goat meat is extremely popular in the DR and is presented in many different ways. Two of the best are *pierna de chivo asada con ron y cilantro* (roast leg of goat with rum

Typical Dominican Menu Items

Entradas (Appetizers)
 bastoncitos de mero (sea-bass sticks)
 bolitas de queso fritas (fried cheese balls)
 coctel de camarones (shrimp cocktail)

Ensaladas (Salads)
 ensalada de aguacate (avocado salad)
 ensalada de camarones (shrimp salad)
 ensalada de langosta (lobster salad)
 ensalada mixta (mixed salad)
 ensalada rusa (Russian salad)
 ensalada verde (green salad)

Sopas (Soups)
 consume de pollo al jeres (chicken consommé in wine)
 sopa de ajo (garlic soup)
 sopa de cebolla (onion soup)
 sopa de pescado (fish soup)
 sopa de mariscos (seafood soup)
 sopa de pollo criollo (creole chicken soup)
 sopa de vegetales (vegetable soup)

Aves (Poultry)
 guineas al vino (guinea hen in wine)
 pollo al horno (oven-baked chicken)
 pollo en su jugo (lemon-style chicken)

Carnes (Meats)
 chivo al vino (goat cooked in wine)
 filete a la criolla (creole steak)
 filete a la parrilla (broiled steak)
 medallon de filete (beef medallions)

 paticas de cerdo (leg of pork)

Arroces (Rice)
 asopao de camarones (soupy rice with shrimp)
 asopao de langosta (soupy rice with lobster)
 asopao de lambi (soupy rice with conch meat)
 asopao de pollo (soupy rice with chicken)
 asopao de pulpo (soupy rice with octopus)

Pescados y Mariscos (Fish and Seafood)
 camarones a la plancha (grilled shrimp)
 camarones al ajillo (garlic shrimp)
 camarones mariposa (butterfly-style shrimp)
 camarones fritos (fried shrimp)
 camarones enchiladas (broiled shrimp with creole sauce)
 carite al horno (oven-baked kingfish)
 carite frito (fried kingfish)
 cazuela de mariscos (seafood casserole)
 chillo al horno (oven-baked red snapper)
 mero a la criolla (creole sea bass)
 mero a la parrilla (broiled sea bass)
 mero a la plancha (grilled sea bass)
 lambi a la vinagreta (conch meat in vinegar sauce)
 lambi guisado (stewed conch meat)

and coriander) and *chivo guisada en salsa de tomate* (goat stewed in tomato sauce). When the former is prepared properly – with just the right blend of oregano, olive oil, lime juice, garlic, rum and finely chopped coriander leaves – it's absolutely divine.

Even the Dominican version of *picadillo* (beef hash) is a bit exotic, including hard-boiled eggs, raisins, olives and capers. Other Dominican specialties that do not appear on the menus of common restaurants are *locrio de salchichas* (rice with Vienna sausages), *sancocho de rabo de vaca* (oxtail soup) and *patitas de puerco guisadas en salsa de tomate* (pig's feet stewed in tomato sauce).

Desserts

Most Dominican desserts tend to be extremely sweet, so much so that many have 'candy' in their name. The following is a list of the more popular Dominican desserts, given in Spanish and English so that you might recognize them when they appear on a menu:

alegrías (sesame seed and molasses candy)
alfajor (ginger and cassava bread pudding)
arroz con leche (milk and rice pudding)
bizocho de azúcar prieta (brown-sugar cake)
brazo de gitano con crema (cream roll)
canquiñas (sugar candy)
casquitos de guayaba en almíbar (guava shells in syrup)
deditos de piña (pineapple jellies)
dulce de leche cortada (sweetened curdled milk, similar to yogurt)
dulce de naranja en almíbar (orange rinds in sweet syrup)
dulce de tomate en almíbar (tomatoes in sweet syrup)
dulce de toronja en almíbar (grapefruit rinds in sweet syrup)
flan de batata (sweet-potato custard)
flan de leche (milk custard)
flan de piña (pineapple custard)
gofio (sweetened, ground toasted corn)
habichuelas con dulce (sweet red beans)
jalaos (coconut and molasses candy)
lactomarol de batata (sweet-potato compote)

lactomarol de papa (potato compote)
majarete (yellow corn and coconut custard)
malarrabia (tropical fruit compote)
piñonates (coconut bars)
pudín de nevera (trifle pudding)
pudín de pan (bread pudding)
raspadura de leche (milk candy wrapped in royal palm bark)
raspadura de melao (molasses candy wrapped in royal palm bark)
salsa de coco (coconut sauce)
salsa de pasas al ron (raisin and rum sauce)
suspiro o merengue horneados (baked meringue)
suspiro o merengue para lustre (meringue frosting)

Fruit

Dominican produce markets are well stocked with tropical fruits and nuts. The well-known ones include coconuts, cashews, apples, guavas, papayas, oranges, lemons, limes, raspberries, mangoes, avocados, bananas, pineapples, passionfruits and grapefruits. Less well-known tropical fruits found in the DR include:

breadfruit
This large round fruit filled with seeds was brought from the South Pacific to the West Indies during the 18th century by English Captain William Bligh. Today it's found in tropical regions worldwide.

caimito
This fruit is round with a green skin and white pulp. A native of the Caribbean, caimito belongs to the *sapotaceae* family (see sapote, below).

guanábana
This fruit, which comes from a variety of the *anona* (sugar apple) tree, is a native to the West Indies. Its skin is green with tiny thorns, and its delicious, sweet pulp is white with black seeds.

jagua
This fruit comes from one of the various small custard-apple trees native to the American tropics. The fruit is light brown, oval-shaped and has a sweet taste.

mamey
This round fruit with a hard brown seed and bright orange meat is also known as the 'mammee-apple.' It makes a delicious preserve.

plantain
This fruit comes from the banana family but is not edible raw. While still green, it can be boiled,

baked or fried. During cooking, the hard, sour fruit becomes soft and sweet.

sapote

This fruit is oval-shaped and about the size of a human hand. The skin is tough and brown, but the flesh is red and has a sweet, delicate taste.

sour orange

Also called the Seville orange, this citrus fruit is small and acidic. Its juice is usually sprinkled on meats and fish to clean them. It is also used as a substitute for vinegar.

tamarind

This fruit, which comes from a tree native to Asia, is a pod that contains up to 12 large seeds and a soft, flavorful brown pulp that's acidic when eaten raw, and very flavorful when cooked. The pulp is used to make drinks, syrups, jams and sauces.

DRINKS
Nonalcoholic Drinks

All of the usual soft drinks are available (Pepsi, Coke, Sprite, 7-UP), but more often than not you won't have the option of purchasing a diet soft drink. Few Dominicans have weight problems and, therefore, they don't see any reason to drink diet drinks. Strangely, the directors of resorts and other establishments that cater to tourists – many of whom do have weight problems and prefer diet drinks – have been slow to make diet drinks available to their guests.

Ah, but why drink anything from a can when in the land of *batidas* and *refrescos*? Batidas (smoothies) consist of crushed fruit, water, ice and several tablespoons of sugar. Sometimes they also contain a little milk, which Dominicans substitute for ice cream when making milkshakes; in those instances when milk is included in a batida, *leche* appears in the name (to request the drink without milk, ask for it *sin leche*). Popular batidas include *batida de piña* (pineapple drink), *batida de piña con leche* (pineapple milkshake) and *batida de zapote con leche* (sapote milkshake).

Some batidas have strange local names, such as *morir soñando* (literally, 'to die dreaming'), which is a milkshake made with orange juice; *champola*, which is what locals call a guanábana milkshake; and *piña colada* (literally, 'coconut washing'), which consists

of coconut milk, cubed pineapple, cracked ice and tablespoons of sugar mixed in an electric blender until smooth.

Refrescos are very much like batidas except that they don't contain the fruit's pulp. Popular refrescos include *refresco de chinola* (passionfruit), *refresco de cáscara de piña* (pineapple peel) and *refresco de tamarindo* (tamarind). A four-serving recipe for refresco de chinola, for example, calls for removing the pulp from six passionfruits using a spoon; mixing the pulp with four cups of water in an electric blender, no longer than 30 seconds; straining and discarding the pulp; adding six tablespoons of sugar and mixing until dissolved. Pour into tall glasses filled with cracked ice.

Other popular nonalcoholic Dominican drinks include *ponche de frutas* (fruit punch), *limonada* (lemonade) and *mabí*, a delicious drink made from the bark of the tropical liana vine. Beware that the local name for orange juice is *jugo de China*, although most people will understand you if you ask for *jugo de naranja*.

Alcoholic Drinks

There are a handful of locally brewed beers, including Presidente, Quisquerya, Bohemia and Soberante. How they compare to, say, German beers, depends on who you talk to and, perhaps, who is buying. Local versions of Heineken and Miller are also available, as are some imported brands. No matter which label it's wearing, a bottle of beer here is relatively pricey (never less than US$1).

But when it comes to rum, it's tough to beat the DR for price and quality. Dozens of local brands are available, but the big three are Brugal, Barceló and Bermudez. Even within these three brands, there are many rums from which to choose, depending on whether you want a *blanco* (clear) rum, which means it's relatively young and no extra coloring or flavoring was added; a *dorado* (golden) rum, which means some caramel was added for color and taste; or an *añejo* (aged) rum, which contains caramel and is aged in special wooden casks. Differences in alcohol content also exist within these varieties. No matter which rum you

Green Is Good

Many of the DR's beaches are lined with coconut trees, and their fruit is delicious, as is the refreshing juice. The coconut has a thick husk, beneath which is a hard shell. Lining the interior of the shell is the fruit's white meat, which may be soft or hard depending on the coconut's age. Filling most of the shell is the fruit's sweet juice, which chiefly consists of mineral-rich, naturally filtered water that's said to be very good for the kidneys. Coconut juice and coconut meat are best consumed when the fruit is green; when the fruit is brown, the meat has hardened and the juice has begun to sour. Naturally fallen coconuts are decomposing and should not be eaten.

Tapping the juice and exposing the meat is a tricky matter best attempted with a machete. Machetes can be found throughout the DR and usually cost US$5; a small machete is a wise buy if you intend to spend a lot of time at secluded beaches, where purified water won't be readily available to you.

Stand the coconut on end so that its stem faces the ground. Hack the pointy top of the coconut at a 45° angle, rotate the fruit one-fifth and repeat. Do this until a portion of the shell about the length of your thumb is exposed; the husk will peel out and away from the exposed shell as you hack. Carefully strike the bared shell until you've made a small hole in it, or poke a sharp object into one of its 'eyes' – the three soft spots at one end. Tilt your head back and enjoy the delicious juice. Once the juice is gone, place the coconut on the ground and split it in two to get at the meat. The meat is best scooped out of the shell with a spoon, but fingers work fine, too.

Getting your hands on a coconut can be a problem. The easiest way is to pay someone to climb a tree and pick a few nuts; where there are coconut trees, there is usually a kid around who's happy to liberate a few nuts for US$0.50 or so. If you're on your own, pick up a fallen coconut and heave it, bowling-ball style, at the lowest bunch on the tree. You can drop several coconuts with a well-aimed throw.

SCOTT DOGGETT

A local chops open a coconut to get at its sweet juice.

---

choose, a 750ml bottle will rarely cost more than US$10.

So what is the hard drink of choice in the DR? *Ron y Coke* (rum and Coke). Tourists are fond of ordering *ron punch* (rum punch), which tastes more like a blend of sweet tropical juices than a rum drink (the perfect choice for people who like the effects of rum but not the taste). Rum daiquiris are also popular among the foreign crowd.

Don't like beer or rum? No problem. There are many well drinks from which to choose and several Chilean and American wines, although the wines tend to be high priced and low quality. Among the drinks most bartenders in the DR know how to make are *ruso blanco* (white Russian), *ruso negro* (black Russian), *naran gin* (orange gin), *trago de etiqueta roja* (Johnny Walker Red Label Old Scotch Whisky), *trago de etiqueta blanca* (Dewar's White Label Scotch Whisky), Bloody Mary, margarita, martini and Tom Collins.

While the official drinking age in the DR is 18, it's loosely enforced.

ENTERTAINMENT

In most Dominican towns, traditional nocturnal entertainment is pretty much limited to the local bar or the back seat of a car. Some potentially money-saving advice: There may or may not be a pool table inside the bar, but if someone challenges you to a game for money, don't bet more than you can afford to lose. Hustlers aren't always easy to spot.

In the larger towns and cities – and especially those frequented by tourists – the number of bars is much greater. There are usually at least two dance clubs where you can practice your John Travolta moves to merengue, salsa and American Top 40. Virtually all all-inclusive resorts have bars and dance clubs, and the touristy towns of Boca Chica, Cabarete, Sosúa and Puerto Plata have plenty too. As you might expect, Santo Domingo also has a very active night scene.

In the larger towns and cities you'll find theaters showing the latest Hollywood releases in English. In the more populated communities or those frequented by tourists, you'll also find live music. This is particularly true in Santo Domingo, where there are several clubs that feature the country's top merengue, bachata and salsa bands. There's a national theater for stage productions as well.

SPECTATOR SPORTS
Baseball

The national pastime is in season from October to January. Every major city has professional and amateur teams, many of which include Dominicans who play major league baseball in the USA during the spring and summer. Getting tickets is a bit of a hassle, but certainly not impossible. Virtually all of the games are sold out ahead of time, but there are always scalpers out front of the stadiums on game days; a general admission ticket (which normally costs between US$2 and US$10) can run US$25 when purchased through a scalper. Check with taxi drivers and hotel clerks; many times they can get you tickets through contacts, negating the necessity of dealing with scalpers.

Presidente: The Refrigerator Beer

Presidente outsells all other Dominican beers by a wide margin, but not because of its taste or price. The company has cornered the country's beer market through refrigerator sales. Within weeks of when a developer submits plans to the government to open a restaurant or bar, Presidente representatives pay a visit.

'We want to sell you a big, beautiful refrigerator,' they say, 'only we know you have a lot of expenses now, so we'll give you two years to pay for it.' True to their word, the Presidente refrigerators are big and beautiful – about twice the size of a standard fridge and emblazoned with a huge picture of a sweating bottle of Presidente beer rising out of a sea of ice.

There's just one catch: When you agree to buy the refrigerator, you must also agree to sell only one brand of beer – Presidente. Attracted by the offer to defray costs, most developers will end up doing business with the Presidente reps.

And that's why bars and restaurants throughout the DR contain giant refrigerators adorned with a 6-foot bottle of Presidente beer. And that's also why bartenders throughout the land shake their heads *no* when you ask if they have any other brands.

Basketball

Amateur basketball is played year-round at the Olympic Center in Santo Domingo. If you want to watch the country's top players and some very competitive American players hoping to catch a scout's attention, all you have to do is show up. It's free to watch.

Cockfights

Every major town and city in the DR has a *gallera* (cockfight pit), and these places fill with people every Saturday and Sunday afternoon. There's no fee to enter. In Santo Domingo, the fights occur at the Coliseo Gallístico de Santo Domingo on Av Luperón. Every taxi driver knows where it is.

SHOPPING

Shopping in the Dominican Republic can be lots of fun. The amber found here is arguably the best in the world, and the quality of the jewelry made from it varies from thoroughly mediocre to top-notch. You can also find objects made of horn, wood, leather and larimar, the blue stone unique to Hispaniola.

Also available at reasonable cost are high-quality paintings by local artists that many people consider grossly undervalued. Further details on things to buy are provided in the regional chapters.

Many souvenirs sold in the Dominican Republic are made from endangered plant and animal species that have been acquired illegally. By collecting or purchasing these items you undermine the wildlife conservation efforts of the Dominican government and wildlife organizations.

For example, all eight sea turtle species are endangered. The purchase of any sea turtle product directly contributes to their extinction. These products include combs, bracelets and *carey* (turtle meat), which occasionally appears on menus.

All products made of American crocodile are prohibited, as are black and white coral products, despite what some store owners say. Many plant species, especially orchids, are endemic and are also protected by domestic and international law. You should also avoid buying products made from conch shell.

Getting There & Away

AIR

A very inexpensive way to vacation in the Dominican Republic is to buy a package deal that includes airfare, airport pickup, accommodations and meals. Many travel agencies work with airlines and all-inclusive resorts to be able to offer such packages, and when transportation, lodging and food are purchased together this way, the savings to you can be very substantial.

Airports & Airlines

The Dominican Republic has eight international airports, with Las Américas International Airport outside Santo Domingo handling most of the flights in and out of the country. The other seven are mostly served by charter aircraft.

The following airlines have offices in Santo Domingo:

ACE
(☎ 809-549-6243) 54 Av Gustavo Mejía Ricart

Air Atlantic
(☎ 809-472-1441) Av 27 de Febrero and Av Tiradentes

Air Canada
(☎ 809-567-2236) 54 Av Gustavo Mejía Ricart

Air France
(☎ 809-686-8419) 101 Av George Washington

Air Portugal
(☎ 809-472-1441) Av 27 de Febrero at Av Tiradentes

ALM
(☎ 809-687-4569) 28 Av Leopoldo Navarro

American Airlines
(☎ 809-542-5151) In Tempo Building, Av Winston Churchill

Condor
(☎ 809-682-8133) 353 Av George Washington

Continental Airlines
(☎ 809-562-6688) In Tempo Building, Av Winston Churchill

COPA
(☎ 809-562-5824) In Tempo Building, Av Winston Churchill

Hapag-Lloyd
(☎ 809-682-8133) 353 Av George Washington

Iberia
(☎ 809-686-9191) 401 Calle El Conde

LTU
(☎ 809-541-5151) 54 Av Gustavo Mejía Ricart

TWA
(☎ 809-689-6073) 54 Av Francia

See the introductory Getting There & Away chapter for information on international flights to the Dominican Republic. There are regularly scheduled flights from Santo Domingo to Port-au-Prince, Haiti.

Departure Tax

The DR levies a departure tax of US$10 when you're leaving by land or sea. It is not usually included in the price of your ticket and is payable at the airport.

LAND

There are two main crossing points between Haiti and the Dominican Republic. One is at Jimaní/Malpasse in the south, on the road that links Port-au-Prince to Santo Domingo. The second one is at Dajabón/Ouanaminthe in the north; the border crossing is on a road that connects Cap-Haïtien and Santiago. There is a third crossing – at Elías Piña/Belladere – but it is not commonly used by foreigners.

Crossing the border is a relatively simple procedure. The border opens around 8 am and closes around 4 pm; get there well before 4 pm, however, as Haiti has ceased adjusting to summer daylight saving time and the border could close earlier. Regardless, avoid arriving at the border right at closing time or you may be asked to come back the following day.

When you leave Haiti, you must have your passport and the yellow entry card you received upon arrival. When entering the Dominican Republic, travelers of certain nationalities must purchase a tourist card, which costs US$10; others need not pay any-

Fly the Safer Skies

Unfortunately, some of the airlines allowed to land in the DR have very poor safety records; so poor, in fact, that the US Federal Aviation Administration has ruled that the country does not comply with International Civil Aviation Organization standards. In other words, airlines that aren't allowed to operate in most other countries due to their safety records are able to fly in and out of the Dominican Republic on a regular basis.

Although the risk of being involved in an air disaster is quite small, it's good to know something about the airline you are considering taking. A case in point: On February 6, 1996, a charter airline loaded with German tourists bound for Berlin and Frankfurt plunged into the Atlantic Ocean minutes after taking off from the Puerto Plata airport, killing all 189 people aboard. Safety authorities ruled the aircraft's pilots were to blame for the crash.

It's likely some of the victims would not have been aboard that plane had they known that the airline operating it, the now-defunct Dominican carrier Alas de Transporte Internacional, had been shut down temporarily in 1993 after failing to meet international safety standards. Unfortunately, no agency that investigates airline safety issues is willing to grade airlines; such agencies fear they'd be sued by the airlines they gave poor grades to, and they probably would.

However, if you have access to the Internet you might want to visit the nongovernmental *AirSafe Journal* (airsafe.com/airline.htm) for a list of 'fatal events rates' that have been compiled for scores of airlines. If the airline you are considering flying with has had an accident since 1970 that resulted in loss of life, you will be able to obtain information on that accident here.

Often included in such accident reports is a recommendation made by the US National Transportation Safety Board (unfortunately, not all airline mishaps are investigated by the NTSB). If the NTSB report indicates pilot error was a factor in the fatal event, you should assume that the pilot wasn't as well trained as he or she should have been, and you might want to consider flying with another carrier.

---

thing. See each country's Facts for the Visitor chapter for further information on tourist cards, visas and other documents.

Private motor vehicles must obtain government permission from the country of origin before they can cross the border. Rental vehicles are not allowed to cross from one country into the other.

SEA

The only way to get to the DR by sea is by cruise ship. No one in their right mind would recommend it, if the purpose of your trip is to see some of the country. See the introductory Getting There & Away chapter for information about cruise boats calling on the Dominican Republic.

AIR

Air Santo Domingo (☎ 809-683-8020) is the only carrier providing service within the Dominican Republic. The pros and cons of using the airline to get around the DR are discussed in the Getting Around Hispaniola chapter. Here are the various domestic flights available and their one-way fares.

Route	Duration	Cost
Santo Domingo – Puerto Plata	40 min	US$54
Santo Domingo – El Portillo	30 min	US$49
Santo Domingo – Punta Cana	45 min	US$54
La Romana – Puerto Plata	50 min	US$59
La Romana – Punta Cana	20 min	US$27
Puerto Plata – Punta Cana	1 hour	US$59
Puerto Plata – El Portillo	30 min	US$49
El Portillo – Punta Cana	40 min	US$54

Contact Air Santo Domingo for current departure and arrival times. Spanish and English are spoken.

BUS

Bus travel is a great way to see the country. It's cheap, it's convenient and if you take either a Metro Bus or Caribe Tours bus, it's cool and comfortable. Smoking is not permitted on these or any other public buses in the DR.

Although greater detail will be provided in the destination chapters, here are some routes and one-way fares from Santo Domingo served by the country's largest bus companies:

Destination	Metro Bus	Caribe Tours
Castillo	US$4	US$4.50
La Vega	US$3.50	US$3.50
Moca	——	US$4.50
Monte Cristi	US$5.50	——
Puerto Plata	US$5.50	US$6
San Francisco	US$3.75	US$3.50
Santiago	US$4.50	US$5

Other buses travel the major highways and thoroughfares of the country, and to board one all you have to do is flag it down. Following is information on these smaller buses.

Gua-Guas

What the *taptap* is to Haiti – the workhorse bus of the Haitian masses – the *gua-gua* (pronounced 'gwah-gwah') is to the Dominican Republic. Smaller and less comfortable than the behemoths of Metro Bus and Caribe Tours, gua-guas are usually mid-size Toyota Coaster buses built to hold 28 passengers but which sometimes hold 35 or more. These buses continuously cruise the country's various highways, and to catch one you simply go to the highway's edge and flag one down.

Gua-guas are a great way to scoot from one place to another within the same region – from Boca Chica to La Romana, for example. If, for instance, you are staying at a resort in Boca Chica and want to spend midday in La Romana, you would walk to the edge of Hwy 4 and, at the sight of any eastbound bus, extend your arm toward the center of the road in the universal I-want-a-ride gesture. If the oncoming bus is a gua-gua, the driver will slow down and let you board. If it isn't, the driver will just ignore you.

It's important to try to hail all of the eastbound buses because it's difficult to tell a gua-gua from a Metro Bus from a Caribe Tours bus when it's coming toward you at a good speed. If you wait to identify whether a bus is a gua-gua or some other type of bus and then hail it, you won't give the driver time to stop for you.

Soon after you've boarded the gua-gua and taken your seat, a conductor will ask you for the fare, which for Boca Chica to La Romana is less than US$1 in Dominican pesos. You really don't need to know any Spanish to travel on gua-guas, but if you simply tell the conductor 'La Romana, por *favor,'* he will inform you when you've reached the city. Gua-gua fares, incidentally, are rarely more than the Dominican equivalent of US$2.

Públicos

Less obvious than Metro Bus and Caribe Tours buses and gua-guas are the *públicos*, which usually appear in the form of banged-up minivans or small pickup trucks. These vehicles are privately owned and operated and generally cruise up and down the major boulevards of Dominican cities and towns. You can usually only tell that they're públicos because of the number of people in them – seemingly as many as will fit. Públicos rarely have signs identifying themselves as such.

If you find yourself on a major street and would like to go a fair distance up or down it, you might stand at curbside and keep an eye out for a crowded, slow-moving vehicle traveling in the lane closest to the curb. If you see such a creature, look the driver in the eye and point to the ground just in front of you; this is the customary signal indicating you want a ride. To get out, simply say, '*¡Déjame, por favor!*' (Let me out, please!), and the driver will let you out at the earliest safe opportunity. A público ride rarely costs more than the Dominican equivalent of US$1.

CAR & MOTORCYCLE
Road Rules

There are few road rules in the Dominican Republic and those that exist are rarely enforced. Moreover, Dominican traffic police are notoriously corrupt; you could be driving to the letter of the law, never exceeding posted speed limits, and still be stopped by a police officer seeking US$5 to $10 on a trumped-up charge. Crooked traffic cops are a major frustration for motorists in the Dominican Republic.

While it's important not to exceed posted speed limits or otherwise violate traffic laws, it's much more important to proceed cautiously. There's no law against driving at night in the Dominican Republic, just like there's no law against playing Russian rou-

Police Etiquette

Run-ins with Dominican traffic police nearly always happen as follows: You'll be driving down a road and well ahead of you a police officer will step into your lane and wave for you to stop. Usually, the officer will accuse you of speeding, but some drivers have been stopped for 'driving a dirty car' or 'failing to brake fast enough.' One Lonely Planet writer was told simply: 'Give me money. I want to buy beer.' In the DR, a police officer does not need just cause to arrest you.

The best way to act in this situation is to be polite. Never be unfriendly or hostile. Your options are many, but accepting the fact that you're being ripped off and minimizing your losses is the best one. Tell the officer you're sorry for breaking the law and say you'd like to make amends. It doesn't matter if you don't speak Spanish; the officer will know enough English to communicate that he wants money. If you keep only a few dollars' worth of Dominican pesos in a wallet and the rest of your money elsewhere, you can withdraw the small sum and give it to the officer. If he sees that there's nothing more in your wallet, he likely won't trouble you further.

However, if he asks for more money, simply say several times that the rest of your money is at your hotel. Say it very slowly. Smile a lot. Then pleasantly say good-bye. He will let you go, satisfied that he got something from you.

lette, but both will kill you if given enough time. There are just too many pedestrians, animals and dangerous objects on the roads to permit safe driving after sunset. Potholes you could shoot a basketball into are not uncommon.

Foreigners in the DR commonly assume that the local motorists follow the same rules that they do. That's generally a bad assumption. Dominican drivers usually prefer not to signal before turning. They typically think nothing of tailgating, even at high speeds. Throwing litter from a moving vehicle, braking for no apparent reason, passing on blind corners, driving at dangerous speeds – all are common Dominican driving habits. Smart drivers exercise extreme caution while driving in the Dominican Republic.

The big difference between driving a car and riding a motorcycle in the DR is that you're much less likely to get yourself into trouble on a motorcycle. With the exception of some bullet bikes offered by one rental agency, all of the motorcycles available are relatively slow dirt bikes, such as the Yamaha DT 125cc. With a top speed of 100km/h (about 60mph), it's pretty much the fastest Dominican bike you can rent. Also, while you might be tempted to drive a car during a downpour, when visibility is poor and the risk of an accident is great, you'd have to be crazy to ride a motorcycle.

What's more, fewer than half of the roads in the Dominican Republic are paved. On a badly rutted dirt road where you could only manage 15km/h safely in a car, you could perhaps manage three times that speed safely on a dirt bike. Because motorcycles are so popular in the DR, there is no shortage of repair shops; there's at least one in even the smallest Dominican town. The cost of service – such as fixing or even replacing a flat tire – is incredibly cheap.

If you have lots of experience – you can handle a bike with finesse and drive defensively – getting around on a motorcycle is a great way to see the Dominican Republic. However, less-experienced motorcyclists would be unwise to saddle up here, due to the number of undisciplined drivers and the amount of pedestrian and animal traffic on the roads.

Rental

Rental cars are expensive in the Dominican Republic, and the Dominican driver is not known for defensive driving. Buses and taxis – a much safer alternative to driving an unfamiliar car in an unfamiliar land – can take you most anywhere in the DR.

If you insist on renting a car, expect to pay at least US$50 a day (plus US$10 for limited insurance coverage) for an economy car. A major credit card and a valid driver's license from your home country or an international driver's license (a good idea if you're from a country most Dominicans likely have never heard of) are required. Also, you must be at least 25 years old to rent a car here.

Most of the major car-rental companies are represented in Santo Domingo, particularly at Las Américas International Airport, and you'd be advised to rent from them to avoid getting a car that's well past its prime. If you're arriving between mid-December and the end of January, consider reserving a car in advance.

Motorcycles will allow you to get to many places you can't get to by car or bus. To rent one, you should be 25 and have a valid driver's license and a major credit card. It's best to bring your own helmet as you can't rent them here. The cost to rent a motorcycle is around US$16 per day, and there's no insurance available.

BICYCLE

It's not possible to rent bicycles in Santo Domingo, and even if you could you probably wouldn't want to due to the heavy vehicular traffic here and the risk of theft. But it is possible to rent bikes in Cabarete, and seeing the north coast of the DR by bike is an excellent way to pass time. For details on bike rental in Cabarete, see the section that discusses that exciting beachside town.

HITCHHIKING

In the Dominican Republic, hitching is rarely a way to get a free ride, and most people are expected to pitch in toward the driver's costs.

See the warning about hitching, and other information regarding it, in the Getting Around Hispaniola chapter.

WALKING

The Dominican Republic lends itself well to long walks, as it is safe (at least during daylight hours) and generally you're not too far from a bus route if you tire and decide you don't want to walk much more. Be aware that the tropical heat has a way of sneaking up on people who aren't used to it. If you're planning on taking a long walk, or even just a stroll from one end of a beach to the other, consider carrying a bottle of water with you.

BOAT

A daily ferry service links Samaná and Sabana de la Mar. It's limited to people, bicycles and motorcycles (so long as the motorcycles are dirt bikes and not the much heavier street bikes above 125cc). Motorists trying to get between these two cities have to circumvent a rather large area. The trip can take up to four hours by car.

There are other times when you might like to take a boat ride in the DR, such as for whale watching or scuba diving, and the only practical way to get to the islands of Catalina and Saona (there are others) is by boat. Several tour operators offer boat rides up the Río Chavon and the Río Soco, which flank La Romana. Parque Nacional Los Haïtises is best explored by small boat, and you'd feel a little nude in croc-inhabited Lago Enriquillo without a boat.

In most instances, you don't need to use a tour operator to take a boat ride. To get to Isla Saona, for example, it's possible to hire a small boat at water's edge in Bayahibe; there are lots of them there, and there are generally a half-dozen captains nearby willing to take you for a ride.

LOCAL TRANSPORT

Local buses in larger cities and towns provide inexpensive transportation. Most routes operate very frequently and cost very little.

With only a couple of exceptions, taxis in the Dominican Republic are not metered, so it's important to agree on a fare before you climb into the cab. Local people often warn tourists about taking taxis at night, particularly if the tourist is a young woman. If possible, avoid going out at night alone. At the very least, try to catch a taxi in a well-lit place with people looking on. Try to size up the driver before you enter the taxi. If the driver is looking around furtively or seems anxious for you to get in quickly, say thank you and walk away from the car. It's better to be safe than sorry.

Another mode of public transportation is the *motoconcho*, or motorcycle taxi. Motoconcho drivers resemble motorcycle gang members: tough-looking bikers straddling their minihogs beside busy intersections, seemingly hanging out for lack of anything better to do.

In fact, they're friendly lads poised to take you anywhere you want to go. Just give them a destination, agree on a price, hop on, and away you go. Because they don't consume gasoline nearly as quickly as a car or cost nearly as much to maintain, their drivers are able to offer rides for generally half or less what the drivers of auto taxis charge. Do motoconcho drivers ever crash, injuring their passengers? Yes, all the time. If a motoconcho driver begins traveling too fast for your liking, don't hesitate to say, *'¡Más despacio, por favor!'* (Slower, please!).

ORGANIZED TOURS

Most of the all-inclusive resorts offer organized tours to Santo Domingo's Zona Colonial; to the waterfalls and rafting river near the mountain town of Jarabacoa; and to many other sites. For the most part they're a great way to see some of the best the country has to offer without doing much thinking. Just get to the tour bus on time and follow the directions given. You needn't worry about catching the correct public bus and communicating in Spanish; all you need to do is remember to return to the tour bus at a certain time.

The prices for such tours vary widely depending on the popularity of the tour, the amount of driving involved, and numerous other factors. For up-to-date prices and a complete selection of tours offered, speak with the concierge at your hotel. In some tourist areas such as Sosúa and Cabarete, you'll find tour offices located on the main streets. These are operated by the same companies that have offices at the big resorts, and offer the same level of service.

Santo Domingo

Few expressions are more overworked by travel writers than 'land of contrasts,' but in the case of Santo Domingo the disparities are so pronounced that it is transcendentally apt. The city's 2 million inhabitants maintain many traditions, revering their city's rich history and preserving its colonial buildings, yet most Santo Domingans watch American TV with awe and readily adopt the latest American trend. It is a city of immense wealth and grinding poverty, where men in suits who carry cellular phones and those in rags who eke out a living selling lottery tickets are equally common sights. It's a city of Catholics, yet it has no shortage of brothels; of five-star hotels and frequent power outages; of oppressive heat but optimistic people who seldom complain about it or anything else.

Santo Domingo, like the Dominican spirit, is profoundly festive. The city holds not one but two Carnivals a year. It has a Merengue Festival and a Latin Music Festival. Its dance clubs are packed with youths dancing till dawn, its cockfight arena and its baseball stadium attract people from all neighborhoods and its art scene is as rich as any in the Caribbean. It's a city with buses belching long trails of spent diesel, of gorgeous green-blue waters crashing against its cliff-lined coast, of couples overlooking the surf in deep embrace and whispering sweet everythings to each other. It's an urban city with a vast cave system beneath it, a huge old fort and a park that fills daily with hundreds of joggers and cyclists.

Most of all, from the traveler's perspective, Santo Domingo is where the European settlement of the New World began. It is here that the earliest Spanish colonists established a foothold in a part of the world so unknown to them that for many years they believed they were in Asia. It was from the present site of Santo Domingo that the Spanish conquest of South and Central America initially began. It was from the area that is now known as the Zona Colonial that

Christopher Columbus – and later his sons – ruled Spain's newest colony.

The Zona Colonial is a treasure-trove of early colonial architecture. The district, which today represents only a tiny part of the fastest-growing city in the Caribbean, contains the oldest church and the first paved road in the New World, as well as the oldest monastery, the ruins of the first hospital and the oldest surviving European fortress. It also has one of the first European residences in the New World with two floors. The list goes on and on, as do your reasons to spend time exploring this colorful, historic city.

HISTORY

In a way, it can be said that the founding of Santo Domingo was an act of desperation. Columbus initially claimed La Villa de Navidad, in present-day Haiti, as the first site for Spanish colonization of the New World. But when he returned from Spain on his second voyage and found that the settlement and settlers had been destroyed by Taíno Indians, he reluctantly pulled up stakes and went searching for a new place to call home away from home.

He didn't go very far. Just 110km east of abandoned La Villa de Navidad, Columbus spied a quiet bay and established a settlement along its shores. He named it La Isabela in honor of the reigning Spanish queen. Despite Columbus' hopes, La Isabela was beset by problems from the beginning. Many of the colonialists grew sick and died of maladies they'd never known in Europe. Food was scarce. A fire destroyed many buildings, and a hurricane soon knocked down many others.

Despite the troubles, Columbus returned to Spain to give the monarchs an account of his discoveries in Cuba and Jamaica. In his absence, many workers revolted against his brother, Bartholomew, who'd been left in charge. In short order the rebels went elsewhere to live, and the situation at La Isabela became even more dire.

With little reason to remain at the trouble-plagued settlement, Bartholomew led his followers south – to an oceanside site beside a large river and facing a natural harbor. There he founded Nueva Isabela, which he would later rename Santo Domingo.

An interesting though little-known fact about Santo Domingo is that it was originally founded on the east bank of the Río Ozama, where a bread factory, a port and a naval base are located today. In 1502, following a hurricane that destroyed most of the young colony, its new governor, Nicolás de Ovando, elected to rebuild it on the west bank of the river. Six years later the settlement received its royal charter from Spain, making it the first European city in the New World.

Columbus' oldest son, Diego, was named the governor of the colony in 1509, and quickly set about having a splendid house built for his family. Today the former residence is the Museo Alcázar de Colón (Citadel of Columbus Museum). It's a fascinating place, as it contains many pieces of furniture and personal effects said to have been used by Diego and his wife, Doña María de Toledo. From the southern windows of the museum you can see where Christopher Columbus used to moor his ships.

In 1511 the Spanish Crown established a new political institution – the *audiencia*, or audience – intended to check the power of the governor. This high court of three judges gained enormous power and in 1524 it was designated the Audiencia Real (Royal Audience) of Santo Domingo, with jurisdiction in the Caribbean, the Atlantic coast of Mexico and Central America and the northern coast of South America. Its powers encompassed administrative, legislative and consultative functions. In criminal cases, its decisions were final. Today the building in which the tribunal exercised its vast powers is home to a museum featuring colonial-era items.

The capital city's prestige began to decline in the first part of the 16th century with the conquest of Mexico by Hernán Cortés and the discovery there, and later in Peru, of mines containing enormous quantities of gold and silver. This discovery coincided with the exhaustion of the gold deposits and Taíno slave population on Hispaniola. As a result, many colonists left the island to seek their fortunes in Mexico and Peru, and new immigrants from Spain mostly bypassed Santo Domingo.

From the mid-16th century onward, neither Santo Domingo nor the island as a whole recovered so much as a fraction of the influence it had at the start of the conquest. Until Spain repealed the annexation of Santo Domingo in 1865, the colony was mostly mired in economic stagnation. Which is not to say that life there was dull; in 1586, for example, the English buccaneer Sir Francis Drake captured the city and collected a ransom for its return to Spanish control. In 1655 an English fleet commanded by William Penn attempted to take Santo Domingo but retreated after encountering heavy resistance.

In 1801 a brazen ex-slave and Haitian leader by the name of Toussaint L'Ouverture marched into Santo Domingo with his troops and took control of the city without any resistance at all; the city's inhabitants knew they were no match for Toussaint's army of former slaves and wisely didn't try to defeat it. During the occupation, many of the city's residents fled to Venezuela or neighboring islands.

The significance of Toussaint's invasion was that it ended, temporarily, Spanish domination over the eastern part of the island (the western part had been under French, and then Haitian, control for some time; see the Facts about Hispaniola chapter for details). However, Toussaint's control over the city was short-lived. A year after his army entered Santo Domingo, a massive French expedition sent by Napoléon Bonaparte reached the city and expelled the Haitians.

The arrival of the French troops didn't diminish the Haitians' hopes of controlling all of Hispaniola. In the few years that followed, the size of the Haitian army grew and France's desire to support its colonial efforts in the Caribbean diminished. On March 8, 1805, a Haitian force of 21,000 hardened troops attacked the walled city of Santo Domingo, within which were 2000 defiant

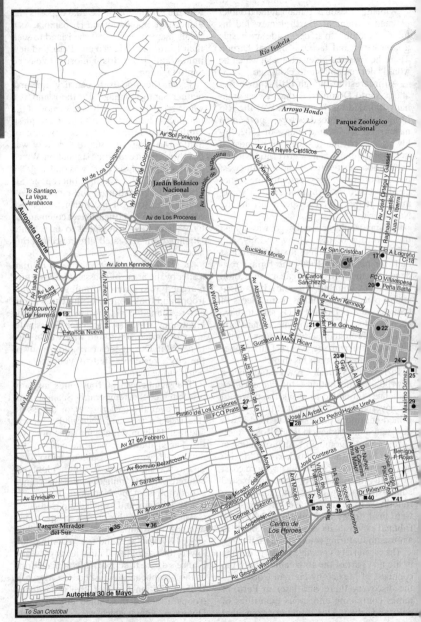

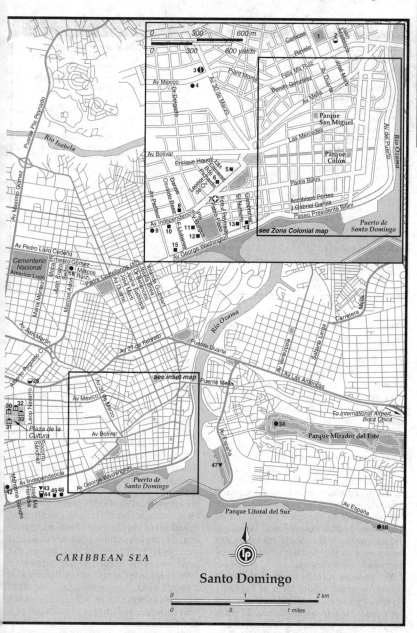

Santo Domingo

DOMINICAN REPUBLIC

SANTO DOMINGO

PLACES TO STAY
5　Hotel Rafael
6　Hotel Antillas
8　La Casona Dorada
10　Hostal Duque de Wellington
11　Hotel El Señorial
12　Hotel Kara
13　Apart-Hotel Sea View
14　Hotel El Napolitano
15　Hotel Inter-Continental
25　Gran Hotel Lina
37　Hispaniola Hotel
38　Hotel Santo Domingo
40　Hotel Villa Italia
45　Renaissance Jaragua Hotel
46　Meliá Santo Domingo Hotel

PLACES TO EAT
25　Restaurante Lina
36　El Mesón de la Cava
38　Alcázar, El Cafetal
40　Costa Azurra
41　Restaurant Vesuvio
43　Restaurant El Fran' Boyan

45　Manhattan Grill, Latino,
　　Café Jaragua
46　La Terraza, Antoine,
　　La Canasta
47　Restaurant Bucanero

OTHER
1　Parque Enriquillo
2　Gua-Guas to Baní,
　　Palmar de Ocoa
3　Secretaría de Estado de
　　Turismo
4　Palacio Nacional
7　Clínica Abreu
9　Galería de Arte Nouveau
16　Quisqueya Stadium
17　Casa Teresa
19　Coliseo Gallístico
21　Galería de Arte El Greco
22　Olympic Stadium
23　Galería de Arte El Pincel
24　Terra Bus
26　Caribe Tours
27　Metro Buses

30　Museo de Arte Moderno
31　Museo Nacional de Historia
　　Natural
32　Museo Nacional de Historia
　　y Geográfia
33　Museo del Hombre
　　Dominicano
34　Faro a Colón
35　Guácara Taíno
39　Secretaria de Estado de
　　Relaciones Exteriores
42　Palacio de Bellas Artes
48　Acuario Nacional

ENTERTAINMENT
18　Penthouse
20　Disco Free
28　Cafe Atlántico
29　Teatro Nacional
38　Marrakesh Bar & Cafe,
　　Las Palmas Bar
44　La Ruta Cerveza
46　El Yarey Piano Bar

French troops and 6000 residents. The siege lasted three weeks, during which time the residents – who had long finished their stored food – were forced to consume their horses, donkeys, dogs, cats and rats.

Despite the efforts of the far-larger Haitian force to wipe out any vestige of French power on the island, the blockade held long enough for French reinforcements to appear on the horizon. When the Haitians noticed that the French ships were continuing past Santo Domingo and heading west toward Haiti, they gave up their battle and began a long trek back home, where they fully expected they'd find French troops occupying their undefended cities. Instead, the French ships sailed along the coast only as far as Azua, some 100km west of Santo Domingo, and then made for the capital. History books do not explain the peculiar route taken by the French reinforcements.

Yet another turning point in the city's history occurred on the night of February 27, 1844, by which time all of Hispaniola had been under Haitian domination for 22 years. Buoyed by a groundswell of Dominican sentiment to separate itself from Haiti, a group of Dominican separatists, headed by Francisco del Rosario Sánchez, executed a bloodless coup and seized control of the city. Convinced that they couldn't oppose the popular insurrection, Haitian authorities agreed to a peaceful surrender of power to the Dominicans and the departure of all deposed Haitians under honorable conditions. Dominicans have since celebrated February 27 as Independence Day.

Much of Santo Domingo's history is discussed in the Facts about Hispaniola chapter, but worth mentioning here is the fact that challenges facing the city's residents aren't always political. In 1930, a brutal hurricane blew through Santo Domingo, destroying thousands of wooden houses and causing the loss of many lives. Other killer storms passed through in 1978 and 1987, and just as this book was being finished in late September 1998, Hurricane Georges struck the city with 200km/h winds. Among the ever-rising death toll were looters shot by police, and inmates who drowned while trying to swim out of a flooded prison.

ORIENTATION

The Santo Domingo of early colonial times was a small, walled community shaped like a pear on the west bank of the Río Ozama. During the late 19th century, overcrowding led to development outside the massive walls that had been erected 200 years earlier to ward off invading pirates. The development was gradual and unremarkable for the first half of the 20th century, but from the mid-1960s up to the present, Santo Domingo has seen enormous growth in population and in geographical extent. Today the Zona Colonial represents a mere 1% of the surface area of the capital city.

Despite the size of the city, it's a fairly easy one in which to maneuver. Most of the city's streets are grouped in grid patterns; some groupings contain streets that run east-west and north-south, while other groupings contain streets that run diagonal to the four cardinal points. Bisecting and separating the clusters of city streets are major boulevards. It has only 10 or so major ones and if you acquaint yourself with them, you'll never feel like you're in a maze. With one glance at the Santo Domingo map you'll quickly recognize the major north-south and east-west thoroughfares.

There are two things to keep in mind when orienting yourself in Santo Domingo. The first is that Av George Washington, which is one of the city's main boulevards and hugs the edge of the Caribbean Sea for 8km, is commonly referred to as the *malecón* ('pier' or 'jetty'). The second is that Dominicans rarely use addresses, but instead describe a site's location relative to a major intersection or landmark; if you're asking someone for directions, it'll help a lot to show them a city map and politely ask them to point out the location of your destination.

Tourists tend to stay in one of two areas: the Zona Colonial and along the malecón between Av Abraham Lincoln and the Zona Colonial. Which is better is a matter of personal choice. On the malecón you'll find large luxury hotels with sea views and all the amenities you'd find in downtown hotels in San Francisco, Paris and Tokyo that cater to businesspeople. Although there are some smaller, lovely hotels in the Zona Colonial, none have sea views or offer many amenities. However, the Zona Colonial – home to streets once strolled by the likes of Christopher Columbus and Sir Francis Drake – offers a strong sense of history found nowhere else in the country.

There are a couple of sections of the city that really should be avoided. These are slum areas as bad as any you'd find in Central America. One of them is along the west bank of the Río Ozama just north of Puente Duarte (Duarte Bridge). The other is on the east side of Av Máximo Gómez north of the Río Isabela. That said, violent crime against tourists is uncommon in the Dominican Republic and is no reason not to explore one of the most historic cities in the Americas.

Maps

There's one map that contains a very good map of Santo Domingo, produced locally by Mapas Triunfo (☎ 809-566-0959, fax 689-1970), PO Box 21388. The map, entitled simply *Dominican Republic*, also contains detailed maps of Santiago, San Pedro de Macorís and Higüey; plus there's a fairly good country map on the back side. It can be found in bookstores and gift shops around town and is fairly well distributed outside the DR; check with a map store in your area.

INFORMATION
Tourist Offices

The city's main tourist office is the Secretaría de Estado de Turismo (☎ 809-221-4660, fax 682-3806), Oficinas Gubernmentales, Bloque D, at the intersection of Av México and Av 30 de Marzo. The tourist office is located on the ground floor of the building at the northwest corner of the intersection. The staff isn't as helpful as it could be, and the literature it occasionally provides contains many inaccuracies. Small maps of the city and Zona Colonial are sometimes available. The office is open 9 am to 5 pm weekdays.

There's also a tourist office in the heart of the Zona Colonial, on Calle Isabel la Católica beside Parque Colón. It's open 9 am to 5 pm daily. Depending on who is staffing the office when you arrive, you may or may

DOMINICAN REPUBLIC

not be greeted by a bilingual person; this is also true in the main tourist office.

Additionally, there are tourist information counters at Las Américas International Airport and at Aeropuerto Gregorio Luperón near Puerto Plata. In addition to speaking Spanish and English, the people attending these counters often understand German.

Money

There is no shortage of places to change money in Santo Domingo, provided you're not trying to change currency that's very exotic; for information on commonly exchanged currencies, exchange rates, Dominican currency and other money matters, see the Money section in the Facts for the Visitor chapter for the DR.

It's possible to exchange major currencies at any of the banks along the malecón; many have ATMs that allow you to withdraw funds from your checking account or against your credit card as long as it's linked to the Plus or Star systems and you have a personal identification number (a PIN, which you have to obtain in your home country). The luxury hotels will exchange currency as well, though usually at a lower rate than the banks.

In the Zona Colonial, there's a money exchange office on Calle Hostos near the Calle El Conde promenade. It is open 9 am till 5 pm Monday through Saturday. Baninter bank, beside the Parque Colón, also offers a currency exchange service. The bank is open 9 am to 5 pm weekdays.

If you find yourself in the Zona Colonial after hours without any Dominican money and are anxious to obtain some, approach one of the guides at Parque Colón and ask him to exchange some money; chances are he will, or he will offer to take you to a nearby money changer. If you do this, make sure you are carrying only the amount of money you want to convert – plus US$5 to give to the guide if he leads you to a money changer. You should change no more than US$40 this way to avoid setting yourself up to get mugged.

Post

The Dominican postal service is very unreliable and slow; mail sent from Santo Domingo to Europe can take up to six weeks to arrive – if it ever does (about half the time it does not). Dominicans residents say mail coming from the USA and elsewhere – possibly containing money sent from relatives living overseas – seldom arrives. Anything of importance must be sent via DHL or Federal Express. DHL (☎ 809-534-7888) has its main office at 26 Av Sarasota, at Av Winston Churchill. Federal Express (☎ 809-565-3636) has its principle office on Av de los Próceres at Camino del Oeste.

If you feel like taking a chance, there's a post office beside Parque Colón in the Zona Colonial. It's open 8 am to 5 pm weekdays and 9 am to noon Saturday.

Telephone

There is a Codetel office and a Tricom office on the Calle El Conde promenade. There's also a Codetel office on Calle General Luperón near Av Duarte. The Codetel offices are open 8 am to 10 pm daily, and the Tricom office is open 9 am to 5 pm Monday through Saturday. At the Codetel offices you can buy a Comuni card that can be used at any of the public telephones, 24 hours a day.

Fax, Email & Internet Access

It is possible to send faxes and send and receive email from the Codetel and Tricom offices. Codetel is usually less expensive and more reliable in performing fax service than Tricom. The per-hour rate for email/Internet access at both offices is about US$2.50. For more information about this service, see the Email section of the Facts for the Visitor chapter for the DR.

Travel Agencies

Located on Calle Arzobispo Mériño, a few meters north of Calle El Conde promenade, is Colonial Tour & Travel (☎ 809-688-5285, fax 682-0964), which has been around many years and enjoys a strong reputation locally. This is a good place to get domestic and international airline tickets. English and

Spanish are spoken. The agency is open 10 am to 6 pm weekdays and 9 am to noon Saturday.

Bookstores

About midway on the Calle El Conde promenade are the Librería Pichaldo and the Librería Daniel. Neither bookstore is very large, nor does either have many new books. Mostly these stores specialize in dusty, out-of-print books, nearly all of which are written in Spanish. These stores are best suited for colonial historians; not only can the buyer find rare, locally published titles about Santo Domingo, the country and the island, but the stores' owners will search their warehouses and private resources for titles if they don't have what you're looking for in stock. Chances are the book they turn up will be used, maybe a bit beat up, and the asking price will be high. But the price is very negotiable (start bargaining at 50% of the asking price) and you may not be able to find the book anywhere else. Both bookstores are open from 9 am to 6 pm Monday through Saturday.

Elsewhere in the Zona Colonial is the Casa Weber, a small bookstore specializing in literature written by Dominicans. If you'd like a book of poems by a Dominican writer or a novel by one of the country's foremost authors, this is the place to come. The store is open 10 am to 5 pm daily except Sunday.

Libraries

Scholars of colonial history will find two libraries to be quite helpful: the Helen Kellogg Library at the Episcopal Union Church on Av Independencia, which has a large selection of English-language books, and the Librería Nacional at the Plaza de la Cultura. Both are open 9 am to 5 pm Monday through Saturday. Memberships are limited to scholars and persons with residency status.

Laundry

There is no shortage of laundromats in Santo Domingo. Many announce their presence with a small sign with the word *lavandería* (laundry) prominently displayed. About half of these places are no more than a home whose owner has a couple of washing machines and a dryer. Customers leave their clothes and pick them up later, often the same day if the clothes arrive before noon. A load of laundry washed, dried and folded typically costs US$3. Due to the nature of these places, they appear and disappear with great frequency. You'd be wise to ask hotel staff for the location of the nearest laundromat. Or, simply ask the front desk if hotel staff can do your laundry for you. In a country where most maids make less than US$10 a day, finding one willing to do a load of laundry for US$3 or US$4 isn't difficult.

Medical Services

Clinica Abreu (☎ 809-688-4411), at Calle Beller 42, near the intersection with Av Independencia, has an emergency room and is widely regarded as the best hospital in the city. It is, for example, the medical facility used by members of the US, Japanese and German embassies. Quite a few staff members received their training at American medical schools and, obviously, speak English. The hospital's doors are open 24 hours for urgent care.

The government hospitals do not compare favorably to Clinica Abreu and are best avoided. They suffer from chronic underfunding, an overworked staff and a lack of modern equipment and supplies. Their waiting rooms tend to be filled with people, many of whom are there to be treated for infectious diseases. If you didn't arrive with a cold or other health problem, there's a good chance you'll leave with one.

Emergency

It used to be that if you needed an ambulance, the fire department or a police officer, you had to know a separate seven-digit phone number for each of them. Today, if you need emergency medical assistance or you want to report a fire or a crime, all you need to dial is ☎ 911 and you will be in contact with a Spanish- and English-speaking person who can dispatch authorities. Public phones will also patch you through to a dispatcher free of charge so long as you dial ☎ 911.

Dangers & Annoyances

Is there a city in the world with more than a million people that doesn't have any muggers? Certainly Santo Domingo isn't such a place. Unfortunately, people get mugged here every day. You can greatly lower your risk by demonstrating a little sense – don't walk down the street with your wallet hanging out of your back pocket, don't wear expensive or flashy jewelry in public, leave the Rolex at home. If you're carrying a camera, keep a firm grip on it at all times. Many muggers are grab-and-run types; if you've got a camera bag slung over a shoulder and a tight grip on its handle, you've basically thwarted any attempt by a grab-and-run mugger.

It's safe to walk downtown in the evening, but avoid streets that appear empty or are poorly lit. If your destination is many blocks away and it's nighttime, hail a taxi. Keep alert. Look behind you frequently to see if someone is following you or eyeing your shopping bag with particularly keen interest. Getting mugged can happen to anyone. If you exercise caution, you shouldn't have any problems. But even if you do, remember: nothing you're wearing or carrying in your purse or wallet is worth dying for. If someone threatens you with a knife or a gun, do what that person says and you will likely live to tell about it.

THINGS TO SEE & DO
Zona Colonial

In physical terms, the Zona Colonial is a slightly hilly area on the west bank of the Río Ozama, where the deep river meets the Caribbean Sea. It averages 11 city blocks from east to west and 11 city blocks from south to north, and its mix of cobblestoned and paved streets follow the classic European grid pattern. By law, none of the buildings in the Zona Colonial are more than three stories tall.

In historical terms, Santo Domingo was the first European city in the Americas, and for years it held unrivaled importance in the New World as the seat of Spanish power in the West Indies and thereabouts. For three decades the area now known as the Zona

Colonial (which then comprised the whole city) was the point of debarkation for Spain's exploration of the Western Hemisphere. Today it stands as a monument to Spain's era as a world superpower.

Most of the structures in the colonial district contain walls that were erected in the 16th century. Many of the buildings' façades have been altered, and in some instances floors have been added, as might be expected with changes in style, usage and materials (few of the buildings, for example, bear tile roofs as they initially did). Those buildings and other colonial attractions that warrant special attention are described here, in the order that you would come upon them in a walking tour.

Fuerte de Santa Bárbara The Fuerte de Santa Bárbara (Fort of Saint Barbara), built during the 1570s, served as one of the city's main points of defense. But it proved no match for Sir Francis Drake and his fleet of 23 ships packed with pirates, who captured the fort in 1586. Today the fort lies in ruin. A garden and small square occupy what was its courtyard. There isn't much to see here anymore, but the view from the elevated site makes for a captivating picture.

Iglesia de Santa Bárbara This well-restored church was built in 1574 in honor of the patron saint of the military. Baroque in style, it is unusual for its lack of proportion: its towers are quite different in height and design, and it is crowned by a capital that is outrageously small for the building. Perhaps because it was sacked by Drake, when it was rebuilt many years later two of its three arches were made windowless while the third one frames an unusually sturdy door; gaining entry to the church wouldn't be so easy if it came under attack again. It also was likely rebuilt with hurricanes in mind.

Museo de las Atarazanas This building, constructed during the early 16th century, initially served as a customs depot and later as a warehouse. Today it houses a little-visited naval museum that's really quite a treat. In it you'll find items recovered from

Museo Alcázar de Colón in Santo Domingo's Zona Colonial, Dominican Republic

GIANFRANCO LANZETTI

Avenida Mella, a typically busy street in Santo Domingo

GIANFRANCO LANZETTI

Iglesia de San Cristóbal, known for a mural by Spanish artist José Vela Zanetti, San Cristóbal, DR

Typical afternoon beach scene in Sosúa, northwestern Dominican Republic

The scene at Club Dominicus Beach, on the southwestern coast of the Dominican Republic

Altos de Chavón, an artists' community near La Romana, southeastern Dominican Republic

Parque Nacional Jaragua, southwestern DR

Rare iguana in Parque Nacional Isla Cabritos, DR

Exploring mangrove forests beside Lago Redonda near Miches, Dominican Republic

ships that wrecked near the Dominican Republic hundreds of years ago. Such items include cannons, crucifixes, silver coins, belt buckles, plates, silver spoons, swords, brandy bottles, pipes and silver bars. The signage is in Spanish and English and contains lots of good information.

Vast information is offered about life aboard the Spanish galleons that plied the Caribbean Sea. One learns, for example, that a common seaman on a galleon sailing between Santo Domingo and Spain during the 16th century earned 20 *reales* (coins) a month; during that period, one real would buy a night's lodging at one of the best inns in Seville.

The museum is open 9 am to 6 pm Monday through Saturday (closed Wednesday), and 9 am to 5 pm Sunday. Admission is US$1.

Monasterio de San Francisco The Monasterio de San Francisco, the first monastery in the New World, belonged to the first order of Franciscan friars who arrived to evangelize the island. Dating from 1508, the monastery originally consisted of three connecting chapels. It was set ablaze by Drake in 1586, rebuilt, devastated by an earthquake in 1673, rebuilt, ruined by another earthquake in 1751 and rebuilt again. From 1881 until the 1930s it was used as an insane asylum, and portions of the chains used to secure inmates can still be seen. A powerful hurricane shut down the asylum, and the buildings have been left to the forces of nature ever since. Today the ruins are occasionally used to stage concerts and artistic performances.

Museo Alcázar de Colón The Citadel of Columbus, designed in Gothic-Mudéjar transitional style, was used as a residence by Columbus' son, Diego Columbus, and his wife, Doña María de Toledo, during the early 16th century. Today it houses a museum featuring many pieces said to have belonged to them.

The palace/fortress was used by the couple until 1523, when Diego was recalled to Spain, and relatives occupied the handsome building for the next hundred years. It was subsequently allowed to deteriorate,

then was used as a prison and a warehouse before it was finally abandoned. By 1775 it was a vandalized shell of its former self and served as the unofficial city dump. Less than a hundred years later, only two of its walls remained at right angles. The magnificent building we see today is the result of three restorations: one in 1957, another in 1971 and a third in 1992. Although every attempt to rebuild the Alcázar to its original specifications was made, it is extremely unlikely any of the period pieces found inside it were ever used by any Columbus family member. Still, the building is definitely worth a look as great pain was taken to adhere to historical authenticity with regard to reconstruction and decor. Admission is US$1.

Plaza de la Hispanidad The plaza in front of the Alcázar de Colón has been made over many times, most recently during the early 1990s in honor of the 500th anniversary of Christopher Columbus's discovery of the New World. The plaza is a large, open area that makes for a lovely stroll on a warm afternoon. Running along its northwest side is Calle La Atarazana, fronted by numerous restaurants, bars and shops in buildings that served as warehouses through most of the 16th and 17th centuries. The street is closed to vehicular traffic and lining much of it every afternoon are dozens of tables set up by the restaurants and bars. This is a very popular place to sip a soda or a beer in the late afternoon and look out across the plaza to the Alcázar and beyond.

Puerto de San Diego Downhill from the Alcázar de Colón is this imposing entryway built in 1571. For a time it was the main gate into the city. Beside it you can still see some of the original wall. This portion was erected to protect the city from an assault launched from the river's edge.

Casa del Cordón The 'House of Cord' – so named because its imposing stone façade is adorned with the chiseled sash-and-cord symbol of the Franciscan order – is said to be not only one of the first European residences in the Americas, but also one of the

DOMINICAN REPUBLIC

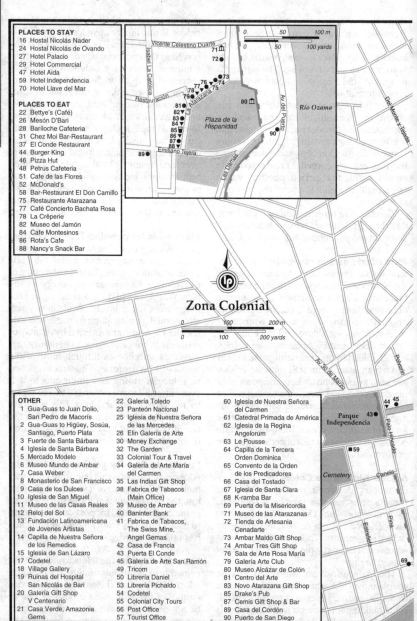

PLACES TO STAY
16 Hostal Nicolás Nader
24 Hostal Nicolás de Ovando
27 Hotel Palacio
29 Hotel Commercial
47 Hotel Aida
59 Hotel Independencia
70 Hotel Llave del Mar

PLACES TO EAT
22 Bettye's (Café)
26 Mesón D'Bari
28 Bariloche Cafeteria
31 Chez Moi Bar-Restaurant
37 El Conde Restaurant
44 Burger King
46 Pizza Hut
48 Petrus Cafeteria
51 Cafe de las Flores
52 McDonald's
58 Bar-Restaurant El Don Camillo
75 Restaurante Atarazana
77 Café Concierto Bachata Rosa
78 La Crêperie
82 Museo del Jamón
84 Cafe Montesinos
86 Rota's Cafe
88 Nancy's Snack Bar

Zona Colonial

OTHER
1   Gua-Guas to Juan Dolio,
    San Pedro de Macorís
2   Gua-Guas to Higüey, Sosúa,
    Santiago, Puerto Plata
3   Fuerte de Santa Bárbara
4   Iglesia de Santa Bárbara
5   Mercado Modelo
6   Museo Mundo de Ambar
7   Casa Weber
8   Monasterio de San Francisco
9   Casa de los Dulces
10 Iglesia de San Miguel
11 Museo de las Casas Reales
12 Reloj del Sol
13 Fundación Latinoamericana
    de Jovenes Artistas
14 Capilla de Nuestra Señora
    de los Remedios
15 Iglesia de San Lázaro
17 Codetel
18 Village Gallery
19 Ruinas del Hospital
    San Nicolás de Bari
20 Galería Gift Shop
    V Centenario
21 Casa Verde, Amazonia
    Gems
22 Galería Toledo
23 Panteón Nacional
25 Iglesia de Nuestra Señora
    de las Mercedes
26 Elin Galería de Arte
30 Money Exchange
32 The Garden
33 Colonial Tour & Travel
34 Galería de Arte María
    del Carmen
35 Las Indias Gift Shop
38 Fabrica de Tabacos
    (Main Office)
39 Museo de Ambar
40 Baninter Bank
41 Fabrica de Tabacos,
    The Swiss Mine,
    Angel Gemas
42 Casa de Francia
43 Puerta El Conde
45 Galería de Arte San Ramón
49 Tricom
50 Librería Daniel
53 Librería Pichaldo
54 Codetel
55 Colonial City Tours
56 Post Office
57 Tourist Office
60 Iglesia de Nuestra Señora
    del Carmen
61 Catedral Primada de América
62 Iglesia de la Regina
    Angelorum
63 Le Pousse
64 Capilla de la Tercera
    Orden Dominica
65 Convento de la Orden
    de los Predicadores
66 Casa del Tostado
67 Iglesia de Santa Clara
68 K-ramba Bar
69 Puerta de la Misericordia
71 Museo de las Atarazanas
72 Tienda de Artesania
    Cenadarte
73 Ambar Maldo Gift Shop
74 Ambar Tres Gift Shop
76 Sala de Arte Rosa María
79 Galería Arte Club
80 Museo Alcázar de Colón
81 Centro del Arte
83 Novo Atarazana Gift Shop
85 Drake's Pub
87 Cemis Gift Shop & Bar
89 Casa del Cordón
90 Puerto de San Diego

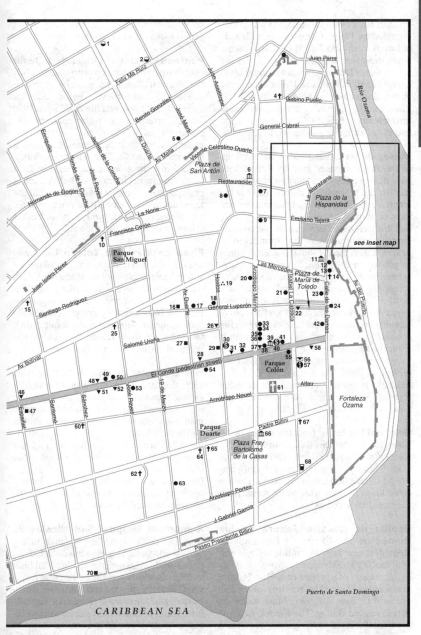

first residences with two floors. It was briefly occupied by Diego Columbus and his wife before they moved into their stately home down the street. It is also said to be the site where Santo Domingo's women lined up to hand over their jewels to Drake during the month he and his men held the city hostage. The building housed a commercial bank through most of the 1990s, but it was vacant and plans for it were unknown in late 1998.

Museo de las Casas Reales The Museum of the Royal Houses, built in Renaissance style during the 16th century and once occupied by the powerful Audiencia Real, is the country's finest museum. It showcases objects of 16th-, 17th- and 18th-century colonial life, including many treasures recovered from Spanish galleons that foundered in nearby waters. Each room has been restored to gilt-trimmed opulence, and the displays range from exquisitely crafted antique weaponry to dozens of hand-blown wine bottles and many thousands of deeply engraved Spanish pieces of eight (coins). Leaning against the southern exterior of the museum is an enormous rusting anchor from the Spanish galleon *Nuetra Señora de Guadalupe*, which sank in a storm near the mouth of Bahía de Samaná in 1724. The museum is open 9 am to 5 pm Tuesday through Saturday, and 10 am to 1:30 pm Sunday. Admission is US$1.50.

Reloj del Sol Across from the Museo de las Casas Reales, the sun clock, or sundial as it is also known, was built by Governor Francisco Rubio y Peñaranda in 1753 and positioned so that officials in the Royal Houses could know the time with only a glance from their eastern windows.

Capilla de Nuestra Señora de los Remedios The Chapel of Our Lady of Remedies was built in Gothic style in the 16th century by alderman Francisco de Avila in the manner of a private chapel and family mausoleum. The earliest residents of the city are said to have attended Mass under its barrel-vaulted ceiling. The chapel, which is occasionally open to the public, contains a series of blind arches on the sides. After years of wear, it was rebuilt in 1884.

Panteón Nacional Originally a Jesuit church when was it was constructed in 1747, the National Mausoleum was also a tobacco warehouse and a theater before dictator Rafael Trujillo restored the building in 1958 for its current usage. Today many of the country's most illustrious persons are honored here, their remains sealed behind two marble walls. The entire building, including its neoclassical façade, is built of large limestone blocks. As befits such a place, an armed soldier is ever present at the mausoleum's entrance. There is no price for admission, but shorts, tank tops and other skimpy apparel are not allowed.

Plaza de María de Toledo This small square named in honor of Diego Columbus' wife is remarkable for two arches that were once part of the Jesuits' residence in the 17th century. Note the buttresses that support the Panteón Nacional; they are original, dating back to the construction of the Jesuit church in 1747, and a likely reason the building has survived earthquakes and hurricanes since.

Hostal Nicolás de Ovando Dating from 1509, this large structure with a handsome Gothic façade was originally the residence of Governor Nicolas de Ovando. He was the man who ordered Santo Domingo rebuilt on the west bank of the Río Ozama following a hurricane that leveled most of the colony while it stood on the east bank of the river. Most recently it served as an inn (*hostal* means 'inn'). In late 1998 a French company was in the process of restoring the building and had plans to reopen the inn.

Ruinas del Hospital San Nicolás de Bari The ruins of the first hospital in the New World stand as a monument to Governor Ovando, who ordered the hospital built in 1503. So sturdy was the edifice that it survived Drake's invasion and numerous earthquakes and hurricanes, remaining virtually intact until a thoughtless public-works official ordered much of it knocked down in

GIANFRANCO LANZETTI

Ruinas del Hospital San Nicolás de Bari

1911 so it wouldn't pose a threat to pedestrians. Even today, visitors can still see several of its high walls and Moorish arches and note that the hospital's floor plan followed the form of a Latin cross.

Iglesia de San Miguel The Church of Michael the Archangel, who was the protector against smallpox, is notable for two reasons: first, the juxtaposition of the rectangular doorway formed by carved blocks of rock stands in sharp but appealing contrast to the structure's curved exterior. Second, a code established in 1784 ordered that all religious brotherhoods of blacks be transferred to this church, which would be equipped with medical facilities to treat their diseases. There is evidence that the code existed, but there is no proof that it was ever acted upon.

Iglesia de Nuestra Señora de las Mercedes The Iglesia de Nuestra Señora de las Mercedes (Church of Our Lady of Mercy), constructed during the first half of the 16th century, was sacked by Drake and his men and reconstructed on numerous occasions following earthquakes and hurricanes. The church is remarkable for its pulpit, which is sustained by a support in the shape of a serpent demon. The intricate Baroque altarpiece is carved from tropical hardwood. Of the group of buildings that pay homage to the Virgin Mary, only the cloister adjacent to the church is in original condition.

Iglesia de San Lázaro The Gothic Iglesia de San Lázaro (Church of Saint Lazarus) was erected in 1650, but has since been altered in so many ways that today it's an unattractive, architecturally unbalanced structure. But its rich history more than offsets its apparent faults. Built beside a hospital from the late 16th century that specifically treated people with infectious diseases, the church was constructed to give the patients hope – a commodity that no doubt was in short supply, especially given that effective treatments for tuberculosis, leprosy and other common diseases of colonial times remained hundreds of years away. In the dim lighting of the church it's not hard to imagine masses of sick people filling the church, staring up at the depictions of Jesus and the Virgin Mary and praying for an end to their suffering.

Casa de Francia The French House, as it is known today, was originally the house of Hernán Cortés, conqueror of Mexico. It was in this building that Cortés is said to have resided and organized his triumphant expedition. From its construction in the early 16th century until the 19th century, it served as a residence for many important people. During the 19th century it was converted into government offices; in 1917 it was remodeled and occupied by the Banco Nacional de Santo Domingo; and in 1932 it lodged the court that settled land disputes. In 1950 it became quarters for the Dominican income tax service. Today it houses the cultural division of the French Embassy.

Visitors are welcome to come in and take a look at this marvel of masonry. Experts believe the Casa de Francia and the Museo de las Casas Reales were designed by the same masters, since they share similar main elements: a flat façade; a double bay in the upper and lower stories; repeating patterns of doors and windows on both floors; and top-notch stone rubblework masonry around the windows, doors and corner shorings.

Fortaleza Ozama Variously called Ozama Fortress, the Fortress of Santo Domingo and simply the Fortress, Fortaleza Ozama is the oldest colonial military edifice in the New World. It was so well constructed when it was erected in 1505 that it continued to serve as a military garrison and prison until the 1960s, when it was opened to the public for touring.

The main gate gives way to the enclosure's esplanade, where massively walled buildings were erected. The most impressive, and clearly visible from the entryway, is the Torre del Homenaje (Tower of Homage), which is very reminiscent of Spanish castles. Its 2m-thick walls contain dozens of riflemen's embrasures. The roof of the tower, reached by an interior spiral staircase, offers 360° views of the city. Off to the side, solid and windowless, stands the old powder house; notice the statue of the Virgin Mary over the door, seemingly standing guard over the fort's supply of gunpowder.

Also on the esplanade is a statue of Gonzalo Fernández de Oviedo, perhaps the best-known military chronicler of the New World. The fort is open 9 am to 5 pm daily. Admission is US$1.

Near the door you'll find several guides, whose knowledge of the fort generally is quite impressive; be sure to agree on a fee before hiring one of them.

Calle de las Damas Heading north and south in front of the fortress is Calle de las Damas (the Ladies' Street), the first paved street in the Americas. Laid in 1502, the street acquired its name from the wife of Diego Columbus and her lady friends, who made a habit of strolling the road every afternoon, weather permitting.

Iglesia de Santa Clara Iglesia de Santa Clara (the Church of Saint Claire) was built in 1552 and was home to the first nunnery in the New World. Thirty years later it, too, was sacked by Drake and his men, who quite apparently hated all things Catholic. It was later rebuilt with funds from the Spanish Crown. This simple, discreet church has a severe Renaissance-style portal with a gable containing a bust of Saint Claire. The doors of the church remain closed except on Sunday mornings for Mass.

Casa del Tostado The house of the writer Francisco Tostado was built in the 16th century and is an architectural gem combining Gothic and Moorish elements. After the scribe died, the house was left to an heir who was sadly struck dead by a cannonball on Calle de las Damas during Drake's attack on Santo Domingo. Today the pridefully restored Casa del Tostado is home to a little-visited museum that honors 19th-century Dominican life by housing furniture, tools and other household objects from that time. The museum is open 9 am to 2 pm daily except Wednesday. Admission is US$1.

Convento de la Orden de los Predicadores The Convent of the Order of Preachers is the oldest still-standing church in the New World and is also the first convent of the Dominican order founded in the Americas. Constructed in 1510, this is the convent where Father Bartolomé de las Casas, the famous chronicler of Spanish atrocities committed against Indians, did much of his writing. The convent and adjacent church were gifts of Charles V. The vault of the chapel is remarkable for its mythological and astrological representations, which are carved in stone and may be unique in Spanish America. On the walls are paintings of the life of Santo Domingo and Pope Saint Pius V.

Capilla de la Tercera Orden Dominica The Chapel of the Third Dominican Order was built in 1729 and is the only colonial monument in all of Santo Domingo to reach the present fully intact. Today the building, with a very graceful Baroque façade, is used by the office of the archbishop of Santo Domingo.

Catedral Primada de América Diego Columbus, son of the great explorer, set the first stone of the Primate Cathedral of America in 1514, but construction didn't begin in earnest until the arrival of the first bishop, Alejandro Geraldini, in 1521. From then up until 1540, numerous architects working at varying times designed portions of the church and adjoining buildings, which is why its vault is Gothic, its arches are Romanesque and its ornamentation is Baroque. It's anyone's guess what the planned bell tower would have looked like; a shortage of funds curtailed construction, and the steeple, which undoubtedly would have offered a commanding view of the city, never was built.

Although Santo Domingo residents like to say their cathedral was the first in the Western Hemisphere, Mexico City in fact built one between 1524 and 1532; it stood for four decades, up until 1573, when it was knocked down and replaced by the Catedral Metropolitano, which is arguably Mexico's most imposing structure. It can accurately be said that Santo Domingo's cathedral is the oldest cathedral in operation, which is something, for sure, but its current interior is a far cry from the original – thanks again to Drake and his crew of pirates, who used the basilica as their headquarters during their 1586 assault on the city. While there, they stole everything of value that could be carried away and extensively vandalized the church before departing. The cathedral was being restored in late 1998. Among its more impressive features are its awesome vaulted ceiling and its 14 interior chapels. Signs in English and Spanish beside each chapel and other features describe their rich histories. The cathedral is open 9 am to 4 pm daily; there's no admission fee but shorts, bikini tops and other inappropriate attire are strictly prohibited.

Parque Colón Beside the cathedral is this historic park containing several popular shade trees and a large statue of the Admiral himself. It is *the* meeting place for area residents, and it's alive with tourists, townsfolk, hawkers, guides, taxi drivers, shoeshine boys and tourist police all day long. El Conde Restaurant, at the corner of Calle El Conde and Calle Arzobispo Mériño, has seating inside and out and lends itself particularly well to people watching. Next door is Fabrica de Tabacos, a cigar factory and showroom. If you've been meaning to sample an excellent Dominican cigar, you might consider buying one at the factory and smoking it at one of the restaurant's outdoor tables – a lot of people do.

Less popular plazas dating from the colonial era include Parque María Trinidad Sánchez, Plaza de San Antón, Plazoleta Padre Billini and Plaza Fray Bartolomé, to name a few; all appear on the Zona Colonial map.

A view of Parque Colón with Santo Domingo's cathedral in the background

GIANFRANCO LANZETTI

DOMINICAN REPUBLIC

Iglesia Nuestra Señora del Carmen Our Lady of Carmen Church was built during the mid-16th century and is famous for its carved-mahogany figure of Jesus, which is worshipped during ceremonies every Holy Wednesday, during Easter Holy Week. The small church was originally built of stone, then of brick. During colonial times its small square was used to stage comedies. The church was set aflame by Drake in 1586 and variously served as a hospital, a church, a jail and an inn after its rebuilding.

Iglesia de la Regina Angelorum This somewhat haunted-looking church, the Queen of the Angels, was built toward the end of the 16th century by a woman who donated her entire fortune to construct this monument for the cloistered Dominican Sisters. In addition to its imposing – even disturbing – façade, with what appears to be the head of a demon above the portal, the church is known for its elaborate 18th-century Baroque altar, which is crowned with the king's coat of arms.

Puerta El Conde The Gate of the Count owes its name to Bernardo de Meneses y Bracamonte, Count of Peñalba, who in 1655 led the successful defense of Santo Domingo against an invading force of 13,000 British troops. The gate is the supreme symbol of Dominican patriotism because right beside it, in February 1844, a handful of brave Dominicans executed a bloodless coup against occupying Haitian forces; their actions resulted in the creation of a wholly independent Dominican Republic. It was atop the gate that the very first Dominican flag was raised. Just west of the gate is a mausoleum with the remains of three national heroes: Juan Pablo Duarte, Francisco del Rosario Sánchez and Ramón Matías Mella.

Persistent Prehistoric Bacteria

From the belly of a honeybee that bumbled when saber-toothed cats prowled the planet, two American researchers have brought back to life dormant bacteria that were alive more than 25 million years ago.

Preserved inside an insect trapped in the sap of one of the island's flowering trees, these living fossils are the first proof that any organism of such antiquity can be revived, according to research made public in the journal *Science* in May 1995.

Thriving now in a laboratory under lock and key at California Polytechnic State University in San Luis Obispo, California, the ancient bacteria promise new insights into the pace of evolution and may even prove to be a source of potentially useful new medicines.

The age of the bacteria was determined by dating microscopic fossils from the rocks in the Dominican Republic where the amber was found. A limited history of the bacteria may be described in three steps:

1. A stingless bee, most likely lured by a fallen flower, was caught in sticky tree sap that later fossilized into amber.
2. As the amber dried, bacteria inside the bee formed themselves into protective spores that could survive extreme dehydration and lack of food.
3. Scientists extracted the spores from the amber and bathed them in nutrients, and the bacteria began to grow again.

Researchers are now testing the bacteria to see if they produce useful antibiotics or other medicinal compounds. Until 1995, the longest-surviving spore was known to have lasted only 70 years.

Puerta de la Misericordia The Gate of Mercy was erected during the 16th century and for many decades served as the main entryway into the city from the west. The gate obtained its name after a major earthquake in 1842, when a large tent was erected beside it to provide temporary shelter for the homeless.

Amber Museums Not every attraction in the Zona Colonial is historic. The finest amber in the world is found in the Dominican Republic, and there are two museums in the old district that feature the prized fossil resin. Perhaps the better of the two is the **Museo Mundo de Ambar** (☎ 809-682-3309, fax 688-1142), which contains sections describing in Spanish and English the history of amber, amber of the world and Dominican amber. The collection on display, which includes fine amber jewelry and amber samples from around the planet, is quite impressive. Between the exhibits' thorough signage and the audio-visual displays showing amber being mined and made into jewelry, the museum likely answers whatever questions you might have concerning the stuff.

The **Museo de Ambar** (☎ 809-686-4471, fax 682-5101), beside the Parque Colón, also does a good job of informing visitors about amber. It contains many dozens of high-quality close-ups of amber with its many inclusions ('inclusions' usually means insects, but it can also mean leaves, baby reptiles and so on – anything that could have gotten caught in tree sap millions of years ago and fossilized along with the sap).

Both museums are privately owned and contain gift shops that sell lovely pieces of amber jewelry. Both are open 9 am to 5 pm daily. There is no cost to visit the gift shops, but the price of admission to each museum is US$1.

Plaza de la Cultura

Located near the center of the city is the Plaza de la Cultura (Cultural Plaza), a complex of modern buildings in a parklike setting on land once owned by the dictator Trujillo and 'donated' to the public after his assassination in 1961. As its name implies,

the site is home to cultural attractions, in this case four museums and the national theater. All of the museums are open 10 am to 5 pm Tuesday through Sunday; informational signs are in Spanish only, and the cost of admission is US$1.50 for each.

Museo del Hombre Dominicano Of the four museums, by far the most spectacular is the Museo del Hombre Dominicano (Museum of Dominican Man). It houses exhibits featuring Hispaniola's pre-Columbian peoples – how they lived, the tools they used, the stuff they left behind. Another section focuses on the Conquest and emphasizes the brutality the slaves experienced at the hands of the Spanish. Perhaps the most interesting section of this museum is the one dealing with the typical Dominican peasants of the here and now – their way of life, their religious artifacts. A typical country house has been reconstructed so the visitor can see the simplicity of the farmer's home, down to the beds he and his family use. There are many captivating photos of today's rural Dominicans. A very pleasant surprise is the wing devoted to Dominican Carnival costumes and masks.

Museo de Arte Moderno The Museo de Arte Moderno (Museum of Modern Art) will come as a shock to those of you who readily associate Dominican art with primitive painters. Some surely are primitivists, influenced by primitive art in Paris some 50 years ago. But as the works in the museum attest, most Dominican artists are not of that school. This becomes abundantly clear as the visitor passes from painting to painting and room to room in the four-story building, which maintains a permanent collection of Dominican art, temporary international exhibits and temporary local and Caribbean exhibits. Among the big names in Dominican fine art whose work is represented in the permanent collection are Luís Desangles, Adriana Billini, Celeste Woss y Gil, Jose Vela Zanetti, Dario Suro and Martin Santos.

Museo Nacional de Historia Natural The Museum of Natural History contains some interesting exhibits, but unless you can read Spanish, the signage (and the museum) won't prove terribly informative to you. The 1st floor features amber – how it came to be, how it's mined, and so on – and exhibits that explain the island's biogeographic history. The exhibits on the 2nd floor focus on the country's many life zones and its wildlife; there are plenty of stuffed birds and fish. The 3rd and uppermost floor is also dedicated to endemic Dominican species, although one room contains a stuffed lion and other animals native to other parts of the world. As far as natural history museums go, this one is nothing special.

Museo Nacional de Historia y Geográfia

The National Museum of History and Geography is divided into three wings, with each containing exhibits particular to a time period – specifically, 1822-61, 1861-1916, and 1916-61. In chronological order, the first wing focuses on the battles between Haitians and Dominicans; many weapons of the period are displayed, along with lots of patriotic art. The second wing is mostly devoted to General Ulises Heureaux, the country's most prominent dictator during the 19th century. The third wing concentrates on Trujillo, the country's most prominent dictator during the 20th century, and the emphasis seems to be on his personal effects (his combs, razor, wallet, etc, are displayed with an air of great import). The National Museum of History and Geography isn't what it could be, and few tourists who enter it stay longer than 30 minutes.

Acuario Nacional

Few foreigners who visit the National Aquarium (☎ 809-592-1509), on Av 28 de Enero across the Río Ozama from the Zona Colonial and on the way to the international airport, leave without being enormously impressed. The aquarium is every bit as impressive as some of the best aquariums found in Europe and the USA, and the amount of money spent on it during the Balaguer administration – money that could have been spent on public education, health care or on a number of other badly funded

areas – sparked much debate about the president's priorities.

Among the remarkable attractions at the aquarium are an enormous Plexiglas tank with an underwater walkway where sharks and other large fish pass overhead; a playful manatee that was rescued as a baby near the coast of Barahona after a thoughtless fisherman killed its mother; and a pool where you can reach down and pet an endangered slider turtle (the turtles are part of a breeding project). The aquarium's one weakness is that the signage is in Spanish only. Hours are 9:30 am to 6:30 pm Tuesday through Sunday.

Jardín Botánico Nacional

Although severely damaged by Hurricane Georges in September 1998, the National Botanical Garden (☎ 809-567-6211, 567-6213), on Av República de Colombia, northeast of downtown, remains a splendid treat for plant lovers.

On the sprawling grounds, which can be strolled or toured by shuttle, are vast areas devoted to aquatic plants, orchids, bromeliads, ferns, endemic plants, palm trees, a Japanese garden and much more. Unlike many littered parts of the city and countryside, here at the Botanical Garden some people have taken great care to keep the grounds spotless and the plants well tended. The garden, another of Balaguer's controversial developments, certainly doesn't feel like it's ringed by 2 million people. If you're the type of person who appreciates a quiet stroll in the country, taking in the natural beauty at every turn, you should not miss this vegetative treasure-trove. The garden is open 9 am to 6 pm Tuesday through Sunday. Admission is US$1; the cost of the shuttle ride is an additional US$1, and well worth it.

Mercado Modelo

Located in and about an aging two-story building on Av Mella, near Calle Santome just north of the Zona Colonial (see the Zona Colonial map), this lively trading center offers superb people watching – and some great buys *if* you are accomplished in the art of bargaining. Just a few blocks west of Santo Domingo's Little Haiti, the market is a carnival of woodcarvings, amber jewelry, musical instruments, love potions, Vodou objects, wicker and much more – all offered in a bustling setting that could have been cribbed from the pages of a Hollywood script. But just as such Hollywood sets are cast with thieves and pickpockets, so too, say the tourist police, is this bazaar. If you decide to check it out, leave your jewelry and fancy camera bag at home, avoid side streets when leaving in case you're being followed and don't bring all of your trip money with you. The market is open 9 am to 6 pm daily.

Parque Zoológico Nacional

The National Zoological Park (☎ 809-562-3149), on Av los Reyes Católicos in the northwest corner of the city, is much more tame than the 'zoo' one usually encounters at Mercado Modelo. Even on a beautiful Saturday afternoon, the number of visitors in the park at any one time rarely exceeds 50, and the reason is simple: the entrance is difficult to find. The zoo is located in a poor neighborhood with many winding streets, and unless you know the way to the ticket office you could easily get lost among the residential streets. For this reason it is best to go by taxi. Once you arrive, you'll be in for a pleasant surprise. There's a lovely flamingo-filled pond, a very spacious and bar-less tiger compound, lots of African wildlife in roomy enclosures and many endemic birds on display. For a nominal fee you can cruise the large grounds by shuttle. The zoo is open 9 am to 5 pm Tuesday through Saturday; admission is US$1.

Parks

Parque Mirador del Sur When most people imagine an urban park, they think of benches, some large shade trees, a group of pigeons strutting about and old people feeding them from the benches. Well, Parque Mirador del Sur (Southern Lookout Park) doesn't fit that mold. It's a spacious area in the southwest part of the city, with thousands of trees, and is very popular with the thirty-something crowd. In the morning before work, hundreds of yuppies slip into exercise clothes and head to Av Mirador del Sur, where they jog, rollerblade and bicycle up and down the avenue. The tree-lined thoroughfare fills again with hard-body types in the evening. So popular have these routines become that police now close the road to vehicular traffic from 6 to 9 am and 4 to 8 pm every day. Also making regular appearances are portable juice bars and snack stands to serve the athletes.

The park is on an enormous limestone ridge which is riddled with caves. Some are no larger than a small house, while others are the size of airplane hangars. One of the caves has been converted into a dance club that frequently accommodates up to several thousand people at one time; another is home to a fine restaurant and bar (see the following Entertainment and Places to Eat sections).

Parque Mirador del Este Another huge urban park, also popular with joggers and riddled with caves, is Parque Mirador del Este (Eastern Lookout Park), across the Río Ozama from the Zona Colonial. Inside the park is an extremely controversial monument to Christopher Columbus (Faro a Colón, discussed below), and there are three deep, very humid open-ceiling caves, Los Tres Ojos (The Three Eyes), accessible by a long staircase carved into the side of one of the caves many years ago.

The caves are limestone sinkholes, which means they were created over a period of many thousands of years by water runoff from the mountains north of the city. The water found its way into crevices and gradually eroded them away until they created the caves we see today; modern development has redirected the runoff and put an end to the caves' natural enlargement. Because the caves are so close to the sea, one actually contains saltwater while the other two contain fresh water (although you might be tempted to sip from one of the freshwater pools, beware that both have an unusually high sulfur content). Unfortunately, the tranquility of the setting is usually hampered by hawkers who pester tourists to buy postcards, jewelry, guide services and so on.

However, one useful service not included in the US$1 admission fee to the caves is the raft shuttle. For US$1, a young boy will gladly shuttle you from one freshwater cave to the other, and the second one is the nicer of the two. It contains a lovely pond of clear water ringed by lush vegetation. Due to the high humidity in the caves, you are encouraged to arrive early. Photographers shooting low-ASA film will need a tripod here.

Faro a Colón Under President Joaquín Balaguer's leadership, the Dominican peasant class grew poorer, its rich class grew even richer and its middle class gradually succumbed to poverty. During Balaguer's shift, as it were, the republic's educational and health-care systems suffered tremendously. Insufficient funds were set aside for social programs, and due to corrupt officials most of these funds weren't spent as intended. But Balaguer never shied away from spending taxpayers' money on projects he wanted to be remembered by, and foremost among them is the Faro a Colón (Lighthouse to Columbus).

At a cost of US$200 million, the block-long monument – with lasers on its roof that can form a blinding white cross on a cloudy night sky – contains numerous exhibition halls, the majority of which feature the Admiral and the island's conquest by Spaniards. However, nearly all of the documents in the building are reproductions (you have to go to Spain to see the real deals), the exhibits are poorly organized and few signs are in English. To top things off, the centerpiece of the 'lighthouse' (due to energy costs, the light is infrequently lit) is a tomb that's supposed to contain Columbus' remains, but there's much debate over whether the bones inside are even his (the Spaniards and the Italians both claim title to the great explorer's skeleton). Ironically, one of the best exhibits in the five-story Faro is dedicated to peoples the conquistadors wiped out. Included in the displays are arrows from Peru and golden animal figurines from Panama. The monument is open 10 am to 5 pm Tuesday through Sunday; admission is US$1.

Palacio Nacional

The National Palace, the Dominican seat of government, was designed by Italian architect Guido D'Alessandro and inaugurated in 1947. Near the Zona Colonial on Av México, the palace is built of Samaná roseate marble in a neoclassical design and is outfitted in grand style with lots of old mahogany furniture, paintings from prominent Dominican artists, magnificent mirrors inlaid with gold and a proportionate amount of imported crystal. Of special note is the Room of the Caryatids, in which 44 sculpted draped women rise like columns in a hall lined with French mirrors and Baccarat chandeliers.

The building covers most of a city block and houses executive and administrative offices and visiting dignitaries. However, it has never housed a Dominican president; they are expected to live in their own homes. The palace is not open to everyone, but with good enough reason you may be able to wrangle a VIP tour; they are offered free of charge Monday, Wednesday and Friday, by appointment only (☎ 809-686-4771, ext 340 or 360). Make sure to dress up if you are granted a tour.

Palacio de Bellas Artes

The Palace of Fine Arts, located on Av Máximo Gómez just north of Av Independencia, is a large beige building with a red tile roof that is considerably more grand in appearance than it is in use. Occasionally an exhibition or performance is held here, but these are surprisingly infrequent given the number of artists in the country. When something is happening at the palace, an announcement generally appears in the weekend editions of the local papers.

ORGANIZED TOURS

Colonial City Tours (☎ 809-687-5245) operates an open-sided trolley from the northeast corner of Parque Colón. The trolley runs up and down the streets of the Zona Colonial at a cost of US$4 per person for the 'panoramic tour' and US$12 per person for the 'monuments tour.' Tours are available in English, Spanish or French. No reservation is required. The trolley departs hourly from

9 am to 5 pm daily, more frequently if the number of passengers warrants it.

Most of the better-class hotels in Santo Domingo are affiliated with tour operators and can arrange a guided tour of the city with one day's notice or less. These tours tend to be expensive because you end up paying a fee to the hotel in addition to the cost of the tour (the hotel's fee is generally added to the price of the tour and discreetly kicked back). The level of this service, however, is usually very good because the operator cannot afford to have tourists give unfavorable reports about his service to the hotels.

Another option is to hire any of the official guides who hang out under the shade tree in front of El Conde Restaurant, beside Parque Colón. The advantage of hiring one of these guides is that they all had to take a history course and pass a test to obtain their tourist-guide license; such licenses are not issued to individuals who have criminal records. Always negotiate the cost of the tour beforehand; US$10 per hour is the standard fare for a private walking tour of the colonial district. One guide who enjoys a particularly favorable reputation is Eddy Antonio Ortega, who speaks Spanish, English, French and Italian.

Outside of Santo Domingo, virtually all of the all-inclusive resorts work with agencies who provide guided tours of the city with a special emphasis on the Zona Colonial. For example, Prieto Tours (☎ 809-685-0102), 125 Av Francia, represents El Portillo Beach Resort in Samaná, Barceló Viajes (☎ 809-541-4994), Av Máximo Gómez at Av 27 de Febrero, represents Bávaro Beach Resort at Playa Bávaro, and Omni Tours (☎ 809-565-6591), 204 Calle Roberto Pastoriza, represents Club Dominicus Beach Resort at Bayahibe. For current prices and tour offerings, check with your hotel or call them directly. Even if you're not staying at an all-inclusive, you may book tours with these agencies.

SPECIAL EVENTS
Carnivals
There are two Carnivals held in Santo Domingo each year. The first one takes place around the anniversary of Dominican independence from Haiti, February 27, beginning two or three days before and ending two or three days after. The second one coincides with the anniversary of the DR's declaration of war against Spain, August 16, beginning the day before and ending the day after.

During both Carnivals, Av George Washington is closed to vehicular traffic and it becomes an enormous party scene that's vibrant all day and night. The only vehicles allowed on the malecón during this time are tractors pulling floats, and there are plenty of those.

The main costumed figures are the same as those encountered at Carnivals elsewhere in the country, but there are a few that are unique to the south; one such character is Roba La Gallina, a man dressed like a woman with an overly painted face, his behind and breasts stuffed to exaggeration, wearing a wig and carrying an open umbrella. Ask five men decked out like this what the meaning is behind Roba La Gallina and you'll get five different answers.

Merengue Festival
Just a little less wild than Carnival (unless you're a big fan of merengue) is Santo Domingo's annual Merengue Festival, held the last week of July and the first week of August on the marvelous malecón. All along the strip, the world's top merengue bands play to the world's top merengue dancers. Exact dates vary from year to year. Check with the nearest Dominican tourism office or diplomatic mission for precise dates. Be sure to make hotel reservations months in advance.

Latin Music Festival
Held at the Olympic Stadium every June, this huge three-day event attracts the top names in Latin music – jazz, salsa, merengue and bachata. Salsa king Tito Rojas and merengue living legend Fernando Villalona are among the dozens of featured artists that regularly attend. The exact dates of this event vary; if you're interested, contact the nearest Dominican tourism office or diplomatic mission for specifics.

PLACES TO STAY

Most visitors to Santo Domingo stay either in one of the hotels in the Zona Colonial that were once grand colonial residences or in one of the modern hotels along the malecón that offer lodging, a restaurant, bar and casino under one roof. If you are mainly in town to see the historic old city and lovely colonial structures, chances are a hotel in the Zona Colonial would be best for you. If being where 'all the action is' – the gaming tables and the nightclubs – is a primary concern, you'll probably want to stay along or near the malecón.

Of course, you could gamble and dance up a storm in a hotel along the malecón until the wee hours of the morning and then spend what remains of the night in a hotel in the Zona Colonial, but returning to a hotel several kilometers away instead of simply going upstairs isn't a great alternative. And leaving a casino in the middle of the night or stumbling out of a nightclub at a time when there are few witnesses around greatly increases your odds of being robbed during your stay in Santo Domingo.

Zona Colonial

Budget Near the western edge of the old city, *Hotel Independencia* (☎ 809-686-1763), on Calle Arzobispo Nouel, offers the best value of this area's budget hotels. The mattresses are firm, the rooms are clean and the ones with air con go for just US$14 for one person and US$16 for two. If you don't mind going without, you can save US$3 a room. The Independencia has its own generator for those frequent times when the government-supplied electricity is shut off – a big plus.

Located beside the popular Calle El Conde promenade is the *Hotel Aida* (☎ 809-685-7692), which has a generator and 2nd-floor-only rooms in three price categories: rooms with a fan and no balcony go for US$19, rooms with a fan and a balcony go for US$21, and rooms with air con and a balcony go for US$24. All prices are for one or two persons. Some people won't care for the showers, which have an electric water heater attached to the shower head. If these

gadgets, which have a tendency to shock, upset you, either take cold showers or stay elsewhere at a different hotel.

On the southwest edge of the Zona Colonial, actually on the malecón but a fair walk to the big hotels, is the *Hotel Llave del Mar* (☎ 809-682-5761). At the time of writing, the Llave wasn't much to look at – if fact, its rooms were pretty worn – but it has the advantage of being seaside and it's about halfway from Parque Colón and the executive hotels down the road. All rooms have air con and a private hot-water bathroom. At US$14 a night for one bed and US$30 a night for two beds, it's reasonably priced. Beware: The hotel does not have a generator, so when the power goes off it stays off until the government turns it back on (that could be in one hour or seven).

Mid-Range At the time of writing there was perhaps only one hotel in the US$30 to US$50 price range, and it was the *Hotel Commercial*, on Calle Hostos near the Calle El Conde promenade. It had just been acquired by a French company and was in the midst of being renovated. Depending on the extent of the renovations, the Commercial could remain in the US$40 range or enter the top-end market. Check a Santo Domingo telephone directory or contact directory assistance (☎ 411) for the hotel's current telephone number.

Top End For the experience of staying in a beautifully restored colonial residence furnished with lots of dark wood and crushed dark-red velvet, look no farther than the *Hotel Palacio* (☎ 809-682-4730, fax 687-5535, www.codetel.net.do/hotel_palacio/welcome .html), centrally located on Calle Duarte one block north of the Calle El Conde promenade. Built during the 17th century and once occupied by the children of 19th-century President Buenaventura Báez, the German-owned and -operated Palacio offers 16 standard rooms and two suites with central air con, fridge and satellite TV ranging from US$50/60 to US$65/70 for a single/double. Substantial discounts are available for stays of a week or more. There is a pleasing courtyard where breakfast is served, and a small bar as well. Reservations are strongly recommended.

An even better value is the *Hostal Nicolás Nader* (☎ *809-687-7887, fax 687-6674*), on Calle General Luperón at Calle Duarte. All of the hotel's 10 rooms are spacious and have tall ceilings, central air conditioning, cable TV and bathrooms with bathtubs (an oddity here). Unlike the Palacio, the Hostal's guestrooms are adorned with contemporary furniture and decorated in cheerful colors. The rooms in this stunning, Dutch-owned and -operated two-story structure surround a beautiful courtyard ringed by hearty tropical plants and paintings produced by top local artists; breakfast is offered in this lovely setting daily. The rates are US$50/60. If you absolutely must have one of the paintings, you'll be glad to know they are all for sale (the hotel doubles as a gallery). Spanish and Dutch are spoken. If you send a brief fax in very simple English, you will receive a reply.

Modern Santo Domingo

Budget The best of the US$30-and-under crowd outside the old city is the *Apart-Hotel Sea View* (☎ *809-221-4420, fax 688-3207*), on Calle El Numero, 50m north of the malecón. Although it specializes in apartments that rent for US$50 a night, it also offers some small, clean guestrooms with good beds, air con and private hot-water bathroom for US$25 for one or two persons. The hotel is equipped with a generator, near the casinos and clubs and within walking distance of the Zona Colonial as well as the Mercado Modelo.

Another good value is the *Hotel Antillas* (☎ *809-686-8383*), on Av Independencia, a few blocks west of the Zona Colonial. At the time of writing the hotel was open for business but it was up for sale, which means the telephone number and even the name may have changed. Hopefully the facility itself will not. Clean air-conditioned rooms with hot-water private bathrooms are US$15 for one or two persons; with fan only, a similar

room goes for US$12. Unfortunately, the Antillas does not have a generator.

Also on Av Independencia, one block to the east, is the *Hotel Rafael* (☎ *809-685-0084*), which has OK rooms with air con, TV and private bathroom for US$20. However, the tap water isn't hot and the establishment doesn't own a generator. If all you really want is a bed and you don't mind sharing a bathroom, the Rafael has a couple of tiny rooms for US$10.

Mid-Range All of the hotels in this category are quite nice and near the malecón, with the first three being quite comparable and the fourth and fifth being a notch above in price as well as amenities. All are far superior to the budget and mid-range hotels found in the Zona Colonial.

The classiest is *Hostal Duque de Wellington* (☎ *809-685-4525, 688-2844, hotelduque@codetel.net.do*) on Av Independencia near Av Pasteur. All of the rooms come with air con, private telephone and hot-water bathroom. The decor is very tasteful, elegant even, and there are just enough tropical plants thriving about to remind you that you are in an exotic locale. The hotel openly welcomes gay and lesbian clients (some hotels in the DR still give a cool reception to homosexual couples), and is a fine bargain at US$32/35.

The *Hotel Kara* (☎ *809-685-3837, 221-1706*), on Pdte Vicini Burgos, opened in 1997 and has very acceptable rooms with air con, TV and private hot-water bathroom for US$30 for one person and US$34 for two, including breakfast. The Kara has its own generator. This is a few-frills, fairly utilitarian place, with everything most people need at an affordable price. It is quite popular with German and American tourists, particularly those in their thirties.

Also on Pdte Vicini Burgos, a few doors north of the Kara, the *Hotel El Señorial* (☎ *809-687-4367, fax 687-0600*) is a relatively large, two-story place with the feel of a big old house that has been pridefully maintained. All rooms have air con, private hot-water bathroom, telephone and cable TV. Rates are

US$33/35. If this area appeals to you, consider asking to see rooms at the Duque, the Kara and the Señorial before deciding on one. All three are quite comfortable.

La Casona Dorada (☎ 809-689-1941), on Av Independencia, is a two-story former residence built in 1844 and renovated several times since. The guest rooms have air con, a fridge, cable TV, private hot-water bathroom (several with bathtubs) and telephone. Outside there's a pool for hot afternoons and a Jacuzzi for cool nights. And at the time this was written, a restaurant was being added. Rates are US$40/53.

Also quite lovely is the Italian-owned *Hotel Villa Italia* (☎ 809-682-3373, fax 412-7685), on Av Independencia near Av Alma Mater, featuring 25 cheerful and comfortable rooms, three executive suites, one apartment with kitchen designed for a family, and a great guest room with a seaview and Jacuzzi that can accommodate six people. All rooms have air con, private bathroom and telephone. Very tasteful. Rates are US$44/53 for singles/doubles and US$65 for the suites. Spanish, English and Italian are spoken.

Top End With the exception of the second hotel, all of the establishments mentioned here are located on or near the malecón. All are large, have guestrooms with all the amenities, their own restaurant and a swimming pool, and all but the Inter-Continental have a casino. Several of them spice things up with dance clubs.

A very good value is the *Hotel El Napolitano* (☎ 809-687-1131, fax 687-6814), which is close to the Zona Colonial and the restaurants and bars of the Jaragua and Meliá hotels. The 72-room Napolitano has a very popular restaurant that looks out upon the malecón, and its casino and dance club are both open 4 pm to 4 am daily. The rate for standard rooms is US$62 for one or two persons, and for superior rooms – which are newer and nicer and definitely worth the additional cost – the rate jumps to US$67. Reservations for this popular hotel are strongly recommended.

Off the beaten path a bit is the multilevel *Gran Hotel Lina* (☎ 809-563-5000, fax 686-5521, www.barcelo.com), on Av Máximo Gómez. Standard rooms for either one or two persons are US$80, larger rooms are US$95/100 and suites start at US$145/160. This 202-room hotel is part of the successful Barceló chain, which has many hotels in Spain and Latin America. The highlight of this hotel is the restaurant, which is quite possibly the best in the country (see Places to Eat, below, for details).

Of the hotels along the malecón, the *Meliá Santo Domingo Hotel* (☎ 800-336-3542, 809-221-6666, fax 687-8150) is certainly one of the best, as top honors vary with personal taste. In addition to the features mentioned above, the Meliá also has tennis courts and a dance club that's very popular late Friday and Saturday nights. Rates are US$145/165. Be sure to request an ocean-view room.

For many DR visitors, the *Renaissance Jaragua Hotel* (☎ 809-221-2222, fax 686-0528) is the pick of the litter. This very modern, very glitzy hotel has all the amenities plus a goose-filled indoor lagoon, color TVs in all of the guest bathrooms, exclusive use of the exercise club, complimentary champagne on arrival, complimentary Continental breakfast and hors d'oeuvres – the works. Rates start at US$140 for one or two people and shoot to US$800 for the penthouse apartment.

The *Hispaniola Hotel* (☎ 800-877-3643, 809-221-1511, fax 533-7455) is older and less appealing than either the Jaragua or the Inter-Continental (see below), but it's also less expensive with rates of US$120/130 through most of the year. Many people find the guestroom decor a bit cheesy. The hotel is owned by the same company that owns the Hotel Santo Domingo directly across the street, and the two hotels share a casino. Considerably nicer is the much newer *Hotel Santo Domingo* (☎ 800-877-3643, 809-221-1511, 221-7111), which features larger guestrooms with slightly more tasteful decor (though still cheap and tacky). The rate of US$190 for one or two persons becomes a more economical corporate rate of US$135 for stays of three or more days. Both the Hispaniola and the Santo Domingo are rather far from most tourist attractions.

A completely modern, comfortable hotel with all the amenities, tennis, a karaoke bar and a facility to practice golf is the *Hotel Inter-Continental* (☎ 809-221-0000, fax 221-2020). Singles/doubles are US$230/240.

PLACES TO EAT
Zona Colonial

Located near the Alcázar de Colón is one of the best restaurants in the country, *Restaurante Atarazana*, which would see many more customers than it currently does if its tables weren't located in an open-air courtyard – out of reach of the air conditioning. The chairs are of the plastic patio furniture variety, and the close walls of the courtyard are a tad stifling, but one bite of the *mero relleno de gambas* (sea bass stuffed with shrimp), served with a white wine sauce, and you know you've come to the right place. The dish, which comes with vegetables and a choice of rice or french fries, costs US$13.50 (the same dish in a New York restaurant would cost at least twice as much). Other delicious dishes include *fetucines Portofino* (US$13), which features shrimp in a creamy white sauce, and the *filete Atarazana* (US$8), a beef filet stuffed with ham and served with cheese and a special sauce.

Just a few doors west of the Atarazana is *La Crêperie*, which opened in 1998 and specializes in two types of crêpes: the traditional French variety and dessert crêpes. Among the first group are *la Classic* (ham and cheese; US$3.75) and *la Raffinée* (salmon, asparagus points and a creamy white sauce; US$6.50). The other variety – the *crêpes dulces*, or sweet crêpes – are stuffed with such terribly decadent treats as chocolate with grated coconut and homemade orange marmalade. Don't forget to leave room for a cup of ice cream to finish your meal; among the selection is *sorbet des isles*, which consists of one scoop each of pineapple, coconut and mango ice cream, and the *colonel* – two scoops of lime sherbet in vodka. If all you're

in the mood for is something light, La Crêperie excels in salads as well. Try the *Montagnarde*, with fresh lettuce, walnuts, prosciutto, bleu cheese, tomato, croutons and a tangy vinaigrette (US$5).

The *Mesón D'Bari,* at the corner of Calle Salomé Ureña and Calle Hostos, is a fine place to dine. The restaurant is in a beautifully restored colonial building and upon its walls are impressive paintings (for sale) by top local artists. Among the establishment's better dishes are the *filete al la criolla* (filet of beef served Creole style; US$8.50), *pescado a la plancha* (grilled fish of the day; US$8) and *chivo guisado* (stewed goat; US$8).

Beside the Parque Colón, and prime for people watching, is *El Conde Restaurant*. About half of its tables are in a fan-cooled room and the rest are under umbrellas out in front of the longtime establishment. Almost everyone prefers the pleasantly breezy sidewalk tables, where you can watch street vendors hawking fresh coconut milk and, with a turn of your head, rich, stylish Dominicans chatting it up with each other when they aren't chatting into a cell phone. If you're there long enough you'll be asked if you'd like your shoes shined, if you'd like to buy some taped merengue music or if you'd like to be sketched. All of the hawkers politely accept 'no' for an answer. The food at the Conde is quite good, and the waiters – many of whom have been working there since the 1970s – are attentive and friendly. Among the specialties are *pollo al ajillo* (chicken with garlic; US$4.75) and *sopa de pescado* (seafood soup; US$2.75).

Also near Parque Colón is the French *Bar-Restaurant El Don Camillo*, which is the best of several indoor-outdoor restaurants on Calle El Conde between Parque Colón and Calle de las Damas. El Don Camillo specializes in Creole cooking and does it right. Among the wise choices are the *chivo a la criolla* (goat stew; US$5.50), seafood paella for two persons (US$17) and the *filete de mero salsa criolla* (filet of sea bass in Creole-style salsa; US$10). Also on the menu are a slew of beef dishes, several pasta dishes and salads. The service here is first rate.

Along Calle La Atarazana, opposite the Alcázar de Colón, are five places that offer food, none of which are particularly good but most of which look tempting and lure in many tourists due to their location. *Cafe Montesinos*, the best of the bunch, is a pleasant bar/restaurant that's overpriced; the best item on the menu is the *mero a la criolla* (sea bass served Creole style; US$8.50). The *camarones a la criolla* (Creole shrimp; US$8.50) are tasty too. The *Museo del Jamón* (Museum of Ham) is as poor as its choice of name. *Drake's Pub*, where the English pirate never spent a night despite the bar's hype, mostly serves wayward Americans, and *Rota's Cafe* is nothing to write home about. *Nancy's Snack Bar* is OK for a cheap sandwich, and that's about it.

There's no shortage of fast-food places in the Zona Colonial, and all of them seem to be on the Calle El Conde promenade. For better or worse, *Burger King*, *Pizza Hut* and *McDonald's* are there. Far wiser choices for budget food are *Petrus Cafeteria*, which serves high-quality pizza by the slice and reasonably priced meaty sandwiches; *Chez Moi Bar-Restaurant*, which serves inexpensive *comida del día* (daily specials); *Bariloche Cafeteria*, which offers so-so quality local food, buffet style; and *Cafe de las Flores*, which serves sandwiches and omelettes and has a long cocktail menu.

Last, but by no means least, is a pseudo-restaurant in a small plaza beside Calle Isabel la Católica, one block north of Parque Colón. This establishment consists of a handful of attractive tables under a handsome white tarp, but what it lacks in standard restaurant trappings (such as a front door and even a name) it makes up for in food. Run by Bettye Marshall, a very likeable ex-Texan who owns the smart Galería Toledo just a few meters away, *Bettye's café* (for lack of a better name) is open 11 am to 7 pm daily and gives you more than your money's worth. The daily three-course meal, for about US$10, is always as treat. All of the beef filets are pre-cut from the USA, her fettuccine is imported from Italy and her gazpacho is sent down from heaven. And don't

even think about leaving without trying the Chocolate Decadence. It's simply divine.

Modern Santo Domingo

The best restaurants outside the old city are mostly located inside Santo Domingo's large hotels. In fact, arguably the finest restaurant in the entire country is the *Restaurante Lina* (☎ 809-563-5000) at the Gran Hotel Lina. It is certainly the most elegant restaurant in the republic, and yet if you keep to the pasta dishes, it's quite affordable. The decor is pure tropics in pattern and color. All about the dining room are huge and exquisite floral arrangements. A pianist plays romantic songs every evening. The waiters wear their black ties with pride and their service is superb. Desserts, condiments and cheeses are brought to your table on rolling trays.

The head chef, Luiz Salidia, trained under Lina Aguado, a Spanish master who was dictator Trujillo's personal chef and who opened this restaurant soon after Trujillo's death. The English and Spanish menu includes among its appetizers oysters on the half shell (14 for US$8) and smoked salmon (US$12). The pastas include lasagna and spaghetti Bolognese (US$7). The seafood dishes include filet of grouper, filet of red snapper and grilled lobster (US$14 to US$20). Among the red meat and poultry dishes are medallions of veal with lemon and sautéed chicken in a garlic sauce (US$9 to US$12). Reservations are recommended. Dress appropriately.

At the Renaissance Jaragua Hotel, you'll find three restaurants. The *Manhattan Grill* specializes in – you guessed it – grilled items, including sirloin steak, filet mignon, grilled fish and lobster thermidor (US$14 to US$24). At the hotel's *Latino* restaurant you'll find among the main courses *paella Valenciana* (seafood with rice; US$13), *chivo guisado* (goat stew; US$11), *chuletas de cerdo a la parrilla* (grilled pork chops) and *churrasco de res* (Argentine-style beef steak), both for US$12, and *parrillada de carnes variadas* (grilled mixed platter; US$17). Also at the Jaragua is the *Café Jaragua*, a very pricey cafeteria that's open 24 hours; among the best items there are the Dominican *sancocho* (soup) with rice for US$15 and the Southern fried chicken served with a honey-mustard sauce for US$8.

There are two restaurants at the Hotel Santo Domingo. The **Alcázar** opens for a buffet only, served from noon to 3 pm Monday through Saturday. The cost is US$12 and typical items include two or three meat dishes, two seafood dishes and a pasta dish. There's generally a good selection of salad as well. **El Cafetal** is the hotel's other restaurant, and it's open from 6 am until 1 am daily. A breakfast buffet is offered 6 to 11:30 am for US$8.50. From noon until 5 pm the restaurant has a fixed menu that includes several choices of soup at US$4 each, typical Dominican dishes from US$5 to US$12 and numerous seafood dishes from US$12 on up. The restaurant offers only Italian cuisine after 5 pm. The *penne arrabiata* is delicious. Most of the pastas are priced between US$8 and US$12.

The Meliá Santo Domingo Hotel boasts three restaurants, all of which offer fair value for the money. **La Terraza** is open from 6:30 am to midnight seven days a week and features a US$12 buffet breakfast from sunrise up until 11:30 am, when a single lunch/dinner menu is offered. Among the items on that menu are sandwiches (US$6), meat dishes (for US$14.50 and up), poultry dishes (US$8.50 and up) and seafood (US$13.50 and up). The **Antoine** is open from 11 am to 3 pm weekdays and puts out a different buffet every day; the cost is always US$15. **La Canasta** serves night owls, opening at 8 pm and closing at 6 am daily. It's a great place to come if you've been out dancing and want good food and service at a good price before retiring. Typical items include a chef salad, Cuban sandwich or Dominican stew (all about US$5), filet mignon (US$13), conch with Creole sauce (US$6) and fish sticks (US$9).

A highly regarded Italian restaurant that is not part of a hotel is the **Restaurant Vesuvio** on Av George Washington just west of Av Máximo Gómez. Its long menu includes an impressive list of hot and cold antipasti and many pasta dishes. The restaurant is formal with corresponding prices. Among its pastas are green tortellini in porcini sauce (US$12.50), *spaghetti alla Pertsovka* (spaghetti smothered in a creamy sauce made with mushrooms, proscuitto and pepper-flavored vodka; for US$9) and *penne all'Arrabiata* (US$8). Also available are numerous fish and shellfish dishes, the most popular of which is the red snapper *à l'orange* for US$16. The most expensive item on the menu is crab meat served Creole style for US$25. Additionally, two dozen beef dishes and 17 veal dishes are available. The beef is not imported; it's range fed and therefore may taste a bit different than beef you are used to eating.

Considerably less fancy than the Vesuvio and simply in another, smaller league is the **Costa Azurra**, located at the Hotel Villa Italia on Av Independencia. The decor is charming and the owner is Italian, but the food is only mediocre. Among the offerings are breakfast dishes, a host of antipasti, pastas, soups, salads, sandwiches, meat dishes, seafood, Creole dishes, juices and desserts.

If you're looking for something completely different, look no farther than **El Mesón de la Cava** (The House in the Cave), located on Av Mirador del Sur in the park of the same name. A number of years ago, a gentleman entered one of the park's stinking, bat-filled limestone caves and thought, 'This is a fine place for a fancy restaurant.' If you've never had the occasion to dine inside a tastefully appointed bat cave, your big chance is here at last. Yes, the stalactites are still there. The walls are *au naturel*, but an elegant bar graces half of the two-cavern facility, and formally set tables, under the watchful eye of waiters in black tie, fill the other half. Amazingly, there's absolutely nothing tacky about this place – and the food is top notch. The chef recommends the grilled salmon filet in a creamed sauce of charbroiled red bell peppers, the veal cutlets in brandy and creamed porcini mushroom sauce or the fresh red snapper filet in a medium-spicy tomato sauce served over a bed of linguini (all around US$12). Open noon to 4 pm and 6 pm to 1 am every day.

Just behind La Ruta Cerveza, a highly conspicuous bar known by all of Santo Domingo, you'll find the far less conspicuous *Restaurant El Fran' Boyan,* a very popular restaurant that serves Creole cuisine. Its long menu includes half a dozen salads, among them *ensalada de camarones* (shrimp salad; US$10) and *ensalada de aguacate* (avocado salad; US$1); and soups such as *sopa de cebolla* (onion soup; US$2) and *sopa de pollo criollo* (Creole chicken soup; US$3). Among the other offerings are *guineas al vino* (guinea hen in wine; US$5.50), *pollo al horno* (oven-baked chicken; US$4.50) and *carite frito* (fried kingfish; US$8). Open 8 am to 2 am daily.

On the east bank of the Río Ozama, on the 2nd floor of the single large building at the Puerto de Santo Domingo (Port of Santo Domingo), is the *Restaurant Bucanero.* This semiformal restaurant, which opened in 1981, has a strong following and a great view, as it faces the Zona Colonial across the mouth of the Río Ozama. The food is quite good, and the selection of dishes includes *mero bucanero* (sea bass stuffed with lobster, shrimp and crab; US$14.50), *centollo al gusto* (king crab, as you like it; US$17) and *filete de res bucanero* (beef tenderloin in a red wine sauce; US$10). The Bucanero is open daily from 11 am till midnight.

ENTERTAINMENT
Dance Clubs
There are five vibrant dance clubs in Santo Domingo, and all are attached to big hotels: the *Hotel Santo Domingo*, the *Hispaniola Hotel*, the *Meliá Santo Domingo Hotel*, the *Gran Hotel Lina* and *El Napolitano*. The discos, which operate Tuesday through Saturday, tend to open their doors around 9 pm but don't usually show strong signs of life much before midnight or 1 am. They close around 4 am. Admission is usually US$2 when the music is recorded and US$10 when there's a band. These clubs attract the wealthiest young Dominicans in the capital city, and they dress up when they go dancing. Short-sleeve shirts, tennis shoes and jeans

are not allowed. Men: wear a jacket if you brought one. Women: dresses are the norm.

Classical Music & Dance
The 1600-seat *Teatro Nacional* (National Theater; ☎ 809-682-7255), in the Plaza de la Cultura, hosts opera, ballet and symphonic performances. Concert tickets range from US$2 to US$10, and can be purchased in advance at the theater between 9:30 am and 12:30 pm and 3:30 and 6:30 pm every day. For show dates and times, call the theater or check the weekend editions of the local newspapers. Regardless of the show, the Teatro Nacional requires that you dress up: no jeans, no tennis shoes, no tank tops. In short, dress your best.

Live Music
The same hotels listed under Dance Clubs (above) also have piano bars, where live music can usually be heard from 7 to 9 pm nightly. Perhaps the best of the lounge acts is found at the *Marrakesh Bar & Café* at the Hotel Santo Domingo and at *El Yarey Piano Bar* at the Meliá Santo Domingo Hotel. There's no price for admission or for the entertainment, and to top it off, most of the acts are accompanied by happy hour. Free entertainment and booze at half price; not bad at all.

In the land of merengue, one would expect its capital to offer more than discos and lounge performers, and Santo Domingo doesn't disappoint. At *Las Palmas Bar* in the Hotel Santo Domingo, there's live merengue or salsa nightly from 6:30 pm to 1 am except Sunday. There's no cover charge. In the Zona Colonial, near the Alcázar de Colón, the *Cafe Concierto Bachata Rosa* is home to live merengue and bachata. In fact, the country's best merengue and bachata bands perform here. The club is open Wednesday through Saturday from 9 pm till 5 am. Admission is usually US$10.

By far the most unique and exciting place to hear live merengue or salsa is the *Guácara Taína* on Av Mirador del Sur in the park of the same name. This giant club is entirely located inside a bat cave. It's so big that it frequently holds more than 2000 people on Friday and Saturday nights. On

Casas de Chicas

Prostitution is legal in the Dominican Republic and, despite the moral issues and risk of contracting AIDS and other sexual diseases, business is booming in the *casas de chicas*, as such places are called. The information given here is intended to inform, not to promote.

In Santo Domingo there are two kinds of prostitutes: those who walk the streets and those who work in brothels. The ones who work in brothels are regularly checked for diseases and therefore are healthier than the street walkers. The typical brothel is a rather nice structure, usually a converted two-story house with a bar and lounge areas downstairs and guestrooms above. The front door is usually barred or made of steel and clients are usually asked to check any weapons with the shotgun-toting doorman before they enter. There's no cost to enter.

Casa Teresa, on Av José Ortega y Gasset just north of the Olympic Center, is considered one of the better casas de chicas in the city. In accordance with house rules, all of the women dress in black and waiters – who wear black tie and are very professional in their demeanor – move through the crowd filling drink orders and answering questions about the women. Most of the men who visit Casa Teresa only chat with the women and buy them drinks; some bring little gifts. Be advised that beers in these places tend to be expensive. At Casa Teresa they are US$3 apiece, and hard drinks are twice as much. But the price of a 'date' – US$80 in-house and US$100 outside the casa – is prohibitive, and hardly worth the health risk.

occasion it's held twice that number. The club is very difficult to find, but every taxi driver in the city knows where it is. Admission is US$10. The club is vivacious from midnight till about 5 am.

Pubs/Bars

Finding a bar in Santo Domingo is no difficult feat; they're everywhere. In the Zona Colonial, the Austrian-owned *K-ramba Bar*, near the southern end of Calle Isabel la Católica, features English/American rock 'n' roll, occasional live music, snacks and salads. It's a great place to meet other travelers. K-ramba is open daily except Tuesday from 5:30 pm till 3 am. Happy hour, when you get two drinks for the price of one, is from 6 to 9 pm.

Opposite the Alcázar de Colón is *Drake's Pub*, which was the first bar in the old city to feature English/American rock 'n' roll when it opened during the 1970s. The pub generally attracts a middle-aged expatriate American crowd. It's an all-right place to have a beer and watch the sun's final rays of the day paint the Alcázar in lovely shades of yellow

and then pink, but if you're watching your money, the drinks at El Conde Restaurant, near Parque Colón, are cheaper.

An extremely popular bar right on the malecón is *La Ruta Cerveza*, which attracts scores of Dominican yuppies from around 6 o'clock each night. Only beer and a few snacks are served in this large, inviting, open-sided establishment. Here, visitors can enjoy the atmosphere and comfort of a restaurant without the pressure of eating a meal that may be outside their means.

Gay & Lesbian Venues

There are lots of gay and lesbian bars in Santo Domingo. Among the more happening ones is *Penthouse*, on Calle Seibo near Calle Marcos Ruíz. This club is open daily except Tuesday and has nightly shows; on Thursday expect male strippers, on Friday transvestites, on Saturday drag queens, on Sunday there's a wet T-shirt contest – beautiful men wearing only T-shirts doused with water (largest erection wins) – and on Monday expect more transvestites. Penthouse also features occasional fantasy acts, such as young men taking showers and the like. This is a very cheerful place with lots of dancing (great sound system, mostly American dance music but also lots of merengue) and a very friendly owner. The 2nd-story club is quite popular with gays and straights. Arrive very late, as the club closes around sunrise. All taxi drivers know its location. Don't let the look of the neighborhood throw you.

Café Atlántico, on Calle José A Aybar near Av Abraham Lincoln, is a very upscale club that's popular with gays, lesbians and straights. It's a multi-level place with three bars, stainless-steel tables and a large foreign clientele and it looks a lot like an art gallery – very stylish. The music is mostly English rock 'n' roll. There are big-screen TVs everywhere, usually showing baseball or another sport if baseball isn't being played. It's open daily except Sunday, and the most popular day for this nightclub is Monday. Café Atlántico attracts lots of rich twenty-somethings, all dressed to the nines. Be sure to follow suit. All taxi drivers know this place.

Le Pousse, on Calle 19 de Marzo in the Zona Colonial is a neighborhood bar that's open Tuesday through Sunday from 9 pm to 3 am. It's not nearly as popular as Penthouse or Café Atlántico, but its patrons are every bit as friendly. There's a dance floor, of course, and lots of tiny square tables. The walls are painted bright red, with framed posters of Elvis and shirtless muscular men, and there's a large painting of Marilyn Monroe behind the bar. The music is mainly merengue and salsa with some English beat. There are male and female strippers on Saturday. Be advised that this place is mellow until very late.

Those are the top gay and lesbian places in Santo Domingo. There are others, but they aren't nearly as nice nor do they draw good crowds. If all you really want is to watch a stage show featuring some gorgeous transvestites, check out *Disco Free* on Av José Ortega y Gasset, two blocks north of Av John F Kennedy. Admission is US$2 to US$5, depending on the show. The club is open 11:30 pm to 6 am, Thursday through Sunday.

Gambling

There are casinos at Hotel Santo Domingo, the Hispaniola Hotel, the Meliá Santo Domingo Hotel, the Gran Hotel Lina and El Napolitano. They generally open at 4 pm and close at 4 am. Bets may be placed in Dominican pesos or US dollars. Las Vegas odds and rules generally apply, though there are some slight variations; it doesn't hurt to ask the dealer what differences he or she is aware of before you start laying down money. All of the dealers at these casinos speak Spanish and English.

SPECTATOR SPORTS
Baseball

Béisbol isn't just big in the Dominican Republic, it's *huge*. Dominicans follow American and Dominican teams closer than investment bankers follow stock markets during a bull run. And that means they follow team and player standings nearly all year round, because while the American baseball season runs from April on into October, the Dominican season runs from mid-November till early February.

In Santo Domingo, the country's professional teams play at Quisqueya Stadium (☎ 809-565-5565), off Av Tiradentes just north of Av John F Kennedy. Because the seasons don't overlap, the Dominicans who play on American teams – people who are full-fledged national heroes in their native land – also often play on Dominican teams. This means that getting a ticket to some games can be especially tough; you'd be wise to show up at the stadium at least an hour early to buy a ticket.

If the game is sold out, look for a scalper; there are usually plenty around the stadium. Officially, you'd pay US$1 for an outfield ticket, US$3 to sit in the main stands, US$5 to sit in a choice reserved seat and US$10 to sit in the clubhouse. But expect to pay at least US$20 to a scalper. Remember: their prices are negotiable. Afternoon and weekend games start at 4 pm; evening games begin at 7:30 pm. You can try calling the stadium for information, but you'll likely learn the game time sooner by just asking around.

Quisqueya Culture

Santo Domingo's Quisqueya Stadium, built in 1955 (and in need of a major facelift), may be the best place in the Western Hemisphere to watch baseball. Indeed, one can pass an extremely entertaining afternoon at the ballpark without watching the game at all.

The atmosphere is a blend of Carnival, a sports bar and the deciding game of the World Series. Icy beer, barbecued chicken and chunks of three varieties of cheese are available. Rum at US$1.50 a bottle comes in plastic flasks. Unless you look dishonest, you won't be expected to pay until near the end of the game.

Vendors not only allow you to run up a tab, but they also return periodically with fresh ice and the latest odds offered by bookies, who cruise 'Wall Street' – the nickname given to the uppermost tier of the grandstand. The bookies, who usually number about 50, are hard to miss; they stand throughout the game, yelling out bets and having bets yelled to them. Taking book is illegal, yet it goes on in full view of all those present, including the police.

If you really enjoy gambling, the bookies at Quisqueya are your kind of people. They accept bets on most anything – the next inning, the next pitch, the direction of the next hit – and they do it in a frenzy, shouting at the top of their lungs, each bookie trying to be heard over the other bookies and the customers.

Vendors, like the bookies, are also part of the entertainment at Quisqueya. When a customer orders a drink, typically the vendor will use a bottle of soda or beer to smash a large chunk of ice, fragments of which shower the customers (a welcome event in the heat), then fill a plastic cup with the ice and the drink. The vendor will wait until the customer has emptied the bottle, so that the customer can return it to him. It's not uncommon for vendors to strike up conversations after a sale; that's also part of the culture at Quisqueya.

The most important people in the stands are, of course, the fans (or more accurately, the *fanáticos*). Fans at the 16,000-seat stadium take baseball very seriously, but not so much that they allow it to spoil their fun. They dance to marimba between innings and embrace the closest stranger with the slightest provocation. Even the city's most powerful business leaders can be seen sucking on lollipops and slurping down piña coladas in the grandstand.

In the USA and Canada, baseball fans might high-five one another after an exciting play; in the DR, they tend to jump up and down excitedly, hug those nearest to them and chatter effusively about what just happened. But when hitters strike out or balls are dropped at crucial moments, they'll slump down in their seats or even cry in profound disappointment.

Then again, opposing fans will quickly take to slinging insults at each other, and they often square off, separated by only the visors of their baseball caps. Remarkably, fights rarely break out at Quisqueya. Emotions run high, rum flows in torrents, everybody's pumped up – but fighting is not part of the Quisqueya culture. Excitement, not violence, is the Dominican way.

Cockfights

While baseball has been the great Dominican national pastime for more than four decades, cockfighting is the traditional Dominican spectator sport. This is particularly true in the countryside, where men have been pitting their fighting birds against those of others for generations, but the sport has many fans in Santo Domingo as well.

In the Dominican capital, cockfights have been elevated to something approaching high-society events. And to keep out the 'riff-raff' (as the elite view the peasants to whom the sport really belongs), admission is charged at the most prominent of the city's hundred or so *galleras*, the Coliseo Gallístico de Santo Domingo (☎ 809-565-3844), on Av Luperón near the Aeropuerto de Herrera, on the western edge of town. Ticket prices here start at US$2. The fights are held every Saturday and Sunday.

Horse Racing

Not nearly as popular as baseball or cock-fights, horse racing does have its fans in the Dominican Republic, and probably more attend the new Race Track V Centenario (☎ 809-687-6060), just outside Santo Domingo, than attend any of the country's other tracks. Devotees of the turf will be glad to know that the major newspapers employ handicappers who publish their 'daily picks.' The race track is off Las Américas Hwy, about halfway between downtown Santo Domingo and the international airport. Admission to the grandstand is US$1; the fee to enter the clubhouse is twice that. Check the local papers or call the track for start times.

Greyhound Racing

If the tropical heat has made you hungry for some good old-fashioned dog races, Santo Domingo won't leave you slack-jawed and downtrodden. Every Wednesday through Saturday evening and every Sunday afternoon, packs of greyhounds at Canodromo El Coco (☎ 809-567-4461) run as fast as they can after a mechanical rabbit that's always just a bit quicker than the lead dog. The track is beside the Duarte Hwy, about 15 minutes' drive north of downtown.

SHOPPING
Amber & Larimar

Dominican amber is fossilized resin that was produced by a tree that apparently slipped into extinction 25 million years ago. It is widely regarded as the world's finest, both for its color and for its quantity of inclusions such as trapped insects, tiny frogs and even tiny lizards. Blue amber is found nowhere else. Black amber, which is the oldest variety at about 50 million years, is absolutely stunning. Red Dominican amber has better color than the famous amber of the Baltics. Do-

minican honey-colored amber is comparable to the yellow amber of Egypt but contains far more inclusions, which add character and greatly increase the value.

Larimar is a semiprecious ocean-blue gemstone found only on a remote mountain in the southwestern region of the Dominican Republic. The Smithsonian Institution in Washington, DC, has identified larimar as a blue pectolite, found nowhere else in the world. It received its name from a lapidary artisan who first worked with the gemstone. He fused the name of his daughter, Larissa, with the Spanish word for sea, *mar*, and thus larimar was born. So goes the story told by larimar salespeople throughout the country.

If you are thinking of purchasing a beautiful gift that's unique to the Dominican Republic, you'd be wise to consider buying a piece of jewelry made of amber or larimar. And there is no better place in the republic to go shopping for either than the Zona Colonial in Santo Domingo. Here, there are literally *dozens* of stores that sell amber and larimar products, but the quality of the jewelry varies enormously.

Absolutely the best place in the old city to buy jewelry made of amber or larimar is The Swiss Mine (☎/fax 809-221-1897), beside the Parque Colón. Not only does the Swiss-owned and -operated shop sell the finest quality amber and larimar in the area, but the designs of its jewelry is unsurpassed. And the prices are remarkably low – about a third or less than what you'd pay in New York, and a quarter of what things go for in Paris. English, French, Italian, German, Russian and Spanish are spoken here.

Both of old town's amber museums – the Museo Mundo de Ambar on Calle Arzobispo Mériño and Museo de Ambar on the Calle El Conde promenade – have gift shops that sell some excellent pieces of amber and larimar jewelry. However, their prices, though open to negotiation, are generally much higher than the sticker prices at The Swiss Mine. Still, because the prices aren't set in stone you may be able to get an item you want at a price you could tolerate.

Las Indias Gift Shop, on Calle Arzobispo Mériño, near the Parque Colón, sells larimar of a particularly high quality. Likewise, the quality of the amber and gold jewelry is quite high. And the prices, which are open to negotiation, are very reasonable.

Galería Gift Shop V Centenario, also on Calle Arzobispo Mériño, contains lots of low-to medium-quality jewelry at competitive prices. Other Zona Colonial stores where bargains in amber and larimar can be found include Casa Verde, Ambar Maldo Gift Shop, Ambar Tres Gift Shop, Novo Atarazana Gift Shop and Cemis Gift Shop and Bar. For information on where to buy antique jewelry, see the passage concerning the Galería Toledo in the Paintings section, below.

Silver Coins

During the 16th, 17th and 18th centuries, the predominant currency in the Dominican Republic was Spanish, and it arrived from Spain and New World mints in the form of silver coins (there were some gold ones as well, but the vast majority were made of silver). The unit of measurement was the *reale*, and the coins mostly arrived in half-reale, one-reale, two-reale and eight-reale denominations. During the 17th century, one reale was what a crewman aboard a Spanish galleon could expect to be paid for two days' perilous work; it would buy a night at the best inn in Seville.

Reales from a sunken galleon

The eight-reale coin is more widely known today as a 'piece of eight.' About the width of a golf ball and half as thick as a Belgian waffle, a piece of eight was made of pure silver and was made very crudely. The method was to pour a long narrow strip from a ladle of molten silver and then pound the strip flat with hammers. From this strip of silver, pieces of eight about the length of an adult's middle finger were chiseled off. These pieces were weighed and small pieces were cut off the corners until the blank coin weighed one Spanish ounce. The coinmaker would then stamp each side of the coin with designs, usually the king's coat of arms on one side and the Spanish cross on the other.

Today, pieces of eight that have been salvaged from 16th- and 17th-century wrecks can be purchased for US$100 at the rarely visited Museo de las Atarazanas. The Dominican government, being poor, allows the naval museum to sell the historic coins to pay the museum's gas and electric bills. The coins are also available at certain area stores, including the gift shop in the Museo de Ambar. A piece of eight makes a great conversation piece when set in a gold frame and worn as a pendant.

Paintings

Haitian primitive art is famous throughout the world, and galleries in Europe have been known to sell Dominican paintings, which tend to be impressionist, figurative and cubist in style, for twentyfold their price on Hispaniola. Both Haitian and Dominican paintings are available in galleries in the Zona Colonial, and due to intense competition, the prices are very reasonable.

Certainly one of the best places to begin the search for a captivating piece of Caribbean artwork is the Galería Toledo along Calle Isabel la Católica, one block north of the Parque Colón. The gallery is owned by Bettye Marshall, a Texas transplant who fell in love with Dominican art during the 1970s and stayed here. Not only does Bettye stock Haitian and Dominican paintings covering a wide price range (from US$50 to US$5000), but she really knows the market and doesn't overcharge. The Galería Toledo is also a good place to look for antique jewelry. You'd think that colonial pieces would be easy to come by in Santo Domingo, but that simply isn't the case. Most of it was taken off the island long ago. But Bettye makes an effort to locate antique jewelry, and her gallery is one of the few places in the city you'll find it.

Works by famous Dominican artists can also be found for sale at the Mesón D'Bari restaurant and the Hostal Nicolás Nader. Likewise, the Galería de Arte San Ramón, at the west end of the Calle El Conde promenade, carries a few high-quality Dominican paintings. The Garden, situated on the Calle El Conde promenade near Parque Colón, specializes in high-quality, low-priced Haitian art, as does the nearby Elin Galería de Arte.

Other worthwhile stops for the Dominican and Haitian art aficionado include the Sala de Arte Rosa María, Galería Arte Club, Tienda de Artesania Cenadarte, Centro del Arte, Village Gallery and the Galería de Arte María del Carmen.

If all you really want from the Dominican art scene is the company of some young Dominican artists, you might want to visit the building on Calle Las Damas used as a meeting and exposition hall by the Fundación Latinoamericana de Jovenes Artistas (Foundation of Young Latin American Artists; see the Zona Colonial map for the exact location). The foundation doesn't maintain regular hours, but it's often open from 8 to 10 pm.

Outside of the Zona Colonial are dozens of other galleries that feature Haitian and Dominican art. Among the top ones are the Galería de Arte El Greco at Av Tiradentes 16 and the Galería de Arte El Pincel at Av Gustavo Mejía Ricart 24; beware that both close for lunch from 1 to 3 pm. One gallery that displays high-quality Dominican paintings and 'new art' that, to be generous, exhibits wide ranges of styles and talent is the Galería de Arte Nouveau on Av Independencia near Av Pasteur.

For a plethora of information on Dominican art and artists, get your hands on a copy of the *Enciclopedia de las Artes Plasticas Dominicanas* by Candido Geron. This 400-page book, which contains 200 pages in Spanish followed by a direct translation into English, is the bible of Dominican art. The book is out of print but can often be found in the used bookstores of the Zona Colonial. Be sure to tell the stores' salespeople you are looking for it. If they haven't got a copy on hand, more than likely they will be able obtain one within hours.

Cigars

Before Fidel Castro came to power, Cuba was *the* name in cigars. But his brand of politics didn't suit wealthy Cubans, among them the owners of the famous cigar companies. Most packed up and moved to the DR. Today, the finest cigar makers are at work in the Dominican Republic. Virtually all of the prestigious brands – among them Davidoff, Avo, Arturo Fuente, Fonseca and Romeo y Julieta – contain tobacco grown in rich Dominican soil.

Needless to say, cigar shops are plentiful in Santo Domingo. There are several on the Calle El Conde promenade offering their goods at very reasonable prices (these sellers aren't hampered by international shipping fees or import taxes), and the duty-free shops at Las Américas International Airport outside Santo Domingo carry all the big Dominican names at very competitive prices. If you enjoy a good cigar, you are in the right place – rather, you are in the *best* place – to find them.

Beside the Parque Colón are two shops owned by the same tobacco company, Monte Cristi de Tabacos, which produces such cigars as the non-Cuban Montecristo, Cohiba and Caoba brands. At both you can watch cigars being made by one or two individuals. It might interest you to know that on the 2nd floor of the shop nearest El Conde Restaurant, 45 employees spend their days rolling cigars for Monte Cristi de Tabacos; the factory usually is not open for touring, but it doesn't hurt to ask. English, French, Italian and Spanish are spoken at the shop.

Gems

The Dominican Republic is not known for its gems, and indeed it can't compete with world-leading Brazil in quality, quantity or variety of gemstones. But just as the DR has lured scores of European and North American expatriates, so too has it drawn a couple of Brazilians, both of whom sell Brazilian gems from shops near the Parque Colón.

Angel Bellver Muñoz owns and runs Angel Gemas, near the Parque Colón, on the 3rd floor of the modern building that houses The Swiss Mine jewelry store and a Monte Cristi de Tabacos cigar shop. Angel has been in the gem business for more than three decades, and his selection of gemstones, particularly his inventories of aquamarines and blue topaz, is outstanding. The gems sold at Angel Gemas are of the same quality as those sold by Hans Stern and Amsterdam Sauer (they even come from the same Brazilian mines), but are considerably less expensive.

Around the corner from Angel Gemas, Gemas José De Ferrari owns and runs Amazonia Gems, which also stocks an impressive assortment of gemstones. Because José also owns the adjacent Casa Verde jewelry store and factory, if you see a gem you like at Amazonia, he can arrange to have it included in a setting of your choice. Beware, however, that the quality of gold work in the Dominican Republic – and even the quality of the gold – does not compare favorably to that found in Europe, the USA and elsewhere. However, the quality is good for the relatively low price that you pay.

Warning: When looking at jewelry in the Dominican Republic, pay special attention to the pins and clasps that are used. At The Swiss Mine, the gift shop at the Museo de Ambar, and elsewhere, the pins and clasps are imported from Europe and the USA because they contain titanium or steel and are particularly sturdy. Dominican pins and clasps contain only gold, which is a soft metal that bends easily and shouldn't be used in this manner. Some places actually use wire when a gold-plated steel pin should be used.

Sweets

In the Dominican Republic, as in most of Latin America, *dulces* are very popular. The word is generic for candy, fudge, various desserts and assorted sugared fruits. It also refers to a smooth, sugary stuff sold in 1lb slabs that are often flavored with coconut or filled with preserved fruit. An excellent place to find some traditional Dominican sweets is Casa de los Dulces (House of Sweets), on the corner of Calle Emiliano Tejera and Calle Arzobispo Mériño in the Zona Colonial. This is also a good place to go for low-priced domestic rum. Rum and sweets – *delicioso!*

GETTING THERE & AWAY
Air
International The following airlines have offices in Santo Domingo; the rest provide customer service at the airport only.

ACE
  (☎ 809-549-6243) 54 Av Gustavo Mejía Ricart

Air Atlantic
  (☎ 809-472-1441) Av 27 de Febrero and
  Av Tiradentes

Air Canada
  (☎ 809-567-2236) 54 Av Gustavo Mejía Ricart

Air France
  (☎ 809-686-8419) 101 Av George Washington

Air Portugal
  (☎ 809-472-1441) Av 27 de Febrero at
  Av Tiradentes

ALM
  (☎ 809-687-4569) 28 Av Leopoldo Navarro

American Airlines
  (☎ 809-542-5151) In Tempo Building,
  Av Winston Churchill

Condor
  (☎ 809-682-8133) 353 Av George Washington

Continental Airlines
  (☎ 809-562-6688) In Tempo Building,
  Av Winston Churchill

COPA
  (☎ 809-562-5824) In Tempo Building,
  Av Winston Churchill

Hapag-Lloyd
  (☎ 809-682-8133) 353 Av George Washington

Iberia
  (☎ 809-686-9191) 401 Calle El Conde

LTU
  (☎ 809-541-5151) 54 Av Gustavo Mejía Ricart

TWA
  (☎ 809-689-6073) 54 Av Francia

Information concerning airline destinations, schedules and prices is subject to change and often does. Airlines add and drop routes with surprising frequency. Be sure to contact a travel agent or check current flight schedules yourself for the very latest information. If you have Internet access and would like to see flight schedules, you'll be glad to know that most airlines have websites that can provide you with arrival and departure information.

For more details on international air travel to and from the Santo Domingo area, see the introductory Getting There & Away chapter.

Domestic Air Santo Domingo (☎ 809-683-8020) is the only airline providing service solely within the Dominican Republic. In and about Santo Domingo, it operates from two airports: Aeropuerto de Herrera (☎ 809-

567-3900), beside Av Luperón near the western edge of the capital city; and Las Américas International Airport (☎ 809-549-0450), beside Las Américas Hwy about 35 minutes' drive east of the Zona Colonial.

There are daily flights from Aeropuerto de Herrera to Puerto Plata, Las Terrenas (served by nearby Aeropuerto El Portillo) and Punta Cana:

Destination & Departures	Duration	Cost
Puerto Plata 7:50 & 10:45 am, 2:15 & 8:50 pm	40 min	US$54
Las Terrenas 5:10 pm	30 min	US$49
Punta Cana 7:30 & 10:50 am, 7:35 pm	45 min	US$54

Bus Schedules

The following is route information for Caribe Tours (☎ 809-221-4422), located at the intersection of Av 27 de Febrero and Av Leopoldo Navarro, and for Metro Buses (☎ 809-566-7126), on Calle Francisco Prats, 50m east of Av Winston Churchill and one long block north of Av 27 de Febrero. Unless Metro Buses is indicated, the route information is for Caribe Tours.

Destination	Distance	Cost	Departures
Azua	120km	US$3	6:45, 7 & 10 am, 1:30, 2:30 & 4 pm
Barahona	200km	US$4	7 am, 2:30 pm
Bonao	85km	US$3	7, 7:30, 9:30, 10, 10:30 & 11 am, 12, 2, 2:45, 5 & 5:45 pm
Cabrera	208km	US$5	7:30 & 9 am, 3 pm
Castillo	150km	US$4	7:15, 7:30, 9 & 10:30 am, 1:30, 3 & 3:45 pm
		US$4	7 & 10 am, 2:30 & 3:30 pm (Metro Buses)
Copey	270km	US$6	6:30 & 8 am, 2, 2:45 & 3:30 pm
Cotuí	105km	US$3	9 & 10:30 am, 5:30 pm
Dajabón	305km	US$6	6:30 & 8 am, 2 & 3:30 pm
Esperanza	200km	US$5	7:30 & 9 am, 1 & 3 pm
Guayacanes	39km	US$5	6:30 & 8 am, 2 & 3:30 pm
Guayubín	238km	US$5	7:15 am, 2:30 pm
Imbert	195km	US$6	7, 8:30, 9:30, 10:30 & 11:30 am, 1, 1:45, 2:45, 4 & 5:30 pm
Jarabacoa	155km	US$4	7:30 & 10 am, 1:30 & 4:30 pm
La Vega	125km	US$3.50	every 30 min from 6:30 am to 7 pm
		US$3.75	7 & 11 am, 4 pm (Metro Buses)
Las Matas de Santa Cruz	250km	US$5	7:15 am, 2:30 pm
Loma de Cabrera	268km	US$6	7:30 am, 1:30 pm
Maimón	235km	US$3	9 & 10:30 am, 5:30 pm

Three domestic flights leave Las Américas International Airport daily, two bound for Punta Cana and one for Puerto Plata:

Destination & Departures	Duration	Cost
Punta Cana	40 min	US$54
11:00 am, 4:45 pm		
Puerto Plata	45 min	US$54
4:45 pm		

Be advised that Air Santo Domingo adds and drops routes and adjusts fares according to demand. For the most up-to-date flight and fare information, call the airline; the ticketing agents speak Spanish and English.

Bus

Santo Domingo has no central bus terminal, but its two major bus companies – Metro Buses and Caribe Tours – each have their own station near the city's center. Both carriers feature large, comfortable buses, the same as you'd find in Europe and the USA. Reservations are a good idea, especially on holidays and during festivals.

There are also several small carriers offering service from depots near Parque Enriquillo, 12 city blocks north of the Calle El Conde promenade. Their buses are the smaller, crowded but generally comfortable vehicles known as *gua-guas*. Reservations are not taken.

Additionally, in the immediate vicinity of Parque Enriquillo there are three small bus depots from which gua-guas frequently depart for the following cities: Baní (US$1.50), Higüey (US$4), Juan Dolio (US$1), Palmar de Ocoa (US$2.50), Puerto Plata (US$4),

Destination	Distance	Cost	Departures
Mao	205km	US$5	7:30 & 9 am, 1 & 3 pm
Moca	145km	US$4	7 & 11 am, 4 pm (Metro Buses)
Monte Cristi	270km	US$6	6:30 & 8 am, 2 & 3:30 pm
Nagua	180km	US$4.50	7:15, 7:30 & 9 am, 1:30, 3 & 3:45 pm
		US$5	7 & 10 am, 2:30 & 3:30 pm (Metro Buses)
Partido	245km	US$6	7:30 am & 1:30 pm
Pimentel	82km	US$3	9 & 10:30 am, 5:30 pm
Puerto Plata	215km	US$6	7, 8:30, 9:30, 10:30 & 11:30 am, 1, 1:45, 2:45, 4 & 5 pm
		US$5.75	7, 8 & 11 am, 2, 4, 6:30 & 7 pm (Metro Buses)
Río San Juan	215km	US$5	7:30 & 9:30 am, 3 pm
Salcedo	160km	US$4	7 & 10:30 am, 2 & 5:45 pm
Samaná	245km	US$5	7:15 & 9 am, 1:30 & 3:45 pm
		US$5.25	7 am & 2:30 pm (Metro Buses)
Sánchez	211km	US$5	7:15 & 9 am, 1:30 & 3:45 pm
San Francisco de Macorís	135km	US$3.50	7, 7:15, 7:30, 9, 10 & 11 am, 1:30, 2, 3, 3:45 & 5 pm
		US$4	7 & 10 am, 2:30, 3:30 & 6 pm (Metro Buses)
San Juan de la Maguana	163km	US$3.50	6:45 & 10 am, 1:30 & 4 pm
Santiago	155km	US$4	every 30 min from 6:30 am to 7 pm
		US$4.50	hourly from 6 am to 7 pm (Metro Buses)
Santiago Rodríguez	258km	US$5	7:30 & 9 am, 1 & 3 pm
Sosúa	240km	US$6	7, 8:30, 9:30, 10:30 & 11:30 am, 1, 1:45, 2:45, 4 & 5:30 pm
Tenares	160km	US$4	6 & 10:30 am, 2 & 5:45 pm
Villa Tapia	142km	US$4	7 & 10:30 am, 2 & 5:45 pm
Villa Vásquez	244km	US$5	6:30 & 8 am, 2 & 3:30 pm

San Pedro de Macorís (US$1.50), Santiago (US$2.50) and Sosúa (US$5). Be advised that gua-guas, unless full, generally make numerous stops along the way.

Lastly, Terra Bus (☎ 809-472-1080), at the intersection of Av 27 de Febrero and Av Máximo Gómez beside the Plaza Criolla, offers bus service to Port-au-Prince Monday through Saturday, departing at 6 am and again at 6:45 am. The trip, in a comfortable, air-conditioned coach, takes about 8½ hours. The vehicle arrives at the Steak Inn Restaurant (☎ 57-2161, 57-2153), 37 Rue Magny, Pétionville. You'd be wise to make a reservation at least two days in advance as this trip is fairly popular.

GETTING AROUND
To/From the Airport
The local taxi union has managed to prevent buses from conducting business between the country's largest airport, Las Américas International, and the country's largest city. So, unless you have a car of your own or someone is meeting you at the airport, you'll be stuck taking a taxi into town, which isn't ideal if you're on a tight budget. The one-way trip is US$20, but be sure to agree on the price before getting in a taxi. Taxis are available at the airport 24 hours a day.

Just as public buses don't serve Las Américas International Airport, neither do they serve Aeropuerto de Herrera. However, a taxi from here to most any part of the city won't cost more than US$10, and is usually a bit less. Taxis are not always available at the airport, but a certain number of drivers know when regular flights arrive and are always there to greet them. If, for whatever reason, there are no taxis around when you arrive, request one from one of the companies mentioned in the following Taxi section.

Bus
The Santo Domingo bus system is very simple to use (and very cheap – the cost of a bus ride from one end of the city to the other is less than US$1). Public buses run up and down the major avenues from sunrise to

sunset, and to catch one all you have to do is stand on the side of the road and hail it. If you're trying to get across town, just look at a map and note the major intersections along the way and plan your transfers accordingly. Knowing your next move before you get on the first bus can prove a blessing if the bus is crowded and seeing out a window proves difficult; if you know before you get on the bus that you want to cross three major intersections before getting off at the next one and transferring to another bus, you won't really need to see any road signs.

In addition to the exhaust-belching buses that labor up and down Santo Domingo's avenues all day long, there's another inexpensive form of public transportation, appropriately called *públicos*. These come in different forms – usually beat-up minivans and cars that are well past their prime – but they usually have three things in common: a license plate with 'público' on it, an inordinate number of occupants and a driver who likes to hug the curb, ready to take on or unload passengers. Like the buses, these vehicles cruise the major avenues. They cost a little more, but people take them when there are no buses in sight.

Car
Major international car rental companies have offices both at Las Américas International Airport and in Santo Domingo. For information pertaining to costs, rental requirements and so on, see the Getting Around the Dominican Republic chapter. Many of the companies mentioned here have toll-free reservations numbers in countries worldwide. You may want to check your local telephone directory or call directory assistance for such numbers to avoid an unnecessary international toll.

American International
 (☎ 809-687-0906) 1069 Av Independencia
 (☎ 809-687-0622) Airport
Avis
 (☎ 809-535-7191) Av Abraham Lincoln
 (☎ 809-549-0468) Airport

Budget
(☎ 809-562-6812) Av John F Kennedy
(☎ 809-567-0175) Airport

Dollar
(☎ 809-541-6801) 253 Av San Martín
(☎ 809-549-0738) Airport

Hertz
(☎ 809-221-5333) 454 Av Independencia
(☎ 809-549-0454) Airport

McDeal
(☎ 809-688-6518) 105 Av George Washington
(☎ 809-549-0373) Airport

National
(☎ 809-562-1444) 1056 Av Abraham Lincoln
(☎ 809-549-8303) Airport

Nelly
(☎ 809-688-3366) 654 Av Independencia
(☎ 809-549-0505) Airport

Thrifty
(☎ 809-685-9191) 1 Av José María Heredia
(☎ 809-549-0717) Airport

Taxi

None of the taxis in Santo Domingo have meters, which means the most important thing to keep in mind is to agree on a price before heading off in one. Another thing to remember is that the taxis parked in front of the luxury hotels on the malecón always charge more than other taxis. Dominican taxi drivers, incidentally, don't cruise the streets looking for rides; they park, and wait for customers to come to them. Most of them speak at least a smattering of English as well as Spanish.

Also bear in mind that when you enter a taxi you are entrusting its driver with your life. To protect yourself, use radio taxis at night and when you are going a fair distance. A particularly reputable taxi is Lino Taxi (☎ 809-687-3333), which, like all of the taxi companies listed below, dispatches cars around the clock.

Other radio-taxi companies serving Santo Domingo are Apolo Taxi (☎ 809-537-7771), El Conde Taxi (☎ 809-563-6131), Mella Taxi (☎ 809-541-5989), Santo Domingo Taxi (☎ 809-541-9032), Super Taxi (☎ 809-536-7014) and Taxi Oriental (☎ 809-549-5555).

Around Santo Domingo

Within easy striking distance of Santo Domingo are numerous towns and cities that offer tourists a relaxing respite from the frenetic pace of the big city. To the east of the capital lies Boca Chica, a popular weekend escape for Santo Domingans since the 1930s; Juan Dolio, home to many all-inclusive seaside resorts where life is just a breeze, a dip in the aquamarine and one delicious tropical drink after another; and San Pedro de Macorís, which in recent decades has produced more major-league baseball players than any other city in the world.

Just west of Santo Domingo are a string of historic cities such as San Cristóbal, birthplace of Rafael Trujillo, who ruled the country with an iron fist for 31 years until his violent death in 1961; and Baní, a bustling city best known as the birthplace of Generalísimo Máximo Gómez y Báez, leader of Cuba's struggle for independence from Spain. Also west of Santo Domingo and an easy drive away is San José de Ocoa, a cool foothills town that offers visitors an intimate look at life in a prosperous Dominican small town.

East of Santo Domingo

From Santo Domingo, Hwy 3 runs east along the coast toward the beach towns of Boca Chica and Juan Dolio and the sugarcane port of San Pedro de Macorís, while the larger Hwy 4 runs the inland route.

PARQUE NACIONAL SUBMARINO LA CALETA

This national park is 22km southeast of Santo Domingo and 12km west of Boca Chica. Its main attraction is the underwater section that contains a number of supposedly protected coral reefs, but the park also includes a stretch of shoreline. 'Supposedly protected' refers to the sad fact that trapping

and fishing occur in the national marine park unabated despite its protected status.

Although the smallest of the country's national parks at only 10 sq km, La Caleta is one of the country's most popular. The marine park has a maximum depth of 180m, but it usually ranges from 10m to 50m. There are many coral reefs here, with a fair number of colorful fish, octopi and eels. In 1984, the year the park was created, the salvage ship *Hickory* was scuttled in park waters to create an attraction for divers (see The *Hickory*'s Colorful Past boxed text). Because the boat's in shallow, calm water, it's a fine site for beginning divers.

The park rates fairly high compared to other dive sites around the DR. Most of the time the visibility is good, and because the *Hickory* is in relatively shallow water, divers can spend a lot of time studying the critters that have made the boat their home. Unfortunately, lobster trapping and spear fishing have taken a real toll on the area's marine life, and Hurricane Georges damaged a lot of La Caleta coral in 1998.

BOCA CHICA

Located 30km east of Santo Domingo, Boca Chica has been a popular weekend escape for residents of the capital city for more than 60 years. During dictator Trujillo's tenure, members of the moneyed class built vacation homes in the sleepy port town and did much of their entertaining there. By the 1960s, a few bayside hotels were in place and the international jet set added Boca Chica to its expanding list of Caribbean party destinations.

But with the development of Puerto Plata and Sosúa on the North Coast during the 1970s, Boca Chica lost much of its appeal among globe-trotters. The once-bustling resort, with its calm, shallow bay and its long white sandy beach, became a tranquil port town again. It stayed that way for nearly 20 years, until a spate of hotel building in the early 1990s sparked a rekindling of interest in Boca Chica. Today, the gently sloping

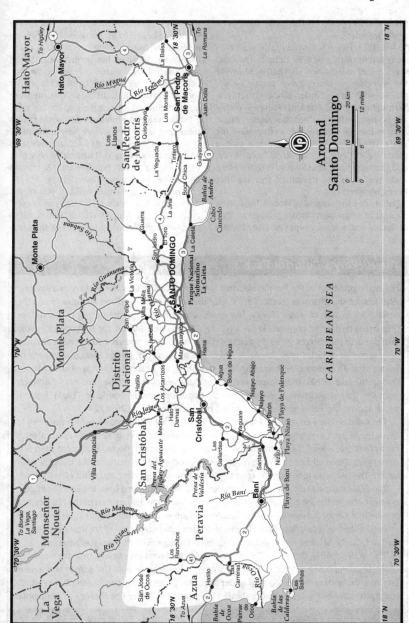

Around
Santo Domingo

town again appears on the radar screens of world travelers.

Whether Boca Chica actually deserves such attention is open to debate. In some ways it has maintained its charm. Many of the wooden buildings have yet to be replaced with drab cinder-block structures. Wrinkled longtime residents still pass pleasant hours chatting on benches under shade trees in Parque Central, just as they have for years. The Bahía de Andrés remains only a meter or so deep a good stroll from shore, and the waves are usually gentle thanks to a coral reef near the mouth of the bay that keeps breakers out.

But today the streets of Boca Chica often contain as many pasty-white *gringos* as they do locals, and a luxury hotel catering mostly to Americans denies access to a lovely stretch of beach to all nonguests, stirring up resentment among locals as well as many foreigners. Most of the quaint older shops and colorful local watering holes on the key oceanfront streets have been replaced by touristy restaurants and bars. Prostitutes are out in numbers, aggressively soliciting men.

Still, the strand has kept its swaying palm trees, and Boca Chica *does* have a nightlife. It offers a wide selection of accommodations and there are many restaurants from which to choose, and the beach scene is vibrant and makes for fun people watching.

Oh, longtime visitors will tell you of the days when there wasn't a single noisy motorcycle on Boca Chica's streets nor were so many establishments poured from the same

The *Hickory*'s Colorful Past

The main attraction in the Parque Nacional Submarino La Caleta is the *Hickory*, a 39m-long steel salvage ship that was scuttled in 1984 for the benefit of scuba divers and now lies on the ocean floor in 10m of water. Today, few divers who kick down to the rusting ship and poke their heads through its portholes know anything about its past. Indeed, the tour operators who take divers to the *Hickory* generally describe it as a 'wreck dive' and say nothing more about it.

As a matter of fact, the *Hickory* was laid to rest by its owner, Caribe Salvage Company of Texas, after an enormously rewarding life – rewarding for history buffs as well as its owner. During the late 1970s, the *Hickory* was the primary vessel used in the recovery of artifacts from the Spanish galleons *Nuestra Señora de Guadalupe* and *El Conde de Tolosa*, both of which sank in the Bahía de Samaná during a hurricane on August 25, 1724.

The galleons were en route to Mexico from Spain loaded with mercury (which was used to extract gold from ore) when howling winds and a violent sea forced the ships into coral reefs far from shore, where they were battered to pieces. Survivors reported that more than 600 passengers drowned during the storm or were ripped apart by sharks in the days that followed. The few who survived managed to save themselves by riding makeshift rafts to shore.

The *Guadalupe* was discovered by fishermen in 1976. A short time later, the Dominican government offered the job of salvaging the galleon to Tracy Bowden, captain of the *Hickory* and president of Caribe Salvage Company. Bowden had ample experience salvaging vessels and he enjoyed a sterling reputation; Santo Domingo trusted him to report all of the articles found. By contract, Caribe Salvage would assume all costs and receive 50% of the pieces salvaged.

The work began in October 1976, when Bowden anchored the *Hickory* over the wreckage of the *Guadalupe* and secured the salvage ship with four large buoys. The galleon was a mere 6m from the surface but was buried under tons of sediment. Only the fragments of earthen jars scattered over the sea bottom indicated the wreck was there. The *Hickory* was equipped

tacky-bar mold. But back then there also weren't so many choices, creature comforts and English speakers, nor so many foreigners with whom to share tales of travel. Certainly one can do much worse than to spend time in this touristy town with a popular beach beside a strollable bay.

Orientation

Boca Chica comprises a 10-by-15-block area between Hwy 3 and Bahía de Andrés, a bay so shallow and calm that it feels more like a lagoon than a large body of seawater. From Hwy 3 there are three main avenues – Avs 24 de Julio, Juan Bautista Vicini and Caracol – that directly link the highway to the key oceanfront roads of Avs San Rafael and Duarte.

The town, which follows a grid pattern and is easy to negotiate, slopes from the highway to the sea. For this reason, visitors with bad knees, bad backs or bad hearts would be wise to find a hotel on or near Av Duarte, if enjoying the beach or the many nearby restaurants and bars is important to them. In fact, during daylight hours and well into the evening, three-quarters of the town's visitors can be found at the beach or on nearby Av Duarte.

Information

Tourist Offices Despite Boca Chica's popularity, the government has yet to open a tourist office here. If you've got questions about Boca Chica – questions concerning relocating to Boca Chica, for example – consider paying

---

with a curved iron shaft that, when placed over the propeller, directed a powerful stream of water straight down. The ship's crew rigged a tube to the shaft, creating a powerful hose that they used to blow much of the sediment away.

The 'water jet,' as the *Hickory's* crew called the device, wasn't the only nifty feature of the salvage ship. On its stern was a large air compressor that crew members jury-rigged to act as a giant vacuum; four hoses extended from the machine, each with its own suction regulator. These were used to gently remove sand and mud without damaging artifacts. Also on the *Hickory* was a crane used to hoist heavy objects; a decompression chamber that saved the lives of several Dominican divers who suffered the bends while working elsewhere in the bay; a laboratory where most of the artifacts were identified; diving equipment for 12 divers as well as a compressor to fill the tanks; and a shark cage that – much to the relief of the crew – wasn't needed.

It took Bowden and his crew one year to carefully excavate the area in which the *Guadalupe* had settled. Knowing from Spanish records that the *Guadalupe* was sailing with the *Tolosa* and that both ships were lost within hours of each other, the salvagers painstakingly searched the section of the Bahía de Samaná northwest of Miches using a magnetometer. It took the team six months, but they found the *Tolosa* and recovered objects from that quicksilver galleon as well.

Among the thousands of items recovered from the two ships were hundreds of silver and gold coins minted in Spain during the early 18th century, a king's ransom in jewelry, and hundreds of crystal glasses. Many of these items, as well as dozens of fascinating photographs of the excavation, are on permanent display at the Museo de las Atarazanas in the Zona Colonial of Santo Domingo. Signs are in English and Spanish. The museum, though astonishingly seldom visited (it's slightly off the beaten track), is one of the finest in the Caribbean.

a visit to the Romagna Mia Ristorante, whose owners/managers are very knowledgeable, friendly and helpful. The restaurant is near the eastern end of Av San Rafael.

Money There are several places in Boca Chica to exchange foreign currency for Dominican pesos, the most popular of which is the Banco de Reservas at the corner of Avs 20 de Diciembre and Juan Bautista Vicini. It's possible to exchange money there 9 am to 8 pm daily. In late 1998 the bank was accepting US and Canadian dollars, German marks, Japanese yen, Swiss francs, Italian lira and Spanish pesetas.

Closer to the restaurants, bars and beach are two other places to swap your money for local currency: the Tricom office on Av Duarte just west of Av Juan Bautista Vicini, and the Banco Popular on Av Duarte, a half block east of the Parque Central. The Tricom office is open daily 9 am to 6 pm. The bank is open Monday through Friday from 9 am to 4 pm, and Saturday from 9 am to 1 pm.

Post & Communications The city's sole post office is on Av Duarte just west of Av Juan Bautista Vicini.

International calls can be made from most hotels, but it's much less expensive to place them from a Tricom office (there's one opposite the post office and another on Av Duarte near Av del Sur) or the Codetel office at the east end of Av Duarte. The Tricom office near the post office is open 9 am to 6 pm daily, while the other Tricom office keeps shorter hours and is closed Sunday. The Codetel office is open 8 am to 10 pm daily.

The Codetel office has computers with Internet access for public use. The per-hour rate for computer use, including access to the Internet, is about US$2.50 an hour.

Laundry Many hotels will provide laundry service if you ask, or their receptionists can steer you toward the closest laundromat.

Playa Boca Chica

Boca Chica's only real tourist sight – its beach – is the site of most of the town's activities, chief of which is spreading out a towel on the sand and paying homage to the skin-cancer god. Although it should go without saying, if you're fair-skinned and unaccustomed to the tropical sun, wear *lots* of sunscreen. Fifteen minutes without it, even on an overcast day, is enough to give many people second-degree burns. The sunscreens that advertise 'waterproof' on their labels and have a protection factor of 15 or greater are best.

The lovely, white-sand Playa Boca Chica has long attracted Santo Domingans (who have no beaches of their own) and foreigners. The wide beach is lined with coconut palms, behind which are numerous bars, restaurants and food stands. In front of the beach is the Bahía de Andrés, which is quite shallow immediately south of Av San Rafael and Av Duarte. There is a marina a few kilometers to the west.

Most of the beach is quite lively, filled every day with locals and foreigners sunning themselves, vendors selling fruit from pushcarts and mariachi bands performing lovely music for a couple of dollars a song. About 100m from shore is a small shrub-covered island that one can wade to; farther toward the mouth of the bay is a second, larger island that cannot be easily reached and is in fact privately owned.

Physically, Playa Boca Chica is one long beach, although it actually has three distinct sections. Near its eastern end, the wide tract of sand is broken by a wall which was erected by the enormous Coral Hamaca Beach Hotel & Casino. The hotel has its main entrance on Calle Duarte and is situated between the street and the beach. Although Dominican law states that all beaches are open to the public, resort hotels frequently ignore the law and post guards to drive nonguests away from 'their' beaches. Some, including the Coral Hamaca, have gone so far as to build walls and check identifications.

West several hundred meters from the Coral Hamaca's wall, to just beyond the point where Calle Hungria ends, is a lovely stretch of sand bordered by establishments catering to tourists. Continuing farther west,

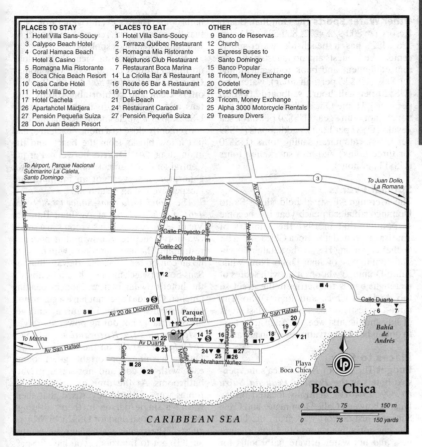

PLACES TO STAY	PLACES TO EAT	OTHER
1 Hotel Villa Sans-Soucy	1 Hotel Villa Sans-Soucy	9 Banco de Reservas
3 Calypso Beach Hotel	2 Terraza Québec Restaurant	12 Church
4 Coral Hamaca Beach	5 Romagna Mia Ristorante	13 Express Buses to
Hotel & Casino	6 Neptunos Club Restaurant	Santo Domingo
5 Romagna Mia Ristorante	7 Restaurant Boca Marina	15 Banco Popular
8 Boca Chica Beach Resort	14 La Criolla Bar & Restaurant	18 Tricom, Money Exchange
10 Casa Caribe Hotel	16 Route 66 Bar & Restaurant	20 Codetel
11 Hotel Villa Don	19 D'Lucien Cucina Italiana	22 Post Office
17 Hotel Cachela	21 Deli-Beach	23 Tricom, Money Exchange
26 Apartahotel Madjera	24 Restaurant Caracol	25 Alpha 3000 Motorcycle Rentals
27 Pensión Pequeña Suiza	27 Pensión Pequeña Suiza	29 Treasure Divers
28 Don Juan Beach Resort		

Boca Chica

CARIBBEAN SEA

the number of touristy places drops off substantially and eventually gives way to a dirt parking lot and a row of food stalls selling cheap local food. This stretch of sand, in front of which the water is somewhat muddy, is used almost exclusively by Dominican families.

Activities

Scuba Diving Treasure Divers (☎ 809-523-5320, fax 523-4819, treasuredivers@hotmail.com, www.netwing.at/business/boca-chica) operates out of a building on the beach

behind Don Juan Beach Resort. It offers day and night dives to many canyon sites, as well as cave diving and wall diving for qualified divers. High-quality rental equipment and PADI certification are available. Treasure Divers also offers dives at nearby Parque Nacional Submarino La Caleta; see earlier in this chapter for information on the park. Additionally, the company offers a special, weeklong whale-watching adventure at Bahía de Samaná. Contact Treasure Divers for further details, including current prices. English, Spanish and German are spoken.

Other Water Sports The Don Juan Beach Resort (☎ 800-922-4272, 809-523-4511, fax 523-6422) has a beachside water-sports center where guests and nonguests alike can rent equipment and book tours, including: Jet Skis (US$22 per half hour), water skis (US$20 per half hour), sailboards (US$20 per hour), Hobie One sailboats (US$20 per hour), snorkeling gear (US$20 per day), sea kayaks (US$7 per hour), paddleboats (US$9 per hour), catamaran sailing tours (US$20 for three hours) and also snorkeling tours (US$14 per hour).

Special Events
The Merengue Festival held along Santo Domingo's malecón each year has become so popular that in 1997 the Ministry of Tourism extended it to Boca Chica and, a bit farther east along Hwy 3, the smaller beach-side community of Juan Dolio. Now, while Santo Domingo whoops it up with scores of merengue bands and parties in the street, so too do Boca Chica and Juan Dolio. The three-city festival takes place the last week of July and the first week of August. Be sure to obtain hotel reservations well in advance.

Places to Stay
Budget The best of Boca Chica's inexpensive hotels is the *Pensión Pequeña Suiza* (☎ 809-523-4619), centrally located on Av Duarte between Calle Dominguez and Calle Sánchez, just a short walk from the beach. The pension's five rooms offer fans, cleanliness and hot-water private bathrooms for US$20 per room. The Pequeña Suiza has its own generator to deal with nagging power outages. For the price, this place is a great value. Reservations are a very good idea. Only Spanish is spoken.

The *Hotel Cachela* (☎ 809-523-5454) is easily overlooked (and usually is) but it's an excellent value at US$26 for one bed and US$40 for two. The Cachela is right in the midst of things on Av Duarte a half block from Calle Sánchez but, because it's above a store and the staircase leading up to it is unpronounced, few passersby ever notice it. Too bad, because its rooms are clean and have fans, air con and hot-water private

bathrooms. There's even a generator. Now that the secret is out, reservations would be wise. Only Spanish is spoken.

On Av Juan Bautista Vicini, half a block north of Parque Central, is the very homey *Casa Caribe Hotel* (☎ 809-523-6724), which offers clean and comfortable rooms with fans and hot-water private bathrooms for US$25/30 for singles/doubles. The hotel is conveniently close to a money exchange and just a few blocks from the beach and the main drag (Av Duarte between Parque Central and Av Caracol), *and* it has its own generator. It's even got an intimate and inexpensive Italian restaurant.

The *Hotel Villa Sans-Soucy* (☎ 809-523-4461, fax 523-4136), at Av Juan Bautista Vicini 48, has a dozen or so rooms in a small, two-story structure with swimming pool and restaurant. The pleasant rooms, with fans but no air con, go for US$25/42. Beware that the Sans-Soucy (which means 'without troubles' – the hotel's owner is from French-speaking Quebec, Canada) does not have a generator; guest rooms and the restaurant can get uncomfortably hot during power shortages.

Romagna Mia Ristorante (☎ 809-523-4647, fax 523-4175), on the east end of Av Duarte, has nine comfortable guest rooms, each with air con and hot-water private bathrooms. At the time of writing these rooms were so little advertised that there wasn't a single person in them, although they were a great deal for US$25/40. Why no guests? The owner wasn't sure he wanted any! To get to the rooms you have to pass through a fairly formal restaurant, and the owner is very concerned about guests making too much noise, looking grungy or bringing prostitutes back to their rooms. However, if you are quiet, well dressed and clean-cut, you probably can stay here. And if so, you're in for a treat: Not only are the rooms very reasonably priced, but the rate includes use of the pool and a hearty breakfast. And, this restaurant-with-rooms has a generator.

Mid-Range Stepping up a level in comfort is the three-story *Calypso Beach Hotel* (☎ 809-523-466, fax 523-4829) on Av 20 de Diciembre near Av Caracol. All of its 40 spacious, attractive rooms have cable TV, a ceiling fan, air con, a safe in the closet and even a hair drier in the bathroom. There's also a pool with a small restaurant beside it. The rate is very reasonable: US$35 for one or two persons. Reservations are a very good idea. English and Spanish are spoken.

The four-story *Apartahotel Madjera* (☎ 809-523-4434, fax 523-4532), on Calle Dominguez, a crab's throw from the beach, is as popular as the Calypso Beach Hotel, but it's very different. Whereas the Calypso has predictable floral-print bedspreads and rectangular rooms, the rooms at the Madjera contain a lot of purple and black and are five-sided, with a small balcony and long dark curtains. None of the 16 rooms have air con, but they tend to be cool and the ceiling fan is sufficient. If you prefer quiche to a hamburger, you'd likely prefer this place. Rates are US$30/40/50 for a single/double/triple. There is a generator.

The *Hotel Villa Don* (☎/fax 809-523-4679), on Av Juan Bautista Vicini, just around the corner from the town's main church, offers decent rooms with fan only for US$30/35. Its chief selling point is its swimming pool. There is a generator at the Villa Don.

Top End A major leap in price and size over Boca Chica's mid-range hotels are the town's resort hotels. Away from the beach and the bustling Av Duarte (and, in most people's minds, therefore less desirable) is the *Boca Chica Beach Resort* (☎ 809-523-4521, fax 523-4438) on Av 20 de Diciembre. The resort covers an entire city block and boasts more than 200 apartments, lovely grounds, a swimming pool and tennis courts. Its all-inclusive rates run upwards of US$60/85, varying with demand. Expect to pay quite a bit more around the Christmas holiday.

The *Don Juan Beach Resort* (☎ 809-523-4511, fax 523-6422), on Av Abraham Nuñez, offers 124 comfortable rooms in a multilevel structure overlooking the beach. Though not quite as nice as the Coral Hamaca, it's also quite popular, particularly with French tourists. Its facilities include a swimming pool and a large restaurant. The rate of US$75 to US$100 per person, varying with

room and season, includes all meals. Generally speaking, this resort is preferred by those who like to mingle with the local population, while it can quite fairly be said that the Coral Hamaca (see below) is designed to separate its guests from everyone else.

The 454-room *Coral Hamaca Beach Hotel & Casino* (☎ 800-945-0792, 809-523-4611, fax 523-6767, coral.h@codetel.net.do, www.coralhotels.com), on Calle Duarte on the east side of town, is the nicest and most expensive resort. It has its own private beach, a popular dance club, a casino, very nice guest rooms, a Jacuzzi, swimming pool and game room – the works. All meals are included in the rates of US$175/270 for a standard room and US$235/390 for a suite.

Places to Eat

Certainly one of the most enjoyable places to eat in Boca Chica is the *Restaurant Boca Marina,* on Calle Duarte on the east side of town. It features lots of wooden tables on several open-air and covered decks facing the Caribbean; some tables are actually over the water. The ambiance is made all the more pleasant by breezes blowing in from the sea. If you don't feel like eating, there's a long bar as well. The Boca Marina specializes in seafood, and the long menu includes shrimp cocktail (US$10.50), fish ceviche (US$4), shrimp in thermidor sauce (US$13.50), lasagna Bolognese (US$5.75), lobster thermidor (US$15), rice with mixed seafood (US$13) and several pasta dishes ranging in price from US$5.50 to US$13. Dress is casual during the day, conservative at night.

A brief stroll west from the Boca Marina is the equally popular, similarly situated *Neptunos Club Restaurant*, which also specializes in seafood. This restaurant offers a bit more shade than the Boca Marina and half of its tables are on decks that extend over the surf. There's always a festive atmosphere in the air, and there's usually a seat at the bar if you have to wait for a table. The food is well worth waiting for. Delicious dishes include the seafood casserole (the house specialty, US$24), lobster lasagna (US$12), lobster thermidor (US$14) and spaghetti with seafood (US$18). There are also a variety of beef dishes listed for around US$9, and chicken breast cordon bleu for US$7.50.

An excellent, somewhat formal Italian restaurant that's routinely patronized by Santo Domingo's movers and shakers is **Romagna Mia Ristorante** (☎ 809-523-4647, fax 523-4175), at the eastern end of Av Duarte. The pasta, made fresh daily, ranges from US$6 to US$10. The breaded veal cutlet, a specialty, is US$9. Seafood dishes are US$10 to US$14. The pizzas, from US$5 to US$10, depending on the toppings, are to die for; the shrimp pizza and the anchovies-and-capers pizza are delicious. The restaurant does not allow beachwear and is open noon to 11 pm daily. English, Italian and Spanish are spoken.

One of the best and certainly the most understated restaurant in town may be found at the **Pensión Pequeña Suiza**, on Av Duarte. It's so understated it doesn't even have a name. Specializing in fondue, the restaurant has many from which to choose, all for US$10 to US$12. You won't be disappointed. This unnamed restaurant also serves a delicious breakfast. It's open from 9 am until very late every day.

There are a lot of mediocre restaurants on Av Duarte between Calle Pedro Mella and Av Caracol; **D'Lucien Cucina Italiana** isn't one of them. Like Romagna Mia Ristorante, 100m to the east, D'Lucien has managed to locate the ingredients needed for fine Italian cuisine – no easy feat in the Dominican Republic. Among the many offerings are a variety of tortellini, ravioli and panzeroti dishes, all priced at US$7.50; spaghetti with a choice of 12 sauces and toppings, from US$5 to US$9; and numerous seafood dishes, vegetarian plates and thin-crust pizzas. Unlike Romagna Mia, the dress code here is lax.

The restaurant at the **Hotel Villa Sans-Soucy** is inexpensive and popular, offering breakfast for US$2, a number of sandwiches and burgers for US$2 to US$4 and a daily special – the pride of the house – which might consist of fine roast beef or a deliciously prepared chicken for about US$7.

Opposite the Sans-Soucy, the **Terraza Québec Restaurant** is very good and fairly popular. Its lengthy international menu includes grilled beef filet (US$9), snails with a garlic sauce (US$3), spaghetti with meat sauce (US$6), fish kabob (US$7.50) and grilled lobster (US$14). Many locals will tell you the Terraza Québec is the finest restaurant in town.

Just looking for a cheap lunch? The **Deli-Beach** on Av Duarte does a fair job with a cheeseburger (US$3), its chicken sandwiches are tasty (US$2.75) and the club sandwiches are a bargain for US$3. More substantial plates go for US$3 to US$6. Continental breakfast here is a mere US$1.50. A good thing about the Deli-Beach is its central location; it makes for fine people-watching.

If you're searching for a bar with that special tropical 'seedy' feel, look no further than the **Restaurant Caracol** on Av Duarte. It's mostly a bar, but is also a hangout for prostitutes and their johns. If nothing else, this place can provide some interesting people-watching. It attracts its share of lowlifes, mainly middle-aged foreign men cruising for *chicas* and intrigued by a sign that reads: 'two-for-one Happy Hour' – the hour lasts from 3 to 7 pm daily. Don't bother with the food, but the place has a fine selection of cigars.

About midway down Av Duarte is a place you can't miss called **Route 66 Bar & Restaurant**; it's got a big sign, and loud rock 'n' roll pours out of it most of the day. This Dominican restaurant named after a bygone American highway serves only mediocre Indonesian food. A much better bet than Route 66 is **La Criolla Bar & Restaurant**, just a couple of doors to the west. It's not about to win any awards for its cuisine, but it offers Creole-style food at reasonable prices.

Entertainment

Frankly speaking, entertainment in Boca Chica caters more to the lowbrow than the highbrow. In other words, it tends to attract and serve a crowd whose idea of an excellent time is drinking to the verge of vomiting at such places as Route 66 Bar & Restaurant and the equally classy Restaurant Caracol – *please* don't get sick inside the restaurant. There are many such bars in the area as well as many prostitutes – so many that the town's reputation is attracting foreigners whose chief purpose for being in the country is Boca's chicas.

But there is at least one classy place to dance the night away – the dance club at the **Coral Hamaca Beach Hotel & Casino**. The dance club there is open 11 pm until 4 am daily, and nonguests are welcome. The cover charge is usually US$5, but it can be twice that on the occasional nights when there's live music. The casino is also open to nonguests; appropriate attire (no beachwear, halter tops, shorts, etc) is required.

Getting There & Away

Getting to and away from Boca Chica is easy. About every 30 minutes during daylight hours an express bus to Santo Domingo appears on the north side of Parque Central; the fare to the capital city on one of these buses is a mere US$1.50. Another option is just to go up to Hwy 3 and flag down a guagua that's traveling in the direction you want to go. It's that simple.

If you've got the money, you can travel by taxi. You'll find taxis near the intersection of Av San Rafael and Av Caracol, and sometimes on Av Duarte opposite the Codetel office. Widely accepted one-way taxi prices from Boca Chica in late 1998 included: Las Américas International Airport (US$10), Santo Domingo (US$20), La Romana (US$50), Punta Cana (US$100) and Puerto Plata (US$150). Of course, a taxi driver can charge whatever he wants; you may have to negotiate his asking price down to the fares mentioned here.

Getting Around

Boca Chica is small and easily walked. Still, if you don't feel like walking or if you just feel like cruising around, you can always take a *motoconcho* (motorcycle taxi). They're cheap and abundant. Just look for young men standing beside their mopeds or motorcycles. You'll find them near Parque Central, near the Codetel office, and cruising Av Duarte honking at prospective customers.

Motorcycles are a great way to see the area if you are an experienced motorcyclist

and a defensive driver. Alpha 3000 Motorcycle Rentals (☎ 809-523-6222, cellular 1-280-5879), on Av Duarte near Calle Dominguez, has dozens of motorcycles available for rent at the country's lowest prices. A Yamaha DT 125, for example, rents for a flat US$16 per day. You'd be wise to call ahead and reserve one of these popular and rugged bikes. Owner Eric Lessard speaks English, French and Spanish. Be sure to bring a helmet with you, as they are required by law and they are not available for rent anywhere.

GUAYACANES

A few kilometers west of Juan Dolio is Playa Guayacanes, a beach that is home to a small community called, simply, Guayacanes. In the vicinity of this community are four hotels, all of which can be easily seen from Hwy 3. The strength of these hotels is a reason Guayacanes won't likely remain unheard of for long. If you don't need the noise, tackiness or pushiness of Boca Chica (and probably Juan Dolio a few years from now), any of the hotels at Guayacanes would likely be enjoyable and relaxing places to stay.

Coming from Santo Domingo or Boca Chica, the first of the four hotels you'll see is the **Coco Village** (☎ 809-526-1065, fax 526-1309), which offers spacious villas with kitchens on lush grounds. It has very reasonable prices for what you get: US$30/60/90 singles/doubles/triples (add 20% during the high season – January, February and August). Lower weekly rates are available. The hotel is three minutes' walk from a nice beach, and on the premises is a large, cool natural bathing pool that is very refreshing on a hot day. Never mind the freshwater turtles; they won't attack you.

The next place to the east is the **Hotel Embassy Beach Resort** (☎ 809-526-1246, fax 535-5292), a big, popular all-inclusive place with lovely standard rooms and spacious bungalows, pool, Jacuzzi, free horseback riding, free barbecue on the beach nightly, buffet breakfasts, lunches and dinners, even free transport to and from Boca Chica. The beach is lovely but the surf is dangerous – the hotel's one drawback. Year-round rates are US$65/100 singles/doubles or bungalow. Spanish lessons, aerobics classes, water games, merengue instruction and even bingo are provided here.

A very different place appears alongside Hwy 3 a little farther to the east. It's the 25-room *Hotel Sueño Tropical* (no phone), which has very attractive rooms with air con, fans, TVs and refrigerators, from US$40 to US$100 for the grand suite with a Jacuzzi. All the guest rooms in this architecturally pleasing two-story hotel face the sea. Also on the premises are an inviting swimming pool (a good thing, because the surf here is unsafe), a café with a spotless kitchen that prepares an assortment of international dishes (most between US$7 and US$10) and a poolside bar where most people could easily sip the day away. The French Canadian owner rents jeeps from the hotel as well.

The last hotel before you leave Guayacanes and make your approach into Juan Dolio is *Playa Esmeralda Beach Resort* (☎ 809-526-3434, fax 809-526-1744), which is a mid-size, all-inclusive resort with beautiful grounds that contain a poolside restaurant and bar, and modern guest rooms in four two-story structures. The resort is adjacent to a large beach with swimmable water. This hotel is particularly popular with Germans. Rates are US$75/110.

JUAN DOLIO

Juan Dolio isn't so much a seaside town as it is a tourist development beside the sea – or rather a 'string' of tourist developments. During the late 1980s several developers looked at lovely Playa Juan Dolio, 50km east of Santo Domingo, and began building hotels between Hwy 3 and the Caribbean. Today, for a stretch of more than 5km, there are many hotels, some right next to each other, some a good distance away from their nearest neighbor. New hotels are under construction all the time, while others are being planned. By the time you read this, at least two new hotels will have opened.

Whether you enjoy your time in Juan Dolio will likely depend on your selection of accommodations, because you will spend nearly all of your time at your hotel. There simply aren't a lot of other places to visit in town. People who leave their hotels tend to walk down the frontage road a ways, look about and then head back. So, choose your hotel carefully!

Orientation

Juan Dolio consists of a fairly large sliver of developed land between Hwy 3 and Playas Juan Dolio and Real. It also incorporates some noncommercial development that is occurring north of the highway, mostly squatters who hawk goods on the beaches during the day or are otherwise trying to benefit from the tourist industry.

The land between the highway and the beaches is bisected by a frontage road variously called Carretera Vieja (Old Hwy) and Carretera Local (Local Hwy). Regardless of what it's called, it's more a quiet lane with speed bumps than a highway, as pedestrians greatly outnumber the motorized vehicles on it. Some portions of the road are paved; others are not.

The two beaches and a third, Playa Guayacanes to the west, are of moderate width and are attractive enough. The water is safe for swimming in some places and quite obviously unsafe in others. Not surprisingly, nearly all of the seaside hotels are beside lovely patches of sand and swimmable water.

If you're approaching Juan Dolio from Santo Domingo, the first hotels you will likely associate with Juan Dolio are actually in Guayacanes, a tiny, poorly signed community that is often mistaken for Juan Dolio, a few kilometers to the east. There are four hotels in the vicinity of Guayacanes, which are mentioned above under that section.

The exits for Juan Dolio from Hwy 3 are not clearly marked. A good turnoff to the frontage road is nearly opposite the only Shell station on this stretch of Hwy 3. This turnoff will bring you to an intersection of two dirt roads, on one corner of which you'll see the white, architecturally eccentric Hotel Fior di Loto. Only the back side of the Hotel Costa Linda is on the frontage road to the west of here; most hotels and restaurants located in the town of Juan Dolio are on the frontage road to the east.

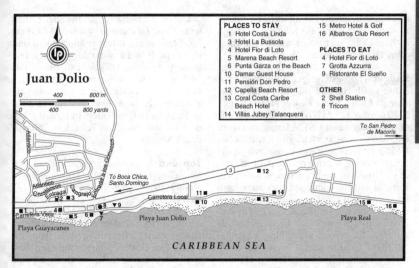

PLACES TO STAY
1 Hotel Costa Linda
3 Hotel La Bussola
4 Hotel Fior di Loto
5 Marena Beach Resort
6 Punta Garza on the Beach
10 Damar Guest House
11 Pensión Don Pedro
12 Capella Beach Resort
13 Coral Costa Caribe
   Beach Hotel
14 Villas Jubey Talanquera

15 Metro Hotel & Golf
16 Albatros Club Resort

PLACES TO EAT
4 Hotel Fior di Loto
7 Grotta Azzurra
9 Ristorante El Sueño

OTHER
2 Shell Station
8 Tricom

Information

Tourist Offices There is no tourist office in Juan Dolio, and given its size there's no real need for one. If you have questions, Mara Sandri, owner of the Hotel Fior di Loto (see below), is very knowledgeable and helpful, and she speaks six languages, including English.

Money Most hotels will gladly change US and Canadian dollars, but might not if they're running low on Dominican pesos. If you're going to be in the area for a while, you'd be wise to change at least as much money as you think you'll need beforehand.

Post & Communications All of the hotels in Juan Dolio will pass mail given them by their guests to the mail carriers who serve the area. However, unless you're staying at one of Juan Dolio's all-inclusive resorts, don't expect to be able to buy stamps in Juan Dolio.

You can, of course, place long-distance calls from your hotel, but those calls will cost you plenty – the long-distance toll plus a significant service fee added by your hotel. If you plan to talk a while, you'd be wise to call

from the Tricom near the center of town. It's open 9 am to 5 pm daily.

Laundry Most hotels in Juan Dolio offer laundry service; the few that don't will provide it if you ask and sound a little desperate.

Activities

At the all-inclusive resorts, guests have access to water sports, including scuba diving and snorkeling trips that can be arranged by hotel staff (such trips are extra). Motorcycle and bicycle rentals are also an option for guests at some of the resorts.

Special Events

The success of Santo Domingo's Merengue Festival has in recent years led to a similar and simultaneous festival in Juan Dolio. While Santo Domingo's malecón shakes its booty to live merengue in the last week of July and the first week of August, merengue bands also perform at various venues in Juan Dolio.

Places to Stay

At the time of writing, options for accommodations in Juan Dolio were limited to budget hotels (most of which were actually mid-range in quality) or all-inclusive hotels, most of which were also reasonably priced, as Juan Dolio isn't yet as widely known as other Dominican resort towns.

Budget The best budget hotel along the entire south coast of the DR is the *Hotel Fior di Loto* ('*Lotus Flower Hotel*'; ☎ 809-526-1146, fax 526-3332). Small rooms for one or two persons cost US$20, larger rooms are US$30 and an apartment with kitchen costs US$40. A dormitory was being built at the time of writing, with a tentative per-bed price of US$10. All of the 19 guest rooms are comfortable and charming, and they come with fans and private hot-water bathrooms. Laundry service is available. Gay and mixed-race couples are welcome. Facilities include a terrace for private sunbathing, a popular bar that's open to guests 'round the clock, and a restaurant that serves Italian, Dominican and vegetarian cuisine. The hotel also offers a variety of classes; see the Entertainment section, below. On top of everything else, it has a generator. Reservations are a good idea.

If the Fior di Loto is full, the next-best budget place in Juan Dolio is the *Damar Guest House* (☎ 809-526-3310, fax 526-2512), on the frontage road 1.5km to the east. Located beside the sea, the Italian-run guest house offers a handful of rooms, each with refrigerator, stove, fan and hot-water private bathroom for US$30, with a minimum stay of four days. This excellent place is particularly popular with people in their twenties. The guest house is amid a strip of funky shops, bars and food stands, which add to its appeal. There is a generator here, as well as an Italian restaurant. Call ahead to reserve a room. English, Italian and Spanish are spoken.

Near the Damar Guest House and also very popular with budget travelers is the *Pensión Don Pedro* (☎ 809-526-2147). It's a bit more mellow than the guest house and a bit cheaper at US$16/24 for singles/doubles. Its 40 rooms have fans and hot-water private bathrooms, and there's a nice dining area and a kitchen that guests are free to use. A grocery store is across the street.

Out on the highway near the Shell station is the *Hotel La Bussola* (☎ 809-526-1320, fax 526-1450), which offers comfortable rooms with fan only and a swimming pool. It is reasonably priced at US$25/30/40, but in late 1998 it was struggling due to its location away from the beach. Low monthly rates are available. The hotel has a restaurant, a bar and a generator, and offers free guest transport to and from Las Américas International Airport.

Top End A very inexpensive and popular all-inclusive hotel is the *Marena Beach Resort* (☎ 809-526-2121, fax 526-1213), located between a lovely stretch of beach and the frontage road. The Marena Beach consists of four clusters of guest rooms, each cluster quite different in style from the others: One cluster features rooms in a short tower, another a number of charming bungalows, a third is comprised of *casitas* with kitchens, and a fourth cluster is made up of standard modern hotel rooms. There are several pools and bars within the facility, open to guests only. All meals are served buffet style. Rates are a very modest US$60/70 singles/doubles. Of the local all-inclusives, the Marena Beach clearly offers the best value for the money.

After the Marena Beach, the value-for-money waters become murky. Clearly the less-expensive places aren't as desirable as the more-expensive places, as they tend to have less-attractive rooms, less-appealing food and fewer facilities. But guests at the such places seem to think they're a great deal; so instead of trying to compare apples to oranges, the following top-end hotels are presented as they appear from west to east.

The *Hotel Costa Linda* (☎ 809-526-2161, fax 526-1212) is the first hotel you'll see in Juan Dolio if you're coming from Santo Domingo. Its rooms come with air con and hot-water private bathrooms, but are otherwise fairly unattractive as all-inclusives go. The food at the poolside restaurant is purely mediocre; the food at the beachside restaurant, which requires reservations, is much more palatable. The beach is attractive and the surf is safe enough for most people. The

Costa Linda's guests, mostly Canadian and British tourists, spend their days catching sun on the beach; few aren't more than happy to pay the US$80/100 rates.

The next all-inclusive to the east, *Punta Garza on the Beach*, looks appealing enough from the street but its unfriendly staff didn't allow for a review.

The 492-room *Coral Costa Caribe Beach Hotel* (☎ 809-526-2244, fax 526-3141) offers what most people hope to find at a tropical resort: lovely guest rooms with all the amenities; a restaurant and bar open 24 hours; massage, a steam bath, dance club, Jacuzzi, pretty beach, inviting swimming pool and lots of healthy-looking people soaking up the sun. The Coral Costa Caribe has four restaurants, a day-care center for the kiddies, a casino, gift shop, jewelry store, tennis courts and even a basketball court. There's a water-sports center, and in front of the long, wide beach there's a small protected bay that's very safe for swimming. This all-inclusive resort charges US$150/220 singles/doubles.

The *Capella Beach Resort* (☎ 809-526-1080, fax 526-1088) is newer than the Coral Costa Caribe and offers 283 luxury rooms and similar facilities for around US$70/100. The nearby *Villas Jubey Talanquera* (☎ 809-541-1166, fax 541-1292) has 320 luxury rooms amid beautifully landscaped grounds, with several swimming pools, a gorgeous dining room, a lovely beach and a water-sports center. The rates are US$98/148.

Continuing east, the *Metro Hotel & Golf* (☎ 809-526-2811, fax 526-1808) resort has 236 rooms, all of which face the sea, tennis courts, Jacuzzi, pool, water sports and as the name implies, access to a golf course. The rates are US$80/120, excluding golf fees.

The resort farthest to the east (at the time of this writing) is the *Albatros Club Resort* (☎ 809-526-1314, fax 526-1555), the least appealing of the bunch. The boxy rooms are lacking in decor, many don't have ocean views, and the swimming pool is not very inviting. Rates are US$68/80.

Places to Eat

Most of the hotels in Juan Dolio are all-inclusives, satisfying the food needs of their guests and closed to outsiders. But there are some good restaurants in the area that are open to the general public, and among them is the restaurant at *Hotel Fior di Loto*. Its Italian restaurant whips up some delicious food at reasonable prices: 12 varieties of pasta (US$4 to US$5.50), fried calamari (US$5.50) and beef filet served with one side dish (US$7). There are other items, among them Dominican fried chicken for US$5.

The *Ristorante El Sueño* is also Italian-owned and managed and serves delicious Italian food, including various spaghettis for US$4 to US$8, meat and chicken dishes for about US$6 to US$9, fish for US$7.50 to US$12, various shrimp dishes for US$9, and a large selection of pizzas, from US$4 for a tomato and mozzarella pizza to US$8 for one topped with octopus, shrimp, squid and mozzarella.

Also on the frontage road is the *Grotta Azzurra*, a small but charming restaurant beside the sea with a very capable chef. Among his specialties are grilled beef filet with green-pepper sauce (US$7.50), baked chicken (US$5.50) and a grilled fish filet (US$7.50). The easy-to-miss Grotta Azzurra is beside the more-visible Mini Market Lucas.

Entertainment

The forms of entertainment in Juan Dolio are rather varied. The worldly owner of Hotel Fior di Loto teaches yoga, meditation and language classes in Italian, German, English, Spanish, Japanese, Russian and Hindi. She can arrange for a masseuse, a martial arts instructor or an acupuncturist. If you so desire, you may also have a 'therapeutic sacred dance' performed for you by Dominican experts in that area.

If all that sounds a bit much, there are some simple bars in the vicinity of Damar Guest House; most play merengue and at least one favors American rock 'n' roll. Far fancier watering holes are found in the all-inclusive hotels, and if you're staying at one you'll have access.

Getting There & Away

Traveling to and from Juan Dolio is easy. Juan Dolio is beside Hwy 3, the coastal highway linking Santo Domingo and La Romana and all the towns in between. In Santo Domingo, go to Parque Enriquillo and look for the small bus depots near the southeast corner of the park. One of them has buses that make the one-hour journey to Juan Dolio about every 30 minutes for US$1. If you're in Boca Chica or another town to the west of Juan Dolio, all you'd do is walk to the edge of two-lane Hwy 3 and hail an eastbound bus; the express buses will flash their lights and blow past you, but most of the buses are gua-guas and this is how they pick people up – on the edge of the road. Just hop in and enjoy the ride; no matter where you go in a gua-gua, the fare is never very much.

Likewise, to leave Juan Dolio, just walk out to the edge of the highway and hail any bus going in the direction you want to go. How you hail – by sticking your thumb out like a hitchhiker, pointing to the center of the road or waving frantically and jumping up and down – is up to you. As long as you get the driver's attention, he'll stop if his bus isn't an express (ie, a Metro bus or Caribe Tours bus).

Of course, you can also take a taxi. Taxis can be found near the Villas Jubey Talanquera, or ask the reception desk at your hotel to call one for you.

Getting Around

Juan Dolio is easily walked. The frontage road is used mainly by pedestrians, but if you'd rather ride there are plenty of motoconchos (motorcycle taxis) around. If you stand at the road's edge, not 10 minutes will pass before a young man on a motoconcho will scoot up. Just hail him and get on board. Anywhere you want to go in the vicinity of Juan Dolio will cost less than US$5. Car taxis cost more, but they are also safer.

SAN PEDRO DE MACORÍS

Fifty years ago, San Pedro de Macorís was a sight to behold. Back then, as it is today, the provincial seaside city was ringed with sugar plantations. And moving slowly through the fields of tall, dense cane were 19th-century locomotives with wide, funnel-shaped stacks that belched steam in small thick clouds. Half the size of conventional locomotives, these pridefully polished engines puffed busily as machete-wielding workers piled long stalks of green cane onto railroad cars specially built for the task. From the fields, the locomotives carried millions of tons of cane to giant grinders that mashed the cane into pulp that was then refined into sugar. Not far away, Pan Am landed its American Clipper hydroplanes on the Río Higuamo for sugar hauls bound for the USA.

Today those wonderful locomotives and planes are gone, as are the stately mansions of the rich plantation owners. The same relentless humidity that turned the locomotives to heaps of rusting parts transformed the elegant wooden homes into monuments of dry rot for termites to feast upon. The humidity also fed mold that destroyed whatever furnishings remained.

Sugar is still the basis of San Pedro's existence, the cane is still cut by machete, and the sweet substance continues to be loaded onto ships at San Pedro's port, just as it has been for more than a century. But unlike other Dominican cities, this provincial capital of 300,000 souls, some 65km east of Santo Domingo, was repeatedly passed over for public improvements. Trujillo did little for the city, and Joaquín Balaguer, who was president during most of the years following the death of the dictator in 1961, never cared much for Macorís residents because of their repeated opposition to his regime.

San Pedro's glory has risen and fallen with international sugar prices, and its past was never more glorious than in the years immediately following WWI. Worldwide shortages of tropical raw materials caused prices of Dominican products such as sugar and tobacco to soar. The price of a hundredweight of sugar surged from US$5.50 in 1914 to US$12.50 in 1918, then to US$22.50 in 1920. It was then that the great estates were built and San Pedro's future seemed destined to sparkle. But sugar prices soon plunged, and with equal speed unemployment rose. The city is still waiting for the majority of its streets to be paved.

It's hard to believe, as you drive past the harbor's crumbling balustrades, that San Pedro was once a cultural showplace of the Caribbean, with an opera hall where Jenny Lind (the 'Swedish nightingale') sang. This has become even more difficult to believe since Hurricane Georges paid its visit in 1998. The city was among those hardest hit by the storm. Although there were few fatalities in San Pedro, government officials said it had the country's largest concentration of victims. Homes and businesses throughout the city were completely demolished. More than a third of the city's residents were homeless by the time the hurricane had moved into the hills, en route to unprepared Haiti. If San Pedro native and Chicago Cubs slugger Sammy Sosa hadn't smashed one of the most coveted records in major-league baseball history the day before the hurricane – lifting the Dominican spirit to new heights – Georges might have destroyed hope there as well.

Places to Stay

If you plan to spend the night in the city, the **Hotel Macorix-UCE** (☎ 809-529-3950), on Calle Gaston Deligne near the malecón, is the best hotel in San Pedro. It offers fan-only rooms for US$20 a night and air-con rooms for US$25, one person or two. A taxi ride from the hotel to the ballpark will cost about US$5.

Baseball Games

There's really nothing worth seeing in San Pedro de Macorís today except baseball games, held in the city's most prominent building – **Estadio Tetelo Vargas**. The stadium appears on the north side of Hwy 3 if you're coming from Santo Domingo, just beyond a large billboard that reads: 'Welcome to San Pedro de Macorís. The City Which Has

Given the Most Major Leaguers to the World.'

Truer words have never been plastered. At any given moment there are usually about 60 Dominicans in the majors, and upwards of 500 Dominicans in the minor-league system. At least a third of those players grew up playing stickball in the streets of San Pedro, and most attended a training camp in or near San Pedro run by a major-league team before signing on. In other words, the level of play at Tetelo Vargas Stadium is very high.

Throughout the Dominican Republic, but particularly in San Pedro – which has seen dozens of its residents go from being dollar-a-day shoeshine boys to millionaire big-league players – béisbol (baseball) is regarded as an opportunity to escape a life of poverty. For Dominicans, baseball is what dreams are made of; an arduous adulthood as a cane cutter is what's in store for the vast majority. For the fortunate few, adulthood will be spent playing pelota and wondering what to do with so much money.

If you happen to be in San Pedro de Macorís anytime from mid-November till early February, try to catch a game. Arrive at the stadium early and, if the game is sold out, buy a ticket from a scalper. The official cost of a ticket is US$2; expect to pay five times that to a scalper.

Sammy Sosa

West of Santo Domingo

To the west of Santo Domingo, Hwy 2 runs along the coast as far as Haina, where it cuts inland to the provincial capital of San Cristóbal. From there it continues south to the city of Baní, then west, while Hwy 41 branches off to the town of San José de Ocoa, in the foothills of the Cordillera Central.

SAN CRISTÓBAL

This provincial capital of 140,000 people, 30km west of Santo Domingo, is the birthplace of Rafael Trujillo, the strongman who ruled the country through fear from 1930 until his assassination in 1961. During his rule, San Cristóbal became a sort of a national shrine to the dictator; in fact its name was officially changed in 1934 to Meritorious City. People stopped using 'Meritorious City' as soon as the *generalísimo* died. City officials contend San Cristóbal was named by Christopher Columbus. History books make no mention of how the city got its name.

Trujillo lived mostly in an enormous house in Santo Domingo that he had built next door to the American Embassy, but he had other residences. The most impressive is a palace high on a mountain overlooking San Cristóbal. Rumor has it Trujillo never used the place, which he aptly named Castillo del Cerro (Castle on the Hill). On the day of its grand opening, it is said Trujillo asked a European ambassador what he thought of it. After the ambassador replied, 'What awful taste!' Trujillo never returned.

Not surprisingly, there is a church in San Cristóbal that houses Trujillo's official tomb, although his actual remains have been removed and are now said to reside in France. The church is fairly impressive, as was the public square in front of it. Trujillo created both the church and the square as memorials to himself, sparing no expense. Today, as a result of the country's poverty, which can be linked to years of corruption

under Trujillo, there's no water for the plaza's fountains and a chronic power shortage that frequently means there's no electricity to keep the plaza lit at night.

Some gun historians may recall hearing of the San Cristóbal carbine, which was famous in its day (the late 1950s). Trujillo was fond of importing experts to help him maintain power; he called upon a former Luftwaffe officer to help create an air force, which Trujillo kept at San Isidro Air Base outside the capital. He also hired armaments experts from Eastern Europe to help build an excellent small-arms factory at San Cristóbal. The San Cristóbal carbine was a rapid-fire weapon considered better than the carbine used by the US military. Trujillo supplied thousands of them to the Cuban dictator Fulgencio Batista, who was overthrown by Fidel Castro in 1959.

San Cristóbal is also known as the site where the first constitution of the Dominican Republic was signed, on November 6, 1844. The constitution was based on the Haitian constitution of 1843 and on the US constitution of 1776, both of which established the separation of powers and the dominance of the legislative branch over the executive. In the years since 1844, the Dominican constitution has been redrafted on several occasions to suit the current executive.

Despite being of some historical interest, San Cristóbal offers the tourist few attractions, and none of its hotels are very appealing. While many Dominican towns and cities are trying to lure tourists by promoting attractions and building new hotels or upgrading existing ones, San Cristóbal certainly isn't doing either with any sense of urgency. The city is best visited as a break in a journey rather than as a destination in itself.

Orientation

As you enter San Cristóbal from the east, you'll cross Río Nigua and immediately come to a traffic roundabout. On the opposite side of the roundabout is the run-down, government-owned Hotel Las Terrazas. Take the road to the right of it and then the first left at the sign indicating the town of Baní ahead. In another block you'll be at the bustling heart of the city. You'll know you're there when you see a church on your right and a large plaza (Parque Independencia), which was beautifully renovated in 1998, on your left. At this point, the road you're on has become Calle Padre Brown. (Take Calle Padre Brown west to get to Baní and beyond, and take it east to return to Santo Domingo.)

The city, settled during the early 17th century, follows a grid pattern, with the plaza at the heart of things. Beside the plaza is the busiest intersection in town – where Calle Padre Brown crosses Av Constitución. At one corner of the intersection you'll notice a very handsome building with a clock tower. It contains municipal offices and was built with funds provided by Trujillo. On the ground floor is a large bronze plaque with the names of the people who signed the republic's first constitution.

Information
There is no tourist office in town. If you have questions about accommodations and services, you might direct them to the receptionist on the ground floor of the municipal building. Otherwise, just ask around.

Iglesia de San Cristóbal
Since he took great pride in his home town, the egomaniacal Trujillo lavished a small fortune on San Cristóbal. This church, as well as the plaza opposite it, the art-deco Hotel San Cristóbal, the town's concert hall and many other structures and sites (most now in disrepair) were built with government funds during the dictatorship. When Trujillo had this church erected, he spared no expense, for this was supposed to be his final resting place.

The highly decorated church, built at the staggering cost of US$4 million in 1946, contains a monumental work by famous Spanish muralist José Vela Zanetti, whose murals also appear in the Palace of Justice in Santo Domingo and in the United Nations Building in New York. Topping each of the two steeples is a lovely winged angel, and behind them is a dome crowned with a large white cross. The church is open 6 to 8 am and 5:30 to 8 pm daily.

To reach it from the Parque Independencia, proceed south on Av Constitución for four blocks. The square and then the church will appear on your right.

Castillo del Cerro
Trujillo owned a beautiful house in San Cristóbal made almost entirely of mahogany (a much coveted jungle hardwood) at the time he ordered the construction of Castillo del Cerro (Castle on the Hill). The six-story residence, which cost US$3 million to construct, was so lavish in its design that it looked ridiculous, and the few people who didn't fear Trujillo told him so.

Trujillo – who had a house and an office in nearly every provincial capital, each of which was adorned with the five-star emblem of the only generalísimo in the land, and who doted on uniforms, many of which he supposedly designed himself – detested the notion that others might think he had bad taste. Consequently, he never lived in his Castle on the Hill, and he told people whose opinions mattered to him that the mansion was a gift from the residents of San Cristóbal – not something of his own design.

Today, the Castillo is in the midst of a slow renovation, in its 10th year at the time of writing, and is far from completion. If you'd like to look at what just might be the ugliest multimillion-dollar structure in the Americas, ask a taxi driver to take you there. Directions are convoluted and the chance of getting lost trying to get there on your own is great.

Casa de Caoba
Located on a hill at the edge of town, the Casa de Caoba (Mahogany House) is one of Trujillo's former homes and, unlike the Castillo del Cerro, the dictator actually lived in it. After Trujillo's death, the home fell into ruin. Then, in the early 1980s, an effort was made to return the structure to a usable condition so that it might be made into a restaurant. Unfortunately, instead of replacing rotten mahogany with new mahogany, concrete was used. The house today isn't what it once was, and only Trujillo scholars would likely get much out of a visit here.

Like the Castillo, a trip to Casa de Caoba is best done via taxi to avoid getting lost, but directions here are less complicated: From the Parque Independencia, head north along Av Constitución for 2.7km. Turn right at an intersection indicating the way to La Toma, and proceed nearly 1km farther to a sign for Casa de Caoba. From the gate, it's nearly 1km farther uphill to the old residence. A groundskeeper will let you inside for US$2.

Mercado

San Cristóbal's main market is housed in a huge building on Calle Padre Brown two blocks west of Av Constitución. Here you'll find lots of images of Jesus, bottles of rum at bargain prices, inexpensive clothing and workers playing cards all day long. If you've been wanting to buy a cassette tape featuring popular merengue artists, this is a good place to do it.

Places to Stay & Eat

San Cristóbal isn't visited by many tourists, and has few accommodations to offer them. At the time of this writing, the centrally located *Hotel Constitución* (☎ 809-538-3309) offered basic but clean rooms for US$18 for one or two people. There are several decent places to eat in the vicinity of Parque Independencia.

Getting There & Away

To get to San Cristóbal from Santo Domingo, go to the bus depots near the southeast corner of Parque Enriquillo and look for a bus with 'Baní' posted in the front window, or ask around. The Baní bus makes a stop beside Parque Independencia in San Cristóbal. The cost of the trip is US$1 each way.

To return to Santo Domingo by bus, go to the opposite side of the park and catch any of the eastbound gua-guas. To continue west, go to where the Baní bus dropped you and catch any of the westbound buses.

Getting Around

There are taxis and motoconchos in the vicinity of Parque Independencia from sunrise until late at night.

SAN CRISTÓBAL TO BANÍ

A well-paved, two-lane highway links San Cristóbal and Baní, and the scenery likely hasn't changed much since the road was completed in the early 1920s. For most of the way, a traveler passes kilometer after kilometer of sugarcane. At certain times of the year, the tall sweet grass forms a wall at the highway's edge, broken up every so often by train tracks that seem to slice through the fields for a ways before being enveloped by them.

When the cane's ready to be cut, small diesel locomotives and scores of container cars traverse the fields. Workers on each side of the cars chop the cane down with machetes and pile it on the container cars. The locomotives pull the filled cars off to a huge refinery you can't help but notice on the south side of the highway. These are the last cane fields you'll see for a while if you're on your way to Barahona or places farther west.

BANÍ

Thirty-six kilometers west of San Cristóbal is this prosperous city of about 110,000 people, whose production of coffee, sugarcane, vegetables and salt makes it one of the wealthiest communities in the country.

Baní is best known as the birthplace of Generalísimo Máximo Gómez y Báez. As a young man Gómez served in the Spanish army in Santo Domingo. He later moved to Cuba and took up farming, an occupation that made him subject to Spanish taxation.

Sugarcane train

During the 1860s, Gómez joined the insurgents opposed to Spanish rule, rose to the rank of general of the Cuban forces and, together with José Martí, led the revolution of 1868-78 that culminated in Cuba's independence from Spain.

Seven decades before Gómez was born, the hot, dusty area that would come to be known as Baní didn't yet have a name – or even a population, although that would change soon enough. During the mid-18th century, France and Spain shared Hispaniola and both countries sought to control as much of the island as possible. No formal border existed and the French colonists outnumbered Spanish colonists by a margin of four to one.

Fearing that the French colony would eventually overrun the Spanish colony, Spain resumed the importation of families from the Canary Islands to Santo Domingo (the importation had started a century earlier but was halted during the War of Spanish Succession from 1702 to 1713). In 1763, Spanish authorities relocated some 100 or so Canarians and founded Baní – a Taíno word meaning 'plenty of water' – beside the Río Baní.

During the next 100 years the people of Baní prospered. They exploited nearby salt ponds, raised goats and cattle, and cut mahogany for export. Life was very good to the descendants of the Canarians. But the houses in Baní were usually constructed of palmwood with thatched roofs, making them vulnerable to fire, such as the one in 1882 that leveled most of the town.

As a result of the fire, Francisco Gregorio Billini, who was president of the republic from September 1884 to May 1885, arranged to have plain roof tiles imported from France. The 'French tiles,' as they were known in the DR, were installed on buildings throughout Baní. More than 100 years after their arrival, the plain roof tiles from France can still be seen on some of the town's old Victorian-style homes and businesses.

Orientation & Information
At Baní's heart is Parque Duarte, a spacious, clean and attractive park – one of the loveli-

est in the country. To reach it coming from the east, turn right just after crossing the Río Baní and just in front of the oncoming one-way street that greets you almost at the foot of the bridge. Go two blocks and make a left onto Calle Máximo Gómez. Go six or seven blocks and make a left onto Calle Mella. After half a block you'll be at the intersection of Calle Sánchez and Calle Mella, in front of the Iglesia Nuestra Señora de Regla (the city's main church).

To get to Parque Duarte from the west, turn right where Hwy 2 (also known as Sánchez Hwy) confronts an opposing one-way street. Turn left at the first opportunity (Calle Sánchez) and follow that street six blocks until it ends at Parque Duarte. At the point where Calle Sánchez meets the park, you can look to your right and see a large concrete building with 'Palacio del Ayuntamiento' written on it in block letters; the building is Baní's city hall.

There's no tourist office here, but there's a Codetel office at Calle Padre Billini 3, near Casa de Máximo Gómez (see below).

Things to See
In addition to being Máximo Gómez's hometown, Baní is know for its mangos, which are smaller than most, pale pink and sweet as can be. They are in season from late May till early July, and are worth stopping for if you happen to be passing through Baní at that time.

But as a tourist destination, Baní hasn't got a lot to offer. Its chief attraction is the **Casa de Máximo Gómez**, which was the site of his childhood home as well as his birthplace. Today, beneath flags of Cuba and the Dominican Republic, there's a bust of the man. Nearby, set in concrete and covered with a small roof, is a beat-up wooden post – all that's left of the simple home in which el generalísimo was raised. Nearby, on a wall that acts as a boundary marker, there's a mural of the Cuban independence leader with his sword raised high and a defiant expression on his face. He is riding a white stallion along a beach at full gallop. The park is kept very clean and, because of the many mature shade trees, is pleasantly cool even on an otherwise hot day.

To get to the site from Parque Duarte, turn right at the intersection of Calle Sánchez and Parque Duarte, go to the end of the park and turn left. Drive alongside the park 100m and turn left onto the road that'll take you past the church. Proceed one block to Calle Máximo Gómez, then turn right. Go two blocks and look for a small park on the right side of the road with the large bust of the Cuban revolutionary hero.

Also worth a look, if you're in no great hurry, is the **Museo Municipal**, on the ground floor of the Palacio del Ayuntamiento. The small history museum is open weekdays from 8 am till noon. There is no charge for admission.

If you've got some time on your hands, check out the **Iglesia Nuestra Señora de Regla**, which hosts a patron saint festival every year on November 21.

Places to Stay & Eat

One block south of Parque Duarte is **Hotel Caribani** (☎ 809-522-5281, fax 522-5024), on Calle Sánchez, the best place in town although its dark rooms are wearing fast. There is no hot water in the private bathrooms, but each room does have air con (a must in Baní), cable TV, a fan, firm mattress and a phone. The rate is US$25 for one or two people.

For food and drinks in Baní, try **Santana's Cafeteria-Restaurant** on the corner of Calle Mella and Calle Máximo Gómez. Santana specializes in barbecue and booze – a full bar and a big grill where all cuts of meat are cooked in various ways. Meat dishes run from US$3 to US$9. The house specialty is *churrasco*, which is thinly sliced grilled beef served with salsa. Fish, pasta, sandwiches and soups are also available.

Getting There & Away

The bus station is at the west end of town. Here, you can hop on any gua-gua headed east to get to Santo Domingo. If you're heading west, hop aboard any bus headed for Barahona or points farther west.

SAN JOSÉ DE OCOA

Sometimes the journey is as good as the destination, and that's the case with San José de Ocoa, a cool foothills town at the end of a well-paved road that stretches 28km from the turnoff at Hwy 2 to the town's central square. The road winds through mostly undeveloped countryside as it rises from 200m above sea level to nearly 2000m. It is one of the best in the country for bicyclists – particularly when coming down out of the foothills, when picturesque views of cliffs and crops, hillsides and the Caribbean appear before you.

But the closer approach to San José de Ocoa is spectacular as well. Each ridgeline is followed by another, higher and higher, and from various points on the road you can see 10 or more sets of peaks simultaneously. Above them the sky is filled with the prettiest blues and grandiose cumulus clouds. To your immediate right and left are numerous small farms, although much virgin brush still remains. The landscape is also pleasantly dappled with royal palms. Once in town, you'll find the quality of the roads doesn't change; all are well paved and easy on bicycle tires.

San José de Ocoa receives very few foreign visitors, and that's a pity. With a population of 70,000, mainly merchants and farmers, it offers visitors a nice look at life in a small, prosperous Dominican town on the lower slopes of the Cordillera Central. Here, the roads are kept in good condition, the buildings are mostly well maintained, and the town square fills with playful children at the end of each school day. And all around the hilly town are magnificent peaks that belong to the largest mountain range in the Caribbean.

Unlike most Dominican plazas, which have a few large shade trees around a gazebo and feel very urban despite any attempt to 'naturalize' the environment, the one in San José de Ocoa has a true tropical-jungle feel. Dozens of broadleaf trees and thick hedges are enhanced by the tinkle of water from one of four low-profile fountains. In several trees, the townspeople have placed enormous birdhouses that can hold more than 20 white pigeons at any given time, and often do. They are regular bird condos, very much appreciated by their tenants. This plaza/park/playground provides a perfect setting for a game of hide 'n' seek, as the children here well know.

Places to Stay & Eat

The best hotel in town is the *Hotel Marien* (☎ *809-558-3800)*, beside the plaza. Rooms have air con, hot-water private bathrooms and cable TV. A room with one twin bed costs US$14 per night; rooms with two beds are a little more. The hotel's 11 rooms are above its restaurant, which is also the best place in town.

In the unlikely event that the Marien is full, the next-best place is the *Casa de Huespedes San Francisco* (☎ *809-558-2741)*, which offers eight guest rooms with cold-water-only private bathrooms, but firm mattresses, air con and cable TV. This very clean hotel charges US$17 per room. The hotel is on Calle Andres Pimentel (same as Hotel Marien), three blocks north of the plaza.

Steer clear of the Rancho Francisco, the first hotel that many visitors see on the main road into town; it's nestled among lots of trees, which is good, but none of its nine cabins have screened windows and they fill with hungry mosquitoes nightly. The rooms are also dark and damp, and guests are expected to sleep on rusty, squeaking bunk beds.

Getting There & Away

Gua-guas run up and down Hwy 2 from sunrise till 7 pm, and to get to San José de Ocoa, simply take one to the Hwy 2 turnoff for the town. At the turnoff, about 7km from Baní, there is a simple snack bar that offers shade and refreshments. It is also the bus stop for gua-guas that travel between the turnoff and the town throughout the day. The cost is US$1 each way.

Southeastern Dominican Republic

Simply put, the southeast consists of seaside property and property that is not seaside. The seaside property can be further divided into three sections: La Costa Caribe (Caribbean Coast), which in the southeast extends from the Río Soco to Parque Nacional del Este; La Costa del Coco (Coconut Coast), which runs from Parque Nacional del Este north to the Punta Gorda that's just east of Miches (there are two Punta Gordas on the bay); and the entire southern coast of the Bahía de Samaná, from Punta Gorda up to and including the shoreline of Parque Nacional Los Haïtises.

Dominicans refer to all of their country that's not within a few kilometers of the coast as the 'interior.' With respect to the southeast, the major interior cities are Higüey, El Seibo and Hato Mayor. These cities and the seaside communities of, say, Bayahibe, Punta Cana and Bávaro are as different as a thong bikini and an ox-drawn cart – objects that partially convey the essence of the two very different worlds of the southeast.

Historically, communities in the southeast developed much more slowly than did the cities of Santo Domingo, Puerto Plata and Santiago, all three of which were well established and prosperous as early as the 16th century. In fact, at the time the Dominican Republic gained its independence from Haiti, in 1844, the people of El Seibo and Higüey were barely eking out a living from the cattle herds that roamed freely on the vast southeastern savannas. They were mere villages when compared to the Big Three. As for the seaside communities of Bávaro and Punta Cana, they wouldn't exist for another century and a quarter.

Today, the interior cities, as well as the longtime port city of La Romana, continue on much as they have for years. In these cities, people still wake before dawn and walk to the cane fields, where they continue to rely heavily on oxen to pull the sweet grass to mills. Here, people continue to raise cattle, tending to their needs until the time comes for the cattle to tend to the financial needs of their owners. Until recently – when mopeds became wildly popular in the DR – horses were still the primary mode of transportation here.

Increasingly, the residents of these interior cities are heading to the coast, where employment opportunities await many at tourist resorts. Although some have been around since the 1960s and 1970s, the vast majority of the southeast's hotels were built after 1990. In 1998, government officials estimated there were 15,000 hotel rooms in the southeast. At least one resort opens in this region every three months. Even Hurricane Georges, which hit the southeast particularly hard in September 1998, didn't damper developers' enthusiasm for the region. Sites that were under construction before the killer storm were back under construction two weeks later.

Near La Romana, Bayahibe and all along the Costa del Coco are all-inclusive hotels beside white-sand beaches where Euro babes and Euro hunks lounge about in itty bitty articles of clothing. Most of the tourists visiting the southeast are European, the majority from Germany or Switzerland. About 10% of the region's foreign tourists are from Canada, and even fewer hail from the USA.

Also in the southeast are two large national parks, both of which offer excellent opportunities for exploring. The Parque Nacional Los Haïtises, beside the Bahía de Samaná, is best experienced by boat due to its scores of tiny islands and kilometers of mangrove forest. In Los Haïtises, it's easy to imagine how the earth looked when dinosaurs roamed the planet. Parque Nacional del Este, which receives much less rain than Los Haïtises and therefore contains vastly different animals and plants, lends itself best to long walks.

With its national parks, all-inclusive resorts and traditional ways of the interior

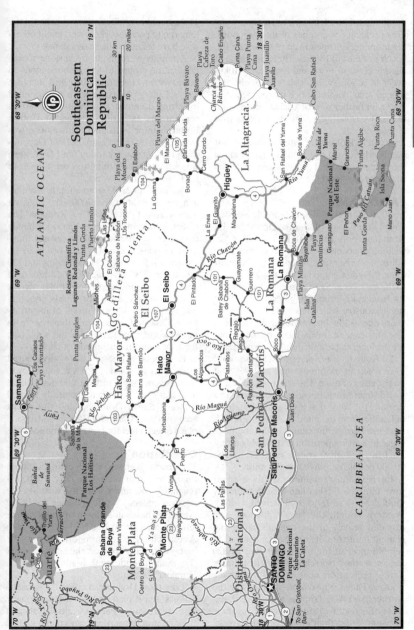

Southeastern Dominican Republic

the southeast is rich in variety. But many visitors prefer it for another of its attractions: the intimate, European-run pensions on the beach just east of Miches. There are three in all, one close to town and two nearly 10km away in a somewhat isolated, jungly and rugged area. Another such place opened in 1998 a bit farther west of Miches and, despite its relative isolation, has modern rooms with air con.

If you're looking for intimate beachfront hotels, where you can actually get to know the owner and other guests fairly well, the southeast has got them too.

LA ROMANA

Located 37km east of San Pedro de Macorís and 114km east of Santo Domingo, La Romana (pop 135,000) is a smaller yet wealthier version of San Pedro, thanks to an influx of tourist money supplied by the enormous Casa de Campo resort a few kilometers to the east. As in San Pedro, the economy of La Romana is primarily based on the local sugar industry, which has suffered in recent years due to low international sugar prices. The hurricane of 1998, which ripped the roof off the local sugar mill, didn't help matters.

La Romana was a sleepy backwater until 1917, when an enormous sugar mill was built on the edge of town. The mill opened just as world sugar prices began to soar, sparking a demand for labor that drew many hundreds of families from the interior. As years passed, the town became the center of the country's sugar industry, a position it still holds today. That fact is a great source of pride for the 20,000 people employed by the mill.

La Romana remained strictly a sugar town until the 1960s, when the US company Gulf & Western Industries arrived. Gulf & Western bought the sugar mill and also invested heavily in the region's cattle and cement industries. Its executives decided to rebuild most of the town, spending US$20 million on the city's schools, churches, clinics, parks, recreation centers and employee houses. These improvements pleased the workers and their families a great deal, but were the result of an economic business decision rather than an act of compassion.

The executives realized it was cheaper in the long run to pacify workers who might otherwise have asked for increases in pay.

Attempts were made by various social-democratic groups to form labor unions to improve working conditions and increase wages; Gulf & Western executives responded by hiring administrators who had earned reputations as ruthless thugs of Cuba's brutal dictator Fulgencio Batista, who was overthrown by Fidel Castro in 1959. Depending on whom you ask today, Gulf & Western was either the best thing to ever happen to La Romana, or the worst.

Before Gulf & Western sold its Dominican assets, it built the 7000-acre Casa de Campo resort just east of La Romana. The resort, owned by a Cuban-American family that lives in Miami, employs several thousand workers, most of whom reside in La Romana. It features 275 hotel rooms and 150 villas, two Pete Dye-designed 18-hole golf courses, long stretches of beautiful beach for sunbathing, and areas for tennis, shooting and horseback riding. With all of its attractions, Casa de Campo is another reason so many world travelers make the southeast their Dominican destination of choice.

La Romana doesn't have any tourist attractions to speak of. It's a sugar town, more prosperous than most, and that's about it. But it's quite pleasant, centrally located between Santo Domingo and the resort areas of Punta Cana and Bávaro, and a good place to get a feel for typical Dominican life.

Orientation

The coastal highway, which changes names for no apparent reason, is Hwy 3 when it reaches La Romana from the west. As the highway enters town it becomes Av Padre Abreu. A baseball stadium appears on the left and, after about 10 city blocks, Av Padre Abreu splits. The northern fork becomes the highway to Hato Mayor, the southern fork the main avenue that leads toward La Romana's downtown.

Like most Dominican cities, La Romana follows a grid plan and has a town square. The square, called Parque Central, truly is at the center of things; the town's major church

DOMINICAN REPUBLIC

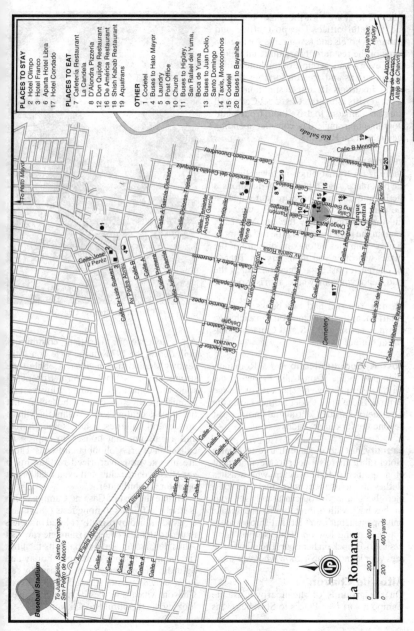

PLACES TO STAY
2 Hotel Olimpo
3 Hotel Franco
6 Aparta Hotel Libra
17 Hotel Condado

PLACES TO EAT
7 Cafetería Restaurant La Candela
8 D'Alondra Pizzería
12 Don Quijote Restaurant
16 De América Restaurant
18 Shish Kabab Restaurant
19 Aquatrans

OTHER
1 Codetel
4 Buses to Hato Mayor
5 Laundry
9 Post Office
10 Church
11 Buses to Higüey, San Rafael del Yuma, Boca de Yuma
13 Buses to Juan Dolio, Santo Domingo
14 Taxis, Motoconchos
15 Codetel
20 Buses to Bayahibe

La Romana

0   200   400 m
0   200   400 yards

is beside it, along with the major bus stops and Codetel office. The post office and numerous hotels and restaurants are nearby. Some of the restaurants are quite all right – fancy even – and a couple of the hotels have air-con rooms and are comfortable, though hardly luxurious. If your destination is one of the resorts along the Costa del Coco, and you're not anxious to drive there from Santo Domingo in a single day, consider spending the night in La Romana.

Information

There is no tourist office in town. Perhaps the best place to go if you've got questions is the Parque Central. There are tour guides in the park from sunrise to sunset every day, and these people know the city. You can't stand in the park looking a little lost for more than two minutes before one or more of the guides will offer you their services. There's no charge for asking a question, but if the guide leads you somewhere, a tip is expected.

Money You will find two banks on Calle Duarte near the park, and you can exchange German marks and US and Canadian dollars at both of them.

Post & Communications La Romana's main post office is on Calle Francisco del Castillo Marquéz, two blocks north of Parque Central. There's one Codetel office facing the east side of Parque Central and another just beyond the fork in Av Padre Abreu.

Laundry Just left of the entrance to Aparta Hotel Libra, there's a door to the apartment of a spunky elderly woman who washes clothes and folds them with great care for a mere US$2 a load. You can usually get your clothes back within three hours. She speaks only Spanish, but don't let that throw you. If you're running low on clean clothes, don't hesitate to knock on her door. The minute she sees your laundry, she'll know what you want.

Altos de Chavón

On the grounds of the nearby Casa de Campo resort (see Places to Stay, below) is

PAUL GERACE

Church at Altos de Chavón

Altos de Chavón, an artists' community built during the 1970s in the style of a 16th-century Mediterranean village. Cobblestone streets, stone carvings, several European-style old fountains, shady pathways and Spanish architecture convey the feeling that the place is centuries old. Within the village are several galleries, a handsome church, and a museum that houses an impressive collection of pre-Columbian artifacts. There are also several overpriced restaurants, a very flashy dance club and even a 5000-seat open-air amphitheater.

Unlike the rest of Casa de Campo, which is strictly off-limits to nonguests (guests are easily identified by brightly colored bracelets issued to them at check-in), anyone can visit Altos de Chavón and patronize its facilities (including the dance club, open Friday and Saturday). However, you must arrive by car; *motoconchos* are not allowed up to Altos de Chavón, which is set beside high cliffs overlooking the beautiful Río Chavón.

There are two roads that serve Altos de Chavón. The first, as you drive east on the main road into the resort (that is, the road coming from La Romana), is gated and only guests are allowed to use it. The second road up the hill to Altos de Chavón is at least 5km farther east on the main road. The turnoff will appear on your left, marked with an 'Altos de Chavón' sign, and is beyond the large golf clubhouse on the southern side of the road.

A taxi ride from Parque Central to Altos de Chavón will set you back US$12 each direction, more at night.

Places to Stay

Budget The best and most popular place to stay in La Romana is the *Aparta Hotel Libra* (☎ 809-556-8820, fax 556-4833), three blocks north of Parque Central. It's within walking distance of the Av Padre Abreu fork unless you're hauling a lot of stuff (in which case you can usually find a taxi near the intersection). The rooms come in different sizes and with a variety of features, although most have air con, kitchens, refrigerators and hot-water private bathrooms. The rates are US$15 to US$26 for a single, and US$30 for a double. Call ahead to reserve a room.

Next best is the *Hotel Olimpo* (☎ 809-550-7646, fax 550-7647), beside the big fork in the road. This place looks a lot nicer from the roadside than it does inside. Still, every room is equipped with air con and a private hot-water bathroom. There is a swimming pool and a simple restaurant on the premises. Singles and doubles are US$28.

A few doors down is the *Hotel Franco* (☎ 809-550-4744), which is a bit run-down but priced right at US$18 for a room with air con and private hot-water bathroom.

If you're counting your pennies, the *Hotel Condado* (☎ 809-556-3010), on Calle Altagracia near the cemetery, offers 24 rooms with decent beds in a clean, two-story building. The rates vary between US$13 and US$33 depending on the number of beds and whether you want air con or are willing to tolerate fan only. There is room to negotiate the price.

Top End Several kilometers east of downtown La Romana, *Casa de Campo* (☎ 800-877-3643, 809-523-3333, fax 523-8548) is a sprawling resort that's best known for its two Pete Dye-designed golf courses, 'The Teeth of the Dog' and 'Links.' The former is widely regarded as the finest golf course in the Caribbean and is often rated as one of the top 25 golf courses in the world. Half of its 18 holes hug the coast and are as beautiful to look at as they are difficult to play. For details on each of the holes, contact the resort and request a copy of *The Golfer* magazine article on The Teeth of the Dog.

The resort is also known for its Sporting Clays Centre, which covers 98 hectares and contains 245 shooting positions. These stations stand in the shadow of a high tower that serves as the center of a sporting clays course that spreads in concentric circles woven together by dirt paths. The center offers skeet, trapshooting and two live pigeon rings. For more information, request a copy of the September-October issue of *Sporting Clays: The Shotgun Hunter's Magazine* from the resort.

On the grounds, but a good distance from the beach and most of the facilities, is the artists' community Altos de Chavón (see earlier in this section).

The eye of Hurricane Georges passed directly over the 7000-acre resort in September 1998, inflicting heavy damage on the 275-room hotel, 150 outlying villas and the golf courses. Most of the resort's trees had been knocked down and only 50 of the rooms in the hotel remained habitable by the time the 202km/hr winds left the area. However, most of the trees will have been righted and facilities repaired by the time this book is published.

Rates, which include three meals daily, all drinks, horseback riding, tennis, use of non-motorized water-sports equipment, and gym access, range from US$225 to US$400 per person (double occupancy). Green fees are US$125 for The Teeth of the Dog, US$85 for Links. Massage, facials, manicures and other pampering are available at additional cost. Towels are provided at the gorgeous beach and at the many swimming pools. Also on the grounds are nine restaurants, a dance club and a private airport. Reservations are required six months in advance.

Be advised that while the facilities are very appealing, the service throughout the resort is absolutely dreadful. One of the major complaints is that mid-size buses that are supposed to pass by designated pickup points every 15 minutes often don't appear for 45 minutes or more, leaving guests to bake under the tropical sun all that time.

The vast majority of the resort's guests arrive by air, either at the private landing strip or the airport that serves La Romana. In both cases, the guests are shuttled to the reception area in waiting buses.

If you are among the minority who arrive by car, a simple way to get here is to take Av Padre Abreu to the major fork in the road, turn right onto Av Santa Rosa, proceed 17 or 18 blocks to Av Libertad, turn left on Av Libertad, and stay in the right lane (the left lane veers off to Higüey and Bayahibe just beyond the river). Av Libertad will lead you straight into Casa de Campo after several kilometers and becomes the resort's principal road.

Places to Eat

Surely the finest value in dining in La Romana is *De América Restaurant*, one block east of Parque Central on Calle Reales. The semiformal setting suggests high prices, but instead they are quite reasonable and the quality of food and service is commendable. The long menu at De América includes a fair selection of appetizers and salads, and an impressive list of main dishes. Among them are sweet-and-sour chicken (US$7), beef filet with your choice of several sauces (US$7.50), conch in a vinaigrette dressing (US$7) and shrimp-and-rice stew (US$11). The margaritas and piña coladas (at US$4 each) are so delicious some people might be tempted to drink several at one sitting.

On the west side of Parque Central, the *Don Quijote Restaurant* probably has the best chef in town but the prices are substantially higher than those at the De América. Among the appetizers are seafood cocktail (US$7) and lobster cocktail (US$6.50). Main dishes include a fettuccine with shrimp (US$12), chicken breast sautéed in lobster sauce, and beef filet (both US$13).

If all you really want is a tasty hamburger or a chicken sandwich, the *Cafetería Restaurant La Candela*, on Calle Gregoria Luperón a few blocks west of Aparta Hotel Libra, has got them for US$2 and US$2.50, respectively. The Candela also serves inexpensive typical Dominican food, as well as a host of traditional Dominican fruit drinks.

Wondering if you can get a decent pizza on the island? Wonder no more. *D'Alondra Pizzeria*, around the corner from the post office, makes them just like Mama, if you were a really fortunate child. Their topping combinations include ham, pineapple and cherry (US$7); ham and corn (US$6.50); mozzarella and sweet corn (US$6.50); and mushroom, ham and sweet corn (US$7). A pizza with the works costs US$13. If it's raining, don't rush to D'Alondra; all of the tables are outside.

Last but far from being least in anyone's mind is the *Shish Kabab Restaurant*, on Calle Reales one block southeast of the Parque Central. Among the restaurant's Middle Eastern specialties are *baba ghanoush* (US$5), which consists of mashed eggplant with parsley, sesame paste, garlic, lemon and olive oil; *warak-inab*, or stuffed grape leaves (US$5); and beef shish kebab (US$8). Also served are fish stew (US$8), garlic lobster (US$17), pepper steak and filet mignon (US$8.50 each). The Shish Kabab is open for breakfast and serves many traditional Dominican fruit beverages.

Shopping

If you like to shop, you might want to visit the Yina Bambu Shop, on Av Padre Abreu west of the baseball stadium and on the south side of the road. It caters to tourists, but it does it well. Possibly every kind of Dominican handicraft is represented here, and the quality is quite high. Check out the amber necklaces and bracelets; they aren't as fine as you'd find at the better stores in the Zona Colonial of Santo Domingo, but these things aren't junk, either.

Most of the silver coins on display are not authentic Spanish *reales* from colonial times, but they are high-quality duplicates and much less expensive than the real deal. Occasionally there are antique coins displayed, but unless they come with stamped papers from the government attesting to their authenticity, you'd be wise to treat them as replicas. Also available are large selections of cigars, music tapes, liquor, bathing suits, hats and T-shirts.

And what would a Dominican crafts market be if it didn't include *lots* of paintings, wind chimes, Carnival masks, woodcarvings and ceramic dolls? There's also a pharmacy and a bar, film and camera batteries, dozens of books and scores of postcards for sale. In the mood for something sweet? There's no shortage of Dominican popsicles and candies at the Yina Bambu.

Getting There & Away

Air It's possible to reach La Romana by air from Puerto Plata and Punta Cana. There is daily service to and from both places. The flight between La Romana and Puerto Plata costs US$59 each way and lasts 50 minutes. The flight between La Romana and Punta Cana costs US$27 each way and lasts 20 minutes. Contact Air Santo Domingo (☎ 809-683-8020) for current departure and arrival times and to book a reservation. Spanish and English are spoken. The cost of a taxi ride between La Romana and the airport is US$10.

Take note that while the official name of the airport outside La Romana is Aeropuerto Punta Aguila, it's often referred to as La Romana International Airport.

Bus The same bus going to Higüey from one of the three small depots near the southeast corner of Parque Enriquillo in Santo Domingo passes through La Romana and will gladly drop you there if you ask. The cost is US$3. To return to Santo Domingo, go to the northwest corner of Parque Central and board one of the buses with 'Santo Domingo' scrawled on the window. Or, walk back up to Av Padre Abreu and hail any westbound *gua-gua*.

To catch a bus to Higüey, go to the station just north of Parque Central, ask for a ticket, and wait for the next departure; Higüey-bound buses usually leave about every 30 minutes. The ride costs US$2.50. This is also the place to catch buses bound for San Rafael del Yuma (US$1.50) and Boca de Yuma (US$2).

To catch a bus to Bayahibe, walk three blocks south of Parque Central to Av Libertad and then three blocks east. Then look for a minivan parked along the side of the road; it leaves whenever it's full, usually about every 45 minutes. The cost is US$1. Or, you could take a taxi. There are plenty of them around the Parque Central. The cost of a taxi to Bayahibe is US$14.

To catch a bus to Hato Mayor, walk or take a motoconcho or taxi to the Av Padre Abreu fork and wait for a gua-gua on the side of the road, directly south of the Hotel Olimpo. If you see a gua-gua approaching from the west, hail it and ask, '¿A Hato Mayor?' If the answer is 'Sí,' you're in luck. The cost of the ride is US$1.50.

Getting Around

Taxis and motoconchos are found near the northeast corner of Parque Central. The cost of a motoconcho ride to anywhere within La Romana will be US$3 or less. The cost of a taxi ride to anywhere within La Romana will be US$6 or less.

RÍO SOCO

Located 17km west of La Romana, the Río Soco is a wide, lazy river that winds 16km from the Caribbean Sea up into cattle-and-cane country. The La Romana-based tour operator Aquatrans (☎ 809-556-4000, 556-3146, cellular 204-1258, fax 476-8737), one block north of Av Libertad at the Río Salado, offers half-day **river trips** aboard a barge designed to look like a school bus. The barge is quite comfortable, with plenty of shade, chairs, merengue, rum and sodas.

The 'bus' pushes off from a point just above the river's mouth and travels 9km to the edge of the town of Sindico, where there's a large corral and the chief attraction seems to be watching burros mate. Fortunately, as the barge cruises past 2km of lush mangrove forest and 7km of semi-steep banks lined with foraging cattle and coconut trees, it makes two other stops, both more rewarding than the turnaround point.

The first stop is at a typical Dominican farm, where a family ekes out a living tending to several crops, raising chickens, and preparing and serving lunches for a 'busload' of tourists. The lunch is served buffet style and generally includes a hearty selection of salad, vegetables and meat. And, this being a Caribbean country, there's no shortage of rum either here or on the barge. Also available here are a number of kayaks, which visitors can use before or after lunch.

The Río Soco is lined with lush mangroves.

The second stop is at a small coffee farm, where the owner will demonstrate how the beans are picked and roasted, after which, of course, samples of his delicious coffee are provided. Be sure to slip on some long pants and a long-sleeve shirt before making this stop, as the coffee farm is home to many tiny biting flies about half of the year.

When the Taínos ruled the island, the banks of the Río Soco were lined from end to end with forest. Sadly, there's no heart-of-darkness feel to the river anymore. However, the trip is still quite enjoyable, made all the more pleasant by the barge's fun-loving crew, who love to dance to merengue and help themselves to the rum as the bus barge gently cruises up and down one of the cleanest rivers in the southeast. The cost of the trip is US$32, and that includes all the food and drink you consume. Many people choose the option of adding an excursion to a sugar plantation to their river adventure for an additional US$16.

BAYAHIBE

Thirty kilometers east of La Romana and 144km east of Santo Domingo is this sleepy little seaside town of less than 1000 people. With its inexpensive hotels and restaurants only a short walk from a Caribbean beach, Bayahibe is what many independent travelers had in mind when they set out for the DR. Until recently there wasn't a sprawling, exclusive resort in sight.

The scene changed significantly in 1998 with the opening of an all-inclusive resort less than 1km from the heart of tiny Bayahibe. No sooner had Casa del Mar opened than it posted armed guards at both ends of the area's loveliest beach – Playa Bayahibe – and illegally privatized it for guests' use only. When reminded that Dominican law guarantees public access to all of the country's beaches, the resort's managers say that the guards are only intended to deter thieves.

Despite the theft of the area's top beach by the AMHSA Hotels chain (owner of Casa del Mar), Bayahibe's peaceful nature, its remaining stretch of public beach and its easy access to two intriguing islands and a national park make it a fine place to spend a few days when you're trying to take life easy.

Orientation

A single dirt road not more than a kilometer or two in length connects the coastal highway with Bayahibe. Once the dirt road enters the town, it continues on for a couple of hundred meters, passing by the ocean's edge and looping around a restaurant and past a couple of hotels before heading back out to the highway. Another dirt road runs off the main road near the water's edge and proceeds east a hundred meters or so. Orienting yourself to Bayahibe takes about 10 seconds, 12 if you're on the slow side.

Information

There is no tourist office, bank, post office or Codetel office in Bayahibe, although there are public telephones that can be used with Comuni cards and for collect calls. Most of the hotels will provide laundry service when their guests request it. Bear in mind that Bayahibe is a fishing village, accustomed to seeing tourists but not necessarily used to accommodating them. If you're low on film, sunscreen or Dominican pesos, reload before arriving or you may be sorry.

Isla Catalina

This uninhabited island, 3.5km south of La Romana and 18km west of Bayahibe, offers divers and snorkelers some colorful reef and wall diving, although Hurricane Georges left a lot of dead coral in its wake. There are no facilities on the island, which means anyone planning a trip there would be well advised to take plenty of fresh water along.

One thing you will find on Isla Catalina is monkeys, placed there years ago by a fellow who – correctly – thought they would help promote the island. As the story goes, the man hoped to turn the island into a kind of zoo without bars. However, after spending enough time there, he became convinced the island's thriving mosquito population would thwart any efforts to make it a real money-maker. The dream is gone, but the monkeys and mosquitoes remain, as do the sand flies.

Although Isla Catalina is close to La Romana, the nearest boatmen serving it are the part-time fishermen, part-time marine chauffeurs who anchor their vessels 100m west of Bayahibe. For US$60 to US$100, depending on the size of the boat, a captain will take a party to the island or to a lovely reef nearby, wait for his passengers to do some exploring on foot or in fins, and return

them to the point of embarkation. The more people in the party, the less costly the trip is per person.

Isla Saona

Boats can be hired from Bayahibe to go to Isla Saona, part of the Parque Nacional del Este (see below). Unlike Isla Catalina, under the shade of this island's coconut trees the visitor will find a small fishing village with a simple store that sells beverages. The prime attractions here are the beaches for sunbathing and the water for snorkeling. Keep an eye out for manatees; they're about, as are bottlenose dolphins.

No-Name Beach

As mentioned above, the Casa del Mar resort has usurped the finest beach within 5km of Bayahibe. Unless you're a guest of the hotel, and wearing one of its brightly colored identification bracelets, you'll be run off Playa Bayahibe by security guards faster than you can shout '¡Bandidos!'

But between 'their' wide, gorgeous beach and the town of Bayahibe there's a narrow, 150m stretch of sand that an all-inclusive resort has yet to pilfer from the public kitty. It's not exactly beautiful Playa Bayahibe, but it's no toxic waste dump either. Pitch a folding chair beneath a lilting palm, settle your toes amid dying waves, grip an ice-cold brewski in each hand and slide a pair of shades onto your face. Before you know it, you could be mistaken for a beer ad.

Places to Stay

Budget The best place in town is the ***Hotel Bayahibe*** (*☎ 809-707-3684, fax 556-4513*), which opened in 1998 and is only 50m from the water's edge. Each of the 17 rooms has a ceiling fan, private hot-water bathroom and telephone. Some have balconies. There's a piano bar and a generator on the premises. A room with one bed rents for US$13 and a room with two beds is US$20. Call ahead to reserve.

Another very pleasant place to stay, next door to the Hotel Bayahibe, is the ***Cabañas Trip Town*** (*☎ 809-707-3640*), whose owner is about the nicest lady you'll ever meet. Trip Town consists of 15 cabins with fans and private hot-water bathrooms, and it's only 30m from the water. Its one downfall is that it doesn't have a generator, which means the cabins will get hot during a blackout. The cabins rent for US$16, and each comes with a double bed and a single bed.

If both of the above are full, turn to **Cabañas Gladis** (no phone), which is toward the east end of town, set back 50m from the frontage road. The cabins aren't quite as nice as Trip Town's, and there's no hot water and only a small fan in each. There's also no generator on the premises. The cabins rent for US$16 a night. They're a little difficult to find; don't hesitate to ask around.

Top End Leaping over the mid-range category (due to the absence of mid-range hotels in Bayahibe) and well into the top end is the 536-room, 32-junior-suite **Casa del Mar** all-inclusive resort (☎ 800-472-3985, 809-221-8880, fax 221-8881). It has a nicely paved driveway on the coastal highway just before the dirt road leading into central Bayahibe. Facilities include four tennis courts, a swimming pool and massage parlor. Archery and scuba diving lessons are available. Standard rooms without an ocean view are US$160/260 for a single/double, standard rooms with ocean view are US$180/300, and the junior suites (all with ocean view) are US$200/340.

Five kilometers east of Bayahibe, set beside a spectacular beach with very swimmable surf, is the immensely appealing **Club Dominicus Beach** (☎ 800-742-4276, 809-221-6582, fax 687-8583), an all-inclusive resort. The Dominicus allows you to choose a standard or superior room with a terrace or balcony, or a stone bungalow with a garden or ocean view. There were 500 rooms in 1998, and more were being built. Facilities include three pools, six bars and three restaurants – all facing the ocean. The staff does an excellent job of keeping active guests busy day and night, offering them numerous activities (volleyball, archery, aerobics, theme parties, dancing, etc). Optional activities include scuba diving, waterskiing, fishing, horseback riding and more. Rates are US$182/260 for a

standard room and US$224/320 for a superior room. Reservations are required at least three months in advance. This place is a huge cut above Casa del Mar.

Places to Eat

The **Restaurant Bayahibe**, a stone's toss from the water and the town's landmark if ever it had one, is open-sided, spacious, very casual and very popular. Its menu advertises pastas ranging in price from US$2.50 for spaghetti pomodoro to US$9 for spaghetti with lobster. The beef filets are all priced around US$7, the seafood ranges from US$5 to US$13 and chicken with rice is US$5.

Fifty or so meters east of the Bayahibe is the **Cafetería Julissa**, which specializes in juices – orange, banana, papaya, pineapple and melon – and sandwiches – cheese, ham, tuna and chicken. The juices will set you back US$1.30 apiece, the sandwiches US$1.70. The Julissa serves breakfasts as well, all for under US$2.50. This is a pleasant place to begin your day.

Getting There & Away

Minivans make the trip to Bayahibe from La Romana during daylight hours for US$1 each way. A minivan departs when it is full. Sometimes the wait is two minutes, sometimes it's 40. You never can know for sure until you arrive at the bus stop, which appears on the La Romana map. Be advised that, while the minivans are supposed to go into Bayahibe, sometimes their drivers, fearing a flat tire, leave passengers out at the start of the dirt road. If you're left at roadside, don't fret; the walk into town is downhill and doesn't take more than 20 minutes.

Buses also depart for Bayahibe from Higüey; see the Higüey map for the location of the bus depot there. The one-way cost is US$1. A taxi ride to or from Higüey or La Romana would run you about US$20.

Getting Around

Most everyone walks in Bayahibe, but there are a couple of motoconchos and at least one taxi stationed in town. The motoconchos mainly shuttle people to and from the coastal highway, where they then catch

Cellars of the Barcelo Rum Company, Santo Domingo, Dominican Republic

Sugarcane worker with machete, DR

Semiprecious larimar is found only on Hispaniola.

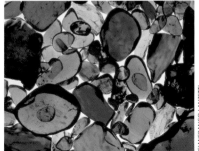

Dominican amber is famous for its trapped insects.

Tobacco growers hang out their harvest to dry near Santiago, Dominican Republic.

A cigar-maker enjoys a smoke at the Davidoff factory in Santiago.

Rafters on Río Yaque del Norte, Jarabacoa, DR

Salto de Limón near Las Terrenas, DR

Tourists gawk at an American crocodile in Lago Enriquillo, Parque Nacional Isla Cabritos, DR.

Holy Week procession in Santo Domingo, DR

Feathery Carnival costumes in Cabral, DR

Well-known artisan Puello Cambita at work in San Cristóbal, southwestern Dominican Republic

Taíno Massacre Site

In 1997 in the Parque Nacional del Este, researchers discovered a settlement that was the site of one of the most brutal and bloody massacres of American Indians by Spanish conquistadors. The battle was well documented in Spanish texts, but the discovery of the settlement's remains provided the first archaeological documentation of the episode and of the Taíno people who lived there.

Only 11 years after Christopher Columbus reached the New World, a Spanish army destroyed the Taíno settlement, slaughtering about 7000 residents. The barbaric incident was one of the first in a 25-year period of conquest in which disease and brutality wiped out the Taíno population of Hispaniola.

Exploring the forest around a sinkhole so isolated that it could be reached only by mule train or helicopter, an archaeological team from the USA discovered the remains of the city, which once may have been home to tens of thousands of people.

Following up on a tip from the head of the national park, the Americans came upon a 5.5m-long mural on a cave wall, commemorating the signing of a treaty under which the Spaniards purchased bread from the Taíno. The detailed display even showed the Spanish galleons that shipped the bread to Santo Domingo. Other pictographs showed Taíno daily life.

But the most significant find was a nearby sinkhole harboring a freshwater well. From the well, the team of scientists recovered baskets, wooden war clubs, carved and decorated gourds and a variety of pottery – one piece was a clear melding of Taíno and Spanish styles.

The archaeologists believe that the well was used during ceremonies for sacrificial offerings. Although such ceremonial wells are not rare in South and Central America, this was the first Taíno ceremonial well ever

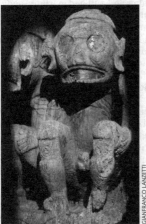

Taíno carving on display at the Museo del Hombre Dominicano, Santo Domingo

discovered. Soon after finding it, the team discovered four large, ceremonial plazas.

The scientists believe the city was the site of a 1503 massacre reported by the Spanish missionary Bartolomé de las Casas. That incident marked one of the first major clashes between the Taíno and the Spaniards, setting the Indians on the path to eventual annihilation.

De las Casas described watching Indians loading bread onto a Spanish ship – fulfilling the treaty commemorated in the nearby cave. A Spanish officer standing nearby had an attack dog on a leash, and when the dog began acting up, a nearby officer jokingly suggested that the dog attack one of the Indians. '¡Tomalo!' he said. 'Take him.'

The dog escaped from his handler and promptly disemboweled the Taíno, who happened to be a minor chieftain. The Indians retaliated later by killing a few Spaniards.

The Spaniards in turn responded by sending hundreds of heavily armed soldiers, many on horseback, from the garrison in Santo Domingo. Over the course of a few hours, they killed about 7000 of the Taíno inhabitants and ran others off into the forest. They cut off the hands of those they captured and lined the bodies up in long rows.

buses heading west toward La Romana or north toward Higüey.

PARQUE NACIONAL DEL ESTE

In the extreme southeastern portion of the republic, the Parque Nacional del Este (National Park of the East) is comprised of 310 sq km of dry forest, subtropical humid forest and a transitional forest type that falls between the two. It also includes 110 sq km of island territory covered mostly with palms and outlined in white, sandy beach. In other words, there are a lot of trees – mainly zamia, copey, gumbo-limbo and Hispaniola mahogany – and bushes on the mainland portion of the park, but there's no triple-canopy jungle dripping with snakes. The island, **Isla Saona**, makes for great sunbathing and snorkeling (see Bayahibe, above).

The park is home to 112 known species of bird, eight of which are endemic to the island, and a rather unimpressive variety of mammals. However, if you come across a critter that looks like a sick rat – rather pale and bony with a long snout and tiny eyes – consider yourself very fortunate: You've witnessed a Hispaniolan solenodon, which is both endemic to the DR and quite rare. Also endangered are the West Indian manatees and the bottlenose dolphins that ply the strait between Isla Saona and the peninsula.

Large, remote Isla Saona is famous throughout the country for its white-sand beaches and crystal-clear water. This is a beautiful spot for sunbathing and snorkeling. There is also a fishing village on the island with a store that sells beverages and a few locally made handicrafts, but none that are particularly nice. Hardcore travelers with light sleeping bags, a grasp of the Spanish language and time on their hands might want to consider staying on the island for a while. Many of the captains at Bayahibe have friends on Isla Saona and could possibly guarantee you a family to stay with for US$10 a night before you commit to making the trip.

Also in the park are many **caves**, some of which contain pre-Columbian pictographs (drawings) and petrographs (rock carvings). Frankly, they are none too spectacular,

either in their complexity or number. Park rangers can lead you to them.

Beware that the park's rangers often tell foreign visitors that they *must* be accompanied by a ranger while in the protected area and, of course, there's a service fee. This simply isn't true, but if you want to stay in the park, you may find yourself having to agree to this fee. The sad truth of it is that the rangers are so poorly paid that they sometimes supplement their salaries in this way.

Getting There & Away

The park can be accessed in three ways: from the dirt road that winds past Club Dominicus Beach (see Bayahibe, above); via a dirt road that winds south from Boca de Yuma on the eastern side of the peninsula; and by boat. Both of these roads require 4WD vehicles. However, there were plans to build an all-weather road from Bayahibe to the western entrance of the park in 1999. Regardless of how you get there, there is a small entrance fee.

Isla Saona is a good 20km each way from Playa Bayahibe, where you hire a boatman for the trip, which means it can't be done on the cheap unless you get a group together. At the time of writing, most boatmen were unwilling to make the round trip for less than US$120.

HIGÜEY

This city of 120,000 people, ringed by sugar-cane fields as far as the eye can see, is most famous for its giant concrete basilica, which is said to contain a miracle-dispensing shrine. Such a thing seems fitting for Higüey, 40km northeast of La Romana and 154km from Santo Domingo, when you consider that *higuey* is a Taíno word meaning 'land where the sun shines.'

It was, no doubt, under a burning sun that the city was founded by Conquistador Juan de Esquivel in 1494. Among the stories one hears in Higüey today is the tale of how a ferocious band of Taíno warriors would have wiped out Columbus and his men had it not been for the Virgin Mary. As the story goes, the European explorers found themselves pitted in battle against a

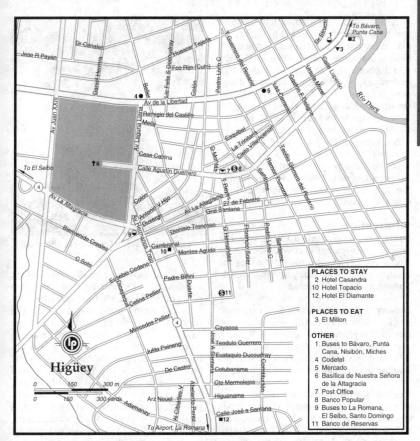

Higüey

PLACES TO STAY
2 Hotel Casandra
10 Hotel Topacio
12 Hotel El Diamante

PLACES TO EAT
3 El Millon

OTHER
1 Buses to Bávaro, Punta
  Cana, Nisibón, Miches
4 Codetel
5 Mercado
6 Basílica de Nuestra Señora
  de la Altagracia
7 Post Office
8 Banco Popular
9 Buses to La Romana,
  El Seibo, Santo Domingo
11 Banco de Reservas

numerically superior Taíno force when the Virgin Mary made an appearance and inspired the conquistadors to vanquish the Indians.

Regardless of the veracity of that report, it is a fact that Juan Ponce de León, the first European in Florida, was among Higüey's early leaders and governed the town from 1502 to 1508. (For more on the life of Ponce de León, see the San Rafael del Yuma section, later in this chapter.)

Today, Higüey is a very busy city, with scores of people coming in from many kilometers away to do their shopping and otherwise take care of business. But from the tourist's perspective, visiting the basilica is about the only reason to stop in Higüey. The one other reason for stopping here is to transfer buses.

Orientation

Relative to most Dominican cities, which are rather neatly laid out, Higüey appears to have been planned by someone preoccupied with thoughts of cooked spaghetti. Looking at a map of the city's streets, you can almost hear its planner say, 'Instead of the usual grid pattern, let's do something completely different . . . .'

As a result, the city's major thoroughfares appear as if they were added to the master plan at the last moment. If you find yourself behind a steering wheel when in Higüey, you'll notice that at times it seems like motorists appear out of nowhere and disappear as rapidly. That's because so many of the streets relate to each other at odd angles.

Some streets to keep in mind while in Higüey are southbound Av Hermanos Trejo, which becomes Hwy 4 headed toward La Romana; westbound Av La Altagracia, which becomes Hwy 4 toward El Seibo; and eastbound Av de la Libertad, which becomes the highway that connects Higüey and the Costa del Coco.

Information

There's no tourist office in the city. For general town-related questions, speak with any of the guides who hang out along the basilica's driveway. They speak English, Spanish and a little German.

Money There's a Banco de Reservas, eight blocks southeast of the basilica, where you can exchange the most common Western currencies for Dominican pesos. There's also a Banco Popular five city blocks east of the basilica; see the map for exact locations.

Post & Communications Higüey's post office is on Calle Agustín Guerrero, six blocks east of the basilica. Its hours are 8 am to 5 pm weekdays, and 9 am to 1 pm Saturday.

There is a Codetel office at the convenient location of Av de la Libertad and Av Laguna Llana, opposite the northeast corner of the basilica compound. It is open 8 am to 10 pm daily.

Basílica de Nuestra Señora de la Altagracia

Higüey's basilica, the 'Cathedral of the Virgin of Altagracia,' isn't like anything you've ever seen before. That was the intention when church leaders in 1951 met with architects from the DR, Chile, Cuba, Ecuador, Haiti, Paraguay, Peru, Belgium, Spain, France, Holland and Italy, and then decided on a design submitted by the Frenchmen Pierre

Basílica de Nuestra Señora de la Altagracia

Dupré and Dovnoyer de Segonzac. Work commenced in October 1954, and the doors of the cathedral opened two years later.

In explaining their design choice, the church leaders said the architecture of the basilica was meant to correspond to modern times. While the floor plan does follow the traditional outline of the Latin cross, everything else about the church is indeed modern; it is made almost entirely of concrete, tons upon tons of it. From the main gate, it appears mostly rectangular but is topped with a set of centrally aligned cone-shaped domes that are intended to represent hands placed together in prayer.

Inside, the long walls consist mostly of bare concrete and approach each other as they rise, connecting at a rounded point directly over the center aisle. The entire wall opposite the front door consists of stained glass and is quite striking. Most foreign visitors, unaccustomed to such daring architecture, especially in a church, are a bit repulsed by it. However, few engineers leave the building unimpressed.

But it isn't the architecture of the church that attracts Dominicans here from across the country. Rather, it's a small, glass-encased image of the Virgin of Altagracia. According to legend, a sick child in Higüey was healed when an old man (later suspected to have been one of the Apostles) asked for a meal and shelter at the city's original church. On departing the following day, he left a small print of Our Lady of Grace in a modest frame. Since that day, the 16th-century image has been venerated by countless devotees, upon whom the Virgin is said to have bestowed miraculous cures.

Mercado

As the big city at the center of a vast agricultural region, Higüey is a beehive of commercial activity. This is particularly true of Av de la Libertad between Calle Colón and Calle Luperón. Midway along this busy stretch is the town's central *mercado* (market), where you can find a few things you could use and lot of stuff you don't need. What makes the market interesting is the people-watching. This is where the DR's people of the earth – good, hard-working folks with friendly dispositions, such as the soil toilers and cattle hands – do their shopping. And it's where the city folk, particularly new arrivals from the rural areas, come to buy their produce. You'll see all kinds of people at Higüey's mercado.

The market's just a few blocks up from the main bus depot, and if you've got some time to kill between buses, you might enjoy a look around. It's open 8 am to 5 pm daily.

Special Events

Every January 21, thousands of people travel to the basilica to pay homage to the Virgin. On this day the church is filled with the country's most devout, all dressed in their best. Bathed in colored light from the stained-glass window, the pilgrims file past the Virgin's image, seeking little miracles and giving profound thanks. The outpouring of faith, when seen in this light, is quite moving even to the nonbeliever, and the church's many tuned bells, sounded by hammers controlled from a keyboard, chime throughout the day.

Places to Stay

Higüey sees quite a few foreign visitors during the day and almost none at night.

That's because the vast majority of foreigners come only to see the basilica, and they arrive in shuttle buses operated by their fancy resorts along the Costa del Coco. After 30 minutes or so at the church, the tourists board their air-conditioned shuttle buses and return to their resorts.

The number of domestic visitors to Higüey who actually spend the night in the city is also quite low, except for the one day out of the year when thousands of pilgrims descend on the city. As a result of the low demand for hotels, there are few in Higüey, all of which fall within the budget category.

The best of the few is the ***Hotel Topacio*** (☎ *809-554-5892, fax 554-4744*), on Calle Cambronal a few blocks southeast of the basilica. The hotel is also close to the bus stop for buses to Santo Domingo, La Romana and El Seibo. All of the Topacio's 24 rooms have air con and private hot-water bathrooms, and this new hotel (built in 1997) has a generator to offset the city's frequent power outages. The rates are US$25/28 for a single/double.

The ***Hotel Casandra*** (no phone) is very near the bus depot that serves Miches, Nisibón, Bávaro and Punta Cana. That's its chief selling point. The rooms at this small, one-story, family-owned hotel are clean and seem secure, but they are fan-only, completely colorless, and the water always runs cold. In addition to a hot-water heater, the place also could use a generator and some screens for the windows; you will get a few mosquito bites here. The rate is US$10/15.

The only other decent budget place in town is the ***Hotel El Diamante*** (☎ *809-554-2754*), beside the intersection of Av Hermanos Trejo and Calle José a Santana. All rooms are worn and not very secure (they can be easily broken into), but they do have air con and decent beds. The shower is cold water only. The rate is US$17.50 per room. There's also a restaurant and a bar at the hotel.

Places to Eat

There are numerous restaurants around town, none of which, according to local residents, is particularly good. However, directly across the street from the bus depot that serves Miches is *El Millon,* a restaurant that consists mainly of a long counter with a cash register and kitchen behind it. It's one of the most popular places in town, known for its fancy fruit drinks. Among the better ones are *bomba*, mixed fruit blended with milk for US$1; *matira*, rose wine blended with milk for US$0.50; and papaya, mango, orange, pineapple and zapote smoothies blended separately with milk or purified ice, or in some combination – for US$0.80 per glass. Also very popular are the equally inexpensive ham-and-cheese sandwiches. The restaurant is open late every day.

Getting There & Away

On Av de la Libertad is a bus station that offers regular and fairly frequent daily service to Miches (fare US$3), Nisibón (US$1.50), Bávaro (US$1.50) and Punta Cana (US$1.50). The last buses depart around sunset. Be aware that the last bus to Punta Cana leaves around 5 pm; thereafter, you take the bus going to Bávaro and get off where the road splits, with the north fork going to Bávaro and the south fork going to Punta Cana. Beside the fork in the road, you'll always find a taxi or motoconcho that you can take you the rest of the way.

Near the southeast corner of the basilica compound is a major intersection where you'll see a ticket booth, people milling around and buses pulling up to and leaving from the curb. This is where you can catch buses bound for La Romana (US$1.50), Santo Domingo (US$3.50 for a regular bus, US$1 more for an express bus), Bayahibe (US$1), El Seibo (US$1.50), San Rafael del Yuma (US$1) and Boca de Yuma (US$1.50). Buses leave frequently during daylight hours, but service is very restricted after sunset.

In general, Dominicans do not like to travel after the sun has gone down, due to the number of animals on the road and the absence of street lights. To leave Higüey at night, plan on taking a taxi.

Getting Around

There are lots of taxis and motoconchos around during the day. If you're up for it, a ride to Bávaro or Punta Cana is much more exhilarating on the back of a moped or motorcycle than on a bus. Be advised that taking a motoconcho at night is particularly dangerous, since drivers tend to drive just as fast as they do during the day.

SAN RAFAEL DEL YUMA

Approximately 22km south of Higüey is this quiet little town of perhaps 5000 people, at the center of which is a proudly maintained plaza with shade trees and benches. There's a Codetel office beside the plaza as well as a small white church.

San Rafael del Yuma, just east of the two-lane highway linking Higüey to Boca de Yuma, is a fine rural Dominican town surrounded by fields in all directions, with dirt roads and nondescript houses varying little from one to the other. The streets fill with schoolchildren in uniforms every afternoon. People can always be seen sweeping their porches, and if you stop to chat, invariably they will be glad you did. They are friendly, outgoing people.

But no one visits this splendid little town for any of the reasons just mentioned. Rather, they pass by on their way to Boca de Yuma or to the nearby former residence of the Spanish explorer Juan Ponce de León. And perhaps that's just as well. Here, no child would dare approach a visitor to say, 'Give me a dollar,' as they do in tourist haunts. Here, the people have yet to view visitors as money-dispensing machines.

Be advised that there's only one really rustic hotel and a few lousy food stands in San Rafael del Yuma.

Orientation

If you're coming by car south on Hwy 4, a few kilometers after passing Los Muertos, keep an eye out for a welcome sign on the east side of the road that reads 'Bienvenidos a San Rafael del Yuma.' When you see it, veer to the left; this road will take you directly into town in 400m or so.

If you're going to the museum instead (see below), after only 100m, look for a dirt road on the left side of the street (it's just before the town's cemetery, which has a tall wall around it). Stay on the winding dirt road for about 400m; after about 300m, start looking for a large stone structure on the right side of the road (Ponce's old place). An unmarked 100m-long dirt driveway will appear on the right, which you'll want to take up to the museum. You've arrived! If you arrive at the bus depot, you can walk to the museum by going to the dirt road on the west side of the nearby cemetery and following the instructions above.

La Casa de Juan Ponce de León

Juan Ponce de León had a residence built in the countryside near San Rafael del Yuma and used it on occasion during the time he governed Higüey for the Spanish Crown. Nearly 500 years later, his stone, two-story residence still stands, now as a museum to a man who led a momentous life.

Ponce de León was born in Spain in 1460. In 1493 he accompanied Christopher Columbus on his second voyage to America. As time passed he became increasingly important to the Spanish monarchy, which made him governor of Higüey from 1502 to 1508. In 1508, with ships and men supplied by the Crown, Ponce de León conquered Boriquén (what today is Puerto Rico). He was governor of the island from 1510 to 1512.

From Indians he heard reports of an island called Bimini, somewhere north of Cuba, which reputedly possessed the fabled fountain of youth, a spring whose waters had the power to reverse the aging process. Believing these reports, Ponce de León in 1512 obtained permission from the Spanish king to find, conquer and colonize Bimini.

The next year, Ponce de León led an exploratory expedition. On March 27 he sighted the eastern shore of the present state of Florida, which he believed to be the legendary Bimini. He landed north of present-day St Augustine on April 2, naming the region Florida because he sighted it on Easter Sunday (*Pascua Florida*, literally 'Flowery Easter'). Believing Florida was an island, he tried to sail around it, going south to what is now Key West, up the west coast of Florida, then south again. He reached Puerto Rico again in September 1513.

The conquistador spent most of the next seven years enslaving Puerto Rico's Indians and violently crushing rebellions, but he never stopped thinking about the supposed fountain of youth. In 1521 circumstances allowed him to resume the search, and he set out to colonize Florida with about 200 people. The party landed on the west coast of Florida, where it came under fierce attack from Indians and Ponce de León was severely wounded by an arrow. The expedition withdrew and sailed to Cuba, where he died shortly after landing.

The residence-turned-museum is at the end of a dirt road that, during the 16th century, passed through dense forest. Today the forest is gone, and from the former residence one can see only rolling pastures and large homes belonging to wealthy local landowners.

The explorer's home was built with security in mind. The stone walls are nearly a meter thick and the windows are too small for a person to squeeze through; from the inside they can be latched shut behind a slab of mahogany. The sole exterior door is made of multiple layers of riveted hardwood. The home's roof is made of Spanish tiles, which were replaced when the building was restored in 1997.

Inside, the building still contains many original items belonging to Ponce de León, including his armor and much of his furniture. Also original are the candelabra and his bed; his coat of arms is carved into the headboard. The floors are made of pure mahogany and are said to be original.

The cost of admission is US$1. All visitors are guided to prevent theft and vandalism; a tip of US$2 is extremely appreciated. The guide speaks Spanish only. The building is open 9 am to 4 pm Monday through Saturday.

Getting There & Away

Because you cannot count on there being a taxi in San Rafael del Yuma, you pretty much have to arrive in one, have your own wheels or plan on walking approximately 600m to and from the bus stop (which really isn't all that far if you're in any kind of shape and aren't hauling lots of stuff).

A bus leaves the bus depot, on the main road into town just beyond the cemetery, every 30 minutes from 6 am to 5 pm bound for La Romana (US$1.50). Buses leave every 20 minutes from 6 am to 5 pm bound for Higüey (US$1). To catch a bus for Boca de Yuma, walk out to the highway and flag down any southbound bus.

BOCA DE YUMA

Beside the mouth of the Río Yuma, tucked way back in the throat of the Bahía de Yuma, is this still-sleepy fishing village. Boca de Yuma has been spared the character-changing effects of a sprawling all-inclusive resort due to its lack of a wide beach and easy sea. Instead, its shoreline may accurately be described as rocky cliffs pounded by heavy surf.

Boca de Yuma offers the visitor four attractions: lovely coastal views, at least one pleasant place to stay, a cave and access to the Parque Nacional del Este. There are no banks in town, nor is there a post office or a Codetel office, so if you think you might be staying a while, plan ahead.

Orientation

As Hwy 4 approaches its eastern terminus, stunning views of the Caribbean appear in the distance. The last stretch of highway gives way to a gas station on the left, a cliff to the right and bad pavement for the remaining several hundred meters to oceanside.

When you come to the end of the road, to your left you'll see some colonial cannon emplacements and a couple of mediocre open-sided restaurants. If you turn right, after a couple of hundred meters the Hotel Saina will appear at shore's edge. Continuing on 200m more, the road turns to dirt/mud, and 30m before you come to the entrance of the national park, you'll see a dirt road to the right; this road winds 200m to the entrance of the Cueva de Bernard (Bernard's Cave).

Cueva de Bernard

This large walk-in cave does not have particularly impressive stalactites or stalagmites. All it apparently has is a big mouth. It's probable that the cave goes back a ways, but exploration is prohibited beyond the initial cavern. At the time of writing, there were no motoconchos or taxis in town, which meant getting to the cave entailed a good walk or using your own vehicle.

Horseback Riding

On the winding road that descends into town is the Hotel Ristorante Italiano Club El 28, which rents out horses for US$7 per hour, less per hour if you're out for several hours or more. It's possible to take horses into the nearby national park, and no one will complain if you ride one through town.

Places to Stay & Eat

A very nice place to stay in Boca de Yuma is the *Hotel Ristorante Italiano Club El 28* (☎ 809-476-8660, fax 223-0503), on the only road into town 200m or so past the town's only gas station. The Italian owner had 11 cabins in late 1998, but more were being built. Each cabin is clean and cool and comes with fan, screened windows and private hot-water bathroom. There is one pool and a second one planned. This, incidentally, is the only place in town where international calls can be placed. Room rates are US$17.75/23 for a single/double.

As the establishment's name implies, there is a restaurant on the premises (as well as a bar and a big-screen TV) and it serves up some excellent Italian cooking at very reasonable prices. Dishes include spaghetti for US$3, conch for US$6 and a large lobster for US$9. The olive oil and wine are imported from Italy.

In 1998, just past the welcome sign at the entrance of Boca de Yuma, was a lovely place that seemed on the brink of closing due to lack of business – largely because it is a bit off the beaten path and probably because its name is hokey: *Club Indiana Jones* (no phone). Except for the name, there is nothing hokey about the Indiana Jones. Its Swiss owners have built four stand-alone cabins beside a cliff with a sweeping view of the town below and the beautiful Caribbean out front. Each *cabaña* is lovingly crafted and features a handsome and cool thatched roof, ceiling fans and natural furniture. A swimming pool was planned. The rate of US$30 per cabin (US$27 per night for a stay of one week or more) includes a hearty breakfast. The restaurant specializes in grilled meats and fish. Prices range from US$6 for spaghetti bolognesa to US$12 for a large piece of grilled beef with whisky sauce. If it's still open, this place is a very nice find. To get to it, follow the signs from the main road, just before it dips into town.

You'd be well advised to steer clear of Hotel Saina on the seaside road approaching the entrance to the national park. Although the hotel has air-con rooms with private hot-water bathrooms, the Saina has not been maintained. Its rooms are dirty, in need of paint and new carpeting, and there were many mosquitoes in the living areas. At the time Lonely Planet paid a visit, in late 1998, the hotel's receptionist was drunk and belligerent.

Getting There & Away
In late 1998, buses from La Romana and Higüey arrived and departed from the end of Hwy 4, just before it becomes a terribly rutted, partially paved road that descends a couple hundred meters into town. The drivers of the buses simply didn't want to go on the bad section of road, claiming it could damage their vehicles. Hopefully, by the time you read this, the road will be repaired and the bus drivers will no longer force passengers to trek up and down the steep, rutted road. Buses for La Romana leave hourly (US$2) and for Higüey about every 30 minutes (US$1.50).

COSTA DEL COCO
Throughout the Dominican Republic, the Costa del Coco (Coconut Coast) is synonymous with 'all-inclusive resort.' From Punta Cana north all the way to Playa del Macao, there's not so much as a single village, let alone a town or city. Instead, there are many all-inclusive resorts, a few hotels and lots of absolutely gorgeous palm-lined beaches. Some of the well-known beaches along the coast include Playa Punta Cana, Playa Cabeza de Toro, Playa Cortesito, Playa del Macao and Playa del Muerto. This is the Caribbean of magazine covers – perfect sand in the foreground, hard-bodied 20-somethings frolicking in water clear as gin, the purest blue sky above and barely a wisp of cloud to be seen.

Most clients of these resorts arrive at Aeropuerto Punta Cana from an international departure point; are transported by private shuttle to a resort where they stay for a week; are transported by private shuttle back to the airport; and return to their international point of origin. Generally speaking, these tourists have considerably more contact with Europeans, Americans and Canadians than they have with Dominicans, and that's just fine with them.

People come here for deep-penetrating sun, spectacular surf, a little romance and the prepaid, all-you-can-eat-and-drink approach to life. They come for the water sports, the nightlife and the massage centers, to look and to be looked at. Most of all, they come to enjoy life, and the staff at these resorts tries its best not to disappoint. As palaces of hedonism, the resorts of La Costa del Coco excel.

La Costa del Coco is divided into two sections – Punta Cana to the south and Bávaro to the north. Separating the two are approximately 20km of roadless territory. At the time of writing, there were two all-inclusive resorts in Punta Cana and nine all-inclusives, one mid-range hotel and one top-end apartment hotel in Bávaro, with additional resorts under construction in both areas.

In deciding whether an all-inclusive is really what you want and, if so, which is most suitable for you, the best approach is to contact all of the resorts and request a brochure from each. In return you'll receive lots of glossy brochures containing photos that will prove helpful in making your decision. Also, if you can provide an anticipated date of travel, you can obtain exact rates.

Beware that rates vary almost weekly at these resorts, and they can vary substantially. For example, the 1999 per-person weekly rates for a standard room at the Club Med in Punta Cana varied from US$820 to US$1660, with the highest rates falling around Christmas. The rates shown in the following pages reflect the rates at the time the resorts were being researched. Also, some resorts give substantial discounts if you stay for two weeks or more.

Furthermore, the rates are always lower when purchased from an agent overseas; expect to pay considerably more if you simply show up unexpectedly and request a room. Much of the time a room won't even be available. Despite the size and number of the resorts along the Coconut Coast, they are often completely booked weeks and even months in advance. Make your reservations early to avoid disappointment.

Between the coast and the two-lane paved road linking Higüey and Nisibón, the countryside is predominantly covered with dry forest sprinkled lightly with small farms. The dirt road connecting El Macao and La Cruz del Isleno, for example, has hardly any houses along it and isn't often used; if you experience trouble with your car or motorcycle, you will likely find yourself far from the nearest home and stuck in the boonies for many hours.

Punta Cana

Located 57km from Higüey and 211km from Santo Domingo, Punta Cana (Gray-Haired Point) contains at least two resorts on gorgeous beaches with swimmable water out front. Both are very appealing.

Places to Stay & Eat Featuring four multi-level U-shaped housing structures, three restaurants, three cocktail lounges and a huge swimming pool, *Club Mediterranée Punta Cana* (☎ 800-258-2633, 809-687-2767, fax 687-2896) is set amid lush gardens and beside an absolutely awesome beach. Included in the weekly rate are three meals daily, beer and/or wine with lunch and dinner, and opportunities for sailing, kayaking, windsurfing, waterskiing, tennis, water exercises, archery, aerobics, volleyball, basketball, softball, ping-pong, picnics and dancing.

Optional excursions include 18-hole golf, horseback riding, scuba diving, deep-sea fishing, Santo Domingo's Zona Colonial (reached by plane), Isla Saona (catamaran sail, picnic and swimming at Playa Bonita), a nature walk, a Zodiac safari up the lovely Río Chavón, and a casino evening in Bávaro.

Rates are for seven nights, per-person double occupancy (singles are required to share rooms), and range from US$820 to US$1660 depending on time of stay. Discounts of 25% to 50% off the second week on a two-week stay apply. There is also a discount available if you book your reservation at least 60 days in advance.

The 400-room *Punta Cana Beach Resort* (☎ 800-972-2139, 809-541-2714, fax 547-2200), 5km south of Club Med, features 800m of beach and villas as well as spacious rooms in three-story buildings, all on the beach. Waterskiing, snorkeling, sailing, windsurfing, paddle boating, kayaking, volleyball, tennis, water polo and aerobics are among the activities included in the rates. Horseback riding, scuba diving and night tennis are the only activities that require an additional charge. Rates vary from US$80 per person per night for a standard room to US$165 for a villa.

Manatí Park

If you get a thrill watching dolphins, or if you've ever wondered what it would be like to swim with some, you should visit this pleasantly unusual amusement park, featuring a variety of animal acts. Located near Bávaro on a well-signed loop road several kilometers from the coast, Manatí Park (☎ 809-552-0807, fax 552-0810) is a great way to pass a couple of hours. The US$21 admission fee permits you to watch a 'dancing horses' show, where the beautiful and well-trained animals perform numerous feats upon command. But most people find more pleasure in the performances by the apparently humorous and obviously fun-loving dolphins and sea lions. For an additional US$44, you can enter the water with the creatures and, most of the time, a dolphin will allow you to hold onto its flippers and give you a little ride. The park is open 9 am to 6:30 pm daily.

Bávaro

Located 55km from Higüey and 209km from Santo Domingo, Bávaro – as in Playa

Bávaro – was until recently simply the name of one of the many beaches along the Costa del Coco. Today, Bávaro refers to the entire area north of Punta Cana and south of El Macao, and the resorts here are collectively the best in the country. There's no other area in the DR where there are so many top-notch resorts with wide, gorgeous beaches and water that's generally safe to swim in all year round (the Playa Dorada complex near Puerto Plata contains a greater number of resorts, but the Atlantic Ocean along their beaches gets a bit dangerous at times). The establishments mentioned here appear in order as you drive north from Punta Cana about 25km along the Bávaro coastal road.

Places to Stay & Eat Owned by Barceló Hotels of Spain, the ***Barceló Bávaro Beach*** (☎ 809-686-5797, fax 686-5859) is not one resort but a complex of five different all-inclusive resorts built between 1985 and 1993. The complex contains 1953 rooms and is bordered by 3km of fine, white-sand beach. A coral reef 800m from the shore stops the breakers, so the waters reaching the shore are usually calm.

Throughout the complex are more than a dozen restaurants and grills serving international and local cuisine, and there are 18 bars. There are also a casino and two dance clubs, one featuring international music and another salsa and merengue. Other facilities include a shopping center, travel agency, two free trains that act as a shuttle around the complex, a church and a medical center.

Guests may participate in the following sports free of charge: tennis, soccer, softball, aerobics, water aerobics, beach volleyball, water volleyball, water polo, darts, badminton and shuffleboard. For an additional cost, guests may take advantage of an 18-hole golf course, sailing, windsurfing, water-skiing, deep-sea fishing, kayaking, scuba diving, and trips on a banana boat and/or glass-bottomed boat.

Many excursions are available (by boat, bus and on horseback), but if you'd rather go it alone, Barceló rents jeeps, cars and vans. Of course, if you'd rather just lie by a swimming pool or on the beach, you can do that too.

Rates at each of the following run from US$116 per person to US$156 per person:

Barceló Bávaro Beach hotel is in the middle of a lush coconut grove on the edge of Playa Bávaro. It was completely renovated in 1994, has 598 rooms and hosts three restaurants, four bars, a swimming pool for adults and one for children, a gift shop, jewelry shop, marine accessories shop, a hair and massage salon and a medical center.

Barceló Bávaro Garden, which opened in 1987, contains 401 rooms and is beside the beach. It's surrounded by palm trees and, as its name suggests, it has a luxuriant tropical garden. The Garden has two restaurants and four bars, two pools, a gift shop and jewelry store.

Barceló Bávaro Golf is a relatively small resort with just 126 rooms, but they range from rooms with four or six beds to different-size suites. It's next to the golf course, 350m from the beach, and is ringed by palm trees and tropical gardens. It was completely renovated in 1995. In addition to boasting two restaurants, two bars and a pool, the hotel has a dance club. Next door there is a handicrafts market, a jewelry shop, a grocer, a gift shop, a film developer, a post office and a boutique.

Barceló Bávaro Casino hotel features 234 rooms and the complex's casino. It has 170 doubles and 64 four-bed rooms, all with views of the adjacent golf course. Renovated in 1995, the hotel is 600m from the beach. It has two restaurants and three bars, two pools, a gift shop and a jewelry store.

Barceló Bávaro Palace, a 594-room hotel, is on the edge of the beach and surrounded by a coconut grove and tropical gardens. With a 1993 inauguration, it is the newest and perhaps the nicest hotel of the five (though none are exactly fleabags to begin with). It has five restaurants, a swimming pool 'wet bar,' a few not-so-wet bars and several shops.

Los Corales Aparta Hotel (☎ 809-221-0801, 221-0274, fax 221-1396) is a great alternative to the all-inclusive resort for people who don't like the impersonal feel of 500-room complexes. Here, there are 36 comfortable and spacious apartments, two per stand-alone villa. Each apartment has an equipped kitchen (there is a grocery store in the area), satellite TV and telephone. The complex, which contains an Italian restaurant, a large swimming pool with Jacuzzi, pool tables and a gym, is nestled amid coconut trees at the edge of the sea. A variety of water toys, including kayaks, are available. Also available for rent are motorcycles, cars and motorboats. Rates around Christmas are US$119/182 for singles/doubles. The rest of the year, the rates tend to be closer to US$75/130, and even less during April, May and June.

The all-inclusive **Hodelpa Bávaro** (☎ 809-683-1000, fax 683-2303) features 336 guest rooms, several restaurants and snack bars, a theater, a dance club, two large swimming pools, a gym, sauna, massage center, dive center, tennis courts, a game room, lots of water toys and, of course, a wonderful beach. Cars, motorcycles, bicycles and even skates are available for rent. Rates are around US$80 per person most of the year, but much higher around Christmas.

The 370-room all-inclusive **Hotel Carabela Bávaro Beach Resort** (☎ 809-221-2728, fax 221-2631) is competing head-on with the Hodelpa, offering just about all the same amenities for the same price. However, the Hodelpa seems a bit livelier.

For those of us hoping to take advantage of the area at more down-to-earth prices, there's **El Cortecito Inn** (☎ 809-552-0639, fax 552-0641), a 20-room inn with a pool and poolside restaurant. Although it's actually 100m from the beach, it offers fine access to it. English, German and Spanish are spoken. Rates are US$30 per person and include breakfast.

A brief walk down from the Cortecito is the equally budget-conscious establishment, **Caribbean Apartahotel** (☎ 809-330-2716), which rents rooms with fan only for US$30 and with air con for US$35. Like the Cortecito, the hotel is not on the beach but does have ready access to it. There are several restaurants in the immediate area, including **Mama Juana**, a very inviting seaside bar/restaurant. Every night its German owners host a bonfire on the beach, and the atmosphere is wonderful.

As its name implies, **Hotel Fiesta Palace Beach Resort** (☎ 809-221-8149, fax 221-8150) is fun, spacious and next to the sandy seashore. It's got two tennis courts, a huge swimming pool with a swim-up bar, a handsome open-sided restaurant and plenty of palm trees. However, it's a good bit tamer than the huge Barceló complex. Rates are US$120 per person for double occupancy, US$144 per person if you arrive solo. Call for reservations.

The **Meliá Bávaro** (☎ 800-336-3542, 809-221-2111, fax 686-5427) was the northernmost resort at the time this was being penned, but others were under construction and will likely be open at the time you read this. However, it's unlikely the new hotels will be as lovely. The beach here is more than 100m wide and nearly 2km long, dotted with hundreds of coconut palms and facing a crystal-clear gentle surf; it's just gorgeous. The design of the hotel, which consists of 750 suites in bungalows built around natural gardens, is superior to anything else in the region. The hotel offers all the amenities, but unlike most of the other resorts mentioned here, its layout conveys both a sense of intimacy and vastness, elegance and casualness.

Of all the resorts on the Coconut Coast, in the author's opinion the Meliá is the only one for honeymooners. Rates range from US$80 to US$175 per room depending on the time of year (the full-board supplement is US$55 extra), US$175 the week between Christmas and New Year's Day. Rates are US$110 most of the rest of the year.

Shopping A large, modern shopping center that caters to wealthy tourists separates the Fiesta Palace Beach and the Meliá. From either resort, the center is an easy walk. On the beach along the northern border of the Barceló complex, at the end of a dirt road marked 'Mercado,' is a huge crafts market under scores of tarps. It's open every day.

Getting There & Away

Air The Coconut Coast is served by Aeropuerto Punta Cana (☎ 809-688-4749), about 5km from where the Higüey-Punta Cana road reaches the coast. The airport is served by dozens of charter airlines and several international carriers, as well as the domestic carrier Air Santo Domingo (☎ 809-221-1184, 552-0675). Check with a travel agent in your area for current international and charter carriers serving Punta Cana.

Following are the various one-way fares for flights from Punta Cana on Air Santo Domingo:

Destination	Duration	Cost
Santo Domingo	45 min	US$54
Las Américas Airport	40 min	US$54
La Romana	20 min	US$27
Puerto Plata	1 hour	US$59
Las Terrenas	40 min	US$54

Contact Air Santo Domingo for current flight times and reservations; Spanish and English are spoken. The cost of a taxi ride between the Punta Cana airport and either of the resort areas is US$5 to US$10.

Bus To reach either Bávaro or Punta Cana by bus, you must first travel to Higüey and then transfer. Of course, bus service is also available from the Coconut Coast to Higüey. See the Higüey section, earlier in this chapter, for information on bus departures and fares in that city. To catch a bus from the coast to Higüey, simply walk (or have your resort shuttle you) to the edge of the coastal highway, and flag down any of the public buses traveling on it. The fare is US$1.50.

Taxi You can also take a taxi to and from the Coconut Coast, but expect to pay a lot more for this option than for the bus. Clerks at the reception desk of your Bávaro or Punta Cana resort can call a taxi for you, or you can walk (or get a ride) to the entrance of a resort, where at least one taxi will be parked.

Getting Around

Bus Gua-guas ply the main coastal road; to catch a ride on one, simply go to road's edge and hail one down. If the bus doesn't stop, it likely wasn't a gua-gua but was instead a resort's shuttle bus. You can generally distinguish a public gua-gua from a private shuttle by the amount of dirt and wear shown on it. Gua-guas usually aren't as fresh-looking as the private buses, to put it gently. The fare along the coast is always US$1 or even less.

Taxi There are numerous taxis in the area, usually parked beside the entrance of the

all-inclusive resorts. Expect to pay at least 10 times what you would pay for a gua-gua ride. However, the gua-guas do not operate at night and the taxi drivers do. That's something to keep in mind if, for example, you decide to go on a long walk late in the day.

HIGÜEY TO MICHES

A well-paved two-lane road (Hwy 104) connects the rural city of Higüey to the port city of Miches on the Bahía de Samaná. Heading north, the road initially passes through flat sugarcane country, and then the land becomes increasingly hilly and the road increasingly windy. The hills, most no more than 50m tall, have mostly been cleared of trees to create pasture for cattle.

But time and again you'll reach the top of a hill and peer across a pretty little valley with patches of forest. And on this road you'll cross many bridges, beneath which run jungle-flanked rivers that are captivating to behold.

The road passes through many hamlets – most not on any maps – that few tourists ever see and that really have very little to offer. Only one, Nisibón, even has a gas station, although you'll pass many poor homes on the route with gallon containers out in front, filled with orange-pink gasoline for sale. Buses frequently ply this route as well.

About 5km west of Nisibón you'll come to the hamlet of El Cedro. When you see it, you should do a U-turn and backtrack 1km, keeping an eye out for a dirt road on the east side of the road you're on. Turn onto the dirt road and proceed 5km until you come to *Cabañas Playa Tortuga* (☎ 809-689-4664). You'll be glad you did.

These directions will place you on an often muddy road between a lovely, overlooked beach and seven cabins, a swimming pool and a restaurant owned and managed by an Austrian who's created something special here. All of the cabins, new in 1998, are very comfortable and smartly designed. All have fans, private hot-water bathrooms and kitchens, and some even have air con – no small feat considering the location. The cabins rent for US$30 to US$60, the price varying with features. One cabin contains several economical rooms that rent for about US$25 (fan) or US$30 (air con). Breakfast and dinner average about US$13 per person each day. The cuisine is European or Dominican, you decide.

In front of the Cabañas is **Playa Limón**, an excellent body-surfing beach, and not far from El Cedro are some statuesque mountains; the owner, Richard Haas, can arrange for you to go there on horseback. There are also two lagoons nearby – the entire area seems to cry out for exploring.

Three species of sea turtle nest on the beach in April and May. You can watch them under the moon's light. Humpback whales migrate off the coast during January and February, and are sometimes visible from the beach. If you may be here then, consider bringing binoculars.

There are frequent buses traveling between Higüey and Miches, so getting to El Cedro isn't a problem. But getting to the cabins can be a bit tricky if you don't have your own wheels. Unless you're in good condition, the 6km to the Cabañas presents a logistical problem because there is no public transportation to them.

You can call Richard to reserve a room and, at that time, alert him to the fact that you'll need a ride from the road to his place. At least a day or two before you are scheduled to arrive, call him again and arrange a time when he can pick you up. It may be that he'll agree to look for you in El Cedro or walking toward his hotel from the roadside hamlet every 30 minutes between, say, noon and 2 pm. Richard speaks English, German and Spanish.

To leave the area, either walk to the Higüey-Miches road or have Richard take you there. From the roadside, hail any of the gua-guas traveling in the direction you are heading. A gua-gua ride to Miches will set you back about US$0.50. A gua-gua ride to Higüey will cost about US$1.

MICHES

The scruffy town of Miches (pop 30,000), on the lower lip of the mouth of the Bahía de Samaná, has nothing to offer the tourist. It's known mainly as a launching point for

Dominicans trying to enter the USA illegally through a back door: the US territory of Puerto Rico. Those who make it across the often-turbulent strait separating the DR from PR are usually able to board flights to the USA without showing a visa or proof of residency.

Just before you enter Miches from the east, you'll cross a bridge over the Río Yaguada. Instead of crossing into Miches, travelers with a spirit of adventure and looking for a place to stay are advised to turn down the paved road that runs beside the east bank of the river.

This road winds down to the city's beach, which is none too spectacular compared to beaches along the Coconut Coast. However, there are three enjoyable places to stay in the area – if you're the kind of person who doesn't mind roughing it a little. Coincidentally, they are owned and managed by Swiss people, all of whom speak English, German and Spanish.

Places to Stay & Eat

The first of the three places, and the least rustic, is the ***Coco Loco Beach Club*** (☎ 809-553-5920, fax 553-5839, www.abatrex.com/cocoloco). The hotel is only 100m or so from the river, and about the same distance from the bay. It consists of a two-story structure in front, with a pleasant and simple restaurant and bar at the top.

Behind the building, in a field of short grass that could do with a few trees, are 10 cabañas, each with private cold-water-only bathroom, a small dining table, two twin beds and a small fan. Each cabin also has a shaded porch. The roofs are made of tin, which are not only unappealing but also transfer the sun's heat right into the cabin.

Coco Loco's selling point is definitely its 2nd-floor bar/restaurant, mostly because of the view and the breeze it catches coming off the bay. Breakfasts run US$2 to US$3.50, pasta US$4 to US$5, and seafood around US$10. The cabins each go for US$25/40 singles/doubles.

A much more attractive option is the ***Campola Concha*** (☎/fax 809-248-5884), but it was tricky to reach in late 1998; one had to drive on a beach for 9km and occasionally turn into the surf to circumvent fallen palm trees; there was even a shallow creek to ford. The likelihood of getting bogged down in sand was very real. However, rumor had it that a nearby resort was planned. If true, a good road would pass very near, making it much easier for people to get to Campola Concha.

Regardless of the road situation, the Campola Concha is a very intimate pension nestled among palms a minute's walk from a secluded beach. There are only four wooden cabins, one used by the friendly couple who run things, and all are charming, rustic and smartly crafted. A carpenter would certainly appreciate them. For starters, all are more than a meter off the ground, which not only frustrates termites but helps keep the cabins pleasantly cool. Likewise, the roofs are made of thatch, which acts as natural insulation. There are numerous windows for cross ventilation, all nicely screened to thwart mosquitoes and sand flies. The bathrooms are communal, but they are so attractive and clean that they give 'shared bathrooms' a good name.

At the center of things is a community dining and chatting area, open-sided except for mosquito screening. It is here that you'll enjoy some delicious European cuisine and perhaps a drink or two; one of the owners is a former bartender. The rates of US$25/40 include breakfast *and* dinner. This place is an excellent value.

If you haven't got your own wheels, be sure to tell the owners, Roger and Eva, when you book your reservation. With a little notice, they can arrange for you to be picked up in Miches and carried here in a mule-drawn cart – a lovely though long (about two hours) way to travel the 9km from town. If you've got your own wheels (a motorcycle or 4WD vehicle; 2WD won't cut it, unless there's a new road), just drive 9km down the beach until you come to the cabins. Drive on the wet sand beside dying waves, because it's easy to spin your wheels in dry sand and get stuck.

Beware that there is a shallow river that cannot be forged when the tide is high. The owners can tell you when that is if you want to drive out. Another option is to park your vehicle in town, locked up and completely empty, and then come in on the cart. That's not a bad idea at all. If you'd like to rent a horse for exploring, that can be easily arranged.

Two hundred meters east of Campola Concha is *Punta El Rey Beach Club* (☎ 809-223-8367), a place that's very similar, only not quite as nice. There are a lot of sand flies in the area and El Rey's owner, a very amusing character named Leo Leu, hasn't been as liberal with mosquito netting as he could be. At times their biting can get fierce. But the owner, a big guy with a big bushy beard, can be so engaging (and he's always got bug spray at hand) that he gets a lot of repeat visitors.

A typical day at El Rey begins with a delicious breakfast and a hearty chat with Leo, a horseback ride, perhaps followed by a walk to a lagoon where Leo keeps a small boat you can use to explore the thick mangroves there. Upon returning, you could lie on the beach or go swimming or snorkeling (there's a coral reef fairly close to shore), or you could walk east 2km to a fantastic body-surfing beach.

If you enjoy music, you'll get along well with the owner; he's got a good sound system and lots of, well, everything. Tell him what you're in the mood for, and chances are he'll have it. He's also got a pool table. If you want to score some points with Leo, show up with a few good cigars for him. You'll be glad you did. Rates, by the way, are US$25/40 and include breakfast and dinner.

Leo's Land Rover was dying a slow, rusty, rattling death in late 1998, but he'll figure out how to get you out to his place if you give him some warning and arrive in Miches by bus. One option, though kind of expensive at US$10 each way, is to hire a moto-concho in town to take you to his place. There are many motoconchos just on the other side of the bridge; all their drivers know Leo and most know how to get to El Rey. If you don't speak Spanish, just say 'Leo' (LEE-oh) several times and make like you're stroking a thick, invisible beard. Then point toward the mouth of the bay. That'll usually do the trick for you.

Getting There & Away

There are two bus stops in Miches. One is on the west side of the bridge that crosses the Río Yaguada. This is where you would catch a bus bound for Higüey. The fare is US$2.50, and a bus departs every 45 minutes or so from 5 am to 5:30 pm daily.

On the same main road that crosses the bridge, but at the other end of town, you'll find minivans that make the trip across a mountain range to the agricultural town of El Seibo. They depart hourly from 7 am to 4 pm. The cost is US$2. Be advised that the often-ridgeline road between Miches and El Seibo is terribly bumpy for at least half of the 44km. However, the views of the coast from the mountains are stunning. If you're on a motorcycle or driving a 4WD vehicle, this route makes for a very scenic road trip.

EL SEIBO & HATO MAYOR

During the early 19th century, French soldiers ruled Santo Domingo and most of the present-day Dominican Republic. However, a much larger Haitian force – led by a former slave and anxious to unite the entire island under Haiti's flag – overran one city after another in central and eastern Hispaniola, in most instances slaughtering the French and Spanish colonists they came across.

After having attacked and burned Monte Plata, Cotuí and La Vega, for example, the Haitians arrived in Moca, where they killed the entire population and burned the town to the ground. The same was done in Santiago, where more than 400 people were massacred. Aside from Santo Domingo, only the towns of El Seibo, Bayaguana and Higüey remained standing by 1806. All the rest were deserted and would remain so for many years.

At the time, El Seibo was a cattle-raising and agricultural center. Today the same can be said about it, and Hato Mayor, 24km to the west, could be its smaller twin. Typical Dominican cities, each is the capital of a province where most workers still earn their living toiling in fields or tending to cattle.

There's little for the tourist in either place, and their only hotels (which are on the road that bisects both cities) are quite unappealing.

The highway to El Seibo becomes its main road and slices through the city. To leave the city, simply hail a gua-gua traveling in the direction you want to go. There is frequent service to Hato Mayor, the next major stop to the west, and to Higüey, the next major stop to the east.

In Hato Mayor, the highway likewise bisects the city, slowing considerably in the process. Just stay on the road if you're continuing west toward Monte Plata or east toward El Seibo. But if you're heading to Sabana de la Mar, presumably to catch the ferry to Samaná on the north shore of the Bahía de Samaná, then you'll want to turn north at the well-marked road. If you're on a gua-gua and it's continuing west, be sure to tell the driver to let you out at the turnoff. If you don't speak Spanish, simply keep an eye out for the Sabana de la Mar turnoff sign, and when you see it, go to the door and tell the driver, '*Alto, por favor*' (Stop, please).

From the turnoff, walk a couple of blocks or so north until you come to a corner gas station on the east side of the road. Alongside the gas station, on the side street, you'll see a bus that goes to Sabana de la Mar. It leaves when it's full, usually about every 20 minutes or so. The cost is US$1.

SABANA DE LA MAR

This town is quite unappealing for a variety of reasons, and one would never recommend its hotels to a friend. Tourists only pass through this town of several thousand people as they head to or from Samaná.

To reach the boat that ferries people to Samaná, simply go to the pier at the north end of town. Near the entrance to the rickety old pier there's a ticket booth, where one-way tickets cost US$2.50.

If you're taking a motorcycle across, beware that the ticketing agent will try to charge you whatever he thinks he can get. The first price he mentions is usually US$50; it's very negotiable. Aim for US$20. If you're on a bicycle, you can usually bring the price down to around US$3. Also be advised not to take motorcycles larger than 125cc. They all have to be lowered by hand from the pier to a small boat, then hoisted up by hand onto the ferry. In other words, the heavier the bike, the greater the likelihood it'll be dropped in the bay. The reason for the shuttle via the little boat to the bigger one is that the water beside the pier is too shallow for the ferry.

Be prepared to pay the three or four men who lift your motorcycle 15 or 20 pesos apiece. Getting the motorcycle on and off the ferry at Samará is a relatively simple process.

The ferry leaves twice daily from each side of the bay. The departure times from Samaná are 9 am and 3 pm. The departure times from Sabana de la Mar are 11 am and 5 pm.

PARQUE NACIONAL LOS HAÏTISES

Just west of Sabana de la Mar is this 208-sq-km park at the throat of Bahía de Samaná. The park contains scores of lush hills that jut out of the ocean and make for excellent exploration by boat. It's believed that the knolls, which consist mostly of marine deposits such as coral, were forced up from the ocean floor about 40 million years ago as one tectonic plate collided with another.

The park receives a tremendous amount of rainfall, which encourages subtropical humid forest plants such as bamboo, ferns and bromeliads to thrive on the knolls. As you head into the park from the bay, you'll first pass through dense mangrove that gives most people a creepy feeling, like they're being watched by a swamp creature or some such beast.

Eventually the mangrove and the waterways fade and you're into an area of rolling hills, 200m to 300m in height. The hills are separated by small valleys packed with vegetation – and mosquitoes. Also in the area are some caves.

The park contains very few mammals (all rodents), but it does contain some lovely birds. Commonly seen species include the brown pelican, the American frigate bird, the little blue heron, the roseate tern and the northern jacana. Less commonly seen is the Hispaniolan parakeet, which is light green except for a splash of red about the upper wing.

At the time of this writing, the only people offering boat tours of the park were in Samaná. See the Northeastern Dominican Republic chapter for details.

Northeastern Dominican Republic

Like the southeast, the northeast has all-inclusive resorts, natural attractions and local communities where people live much the way they have for generations. But unlike in the southeast, the northeast's tourist haunts are also actual towns. And that makes a big difference.

The southeast has plenty of resorts that you're free to enjoy – as long as you're one of their guests. But it hasn't got places like Sosúa, Cabarete, Las Terrenas, Las Galeras and Samaná, where visitors and locals are free to roam from one restaurant to another, one beach to another, one bar to another without any irksome security guards scrutinizing them for hotel-issued identification bracelets and treating the unadorned like criminals.

The northeast offers the best of two worlds: one of restaurants, hotels and tour operators that cater to visitors, and the other of local communities with their unique personalities and charms. These are the same communities where Dominicans from big cities spend their vacations. Here the foreign visitor has the added attraction of watching Dominicans at play.

The towns of the northeast are surrounded by some lovely countryside as well. Most of the towns of interest to tourists are beside the ocean and are linked by a well-paved highway that follows the contours of the coast. Inland, the enormously fertile Valle del Cibao (Cibao Valley) – a vast triangular area that has as its points the cities of La Vega, Santiago and Moca – has little of interest to the tourist except a few quiet farming communities nestled in the picturesque mountains.

Historically, the region has many tales to tell. At various times during the early colonial days, hidden coves and lagoons around the heavily forested Península de Samaná were popular with pirates, who used them to launch attacks, initially against Spanish galleons traveling between the New World and the Old, and later against cargo ships

plying the trade routes between North and South America.

Bahía de Samaná (Samaná Bay) is a veritable graveyard of ships, some ripped apart by horrendous storms, others plundered and scuttled by pirates. On one occasion the notorious pirate Roberto Cofresí sank his own ship near the throat of the bay when he found himself cornered by Spanish patrol boats. Cofresí and his crew are said to have escaped the advancing Spaniards by boarding small skiffs and rowing their way into the area's maze of marshes.

Cofresí's ship went down off Punta Gorda laden with treasure, but to this day the vessel has never been found.

Two other famous sunken ships in Bahía Samaná – the Spanish galleons *Nuestra Señora de Guadalupe* and *El Conde de Tolosa* – remained untouched for more than 250 years until they were discovered in 1976 and 1977, respectively. Both ships were en route to Mexico from Spain loaded with mercury when hurricane-whipped waves forced them into coral reefs, where they broke apart and sank within hours of each other. More than 600 people hoping to start new lives in the New World went down with the ships.

Over the centuries many thousands of people from various countries have arrived in the northeast to pursue their dreams or to escape persecution. Among them was a group of runaway American slaves, shipped to Samaná in the 1820s by two sympathetic white women from Philadelphia. Their descendants – with the last names of Williams, Green and Jones – still live in town. During the late 1930s, at the start of the Holocaust, several hundred Jewish families left Germany and Austria and resettled in Sosúa.

Today, the region continues to attract refugees – mainly the kind seeking a temporary escape from frosty climates, the normal pressures of everyday life back home, or both. For these folks, the northeast offers up sunny days, gorgeous beaches, warm-hearted

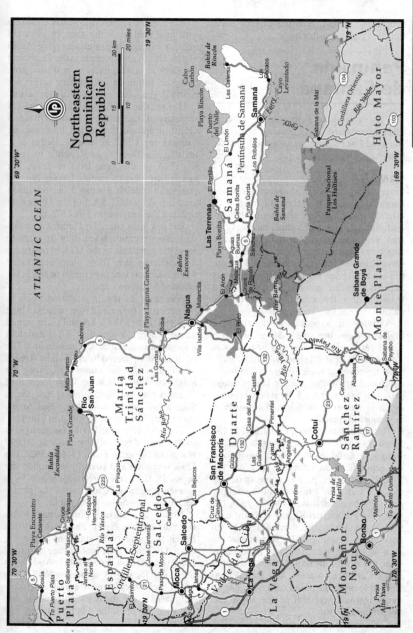

Northeastern Dominican Republic

DOMINICAN REPUBLIC

people and enough activities to keep even the most restless visitor busy.

Península de Samaná

The lushly forested Península de Samaná extends eastward from the coast at Parque Nacional Los Haïtises, creating the Bahía de Samaná to the south.

SAMANÁ

Situated on the north shore of Bahía de Samaná, Samaná is a tranquil town with brightly colored houses clinging to the surrounding hillsides and a small business district near the water. Virtually all of the structures face south – toward the bay and Cayos Linares and Vigia, two islets opposite the town. The sea smells surprisingly sweet here, as does the breeze that comes down from the hills. Tropical plants and majestic palms thrive among the houses.

Arriving at Samaná's dock, across a highway from the small downtown, you might get the impression that Samaná was just another sleepy fishing village beneath swaying coconut trees before it gradually developed into what it is today. The old adage 'You can't judge a book by its cover' once again proves true, as Samaná's history is anything but typical.

The town dates from the 1750s, when the Spanish relocated families from the Canary Islands here and to other new towns around the republic in an effort to keep out the French and other pesky expansionists. In fact, the Canarios' presence did nothing to deter rival colonialists. Over the next 100 years, the French, British and Haitians each took Samaná from the Spanish. The French needed the resources. The British saw the area as having great strategic importance, since it was within striking distance of other major Caribbean islands. And the Haitians wanted to unite the island under one flag. In every instance, control of the town was determined by war.

But it was the USA that nearly ended up with final control of the area. In 1850, US military officials began encouraging Washington, DC, to acquire a site in the Caribbean on which to build a naval base. Washington, however, refrained from taking action for nearly 20 years, fearing European opposition.

However, in 1869 Hamilton Fish, the US secretary of state under President Ulysses S Grant, proposed buying the Península de Samaná for US\$2 million or, better still, inviting the Dominican Republic to enter the USA on the same basis as Texas. For nearly two years thereafter, Dominican and American officials discussed the republic's annexation by the USA, but the US Senate rejected the proposal in July 1871.

Just one year later, the Dominican president, Buenaventura Báez, drew up plans to lease the peninsula to the USA in return for its support of him. Those plans were foiled when Báez was forced to resign or risk being arrested by his own army.

American interest in acquiring rights to the peninsula for a naval base remained high until 1903, when the USA and Cuba signed an agreement allowing the USA to maintain a naval base at Bahía de Guantánamo. The peninsula disappeared from US radar screens for the next 13 years – until 1916, during the height of WWI, when the USA learned of German plans to build a naval base there. Such a base would have threatened America's ability to resupply its forces in Europe.

The USA responded to the German plans swiftly and decisively by sending 20,000 troops to the area. From 1916 to 1924, the USA occupied and virtually controlled the republic. If later efforts were made by a foreign government to control the peninsula, they were never made public.

No longer a strategic port, Samaná today is simply a docile seaside town with only one beach to speak of (a small, not-so-lovely stretch of sand at the foot of the steep road leading to Bahía Escondido). And that's about it in the way of attractions. Well, that's not entirely true; there *are* a couple of pleasant places to eat and drink, from where one can gaze out upon the picturesque bay and

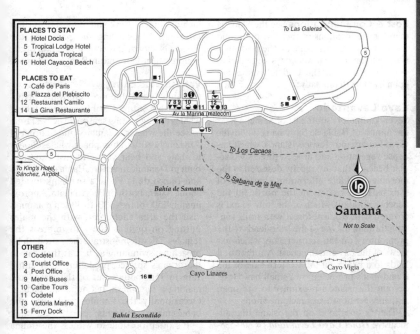

PLACES TO STAY
1 Hotel Docia
5 Tropical Lodge Hotel
6 L'Aguada Tropical
16 Hotel Cayacoa Beach

PLACES TO EAT
7 Café de Paris
8 Piazza del Plebiscito
12 Restaurant Camilo
14 La Gina Restaurante

OTHER
2 Codetel
3 Tourist Office
4 Post Office
9 Metro Buses
10 Caribe Tours
11 Codetel
13 Victoria Marine
15 Ferry Dock

To Las Galeras

Av la Marina (malecón)

To Los Cacaos

To Sabana de la Mar

Bahía de Samaná

Samaná

Not to Scale

Cayo Vigia

Cayo Linares

To King's Hotel,
Sánchez, Airport

Bahía Escondido

imagine the pirate Cofresí sailing off to plunder a treasure-packed galleon.

Orientation
Proceeding north from the dock (as you arrive from the Sabana de la Mar ferry, as most travelers do), the first thing you come to is a wide street.

Simply cross the street to reach the tiny business district: a row of small businesses runs parallel to the water and a divided street runs north. To reach the tourist office, head north on the left side of the divided road until you reach an ugly, concrete government building; the tourist office is on the ground floor. The post office is directly east of the tourist office, on the other side of the wide street divider.

With the exception of the Hotel Cayacoa Beach, which is on a bluff across from the smaller of two islands in the bay, all of the places of interest to the visitor – hotels, restaurants, Codetel offices, bus stations, tour operators, the tourist office, post office and ferry dock – are centrally located and within easy walking distance from one another.

The main road running along the water is Av la Marina, which is more commonly called 'the malecón,' but in general, street addresses are not used. If you turn right onto this street and keep on it for the next 24km, you reach the lovely seaside community of Las Galeras. If you turn left and keep on the road for 34km, you arrive in the dirty port town of Sánchez.

Information
Tourist Offices The tourist office is open 8 am to 4 pm weekdays. Sometimes there is someone on duty who speaks English. There is no literature at the office, but occasionally a simple map of the town is available.

Money There are no banks in Samaná. Be sure to bring enough cash with you, as credit cards are not widely accepted here.

Post & Communications See the Samaná map for the locations of the post office and the town's two Codetel offices. The post office is open 8 am to 5 pm weekdays and 9 am to noon on Saturday. The Codetel offices are open 8 am to 10 pm daily.

Cayo Levantado

Seven kilometers southeast of Samaná near the mouth of Bahía de Samaná is the idyllic Cayo Levantado (Raised Island), which has dense vegetation and at least three spectacular beaches that are mostly deserted in the mornings and late afternoons (busloads of tourists from resorts in the north fill the beaches midday). Much of the hilly island is covered with tropical forest with trails running through it. One of the trails leads to the promontory on the southern tip, which has views of the bay and the coast. Another trail leads to a beach on the western side of the island that's protected by a small bay. Here, despite the island's proximity to the open sea, only gentle waves reach the shore.

There's one hotel on the island, the all-inclusive *Hotel Cayo Levantado* (☎ 809-538-3141), which offers 13 very comfortable rooms and 31 cabins, a swimming pool and a restaurant. Rates are US$46 per person per night, higher during the whale-watching season (for details, see Whale Watching, below). Not surprisingly, the hotel's restaurant specializes in seafood, and it's open to both guests and nonguests. The only other food available on the island at the time of writing was sold at stands on the north side. However, a large hotel was under construction, and presumably it, too, will have a restaurant.

Both the Hotel Cayo Levantado and Victoria Marine (see Whale Watching, below) can arrange year-round transportation to and from the island for about US$20 one way.

Parque Nacional Los Haïtises

This national park, with its scores of tiny, jungly islands and thick mangrove forests, makes for great exploring by boat. Victoria Marine (see Whale Watching, below) offers a boat tour of the park every Thursday from 9 am to 4 pm. The cost of US$35 per person includes lunch, drink and guide. For further information regarding the park, see the Parque Nacional Los Haïtises section of the Southeastern Dominican Republic chapter.

Whale Watching

Certainly one of the most enjoyable activities in the entire Caribbean is watching whales during mating season. (The best time to see the whales is January and February.) Amazingly, 80% of humpback whales choose to mate and bear young at just two sites, both in Dominican waters: Bahía de Samaná and Banco de la Plata, a sea bank located about 100km north of Puerto Plata. Approximately 1500 of these 30- to 40-ton mammals visit the area each year, with the males putting on quite a show to impress the females. They demonstrate their strength by breaching: swimming as fast as they can to the ocean's surface, propelling their entire 12m to 15m bodies out of the water and making a *big* splash. It's quite spectacular. Occasionally the females and even the babies take short flights.

It's often possible to witness the drama from shore using powerful binoculars, but for extreme fun you should make plans to observe the whales' singles club, as it were, in a boat. During whale-watching season it's possible to find captains near Samaná's dock who'll take you for the ride of your life for US$25 to US$40. However, some of these captains do not abide by local regulations intended to prevent observers from spooking the whales and scaring them off. Of course, these same regulations are intended to keep observers out of harm's way; none of the boats used for whale watching would survive a direct hit by an animal the size of a North Korean spy submarine.

For these reasons and others, you'd be better off employing the services of Victoria Marine (☎ 809-538-2588, ☎/fax 538-2494), PO Box 53-2, which has its office on the malecón, Samaná's main street. The company is owned and operated by Canadian marine biologist Kim Beddall, who can tell you more than you'll ever need to know about humpbacks. Also, her tour operators religiously

Salvaging Sunken Galleons

During the Spaniards' colonization of the New World in the 16th, 17th and 18th centuries, galleons left Spain carrying goods to the colonies and returned loaded with gold and silver mined in Colombia, Peru and Mexico. Many of these ships sank in the Caribbean Sea, overcome by pirates or hurricanes. During these years literally thousands of ships – not only Spanish but also English, French, Dutch, pirate and African slave ships – foundered in the green-blue waters of the Caribbean.

The frequency of shipwrecks spurred the Spaniards to organize operations to recover sunken cargo. By the 17th century, Spain maintained salvage flotillas in the ports of Portobelo, Panama; Havana, Cuba; and Veracruz, Mexico. These fleets awaited news of shipwrecks and then proceeded immediately to the wreck sites, where Caribbean and Bahamian divers – and later African slaves – were employed to scour sunken vessels and the sea floor around them. On many occasions great storms wiped out entire fleets, resulting in a tremendous loss of lives and cargo.

As early as the 1620s, salvagers were using bronze diving bells to increase the time they could spend underwater. The bell was submerged vertically from a ship and held air in its upper part. Divers would enter it to breathe, rest and observe. Over time, such divers became very skilled and the salvaging business became very lucrative. So lucrative that the English, who were established in Bermuda and the Bahamas, entered the Caribbean salvage business at the end of the 17th century. And pirates, as you'd expect, were always pleased to come upon a salvage operation.

In recent decades, advances in diving and underwater-recovery equipment have led to a boom in Caribbean salvaging efforts. In most cases salvagers get to keep a portion of the treasure they recover, but the larger share is turned over to the government in whose waters the recovery took place. Among the items most frequently raised from the depths are silver coins minted in Spain and brought to the New World. Such coins are occasionally sold in jewelry stores in Santo Domingo; the real deal will be accompanied by government papers of authenticity.

---

observe the local boat-to-whale distance regulations. Tours leave at 9 am daily and return at 11 am. Cost is US$30 per person. You also have the option of spending the afternoon at Cayo Levantado for an extra US$10.

Places to Stay

Budget The best value for the money in Samaná is *L'Aguada Tropical* (☎ 809-538-2440, fax 538-2541), beside the Tropical

Lodge Hotel but 75m from the main road, on the east side of town. Built in 1997, this two-story hotel has spacious air-conditioned rooms with private hot-water bathroom for US$23/28 for singles/doubles. A superfriendly family owns and operates the hotel and lives on the premises; they will do laundry for a small fee as long as your clothes are not covered with mud or sand (which could damage their washing machine), and if you need to use a phone and the Codetel office is closed, they'll gladly let you use theirs so long as you pay for the call. If it's an international call, you'd best call your party and request a return call.

The *Tropical Lodge Hotel* (☎ 809-538-2840) has a European ambiance and a pleasant restaurant, but its longtime owner has a reputation for being smug. The establishment itself is quite nice and a good value, with air-conditioned rooms with private bathroom for US$26/30. Expect the rates to be higher during the whale-watching months.

Foreigners arriving by ferry are often approached by 'guides' who offer to show you the best hotel bargains in town, and then walk you directly to a friend's hotel or a hotel belonging to a member of their immediate family. These suspect places should be avoided if at all possible. One of them is the *Hotel Docia* (☎ 809-538-2041), which has the look and feel of a prison-cell block and, appropriately, does not have hot water or air conditioning. Still, the hotel seems to be quite popular – with mosquitoes. The rate is US$16/20.

Another place these 'guides' often like to march budget travelers to is the *King's Hotel* (☎ 809-538-2352), which is on the road to Sánchez (just beyond the western border of the Samaná map). The large sign out front tends to attract lots of travelers, but the King's rooms are dumpy and mildewy, and most are reachable only by a hazardous flight of outside stairs. For what you get, the US$20 per-room rate is too steep.

Top End Five hundred meters or so from the dock, on a bluff overlooking downtown and the bay, is the all-inclusive *Hotel Cayacoa Beach* (☎ 809-538-3111, fax 538-2985), which features 82 air-conditioned rooms, a number of cabins, a swimming pool and a restaurant. The hotel even has its own beach, although it's a bit of a walk to get to. At US$50 per person (more during whale-watching season), it's a good deal.

Places to Eat & Drink

All of the restaurants mentioned here are located on the four-lane road that passes through town. Of these establishments, the best is the *Restaurant Camilo*, which serves tasty food and has a prime location overlooking the bay. This is a casual-but-classy place, with cloth tablecloths, plenty of ceiling fans, comfortable chairs and a professional staff. From here you can watch all of the activity at the dock, just across the way. The menu includes a variety of salads, four varieties of spaghetti (US$3 to US$4), 11 red-meat dishes (US$6 to US$10), chicken dishes (around US$5) and seafood and fish (US$5 to US$9). This is also a fine place to sip a cocktail.

Also quite popular is the *Café de Paris*, whose many stools ringing a central bar make it feel more like a place to drink than to eat. Menu items include pancakes (US$2), pizzas (US$4/6.50) and *ensalada niçoise* (US$3.50). Ice cream and crêpes are also available. The drink selection includes piña coladas (US$2), rum punch (US$2), margaritas (US$2.75) and wine by the bottle (US$10).

A short distance from the café you'll find the *Piazza del Plebiscito*, a simple sit-down place with a pleasant ambiance where sandwiches sell for about US$2.50 to US$4 and a cheeseburger and fries will set you back about US$4.

At waterside opposite the Café de Paris is the often-overlooked *La Gina Restaurante*, a casual, open-sided bar/restaurant that catches a refreshing breeze direct from the sea. It's the hangout for resident gringos. The menu includes breakfast and sandwiches from US$2 to US$4, seafood for US$8 to US$13, and spaghetti for around US$4 (the Italian owner makes a lovely sauce). The seafood, which is the house specialty, is also quite good.

Getting There & Away

There are two bus stations in town, both on the main street. Caribe Tours offers bus service to Samaná from Santo Domingo four times daily, at 7:15 and 9 am and 1:30 and 3:45 pm; the cost for the 245km journey is US$5. Departing Samaná for the capital are buses leaving at 7 and 9 am and 2 and 4:30 pm (US$5). Caribe Tours also serves Cotuí from Samaná (one bus daily; 3:30 pm; US$3.50), as well as Puerto Plata (one bus daily; 4 pm; US$5).

Metro Buses offers service to and from Santo Domingo and Samaná. From Santo Domingo, buses leave at 7 am and 2:30 pm; the cost is US$5.25. From Samaná, buses leave at 8 am and 3:30 pm (US$5.25). Before reaching Santo Domingo, the bus makes stops at Sánchez (US$3.50), at Nagua (US$3.50), at Castillo (US$4) and at San Francisco de Macorís (US$4).

Additionally, many gua-guas pass through Samaná on their way between Sánchez and Las Galeras. You can hail them on the main street; for about US$1 a gua-gua will take you to either community or to any point in between.

Getting Around
Samaná is easily walked. However, there are taxis and *motoconchos* in town, usually near the dock and out in front of the Café de Paris.

LAS GALERAS
Before 1990, there were only two simple hotels in this fishing community with zillions of swaying palms and a sweeping beach at the throat of Bahía de Rincón (Rincón Bay), 24km northeast of Samaná. Today there are five hotels, most quite comfortable. The choice of hotel here is more important than elsewhere due to the fact that, except for sunbathing, bodysurfing and horseback riding, there is very little to do in Las Galeras.

Most people come here to relax, in their hotels and at the beach. However, the still-jungly area lends itself superbly to exploring on horseback. For example, the fabulous and secluded Playa Rincón, about 8km to the west, can be reached only by horse trail. Of course, you might be able to get a fisherman to drop you there for about US$25, and then hike back along the horse trail.

Orientation
The road coming from Samaná winds through lovely, often-forested countryside before reaching the outskirts of Las Galeras. Then, within a distance of only a couple of kilometers, homes appear on both sides of the road, then the Hotel Villa Marina, then a simple store or two, then the Paradiso Bun-

galows, and then the paved road ends at the beach. However, from here a dirt road continues for another 250m, gently winding to the east along the shore. The road passes the Club Bonito Hotel and the Todo Blanco, adjacent hotels under the same ownership. The dirt road ends at the Casa Marina Samaná Beach Resort.

Information
There's no tourist office, bank, post office or Codetel office in town, although there are some pay phones beside the main road.

Places to Stay
Camping Although camping in the Dominican Republic is not generally recommended for reasons mentioned in the Facts for the Visitor chapter, the secluded Playa Rincón would be a good place to pitch a tent. You can either hike in, go in by horseback using horses hired in Las Galeras or arrive by boat. If you speak some Spanish, consider making an arrangement with a fisherman to be left at the beach for US$20 and picked up two or three days later for US$30 (the higher amount on your return increases the likelihood that the fisherman will remember you). Because there are no facilities, bring in whatever you think you'd need, including fresh water.

Budget Less than 100m from the beach, *Paradiso Bungalows* (π/fax 809-538-0210) consists of a half-dozen or so cabins, all quite comfortable and all with air conditioning. At US$18/23/28 for a single/double/triple, they are a great value. The prices also make them quite popular; be sure to call or fax ahead. Only Spanish is spoken. If you send a fax in English, keep it very simple: 'My name is (name). I am in (city and country). I need (number) cabins for (dates). My fax number is (number, beginning with country code if you're not calling from the USA or Canada).' You needn't ask the cost, as it will be included in the confirmation, and the more complicated the fax, the greater the likelihood of it being unanswered.

Another great value in town, but located about 500m away from the beach, is the

Hotel Villa Marina (☎ 809-538-0003), which offers seven rooms in one large, attractive two-story structure, and four cabins. The per-person price of US$20, for either a room or a cabin, includes breakfast.

Top End The *Todo Blanco* and the *Club Bonito Hotel* share a reception area and are owned and run by the same European family *(for either hotel, call ☎ 809-538-0203, ☎/fax 696-0082, fax 538-0204)*. The guest rooms of both hotels are decorated in a Southwestern American style. While all are spacious and lovely, only the rooms at the Todo Blanco have balconies with ocean views. There are several very pleasant sitting areas at these hotels as well as a charming Japanese-style fish pond, but there is no swimming pool (to the disappointment of some guests). If you prefer an intimate atmosphere and wonderful personal service over the more lively atmosphere and poor service of, say, the all-inclusive resort just down the road, either of these hotels is an excellent choice. Rates, which include breakfast, range from US$50/60 to US$60/90, depending on the time of year and whether you want air conditioning.

The Dominican-run all-inclusive *Casa Marina Samaná Beach Resort* (☎ 809-682-7609, fax 687-3603) is in a large, parklike setting and is popular with packaged tours. However, its 62 rooms (with 148 more under construction) are in unappealing rows, and service is horrible. At US$60, it's not a bad deal if your main concern is access to a nice beach and swimming pools. Still, even at only 62 rooms, guests can't help but feel they're just a number – there is a sense that the resort's owner is just trying to 'pack them in.'

Places to Eat
If you're on a tight budget – or even if you're not – definitely check out the food stands where the paved road meets the beach. The stands are nothing fancy – a few grills and some tables under tarps strung from palm trees – but the fish and lobster that are offered are caught fresh daily and are delicious and cheap. This is a good place to mingle with the friendly locals in a setting

that is pure Caribbean. In some ways, this is the Dominican Republic at its best.

The *Club Bonito Hotel/Todo Blanco* has a wonderful restaurant that is open to nonguests, though many tourists don't realize it, as the term 'club' leads them to think it's a members-only kind of place. For about US$18 they will serve nonguests a wonderful European dinner. Since the restaurant staff isn't accustomed to preparing meals for nonguests, it's a good idea to stop by the reception desk early in the day and let them know you'd like to return for dinner. You'll be glad you did when the food arrives.

There were also two more restaurants under construction at the time this was penned in late 1998.

Getting There & Away
Gua-guas run between Las Galeras and Samaná all day long. The cost is US$1. Occasionally there are taxis and motoconchos to be found in town as well.

LAS TERRENAS
In 1988 Las Terrenas consisted of nothing more than a very rustic fishing village with one European-owned hotel and several food stands. From a visitor's perspective, it didn't offer much. Then another European moved in and opened a second hotel. Then yet another European arrived and opened still another hotel. Then another and another, until today Las Terrenas has no fewer than 16 hotels and many restaurants, nearly all owned by German, Italian or French entrepreneurs, who considered many Caribbean sites before settling on the still-pleasant Las Terrenas.

For the most part, Las Terrenas has managed to keep its fishing-village feel. Unlike many other resort areas in the DR, this town contains a healthy mix of tourist haunts and local homes and shops. It has a pretty stretch of beach, plenty of hotels and restaurants to choose from, and for the visitor, a sense of inclusion with, instead of exclusion from, the local culture. This is not a strictly tourist development like Punta Cana, where tourists are intentionally kept separate. And Las Terrenas is within easy

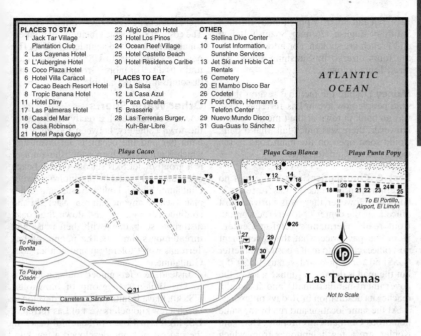

PLACES TO STAY	22	Aligio Beach Hotel	OTHER
1 Jack Tar Village	23	Hotel Los Pinos	4 Stellina Dive Center
Plantation Club	24	Ocean Reef Village	10 Tourist Information,
2 Las Cayenas Hotel	25	Hotel Castello Beach	Sunshine Services
3 L'Aubergine Hotel	30	Hotel Residence Caribe	13 Jet Ski and Hobie Cat
5 Coco Plaza Hotel			Rentals
6 Hotel Villa Caracol	**PLACES TO EAT**		16 Cemetery
7 Cacao Beach Resort Hotel	9	La Salsa	20 El Mambo Disco Bar
8 Tropic Banana Hotel	12	La Casa Azul	26 Codetel
11 Hotel Diny	14	Paca Cabaña	27 Post Office, Hermann's
17 Las Palmeras Hotel	15	Brasserie	Telefon Center
18 Casa del Mar	28	Las Terrenas Burger,	29 Nuevo Mundo Disco
19 Casa Robinson		Kuh-Bar-Libre	31 Gua-Guas to Sánchez
21 Hotel Papa Gayo			

Playa Cacao

ATLANTIC OCEAN

Playa Casa Blanca   Playa Punta Popy

To El Portillo,
Airport, El Limón

To Playa
Bonita

To Playa
Cosón

Carretera a Sánchez

To Sánchez

Las Terrenas

Not to Scale

striking distance of Cabarete, Sosúa and other destinations popular with foreign as well as Dominican vacationers.

Orientation

A well-paved coastal road, known locally as the Carretera a Sánchez (the highway to Sánchez), approaches Las Terrenas from the west, ending at the beach. From the road's eastern terminus, in front of Las Palmeras Hotel, a dirt road proceeds to the east, linking Las Terrenas with the community of El Portillo and the airport there. The badly rutted road continues on to the hamlet of El Limón, near which are some fine waterfalls, and then proceeds over a mountain range and continues to Samaná.

At the time of writing, an effort was being made to pave the entire stretch of dirt road from Las Terrenas to Samaná, but extensive road damage caused by Hurricane Georges in other parts of the country has slowed the work, which was to be completed in mid-1999.

From the paved road, there are two major crossroads: one heads off to Playa Bonita, several kilometers away, and one runs parallel to Playa Cacao. Both roads are unpaved.

As a glance at the map indicates, nearly all the hotels and restaurants in Las Terrenas are near the ocean. Of the area's four beaches, Playas Cacao and Bonita are somewhat prettier than Playas Casa Blanca and Punta Popy. That's because staff at the hotels near Playas Cacao and Bonita frequently comb their beaches for litter, while the staff at the hotels near Playas Casa Blanca and Punta Popy don't.

Information

Tourist Offices There is no government tourist office in town. However, near the center of things is the office of Sunshine Services, a tour operator that generously dispenses good information just for the asking. Look for the large 'Tourist Information' sign posted out front. Sunshine is open 9 am to

12:30 pm and 3:30 to 7 pm Monday through Saturday. English, German, Spanish, Italian and French are spoken. For information on the tours offered by Sunshine, see Organized Tours, below.

Money Despite the fact that several thousand people now live in Las Terrenas, there was no bank in town at the time of writing. However, there was much talk that a bank would soon open on the main road in the vicinity of the Codetel office.

Post & Communications There was no government post office in Las Terrenas in late 1998. However, there was a private post office near the center of town. The sign out front reads 'Hermann's Telefon Center.' Here you pay twice what the government post offices charge to mail a postcard or letter (US$1.50 for a postcard versus US$0.75), but the mail is delivered (unlike a lot of the government-handled mail) and it usually reaches its destination in 10 days or less.

At the same location and run by the same humorous German entrepreneur, Hermann Kobler, are a few telephones from which you can place international calls for considerably less than you'd pay at a Codetel office. How this can be is a great mystery, but so it is. Hermann's is open 9 am to 1 pm and 2 to 6 pm daily. English, Spanish, German and Italian are spoken.

There is a Codetel office with Internet services on the main road 100m or so from the beach. It is open 8 am to 10 pm daily.

Diving
Across a sandy, unpaved street from Playa Cacao is Stellina Dive Center (☎ 809-240-6000, fax 240-6149), which offers dive training and a variety of specialty courses in English, Dutch, German, Italian, Spanish and French. The cost to receive a PADI Open-Water Certificate is a reasonable US$340 and includes all instruction materials and dives. Four to five days are required to complete the instruction. Couple and group rates are available.

Wall and night dives are offered to all certified divers, and cavern dives are offered to those possessing a PADI Cavern Diver card. The cost per dive, which includes all nonpersonal gear, a boat and a guide, is US$35. The per-dive cost drops to US$30 if you decide to do 10 dives or more. Group and monthly discounts are also available.

Other Water Sports
Located on the beach directly northwest of the town cemetery, between the Paca Cabaña bar and the ocean, is Jet Aventura, which is not so much an establishment as it is a group of Jet Skis set out on the beach every day and available for rent from owner Guillaume Serve. Unlike Sosúa and other places where anyone can rent a Jet Ski and continuously race up and down the coast, disturbing sunbathers with their noise and threatening swimmers, the people of Las Terrenas won't tolerate it and neither does Guillaume.

Instead, he offers guided tours on Jet Skis to Las Ballenas (a group of blowholes; US$30), Playa Bonita (a beautiful developed beach a few kilometers west of Las Terrenas; US$40), Playa Cosón (a beautiful beach in the process of being developed a few kilometers west of Playa Bonita; US$50) and Playa Jackson (least developed of all of the area's beautiful beaches; US$60). You and your guide can ride on one Jet Ski or each have your own; it's up to you. Jet Skis are a lot of fun, even if you are racing their engines and bouncing off waves, and exploring the coast on a Jet Ski is definitely exhilarating.

A few meters from Jet Aventura is another officeless water-sports business, one that rents windsurfing equipment (US$7 per hour), surfboards (US$10 per half day), boogie boards (US$7 per half day) and Hobie Cats (as in catamarans) for US$21 per hour. Also available here are one-day guided excursions via Hobie Cats to beautiful secluded beaches (US$55 per person, three-person minimum). Not adventurous enough? Yet another option is a two-day excursion to oceanside caves, blowholes, and a place where you can see giant bullfrogs! The price of this tour, with tents and meals included, is a very reasonable US$80 per person (four-person minimum).

Organized Tours

The friendly folks at Sunshine Services (☎/fax 809-240-6164) work with all of the tour providers in the northeast and offer their many excursions to you from their office in Las Terrenas. Among the more popular excursions are the following: a jeep ride to Cascada El Limón, the waterfalls near El Limón, with the final 4km of the journey on horseback (US$40); a river adventure for US$55 that also promises visits to a mangrove forest and a boat ride across Bahía de Samaná as well as a swim in a freshwater lagoon; and a jeep safari to a beach, a waterfall and a small rubber plantation where you can learn how gum is processed (US$65). Sunshine also rents motorcycles (US$19 a day) and cars (US$50) so you can do your own touring. The motorcycles are Yamaha 125cc DTs, the best motorbikes for the choppy Dominican roads.

Places to Stay

Budget There are eight hotels in Las Terrenas with rooms for US$30 or less, and most of them are a good deal given their proximity to the ocean and the appeal of the town. All are along the beach except for Hotel Residence Caribe.

The French-owned, eight-room *Casa del Mar* (no phone) is a super value at US$18 per room. The rooms are very spacious, clean and charming, and they are surprisingly cool despite having no shade and only ceiling fans. No doubt the tall ceilings help. All of the rooms come equipped with a private hot-water bathroom. This hotel was designed with the budget traveler in mind: there's a smart little area for washing and hanging laundry.

Also at the low end of the budget category is the *Hotel Diny* (☎ 809-240-6113), which offers 26 rooms with a private hot-water bathroom and ceiling fan for US$9 to US$20 per room, depending on the size of the room. The Diny, which dates from the early 1980s, was the first hotel in town. Back then, electricity was years away and fresh water had to be brought into town in trucks. The Diny has been a budget traveler's friend all these years.

Another very good value is the *Las Palmeras Hotel* (☎ 809-707-7263), which has six very comfortable rooms located above a restaurant. Rates for the rooms, each of which is very clean and has a ceiling fan and a private hot-water bathroom, are US$16/23 for a single/double.

Slightly pricier but with considerably more charm is the Italian-owned *Casa Robinson* (☎/fax 809-240-6496). Each room is decorated and maintained with pride and has spotless white walls and lovely tiled bathrooms. Many of the guest rooms are upstairs and have balconies, and quite a few also have kitchens. Rates are US$25/26 for a kitchenless room, and US$5 more for a room with a kitchen.

The *Hotel Los Pinos* (☎/fax 809-240-6168) is, as its name suggests, nestled among the pines. Yet it's still just across the road from the beach. Nice! The rooms vary a great deal from one to another, but they are all very clean, and they all have mosquito nets over the beds (a great addition). Some also have porches, others have kitchens, some have shared bath, some are upstairs, and some have better cross-ventilation. This pleasant, Swiss-owned and -operated hotel looks like a lodge you might come across in the Bavarian woods. The rates for one or two people range from US$24 to US$46.

The multilevel, many-room *Hotel Villa Caracol* (☎ 809-240-6078, fax 240-6342) has few guests due to the fact that it's on a little-used road, but it offers a good value. Most rooms have cable TV and a private hot-water bathroom, and some have air conditioning. Rates range from US$14 for a room with fan and shared bathroom to US$20/23 for fan and private hot-water bathroom to US$26/40 with air con. This is one of the few Dominican-owned hotels in the area.

The *Hotel Papa Gayo* (☎ 809-240-6131) is an older place that could use a bit of fixing up, but it's not without its charm. All rooms come with fan only, a private hot-water bathroom and a safe. Some rooms are definitely much better than others, so ask to see several before making a decision. The rates are US$26 for a standard room and US$33 for a suite.

The least impressive of the budget hotels, mentioned here because of its high profile (on the main road close to the entrance to town), is the *Hotel Residence Caribe* (☎ 809-240-6325), which consists of a dozen or so rooms in one large structure with fans only for US$26 per room. The hotel is located about 400m from the beach.

Mid-Range At the far east end of town is the *Ocean Reef Village* (☎ 809-240-6456, fax 240-6457), an Italian-owned and -operated hotel that opened in the summer of 1998. All 100 rooms are quite attractive, although (surprisingly) none is available with air conditioning – a strange decision for a place that spent plenty of money on two bars, a large and lovely swimming pool and an appealing Italian restaurant. Rates range from US$35 to US$75 per room, depending on size and view.

Under construction at the time of writing and definitely worth investigating is the *Hotel Castello Beach,* near the Ocean Reef Village. Plans call for 16 air-conditioned suites constructed of natural stones from the area, a large swimming pool and a second-story restaurant overlooking Playa Punta Popy and the Atlantic Ocean. Rates were expected to start at US$40 per room.

At the time of writing, both the *Coco Plaza Hotel* and the *L'Aubergine Hotel* (both ☎ 809-240-6167, fax 240-6070) were up for sale but still open for business. These hotels are directly across from each other, and all rooms have air con and a private hot-water bathroom. Rates are US$35 per room, but they are unlikely to stay this low; it's certainly worth confirming them if air conditioning is important to you.

Top End At the time of writing, a *Jack Tar Village Plantation Club* resort was being built; the quality of accommodations and service at Jack Tar resorts is always very high. Until that opens, the best of the town's top-end hotels is definitely the *Tropic Banana Hotel* (☎ 809-240-6110, fax 240-6112, hotel.tropic@codetel.net.do). This French-owned and -managed resort features simple yet elegant rooms, a gorgeous swimming pool and a very classy and exotic bar that is open to nonguests. There are beautiful gardens, as well as tennis courts and billiards tables. Rates are US$50/70/90 for a single/double/triple. Meal plans are available as well.

The *Cacao Beach Resort Hotel* (☎ 809-240-6000, fax 240-6020) is a 181-room all-inclusive resort with a swimming pool, restaurant, travel agency and gift shop, and so much security you'd think you were on the grounds of a mint instead a fancy hotel. Every room has air con, two beds, a phone and a safe. It's quite nice, as well it should be for US$135 per person double occupancy, including three meals daily, or US$90 per person without meals.

The *Aligio Beach Hotel* (☎ 809-240-6255, fax 240-6169), near the east end of town, is a 90-room, all-inclusive resort with spacious rooms with fans only but plenty of cross-ventilation. This Italian-owned resort has a dance club and a cinema, a handsome swimming pool with poolside bar, a restaurant serving Italian and international fare, and a pizzeria. Laundry and fax service are available, and deep-sea fishing and scuba diving are offered. Rates are US$95 for one person, one room, or US$75 per person double occupancy.

A French woman with very refined taste owns and manages *Las Cayenas Hotel* (☎ 809-240-6080, fax 240-6177), a former plantation house turned hotel. This is a no-frills establishment – just plenty of elegance and quiet, facing a lovely beach and the ocean. The rates of US$55/65 include breakfast.

Places to Eat

A great place to get your hands on a hamburger is *Las Terrenas Burger*, which serves the best burgers (US$1.75) and chicken sandwiches (US$2.25) in town. Another great value at this small roadside diner, which has just enough chairs for four or five people, is the orange juice – US$0.75 for a large glass of delicious fresh-squeezed orange juice. The ice here is also safe to consume. There's a breezy, pleasant bar directly above the burger joint called *Kuh-Bar-Libre*. It has a dartboard and is open late every day.

For cheap Dominican food go to the main road: in the vicinity of the Codetel office, you'll find a bunch of places serving local food cheap. Among the better of these restaurants are *El Zapote*, *Sumi* and *El 28*.

The *Paca Cabaña*, the only real beach bar in town, offers a half-dozen sandwiches for about US$2.75 each. Salads, fruit dishes and desserts are similarly priced. There's an adjoining restaurant with more substantial meals: beef kabob (for US$5), filet of beef (for US$8), filet of fish (for US$6) and grilled lobster (for US$8).

One hundred meters west of the Paca Cabaña is *La Casa Azul*, a seaside restaurant and bar with a thatch roof and easy-listening Latin American music. This is a fine place to watch the sunset. Breakfasts here run US$2.75 to US$4, sandwiches US$2 to US$3, pastas US$4.50 to US$8, mussels with garlic US$8, and grilled shrimp US$10. The food here is quite good.

The *Brasserie* is an agreeable, open-sided, fan-cooled gringo hangout with menus in English, Spanish, German and French. The prices are low to moderate for typical international dishes (salads, sandwiches and burgers). The beef filets are imported from Argentina, which produces a higher grade of meat than Dominican cattle. A steak will set you back about US$10.

The oldest bar in town is the beachfront *La Salsa*, which is about 200m west of La Casa Azul. La Salsa's appeal is very similar, but it's more upscale, with wooden floors instead of sand and finer tables and drinks, which arrive in artistic coconut shells. The drink list runs four pages and food is a bit pricey, with many food items over US$8, but it's also the most romantic restaurant in town.

Entertainment

Las Terrenas has two dance clubs featuring Dominican music: *El Mambo Disco Bar*, which faces Playa Punta Popy, and the more popular *Nuevo Mundo Disco*, located on the main road about 200m south of the cemetery. There's a small cover charge at both discos, which don't get hopping much before midnight.

Getting There & Away

Air The Aeropuerto El Portillo is a few kilometers east of Las Terrenas along the coastal road, in the hamlet of El Portillo. Here are the routes, flying times and one-way prices available on Air Santo Domingo:

Destination	Duration	Cost
Santo Domingo	30 min	US$49
Puerto Plata	30 min	US$49
Punta Cana	40 min	US$54

Contact Air Santo Domingo (☎ 809-683-8020) for current departure and arrival times, which change fairly frequently. Spanish and English are spoken.

Bus Las Terrenas is served by pickup trucks, which slowly cruise the town looking for riders to take to Sánchez, and by gua-guas that travel between Sánchez and Las Terrenas. Oddly, the gua-guas barely enter Las Terrenas, going only as far as the bus stop at the intersection of the Carretera a Sánchez and the turnoff for Playa Bonita. The gua-guas operate from dawn till dusk, leaving Sánchez for Las Terrenas and Las Terrenas for Sánchez every 25 minutes. The cost is US$1.25.

Getting Around

There are motoconchos and taxis to take you to and from Aeropuerto El Portillo and Las Terrenas; the cost is US$5. In the town itself few people ever hail a taxi or a motoconcho – it's easy enough to walk the town – but several taxis and motoconchos are around (usually near the cemetery) anyway.

EL PORTILLO

The community of El Portillo consists of fewer than a thousand residents, most of whom are farmers. Excluding the airport, there are no public services of any kind in El Portillo. Few visitors to the northeast would ever think twice about the community if it weren't for its lovely resort.

An all-inclusive resort, *El Portillo Beach Resort* (☎ 809-240-6100, fax 240-6104) features 171 guest rooms – each with ceiling fan, private bathroom and terrace – and two restaurants, five bars, a dance club, two clay tennis courts, a swimming pool, a Jacuzzi and an absolutely gorgeous beach with calm surf. Horseback and bicycle riding, volleyball, Ping-Pong, snorkeling, windsurfing, kayaking, pedal boats and scuba clinics are available. One of the neat things about this all-inclusive resort – as opposed to, say, those at Punta Cana and Bávaro – is that it's just a short distance from a town, in this case Las Terrenas. By the time you read this, it's quite possible that the dirt road that travels past the resort en route to Las Terrenas will be paved, allowing guests to bicycle into town and explore it with ease. Rates are US$75 per person most of the year.

Almost all of the resort's guests arrive by air and are taking advantage of a package deal. Occasionally some arrive by car. If you're coming by car, take the road from Sánchez to Las Terrenas, and from Las Terrenas follow the coastal road east a few kilometers until the resort appears on your left. If you're driving from Samaná, head to Sánchez first, but when you reach the turn-off for Las Terrenas (which appears well before Sánchez), check to see if the road has been paved. If so, take that one instead; you'll save yourself some driving and you can stop at the **waterfalls** at El Limón on the way to the resort. If you're coming by bus, take a bus to Sánchez and from there catch a gua-gua to Las Terrenas. In Las Terrenas, hire a taxi or motoconcho to take you to the resort.

PLAYA BONITA

A few kilometers west of Las Terrenas is Playa Bonita, or 'Beautiful Beach' – and that it is. Playa Bonita consists of a kilometer-long curve of tan sand, scores of swaying coconut trees and an aquamarine surf that's shallower and prettier than that at Las Terrenas. Off the coast but well out of swimming range are several small, palm-lined islands. Behind the C-shaped beach and located within a short distance of each other are a handful of nice hotels. There is no community in Playa Bonita, and the beaches here have far fewer people on them than those at nearby Las Terrenas. By car, Playa Bonita is reachable by a single road that

turns off from the Sánchez-Las Terrenas highway. It is, however, possible to walk from Playa Bonita to Playa Cacao via a coastal dirt/mud trail that is fairly steep at one section. There are far fewer motorcycles and cars in Playa Bonita than there are in Las Terrenas, which is something to consider if you are bothered by the noise of motorized vehicles.

Diving

Out front of the Hotel Acaya is the Acaya Diving Center (☎ 809-240-6161, fax 240-6166), which uses the same telephone and fax numbers as the hotel. The center offers PADI classes (US$350 for open water, US$280 for advanced, and US$350 for rescue) and a host of exciting dive possibilities, the costs of which include all equipment (divers should bring their own personal gear to ensure proper fit). Among the more dramatic offerings are a two-tank dive at a fantastic coral wall 40km from Playa Bonita (US$80); cave diving and shallow-water reef diving at Las Ballenas (The Whales), a cluster of five islands that are often visited by humpback whales during January and February (US$30); and one-tank night dives (US$40).

Also very popular but limited to certified cavern divers is an underwater adventure at Lago Dudu. Here, you dive into the lake and kick through an underground tunnel to another lake. At the second lake you kick through another underground tunnel and pop up inside a cave, the top of which is a mere 3m above the surface of the water. Stalactites hang from the ceiling of the cave, which can only be reached in this manner. The underwater visibility is surprisingly good for lake water, which is often murky. The cost for this very unusual adventure is US$70.

Places to Stay & Eat

The first place to stay you'll come to in Playa Bonita is the *Hotel Acaya* (☎ 809-240-6161, fax 240-6166), which offers 16 spacious guest rooms, each with ocean-facing private balcony, ceiling fan, good cross-ventilation, refrigerator, desk and a private hot-water bathroom. The hotel has a generator to combat frequent power shortages. Rates are US$35/50/60 for a single/double/triple. This family-run hotel, which has half of its rooms in one building and half in another, is a very good value. There's a restaurant on the premises as well.

Continuing west is the German-owned *Casa Grande Beach Resort* (☎/fax 809-240-6349), which resembles a big, two-story house and is also a very good value. There are six rooms and singles/doubles cost US$30/40. The restaurant at the resort serves sandwiches (US$3), salads (US$3 to US$5), pastas (US$5.75 to US$8) and fish (US$8 to US$11). There is also a bar.

Next is the *Punta Bonita Resort* (☎ 809-240-6012, fax 240-6082), which has 45 guest rooms, 10 cabins, eight suites and six studios. Only the suites are air-conditioned, but all of the rooms contain handsome furniture and the two-story cabins are very nice. Most rooms face a lush, manicured courtyard. The half-indoor, half-outdoor restaurant is beautiful. Rates, which include breakfast and dinner, range from US$47/70 to US$90/132.

Last on the strip is the French-owned *Hotel Atlantis* (☎ 809-240-6111, fax 240-6205), which was once quite charming with its architecturally appealing and unique guest rooms. But most of the still-spacious rooms show a lot of wear, and a couple smell of mildew. If the new owner puts some money and tender loving care into the hotel, it would be the kind of place that would draw repeat clients. Rates are a bit steep at US$50/60/70.

Getting There & Away

There is usually one taxi and a couple of motoconchos at the Playa Bonita turnoff from the Sánchez-Las Terrenas highway. The cost to reach any of the hotels mentioned here from that turnoff is US$5 by taxi and US$2 by motoconcho. For the location of the turnoff, see the Getting There & Away section and the map for Las Terrenas.

SÁNCHEZ

Looking at a map, one might suspect that Sánchez, at the uppermost throat of the

Bahía de Samaná and a major crossroads, would have something to offer the tourist, but it really doesn't. With its well-worn buildings and its small port full of rusting fishing boats, it has the feel of a place that time forgot. If you have an itch to explore and you love shrimp, try some at one of the humble restaurants in town; the shrimp in Sánchez are said to be the largest in the country.

North Coast

North of the Peninsula de Samaná, there is little along the coast to draw tourists until one reaches the beaches near Río San Juan and, farther west, the surfing and windsurfing mecca of Cabarete.

NAGUA

On the coastal highway 36km northwest of Sánchez, Nagua is a dusty, hot and stinking town with a super-littered beach. While Sánchez at least has its shrimp, Nagua has nothing to offer the tourist. For some reason, it has three hotels – the *Hotel Brisas del Mar* (US$7), the *Hotel Casa Blanca* (US$15) and the *Hotel Sinai* (US$10). Not surprisingly, they are generally empty.

But the town's history is interesting. During the Trujillo era, the town was named Julia Molina, in honor of the dictator's mother. There was a fort in town as well as several impressive government buildings. And, several kilometers inland, there was a rice mill and a huge plantation where Trujillo had dispossessed thousands of peasants of their rice land (he simply sent in the troops, who drove away the peasants away). Trujillo ran the plantation with slave labor – he used political prisoners to do the work, which they did at the point of a bayonet.

When a prisoner wore out or tried to escape, he was taken away and murdered. The town's oldest residents say that many prisoners were killed at the fort and their bodies tossed into the surf, only to wash ashore later and be fed upon by dogs. Today, the old fort's gone, the rice mill is just a scrap heap, and the peasants have reclaimed their fields.

Getting There & Away

Nagua is at a crossroads. The coastal highway passes through Nagua, heading northwest/ southeast, and is intersected here by an inland highway that links the town to San Francisco de Macorís, Moca, Santiago and other towns in the interior. From Nagua, it's possible to catch a coastal bus by simply walking out to the coastal highway at any point and waving down a gua-gua.

To catch an inland-bound bus, you must go to the intersection of the two highways and hail a bus that is turning off of the coastal highway onto the inland highway. There are usually a few people waiting for an inland bus at the intersection. Don't hesitate to stand near them and utter a hearty *buenos días* (good morning) or *buenas tardes* (good afternoon); their friendly smiles and warm replies will make you glad you spoke up. Gua-guas travel the two highways during daylight hours every day of the year except Easter Sunday; they arrive approximately hourly.

Both Caribe Tours and Metro Buses serve Nagua from Santo Domingo. From the capital, Caribe Tours buses depart at 7:15, 7:30 and 9 am, and 1:30, 3 and 3:45 pm. From Nagua, Santo Domingo-bound buses depart at 2, 3 and 4:30 pm. The cost is US$4.50 each way. From the capital city, Metro buses depart at 7 and 10 am, and 2:30 and 3:30 pm. From Nagua, Metro buses leave at 7 and 9:30 am, and 2 and 4:30 pm. The cost is US$5 each way. Ask around for the location of the bus depots.

CABRERA

Forty-one kilometers north of Nagua is the coastal town of Cabrera, which, like Nagua and Sánchez, has little to offer the tourist. There are no beaches in town, and those closest to it are strewn with litter. The town itself could do with a thorough cleaning and a coat of fresh paint. Cabrera is mentioned here only because of its two hotels, which may be of interest to travelers who are getting around on bicycles or are otherwise making tracks at a leisurely pace.

The better of the two hotels is the five-room *Aparta Hotel Francis* (☎ 809-589-

7496), which opened in 1998. It's 150m from a pounding surf (though there is no beach), and each room comes with ceiling fan and a private hot-water bathroom. The rate is US$20 per room. To find the Francis, first locate the Plaza Central (main square), which is near the west end of town between the coastal highway and the ocean. The entire town is only about five blocks wide, and the plaza is located on one of the busier streets. Once you've found the main square, take the road along the west side of the square two blocks toward the ocean. The hotel will be on the right-hand side.

The town's only other hotel, *Hotel El Dorado* (no phone), consists of four rooms above a pizzeria. The rates range from US$10 to US$24, depending on size and whether you request a private bathroom. None of the rooms has air conditioning. This place is quite OK for a night, possibly two. The hotel is on the coastal highway, near the east end of town.

RÍO SAN JUAN

Thirty-two kilometers west of Cabrera and 51km southeast of the ever-popular Sosúa is the still-sleepy, typical Dominican seaside town of Río San Juan. This longtime fishing and dairy community is known mainly for its mangrove-laden lagoon, which makes for some fun exploring. The town has some decent tourist accommodations, a small beach nearby and a dive center that takes advantage of the interesting coastal area.

Orientation

The main road into town from the coastal highway is Calle Duarte. On this street is a money exchange, a gas station, a Codetel office, a fine hotel and even a tourist office. Perpendicular to and mostly west of Calle Duarte are eight residential streets. The town, containing about 6000 people, is quite small and easily covered on foot.

Information

Tourist Offices There's a government-operated tourist office near the northern end of Calle Duarte. It is staffed with friendly

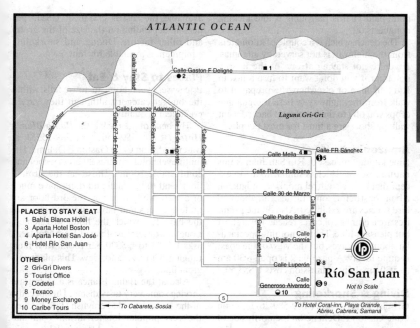

ATLANTIC OCEAN

Laguna Gri-Gri

Calle Gaston F Deligne

Calle Trinidad
Calle Lorenzo Adames
Calle Beller
Calle 27 de Febrero
Calle San Juan
Calle 16 de Agosto
Calle Capotillo

Calle Mella
Calle FR Sánchez
Calle Rufino Bulbuena
Calle 30 de Marzo
Calle Padre Bellini
Calle
Dr Virgilio García
Calle Libertad
Calle Duarte
Calle Luperón
Calle
Generoso Alvarado

Río San Juan
Not to Scale

To Cabarete, Sosúa ←   5

→ To Hotel Coral-inn, Playa Grande,
Abreu, Cabrera, Samaná

PLACES TO STAY & EAT
1 Bahía Blanca Hotel
3 Aparta Hotel Boston
4 Aparta Hotel San José
6 Hotel Río San Juan

OTHER
2 Gri-Gri Divers
5 Tourist Office
7 Codetel
8 Texaco
9 Money Exchange
10 Caribe Tours

people who have maps to offer and can answer questions, though only Spanish is spoken. The office is open 8 am to 3 pm daily.

Money There's a currency exchange on Calle Duarte near Hwy 5 that will swap Dominican pesos for US and Canadian dollars and German marks. It's open 8:30 am to 5 pm Monday through Saturday.

Post & Communications There is no post office in town. However, at the Bahía Blanca Hotel and Hotel Río San Juan, it is possible for guests to buy stamps and mail postcards and letters.

There is a Codetel office on Calle Duarte that is open 8 am to 10 pm daily.

Laguna Gri-Gri

This picturesque lagoon at the northern end of Calle Duarte contains several boats that can be hired for tours of the lagoon and

beyond. The cost of chartering a boat is US$25 an hour per boatload, and you can expect the captain to take you past some healthy mangrove, interesting rock formations and a cave that is home to many swallows. If the timing is right, the captain will ease the boat into the cave for a close-up look.

Playa Grande

The main attraction east of Río San Juan is Playa Grande, the finest beach in the area. Near the beach is also one of the best hotels in or near Río San Juan and a small nature reserve that's worth a stop.

A little more than 5km east of Río San Juan, Playa Grande is a wide, long, tan-sand beach with gorgeous aquamarine water that gently laps the shore during most of the year (at times the waves can become rather unruly and are a hit with surfers). Fortunately, a resort has yet to be built directly behind the beach, which means that there aren't any hotel-paid guards patrolling it and kicking nonguests off.

The beach, which is a couple of kilometers from the highway, is not served by gua-guas. If you're not staying at one of the nearby hotels, or if you don't want to hire a taxi in Río San Juan or elsewhere, be prepared to walk from the highway (where the gua-gua drops you off) to the beach and back; decent walking shoes are a must for most people.

Amazonia 2

Nine kilometers east of Río San Juan is this nature reserve, which is similar to a zoo except that only a squirrel monkey, an iguana, a boa constrictor, some turtles and about 10 bird species are exhibited. Also on the premises are a number of caves reached by a short but pleasant hike. There's nothing spectacular about the caves, but the view of the coast is quite lovely. Amazonia 2 is open 8:30 am to 5:30 pm daily. Admission costs US$3.50.

Diving & Snorkeling

Gri-Gri Divers (☎/fax 809-589-2671), upon Calle Gaston F Deligne on the north side of town, has three boats owned and operated by a very friendly Canadian couple who enjoy taking divers to 15 different dive sites along the northeast coast. Depending on when you're in the area, you stand a chance of seeing humpback whales, octopi, scorpion fish, barracuda, lobsters, sponges, yellow sting rays and even sea turtles. Some swim-throughs and cave dives are available. Dives are open to certified and uncertified divers, but uncertified divers are limited to shallow dives.

The cost of the first dive for an uncertified diver is US$55 and includes hotel pickup and return and a one-tank dive at a nearby reef. The second dive costs US$40. For certified divers, the costs break down like so: one dive, US$40; two dives in one day, US$70; the third dive costs US$35; beginning with the sixth dive, the per-dive cost is US$30. For night dives, add US$15 per dive. PADI Open-Water certification is available (US$378), as is PADI Advanced certification (US$225). Although most outings are geared for divers, Gri-Gri accommodates snorkelers whenever possible. When a snorkeling trip is

available, the cost is US$10 or US$15 per person, depending on the size of the group and other factors. Diving and snorkeling equipment is available for rent.

Places to Stay & Eat

Pricewise, every hotel in town falls within the budget category, although they vary a great deal in quality.

The head of the pack is the **Bahía Blanca Hotel** (☎ 809-589-2563, fax 589-2528), at water's edge on Calle Gaston F Deligne. The multilevel hotel features 20 breezy, cool and comfortable rooms. Those on the ground floor tend to be small and don't have much of a view, while those on the 3rd floor are quite spacious and have sweeping views of the bay after which the hotel was named. Longtime owner Lise Pineau, from Montreal, asks US$13 to US$30 per room, with rates ranging with size and view. This place is a great find.

Also at the Bahía Blanca is a restaurant serving some very tasty dishes. The specialty of the house is grilled crayfish (US$13), and the very popular lobster/shrimp combination goes for US$16. Also available are a number of red-meat dishes (US$5 to US$6) and a selection of pastas (around US$4).

If you absolutely must have air conditioning, the only place to find it in town is the **Hotel Río San Juan** (☎ 809-589-2211, fax 589-2534), on Calle Duarte, which has 40 guest rooms, a swimming pool, a bar and a generator. Because the hotel is away from the ocean and ringed by air-stilling trees, the hotel actually needs air conditioning most of the time. The rates are very reasonable at US$27 for one or two people.

A huge step down in quality is the **Aparta Hotel San José** (no phone) at the corner of Calle Mella and Calle Duarte. The San José has six rooms, each with ceiling fan and private hot-water bathroom. There is a generator on the premises. Rates are US$24 for one or two people.

Two blocks west of the San José, on Calle Mella at Calle 16 de Agosto, is the **Aparta Hotel Boston** (☎ 809-589-2921), which has five rooms, each with kitchenette, fan and private hot-water bathroom for US$20 per room. They have no generator, so this place can get very hot when a power outage strikes.

The **Hotel Coral-inn** (☎ 809-248-5435, fax 248-5437) is 3km east of Río San Juan on the north side of Hwy 5. This very comfortable, Canadian-owned hotel was new in 1998, and it now tops the list over all those in the area. The Coral-inn consists of 18 air-conditioned rooms in a two-story building, an inviting swimming pool, and a very attractive restaurant and bar serving good food, all set in quiet surroundings. Although not on the beach, the hotel is only five minutes' drive from Playa Grande, and hotel staff will drop you there and pick you up at no additional charge. Rooms rent for US$24. The hotel will also provide shuttle service from the Aeropuerto Gregorio Luperón. English, French and Spanish are spoken.

The Coral-inn restaurant's menu includes breakfasts from US$1.50 to US$3, several pastas for about US$3, several steaks priced at around US$6, pork chops for US$5, filet mignon for US$10, half chicken for US$5, seafood and fish for US$7 to US$10, and an assortment of kabobs for about US$5 each.

Five kilometers east of Río San Juan and within walking distance of Playa Grande is the all-inclusive **Caribbean Village Resort** (☎ 809-582-1170, fax 582-6094), which contains a total of 300 guest rooms in five buildings, an 18-hole golf course designed by Robert Trent Jones, one large swimming pool, three tennis courts, one main restaurant and two specialty restaurants, along with lots of activities. The per-person cost is US$120 single occupancy and US$95 double occupancy. Green fees are extra.

Though it's not as close to Playa Grande as the above hotels, you may be tempted to stay at the all-inclusive **Club Bahía Principe** (☎ 809-226-1590, fax 226-1991), which is about 10km east of Río San Juan. Resist the urge. This place would have been nice had the owners kept the number of rooms to fewer than 300, but it consists of 970 guest rooms in more than three dozen structures that are just a tad less utilitarian than a prison compound. The overriding feeling is that you're just part of the herd, and there is almost no sense of romance or intimacy to

the grounds. This resort has all the typical amenities but isn't very attractive. Rates range from US$61/94 to US$104/166.

Getting There & Away

Gua-guas can be hailed at any point along Hwy 5 for travel in either direction.

Caribe Tours provides service between Río San Juan and Santo Domingo. Three buses depart daily from the town to the capital – at 6:30 am and 1 and 3:30 pm. Likewise, three buses depart from Santo Domingo to Río San Juan daily – at 7:30 and 9:30 am and 3 pm. The cost is US$5 each way. The bus depot is located on Hwy 5, just west of Calle Duarte.

Getting Around

There are motoconchos and taxis near the intersection of Calle Duarte and Hwy 5 during daylight hours.

CABARETE

It's hard to believe, but this seaside resort town had only two hotels in 1989. During the 1980s, the explosion in tourist facilities that was occurring in nearby Sosúa and elsewhere somehow missed Cabarete, with its lovely white-sand beach and enormous bay, which is widely regarded as one of the best in the world for windsurfing.

Well, if developers overlooked Cabarete during the previous decade, it sure didn't escape their attention during the 1990s. By 1998, eight more hotels, 10 bars and a dozen restaurants had moved in, replacing the few homes and simple businesses that had previously existed on both sides of the coastal highway as it passes Playa Cabarete. And at the time this was being penned, two more hotels and several more restaurants were being built.

Today, the former fishing village caters solely to tourists. For more than a kilometer on both sides of the slow, two-lane highway, there is nothing but businesses serving the vacation crowd: hotels, restaurants, bars, T-shirt shops, film-developing centers, tour operators, and an office where international calls can be placed. And on the nearby beach are scores of 20-something babes and hunks, most eyeing the many windsurfers on the water when they're not eyeing each other.

DOMINICAN REPUBLIC

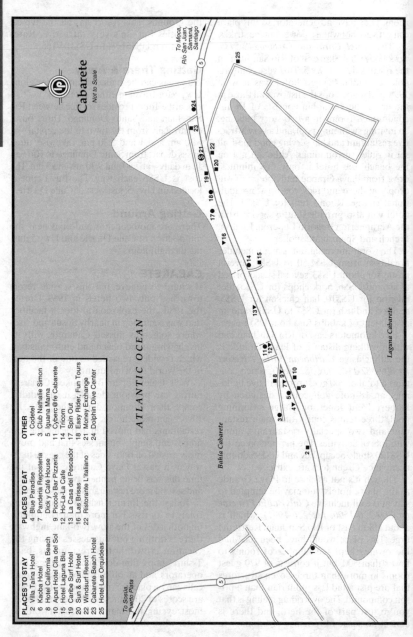

Cabarete

Not to Scale

To Moca,
Río San Juan,
Samaná,
Santiago

25 ■

24 ●

23 ■

$ 21
20 ■ 22 ■

19 ■ 19 ●

18 ● 18 ▼
17 ●

▼16
14 ▼ 15 ■

13 ▼

11 ▼
12 ▼
8 ● 9 ▼
5 ▼ 7 ▼ 10 ■
4 ▼ 6 ■

3 ●

2 ■

1 ●

ATLANTIC OCEAN

Bahía Cabarete

Laguna Cabarete

To Sosúa,
Puerto Plata

PLACES TO STAY
2　Villa Taína Hotel
6　Kaoba Hotel
8　Hotel California Beach
10　Apart Hotel Cita del Sol
15　Caribe Surf Hotel
19　Sun & Surf Hotel
20　Windsurf Resort
22　Cabarete Beach Hotel
25　Hotel Las Orquídeas

PLACES TO EAT
4　Blue Paradise
7　Pandería Repostería
9　Dick y Café House
11　Piccolo Bar Pizzeria
12　Ho-La-La Cafe
13　La Casa del Pescador
16　Las Brisas
22　Ristorante L'Italiano

OTHER
1　Codetel
3　Club Nathalie Simon
11　Cyber@fe Cabarete
14　Tricom
17　Spin Out
18　Easy Rider, Fun Tours
21　Money Exchange
24　Dolphin Dive Center

The ocean view is spectacular. Not only is the water a provocative green-blue with plenty of whitecaps in the distance, but the scene is enlivened by dozens of wind-surfers and their colorful triangular sails zipping across the waves. This is definitely a place for a set of binoculars, or bring along a really powerful camera lens if you enjoy taking action photos. You'll see people enrolled in Windsurfing 101 failing miserably as well as world-class wind-surfers doing 360° flips.

The action doesn't end at sunset. Every night the bars fill with people looking to meet and mingle, and every night (weather permitting) a band plays merengue, salsa, rock and/or reggae on a stage set up on the beach. Join the dancing throng or just sit back with a piña colada and watch the fes-tivities. The choices don't get any tougher at this increasingly popular destination.

Orientation
Cabarete is mostly a one-road town, and that road is the coastal highway, or as the locals call it, the *carretera*. Most of the town's buildings are located beside the highway, although there are a handful of short streets – mostly former driveways – that stem from it. The entire town can be walked in 30 minutes.

Information
It seems the Ministry of Tourism is awaiting a sign from God before it establishes a tourist office in Cabarete. However, many of the bar, restaurant and hotel owners speak English as well as Spanish, and French and German are widely spoken as well. If you've got any questions about Cabarete, don't hes-itate to put that question to any number of people. The folks at Iguana Mama, a tour company specializing in mountain-bike and hiking adventures, are especially friendly and knowledgeable.

Money Opposite and slightly to the east of the Sun & Surf Hotel is a no-name, closet-size money exchange that offers very competitive rates for US and Canadian dollars and German marks. It is open 8 am to 7 pm daily.

Post There is no post office in Cabarete. However, there is Domex, a private postal service, though it only serves the USA, Canada and Europe. Inside several gift shops and at several hotels you'll find a small wooden box with 'Domex' printed on the outside. At these establishments you can buy Domex labels (they look like stamps), affix them to your mail and simply drop your postcard or letter in the Domex box. Later the same day or some time during the next, your mail will be picked up for delivery. In fact, Domex is both faster and more reliable than the government postal service.

Telephone At the time of writing there was only a Tricom office in town, with posted hours of 8 am to 6 pm daily. However, Code-tel had plans to open an office near the west end of town, which should be functioning by the time you read this.

Email In addition to the Codetel office, where email service and Internet access should be available, there's a dedicated Inter-net business in town – Cyberc@fe Cabarete (☎/fax 809-571-0573, www.cybercafe.com, www.cabarete.com). Here, you can send and receive email all day long for US$3 per hour; a variety of dis-counts and private email ad-dresses are available. There is one major drawback: access to Hotmail, Rocketmail and

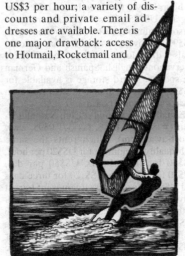

other webmail services was not available at the time of writing.

Activities

Windsurfing Windsurfing is the main reason most foreign tourists visit Cabarete. The combination of strong, steady winds, relatively shallow water and a rockless shore creates perfect conditions for the sport. The best time to be there is May through July, when average wind speeds exceed 15mph and winds in excess of 25mph are common.

The bay is used by beginner, intermediate and advanced windsurfers, and a good number of the people near shore are actually taking lessons. A reef near the mouth of the bay prevents heavy chop from reaching the beach. The waves and wind are considerably more impressive half a kilometer from shore, which is where the advanced windsurfers can be seen doing flips and other athletic feats.

All the equipment needed to windsurf is available for rent on Playa Cabarete, where there are two major rental companies (and several smaller ones), both of which enjoy good solid reputations. Spin Out (☎ 809-571-0805, fax 571-0856, www.velawindsurf.com/cabarete.html) rents equipment for US$20 an hour, US$40 for three hours, US$50 per day and US$250 for a week. Lessons (two-person minimum) cost US$50 for beginners, US$90 for advanced. Spin Out has discount deals with a local hotel as well. Call for reservations. English, Spanish and German are spoken. Board storage is available for US$30 per week. Spin Out also rents sea kayaks and boogie boards.

Equally professional is Club Nathalie Simon (☎ 809-571-0848, fax 571-0595, www.sport-away.com), which rents the same high-quality equipment for US$20 per hour, US$40 for three hours, US$50 per day, US$80 for two days, US$120 for three days and US$210 for a week. If you want to rent only the board or only the sail, you pay 60% of the full rental price. Lessons cost US$36 (US$50 if the student is using a training board). Board storage is available for US$30 per week. English and Spanish are spoken. The Club Nathalie Simon also rents

sea kayaks and boogie boards as well as Hobie Cats, which are always accompanied by an instructor.

Surfing Some of the best waves for surfing on the entire island appear just west of Cabarete, opposite a thin beach locals call Playa Encuentro. The waves are called *El Canal* (The Channel), *Encuentro* (Encounter), *La Barca* (The Launch) and *Preciosa* (Precious One). All are reef breaks. To find them, take the dirt road just west of town toward the ocean.

El Canal breaks primarily to the left, but it also has a short right. Encuentro, which is the most consistent of the waves, breaks both ways, but mostly to the right. Preciosa breaks only to the right. La Barca breaks mostly to the left. When breaking big, the faces of these waves can reach 4m. August to October and December to March are the best months for surfing here.

Surfboards can be rented at Spin Out and at Club Nathalie Simon for US$9 an hour, less per hour for the half day, day and week.

Diving Dolphin Dive Center (☎/fax 809-571-0842, d.divecenter@codetel.net.do) offers a host of dives in the vicinity of Sosúa that leave from Cabarete (there is no diving near Cabarete because of the area's strong winds and choppy seas). A one-tank dive costs US$28 (add US$12 for rental equipment). The per-dive cost falls to US$26 after the first two dives. PADI certification is also offered: Open-Water (US$385), Advanced (US$270), Master (US$895) and Rescue (US$495). The quality of the diving there is only mediocre, due to overfishing and reef damage caused by hurricanes.

Organized Tours

Iguana Mama (☎ 800-849-4720, 809-571-0908, fax 571-0734, www.iguana-mama.com) is a rather unusual tour operator, in that it specializes in mountain-bike rentals and tours in addition to hiking tours. It rents only top-of-the-line bikes, mostly Cannondale F700s and F500s, and its tours are designed to reach places cars and trucks simply can't. Mountain-bike tours range from a host of fun day tours to a five-day 'Dominican Alps' tour to a 10-day, coast-to-coast tour. Among the numerous hiking tours available is the 'Samaná Nature Week,' which includes exploration of Parque Nacional Los Haïtises, whale-watching in the Bahía de Samaná, hiking up to the gorgeous waterfall near El Limón and cycling up to Las Galeras. Run by American-born Tricia Suriel, Iguana Mama is the top adventure-tour operator on the island. You're encouraged to contact the company to request a brochure, which includes current prices, tour dates and other details.

Fun Tours (☎ 809-571-0825), which shares an office with Easy Rider, offers more than a dozen tours from Cabarete, including a two-day trip into Haiti (US$175), a rafting adventure (US$85), a jeep safari (US$50) and horseback riding in Jarabacoa (US$45).

Special Events
Cabarete Alegría Cabarete hosts *alegría* (happiness) month each February. During this month, Iguana Mama and other local businesses hold special weekend events. These events vary from year to year but generally include mountain-bike races, kite-flying contests and sand-castle-building competitions. The fourth weekend of the month always plays host to the Dominican national surfing and windsurfing championships, held at nearby Playa Encuentro.

Encuentro Classic Cabarete is one of the top windsurfing sites in the world, and the best time of the year there for the sport is June, when the region's winds are at their mightiest. Every year during the third week of June, course races are held for various skill classes, from world-class, year-round windsurfers to very good, seasonal windsurfers to a lot of people who are out just to have a great time – and that's what matters most at the Encuentro Classic. Every night of the week there are concerts and parties on the beach.

Places to Stay
Budget The only hotel in town with rates generally under US$30 per single room is

the *Hotel Laguna Blu* (☎ 809-571-0659), which is near the center of town but about 75m off the main road. The Blu has 26 guest rooms in one two-story structure and four studio apartments; they are a bit quieter than most because the hotel is a good distance away from vehicular traffic. Each room features a ceiling fan and private hot-water bathroom. There's also a swimming pool and a generator. For US$24 per room, this place is a great value. Reservations are a good idea.

Mid-Range The *Kaoba Hotel* (☎ 809-571-0837, fax 571-0879) is a major step up in comfort and is the best of the mid-range hotels, so make reservations if you can. It has 25 charming thatch-roof bungalows (US$30/32 for a single/double), 16 standard rooms with TV and fridge (US$35/38) and 15 studio apartments with TV and kitchen (US$40/44). Facilities include an inviting swimming pool, lush grounds, an open-air restaurant/bar and a friendly staff. A safe and a laundry service are available, and there is a generator to combat power outages.

The *Caribe Surf Hotel* (☎/fax 809-571-0788, fax 571-3346, www.hispaniola.com/CaribeSurfHotel/CaribeSurfHotel.html) is very popular and a good value at US$32/39. The hotel features 20 rooms, most of which have a balcony with sea view. All have a ceiling fan and a private hot-water bathroom. There's a swimming pool and a generator, and every Wednesday and Sunday the hotel hosts a barbecue at the poolside bar/restaurant. Like being on top of the world? Inquire about the penthouse (US$50 a night), which comes with a kitchen. The friendly Swiss owner, Teddy Müller, speaks English, Spanish and German.

The *Hotel Las Orquideas* (☎ 809-571-0787, fax 571-0853) is a bit of a walk from the beach, only a slight inconvenience considering what a good value this is for the money. All of its rooms contain a fully equipped kitchen, a safety box, a minibar and a balcony overlooking a swimming pool and gardens. There's a generator and the hotel provides chairs and towels for guests to use at the beach. Rates start at US$32/40 for a single/double.

The French-Canadian-run *Apart Hotel Cita del Sol* (☎ *809-571-0720, fax 571-0795; in Montreal, ☎/fax 514-646-3772*) offers numerous apartments in several multilevel buildings overlooking a large swimming pool. The apartments are privately owned and are rented out when the owners aren't using them. Some are much nicer than others. The Cita del Sol is a fairly good value at US$30/35.

A bit more expensive than the Cita del Sol but a significant step up in luxury is the *Hotel California Beach* (☎ *809-571-0930, fax 571-0931*), which has 28 lovely, beachside rooms with ceiling fan and a private hot-water bathroom. There's a swimming pool, a bar, a restaurant and a generator on the premises. Rates are US$45/55 most of the year.

Also right on the beach is the *Cabarete Beach Hotel* (☎ *809-571-0755, fax 571-0831, beach.hotel@codetel.net.do*), which has 24 comfortable rooms, some with air conditioning. The hotel features a fine restaurant overlooking the ocean, two bars and a gift shop. Services include money exchange, laundry and child care. English, Spanish, German and French are spoken. Rates start at US$40 per room during the low season (July and August) and range up to US$120 from mid-December to mid-January. Reservations are recommended.

Top End The best of Cabarete's high-end places and the only one situated on the beach side of the coastal highway is the stylish *Villa Taína Hotel* (☎ *809-571-0722, fax 571-0883, happy.cabarete@codetel.net .do*). The Villa Taína offers a variety of air-conditioned double rooms, suites and deluxe suites starting at US$53 per room. All rooms have a balcony or a terrace.

The *Sun & Surf Hotel* (☎ *809-571-0522, fax 571-0783*) consists of a three-story structure with air-conditioned rooms, each containing a satellite TV, phone, minibar, safe and a balcony or terrace. There's a swimming pool and some gardens. Rates are US$60 for a single or double.

The *Windsurf Resort* (☎ *809-571-0718, fax 571-0710*) has 50 air-conditioned rooms that range from US$60 to US$150, which makes it a bit overpriced. They provide a swimming pool, two bars (including one swim-up), an international restaurant and a tour office.

Places to Eat

There are lots of places to eat in Cabarete. For Italian, try the *Ristorante L'italiano* in the Windsurf Resort. It serves the best pasta in town, including such dishes as *pennine arrabiata*, *spaghetti alla calabrese*, *fettuccini alfredo* and lasagna, each for about US$6. Also offered are three veal dishes (around US$8) and 17 pizzas cooked in a wood-burning oven (most are around US$6). The restaurant also has a nightly special that is often an excellent value for the money.

A popular beachside bar/restaurant – and an excellent place from which to watch the windsurfers – is *Las Brisas*, which is flanked by windsurfing companies. The food here isn't fancy, but the atmosphere more than makes up for the mundane cuisine, which includes cheeseburgers (US$2.50), club sandwiches (US$4), spaghetti with pesto sauce (US$3) and fish (US$5.50).

While not in the heart of the action, the *Blue Paradise* makes an excellent stop if you're in the mood for inexpensive sandwiches or pizza. The pies are delivered in two sizes, the smallest of which most people would find difficult to finish at one sitting. The sandwiches come in three dozen tasty varieties, and most everything sells for less than US$4. An even better value are the mixed drinks – US$1.75 for a daiquiri, US$2 for rum punches and piña coladas – which arrive filled to the rim in large soft-drink glasses.

Been eating plenty of inexpensive food and want to splurge? Try *La Casa del Pescador*, which serves the best seafood in town. The seaside restaurant, with its little wooden tables and its so-so decor, is none too fancy, but the food is very good. Among the more popular items are the fish of the day (US$8), seafood spaghetti (US$9) and lobster (US$14). For dessert, try the banana flambée (US$3).

If you're in the mood for a Dominican pastry and a cup of java, the *Panaderia Reposteria Dick y Café House* can accommodate you. Other casual and popular places include the *Ho-La-La Cafe* and the *Piccolo Bar Pizzeria*.

Getting There & Away

Cabarete is served by gua-guas that travel the coastal highway all day long, linking the towns of Puerto Plata, Sosúa, Cabarete and points east. To catch a gua-gua, simply stand beside the highway and wave one down. The cost of a ride along the coast rarely exceeds US$1.50.

Getting Around

Taxis and motoconchos can usually be found parked at the roadside. If you need one to take you to the airport, don't hesitate to ask someone at your hotel's reception desk to call one for you; it beats trying to watch your luggage and hail a taxi at the same time.

Motorcycle Easy Rider (☎ 809-571-0825) rents out Yamaha DT 125cc motorcycles (US$25 per day), Yamaha DT 175cc motorcycles (US$28 a day), Honda 100cc scooters (for US$18 a day), Yamaha 600 choppers (US$50 a day) and Honda 600cc bullet bikes (US$57 a day). Insurance is extra. Easy Rider is the only motorcycle-rental company on the island that rents 600s, which are, in fact, incredibly impractical on Hispaniola: These motorcycles do not handle dirt roads well, which greatly limits your exploration options, and only a few mechanics on the island know how to work on them, so flats and other common mishaps are especially debilitating.

That said, what's nice about Easy Rider is that it offers a variety of riding options, from cute scooters to 230km/h low-flying rockets; it provides a list of suggested tours; and its friendly German owner speaks English, German, Spanish and French. What's not so nice is that prices are higher here than most anywhere else on the island.

If you're planning on renting a motorcycle for several weeks or more, it may be worth your while to rent from Alpha 3000 Motorcycle Rentals in Boca Chica, which rents Yamaha DT 125cc motorcycles (an excellent off-road bike for the DR) for US$16 a day.

Be sure to call in advance to reserve a motorcycle, as they are very popular with locals as well as foreigners. See the Boca Chica section of the Around Santo Domingo chapter for details.

SOSÚA

The present-day site of Sosúa was once owned by the United Fruit Company, which covered it with banana plantations. In the late 1920s, these were bought cheaply by the dictator Rafael Trujillo, who a decade or so later sold the land at a profit to Jewish organizations in the USA. These organizations were looking to create a new home for European Jews suffering from a growing wave of anti-Semitism.

In 1940 some 350 Jewish families, mostly from Germany and Austria, were relocated to the Dominican Republic. At first they had a terrible time. Most were from cities and knew nothing about farming, let alone the tropics or the Spanish language. Initially they tried to survive by growing vegetables. But the country's newest colonists discovered the hard way that there was no local market for their produce and the road system was too primitive to safely ship fresh vegetables to Santo Domingo, where there was demand for it. It took more than a week to get from north to south, and in that time the food would perish.

The Jewish settlers hit on a solution: raise cattle and hogs, and make milk, cheese and sausage. They built a slaughterhouse, a sausage factory, a cheese factory and even a milk pasteurization plant. They established markets and trucking systems, first locally and then to Santiago and the capital. Eventually, Sosúa's sausages and cheeses sold well throughout the country, and the Jewish settlement prospered.

But the thriving colony was virtually wiped out during the 1960s. Dominican peasants who resented the colonists' success moved in and overran their grazing lands, built squatters' shacks, cut down splendid timber and planted corn on hillsides so steep that rain washed away the topsoil after a single season. Then the peasants abandoned the land they had ruined and moved deeper

DOMINICAN REPUBLIC

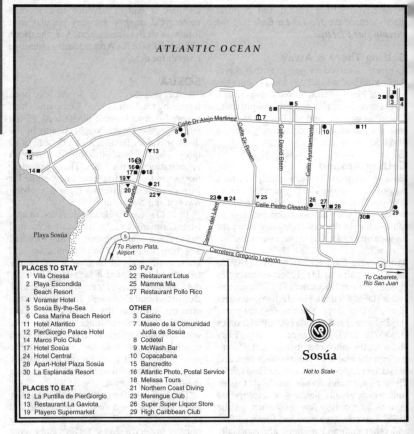

ATLANTIC OCEAN

Playa Sosúa

To Puerto Plata,
Airport

Sosúa

Not to Scale

To Cabarete,
Río San Juan

PLACES TO STAY	
1 Villa Chessa	20 PJ's
2 Playa Escondida	22 Restaurant Lotus
Beach Resort	25 Mamma Mia
4 Voramar Hotel	27 Restaurant Pollo Rico
5 Sosúa By-the-Sea	
6 Casa Marina Beach Resort	**OTHER**
11 Hotel Atlantico	3 Casino
12 PierGiorgio Palace Hotel	7 Museo de la Comunidad
14 Marco Polo Club	Judía de Sosúa
17 Hotel Sosúa	8 Codetel
24 Hotel Central	9 McWash Bar
28 Apart-Hotel Plaza Sosúa	10 Copacabana
30 La Esplanada Resort	15 Bancredito
	16 Atlantic Photo, Postal Service
PLACES TO EAT	18 Melissa Tours
12 La Puntilla de PierGiorgio	21 Northern Coast Diving
13 Restaurant La Gaviota	23 Merengue Club
19 Playero Supermarket	26 Super Super Liquor Store
	29 High Caribbean Club

into the colony's land. At the same time, ominous notes of anti-Semitism began cropping up, and it became clear to the Jewish settlers that the police would offer them little protection.

During the previous decade, most of the colony's children emigrated to the USA or to Israel. By the 1960s, Sosúa's Jewish community consisted mainly of elderly people who wanted only to be left alone to produce sausages, cheeses and milk. But with the encroachment of the Dominican peasants and the threat they felt to their lives, most of the Jews packed what they could

and left. Only a few Jewish families remain in Sosúa.

Today Sosúa reflects little of this past, and some say the town has lost its charm. Certainly there are fewer and fewer old homes in town, and all of its dirt streets are gradually being paved. On the road to the PierGiorgio Palace Hotel and along the western end of Calle Dr Alejo Martínez, you can still find some of the lovely handcrafted houses built by Jewish colonists, but they represent only a fraction of what once existed.

However, the Sosúa of today isn't without its beauty and its comforts. The town is situated beside a spectacular beach about a kilometer long, at both ends of which rock walls rise up and long peninsulas jut out into the Atlantic. The beach is covered with golden-yellow sand and sprinkled with coconut trees. And beneath the trees are scores of sunbathers who find the town a comfortable retreat, with over a dozen hotels, a wide variety of restaurants and bars and a lively nightlife.

Mostly a product of the 1980s and 1990s, present-day Sosúa continues to grow, and its beach and its bay are as pretty as ever.

Orientation

As it passes along the south edge of Sosúa, Hwy 5 becomes Carretera Gregorio Luperón. The main street into town off the highway is Calle Duarte, although Camino del Libre is also a popular turnoff. Calle Pedro Clisante is Sosúa's main drag, lined for much of its length with shops, restaurants and bars.

The heart of the town is around the intersection of Calle Duarte and Calle Pedro Clisante. From here, Playa Sosúa, many restaurants, bars, a bank, a postal service and a Codetel office are only a short walk from one another. Motoconchos serve the hotels on the east edge of town, and at least one hotel (La Esplanada Resort) provides a shuttle service for its guests.

Information

There is no tourist office in Sosúa. Travelers with questions are well advised to visit Melissa Tours (☎ 809-571-2567, fax 571-1733) on Calle Duarte. The first travel agency and tour operator in town, it has an especially knowledgeable and friendly staff. The manager, Manuel A Brito, speaks English, Spanish, German, French, Dutch, Italian and Portuguese. The agency is open 8 am to 8 pm Monday through Saturday, and 9 am to noon and 4 to 8 pm on Sunday.

Money On Calle Duarte, Bancredito is open 8:30 am to 3 pm weekdays. The bank will exchange major currencies for Dominican pesos. There are other banks in town. Many hotels will readily exchange US and Canadian dollars and German marks for pesos.

Post There is a DCS Express Service in the Atlantic Photo shop on Calle Duarte, which promises to deliver your letter or postcard to the destination country in three to five business days. The standard cost of postage is less than US$2. Also at Atlantic Photo is Service Postal Express, which also claims to deliver mail from the DR to the destination country in five business days or less. The cost is US$1.50 per letter.

Telephone There is a large Codetel office where Calle Duarte meets Calle Dr Alejo Martínez. The office is open 8 am to 10 pm daily. There are also numerous Codetel pay phones around town that accept Codetel-issued Comuni cards.

Email At the Codetel office, email can be sent and received. The centrally located Hotel Sosúa, which was undergoing extensive renovation in late 1998, was in the process of installing three computers with Internet and email services for public use (for both guests and nonguests). The computers, in the hotel's stylish bar, were scheduled to be online by the time this book was released.

Laundry The McWash Bar, at the end of a short street just south of the Codetel office, is what its name suggests: an establishment for both cleaning and drinking. From 10 am to 10 pm weekdays, and 10 am to 6 pm weekends, you can wash away your troubles while your clothes slosh it up, spin around and tumble nearby. A load of laundry costs US$2 to wash; to dry it is another US$2.

Museo de la Comunidad Judía de Sosúa

The Jewish Community Museum of Sosúa (☎ 809-571-1386, fax 586-2442 during museum hours only), on Calle Dr Alejo Martínez near Calle Dr Rosen, describes the complete history of the town's Jews and includes an exhibit of photographs. It is open 9 am to 1 pm Monday through Thursday.

Sosúa's Populace in 1948

During the late 1930s, Dominican strong-man Rafael Trujillo sold a large tract of farmland where the town of Sosúa now stands to American Jewish groups seeking to rescue Jews from Nazi Europe. The first group of refugees reached Sosúa in 1940 and laid the groundwork for a colony. Shown here are the results of a survey taken in Sosúa in 1948 – three years after Allied forces defeated the Nazis. The countries indicate the residents' places of origin; the number indicates the number of people from each country. Note that while most of Sosúa's residents were from the key Nazi states of Germany and Austria, Sosúa's makeup was quite international.

Austria	250
Belgium	5
China	7
Czechoslovakia	23
Ecuador	2
England	3
France	7
Germany	259
Hungary	15
Italy	2
Luxembourg	18
Poland, Russia & Lithuania	63
Portugal	2
Romania	2
Switzerland	4
USA	1

In addition, there were 94 Dominican nationals living in Sosúa, consisting of nine wives of settlers, 83 children born in Sosúa and two children with settler parents born elsewhere in the DR.

Next to the museum is the **Sinagoga de la Comunidad Judía de Sosúa** (Synagogue of the Jewish Community of Sosúa), which dates from the 1940s. The following religious services are held here: Kablat Shabat (6:45 pm Friday), Shajarit (10 am Saturday), and Havdalá (6:45 pm Saturday).

Diving

Northern Coast Diving (☎ 809-571-1028, fax 571-3883, northern@codetel.net.do), on Calle Pedro Clisante near Calle Duarte, has been in operation since 1988 and provides excellent service. It's open 8 am to 6 pm daily.

For certified divers, a two-tank boat dive with a PADI divemaster costs US$49; add US$11 to rent a complete set of scuba equipment for a day. Sixteen dives are available in all, including a shallow-wall dive, a canyon dive, a wreck dive and a dive featuring various hard and soft corals. All of the dives are offered as guided tours only – as they should be – with PADI-certified divemasters.

In addition, Northern Coast offers non-certified divers a 90-minute pool lesson followed by a 40-minute, shallow boat dive at a coral reef with your instructor for US$50. This is a great opportunity for people who've always wanted to try scuba diving but haven't wanted to spend the money, or haven't had the chance, to become certified.

Of course, if you'd like to get your PADI Open-Water certificate or receive additional training, that can be arranged as well. The following PADI classes are offered: Open-Water Diver (for US$325), Advanced Open-Water Diver (for US$250), Rescue Diver (US$350), Master Scuba Diver (US$799) and Divemaster (US$475). Instructors speak English, Dutch, Swedish, German and Spanish.

Organized Tours

Melissa Tours (☎ 809-571-2567, fax 571-1733), on Calle Duarte, offers many fun tours, and you should definitely pay them a visit if you are in Sosúa for more than a couple of days. Why? Because most likely you'll end up on an unexpected adventure you wouldn't have been able to arrange yourself.

If, for example, you don't have the cool mountain town of Jarabacoa on your itinerary, Melissa Tours can take you on a one-day trip: You'll ride a horse up to a secluded waterfall for a refreshing dip and back. The price of

US$40 includes breakfast and lunch and pick-up from and return to your Sosúa hotel.

Another Jarabacoa tour includes rafting down the Río Yaque del Norte. They provide all the equipment, including wetsuits, and drive you and five other people up into the mountains to the drop-in point; then you spend the rest of the afternoon paddling down the river. This popular all-day adventure costs US$85 and includes breakfast and lunch.

Among the other good tours offered by Melissa are one- and two-day excursions into Haiti, a road trip to Samaná and a boat ride to the marvelous Cayo Levantado, and a boat ride through mangrove near Río San Juan followed by several hours at Playa Grande. Call for current prices. Spanish, English, German, Dutch, French, Italian and Portuguese are spoken. Melissa Tours is open 8 am to 8 pm Monday through Saturday, and 9 am to noon and 4 to 8 pm Sunday.

Places to Stay

Budget The least-expensive place in town and a rather nice find for the money is the appropriately named *Hotel Central* (no phone), on Calle Pedro Clisante near Camino del Libre. The Central features 27 guest rooms with ceiling fan and private hot-water bathroom, a swimming pool and a generator to do battle with those common, irksome power shortages. The rooms are a bit worn, but the price – US$16 per room – is more than reasonable. The hotel's strongest asset is its location.

On the northeast side of town are three budget places, all of which are good and two of which are excellent. Each has a restaurant and swimming pool, but they are all too far from Playa Sosúa to reach the beach on foot. However, motoconchos are often waiting at the nearby intersection of Calle Dr Alejo Martínez and Calle Pedro Clisante and cost around US$0.50.

The German-owned *Hotel Atlantico* (☎/fax 809-571-2367) is a very pleasant place with 10 fan-cooled rooms and plans to expand to 24. All rooms have a private hot-water bathroom, and there's a pool, a restaurant and a generator. This place is very popular with Germans, particularly in December when the Atlantico reserves the month for repeat customers. Rates are US$20 per room. English, Spanish and German are spoken.

The livelier of the three places is the 20-room, German-owned *Voramar Hotel* (☎ 809-571-3910, fax 571-3076), which features two three-story buildings overlooking a swimming pool. The rooms in one building are fan cooled, while those in the other have air conditioning. All of the rooms are very nice, with satellite TV, telephone, great cross-ventilation and tasteful decor – the bathrooms even have bathtubs (a feature rarely found in the DR). The rooms on the 3rd floor are best because they have terraces large enough for chaise lounges (for that all-over tan you've always wanted). The fan-only rooms are US$25/30 for a single/double, while the air-con rooms are US$30/40. Reserving by fax is a great idea. The restaurant specializes in fine German cuisine at affordable prices. Airport pickup is available. German, English and Spanish are spoken.

The other highly recommended east-side budget hotel is the 32-room *Villa Chessa* (☎ 809-571-3412, fax 571-1020), which features singles for US$25, doubles for US$30 and spacious apartments for US$40. All of the tastefully appointed rooms on the well-maintained grounds are equipped with cable TV and ceiling fan; prices include breakfast. In addition, the English-run Chessa provides hourly shuttle service to and from Playa Sosúa between 9 am and 4 pm. These times are flexible; if you would like to be picked up at, say, 7:45 pm, that can be arranged. The emphasis at the Chessa is personal service.

Mid-Range Just outside of the budget category and a very good mid-range value is the *Apart-Hotel Plaza Sosúa* (☎ 809-571-335, fax 571-1905), on Calle Pedro Clisante a fair walk from the beach. New in 1998, the Plaza Sosúa is a big, three-story place with a courtyard and a swimming pool. All of the apartments are air-conditioned and spacious, with user-friendly kitchens, terraces, cable TV and ceiling fans. If you're looking for a lot of space – if there are two of you with bikes you keep in your room, for example – this is certainly a good value. And the value improves with each night of your stay: One night is US$45 per room; a two-night stay is US$80; a three-night stay is US$99; and if you stay four or more nights, it's only US$32 per night.

The recently remodeled and Italian-owned *Hotel Sosúa* (☎ 809-571-2683, fax 571-2180) is the best deal in town. It's perfectly situated on Calle Duarte. The rooms are quite adequate, with air conditioning, private hot-water bathroom, cable TV, ceiling fan, telephone and good mattresses. The decor, alas, is super tacky, but if you don't mind that, this place is a great find. The hotel has a swimming pool, an Italian restaurant, a bar, a gym, a generator and even computers with Internet access. International calls are available from the bar. The price of US$35/50 includes an American (that is, hearty) breakfast.

Top End Six hotels fall into this category, the loveliest by far being the *PierGiorgio Palace Hotel* (☎ 809-571-2215, fax 571-2786, www.piergiorgio.com), a 51-room, three-story, Victorian-style hotel with all the fixings. Brand new in 1998, the Palace is the realized dream of Italian fashion designer PierGiorgio, who can be found at his fabulously decorated hotel or adjacent restaurant most of the time. Twenty-eight of the guest rooms have wonderful sea views (the hotel and restaurant are within meters of the mouth of Bahía de Sosúa), while the remaining 23 guest rooms face the town. All rooms have air conditioning, cable TV and two telephones (one is in the bathroom). There's an inviting swimming pool and handsome gardens. The rate of US$75 per room includes breakfast. This is a 'wow' kind of place.

The *Casa Marina Beach Resort* (☎ 809-571-3690, 571-3110) is your typical, 300-room all-inclusive hotel: it sits on a beach with as many guest rooms as possible stacked around two large swimming pools. Which isn't to say it's uncomfortable; each room is air-conditioned, has a small balcony and is equipped with cable TV. The beach is

quite attractive, and there are two restaurants – one serving Creole food and other international cuisine. There's a dance club, a game room and plenty of water-sports equipment. Rates are US$105/160 for a single/double.

Next best is the Victorian-style *Marco Polo Club* (☎ 809-571-3128, fax 571-3233), which is at the edge of the bay. It has eight oceanfront apartments (with 16 more under construction), each cheerfully decorated and equipped with an oversize romantic bathtub, air conditioning, balcony and telephone. There's also a fancy restaurant and a popular bar. If the hotel has a weakness, it would be its service. For US$80 per room, it's not what it should be.

Not nearly as large or flashy as the nearby Casa Marina but quite all right is the all-inclusive *Sosúa By-the-Sea* (☎ 809-571-3222, fax 571-3020), which offers a variety of studios, one-bedroom apartments and superior suites for US$60/70/90 per person (double occupancy), respectively, from May through mid-November, and US$75/85/125 per person (double occupancy) from mid-November through April. Rates do not include a 23% tax and service charge. This is not the greatest bargain in the world, but it does have a lovely patch of beach.

The all-inclusive, Spanish-owned *La Esplanada Resort* (☎ 809-571-3333, fax 571-3922) is quite popular with the 20-something crowd. The hotel is a good distance from the shore, but provides frequent shuttle service to and from the beach. It contains 210 rooms in all, including 120 junior suites, as well as two restaurants and a pizzeria, a karaoke pub, a swim-up bar, a swimming pool, two tennis courts and an exchange bank. Rates for most of the year are US$90/160.

The least attractive of the top-end hotels is the *Playa Escondida Beach Resort* (☎ 809-471-5040, fax 571-3110), which is far from Playa Sosúa but does have a tiny beach all to itself. The surf at that beach is, however, too strong for swimming. All of the resort's 90 rooms have air conditioning, cable TV and a view of the so-so swimming pool. Year-round prices are US$60/110.

Places to Eat

A popular and easy-to-recommend indoor/outdoor restaurant-bar is *PJ's*, near the key intersection of Calle Duarte and Calle Pedro Clisante. The very varied menu offers soups (for US$2 to US$3), sandwiches and burgers (all for around US$3), a choice of spaghetti (US$3 to US$5), traditional Dominican fare (US$4 to US$7), pizzas (from US$4), seafood (from US$8), schnitzels (US$6) and beef steaks (US$7 to US$9).

For good Italian food at affordable prices, turn to *Mamma Mia* near the middle of town. Most of the pastas cost around US$5. The pizzas here are particularly good, and the most expensive of the lot is the combination Mamma Mia for only US$6. This is a very pleasant, clean place with a friendly staff. It's a good find.

If you really love Italian food and feel like pampering yourself, go to *La Puntilla de PierGiorgio* (☎ 809-571-2215), next to PierGiorgio's gorgeous hotel and on the edge of a small cliff. The indoor-outdoor La Puntilla has elegant tablesettings and somewhat formal service by a waitstaff in black tie. Surrounded by lush gardens, tables are set far enough apart to give a sense of privacy. Overall, it's quite lovely and romantic, and the food is divine. Perhaps the best items on the long menu are the green tagliatelle with seafood, *gnocchi puntilla* (pasta in tomato sauce with seafood), spaghetti marinara and a combination plate with all three of these dishes. PierGiorgio's favorites are the *cannelloni rossini* (spinach and meat cannelloni) and tortelloni with ricotta. All of the dishes listed here are priced at US$13. Reservations are recommended.

Equally elegant but inferior in quality and service to La Puntilla is the restaurant at the *Marco Polo Club*. If only the dishes tasted as delicious as they read: seafood fettuccini in olive oil and garlic and topped with a white wine sauce (US$12); penne with smoked salmon covered in a vodka and caviar cream sauce (US$10); New York sirloin in a tomato and oregano sauce (US$14); deep-fried squid with tartar sauce (US$8); and lobster served as you wish (US$18).

For Chinese food, try the *Restaurant Lotus*, on Calle Pedro Clisante near Calle Duarte. This pleasant, breezy, open-sided diner has booths, tables and a long bar, and it offers a number of set dinners, one of which consists of wonton soup, egg rolls, steamed rice, vegetable chop suey and Cantonese shrimp (US$12). The Lotus also offers numerous main dishes with rice for around US$6.

The Swiss-owned *Restaurant Pollo Rico*, on Calle Pedro Clisante, offers some items you won't find elsewhere in Sosúa, including escargot (US$7), ox-tail soup (US$4) and cubed chicken with curry sauce (US$7). It also serves a variety of German dishes you can find elsewhere in Sosúa, including Wiener schnitzel (US$6), beef stroganoff (US$10) and meat fondue (US$12). The bar at Pollo Rico is quite popular with the town's German residents.

Restaurant La Gaviota, on Calle Duarte, is nice and airy and less expensive than most of the restaurants in the area: A filling seafood soup costs only US$3, a mixed salad sells for US$2 and the spaghetti carbonara is US$4.50. This is a fine place just to order a glass of fresh-squeezed orange juice and people-watch.

If you're preparing your own food and beverages, the *Playero Supermarket*, on Calle Pedro Clisante near Calle Duarte, is well stocked, inexpensive and open 8 am to 10 pm daily. The *Super Super Liquor Store*, on Calle Pedro Clisante near Calle Ayuntamiento, has a super selection of liquors and wines at super-low prices and is open 8 am to 10 pm Monday through Saturday.

Entertainment

Dance Clubs There are many dance clubs in Sosúa, and they come and go with great regularity. The ones mentioned here were very 'in' at the time of writing and appeared to have staying power. Note that the DR dance scene doesn't start until well into the night. Unless you like to have the dance floor all to yourself, don't bother showing up at any of these places before midnight. Arriving after 2 am is even better.

If you've ever been to Rio de Janeiro, home of the famous Copacabana Beach, you might guess the decor of Sosúa's *Copacabana*: dozens of black tables ringed by beige wicker chairs set on three levels around three sides of the wooden dance floor, giant palm fronds smartly placed to give the illusion of the beach, walls covered with vivid paintings of coconut trees. The music is merengue, salsa and American pop. The club is open 11 pm to 6 am daily, and the cost is US$2 at the door.

The *High Caribbean Club* – with its flashing colored lights, fog machine, American rock, and several bars around the dance floor – wouldn't be at all out of place in Los Angeles (except for the small indoor swimming pool next to the dance floor). Patrons are encouraged to drink and dive, so when you're dressing to go out, consider wearing a bathing suit underneath. If you want to attract attention, wear white; the High Caribbean uses a lot of black lights, making white clothes absolutely eye-catching. The entry fee is US$2.

A much tamer and romantic place is the oceanside bar/disco at the *Marco Polo Club*. With a commanding moonlit view of Playa Sosúa, the small lounge is awash in a sea of soothing colors, mainly tans and browns, and bamboo chic – no ballroom glitter here. The furniture is mostly padded bamboo bar stools, although in several corners sit kingly bamboo reading chairs. This place doesn't get going much before 3 or 4 am. People tend to arrive here after partying elsewhere, to catch the sunrise on the water; it's a smart plan. The music is merengue. Cost is US$2.

Another hot spot is the *Merengue Club*. Because of its central location, it attracts lots of tourists, which in turn attracts lots of locals and a good number of prostitutes. This club offers some superb people-watching; there is no entry fee. Incidentally, most of the prostitutes are quiet, friendly Haitians who visit Sosúa for a month at a time and take home to their families whatever money they are able to earn. A smart and compassionate response to being approached would be to chat for a minute, give them a few dollars, and leave it at that; in addition to ethical

considerations, you should know that HIV incidence is high among island prostitutes.

Casinos There's one casino in town, operated by the Playa Escondida Beach Resort. All of the usual games can be found there. The casino is open 8 pm to 4 am daily.

Getting There & Away

Air Sosúa is served by Aeropuerto Gregorio Luperón, which is about 20km west of town. Numerous charter airlines use the airport, virtually all working in conjunction with the all-inclusive hotels. Check the travel sections of newspapers in your country and contact a local travel agent to learn about any package deals that may be applicable to you. Several major airlines, including American and LTU, also provide service to and from the Aeropuerto Gregorio Luperón from abroad.

Air Santo Domingo (☎ 809-683-8020) is the only carrier providing service to Aeropuerto Gregorio Luperón from other Dominican cities. Be advised that since the airport is nearest to Puerto Plata, it's usually referred to simply as the Puerto Plata airport, and the destination is often referred to as Puerto Plata (instead of Aeropuerto Gregorio Luperón). Here are the various flight options available from Air Santo Domingo; shown are routes, flying times and one-way prices.

Destination	Duration	Cost
Santo Domingo	40 min	US$54
Las Américas Airport	45 min	US$54
La Romana	50 min	US$59
Punta Cana	1 hour	US$59
El Portillo	30 min	US$49

Contact Air Santo Domingo for current flight times and reservations; Spanish and English are spoken. The cost of a taxi ride between the airport and Sosúa is US$10.

Bus Caribe Tours offers bus service to Sosúa from Santo Domingo 10 times daily, at 7, 8:30, 9:30, 10:30 and 11:30 am, and at 1, 1:45, 2:45, 4 and 5:30 pm. Departing Sosúa for the capital are buses leaving at 6, 7, 8:25, 9:25 and 10:25 am, and at 12:25, 2:10, 3:25, 4:25

and 4:55 pm. The cost for the 240km journey is US$6 each way. Caribe Tours has its depot along Hwy 5 in the hamlet of Los Charamicos, which is actually 1.5km southwest of Calle Duarte. Taxis and motoconchos will take you there from Sosúa for US$3 or less.

Additionally, gua-guas pass by Sosúa on Hwy 5 all day long. If your next destination is Puerto Plata, Cabarete or another town on the north coast of the DR, it's easier and quicker just to go to the highway's edge and hail a passing gua-gua headed in the right direction rather than going to the Caribe Tours depot and waiting for a scheduled departure. Also, the cost of the gua-gua won't be more than US$1.50.

Getting Around

There is no shortage of taxis and motoconchos in Sosúa, although it's easy enough to walk to most things in town. A motoconcho ride anywhere in town will never cost you more than US$2, and usually half that. A taxi costs twice or more what a motoconcho costs.

Valle del Cibao

Although the towns in the fertile Valle del Cibao (Cibao Valley) have little to offer the tourist, they have interesting histories and are pleasant enough to pass through, and the countryside is beautiful.

MOCA

The country town of Moca has prospered in recent decades as a result of its production of coffee, cocoa and tobacco. Its sole tourist attraction is its church, the **Iglesia Corazón de Jesus**, which is the tallest building in town and has lots of beautiful stained glass imported from Turin, Italy.

During the 19th century, Moca became one of the Spanish colony's chief cattle centers. Unfortunately for the people of Moca, its distance from Santo Domingo made it a natural target of forces seeking to wrest control of eastern Hispaniola from Spain. In 1805, for example, a Haitian force led by Henri Christophe that was trying to place the entire island under the Haitian flag

entered Moca, killed the entire population and burned the town to the ground.

It took a decade, but people eventually resettled Moca, raising cattle and planting subsistence crops. During the 1840s, they began to raise tobacco as a commercial crop; today, some of the world's best cigars contain tobacco grown on hillsides around the town. At the same time (1844) and after many years of guerrilla fighting, the Spanish colonists were finally able to oust the Haitian army, which no doubt allowed the people of Moca to sleep more soundly.

Today, Moca is one of a number of prosperous communities in the Cibao Valley. Coffee and tobacco plantations abound on the slopes to the north and south, and the town buzzes with cars and mopeds. There's little reason to make Moca a destination, but if you happen to be passing through, you might want to stop by the church, which is beside the main road through town.

SAN FRANCISCO DE MACORÍS

Also in the fertile Valle del Cibao, San Francisco de Macorís is similar to Moca in many ways, and significantly different in others. Although much larger than Moca, with 180,000 inhabitants, San Francisco de Macorís' prosperity is also due to the rich farmland that surrounds it. Like Moca, it developed beside a highway that today pretty much divides the community into even halves. And as in Moca, the visitor to San Francisco de Macorís can still see quite a few examples of Caribbean-colonial architecture, with its high, narrow doorways and windows.

But unlike Moca, which is bounded by mountains, the land around San Francisco de Macorís is flat and is primarily used for growing rice. And San Francisco de Macorís is known throughout the Dominican Republic as the home of the country's drug lords. Even the director of promotions for the country's Ministry of Tourism acknowledged this in a 1998 interview: 'It's true. The drug traffickers own the nicest homes there. Huge places. Mansions.'

The largest homes in San Francisco de Macorís are behind tall walls and heavy gates and may or may not be owned by drug lords. It's not the type of thing you actually inquire about while you're there, and it's probably not a great idea to go searching out such places. Since there really isn't much to draw tourists here in any case, San Francisco de Macorís is best avoided altogether. Bicyclists or others needing a place to stay for the night will find four budget places along the main road through town.

COTUÍ

Like other towns in the Valle del Cibao, Cotuí's earliest recorded history is one of peasants raising cattle and farming mostly to feed themselves. A survey in 1690 showed that Cotuí consisted of 70 families residing in a total of only 20 huts. During the next 100 years, it grew some in size and population but remained a simple rural community struggling to make ends meet.

Like Moca, it had the misfortune of catching the attention of a Haitian ruler, Jean-Jacques Dessalines, who sought to incorporate Cotuí and other towns into Haiti. In early 1804, the residents of Cotuí were forced at bayonet point to leave their homes, their cattle and their fields. However, after several weeks the residents gradually returned, as they had no wish to rebuild their community from scratch elsewhere.

A year later the Haitians returned, led by Henri Christophe, and Cotuí was burned to the ground and most of its residents killed. In fact, aside from Santo Domingo, only the towns of Bayaguana, El Seibo and Higüey, in the easternmost part of the country, remained standing. All the rest were deserted and most would remain so for years.

By the 1850s Cotuí had yet to recover. Its small population of subsistence farmers lived in extreme isolation. More than 140 years later, life may have changed, but it continues to be hard in Cotuí, and locals still struggle for a better life. In 1989, more than 100 peasants were jailed after clashing with the army over protests about their shrinking incomes due to inflation.

The massive infusions of tourist money that have revived towns throughout the republic in recent decades have yet to arrive in Cotuí, which has no attractions to speak of. However, the road to Cotuí from the Hwy Duarte and via the hamlet of Maimón is very pleasant and scenic, winding through lush canyons and atop a ridge beside a beautiful river. If you decide to make the trip, you'll find that the residents of Cotuí are very welcoming.

If you need somewhere to overnight, the best place in town is the **Cabañas Turistica del Yuna** (☎ 809-585-3021), near the north end of town. New in 1998, it's a bargain at US$20 for an air-conditioned room with private hot-water bathroom, parking and security.

Another option, on the main road downhill from the town square, is the **Hotel El Rey** (no phone), which offers decent, fan-only rooms for US$10 per room.

Northwestern Dominican Republic

When Christopher Columbus made his second voyage to the New World in 1493, he landed at La Isabela in the Dominican Northwest, founding the colony that would give the Old World its first successful foothold in the New. The Spanish settlement at La Isabela, the ruins of which are the primary attraction of the DR's youngest national park, suffered through two epidemics – a hurricane and a fire – barely surviving for five years. From this struggling port, approximately 55km northwest of Puerto Plata, Europeans commenced their assault on the people and territory of the Western Hemisphere.

Today, more than 500 years since the founding of La Isabela on the shore of a calm bay along Hispaniola's Atlantic coast, the Northwest in many ways still remains unsettled territory. Yes, it's changed: Puerto Plata has become a tourist destination; Santiago is the country's second-largest city; and Dajabón is a bustling border town. But most of the Northwest is wide-open, undeveloped land, and most of the region's cities are scarcely more than provincial towns with no real tourist attractions. Surrounding Santiago are fields of tobacco and other crops, but west of the city remain large tracts of untouched subtropical dry forest. Along the 115km Santiago-to-Monte Cristi highway, a half-dozen or so small towns quickly appear and disappear, with much of the drive dominated by the gorgeous slopes of the Cordillera Septentrional to the north.

More than 95% of the Northwest's foreign visitors stay at all-inclusive resorts in the vicinity of Puerto Plata and confine their exploration to their resorts and to the ride to and from the Aeropuerto Gregorio Luperón, the airport serving Puerto Plata. That's a pity because most of the towns in the Northwest typify towns found throughout the Dominican heartland; a day spent in any of them will teach the traveler more about the DR than a month at a Puerto Plata resort.

PUERTO PLATA

At the ocean's edge in the shadow of a majestic mountain, Puerto Plata (Port of Silver) was named by Columbus – but not for the obvious reason. When the great explorer first set eyes on the area, it was from the deck of a ship. On January 11, 1493, Columbus approached the Bahía de Puerto Plata, its verdant shore and the 800m peak behind it, and the sunlight reflected off the bay so brilliantly it resembled a sea of sparkling silver coins. Hence the admiral named the area Puerto Plata, and to the mountain he gave the name Pico Isabel de Torres, in honor of the Spanish queen who'd sent him.

Since then, Puerto Plata has known very good times and very bad, and it is currently struggling through another difficult stretch. While nearby all-inclusive resorts are capitalizing on an enormous influx of tourists, the town itself has difficulty drawing visitors. However, it's a friendly, low-key place with an interesting history and a beautiful oceanside promenade, called the *malecón*. From here you can often spot dolphins frolicking in the waves or a passing humpback whale (during January and February). A lovely lawn by the historic fort, with splendid ocean views, also cries out for a picnic. And if you have any interest in amber, the town contains one of the country's best museums.

Note, however, that the *teleférico,* or cable car, that used to go to the top of Pico Isabel de Torres is no longer functioning. Several other guidebooks on the Dominican Republic still mention it, but it stopped running in 1996 and as of late 1998 there were no plans to put it back on line. At the time of writing, there were no roads or hiking trails to the peak.

History

Despite its optimistic name, and the hopes of the arriving conquistadors, who were coming to the New World in search of riches, Puerto Plata contained few precious metals; its silver was limited to the shimmering waves that lapped its shores. However, the

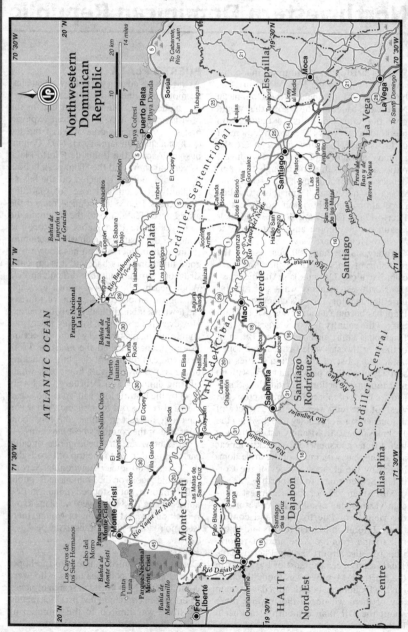

Northwestern Dominican Republic

land proved tremendously fertile. It's a little-known fact that Columbus brought with him on his second voyage stalks of sugarcane, and the sweet perennial grass was first planted on the island near here. From colonial times until the late 20th century, sugar, tobacco and cattle-hide production were Puerto Plata's chief industries.

Puerto Plata began as an enormously important port, since it was the most convenient outlet for the goods produced in the Northwest and the crop-rich Valle del Cibao. Until 1922, when the highway connecting Santiago and Santo Domingo was completed, it made better sense to ship produce from the northern half of the country through the Mona Passage (off the east coast of Hispaniola) to Santo Domingo in the south than to haul the goods to the capital across rugged country on the backs of mules. During the mid-16th century, Fuerte de San Felipe was built at the mouth of Bahía de Puerto Plata to protect the port from pirates, and the fort can be visited today.

Unfortunately for the residents of Puerto Plata, the number of pirates operating in the Atlantic during the late 16th century steadily increased, and Spanish trading ships became reluctant to stop at Puerto Plata. Although the colonists produced plenty of sugar, tobacco and cattle hides, they were sorely lacking in manufactured goods. Since French, Portuguese and English smugglers – all enemies of Spain – were able to supply these goods as well, the colonists began trading with the smugglers even though it was strictly forbidden by the Spanish government. This trade became so intense that in 1598 Spanish authorities estimated that nearly 80,000 hides a year were being sold to their enemies.

By 1605 the Spanish Crown had had enough of the illegal trade. It ordered its troops from the garrison at Puerto Rico to evacuate Puerto Plata – as well as the trading centers of Monte Cristi, La Yaguana and Bayajá – and with little choice the residents of these towns moved their cattle overland to Santo Domingo. Of the estimated 110,000 head of cattle that were rounded up and herded south, only 8000 survived the arduous

journey. Of those animals, another 6000 perished due to poor pasturage in the new area.

Puerto Plata remained abandoned for the next 13 decades – until the Crown decided to repopulate the area to prevent settlers from other countries from moving in. Gradually Puerto Plata regained much of its importance as the major port in the north. But during the late 18th and early 19th centuries its residents were repeatedly victimized by French and Haitian forces seeking to wrest the area from Spanish control. It wouldn't be for yet another hundred years that a generation of Puerto Plata residents would be left alone. Unfortunately for them, the completion of the Hwy Duarte from Santo Domingo to Santiago in 1922 resulted in a major loss of business from their port, and the town's prosperity paid the price.

The years from 1930 to 1961 – during the reign of dictator Rafael Trujillo – were particularly bad for Puerto Plata. Many of the town's residents despised the strongman, and the incidence of clashes between antigovernment demonstrators and Trujillo's troops was much higher there than elsewhere in the country. As a result, Trujillo did nothing to improve the economic situation in the area, and he had many Puerto Plata residents arrested and locked up as enemies of the state. By the time Trujillo was assassinated in 1961, the city looked dead. The town's large dock was sagging, the stores and streets were empty and an air of sullen suffering hung over the city.

But in the early 1990s, Puerto Plata was revived by a new industry: tourism. The town spiffed itself up and quickly grew to accommodate the new visitors. Before long, tourism revenues surpassed those of its three main industries – sugar, tobacco and cattle hides – combined.

But the good times haven't lasted very long. Today, despite the hordes of vacationers who continue to arrive, the town of Puerto Plata itself is struggling again. The reason is simple: Nearly all of the tourists who come to the area stay at all-inclusive resorts at Playa Dorada and Cofresí, both a few kilometers outside of town. Because all of their meals and drinks are prepaid, the

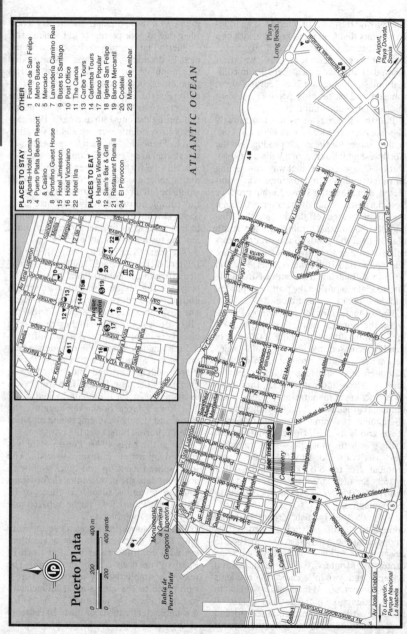

Puerto Plata

0   200   400 m
0   200   400 yards

PLACES TO STAY
3   Aparta-Hotel Lomar
4   Puerto Plata Beach Resort
    & Casino
8   Portofino Guest House
15 Hotel Jimesson
16 Hotel Victoriano
22 Hotel Ilra

PLACES TO EAT
6   Hans's Wienerwald
12 Sam's Bar & Grill
21 Restaurant Roma II
24 El Provocon

OTHER
1   Fuerte de San Felipe
2   Metro Buses
5   Mercado
7   Lavandería Camino Real
9   Buses to Santiago
10 Post Office
11 The Canoa
13 Caribe Tours
14 Catemba Tours
17 Banco Popular
18 Iglesia San Felipe
19 Banco Mercantil
20 Codetel
23 Museo de Ambar

ATLANTIC OCEAN

Bahía de
Puerto Plata

Monumento
a General
Gregorio Luperón

see inset map

guests at these resorts rarely spend money at restaurants or bars in town. And because the resorts abound with gift shops and jewelry stores, few of the guests come to town to shop. In fact, few of 'Puerto Plata's tourists' ever see the town.

But Puerto Plata *does* have a few attractions, not the least of which are its welcoming residents, its small-town charm and the few Victorian-style houses that remain. And if you visit Puerto Plata during one of its annual festivals, you'll find the entire town in a very celebratory mood (see Special Events, below).

Orientation

Puerto Plata is 71km north of Santiago via the excellent Bisonó-Imbert route. This well-maintained stretch of highway winds up and over the Cordillera Septentrional, changing names twice as it reaches Puerto Plata from the east: first it becomes Av José Ginebra and then Av Circunvalación Sur. The town is north of this avenue.

To get to downtown Puerto Plata from Hwy 5, take Av Colón, then a quick right onto Calle Camino Real. Calle Camino Real soon becomes Calle Separación, taking you to the center of town and past the delightful and popular town square, Parque Luperón, beside which is the art-deco Iglesia San Felipe. The main east-west street is Calle Beller. Puerto Plata's sole beach, Playa Long Beach, is several kilometers east of downtown.

Information

Puerto Plata has no tourist office, but there are many English-speaking guides who hang out along the east side of Parque Luperón and are generally anxious to dispense information, especially if there's a tip involved.

Money There is no shortage of banks in Puerto Plata, and it's possible to exchange common currencies at all of them. Banco Mercantil and Banco Popular are near the Parque Luperón. Both are open 8 am to 5 pm weekdays. There's an ATM at the Banco Mercantil.

Post & Communications The downtown post office, on Calle 12 de Julio, two blocks

north of Parque Luperón, is open 8 am to 5 pm weekdays and 9 am to 1 pm Saturday. The Codetel office on Calle Beller, one block east of Parque Luperón, is open 8 am to 10 pm daily. The office has two computers with Internet access for public use.

Travel Agencies If you need the assistance of a travel agency, consider visiting Cafemba Tours (☎ 809-586-2177, fax 586-6313), a half block north of Parque Luperón. Cafemba has been operating in Puerto Plata since 1969 and can assist you with airline tickets and arrange for you to join tours originating at Playa Dorada resorts destined for Isla Saona and elsewhere.

Laundry Unfortunately, there is no laundry right in downtown. Lavandería Camino Real is the closest, on Calle Separación near Calle Camino Real, about 500m from Parque Luperón. This is a laundry service; there are no coin-operated machines. If clothes are left early in the morning, they are usually available for pick up the same day. A large load of laundry – cleaned, dried and folded – costs US$3. Lavandería Camino Real is open 8 am to noon and 2 to 6:30 pm daily.

Museo de Ambar

Dominican amber is widely regarded as the finest in the world. It not only exhibits the largest range of colors – from clear and pale lemon to warm oranges, gold, brown, and even green, blue and black – but it contains the greatest number of inclusions, such as insects, tiny reptiles and plant matter. Such inclusions add character to a piece of amber and increase its value. One variety of amber, the blue, is unique to the island.

At the Amber Museum (☎ 809-320-2215, fax 586-8518, www.ambermuseum.com), on the corner of Calle E Prudhomme and Calle Duarte, the excellent exhibits have information in English and Spanish, and they are as detailed as either of the amber museums in the Zona Colonial of Santo Domingo. This museum will answer just about any question you might have about Dominican amber. In addition, the gift shop has some superior pieces of amber jewelry on sale at good prices (be advised that all of the prices are negotiable). See Shopping, below, for other places to buy amber.

The museum is open 9 am to 6 pm Monday to Saturday. Admission is US$3.

Fuerte de San Felipe

This well-maintained fort on a point at the mouth of Bahía de Puerto Plata was built in the mid-16th century to prevent pirates from sacking the town or from seizing one of only two protected bays on the entire north coast. Perhaps the fort served a useful purpose in deterring attacks that would have occurred without it, but in fact it was never called on to defend the town, and for much of its life it served as a prison.

The fort, with its massive walls and interior moat, is the only remnant from Puerto Plata's early colonial days. In tiny rooms once used to confine prisoners, the government has created a rather unimpressive museum that displays rusty agricultural tools, a few rifle barrels from the 1880s, lots of bayonets and a stack of cannonballs. The few informational signs are in Spanish only. The museum is open from 8 am to 4 pm daily. Admission is US$1.

PAUL GERACE

Fuerte de San Felipe

Mercado

If you've never seen a traditional Latin American market, amble through the interesting one on Calle 2 at Av Isabel de Torres. While it's not nearly as impressive as the much larger market near Santo Domingo's Zona Colonial, it's usually quite lively and a

good place to buy fresh fruit, vegetables and inexpensive clothes. The market is open 8 am to 5 pm Monday through Saturday.

Special Events

Merengue Festival Puerto Plata hosts a popular merengue festival the first week of October. During the festival the entire length of the city's malecón is closed to vehicular traffic, food stalls are set up on both sides of the oceanside boulevard, and a huge stage is erected for merengue performances. Beside the Fuerte de San Felipe and at Parque Luperón, visitors can watch how traditional local dishes are prepared using just-harvested crops, and they can observe local artists making many traditional Dominican crafts.

Cultural Festival Puerto Plata holds the weeklong Cultural Festival during the third week in June, which features merengue, blues, jazz and folk concerts at Fuerte de San Felipe. Troupes from Santo Domingo perform traditional dances that range from African spirituals to sexy salsa steps. At the same time, the town hosts an arts-and-crafts fair for local artisans at the nearby Parque Luperón.

Places to Stay

If you're going to be in town during either the Merengue Festival or the Cultural Festival, be sure to make hotel reservations at least a month in advance. This is particularly true if you would like to stay at the Hotel Victoriano, the Aparta-Hotel Lomar or the Portofino Guest House.

Budget By far the best accommodations in the downtown area are at the 25-room *Hotel Victoriano* (☎ 809-586-9752), on Calle San Felipe two blocks from Parque Luperón. It has rooms with cable TV and private hot-water bathroom on three levels in a clean and well-maintained complex. Rooms with ceiling fans rent for only US$10 per room. An air-conditioned room with one bed rents for US$14, and an air-conditioned room with two beds rents for US$17. The management here is very friendly, and they have a generator to offset power shortages.

Not nearly as nice but also near Parque Luperón is the *Hotel Jimesson* (☎ 809-586-5131), on Calle JF Kennedy, which offers 22 rooms, some on a second floor, for US$20 per room. All rooms have air con, but the bathrooms don't have hot water. The beds are worn, as are the pillows, and there's no shortage of pesky mosquitoes.

The *Hotel Ilra* (☎ 809-586-2337), on Calle Villa Nueva near Calle Beller, offers nine basic rooms, each with a fan on a stand and a mosquito net over the bed, that share a hot-water bathroom. Rooms with one bed are US$10, two beds are US$14. All of the rooms are located on the 2nd floor of an old Victorian-style home, and most have excellent cross-ventilation.

Be especially wary of the Hotel Castilla, two blocks north of Parque Luperón. A lot of people see this place (since it's across from a bus station) and wonder if it's OK. It's not. The rooms look like they haven't been maintained since the building was built – in 1894. In short, avoid this place.

Mid-Range Really more like high-end budget hotels are two very comfortable and recommended places. Neither is close to downtown, but both are quite near the attractive Playa Long Beach – the town's only beach. The two hotels have the same owner, a very friendly man who manages the properties when he's not tending his cattle. He takes a lot of pride in his hotels, and it shows.

The *Portofino Guest House* (☎ 809-586-2858, fax 586-5050), on Av Hermanas Mirabal, has 13 rooms in a one-story building beside an appealing swimming pool. Each room has air con, a private hot-water bathroom and a telephone. There's a generator, secure parking and a pleasant and inexpensive restaurant. Rates are US$26 for singles or doubles.

The *Aparta-Hotel Lomar* (☎ 809-586-2858, fax 586-5050), toward the east end of the malecón, is a bit pricier than the Portofino Guest House. Its very spacious rooms have air con, telephone, cable TV, a private hot-water bathroom and a fridge. If you don't need the air conditioning, try one of

the spacious two-bed rooms with ceiling fan and balcony with sea view for US$26. And the budget-priced Aparta-Hotel Lomar also offers room service.

Top End While many resorts are to the near east and west of town, the all-inclusive *Puerto Plata Beach Resort & Casino* (☎ 800-348-5395, 809-586-4243, fax 586-4377) is the only resort actually in the town; it's near the east end of the malecón. The Puerto Plata Beach Resort consists of 216 rooms in a Victorian-style village that also contains a casino, two restaurants, a swimming pool, an exchange bank, a gift shop, a beauty parlor and massage and baby-sitting services. The vast majority of the guest rooms contain a separate living area; all have a full bathroom with tub.

The Puerto Plata is across the street from the town's only beach, where it operates a guest bar. Activities include scuba diving lessons, a windsurfing clinic and sailing. Room rates are US$145/210 a single/double.

Places to Eat

El Provocon, on Calle Separación a few blocks south of Parque Luperón, is open 24 hours a day and is very popular with the locals. El Provocon is an indoor-outdoor diner specializing in grilled chicken – *very* tasty and inexpensive. An entire *pollo al carbon* – chicken cooked on a barbecue – costs a mere US$4.25. Half a grilled chicken sells for US$2.10. Side orders include yucca, rice or salad at US$0.75 each. A large beer is US$1.35, a glass of real orange juice is US$0.65 and a soft drink US$0.50. No one will think any less of you if you order a chicken to go and eat while gazing upon the ocean from the lawn beside the Fuerte de San Felipe.

Another thoroughly unpretentious place is *Hansi's Wienerwald*, at the east end of the malecón near Av Hermanas Mirabal. This oceanside café with little tables covered in red-checkered tablecloths opens for breakfast and stays open until '10, 11 or midnight or 1 – it all depends,' according to its friendly staff. At Hansi's Wienerwald, where a pleasant breeze is accompanied by classy Spanish music, breakfast will rarely exceed US$3, Wiener schnitzel costs US$6, a cheeseburger is US$2.75, and a strong rum drink is only US$1.30. All of the breakfast jams are home-made, and the Wiener schnitzel is decent.

The restaurant at the **Portofino Guest House** is a major step up from either of the above in terms of presentation and setting, and yet it's still quite inexpensive. It serves spaghetti carbonara (US$2.50), lasagna (US$3), meat dishes (US$3 to US$5) and pizzas (around US$3.50). The restaurant is open-sided, the kitchen is spotless, the tables are clothed, and the roof is thatched. Ceiling fans keep the air circulating. Quite nice.

The best restaurant in town is the **Restaurant Roma II** (☎ 809-586-3404), on Calle Beller two blocks east of Parque Luperón. It offers a variety of pastas, including fettuccine al pesto (US$6), penne thermidor (US$6) and lasagna bolognesa (US$7). Seafood dishes (the house specialty) include broiled lobster in lemon sauce (US$19), shrimp in a garlic-and-brandy sauce (US$14) and sea bass in a lemon-and-wine sauce (US$10). Also delicious and reasonably priced are any of their 17 pizzas, including such exotic choices as tuna fish pizza, shrimp pizza and octopus pizza. Be sure to make reservations if you're visiting town around the Christmas holiday or during a festival; English and Spanish are spoken.

On Calle José del Carmen Ariza just north of Parque Luperón is **Sam's Bar & Grill**, the favorite watering hole of the area's heavy-drinking resident gringos and gringas, who begin wandering in well before noon for the first of many Presidente beers. Like Sam's owners, Al and Joanne from Philadelphia, the music is strictly American – lots of Elvis and Chuck Berry – and the walls are plastered with Humphrey Bogart movie posters. Breakfast items include egg tostada, steak and eggs, and fluffy pancakes. Lunch includes soups, salads and sandwiches (the Philly cheesesteak rules). Few breakfast or lunch items top US$4. Also on the menu are Mom's meatloaf, Sam's ham and several burritos (the chili burritos are much tastier than the chicken burritos and are even more satisfying with hot sauce). It's open late every day.

Shopping

There are lots of gift shops in the vicinity of Parque Luperón, the best of which is The Canoa, on Calle Beller one block northwest of Parque Luperón. The Canoa has a wide variety of handicrafts, including knee-high wooden figures of Haitian peasants carved from avocado, mango and mahogany trees; lots of paintings, most in the 'primitive' style and produced by Haitian artists; and many pieces of jewelry made from black coral, amber and larimar.

Also for sale here and elsewhere are necklaces made of lava. The pieces resemble blued steel. The necklaces, though beautiful, are not locally produced. The finished products are sent to Hawaii from Taiwan, and from Hawaii the necklaces are distributed to jewelry stores throughout the Caribbean. They're quite attractive and rather inexpensive, but if you're looking for a little bit of the Dominican Republic to take back with you, shop for amber or larimar. The Canoa is open 9 am to 6 pm daily.

At the back of the store and easily overlooked is a small factory, where two or three artisans can usually be found making jewelry. Here, you can get a good feel for the amount of work that goes into making a fine necklace or set of amber or larimar earrings. However, for really high-quality jewelry, go to the gift shop at the Museo de Ambar.

Getting There & Away

Air Puerto Plata is served by Aeropuerto Gregorio Luperón, which is about 10km southeast of town. Numerous charter airlines use the airport, mostly in conjunction with the all-inclusive hotels. To find out about available package deals, check the travel sections of your national newspapers and contact a local travel agent. Several major airlines, including American and LTU, also provide international service to and from the airport.

Air Santo Domingo (☎ 809-683-8020) is the only carrier providing service to Aeropuerto Gregorio Luperón from other Dominican cities (although they currently do not serve Santiago). Note that people usually refer to the airport and the destination as

Puerto Plata rather than Aeropuerto Gregorio Luperón, since Puerto Plata is the city nearest to the airport. Here are the various flight options available from Air Santo Domingo; shown are routes, flying times and one-way prices.

Destination	Duration	Cost
Santo Domingo	40 min	US$54
Las Américas Airport	45 min	US$54
La Romana	50 min	US$59
Punta Cana	1 hour	US$59
El Portillo	30 min	US$49

Contact Air Santo Domingo for current flight times and reservations; Spanish and English are spoken. The cost of a taxi ride between the airport and Puerto Plata is US$5.

Bus Caribe Tours (☎ 809-586-4544) has a depot one block north of Parque Luperón on Calle José del Carmen Ariza with service to Santiago, Bonao and Santo Domingo (the same bus makes all three stops). The bus departs every day at 6:30, 7:30 and 9 am, and then every hour on the hour till 6 pm. The cost to Santiago is US$2.50; to Bonao and Santo Domingo it's US$6. Caribe Tour buses from Santo Domingo depart at 7, 8:30, 9:30, 10:30 and 11:30 am, and at 1, 1:45, 2:45, 4 and 5 pm. From Puerto Plata, a bus also goes to Río San Juan, Sánchez and Samaná, departing at 7 am daily; it costs US$2.

Metro Buses (☎ 809-586-6061) has a station eight blocks east of Parque Luperón on Calle Beller. The company serves only one destination: Santiago. Its buses to Santiago depart at 7, 9 and 11 am, and 2, 4 and 6:30 pm. The cost is US$3. Metro buses from Santiago to Puerto Plata leave at 9:15 and 10:15 am, and 1:15, 4:15, 6:15 and 8:45 pm. From Santiago it is possible to catch buses to many destinations; see the Santiago section, later, for details.

Additionally, near the intersection of Avs José Ginebra and Colón is a bus stop for *gua-guas* – the mid-size Toyota buses that are the backbone of the Dominican public transportation system. The gua-guas at this depot only travel between Puerto Plata and Santiago, but, unlike Metro Buses, they

make stops along the way. This means, for instance, that if you're on your way to Parque Nacional La Isabela, you could take a gua-gua to Imbert, hop out, catch another gua-gua to Luperón, and from Luperón take a taxi or a *motoconcho* (motorcycle taxi) the remaining 15km to the national park.

Getting Around

Taxis and motoconchos are common sights in Puerto Plata. They can be found parked beside Parque Luperón and near the entrance most of the day and night.

PLAYA DORADA

A few kilometers east of Puerto Plata along the coastal highway is Playa Dorada, which is both the name of a gorgeous beach *and* a large gated complex beside the beach containing 14 resorts. Guests at all of the resorts have access to the beach, to an 18-hole golf course, to several dance clubs and casinos and to a shopping center. All of these facilities lie within the gated complex, which consists of a simple, single-loop road that winds from one of the two entrances to the other and has driveways to the resorts branching off of it. Note that those who are not guests at one of the resorts are not allowed on the beach or at any of the restaurants, bars, casinos or other facilities. There are only two entrances to the complex from the highway, and the guards are zealous about making sure that only those with reservations drive in.

In deciding which resort to choose, prospective guests should first contact each resort and request a brochure, a map of the complex and a current price list; the brochure will include a comprehensive list of all of the facilities and of everything that's included in the all-inclusive rate. December and January rates will be considerably higher than the rates shown here. Once you know which resort you want, contact a travel agent to arrange a package deal; they can often get better room rates than those quoted here.

Golf

One of the complex's major attractions is its golf course, which was designed by Robert Trent Jones. While guests at any one of the

Playa Dorada resorts have access to the course, green fees are not included in their 'all-inclusive' rates. The green fee for 18 holes runs US$33; for nine holes it's US$19. Some of the resorts offer discounted green fees.

Places to Stay & Eat

Paradise Beach Club & Casino Paradise (☎ 800-752-9236, 809-320-3663, fax 320-4858) consists of 436 guest rooms in 20 four-story buildings set among beautiful gardens and cascading waterfalls. The resort is on the beach and is, in fact, the closest of all the resorts to the surf. The hotel prides itself on the many activities it offers its guests. These include scuba diving lessons at the pool, windsurfing and archery lessons, dancing at its Crazy Moon club, snorkeling and Sunfish sailing, bicycling and volleyball, horseback riding, aerobics and tennis. Room rates are US$150/240 for a single/double.

Playa Naco Golf & Tennis Resort This 418-room resort (☎ 809-541-0484, fax 541-7251) is also quite close to the surf but is not nearly as appealing as the Paradise, a fact that's reflected in the rates: between US$82 and US$93 per person, double occupancy. The hotel prides itself on the fact that it can offer its guests many types of rooms, not simply the usual 'standard' or 'superior.' Despite its proximity to the beach, the Naco emphasizes its golf, tennis and workout (as in weight room) facilities.

Caribbean Village Club on the Green This resort (☎ 809-320-1111, fax 320-5386) contains 336 guest rooms in 45 villa-style buildings. Furnished in Mediterranean decor, each room has a king or two double beds, cable TV and a balcony overlooking the golf course. Meals consist of generous breakfast, lunch and dinner buffets, Dominican specialties and à-la-carte Italian and American fare. Rates are generally US$120 per person, double occupancy.

Dorado Club Resort This 190-room resort (☎ 809-320-2019, fax 320-3608) is near the beach and contains a buffet restaurant, two à-la-carte restaurants, a beach grill, a

pizza counter and three bars. Other facilities include a tour desk, a foreign currency exchange, three gift shops, a beauty salon and a Kids Kamp program run by dedicated counselors. The resort also offers nonmotorized water sports, tennis courts, volleyball, a pool table and table tennis. Room rates are US$125/210.

Gran Ventana Beach Resort The Gran Ventana Beach Resort (☎ 809-412-2525, fax 412-2526) is a mustard-colored group of three-story buildings circling a large, clover-shaped swimming pool with a swim-up bar. The Gran Ventana, or Grand Window, indeed boasts some grand views, but in fact only a fraction of its 365 rooms have windows that face the ocean; most face other rooms. What's particularly nice about this resort is that no matter where you are on its grounds, you're not far from the gorgeous tan sand and inviting surf. Rates are US$130/200.

Puerto Plata Village Caribbean Resort The Puerto Plata Village (☎ 800-753-8260, 809-320-4012, fax 320-5113) contains 390 somewhat tacky rooms and suites, four restaurants, four bars, a large swimming pool with a swim-up bar, a children's pool, four clay tennis courts and volleyball and basketball courts. While it's fairly far from the beach, it's right beside the golf course – it doesn't get much better if you're a golfer. But if your plan is to lay out on the beach, you may want to pick a resort a bit closer to the water. Rates are US$95/160.

Flamenco Beach Resort The newly built Flamenco (☎ 809-320-5084, fax 320-6319) has a total of 582 rooms in numerous attractive three-story buildings grouped around several swimming pools and within easy access of the beach. There's a shopping center on the premises, and a baby-sitting service and motorcycle and car rental are available. There are three à-la-carte restaurants, one buffet restaurant and three bars. Rates are US$180/230.

Playa Dorada Hotel & Casino Despite the proximity of all these resorts to the ocean, the 351-room Playa Dorada Hotel (☎ 809-221-2131, fax 532-4494) is one of the few with more than half of its guest rooms offering a glimpse of it. Facilities include a nicer-than-most swimming pool, three tennis courts, four restaurants and three bars. Rates are US$120/190.

Villas Doradas Beach Resort For most guests, the Villas Doradas Beach Resort (☎ 800-545-8089, 809-320-3000, fax 320-4790) offers the best value for the money in the Playa Dorada complex. The 244-room resort, which was fully redecorated in 1993, has guest rooms that are more spacious and more tastefully decorated than rooms found elsewhere in the complex. The resort offers its patrons direct access to the beach, and the facility's size, while not small, is much more conducive to intimacy than the much larger resorts at Playa Dorada. Rates are US$120/190.

Victoria Resort As its name suggests, this resort (☎ 809-320-1200, fax 320-4862) was built in Victorian style. Its 190 guest rooms, four restaurants and pool (with pool bar) are all beside a lake and ringed on three sides by the immaculate golf course. It's a lovely setting, but it's also a good walk from the beach. That distance is likely the reason the Victoria doesn't charge as much as other Playa Dorada resorts (US$95/140).

Clubs International Fun Royale Even farther from the beach is the Fun Royale (☎ 809-683-5636, fax 227-1506), which features 168 guest rooms, two tennis courts, three swimming pools and a host of activities for children and the child within you. More so than other Playa Dorada resorts, the Fun Royale – and its sister resort, Fun Tropicale, below – appeals to families. Still, there's no shortage of bars, and its dance club is open nightly till 2 am. Tea is served at 4 pm promptly every day. Rates are US$120/160.

Clubs International Fun Tropicale Fun Tropicale is very similar to Fun Royale: It is run by the same Dominican company, is next door, and guests of either can enjoy all

of the facilities offered at both hotels. It also attempts to accommodate couples with small children, offering a number of child-care options. The main difference between the two resorts is that guest rooms at the Tropicale are larger than those of the Royale. Rates are US$140/180.

Heavens A first-class resort with 150 guest rooms and suites, most with balconies, Heavens (☎ 800-835-7697, 809-320-5250, fax 320-4733) is housed in a group of rectangular buildings between the golf course and the beach. Ninety rooms come with separate living quarters and two double beds. There are two restaurants, two bars, a dance club, an exchange bank, a gift shop, a boutique and a beauty parlor. Massage and babysitting are available. Rates are US$140/220.

Jack Tar Village Beach Resort Throughout the Caribbean, 'Jack Tar Village' is synonymous with 'luxury,' and the 285-room Village in Playa Dorada (☎ 809-320-3800, fax 320-4161) doesn't deviate from the rest of the chain in quality or level of service. Each room has a twin, double, queen- or king-size bed, a bathroom with shower and tub, cable TV, telephone and safe. Deluxe rooms additionally offer an in-room coffeemaker, hair dryer and remote-control TV. All rooms have balconies or patio with outdoor furniture. Rates are around US$140 per person, rising and falling with the season.

Entertainment
Dance Clubs Inside the complex are three very chichi dance clubs: *Andromeda* in Heavens resort (the most popular of the three), *Charlie's* in the Jack Tar Village casino and *Crazy Moon* in the Paradise Beach resort. All three dance clubs play a mix of merengue, salsa and international pop music. They are open from 8 pm to 2 am, though no one usually shows up before 10 pm; entrance is US$10 and drinks are extra. The clubs are open to anyone staying at a Playa Dorada resort.

Casinos The complex also has three casinos that are open to all resort guests – at Jack

Tar Village, Playa Dorada Hotel and Paradise Beach Club. The casinos feature blackjack tables, craps, roulette, poker and slot machines.

All games can be played with US dollars or Dominican pesos except the slot machines, which accept US dollars only. If you play in US dollars, your winnings are paid in US dollars; if you play in Dominican pesos, your winnings are paid out in Dominican pesos. If you intend to gamble, determine your personal loss limit before you go in so that you won't need to change any money at the casinos; the exchange rates at all three gambling houses are very unfavorable.

Getting There & Away

Nearly everyone who stays at a Playa Dorada resort purchases a tour package that includes air transportation to the Aeropuerto Gregorio Luperón and a shuttle service from the airport to their resort. If you don't get air transportation as part of a package, see the Puerto Plata Getting There & Away section, above, for information on flights. Regardless of how you get here, don't arrive without a reservation or you'll have trouble getting past the guards at the entrances to the complex.

PLAYA COFRESÍ

Five kilometers west of Puerto Plata, this lovely beach has been flanked by fully staffed vacation villas in recent years. The villas, seven in all, are privately owned homes and they vary in size, design, distance to the beach and rental cost. But one thing they all have in common is quality; these villas are *very* nice. And unlike other beaches, which have become off-limits to nonguests, locals still frolic on Playa Cofresí – particularly on Sundays, when the beach becomes a picnic area with music and barbecues. The fun can last well into the night.

Places to Stay

When compared to similar vacation villas elsewhere in the Caribbean, these villas are cheap. What's also nice about them is that unlike all-inclusive resorts, which are generally designed to pack in as many guests as possible and offer limited privacy, these are actual houses with fully equipped kitchens and ample space between each villa. And all rates quoted here include a live-in maid/cook. However, the rates don't include a 13% tax, which must be added on top of the rental price.

Before you make any decisions, contact the Vacation Villa Referral Center (*VVRC;* ☎ *800-390-1138, 610-896-5815, fax 649-5422, www.ifb.com/vvrc*), 14 Rolling Rd, Wynnewood, PA, USA 19096-3521. They will send you a brochure and confirm rental rates. If you have Internet access, you can do this online: there are photos of the villas and rental rates at VVRC's webpage for Playa Cofresí (*www.puerto-plata.com/index.htm*). Be advised that there are few restaurants in the area and only a small grocery store. Unless you have your own wheels, these villas can be a bit confining.

The *Casa de Sueño* features two levels, an ocean view, three bedrooms (each with a queen-size bed) and three bathrooms. The rates are US$560 per week from April 16 to November 14 and US$945 per week from November 15 to April 15. No pets and no smoking. The seaside villa of *Seis Amigos* contains three bedrooms, two bathrooms, one queen-size bed, one double and two single beds. The weekly rates are US$525 from April 15 to November 14 and US$770 from November 15 to April 14. Pets and smoking are permitted.

The three-level *Villa Carolisol* features ocean views, four bedrooms, 4¹/₂ bathrooms, one queen-size bed, five double beds and one single bed. Rates are US$595 per week from April 16 to December 14 and US$980 per week from December 15 through April 15. Pets and smoking are permitted. The *Villa de la Familia* is a five-bedroom, three-bathroom, single-level villa featuring ocean views, three queen-size beds and four single beds. Rates are US$100 a day from May 1 through December 14 and US$125 a day from December 15 through April. Pets and smoking are OK.

The two-level *Villa del Caribe* has an ocean view, five bedrooms and four bathrooms, and was designed to accommodate

eachside walkway in Sosúa, northwestern DR

Friday market in the border town of Elías Piña, DR

Colorfully painted doors and walls brighten a pedestrian street in Santiago, Dominican Republic.

White-sand beach at Punta Cana, southeastern Dominican Republic

Balneario Los Patos, a river-fed public pool near Paraíso, Dominican Republic

Vodou temple entrance in Port-au-Prince, Haiti

A *taptap* on the streets of Port-au-Prince

Metal sculptor in Croix des Bouquets, Haiti

Street scene in remote Jérémie, southern Haiti

Schoolgirl in Hinche, central Haiti

two families. It can sleep 11 people comfortably in one queen-size bed, three doubles, two twins and one sofa bed. Rates are US$700 a week from May 1 to November 14 and US$1050 from November 15 to April 30. Smoking and pets are allowed. The three-level *Villa del Sol* features ocean views, three bedrooms, two bathrooms, one queen-size bed and two double beds. Rates are US$525 a week from April 16 to December 14 and US$770 a week from December 15 through April 15. Smoking is permitted, but not pets.

Two-level *Villa Vista del Mar* features a swimming pool, five bedrooms, and 3½ bathrooms. The L-shaped pool is surrounded by a walled terrace to facilitate full-body sunbathing and skinny-dipping. The villa contains four queen-size beds, three single beds and one crib. Rates are US$700 a week from May 1 through December 14 and US$2100 the rest of the year. Smoking is permitted, but pets are not allowed.

IMBERT

About 22km southwest of Puerto Plata, connected by a well-maintained two-lane stretch of Hwy 5 that winds through rolling farm and cattle country, is the small roadside community of Imbert. It has a gas station and a typical Dominican restaurant that's popular with locals on weekends, but there are few other establishments of interest to tourists.

Imbert, however, is a significant crossroad. You'll always find a few gua-guas at the turnoff to Luperón: some are headed toward that town, others toward Hwy 1 and Santiago, and yet others toward Puerto Plata. Imbert is the main jumping-off point to the town of Luperón, the Caribbean Village Luperón beach resort and Parque Nacional La Isabela.

Gua-guas from Imbert leave for the Parque Central of Luperón every 30 minutes from sunrise to sunset; the cost is US$1 each way. Likewise, gua-guas bound for Puerto Plata and Santiago leave Imbert about every 20 minutes and cost US$1 and US$2, respectively. To get to Monte Cristi from Imbert, take a gua-gua to the intersection of Hwys 1

and 5 (in the community of Bisonó), and then catch any westbound gua-gua.

If you're exploring the region on bicycle or in a 2WD vehicle, be advised that the only decent road west of Imbert for 40km is the Imbert-Luperón-Parque Nacional road. Despite what several country maps indicate, all roads leading to the small town of La Isabela, for example, are unpaved and badly rutted. Incidentally, La Isabela is not where Columbus founded the historic New World settlement in 1493; that site is to the north at Parque Nacional La Isabela.

LUPERÓN

Luperón is a sleepy town of several thousand people who mostly make their living tending to sugarcane fields. The town is bisected by the road connecting Imbert and the Parque Nacional La Isabela. Its Parque Central, on the southern end of town, is quite visible from the thoroughfare, and this is where you catch transportation to other sites: gua-guas, taxis and motoconchos go to Imbert and taxis and motoconchos go to the Parque Nacional La Isabela.

There are no real attractions in Luperón, although there is an all-inclusive beach resort nearby.

Places to Stay & Eat

If you're traveling by bicycle and need a place to stay in Luperón, try the *Hostal-Restaurant Dally* (☎ 809-571-8034, fax 571-8052). New in 1998, the Dally is on the main road and offers eight clean and secure rooms with ceiling fan and private hot-water bathroom for US$20 per room. The popular restaurant is fairly inexpensive and specializes in seafood.

Across the street from the Dally is a very pleasant bar that doubles as a simple *restaurant*. If you stay at the Dally or are in the mood for an ice-cold beer or a frosty piña colada as you approach Luperón, consider making a pit stop here; you'll be glad you did.

Two and a half kilometers west of Luperón is the *Caribbean Village Luperón* (☎ 809-571-8303, fax 571-8180). This 441-room all-inclusive is perched on a gently sloping hill overlooking a gorgeous tan-sand beach and delightfully calm bay. Every room is air-conditioned and has all the usual amenities, plus a balcony facing the ocean or a garden. Per-person double-occupancy rates for a standard room range from US$85 to US$125, depending on the season. Superior rooms are US$5 more per person; suites are US$10 more. The 15-hectare resort caters to families, and in addition to relaxing poolside or by the beach, guests can try their hand at windsurfing, sailing or horseback riding, and scuba clinics in the pool, all of which are included in the room rate. Among the many facilities are an attractive three-floor restaurant and a dance hall.

PARQUE NACIONAL LA ISABELA

This park contains the remains of Columbus' second settlement upon the island of Hispaniola. Columbus founded the first European settlement in the Americas near present-day Cap-Haïtien, Haiti, on December 25, 1492. In honor of the date, he named the settlement La Villa de Navidad – the Village of Nativity – and it consisted chiefly of a fort, several houses and 39 men, the New World's first colonists. A short time later, Columbus returned to Spain to announce (incorrectly) that he had discovered a shortcut to Asia, or the 'Indies' as the continent was then called.

When the great explorer made his maiden voyage to the New World, he did so as a little-known sailor leading three small ships carrying a total of 90 men. When he left Spain on his second voyage, all of Spain knew the name Christopher Columbus, and placed at his disposal by King Ferdinand and Queen Isabella were 17 fine ships crammed with 1200 men, lots of weapons and even horses. By order of the royal couple, Columbus received the titles 'Admiral of the Ocean Sea' and 'Viceroy and Governor of the Islands Discovered in the Indies.'

Columbus couldn't have been happier. But that happiness came to an abrupt end on November 4, 1493 – the day he returned to La Navidad and discovered that the 39 settlers he'd left behind had been slain and their fort and homes burned to the ground. Gradually, Columbus learned what had hap-

pened to the men, as a few fearful Indians returned to tell the tale. The settlers had taken to kidnapping and raping Indian women, and one of the local chiefs had ordered his warriors to hunt down all the white men and destroy their settlement.

Disappointed but undeterred, Columbus sailed east – toward a place on the island the Indians called Cibao, where gold had been found. After traveling approximately 110km, the admiral established a new settlement. He named it La Isabela, in honor of the queen. Columbus quickly put his men to work constructing cabins, a church, a fortress and other buildings of mud and limestone. And soon after his arrival he organized expeditions into the interior in search of gold. Then he set sail again for the 'mainland of the Indies' – which, in fact, was the south coast of Cuba. He left his brother Diego in charge.

Almost from the moment the settlers arrived at La Isabela, they were beset by hardship. 'One-third of our people have fallen sick within the last four or five days,' wrote physician Alvarez Chanca shortly after construction of La Isabela began. Chanca, who accompanied Columbus on his second voyage, blamed hard work and an unhealthy climate. Historians have since added syphilis, which the Taínos are thought to have had, and intestinal parasites as probable culprits.

The illnesses and hard work did not sit well with the settlers, many of whom had

Royal Trivia

What's in a name? An extra *a* or *l*, if you're a Spanish queen. The queen of Castile from 1474 to 1504 was known to her countrymen as Isabel la Católica I, or (more commonly) Queen Isabel. On Hispaniola, for reasons lost to time, she is Queen Isabela. But if you find yourself in England with an itch to learn more about the woman who aided Columbus, the name to look up is Isabella; it's the favored spelling there.

been wealthy men in Spain and were unaccustomed to manual labor. They had wrongly assumed that the New World would present them with vast quantities of gold and that the Indian population would do all the work. Instead, they were ordered to toil under the tropical sun, they were bitten by insects night and day and they fell ill almost the moment they landed. Tensions rose rapidly. Within one month of La Isabela's founding, Columbus had to put down a revolt led by the expedition's chief accountant. The accountant was jailed and several of his followers were hanged as a warning to others.

While Columbus was searching for the mainland of the Indies, epidemics repeatedly struck the colony, weakening and frustrating the settlers. They maintained their faith in their dream of riches by praying that the admiral would return with much gold, but when Columbus reappeared after five months' absence, he had little gold to show and only one new land to add to his discoveries, an island the Indians called Jamayca. In the meantime, Columbus's other brother, Bartholomew, had arrived, and he and Christopher spent most of the next year trying to salvage La Isabela.

During that year the Spaniards imposed a tax on every Taíno age 14 and older living in gold-mining districts: three ounces of gold every three months. Soon the Indians were in open revolt, and the conquistadors had to resort to cannon and crossbow to fend off attacks. Then a hurricane hit the area with such force that it sank several of the ships anchored in the bay beside the colony. To top things off, carelessness on the part of one settler resulted in an uncontrolled fire that destroyed two-thirds of the settlement's structures.

Before leaving for Spain in March 1496, Columbus named Bartholomew governor and ordered that the capital of the New World be moved in his absence. The building of Santo Domingo was begun in that year. Within five years of La Isabela's founding, the settlement was abandoned. Among the features left to wither away was the first church in the New World and a cemetery filled with men whose avarice got the better of them. At least one of the corpses was buried face down, with his arms tied behind his back. One of the hanged rebels, most likely.

In 1998 the ruins of La Isabela, reached via a paved road 15km west of Luperón, became a national park. Unfortunately, there's little to see at the site today, as the ruins have been plundered many times over the years. In addition, when Generalissimo Rafael Trujillo ordered the site cleaned up several decades ago prior to the arrival of some dignitaries, work crews accidentally pushed a large portion of the ruins into the bay with their tractors.

What's more, national park workers – hoping to turn the site into a major tourist attraction – have re-created some of the ruins so that it's now difficult to tell what has remained untouched since the colonists walked away from La Isabela and what's been added in recent years to give more substance to the site. In other instances, inappropriate 'improvements' were made. The cemetery, for example, had been so thoroughly rifled by grave robbers by 1990 it only appeared as an area of lumpy earth. In recent years, however, more than a dozen white concrete crosses have been added.

For the most part, the authentic remains are limited to the foundations of several buildings, including one that archaeologists believe was Columbus's home. During the life of La Isabela, most of the structures wore thatch roofs. Archaeologists in recent years have found roof tiles in the vicinity of Columbus's house, and across the bay they have found a beehive-shaped kiln where such tiles were probably made. Before the kiln was found, researchers believed that European ceramics had not been produced in the New World until decades later.

The park is open 8 am to 5 pm daily; admission is US$1.50. There's also a museum containing many artifacts purported to have belonged to the earliest colonial Americans, including rings they may have worn and tools they may have used. There are coins dating from 1474 and artists' renditions of what La Isabela looked like. The museum is more impressive than the ruins nearby, but unfortunately all the informational signs are in Spanish, and there are no guides around to translate.

Places to Stay

Only 100m from the entrance to the small national park is the quite decent *Hosteleria Rancho del Sol* (☎ *809-543-8172, fax 696-0325*), which features eight air-conditioned rooms with ocean view and private hot-water bathroom for US$23/30; the price includes breakfast. It has a generator, a swimming pool and a tennis court. There's even a small beach with gentle waves. Guest have free use of kayaks and canoes.

Be advised that the Rancho del Sol uses El Castillo as its address. This is to differentiate the area from the town of La Isabela, a good distance away from the site of the ruins. In fact, a total of three communities within 40km of the ruins call themselves La Isabela. If you stop to ask for directions, specify *el castillo* (the castle) or *las ruinas de La Isabela* (the ruins of La Isabela), or else you'll likely receive directions to a village or town you really didn't want to visit.

Also, at the time of writing several basic rooms were being built within the national park, but no one could say for certain whether they would be budget accommodations for tourists or would only be available for visiting archaeologists and other invited guests. If the Rancho is all booked up, check the status of these rooms.

Getting There & Away

See the Imbert and Luperón sections, above, for details on how to get to the ruins. The cost of a motoconcho ride from Luperón to the park and back is about US$10. The cost of the same trip in a taxi is about US$20, and the drivers will wait for you to see the sights.

PUNTA RUCIA

Most of the coast between Parque Nacional La Isabela and Playa Monte Cristi is not one of fine sandy beaches. Instead, the shoreline is well littered, and where the sand should be there's gravel.

The beach bordering the fishing village of Punta Rucia is an exception, made all the more picturesque by its coconut trees and colorful little fishing boats pulled up onto the sand. The laid-back Caribbean atmosphere is enhanced most Sundays when area musicians play old-school merengue.

Playa Punta Rucia is quite isolated and, not surprisingly, draws few tourists. But if it still isn't isolated enough for you, consider hiring a boatman to take you to Cayo Arenas, a tiny white-sand isle about 10km northwest of Punta Rucia. The cost is about US$35 roundtrip.

As pretty as its beach is, Punta Rucia is actually known for its many wild orchids, which grow on the branches of decaying trees. The trees are inland, beginning a couple of kilometers from the beach and 5km west of Punta Rucia. If you enjoy hiking, the area lends itself well to exploration on foot.

Places to Stay & Eat

Because Punta Rucia receives so few guests, its selection of accommodations is quite limited. You have a choice between two budget hotels: *La Orquidea del Sol* and *Discovery Bay Club*. Both charge around US$20 per room (with air con), and both have simple restaurants.

Getting There & Away

Unfortunately, Punta Rucia is not served by gua-guas. Getting there is a do-it-yourself deal. There are two routes to Punta Rucia – an unpaved road from the town of La Isabela, which shouldn't be tried by 2WD cars, and a paved road from Villa Elisa, off Hwy 1.

SANTIAGO

In contrast to Santo Domingo, Santiago de los Caballeros (Santiago of the Gentlemen; or, more commonly, just Santiago), the nation's second-largest city, retains a relaxed, provincial air. Commercial hub of the Valle del Cibao, the breadbasket of the nation, Santiago has 550,000 inhabitants, many of whom are employed in processing and transporting local agricultural products; the valley yields sugarcane and tobacco, which the city converts into rum, cigarettes and cigars. Santiago boasts a thriving industrial free zone and one of the finest universities in the country.

DOMINICAN REPUBLIC

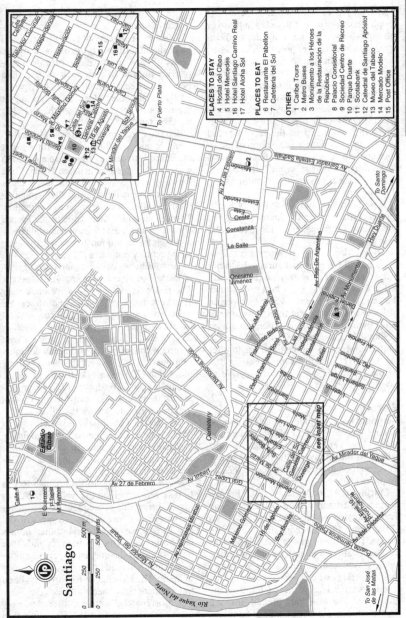

Santiago

PLACES TO STAY
4 Hostal del Cibao
5 Hotel Mercedes
16 Hotel Santiago Camino Real
17 Hotel Aloha Sol

PLACES TO EAT
6 Restaurante El Pabellon
7 Cafetería del Sol

OTHER
1 Caribe Tours
2 Metro Buses
3 Monumento a los Héroes
   de la Restauración de la
   Republica
8 Palacio Consistorial
9 Sociedad Centro de Recreo
10 Parque Duarte
11 Scotiabank
12 Catedral de Santiago Apostol
13 Museo del Tabaco
14 Mercado Modelo
15 Post Office

The tempo of Santiago is leisurely, its people generally more refined than those of the capital city. Even the vehicular traffic in Santiago, which can get pretty thick at times, lacks the frenetic feel so common in much-larger Santo Domingo. Possibly the most popular activity in town is taking a stroll on Calle del Sol, Santiago's main street and one of the country's leading shopping districts. The residents of Santiago consider themselves the aristocrats of the republic, and more than a few have made a point of incorporating into their Sunday routine a ride in a horse-drawn carriage around the central park – a nice tribute to tradition in a fast-changing city.

Despite its size and a rich history, Santiago has little to offer the tourist by way of attractions. Earthquakes in 1562, 1842 and 1946 destroyed many of Santiago's old structures, and 'development' is taking a toll on those fine old houses that survived Mother Nature's whims. Conversely, tourism has had little effect on the city, for better or worse; the central plaza has not yet been overrun with shoeshine boys and foreigners are not beset by bothersome self-appointed guides as they often are in the Zona Colonial of Santo Domingo. What Santiago has to offer the traveler is a pleasant break in the journey from the capital city to the North Coast, or vice versa.

History

Santiago was founded by Bartholomew Columbus, elder brother of the explorer, in 1495. However, the earthquake of 1562 caused so much damage to the city that it was rebuilt on its present site beside the Río Yaque del Norte.

During the 1660s, some 800 French buccaneers-turned-settlers, who had been living along the western and northern coasts of the island, began moving into the central valleys. This expansion was spurred by their indiscriminate slaughter of animals in earlier years, which resulted in scarcity so severe that the pirates, who were not keen on deprivation, actually considered limiting the number of livestock they hunted. Instead, they elected to attack and pillage Santiago,

which was the main Spanish city in the interior at the time.

Tension between local French and Spanish authorities – brought about by the desire of Paris and Seville to rule all of Hispaniola instead of sharing it as they had been – reached a high on July 6, 1690, when 1400 French troops entered Santiago and set fire to nearly 160 homes. Only the churches were spared.

Eventually Spanish colonists returned to Santiago and rebuilt the city, and throughout the entire 18th century they were allowed to go about their business in peace. By the 1780s Santiago was quite prosperous, its residents mostly raising cattle but also supplementing their incomes through tobacco cultivation. The people traded their cattle to the French and others in return for manufactured goods, and their farms and ranches were expanding as the century came to a close.

But old habits die hard, and once again – in 1804 – French colonists attacked Santiago. The residents managed to drive back their attackers, but fear of a second attack led them to abandon their city for several months, during which time many families elected never to return. They made a wise choice: within a year 2000 French colonists reappeared and sacked the town, killing more than 200 Spanish colonists in battle, beheading all of the dozens of Santiago residents they captured, and forcing several hundred others to flee for their lives.

The Spanish eventually regained control of the city, but the people of Santiago finally succeeded over the Spanish colonial power in September 1863, when some 6000 Dominicans from the whole Valle del Cibao area forced 800 well-armed Spanish troops to take refuge behind the walls of the city's fort. During the subsequent battle, a fire broke out that swept through most of the city. The people of Santiago lost their homes and businesses to the fire, but they and other patriots forced the queen of Spain to nullify a pact that had made the republic an annex of Spain. The Dominican Republic has been independent since then.

Unfortunately, Santiago suffered terribly during a civil war in 1912. The city's jails were filled with political prisoners, and governmental executions were carried out by the dozens. Again, battle took its toll on many Santiago neighborhoods. The war did not end until the USA, which viewed instability in the Caribbean as a national security threat, sent a pacification commission to Santo Domingo and forced the two warring sides to negotiate or face US military intervention.

The years immediately following the civil war were some of the city's best. Worldwide shortages of raw tropical materials brought on by WWI caused prices of Dominican products such as sugar, tobacco, cacao and coffee – all of which were being grown around Santiago – to soar. From 1914 through the end of the war and into the 1920s, Santiago's economy exploded. Just how radical were the price increases? The price of a hundredweight of sugar, for example, rose from US$5.50 in 1914 to US$22.50 in 1920. Lovely homes and impressive stores, electric lighting and paved streets appeared throughout town. In May 1922, Hwy Duarte opened, linking Santiago with Bonao, La Vega and Santo Domingo.

The Trujillo years (1930-61) were bad ones for Santiago. By the '30s, the world prices for raw tropical materials decreased as quickly as they had increased. Trujillo, who could have helped Santiago, chose to do nothing because its leading newspaper often reported incidents of corruption within his government, and because the city was a hotbed of antigovernment activity. Out of

spite, Trujillo had a gigantic monument, La Paz de Trujillo (Trujillo's Peace), built atop a hill in the center of town, capping it with a statue of himself. After Trujillo's assassination, the large and ugly memorial was renamed Monumento a los Héroes de la Restauración de la República (Monument to the Heroes of the Restoration of the Republic) in honor of the Dominicans who died during the 1860s in the war to force Spain to relinquish control of the republic. Oddly, the statue of the dictator remains atop the eight-story-high monument.

Today, Santiago still relies on agriculture as its chief source of revenue, but with world prices of sugar and tobacco in the doldrums the city has not maintained itself well. The swank stores and shops that used to line Calle del Sol have been replaced by more utilitarian enterprises. Signs advertising cheap clothes rather than name brands are now the norm. The town's grand dame of hotels needs a facelift and arterial reconstructive surgery (namely, rewiring, new plumbing and earthquake-proofing).

Still, anyone touring the country would make a mistake not spending a day in Santiago, visiting its sights and delighting in its pleasant ambience, maybe even taking a buggy ride around the central square. And if you speak Spanish and enjoy hearing theories, ask residents how Santiago de los Caballeros acquired its name. No one really knows. Historians can't agree on whether Bartholomew Columbus gave the city the lofty name, or whether *de los Caballeros* was added later – and when. It's the type of discussion you'll overhear in the popular, tree-shaded, bench-bedecked central plaza.

Orientation

Santiago is 155km north of Santo Domingo, linked to the capital city by a concrete, four-lane expressway variously called Hwy 1, Hwy Duarte and Autopista Duarte. Coming from Santo Domingo, the expressway ends at the 67m-high Monumento a los Héroes de la Restauración de la República, which looms over the city.

At the monument, the expressway becomes a one-way street (Av Las Carreras)

GIANFRANCO LANZETTI

Sugarcane worker

that flanks the north side of downtown. From Las Carreras, make a left turn onto Calle 30 de Marzo and proceed several blocks to reach Parque Duarte, also known as Centro de la Cultura, which marks the city center. From the plaza, Calle del Sol proceeds east (it's also one-way) and leads back to the monument and Hwy Duarte. All of the city's attractions are near Calle del Sol, but the bus stations are a good distance away to the north and east.

Information

There's no tourist office in town. If you've just arrived by bus, ask the ticketing agents at the bus depot for the information you need. Most speak some English and they are paid to be helpful.

Money There are several banks within 100m of Parque Duarte. Scotiabank, which will exchange currency, is across the street from the park, at the corner of Calle del Sol and Calle 30 de Marzo. The bank is open 8:30 am to 3 pm weekdays.

Post & Communications There's a post office on Calle del Sol four city blocks east of Parque Duarte. It's open 8 am to 5 pm weekdays, and 9 am to 1 pm Saturday. There are no Codetel offices downtown, but it's possible to place international calls from the lobby of the Hotel Mercedes, on Calle 30 de Marzo one block from the central plaza.

Catedral de Santiago Apóstol

Santiago's cathedral, on Calle 16 de Agosto opposite the south side of Parque Duarte, was built between 1868 and 1895 and is a combination of Gothic and Neoclassical styles. The cathedral contains the tomb of the late-19th-century dictator Ulises Heureaux, an elaborately carved mahogany altar and some impressive stained-glass windows. The cathedral was renovated in 1991.

Museo del Tabaco

The Museo del Tabaco, on Calle 30 de Marzo across the street from the cathedral, is devoted to the region's tobacco industry, which features very strongly in Santiago's

economy. The museum describes the history of tobacco as well as the process of how it's grown and prepared, and you can also watch cigars being made. However, signs are in Spanish only. The museum is open 8 am to 5 pm weekdays. Admission costs US$1.

Sociedad Centro de Recreo

This private social club, on Calle Benito Monción across from the park, opened on August 19, 1894, and is the oldest such club in the country. Owned by Bermudez of Bermudez Rum, one of the island's largest producers of the fine sugarcane-based liquor, the club is a throwback to Santiago's boom days. Even though it's open to members only, they will let you in for a look around if you're polite and decently clad (no shorts, tank tops or the like). Among the sights is a scruffy library that contains a custom-made chair Trujillo used when he had his shoes shined. Be sure to see the gorgeous ballroom upstairs, which underwent greatly needed restoration in 1998. If you're lucky, Ramon Consuera will be shooting pool when you visit (the club has two pool tables and a billiards table). Ramon is the club's best billiards player, and he can sink dozens of balls without a miss. The club is open all day, but its members don't start showing up before 5 pm.

Palacio Consistorial

Next door to the Sociedad Centro de Recreo is the former town hall, which now includes a small museum devoted to the city's colorful history. Hours are 9 am to 1 pm weekdays. Admission is free.

Mercado Modelo

Filling a room about the size of a high-school gymnasium is the city's traditional market, on Calle del Sol a couple of blocks east of Parque Duarte. It offers few surprises, but it can be fun to browse the low-end merchandise.

Most of the items here are those you'll see just about anywhere: cheap T-shirts, cheap jewelry, cheap watches, cheap shoes, cheap pants, cheap toys and other – yes – cheap things. You can also find lots of (generally low-quality) handicrafts, including straw hats, ceramic ashtrays, carved serving trays, plastic jewelry boxes and conch shells.

Monumento a los Héroes de la Restauración de la República

There is little to recommend this hideously unattractive, eight-story tower of egoism – despite being rededicated to those who died bringing independence to the Dominican Republic in the 1860s, it is still topped by Trujillo's statue. Not only that, but its tiny elevator broke in 1991 and has yet to be fixed. About the best thing that can be said is that a visit here will provide you with a decent aerobic workout. You must climb up a narrow, winding, five-story staircase to reach the museum and viewing deck of downtown Santiago. Most of the museum's dusty display cases are empty, the signs are in Spanish only, and the displays that there are consist mainly of browning photos of the city from years ago. The monument is open 7 am to 2 pm daily. Admission is free.

Special Events

Carnival in Santiago is said to be quite lively, second only to Santo Domingo's in terms of costumes and party atmosphere. Carnival is celebrated the week preceding Easter Sunday.

Places to Stay & Eat

A couple of blocks from Parque Duarte on Calle Benito Monción, the *Hostal del Cibao* (☎ 809-581-7775) is a clean place with 14 second-floor rooms, all with private hot-water bathroom (be advised that the bathroom is separated from the bedroom by only a hanging bedsheet or two). Each room comes with a fan and a TV. For US$10 per room, this place is an excellent find if you're counting your pesos.

Hotel Mercedes (☎ 809-583-1171, fax 581-5207), at the corner of Calle 30 de Marzo and Calle Máximo Gómez, is the grand old dame of Santiago, built in ornate style during the roaring 1920s. It features a wide marble staircase and quaint balconies off each of its guest rooms, some of which have air con and all of which have TV and private hot-water bathroom. The rooms are well worn but quite OK for US$25. There's a bar, as well as a restaurant with good food; its menu includes sandwiches (US$1.50 to US$3.50), pasta (US$3.50 to US$7.50) and meat dishes (US$5 to US$7).

Making a major leap in price and creature comforts is the 72-room *Hotel Santiago Camino Real* (☎ 809-581-7000, fax 582-4566), on Calle del Sol five blocks east of Parque Duarte. Guest rooms with air con start at US$40 and include all the usual modern-city amenities. This is the best place in town if you want comfortable, up-to-date accommodations and don't mind spending a little extra. The Camino Real also has an excellent restaurant with a view to match.

If you want to be pampered, book a room at the *Hotel Aloha Sol* (☎ 809-583-0090, fax 583-0950), which is next door to the Camino Real on Calle del Sol. New in 1998, this is the kind of place where doormen seemingly can't wait to assist you. While the rooms at the Camino Real are very nice, those at the Aloha Sol are plush. Rates start at US$50/67 for a single/double. The hotel's restaurant offers many national and international dishes.

Santiago is a long way from China, but you wouldn't know it from the quality of the Chinese food served at *Restaurante El Pabellon*, on Calle del Sol opposite Parque Duarte. The prices range from US$2 for soup and even less for an egg roll and other appetizers to US$15 for a variety of lobster dishes. Chicken dishes cost around US$4, and shrimp dishes around US$10. It's open till late every day.

If you're on a tight budget and haven't tired of Dominican food, the *Cafeteria del Sol* serves a fair variety of local specialties at very affordable prices. It's on the corner of Calle del Sol and Calle 30 de Marzo.

Getting There & Away

Air For all practical purposes, there is no air service to or from Santiago. There is an airport, but it's no longer served by Air Santo Domingo, and no international carriers use it. It's only used privately these days. Foreign tourists provide enough business to keep other domestic airports alive, but in mid-1998 there was so little air traffic in and out of Santiago that the domestic airline stopped providing it.

Bus Santiago is a major connecting point for buses. From Santiago, it's possible to take buses to Santo Domingo, Monte Cristi and Puerto Plata, and get there in good time – two hours, 90 minutes and one hour, respectively.

Metro Buses (☎ 809-582-9111) offers bus service between Santiago and Santo Domingo and Puerto Plata. Its depot is on Calle Maimón between Avs 27 de Febrero and Juan Pablo Duarte. Metro Buses offers two services to Santo Domingo: buses for those who have reservations, and buses for those who don't. Reserved-seating buses leave for Santo Domingo at 6, 6:30, 7, 9, 10, 10:20 and 11:30 am, and 1:30, 3, 4:30 and 6:30 pm; there's an additional 5:30 pm departure on Friday and Sunday. Cost is US$4.50. The Santo Domingo-bound buses for those without a reservation depart Santiago at 8:15 and 10:15 am, and 12:30, 3:30, 5:30 and 7:45 pm. Cost is also US$4.50. Metro buses to Puerto Plata leave Santiago daily at 9:15 and at 10:15 am, and 1:15, 4:15, 6:15 and 8:45 pm; the cost is US$2.75, and no reservation is required (although making one is a good idea).

Caribe Tours (☎ 809-576-0790) has a terminal off Av 27 de Febrero just north of Av Imbert and provides service as follows:

Destination	Cost	Departures
Cruce Copey	US$2.35	9 & 9:30 am
Dajabón	US$2.75	10:30 am
Guayubin	US$2	9:30 am
Las Matas de Santa Cruz	US$2.75	9:30 am
Loma de Cabrera	US$2.75	10 am
Mao	US$2	10 am & noon
Monte Cristi	US$2.25	9 & 10:30 am
Partido	US$2.75	10 am
Puerto Plata	US$2.75	9:30, 10:30 & 11:30 am
Santo Domingo	US$4	6, 7, 8, 8:30, 9:15, 9:30, 9:45, 10:30 & 11 am, noon, 1:30, 2:30, 3, 3:30, 3:45, 4:15, 4:45, 5:15, 6 & 7 pm
Sosúa	US$2.75	9:30, 10:30 & 11:30 am
Villa Vásquez	US$2	9 & 10:30 am

Getting Around

There are lots of taxis and motoconchos in Santiago, especially in the vicinity of Parque Duarte. The cost of a taxi ride anywhere in town rarely exceeds US$4; from Parque Duarte to either bus depot is around US$3. The cost of a motoconcho ride anywhere in town rarely exceeds US$2.50.

SANTIAGO TO MONTE CRISTI

The stretch of Hwy 1, also called Hwy Duarte, between Santiago and Monte Cristi is one of the best-maintained roads in the nation. Completed during the Trujillo era, its two lanes run along the northern side of a large valley that is flanked by the Cordillera Septentrional to the north and the much bigger Cordillera Central to the south. At times the mountains of the Cordillera Septentrional, which occasionally are within 5km of the highway, are quite majestic, with sheer silver cliffs and jagged peaks.

Winding its way down the center of the valley, flowing east to west, is the Río Yaque del Norte. The Yaque del Norte is the most significant river in the country. Some 296km long, with a basin area of 7044 sq km, it descends from near Pico Duarte at an altitude of 2580m and empties into the Bahía de Monte Cristi, where it forms a delta. Today all of the delta is contained in Parque Nacional Monte Cristi.

There are numerous small towns along the way, most scarcely more than a few dozen homes, a few simple eateries and occasionally a gas station. In late 1998 not a single one contained a hotel for the weary traveler. There are few signs of development flanking the highway between towns; mostly the land stretching out from the highway consists of tobacco fields, pasture or bush. If you're driving, it's best not to drive this highway at night, as you'll find yourself 'in the middle of nowhere' with little chance of receiving assistance should you experience car or motorcycle trouble.

MONTE CRISTI

In the extreme northwest corner of the Dominican Republic is the city of Monte Cristi, which is the capital of the sparsely populated province of the same name. The province is generally hot, with an average temperature (including nighttime lows) in excess of 28°C. The territory is as dry as it is hot, with average yearly rainfall of only 600mm. Most of the province is covered in subtropical dry forest.

Most of the 22,000 residents of the city of Monte Cristi make their living tending cattle and goats and fishing, just as they have done for generations. Another major source of revenue is salt, which is harvested from salt flats north of town. Tourism accounts for a fraction of the town's income, and that isn't likely to change anytime soon; the city and the surrounding area offer almost nothing in the way of tourist attractions.

One could say that the city was founded twice – during the 16th century, and again in the 18th century. Like many of the towns that were settled in the Northwest, its residents traded cattle hides for manufactured goods, with almost all commerce conducted by sea. When a surge in pirates scared off Spanish galleons at the end of the 16th century, residents began trading with Spain's enemies. In 1605, the king of Spain, furious with what he viewed as treasonous behavior by the Spanish colonists, ordered Monte Cristi abandoned and its people relocated to the Santo Domingo area.

For nearly 150 years, hot, dusty Monte Cristi remained a ghost town. Then, French colonists began settling abandoned areas. Not wanting to lose control of them, the Spanish Crown ordered all of the depopulated towns in the Northwest repopulated. In 1751, Monte Cristi was re-founded with 100 families from the Spanish-ruled Canary Islands.

Initially the Canarios lived almost exclusively from raising cattle and goats that they traded in the northern sections of present-day Haiti. As time passed, Monte Cristi's natural harbor became an important port for export timber felled far inland and floated down the Río Yaque del Norte, which empties into the Bahía de Monte Cristi. The wealthy timber industry attracted Europeans, who settled in the town during the early 19th century.

However, most of the city was destroyed in the 1860s during the three-year Restoration War, in which Dominicans fought Spanish troops to annul annexation of the country to Spain and restore Dominican independence. It's impossible to say what would have become of the city if it hadn't been so devastated. Afterward, due to the influence of Monte Cristi's European citizens, many Victorian-style homes were built, some of which still stand. In 1895, someone bought a large clock in France and had it reassembled in Monte Cristi; today it looms over the town's Parque Central.

Aside from the old houses and the old clock, there isn't really much in Monte Cristi today of interest to travelers, and despite its low level of rainfall the town's got a thriving mosquito population. Most tourists who spend a night in Monte Cristi do so on their way to or from Haiti – Monte Cristi just happens to lie at the junction of two highways linking the north's only border crossing with roads to Puerto Plata, Sosúa and other popular destinations.

Orientation & Information

Downtown is centered around the main crossroad in town, where the two highways meet: Hwy 45 (also called Carretera Vincent) runs north-south to Dajabón, and Hwy 1 (also known as Hwy Duarte) runs east-west to Santiago and ultimately Santo Domingo. A large green road sign clearly indicates which way is which.

Everything a visitor needs is at this major intersection: there are gua-guas, taxis and motoconchos; a Caribe Tours bus depot; a decent hotel; two banks; an adequate restaurant; and a gas station. On Hwy Duarte

100m west of the intersection is a Codetel office where you can make phone calls. The office is open 8 am to 10 pm daily.

Special Events
Monte Cristi is said to celebrate Carnival with admirable gusto in the days leading up to Easter Sunday. Monte Cristi also comes alive every May 30, when the city holds its patron saint festival, in honor of San Fernando.

Places to Stay & Eat
During the early 1990s Monte Cristi had hoped to join Sosúa, Puerto Plata and other northern cities in becoming a major Dominican tourist center. Speculators opened hotels, restaurants and dance clubs along the edge of Bahía de Monte Cristi, but few people patronized them. The problem: generously put, the beaches beside the bay do not compete favorably with beaches elsewhere in the north. There's a national park nearby, but it too is nothing special.

As of now, there is only one decent hotel in town – *Chic Hotel* (☎ 809-579-2316), on the west side of Hwy 45, 75m north of the major intersection. The Chic Hotel offers clean, fan-only rooms with private cold-water bathroom for US$13 and has clean air-conditioned rooms with private hot-water bathroom for US$20. The Chic was for sale at the time of writing.

Next door to the Chic is Monte Cristi's most popular *restaurant*, with tables inside and outside and a long menu. It serves sandwiches (US$1 to US$4), fish prepared 10 different ways (US$4 to US$6), four salads and many rice dishes. A large order of rice with shrimp costs US$8. Lobster is from US$10 to US$15. There are 11 shrimp dishes, as well as a hearty selection of crayfish, octopus, crab and beef dishes. It's open late every day.

Getting There & Away
Caribe Tours (☎ 809-579-2496) has a depot on Hwy 1, 75m east of the major intersection. Its Santiago-bound buses leave at 7:15 and 9 am, and 1:45 and 3:15 pm daily; the cost is US$2.50. There are also several buses each day from Monte Cristi to Dajabón (US$1.50 each way).

Gua-guas also go to Santiago from the major intersection (US$1.50), although this is a much slower option than Caribe Tours due to the number of stops the gua-guas make along the way. However, a gua-gua is a good option if you're headed from Monte Cristi to Dajabón, as they leave about every 20 minutes throughout the day, cost only US$1, and make few stops before reaching the border town. To catch an east-bound or south-bound gua-gua, simply go to the major intersection and hail a gua-gua going the direction you want to go.

Be advised that Hwy 45 between Monte Cristi and Dajabón is flanked on both sides for most of its length by dense dry bush that's said to be popular with Dominican and Haitian fugitives. It's also said to be a stomping ground of zombies released by Vodou priests. In any event, this stretch of road is very dangerous to travel at night.

Getting Around
Most anything you would want to see in Monte Cristi, including the old clock in the Parque Central, is within easy walking distance of the major intersection. If you are traveling on foot and want to see the bay or have a better look at the large plateau 5km or so north of town, you can hire a taxi or motoconcho, which camp out beside the major intersection all day long and well into the night.

PARQUE NACIONAL MONTE CRISTI
This 530-sq-km park, 20km west of Monte Cristi, consists of subtropical dry forest, numerous coastal lagoons and a group of seven small islands called Los Cayos de los Siete Hermanos (The Seven Brothers Islands). Although quite dry for the tropics, the national park is home to many sea birds, including great egrets, brown pelicans and yellow-crowned night herons. American crocodiles are said to inhabit the park's lagoons as well, but don't be surprised if you don't see any; they're being hunted nearly every night.

Unfortunately, the park has been illegally poached for years. According to Dominican fishers, desperate Haitians have poached to local extinction the several sea turtle species that used to lay their eggs on the beaches from the Bahía de Monte Cristi south to the Haitian border. Likewise, the fishers claim that Haitians have illegally ravaged the marine life in the vicinity of the islands, trapping lobsters and spearfishing anything edible. Indeed, you may well see people spearfishing here and the snorkeling certainly isn't what it should be.

The park's chief ranger station is about 3km north of Monte Cristi, on the east side of a paved road that follows the contours of the bay, just beyond a bridge; it's easy to overlook. The station is open 9 am to 5 pm daily, and you can usually find a park ranger or two. The rangers have no maps of the park nor do they speak English, but they can arrange for one of their friends to take you snorkeling at Los Cayos de los Siete Hermanos. The roundtrip cost is US$35 to US$50, depending on the size of the boat used and the number of people involved.

You also need a boat to investigate most of the park's many lagoons, although it is possible to visit one of the park's largest lagoons – Laguna de Marigo – on a motorcycle or in a 4WD vehicle via a long, dirt loop road that stems west from Hwy 45; you can't miss it, as it is the only turnoff to the west from the highway. Be warned that mosquitoes are rampant here; wear light cotton trousers and a loose-fitting long-sleeve shirt and carry lots of insect repellent.

Two kilometers north of the ranger station and within the boundaries of the national park is the huge mesa El Morro, which rises majestically against the bluest sky, its flank barren – at least until recently – except for windblown shrubs, flowering cacti and gnarled thorn-covered trees. Today, despite its so-called protected status, homes are creeping up its southern slopes, which overlook Monte Cristi and beyond.

The foot of the mesa may be reached by paved road – the same road that passes the ranger station. At road's end a steep trail veers up the side of El Morro and gradually works its way to the plateau. Also at road's end a second trail continues due north 100m

or so to a ridge that overlooks a long rocky beach in the northern shadow of the mesa. The rocks, though not large, are too rough to lie upon, and the water looks deep even near the shore.

DAJABÓN

Dajabón is a bustling border town laid out in grid fashion, and most foreigners here are either on their way to or from Haiti. Hwy 45 becomes the main street in town, and it leads the traveler directly to the crossing point. On both sides of this street, or within a short walk of it, are all sites of interest to the tourist, including the Caribe Tours bus depot, a very decent and inexpensive hotel, a couple of restaurants and an open area that becomes a lively Haitian-Dominican trade center every Monday and Friday. This colorful market makes for great people-watching.

Historically, Dajabón was, like so many other northern towns, depopulated during the early 17th century because its Spanish colonists had taken to trading with people from other nations against the king's wishes. It was resettled at the insistence of the Spanish Crown more than 100 years later, when the king realized that French settlers were moving into unoccupied Spanish territory. Today, just as it was hundreds of years ago, trade between the Dajabón residents and people of another nation is the major local business activity.

Places to Stay

Six blocks straight out from the crossing point is the *Hotel Juan Calvo* (☎ 809-579-8285), which features 44 guest rooms, five with air con and cable TV. All of the rooms contain a private cold-water bathroom. The air-conditioned rooms go for US$17 per room, while the fan-only rooms rent for US$14. If you arrive in Dajabón and believe you will be staying the night, rent a room here first thing before getting a bite to eat or seeing the market, as the Juan Calvo is often full well before nightfall.

Getting There & Away
Crossing the Border The Dajabón/Ouanaminthe border crossing is one of only two

that may be used by foreigners; the other is Jimaní/Malpasse, in the southern part of the island. Although there are other crossing points, they may be used by Haitians and Dominicans only.

Crossing the border is a relatively simple affair. The border opens around 8 am and closes around 4 pm; be aware that Haiti sometimes adjusts its clocks according to summer daylight savings time, and sometimes it doesn't. Avoid arriving at the border right at 4 pm or close to it or you may be asked to come back the next day.

When you leave Haiti, you must have your passport and the yellow entry card you received upon arrival. When entering the Dominican Republic, some nationalities must purchase a tourist card, which costs US$10; other nationalities need not pay anything. It's a good idea to contact the nearest Dominican diplomatic mission for information about current entry requirements.

To enter Haiti, no visa is currently required if you are from the USA, the UK, Canada and a host of other countries. However, Haitian entry requirements tend to fluctuate, so you should definitely contact the nearest Haitian diplomatic mission for their current policy. Note also that most foreign residents are required to pay a US$10 exit tax when leaving the Dominican Republic.

Private motor vehicles must obtain government permission from the country of origin before they can cross the border. Rental vehicles are not allowed to cross from one country into the other.

On both sides of the border, there are buses to whisk you away from it. However, there are no decent accommodations in Ouanaminthe; most west-bound travelers head straight for Cap-Haïtien after crossing the border. Unlike several roads on the Dominican side that head out of town, the road from the border to Cap-Haïtien is in very poor condition.

Bus Caribe Tours (☎ 809-579-8293) has a depot five blocks straight out from the crossing point and one block to the north. Buses depart for Santiago every 30 minutes from 7 am to 6 pm. Each of these buses passes through Monte Cristi before heading east on Hwy Duarte to Santiago; if you wish to get off the bus in Monte Cristi, just tell the driver and he'll let you out at the Hwy 45-Hwy 1 intersection.

The cost to Monte Cristi is US$1.50, to Santiago US$2.75. From Dajabón it's also possible to take a Caribe Tours bus to Santo Domingo; such buses depart at 6:30 and 8:30 am, and at 1:30 and 2:30 pm; the cost is US$5.75.

Gua-guas will also take you to Monte Cristi (US$1). They wait a short distance from the border and leave when they are full, usually about every 20 or 30 minutes.

Getting Around
There are taxis and motoconchos near the crossing point every day until the time of closing. After that, taxis and motoconchos may still be found on the main road.

Central Highlands

The backbone of the Dominican Republic is the Cordillera Central, which runs northwest-southeast from the Haitian border to the outskirts of Baní and San Cristóbal. The Cordillera Central is home to the Caribbean's tallest mountains, and at its heart are two large national parks – Armando Bermúdez and José del Carmen Ramírez – that provide incredible hiking opportunities. The parks, which were created two years apart during the 1950s, abut each other, forming what is really a single massive protected mountain area.

Outside the national parks but within the central highlands are the foothill towns of Jarabacoa, La Vega and Constanza to the east, and San José de las Matas, Monción and Sabaneta to the north. While the northern towns have nothing to offer the tourist, the eastern ones have their own particular, unhurried attractions. Jarabacoa is home to several lovely waterfalls, some decent whitewater rafting and a hotel-ranch that offers plenty of outdoor activities for nature lovers. Constanza is a charming valley town, and La Vega has an interesting past. Still, the region's main attraction is, by far, hiking in the national parks.

PARQUES NACIONALES ARMANDO BERMÚDEZ & JOSÉ DEL CARMEN RAMÍREZ

The Dominican government established Parque Nacional Armando Bermúdez in 1956 with the hope of preventing the kind of reckless deforestation that was occurring in neighboring Haiti. The park encompasses 766 sq km of tree-flanked mountains and pristine valleys. Two years later, an adjoining area of 764 sq km was designated Parque Nacional José del Carmen Ramírez. Together, the parks contain the highest peaks in the Caribbean and attract hikers from around the world.

Although puny by Himalayan standards, the Cordillera Central presents wilderness activities found on few other Caribbean islands. For starters, Pico Duarte (3175m), Pico La Pelona (3087m) and Pico La Rucilla (3045m) offer the hiker three significant summits. The Valle del Tetero, at 1500m, is another popular destination with trekkers; the valley is home to some spectacular vegetation, pre-Columbian rock carvings and a sizable wild boar population.

Twelve of the country's major rivers flow from the Cordillera Central, and the headwaters of the nation's only white-water river – the Río Yaque del Norte – are in Parque Nacional Armando Bermúdez. Rafting the Yaque del Norte isn't exactly rafting the Colorado or the Zambezi – in fact, you could safely run its rapids aboard inflatable swimming pool furniture – but it is a very pleasant way to pass an afternoon. Much more unnerving is rappelling down some of the impressive rock cliffs found in the area, an activity called 'canyoning,' offered by at least two tour operators. (See Jarabacoa, below, for information on rafting and canyoning.)

Scientists believe the Cordillera Central began to form more than 60 million years ago, the product of erupting volcanoes and an upward thrust of a continental plate. Most of the rocks found in the central highlands are solidified magma; volcanic limestone, diorites, slate and marble – all igneous rocks – abound in the mountains. In many places you can see magnificent rock cliffs topped by jagged peaks, not unlike portions of the Swiss Alps, only smaller and without ice and snow.

The average temperature in the parks ranges between 12°C and 20°C most of the year, but during December and January lows down to -5°C are not uncommon. The Parque Nacional Armando Bermúdez receives between 2000mm and 4000mm of rain annually, which usually arrives in drenching downpours. Parque Nacional José del Carmen Ramírez, on the southern side of the range, generally receives about one-third as much rain. Cold-weather clothing

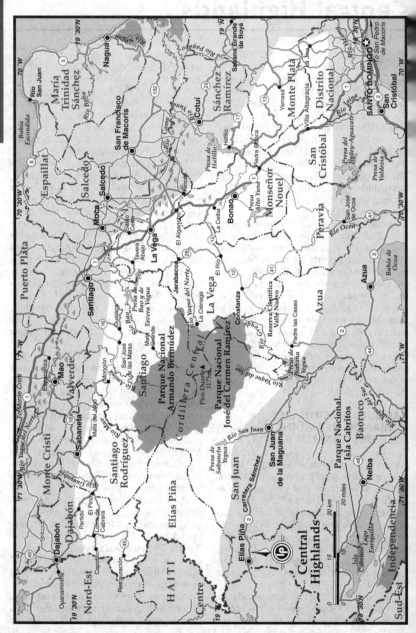

and rain gear are musts for anyone intending to spend a night in either park.

Flora & Fauna

The predominant life zones in the parks are subtropical montane humid forest and subtropical montane rain forest. Up to about 1200m, the flora is mostly West Indian cedar, petitia, mountain wild olive, palo amargo and, close to the rivers, West Indian walnut and wild cane. From 1200m to 1500m, the flora mostly consists of pasture fiddlewood, West Indian laurel cherry, sierra palm, copey oak and lirio. Between 1500m and 2000m, Krug wild avocado, tree ferns, cyrilla, wild braziletto and sumac dominate. Above 2000m, the forest is ruled by Creole pine and a variety of bushes (such as *Garrya fadyenii* and *Baccharis myrsinites*), which aren't terribly exotic, but when viewed as pieces of a panorama add a great deal to the area's visual appeal.

There are 47 known amphibians in the parks and several mammal species, most notably the wild boar, which was introduced. They reside chiefly in areas that are very difficult to access on foot.

Much more impressive is the birdlife. Among the more characteristic species you will find in the parks are the Hispaniolan parrot, the Hispaniolan woodpecker, the white-necked crow, the Hispaniolan trogon, the ruddy quail dove, the red-tailed hawk and the Dominican Republic's national bird, the palm chat.

Orientation & Information

There are ranger stations near the start of the five major trails into the parks – at La Ciénaga, Sabaneta, Mata Grande, Las Lagunas and Constanza (see Hiking, below, for information on how to get to each of these spots). There are no roads into the parks. Every person entering the national parks must obtain a permit (US$3) at one of these ranger stations and must be accompanied by a guide even for a short walk. The guides, who can be found near the ranger stations, are required because it is easy to get lost in the woods. As a matter of fact, the requirement only went into effect after a tourist set off on a trail by himself in January 1988 and was never seen again.

Ranger stations (no phones) are open 8 am to 5 pm daily, and the rangers are friendly and happy to answer questions and provide assistance in hooking you up with a competent, officially approved guide. However, few of the rangers speak English. Posted at each station is a large map of the parks showing trails as well as the location of the free hikers' cabins (see Places to Stay, below), but portable trail maps are generally unavailable.

The free cabins consist of bare one-room wooden structures, each with a nearby (often disgusting) portable toilet and some with sheltered wood-fire grills for cooking. There are no other facilities in the parks, and everything you need must be brought in. Creek water must be boiled or treated before drinking (since it usually contains parasites), so bringing some bottled water is recommended. While Constanza is a city, be advised that the starting points of La Ciénaga, Sabaneta, Mata Grande and Las Lagunas are small communities without so much as a market; be sure to purchase your provisions elsewhere.

Guides & Mule Trips

A guide's fee is negotiable, but at the high end of the scale it's around US$30 per day. Park regulations stipulate one guide for every three tourists for overnight outings; there's no required ratio for day hikes. However, if some members of your party want to maintain a faster pace than others, you might consider hiring two guides. That way one guide can stay with the slower hikers and the other can accompany the speedsters. Avoid leaving any member of your party without a guide at any point.

Guides also have mules available, and most tourists opt to rent one or two of them as well, to carry either their supplies or themselves. The cost per mule is the same whether it's used for transporting provisions or people – generally between US$10 and US$20 per day. The tourist is not expected to pay for a mule used by a guide. So, two people who intend to ride mules much of the time will need two mules for themselves,

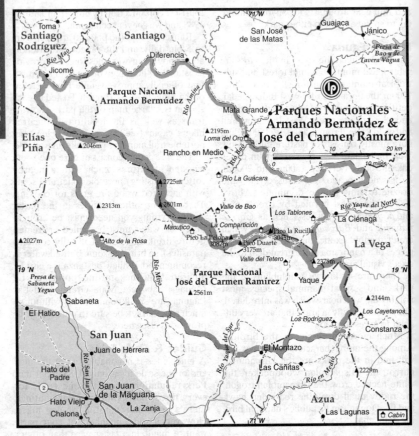

a cargo mule for tent, kitchenware and provisions, and at least one guide and probably two: most guides insist on a second guide when three or more mules are involved – one to guide the lead mule and the other to keep the last mule moving.

For outings that involve one or more nights in the mountainous parks, the beasts are a welcome addition. For one thing, they can carry all the gear; for another, they can carry you if you discover halfway up the mountain that you just aren't in the near-Olympic condition you thought you were. Furthermore, a mule is a godsend to have

around in the event you twist an ankle or develop painful blisters.

In addition to mules, guides have access to pots for cooking and hatchets for chopping wood; they'll bring them *if requested* (don't make any assumptions). You must provide all other equipment: you are expected to bring your own utensils, plates, sleeping bags, toilet paper, matches, lighter fluid, tents, and so on – whatever you intend to use.

You are also expected to provide the food, for yourself as well as for the guide or guides; the usual campsite grub includes rice, beans, eggs, fruit, coffee, bacon, bread, peanut butter, jam, cheese and crackers, which you can buy at a market before heading to the departure towns. However, you may want to consider bringing specialized dehydrated meals from your home country, which are surprisingly tasty, weigh very little and are available at most camping stores; remember to buy some for your guides as well.

If you book your hiking adventure through a tour operator (see Organized Tours, below), all arrangements will be taken care of for you. You will also be accompanied by someone who speaks English; none of the 87 officially approved guides speaks a language other than Spanish. All you'll need to bring with you are cold-weather clothes, a poncho in case it rains, and a broken-in pair of hiking boots. Tipping the guides is optional, but customary. If you can afford to use a tour operator, you'll likely be glad you did.

Hiking

Astonishingly, Pico Duarte – the Caribbean's tallest peak – was not climbed until 1944, as part of a celebration commemorating the 100th anniversary of Dominican independence. During the late 1980s, the government began cutting trails in the parks and erecting cabins, hoping to increase tourism to the country by increasing the accessibility of its peaks. Today, 3000 people a year ascend Pico Duarte, and a fair number of visitors summit the second- and third-highest peaks.

The trails are generally kept free of boulders and falling trees, but little effort is made to fill in deep ruts or otherwise smooth out choppy sections. Over some stretches, compacted dirt gives way to loose rock that's murder on your feet if you're not wearing sturdy boots. In other places, especially after rain, the dirt trails turn to mud and shallow creeks occasionally cross the trails. Where the trails are flanked by embankments, they might even become creek beds for 20m or more. The need for proper footwear – ideally, broken-in hiking boots with steel-reinforced soles – cannot be overemphasized.

An item many hikers forget to pack but one that's especially appreciated by people with weak knees or ankles is a walking stick.

A walking stick permits you to shift stress from your lower extremities to your upper extremities. If one of your main reasons for visiting the DR is to hike in its mountains, consider bringing a walking stick with you. Many are lightweight and collapsible. If you don't bring one, consider finding or making one – using your guide's hatchet – before you head out; that is, before your joints become sore.

There are six major hiking routes in these national parks: three that wind from the edge of the parks to Pico Duarte, two that wind from the parks' edge to Valle del Tetero and one that links Valle del Tetero and Pico Duarte. Here are brief descriptions of each of the six major routes.

La Ciénaga-Pico Duarte This is by far the most popular route. It is 23km in each direction and involves approximately 2275m of vertical ascent en route to the peak; calculated into this figure are the hills and valleys encountered along the way. Most people make the trip in two days, spending one night at La Compartición campground. They begin their final, 5km ascent at 4:30 am, giving them enough time to watch the sunrise from Pico Duarte. La Ciénaga may be reached by público from Jarabacoa. The road between the two communities is mostly paved (see Jarabacoa, below, for more detailed directions).

Sabaneta-Pico Duarte This is the most difficult of the six routes mentioned here. It is 48km in each direction and involves 3802m of vertical ascent, with all the hills and valleys factored in. Most people make the trip in three days, spending the first night in or beside the cabin at Alto de la Rosa and the second in or beside the cabin at Macutico (many people choose to erect a tent near the cabins). Sabaneta may be reached by público and gua-gua from San Juan de la Maguana (see the Southwestern Dominican Republic chapter). The road between the two communities is paved. Note that there is another Sabaneta north of the parks, on the road to Dajabón (see below), so don't confuse the two.

DOMINICAN REPUBLIC

Elevation Profiles for Hiking Routes in Parques Nacionales Armando Bermúdez & José del Carmen Ramírez

⌂ Cabin

La Ciénaga – Pico Duarte Route

Sabaneta – Pico Duarte Route

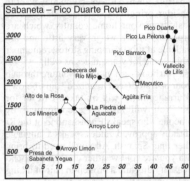

Mata Grande – Pico Duarte Route

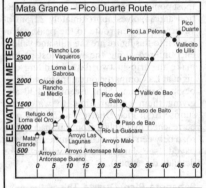

Las Lagunas – Valle del Tetero Route

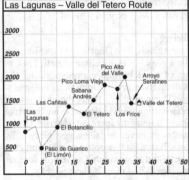

Constanza – Valle del Tetero Route

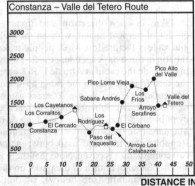

Valle del Tetero – Pico Duarte Route

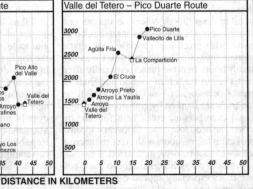

ELEVATION IN METERS

DISTANCE IN KILOMETERS

Mata Grande-Pico Duarte The next most difficult route, this is 45km in each direction and involves approximately 3802m of vertical ascent, including hills and valleys encountered along the way. Most people make the trip in three days, spending the first night at the Río La Guácara campground and the second at the Valle de Bao campground. Mata Grande may be reached by público from San José de la Matas. The road between the two communities is unpaved.

Las Lagunas-Valle del Tetero At the time of writing this route required the use of a tent. It is 36km in each direction and involves approximately 2000m of vertical ascent. Most people make the trip in three days, spending the first night at the campground near the small town of Las Cañitas (rangers plan to build a cabin there in 1999) and the second at the Valle del Tetero campground. Las Lagunas may be reached by público from Padre las Casas. The road between the two communities is unpaved.

Constanza-Valle del Tetero This route passes through lots of farmland before the scenery becomes pristine (encroachment on the parks is a big problem). It is 43km in each direction and involves about 1590m of vertical ascent. Most people make the trip in three days, spending the first night at Los Rodríguez campground and the second at the Valle del Tetero campground. Constanza is a city and may be reached by gua-gua from La Vega, Bonao and the turnoff at Duarte Hwy.

Valle del Tetero-Pico Duarte After a fairly arduous 8km trek, this 20km route connects with the La Ciénaga-Pico Duarte route at a fork in the trail called Agüita Fría. From Agüita Fría to the campground at La Compartición, it's another 3km. Most hikers spend the night at the campground and get a 4:30 am start on the 5km ascent to the summit. Their intent: to watch the sunrise from the highest point on the island. On a clear day, the Caribbean and the Atlantic are visible from the heap of boulders that forms the very top of the Cordillera Central.

Organized Tours

At least two tour operators arrange trips to the top of Pico Duarte, and both of them can be recommended. Maxima Aventura is the name of the adventure center at Rancho Baiguate (☎ 809-574-6890, fax 574-4940, rancho.baiguate@codetel.net.do), which is 5km east of central Jarabacoa. Maxima Aventura offers three Pico Duarte programs: 'Pico Express' includes one night at the ranch and one at the La Compartición campground and a total of seven meals (rates per person are US$450, or US$310/285/270 for groups of two/three/four or more); 'Pico Duarte' includes one night at the ranch and two at La Compartición campground and a total of 10 meals (rates per person are US$755, or US$437/390/322 for groups of two/three/four or more); and 'Pico Duarte y Valle del Tetero' includes one night at the ranch, two nights at the campground at La Compartición and one at the campground at Valle del Tetero and a total of 13 meals (rates per person are US$930, or US$540/495/450 for groups of two/three/four or more). All packages include guide services, pack mules, equipment rental and transportation between La Ciénaga and Rancho Baiguate.

Iguana Mama (☎ 800-849-4720, 809-571-0908, fax 571-0734, www.iguana-mama.com) is in Cabarete (see the Northeastern Dominican Republic chapter) and also uses the La Ciénaga-Pico Duarte route. Iguana Mama offers three hiking programs, all of which involve summiting Pico Duarte. 'Highlights of the Caribbean Alps' includes a night at Los Tablones campground and a night at La Compartición campground (US$350 per person); 'Nature Lovers Trek' includes a night at Los Tablones campground and two nights at La Compartición campground (US$425 per person; it's basically the first program at a more leisurely pace); 'The Full Legend' features summiting Pico Duarte, Pico La Pelona and Pico La Rucilla – the three highest peaks in the Caribbean – and spending six nights in the mountains (US$850 per person). Prices include transportation from Cabarete to La Ciénaga and back. Whereas the costlier tours offered by Maxima Aventura can be arranged at your convenience, those offered by Iguana Mama have fixed dates (often corresponding with the full moon).

Places to Stay

There are approximately 14 campgrounds in the parks, and each one contains a free cabin in which hikers can overnight. Each one-room structure can hold 20 or more people and consists of a wooden floor, wooden walls and a wooden ceiling, and nothing but air in between – no beds, no fireplace, not even a table on which to place a lantern. Because messy campers often leave scraps of food behind, the cabins are frequently visited by tree rats looking for leftovers. Using a pup tent inside a cabin will protect you from rodents and insects.

Cabins are available on a first-come, first-served basis, so it's a good idea to bring along your own tent as well. While it's un-likely that you will find a cabin full, you may decide you don't want to share one with a dozen or so strangers.

Stand-alone portable toilets are near most of the cabins, but they are usually in dire need of cleaning. Many campers gener-ally prefer to slip behind a tree and hope to go unnoticed. To be considerate of others and lessen your impact on the area, bring a small shovel to dig a hole and then cover it over when you're done. Short, lightweight plastic shovels can be purchased at most camping stores.

Beside most of the cabins is also a stand-alone 'kitchen': an open-sided structure with two or three concrete wood-burning stoves. Fallen, dead wood is usually abundant near the campsites, and even if it's been raining, chances are good that if you split the wood, it will fire up pretty well (particularly if you sprinkle it with lighter fluid). Of course, make sure your guide has packed a hatchet for just such a chore.

The only running water in the parks is in the creeks. Creek water is fine for cooking and even for drinking, so long as you boil it for several minutes, but bottled water is safer and tastes better. Unboiled creek water can contain parasites, and should

never be drunk straight from the stream. You can also use water purification tablets, which are simpler, but many people don't like the idea of ingesting chemicals that can kill even the most formidable parasites. As before, you must buy all the bottled water you think you will need before reaching your departure town.

JARABACOA

Residents of Jarabacoa like to describe their mountain town as being 'Switzerland in the tropics.' While the description is hardly accu-rate, the town isn't without character – espe-cially on weekend afternoons, when the Parque Central fills with young people seeking romance. On these afternoons the streets around the park become cruising zones, where young men and women ride mopeds and dirt bikes hour after hour, exchanging coy smiles, suggestive invitations and furtive glances.

Jarabacoa is along the east bank of the Río Yaque del Norte, at the end of a winding paved road that has its eastern terminus at Hwy Duarte just north of La Vega. At 800m above sea level, Jarabacoa's days are warm and its nights cool. The climate is perfect for growing apples, pears, strawberries and cher-ries, which cover the hills that ring the modern town. Jarabacoa's climate is also perfect for people, and many wealthy Dominicans maintain weekend homes along secondary streets flanking Av Independen-cia just north of the post office.

What makes Jarabacoa special are the area's natural attractions. Among them are three impressive sets of waterfalls, all of which have inviting bathing pools at their bases. The nearby Río Yaque del Norte is the country's only white-water river, and at least three tour operators offer rafting trips down its upper portions. Two of the tour operators also offer area canyoning trips, which involve rappelling down steep cliffs and swimming in the lovely Río Jimenoa. Also nearby are the mountain trails of the Parque Nacional Armando Bermúdez (see above).

For the avid hiker, Jarabacoa makes a marvelous base camp. A large variety of accommodations exists in and around town,

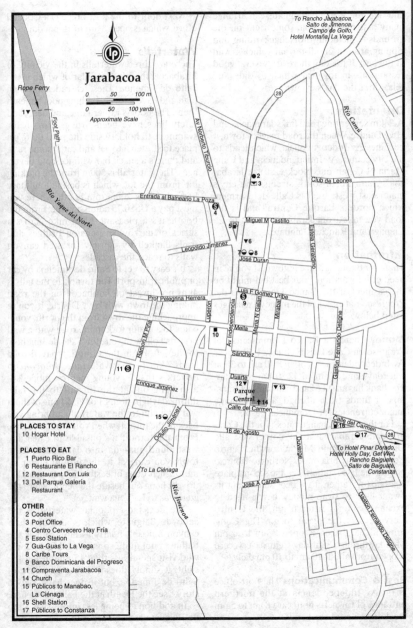

Jarabacoa

0   50   100 m
0   50   100 yards
Approximate Scale

Rope Ferry

Foot Path

To Rancho Jarabacoa,
Salto de Jimenoa,
Campo de Golfo,
Hotel Montaña, La Vega

Río Yaque del Norte

Río Camú

Av Norberto Tiburcio

Entrada al Balneario La Poza

Club de Leones

Miguel M Castillo

Estela Geraldino

Leopoldo Jiménez

José Durán

Luis F Gomez Uribe

Prof Pelegrina Herrera

Malia N Galan

Miraba

Lupeión

Av Independencia

Ramón M Pina

Mella

Sánchez

Enrique Jiménez

Gastón Fernando Deligne

Duarte

Parque
Central

Calle del Carmen

Odulio Jiménez

18 de Agosto

Calle del Carmen

Divarge

To Hotel Pinar Dorado,
Hotel Holly Day, Get Wet,
Rancho Baiguate,
Salto de Baiguate,
Constanza

To La Ciénaga

Río Jimenoa

José A Canela

Gastón Fernando Deligne

PLACES TO STAY
10 Hogar Hotel

PLACES TO EAT
1   Puerto Rico Bar
6   Restaurante El Rancho
12 Restaurant Don Luis
13 Del Parque Galería
    Restaurant

OTHER
2   Codetel
3   Post Office
4   Centro Cervecero Hay Fría
5   Esso Station
7   Gua-Guas to La Vega
8   Caribe Tours
9   Banco Dominicana del Progreso
11 Compraventa Jarabacoa
14 Church
15 Públicos to Manabao,
    La Ciénaga
16 Shell Station
17 Públicos to Constanza

and one, the Rancho Baiguate, can arrange many activities for you, some right on the grounds – including horseback riding and zipping around on all-terrain vehicles. And at the end of the day there are several good restaurants in town at which to dine and relax after the day's events.

Orientation

A 24km serpentine road links Jarabacoa and Hwy Duarte. When the road reaches town, it becomes Av Independencia, which leads to the city center. Av Independencia and Calle Maria N Galan one block east are Jarabacoa's main north-south streets. The city's major east-west street is Calle del Carmen, which borders Parque Central and is the road you take from Jarabacoa to get to La Ciénaga and Rancho Baiguate.

Information

There is no tourist office in town. If you're in need of information, your best bet might be the cashiers at the Banco Dominicana del Progreso or at either of the money exchanges listed below.

Money There's a Banco Dominicana del Progreso on Calle Luis F Gomez Uribe near Av Independencia. It's open 8:30 am to 3 pm weekdays, and 9 am to 12:30 pm Saturday. The bank has an ATM and can conduct transfers of funds from abroad, and exchange major currencies for Dominican pesos.

For the best exchange rates, visit the Compraventa Jarabacoa at the corner of Calle Duarte and Ramon M Piña or the Centro Cervecero Hay Fría on Av Norberto Tiburcio behind the Esso station. Yes, the second place is a bar (or, rather, it's a beer stand), but its owner likes to swap money; if you need to exchange money after 6 pm, the Centro Cervecero is the place to go. The Compraventa Jarabacoa is open 8 am to 6 pm Monday through Saturday. Centro Cervecero is open from about 10 am to 10 pm daily.

Post & Communications The post office is on Av Independencia at the northern entrance of town. Its hours are 8 am to 5 pm weekdays; closed weekends.

Next door to the post office is a Codetel office, which is open 8 am to 10 pm daily.

Waterfalls

There are three waterfalls in the vicinity of Jarabacoa, the most popular of which is the **Salto de Jimenoa**. These cascades are 40m high and have a lovely bathing pool beneath them. The pool is rather large and deep, and safety lines have been strung across it for swimmers to hold. Beside the pool there's a place to stretch a towel and catch some rays, and there's a snack bar with ice-cold beverages. The waterfall is 500m from the parking lot. From the lot, which is beside a military barracks, walk 200m to a booth, where you must pay a US$0.75 admission fee. From the booth, it's a pleasant 300m hike across a series of narrow suspension bridges and trails flanked by densely forested canyon walls to reach the cascades.

It's easy to get to Salto de Jimenoa by car or public transport. The turnoff to the falls is 4km northwest of Jarabacoa on the road linking the town with Hwy Duarte. If you're approaching the town from the north, you'll come to a major fork in the road with a wall of signs. Follow the one for 'Salto de Jimenoa' to the left. From the turnoff, a paved road leads 6km to the waterfall. *Motoconcho* drivers – that is, young men on mopeds – also hang out at the turnoff to the falls during daylight hours. For US$4 one of them will take you to the waterfall and bring you back to the turnoff when you want to return. From the turnoff it's possible to catch any westbound gua-gua into Jarabacoa; from town, you can get to the turnoff either by motoconcho, taxi or eastbound gua-gua. Taxi drivers hang out beside the depot where the gua-guas to La Vega wait.

The next most popular waterfall is the **Salto de Baiguate**, which is also in a lush canyon but isn't nearly as large, nor is the bathing pool quite so inviting. Most people who visit spend less than 15 minutes at the sight; it simply doesn't have the allure of Salto de Jimenoa, but it does have a good story – see the Death at the Falls boxed text.

In addition to being less impressive, Salto de Baiguate is also harder to reach. In fact, the road to this waterfall is so bad in places it's best avoided in a 2WD vehicle; a horse, a motorcycle or a 4WD vehicle are safer bets. To get there, take Calle del Carmen out of Jarabacoa to the east for 3km – until you see a sign for the waterfalls on the right-hand side of the road. From there, a badly rutted dirt road, which at one point is crossed by a shallow creek, leads 3km to a parking lot. From there, a lovely 300m trail cut out of the canyon wall leads to the *salto*. At the time of writing there was no admission fee.

The loveliest waterfall of all doesn't have a formal name and there are no road signs for it. Because this one is the highest (at 60m) of the three cataracts, some people call it **Salto de Jimenoa Uno**. This waterfall is rarely visited, although it is quite gorgeous – and quite unusual: it pours from a gaping hole in an otherwise solid rock cliff. Unseen from the trail's vantage, however, is a lake behind the waterfall; the long, single-stream cataract is the product of a hole in the shore of the lake. The bathing pool is quite enticing on a hot day, especially after climbing down the steep canyon wall that looms over it. But the water isn't for everyone; the Río Jimenoa is cold all year round.

Finding this waterfall is tricky. The Uno is exactly 7.1km from the Shell station in Jarabacoa on the road to Constanza. It's paved and flat at first, and then dirt, winding and rising. You'll pass the hamlet of Pedregal, then the city's garbage dump (it's at roadside; you won't miss it). Then, after another curve, you'll come to a place where bulldozers have taken a huge bite out of the mountain. From this point, the start of the unmarked trail leading down to the bathing hole is exactly 1.1km farther up the road. The trail's entrance appears as an apparent driveway on the left-hand side, and there are no other apparent 'driveways' on this side of the road. Directly opposite the trail's start are a couple of simple wooden homes.

People are always seated on the porches of these homes, so to be sure you are about to go down the correct path, call out to them, '*¿El salto?*' If they say, '*¡Sí!,*' you're on target; otherwise, someone will point you to the trail's starting point. Be sure to wear

The Salto de Jimenoa

SCOTT DOGGETT

hiking boots, as the hike back up the trail is quite steep, although it's perhaps only 400m long. If you don't have wheels, be sure to tell the motoconcho driver or the taxi driver to pick you up in two hours or whenever, unless you don't mind the walk back to town (fortunately, it is nearly all downhill). If you're in no hurry, you can catch a público heading to Constanza and get out near the trail's start; see Getting There & Away, below, for details.

River Rafting

The Río Yaque del Norte is the longest river in the country, and at least three tour operators send rafts down its upper portions on a regular basis. All three offer the same experience. They provide breakfast before loading everyone onto trucks and taking them up the road toward La Ciénaga, where they enter the river; they order their clients to paddle for much of the trip, which can be a turnoff to many adventurers; and they

Death at the Falls

According to local lore, Salto de Baiguate's bathing pool was the sight of a terrible tragedy 200 years ago. Apparently, a wealthy Spaniard had grown tired of being chided by a monk for mistreating his slaves and decided to take matters into his own hands by drowning the monk in the water here. It's said that the spirit of the monk placed a curse upon the vengeful Spaniard and that a short time later his beautiful wife died of an unknown sickness.

Frightened, the Spaniard took his young son and mounted a horse to escape the region forever. But as they passed the cliffs above the Río Baiguate, the roar of the cascades spooked his horse and caused it to lose its footing. The animal and its riders plunged to their deaths. Today, some of the old townsfolk say that if you listen closely as you walk the last 100m to the Salto de Baiguate, you can hear the Spaniard's screams, forever echoing in the canyon.

break for lunch about two-thirds of the way downriver. They also require all of their clients to wear wetsuits, helmets and life jackets, and to participate in a safety lesson.

Anyone who has been through truly fear-inspiring rapids won't be impressed by the mild white water on the Río Yaque del Norte; its best rapids are easily less than half as strong as the mightiest navigable rapids elsewhere. And the scenery, though lovely at times, isn't spectacular. The mountains on either side have mostly been deforested, and the riverbanks also show quite a bit of litter – though far less than is found downstream (since the river guides regularly remove trash from the stretch of river they use). Occasionally you'll pass local people washing their clothes in the river.

Does all this mean that a trip down the Río Yaque del Norte is a bummer? Not at all. The guides are humorous and do a fine job of entertaining, and one could do much

worse than spend an afternoon paddling down a sparkling mountain river. For those who aren't disappointed when their lives aren't placed in serious danger three times in a single day, the few dips and good-size splashes on the Río Yaque del Norte may be just right.

Of the three rafting outfits, Maxima Aventura at Rancho Baiguate (☎ 809-574-6890, fax 574-4940, rancho.baiguate@codetel.net.do) has the most experienced guides and the greatest number of rafts on the river. They charge US$55 per person. Get Wet (☎ 809-586-1170, fax 586-1655, get.wet@codetel.net.do), along Calle del Carmen 2km east of central Jarabacoa, charges US$60 per person. Franz Aventuras (☎ 809-574-2669, fax 574-4815) operates out of Rancho Jarabacoa, which is along the turnoff road to Salto de Jimenoa (see Waterfalls, above, for directions to the turnoff) and charges US$50 per person.

Canyoning

This is definitely not an activity for people who fear heights. Canyoning involves hiking down into a deep canyon just below Salto de Jimenoa Uno, leaping from the top of an enormous boulder into the chilly Río Jimenoa 15m below, swimming down part of the river, then rappelling twice down rocky cliff faces to solid-rock landings. If you've never rappelled before, this is not the time to learn. Instruction is minimal and the cliffs are high. Both Maxima Aventura and Get Wet offer canyoning, in fact using the same boulder and the same cliffs; the only difference is that Maxima Aventura charges US$55 for the adventure while Get Wet charges US$60 (see River Rafting, above, for contact information). Both outfits provide all the equipment you will need. Don't bother taking a camera; it would only get wet.

Hiking

The most popular hiking trail to Pico Duarte begins at La Ciénaga, a hamlet at the eastern edge of Parque Nacional Armando Bermúdez. (For details about the park and the route, see Parques Nacionales Armando Bermúdez & José del Carmen Ramírez, above.) The distance between Jarabacoa and La Ciénaga is 42km, the first 33 of which are paved and end at the small town of Manabao. Nine kilometers of poor, unpaved road separate Manabao and La Ciénaga. However, both of these towns are served by públicos that depart every two hours from Calle Odulio Jiménez near Calle 16 de Agosto in Jarabacoa. The públicos that make the trip are generally small red pickup trucks, and the passengers just climb into the back. The cost to reach Manabao is US$1, and the cost to reach La Ciénaga is US$1.50.

Of course, it is also possible to take a público in the opposite direction. But due to the infrequency of these vehicles, if you've just completed your hike and are anxious to get back to Jarabacoa, don't hesitate to hail down any truck heading toward the city. Chances are the driver, most likely a local farmer, will allow you to hop aboard. It's customary to tip the driver a couple of dollars.

Golf

Just outside Jarabacoa is a well-maintained nine-hole golf course that's open to anyone. The daily greens fee is US$13, and rental equipment is another US$13 a day. Caddies are available for hire as well. To get there, take the turnoff to Salto de Jimenoa at the wall of signs (see Waterfalls, above), and after about 3km you'll come to a sign that reads 'Campo de Golfo.' A driveway heads off to the left and reaches the golf course in another 200m.

Places to Stay

Budget The only hotel that's actually in central Jarabacoa is the *Hogar Hotel* (☎ *809-574-2739*), on Calle Mella one block west of Av Independencia. This place offers eight run-down rooms with swaying beds, seatless toilets and screenless windows. However, it *is* centrally located and its wild garden *is* lovely, and there is hot water in the private bathrooms and several of the rooms catch a nice breeze. The rate for one or two persons is US$12.

A better value is the *Hotel Holly Day* (☎ *809-574-2778*), upon Calle del Carmen about 1km east of the Shell station. The

Holly Day consists of a two-story structure with 14 rooms that are quite OK – *if* you arrive with a mosquito net to place over your bed. The beds here are much better than those at the Hogar, the bathrooms are private and have hot water, and most of the rooms have ceiling fans. The big drawback is the lack of screens on the windows. But for US$7 per room per night, one can hardly complain.

During the 1940s, a hotel that was the talk of the island opened on the road linking Hwy Duarte and Jarabacoa, about a dozen kilometers outside of town. The *Hotel Montaña* was elegant and spacious, the valley views grand, the swimming pool enormous. Steam pipes laid under the dance floor provided radiant heat on chilly nights. Surrounding the hotel were all manner of sports facilities, including hunting grounds and tennis courts. Today, the hotel doesn't even maintain a telephone number. There's a generator, but it doesn't work. The pool's empty. But some of the 25 rooms remain in decent condition. If you've got a vivid imagination, a taste for history and your own wheels (there's no restaurant here and no services within walking distance), it's worth a look. Rates are US$17/20 for a single/double, but even at those prices you might have the place to yourself.

Mid-Range Built in the 1970s, the *Hotel Pinar Dorado* (☎ *809-574-2820, fax 689-7012*), on Calle del Carmen east of town, shows no signs of updating and is not aging well. Yet it is the only place in town that offers air-conditioned rooms; those same 43 guest rooms also have cable TV, a private hot-water bathroom and a telephone. Its strength is its woodsy grounds, although some rooms are much better than others (ask to see several). Rates are US$34/38. There is also a restaurant.

Five kilometers east of central Jarabacoa is *Rancho Baiguate* (☎ *809-574-6890, fax 574-4940, rancho.baiguate@codetel.net.do*), a 72-sq-km ranch bordered by the Ríos Baiguate and Jimenoa. Accommodations include 17 comfortable guest rooms with private hot-water bath, screened windows, ceiling fan and heater. Also on the grounds are a dining room, a swimming pool, volleyball and basketball courts, a soccer field and a gift shop. The Baiguate is known for its many outdoor activities, including horseback riding (US$7), trips to Salto de Jimenoa and Salto de Baiguate (US$20 each) and paragliding (these tandem flights take off from a 200m hill at the edge of the Jarabacoa Valley; US$55). The ranch has even got quad runners (also known as all-terrain vehicles and 'funny bikes') for rent at US$25 for 30 minutes. Single/double room rates are US$35/50 with breakfast only, US$45/66 with just breakfast and lunch, and US$55/80 with three meals. This is a fun place, and most guests leave wishing they'd given themselves more time here.

Places to Eat

The best restaurant in town is the *Restaurant Don Luis*, on the west side of the ever-popular Parque Central. This somewhat charming restaurant offers awesome people-watching from a breezy corner locale, and it serves a delicious guinea fowl with wine sauce (US$7), a generous portion of *pollo Don Luis* (fried chicken with mushroom sauce, US$5) and a very good chicken salad (US$3). The cheese used in their pizzas is popular in the Dominican Republic, but not what you're used to. Good? Bad? You be the judge. Also, because strawberries are locally produced, the *jugo de fresa* (strawberry juice, US$1) served here and elsewhere is quite tasty, as are the pineapple and orange juices.

The *Del Parque Galería Restaurant*, on the east side of the Parque Central, is *the* place to be on a Saturday or Sunday afternoon for people watching. The elevated restaurant and bar areas provide excellent vantage points from which to observe the goings-on in the park and the streets nearby. Feel free just to sip a cocktail and watch the youths of Jarabacoa interact, but if you're hungry, the *mero al ajillo* (grouper in garlic sauce, US$6), the *camarones empanado* (breaded shrimp, US$7) and the *pulpo enchilado* (octopus in hot sauce, US$5) are all

excellent. If *carne al barbeque* (barbecued beef, US$6) is offered, go for it. It's delicious!

Another good restaurant is the *Restaurante El Rancho*, on Av Independencia near the north end of town. Owned by the same couple that owns Rancho Baiguate, El Rancho's long menu contains a host of chicken and beef dishes and pizzas at reasonable prices. The walls of this semi-dressy, open-sided restaurant are graced with handsome local paintings (a fair number of artists live in town), and the ambiance goes well with the selection of wines.

To try something completely different, check out the *Puerto Rico Bar*, in the northwest part of town. This peculiar place is on the bank of the Río Yaque del Norte and is reachable only by a rickety little barge that a young boy operates. The Puerto Rico has been for sale for a couple of years and might well be out of business by the time you read this, but if you like oddball places and have time to kill, you might want to check it out. Pretty much the only people who frequent the narrow, two-story establishment looming over the river are men who have lived in the area for years and like to play cards all afternoon long.

Getting There & Away

Caribe Tours (☎ 809-574-4796) has a depot on Calle José Duran 20m east of Av Independencia. It's possible to reach Jarabacoa from the Caribe Tours depot in Santo Domingo four times a day; buses leave the station at 7:30 and 10 am, and at 1:30 and 4:30 pm. The cost is US$4 and the trip takes a little more than two hours, unless there's traffic leaving the capital. Likewise, from Jarabacoa to Santo Domingo there are four departures daily – at 7 and 10:30 am, and at 1:30 and 4:30 pm.

Gua-guas leave Jarabacoa for La Vega every 30 minutes from the depot on the corner of Calle José Duran and Av Independencia. The cost is US$1. If you'd prefer to take a taxi to La Vega, they can be found at the gua-gua depot during daylight hours and even into the evening. A taxi ride to La Vega will set you back US$12.

It's also possible to take a público to Constanza from Jarabacoa. They leave from the intersection of Calle 16 de Agosto and Calle del Carmen every 90 minutes and cost US$2.50. However, this route to Constanza, while perfectly fine on a motorcycle or in a 4WD vehicle, is a rough ride in the back of a small pickup truck, since the first 29km is·on a badly rutted dirt road that winds around mostly denuded mountains. From El Río the remaining 19km to Constanza is paved and quite OK, passing through a lovely valley and past cattle-speckled mountains.

Getting Around

Central Jarabacoa is easily walked, but to get to Rancho Baiguate and other places that are a bit out of the way, you can hire a taxi at the corner of Calle José Duran and Av Independencia. Or, you can hire a moto-concho (motorcycle taxi); there are many beside major intersections and they are much less expensive than taxis.

LA VEGA

Situated beside the Hwy Duarte 125km north of Santo Domingo is the bustling provincial city of La Vega (pop 200,000), which serves the farming interests of the lower Valle de Cibao. Today La Vega is big, busy, noisy and crowded, with little or nothing of interest to the tourist. But during the late 15th century and the early 16th century, it was making history.

The city's origin dates to the late 1490s, when Christopher Columbus ordered that a fort be built at La Vega's original site to house gold mined in the area. During the next 50 years the first mint in the New World was established in La Vega; the nation's first commercial sugar crop was harvested in the vicinity of La Vega; and the first royally sanctioned brothel in the Western Hemisphere opened its doors for business.

But the city's prosperity came to an abrupt end in 1562, when an earthquake leveled La Vega. So severe was the damage that a decision was made to relocate the city, and it was moved to its present site on the banks of the Río Camú. You can visit what

remains of the old city near the town of Santo Cerro (see that section, below).

Today, La Vega's years of glory are past. Its foremost landmark is its cathedral, a concrete monstrosity. Visitors to La Vega these days are mostly transferring buses – taking gua-guas to and from Jarabacoa – although the city's pre-Lent Carnival celebrations are among the most colorful in the country.

La Vega is served throughout the day by both Metro Buses and Caribe Tours from Santo Domingo and Santiago; see the Santo Domingo chapter for details.

SANTO CERRO

Just north of La Vega is Santo Cerro (Holy Hill), several kilometers east of Hwy Duarte and well-signed from the road. Santo Cerro acquired its godly name the old-fashioned way – through a miracle. Legend has it that Columbus placed a cross he received as a bon voyage gift from Queen Isabella atop the hill, which commands a sweeping view of the Valle de Cibao. During a battle between Spaniards and Taínos, the Indians tried to burn the cross but it wouldn't catch fire. And then, with Taíno warriors looking on, the Virgen de las Mercedes appeared on one of its arms. The Indians are said to have fled in terror, and the Spaniards scored another victory for colonization.

Today the cross is said to be in private hands (although nobody seems to know whose). You can, however, see the **Santo Hoyo** (Holy Hole) in which the cross was allegedly planted by the great explorer. The hole is inside the **Iglesia Las Mercedes**, covered with a small wire grill and illuminated. Just how the hole survived from the 1490s until the church was constructed around it in 1860 is, perhaps, yet another miracle.

In any event, thousands of followers flock to the church every September 24 to celebrate **Nuestra Señora de las Mercedes** (Our Lady of Mercies). The beige-and-white church with its red-tile roof is open every day and the nuns play tape-recorded sermons all day long. Be sure to look for a fenced-off tree near the steps leading to the church – it was apparently planted in 1495.

If you continue a few kilometers on the same road that brought you to Santo Cerro, you'll come to **La Vega Vieja**, the original site of the city. All that's left are the ruins of the fort Columbus ordered built as well as a church; these are mostly the work of restoration crews. Little of either actually survived the great earthquake of 1562. Most of what remained of the structures was taken to the latter-day La Vega, where it was used in construction.

Getting There & Away

The best way to visit Santo Cerro and the ruins is by taxi, which can be hired in La Vega at either of the bus depots or at the Parque Central. The roundtrip taxi ride will set you back about US$20.

CONSTANZA

Like Jarabacoa, Constanza (pop 50,000) is a cool, lush city on the floor of a lovely valley, surrounded by picturesque though mostly deforested mountains. Situated at a very agreeable 1300m, it is the nearest thing to a Swiss grazing meadow in the Caribbean. The busy little city, ringed by farmland, is framed by mountains that appear stacked on one another for as far as the eye can see. The chief crops are potatoes, garlic, strawberries, apples and lettuce.

As recently as 1950, Constanza was as charming as any community in the country, a quiet town where many of the houses were log cabins made from pine plucked from surrounding slopes. Today most of the pine trees are gone, the rustic houses have been replaced by stucco dwellings and a sprawling shanty town has developed on the edge of the city. Within a single kilometer, vacation estates owned by wealthy Santo Domingans give way to shacks without electricity or running water owned by the Haitian laborers who tend the fields.

Also calling Constanza home are a couple of hundred Japanese farmers who arrived during the 1950s at dictator Rafael Trujillo's invitation. In return for providing 50 Japanese families superior farmland at dirt-cheap prices, Trujillo hoped the Japanese would convert the fertile valley into a thriving agri-cultural center. And this they did. Today they own much of the land being worked by Haitians.

As for formal tourist attractions, Constanza doesn't have a magnificent cathedral, an impressive museum or even the foundation of a leveled historical building that it can develop into a tourist-drawing site. Its appeal is in its charm, which, though diminishing, is still substantial. It is also a departure city for one of the major hiking trails into the Parque Nacional José del Carmen Ramírez (see above). And if you've got your own wheels, just getting to Constanza makes a fine excursion: the rolling paved road winds 68km from Hwy Duarte through one lush valley after another. But beware, bicyclists: the first 10km or so are nearly all uphill. The ride back, with views of the Valle de Cibao, makes the grueling climb worth it.

Orientation

Few of Constanza's streets are signed or even have names. Locals use landmarks or well-known businesses to give directions.

The main street is one-way Calle Luperón, which runs from east to west and has a prominent Isla gas station at its eastern end. Most of Constanza's hotels and restaurants are on or near Calle Luperón.

Unlike most Dominican cities, Constanza's Parque Central is not a popular hangout. However, it represents the center of town and may be reached by proceeding eight or nine blocks down Calle Luperón from the

SCOTT DOGGETT

Farmers tending to garlic in Constanza

Isla station and turning left. The adjacent church, which was erected in 1990 and is nothing special, can be seen after you turn left and go two blocks farther.

Places to Stay

Until the mid-1990s Constanza was home to several large and luxurious hotels, including the Nueva Suiza Hotel, which is still mentioned in some guidebooks as a fine place to stay. In fact, all of Constanza's luxury hotels have gone out of business. As Constanza's charm has slipped, so has her number of suitors. Today her appeal is barely able to sustain two budget hotels.

The better of the two is the *Hotel Margarita* (☎ 809-539-2943), which is just off Calle Luperón three blocks west of the Isla gas station. The Margarita rents only two rooms (the rest are used by family members), but both have a private hot-water bathroom. Neither room has a window, there's only one bed in each, and the walls are cold concrete. However, there is a mosquito net over each bed (a big plus!), the rooms are clean and the mattresses decent. For US$7 per room, the Margarita is a good value.

A major drop in quality are the rooms at the only other hotel in town – the *Hotel Restaurant Mi Casa* (☎ 809-539-2794), which does fairly brisk business due to its high-visibility location directly on Calle Luperón a mere 100m west of the Isla station. All of the guest rooms have a private hot-water bathroom. Rates vary with the room. A room for one person with one bed goes for US$12. A room with two beds costs US$18. The restaurant is quite OK but is nothing special.

Places to Eat

Six blocks down Calle Luperón from the Isla station is *Lorenzo's Restaurant Café*, which, when they turn off the usually blaring TV, is quite nice. The restaurant is the most formal in town, which isn't saying much, but it's a welcome change from most Dominican restaurants. The food is quite good. Lorenzo's offers the usual sandwiches (for US$1.50 to US$3.50), several chop sueys (from US$6 to US$8) and a variety of pastas (US$3 to

US$5). But it excels at two delicious dishes: *guinea al vino* (guinea fowl in wine, US$8) and *conejo al vino* (wild rabbit in wine, for US$6).

Facing the Parque Central is another good restaurant, the *Restaurant Cafetería Rey*. Like many upscale restaurants in the DR, the Cafetería Rey isn't much to look at, but it does serve tasty food. Among the establishment's long list of offerings is *pechuga de pollo champiñón* (chicken breast in a mushroom sauce, US$5), pizza with *hongo y longaniza* (mushrooms and sausage, US$6) and *conejo guisado* (stewed wild rabbit in a salsa, US$5).

Getting There & Away

Constanza can be reached by público from Jarabacoa and by gua-gua from La Ceiba, which is a small community near the intersection of Hwy Duarte and the road to Constanza. Constanza is also linked to Padres las Casas by regular gua-gua service. The roads between each of these communities is paved and maintained.

However, the 89km road between Constanza and San José de Ocoa is rocky, badly rutted and little traveled; for these reasons, and because nighttime temperatures often dip below freezing, it ought to be avoided. It's a shame that the road is in such terrible condition, because much of it winds through the Reserva Científica Valle Nuevo (the New Valley Scientific Reserve), which was created in 1983 and contains an enormous tract of virgin forest, most of which is above 1500m.

Getting Around

Motoconchos and taxis may be found near the Isla gas station.

BONAO

Bonao, a commercial city of 30,000 people along the Hwy Duarte, is a struggling, unappealing mining town at the center of rich deposits of nickel, bauxite and silver. It has nothing to offer the tourist and is only mentioned here because, halfway between Santo Domingo and Santiago, it might be of interest to bicyclists planning their itineraries.

The town's hardened and cash-strapped residents make it a somewhat unsafe place to roam. However, beside Hwy Duarte is the new-in-'98 *Hotel Jacaranda* (☎ *809-525-5590, fax 525-5078)*, which offers 22 guest rooms with all the desirable creature comforts. Rates are US$25 for one person or two, and US$30 for three or four people. The hotel is next to the Plaza Jacaranda, a small shopping complex that contains two fast-food restaurants, a Codetel office, a music store, a candy store and a counter where suntan lotion, film and toys are sold.

NORTHERN FOOTHILLS

The towns along the northern foothills of the Cordillera Central are small, quiet communities that are ill-served by a winding, mostly unpaved road connecting Santiago and Dajabón. Except in the towns of San José de las Matas, Monción, Sabaneta and Partido, the way is devoid of any services, and for speed as well as safety, the Santiago-Monte Cristi-Dajabón route is the better choice for getting to and from the border.

Several maps incorrectly show this as a paved, primary road. For many kilometers it is in fact a dirt road that passes through rolling, arid country that was deforested long ago and mostly serves ranchers who raise cattle in the region. The remainder of this chapter is intended for those who elect to make the drive, which should only be attempted in a 4WD vehicle or on a reliable motorcycle with good tires. The road is also served daily (usually in the mornings) by públicos.

San José de las Matas

This attractive mountain city of 70,000 people is 38km west of Santiago, and it is a jumping-off point for one of the major hiking trails (from Mata Grande) in the Parque National Armando Bermúdez (see above).

The road to San José de las Matas is alternately paved and unpaved: one minute you're moving along at a good clip, the next you're on dirt and gravel, wondering what happened to the pavement. The road is seldom used, and you can go many kilo-meters without seeing another person. Seven kilometers before reaching San José de las Matas, you'll come upon Pedregal, which has no hotel or gas station or mechanic – just a few roadside stands selling warm sodas and the like.

The residents of San José de las Matas have been raising cattle, growing tobacco and practicing subsistence agriculture since the 18th century, as they do today. But during the early 1990s the Occidental Hotel chain thought it could turn the sierra town into a major resort. At enormous cost it constructed the Hotel Club Spa La Mansión, complete with 276 air-conditioned rooms, including 50 two-bedroom villas, a gorgeous swimming pool, huge buffets, sprawling gardens and a 12-sq-km pine reserve for horseback riding. In 1998, after years of staggering losses, La Mansión went belly up.

There are several humble hotels in San José de las Matas these days, all on the main road. The best of the bunch is the *Hotel Restaurant Los Samanes* (☎ *809-578-8316)*, which has four very decent rooms with fan, private hot-water bathroom and mosquito net over the bed for US$8 per room. The rooms are above the best restaurant in town; menu items include a variety of sandwiches (most are under US$2), chicken and rice (US$3), several seafood dishes (for around US$6) and several beef dishes (each for around US$6). This place is an excellent find.

Monción

Monción is the next community west of San José de las Matas that has any public services. There are two gas stations (one with a mechanic), many homes made of clapboard or cinder block, a few paved roads, a central park, a couple of simple restaurants and no accommodations.

Sabaneta

Sabaneta is a hot, dry farming town that developed along both sides of the Santiago-Dajabón road. There are several struggling hotels along the road, the best of the lot being the *Hotel Don Chucho* (☎ *809-580-2431, fax 580-2337)*. The Don Chucho has 12 air-conditioned rooms with TV, telephone and private cold-water bathroom. Do be advised that when there's a power outage and the hotel's generator fires up, it supplies electricity to the hotel's ceiling fans but not to its air conditioners. The Don Chucho charges US$20 per room.

Partido

Partido is the last town on the Santiago-Dajabón road before reaching Dajabón that has any public services. Those services are limited to a couple of places to eat and a gas station with a mechanic on duty during daylight hours.

Southwestern Dominican Republic

The southwestern region of the Dominican Republic is the most ecologically diverse in the country, a vast area of searing deserts and frosty mountains, of pebbly beaches and lush valleys, of freshwater lagoons and saltwater lakes. It is home to the seaside town of Barahona, where wealthy Santo Domingans arrive in spiffy SUVs and frolic on weekends, and to Elías Piña, a scruffy border town where colorfully clad Haitian peasants arrive on foot and on mules twice a week to sell produce and inexpensive household goods.

The region is shaped like a large peninsula, with Haiti along most of the western edge. The northern, interior section contains San Juan de la Maguana, the largest Southwest city with 145,000 residents, while the rest of the Southwest's communities are all much smaller. These agricultural towns see few tourists, and they depend chiefly on farming sugarcane, bananas, corn, rice and cassava. That could be changing soon: at the time of writing, an international airport was being built near Barahona, and the area's second all-inclusive resort had just opened for business.

Boasting three national parks and a separate reserve, the Southwest has the potential to become a major ecotourism destination – at least once it develops the proper facilities. The parks are quite different from one another. One features a saltwater lake that's home to crocodiles and a desert island that's famous for its iguanas. Another, the largest protected area in the country, contains mostly thorn forest and an extensive marine area. The third park, on the slopes of the Sierra de Baoruco, encompasses a range of vegetation zones, from low-lying broad-leafed plants to mountain pine forests.

However, the communities of the Southwest are generally unprepared for tourists, even if they are well-served by paved highways; of the few hotels there are, most are unappealing. The exception to this is Barahona, which contains an amiable range of accommodations and restaurants.

For the resourceful traveler, the Southwest has many appealing attractions off the usual tourist trail. If you have your own wheels, you can easily explore the region by day and sleep in a comfortable hotel room in Barahona, Azua or San Juan de la Maguana at night. Even without a car, you can get most anywhere by *gua-gua*, *público* or taxi, but time constraints will mean at least a couple nights in run-down lodgings.

The Interior

Just west of the Bahía de Ocoa, Hwy 2 heads inland to Azua and then north through the Valle de San Juan to Elías Piña and the Haitian border.

AZUA

Azua is the first and largest town you'll encounter as you approach the Southwest from the east, but it is little more than a pit stop for most travelers.

Azua was founded in 1504 by Diego Velásquez, who reached Hispaniola with Christopher Columbus on the admiral's second voyage to the New World in 1493. Making the months-long journey the following year was Hernán Cortés, who worked in Azua as a notary public. Over a decade later, in 1511, Cortés fought under Velásquez in Cuba, where Velásquez subdued the Indians with legendary brutality. Cortés then led the Spanish invasion of Mexico a decade after that, annihilating the Aztec empire.

Juan Ponce de León also lived in Azua for a brief period. In 1513 he led a fleet of three Spanish galleons in search of Bimini and the mythical fountain of youth and quite unintentionally discovered Florida, where he died eight years later, wounded by an Indian's arrow.

But today, no memorials commemorate Azua's three most famous and infamous residents, though several may have existed at one time: Azua has experienced so much

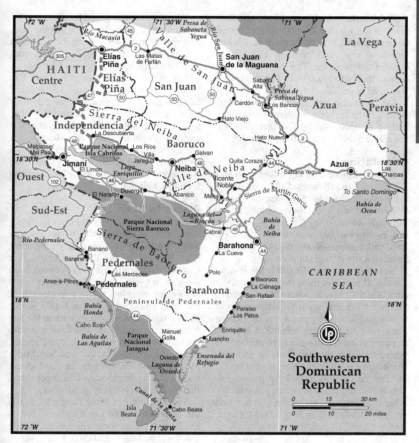

Southwestern Dominican Republic

natural disaster and decimating warfare since its founding that it's impossible to know. The original town was leveled by an earthquake in 1751 and relocated a half dozen kilometers northwest, where the current town now resides. Nothing remains of the Azua Velásquez founded.

In 1760, Spanish authorities settled 26 Canary Island families in Azua 'for its development and defense in case of some insult on the part of enemies in times of war.' In 1844, following a battle between Spanish soldiers and Haitian troops, Azua was briefly abandoned; the Spaniards feared the much

larger Haitian force would encircle them and set the town on fire. Azua consisted mainly of thatched wooden houses, and indeed, after occupying it for a few days, the Haitians put it to the torch.

Azua was resettled and rebuilt, and yet it changed very little from the mid-19th century until the mid-20th century. Its population rose from about 500 residents to about 5000, but people still lived in small square houses built of split palm trunks, chinked with mud or lime, and topped with dry palm-frond roofs. It remained a quiet dusty town stuck in a hot desert plain.

Today, cinder-block homes have replaced many of the wooden homes, and corrugated tin has replaced most of the palm thatch, but the heat and dust remain, and power outages are frequent. This is not a tourist destination, but a place to fuel up and stop if you need a rest. Located halfway between Santo Domingo and the Haitian border, Azua has the feel of a transients' town. This feeling is bolstered by the fact that the Carretera Sánchez runs directly through it.

Orientation

Azua is 120km west of Santo Domingo and 77km east of Barahona, and, some might say, in the middle of nowhere; it's variously ringed by farmland and desert for many kilometers. Through town, the Carretera Sánchez divides into two one-way streets, which are lined with businesses catering mostly to area farmers. Azua is their supply center.

Near the west end of town is the Parque Central. If you're coming from the west, the park and its plaza is where the Carretera Sánchez splits into separate eastbound and westbound lanes. The plaza is a happening place most of the time because it is a key stopping point for gua-guas and públicos. If you're traveling through Azua by gua-gua, chances are it will make a brief stop beside the Parque Central to pick up passengers. This is also the place to switch gua-guas for other destinations. From here, you can find gua-guas headed to San Juan de la Maguana, Barahona and Jimaní, among others.

Beaches

Several guidebooks refer to lovely beaches south of Azua, along the shore of the Bahía de Ocoa. In fact, most of the *playas* are kissed by waves so gentle that they've yet to convert the gravely shore into sand. Hardly deserving of the name, these beaches are also sporadically piled high with garbage, as they've been used as dumping grounds over the years. The cleanest of the area's beaches is the **Playa Río Monte**, but like the others a grain of its 'sand' could easily break a window. There are cabañas at the beach for US$13 a night, but they wouldn't be worth staying in if the price were US$3 a night.

If you've just got to see the shoreline for yourself, you'll be glad to know that the 6km-long road that runs to it from the Carretera Sánchez was paved in 1998. To find this road, look for a large 'Río Monte' sign near the east end of Azua. Once you reach Playa Río Monte, a dirt road hugs the coast for a dozen kilometers or so to the west. The road is rarely traveled and badly rutted; unless you're driving a reliable 4WD vehicle, it's best avoided altogether. Playa Río Monte is not served by gua-gua or público. Taxis and motoconchos, found beside Parque Central, can take you to it. Expect to pay US$10 roundtrip for a taxi, half that for a motoconcho.

Places to Stay

There are only two decent places to stay in Azua, and the better of the two is the *Hotel San Ramon* (no telephone), on Sánchez Hwy 3km east of the Parque Central. It is easy to miss the hotel: if you're coming from the east, it's just before the highway separates going into town, on the opposite side of the road and 75m before a highly visible Texaco station. Most of the rooms at the San Ramon are stand-alone and have a private cold-water bathroom and air conditioning, which is important in the arid Southwest. Most of the mattresses are in good shape, and there is a generator. At US$13 per room, the San Ramon is a very good value.

Two blocks north of the Parque Central is the *Hotel Don Juan* (no telephone), which has 20 drab guest rooms with air con, private hot-water bathroom and cable TV. However, unlike the Hotel San Ramon, the Don Juan doesn't have a generator; this is a huge drawback because Azua experiences many power failures and during them the Don Juan's rooms become unbearably hot. Rates at the Don Juan are US$15/18 for a single/double.

Two kilometers west of Azua, on the northern side of the Sánchez Hwy, is the *Cabañas Paradise* (no telephone), which consists of a half dozen or so rooms, each with an adjacent private garage that you can secure at night. Each of the spacious rooms has a king-size bed facing an oversize mirror and a private warm-water bathroom; rates are US$13/15. The place is equipped with a generator. If you've got your own wheels, this is *the* place to stay in the vicinity of Azua.

Places to Eat

The best restaurant in town, and possibly the only one equipped with a generator, is the ***Restaurant el Gran Segovia*** on the east end of town near the Texaco station. The specialty of the house is *filete de carey* (filet of sea turtle, US$6); if you want to help serve this endangered species, don't order this dish. Also offered and quite tasty are seven lobster dishes, each for US$10. There are also seven shrimp dishes (US$7 each) and a variety of meat dishes, including *chivo al vino* (goat in red wine) for US$4.50. Also quite delicious is the *pulpo guisado* (octopus stew, served in a red salsa) for US$6.

Getting There & Away

Gua-guas ply the Carretera Sánchez from sunrise to sunset. To reach Azua, simply hail any passing gua-gua going that way from any point along the highway. A gua-gua ride to Azua from anywhere in the Southwest won't cost more than US$3. A gua-gua to/from Barahona costs US$1.50.

Azua is also served by Caribe Tours from Santo Domingo and Barahona. Buses going from Santo Domingo to Azua depart at 6:30, 7 and 10 am, and 1:30, 2:30 and 4 pm; the cost is US$3. Buses from Barahona to Azua depart at 7 am and 2:30 pm; the cost is US$4. There is no Caribe Tours depot in Azua. Their buses simply arrive and depart from the Parque Central.

According to area residents, it is unwise to travel the Carretera Sánchez at night due to bandit activity.

CARRETERA SÁNCHEZ

Fifteen kilometers west of Azua is the turnoff to the border town of Elías Piña (formerly known as Comendador, which still appears on some maps). This is an excellent road for seeing a part of the Dominican Republic seldom traveled by outsiders. The entire way is paved and in good condition, and it makes an excellent bicycle trip. There are no steep sections, although there are plenty of rolling hills along the way.

Though it doesn't make much sense, the turn-off road to Elías Piña keeps the name Carretera Sánchez (Sánchez Hwy), while the road that continues to Barahona becomes Hwy 44. It's 124km long and flanked most of the way by small farms and ranches and a dozen or so hamlets. You mainly pass farmers growing corn, cassava, watermelon and cantaloupe. Though the jaunt to the border is a pleasant way to experience life in the DR, there are few sites that qualify as bona fide 'tourist attractions.' The three cities – San Juan de la Maguana, Las Matas de Farfán and Elías Piña – are the only places with lodgings for the traveler.

Elías Piña is a major Haitian-Dominican trading center, particularly on Monday and Friday – the days of market. Another guidebook unfairly refers to Elías Piña as 'a sleepy place, except for the activity of police, soldiers, and smugglers.' In fact, on market days the town is bustling, and tourists are in very little danger from either smugglers, the police or the military, who are common to border towns and generally quite mellow. Since the Elías Piña border may only be used by Haitians and Dominicans, it's not exactly Checkpoint Charlie – for instance, you only know that you've reached the border when you come to the end of the highway and see an old rope stretched across it.

SAN JUAN DE LA MAGUANA

San Juan de la Maguana is an old city, dating to the 16th century. The town takes its name from the combination of San Juan El Bautista (St John the Baptist) and the Maguana Indians, who were one of the Taíno tribes that inhabited Hispaniola at the time of Columbus's arrival. The city of 145,000 is often referred to simply as San Juan.

Being close to Haiti, San Juan was not immune from the fighting that occurred between Haitian and Spanish troops during the 1840s. At that time Haiti tried to wrest control of the eastern two-thirds of Hispaniola from Spain, and though unsuccessful, it did manage to level many of the Dominican communities its troops briefly occupied. One such town was San Juan, which Haitian soldiers burned to the ground in 1845.

The city we see today dates back to the late 1960s, when President Balaguer initiated a countrywide modernization effort to prepare the DR's largest cities for the millions of tourists he hoped the republic would attract. Also, various international development agencies were pouring money into the country at the time, and they required the government to build ports, highways, aqueducts, streets and energy plants, and San Juan benefited handsomely.

Despite the improvements, San Juan hasn't become a tourist destination. In fact the only tourist attraction within its vicinity is **El Corral de los Indios**, 7km north of town on the road to Juan Herrera. The Corral is marked by a government sign and consists solely of a circle of stones defining a 300m area. It is presumed that the Corral was a meeting place of the Taínos and was probably used in rituals – and not, as its name suggests, to confine horses. The Corral existed prior to the arrival of the conquistadors, who introduced horses to the Western Hemisphere.

To get to the Corral, take San Juan's main westbound road, Calle Independencia, to Av Anacaona and turn northward toward Juan Herrera. Beyond that town is Sabaneta, where one of the trails leading to Pico Duarte originates.

Orientation

The Sánchez Hwy becomes the main road through town, where it splits into two one-way streets running east and west. The westbound lane is Calle Independencia, and the eastbound lane is Calle 16 de Agosto. All of the city's hotels and a Caribe Tours bus depot are near the east fork in the highway.

Places to Stay & Eat

There are three hotels in San Juan, all of which are good values. If you're on a tight budget and can do without air conditioning, stay at the **Hotel Maguana** (☎ 809-557-2244), which was built in 1947 and has maintained some of its grandeur. The three-story hotel has 24 spacious rooms, each with ceiling fan, firm mattresses and private hot-water bath. There is a pay phone in the lobby.

The rate for a single or a double is US$11. The Maguana is on the north side of the Carretera Sánchez just before it splits as you're coming from the east.

One hundred meters to the west of the Maguana is the **Hotel Tamarindo** (no telephone), which has 30 boxy but decent rooms, each with private hot-water bathroom; it's US$10 with ceiling fan and US$13 with air conditioning.

New in 1998 and much spiffier is the **Hotel D'Angel** (☎ 809-557-3484, fax 557-5344), on Calle Independencia 200m west of the Hotel Maguana. The D'Angel features 33 guest rooms with air conditioning, private hot-water bathroom, cable TV and private telephone. The rates are US$30/40. The restaurant at the D'Angel is the best in town; of the dozen or so local eateries to choose from, it's the only standout.

Getting There & Away

Seventy-five meters west of the Hotel Maguana is the town's Caribe Tours depot. It offers daily service to Santo Domingo, with buses departing at 6:45 and 10 am, and 1:45 and 5:15 pm. Buses from Santo Domingo to San Juan depart at 6:45 and 10 am, and 1:30 and 4 pm. These buses make one stop in Azua along the way. One-way fares are US$3.50 to Santo Domingo and US$2 to Azua. Gua-guas stop beside the Parque Central, which is near the center of town.

Getting Around

Taxis and motoconchos may be found near the Parque Central.

LAS MATAS DE FARFÁN

Thirty-three kilometers west of San Juan is this much smaller roadside city. Las Matas has nothing special to offer, but its hotels are much cleaner and more secure than those in the border town of Elías Piña, 23km away. The town also has a bank and three gas stations. If you're visiting the Monday or Friday market in Elías Piña and need a bed for the night, you'll be better off staying in Las Matas.

As with San Juan, the Sánchez Hwy splits at each end of town; the westbound lane be-

A Village Swallowed

The village of Mesopotamia was, quite literally, here one minute and gone the next, a tragic victim of Hurricane Georges in 1998.

The village of 1000 people was situated just above the confluence of the Ríos San Juan and Yaque del Sur in the southern foothills of the Cordillera Central. On September 23, 1998, during a 15-second period sometime between 3 and 3:05 am, all of Mesopotamia was washed away – every building, every street, every resident.

Ten hours earlier, Red Cross officials using megaphones had urged the people of Mesopotamia to evacuate. 'A hurricane is coming,' they said. 'Your village could be flooded.' No one listened. Church leaders, urged by the Red Cross, repeated the message. Their pleas were also ignored.

The weather in Mesopotamia told the people all they wanted to know: it wasn't raining, and hurricanes had always brought rain. Besides, no one wanted to leave their possessions unattended, for fear that they would be stolen.

Soldiers arrived an hour later and ordered the people of Mesopotamia to abandon their homes and reach higher ground. No one paid any attention to the soldiers either – which is perhaps less surprising, since Dominican soldiers long ago lost all credibility with the people they're supposed to protect.

What the villagers didn't know was that Hurricane Georges was swirling into the mountain range north of Mesopotamia, having just hammered the Southeast of the DR. Once in the mountains, the hurricane unleashed a deluge. The rain fell so hard it hurt. Mountain brooks became creeks, creeks became rivers, and lazy rivers became frothing white-water torrents.

But rain never fell on Mesopotamia, and feeling safe, the villagers went to sleep that night. As they did, the rivers on both sides of the town swelled to the tops of their levees.

The villagers might have lived to see the sunrise had it not been for a panic-stricken man at the controls of a dam on the Río Yaque del Sur 4km upriver of Mesopotamia. Fearing a break in the structure, he threw open the flood gates and released a catastrophic volume of water into a river poised to burst its banks.

It's unlikely the people of Mesopotamia knew what hit them. One minute they were asleep in their beds, and the next, a wall of water 4m high and traveling at 30km/h was sweeping through town, obliterating everything in its path, including a chunk of the levee separating the Río San Juan from Mesopotamia.

In less than a minute, Mesopotamia was gone, swept downriver by a hurricane-powered deluge that permitted no chance of escape.

Just before daylight, the rivers receded, revealing a landscape covered in mud where a church, businesses and homes had stood hours earlier. The gardens and chicken coops, parked cars and farming tools were all gone. A day later, corpses and debris began appearing in the Bahía de Neiba, 50km downstream.

comes Calle Damian Ortiz and the eastbound lane becomes Calle Independencia. The two streets are separated by a short block.

The city's lush Parque Central is near the east end of town where the highway splits; it's a popular hangout. There are a couple of decent budget hotels on Calle Damian Ortiz, but there are two better budget hotels on Calle Independencia a short walk away from the Parque Central.

The *Hotel Independencia* and the *Hotel Farfán* have ceiling fans only and private cold-water bathrooms, but both are clean and secure; rooms are US$10 for single or double.

Also on Calle Independencia and within 100m or so of the Parque Central is a Codetel office (open 8 am to 10 pm daily), a bus depot that serves gua-guas and públicos and the *Restaurant Gloria*. The Gloria won't inspire you to write postcards home, but it's the best restaurant in the neighborhood.

Five kilometers east of town is the popular Western-style *Cactus Bar*, a big open-sided bar/restaurant with a thatch roof and an assortment of atmospheric odds and ends suspended from the rafters – saddles, a chair, a boot and so on. The dance floor is packed on weekend nights. If you happen to be in Las Matas or San Juan on a Friday or Saturday night, consider saddling up to the Cactus Bar for a glass of Dominican rum over ice with a twist of lemon. If there's not a taxi around when you want to leave, ask the bartender or cashier to call one for you. If you don't speak Spanish, a *'Taxi, por favor'* and a concerned look will get the ball rolling.

ELÍAS PIÑA

Elías Piña – also known by its former name, Comendador – is on the Haitian border, but because there is no immigration office in town, only Haitians and Dominicans are allowed to cross at this remote outpost. And cross they do – especially on the market days of Monday and Friday, when hundreds of Haitians arrive on burros and on foot to sell their wares. The **market** attracts hundreds of Dominicans as well, some from as far away as Azua, Baní and San Cristóbal, who arrive and depart in gua-guas.

The market is impossible to miss; just stay on the major road until you come to streets where people have suspended numerous tarps from trees, road signs and what not. Among the goods laid out on the ground beneath them are cooking utensils, clothing, shoes, fruits and vegetables and some handicrafts. However, the quantity and variety of handicrafts is limited since few tourists attend the market. The sellers sit in the protective shade of tarps; most of the Haitians

are women, many wearing colorful scarves on their heads, cotton blouses and long wraparound skirts. Increasingly, however, the Haitian women arrive in T-shirts and jeans or in light dresses – Western clothing donated by various US-based aid groups.

Also in Elías Piña is a military base and a police headquarters. At times tensions between Haiti and the Dominican Republic mount, with Dominicans accusing Haitians of undercutting their job market with cheap labor and Haitians accusing Dominicans of owning more than their fair share of Hispaniola. Along with performing the usual border duties – occasionally searching vehicles and persons for drugs or other contraband – the soldiers and police are there to ensure the peace during tense times.

Be aware that you may be stopped by soldiers or police who want to search your vehicle or camera bag – such searches often take place a kilometer or two from the border and are quite routine. You'd be wise to be friendly and just let them do their job, *and* to make sure you don't carry anything into town you wouldn't want them to find. If they ask questions you don't understand, politely saying *'Tourista, no comprendo'* will usually end the questioning and result in your being sent on your way. Acting defensive or aggressive is the quickest way to get into trouble; however, treat the police officers or soldiers with respect, and nine times out of 10 they'll treat you the same.

Other than the twice-weekly markets, there's absolutely no reason to visit Elías Piña, and once you've seen the market, there's no reason to spend the night here. The few hotels in town are very worn, and there are a couple of decent places only 23km away in Las Matas de Farfán; see above for descriptions.

Península de Pedernales

With three varied and striking national parks, a scientific reserve and hundreds of kilometers of Caribbean coast, the Península de Pedernales seems at first glance like a can't-miss spot – and one day that may be true. However, the way has not yet been paved smooth for tourists. The beaches on the east coast are mostly made of pebbles, the parks have almost no visitor facilities, and only one town, Barahona, is worth spending the night in. There are two paved, well-maintained highways, both of which are fairly flat and seem inviting to bicyclists, but they pass through an arid, barren country-side that offers little relief. What this means is that dedicated travelers, preferably in a 4WD vehicle, will have most of the incred-ible, sometimes awesome natural splendors almost to themselves.

Although the continuity of the road between Azua and Barahona doesn't physi-cally change, its name does, 15km west of Azua at the turnoff for San Juan de la Maguana. At this point the Sánchez Hwy becomes Hwy 44: it runs to Barahona, fol-lows the east coast of the peninsula till it reaches the Parque Nacional Jaragua, and then heads west across the peninsula to Ped-ernales, the DR's southernmost border town. For its entire 198km length, Hwy 44 is paved and well maintained.

Looking at a map, adventurous bicyclists may be intrigued by Hwy 44, since much of it runs along the Caribbean coast and along the northern boundary of the country's largest national park. However, be aware that there are precious few facilities and sometimes little to see on this route. Bicy-clists especially should be advised that more than 10km of Hwy 44 (the section northwest of Sierra Martin Garcia) is arduous; there's not a single hotel on several 30km-plus stretches; the heat, particularly between Oviedo and Pedernales, can be debilitating; and bicycle repair shops are virtually non-existent south of Barahona.

From the San Juan turnoff to the Vicente Noble turnoff, the terrain flanking Hwy 44 is mostly covered with desert scrub. This section is not unlike 'rattlesnake country' in the US Southwest. Cacti and tumbleweeds abound, and the air seems especially dry and dusty. Vehicles frequently overheat on the portion of Hwy 44 that rolls across the north-ern foothills of the Sierra Martin Garcia, an enormous and beautiful desert mountain.

South of Vicente Noble to Barahona, a tan landscape punctuated by reddish-beige rock formations gives way to verdant fields of sugarcane, which the dictator Rafael Tru-jillo ordered planted and which today play a major role in Barahona's economy. Another anachronism here is the appearance of several large banana plantations, fed by an extensive irrigation system that taps the Río Yaque del Sur.

At Barahona the highway becomes Av Casandra Damiron and then Av Luis E Del-monte before reemerging as Hwy 44 at the southern end of town. Paved in 1991, the highway south of Barahona winds over hills and hugs a coastline that's variously adorned with pebbly beaches and rocky shore. Every so many kilometers it bisects a small com-munity or town. However, the two largest towns here, Paraíso and Enriquillo, contain neither anything to see nor a decent place to stay.

Just south of Juancho the highway swerves inland, and the air becomes noticeably hotter and drier all the way to Pedernales, a sprawling, unattractive border town without a single adequate hotel. Most of the 60km of highway linking Oviedo and Pedernales forms the northern border of Parque Nacional Jaragua, and on both sides of the pavement there's nothing but thorn forest for as far as the eye can see. Traveling this awesome and desolate stretch of highway inspires the desire not to become stranded in this unforgiving environment.

RESERVA CIENTÍFICA LAGUNA RINCÓN

The 47-sq-km Reserva Científica Laguna Rincón (Corner Lagoon Scientific Reserve) is the largest freshwater lagoon in the Dominican Republic and is known for its healthy population of Hispaniolan fresh-water slider turtles, which are endemic to the island. Freshwater shrimp and several endemic fish species also reside in the lake. Its aquatic vegetation consists mostly of water lily, coontail and yellow nelumbo. Among the bird species here are the masked duck, the ruddy duck, the Louisiana heron, the blue-winged teal and Florida flamingo.

The reserve is seldom visited, but with the handsome peaks of the Sierra de Neiba in the background it certainly isn't without photographic appeal. Anyone taking a taxi from Barahona to Parque Nacional Isla Cabritos would do well to sneak a peek at the lagoon, which has a dirt access road from the town of Cabral. From Barahona, a taxi ride to the lagoon and back will cost about US$20 per party. Gua-guas only go as far as Cabral (roundtrip is less than US$4), and from Cabral transportation options to and from the lagoon are very limited.

BARAHONA

Barahona is a pleasant city, a windswept seaside community that seems to have developed with little planning or architectural uniformity. It might be ideal except that there's no beach. Instead, where the city's main street meets the sea, there's only a big, ugly mining operation. But Barahona does offer a variety of hotels and restaurants, and it makes a good home base for exploring the nearby national parks. It is becoming increasingly popular with Dominican and foreign tourists for just that reason.

With a population of 90,000, Barahona is the largest community on the Península de Pedernales. Its economy is based chiefly on sugarcane farming and on salt, gypsum and bauxite mining. Developers are trying to change that by adding seaside hotels, but whether they can compete successfully against those areas – such as Punta Cana, Boca Chica and elsewhere – that boast picturesque beaches remains to be seen.

By Dominican standards, Barahona is a young city, founded in 1802 by Haitian general Toussaint L'Ouverture. For over a century, residents mostly made their living taking what they could from the Caribbean, but today, fishing accounts for only a small part of Barahona's economy. The dictator Rafael Trujillo changed everything when he ordered many square kilometers of desert north of town converted into sugarcane fields for his family's financial benefit. More than three decades after his assassination,

the thousands of hectares of sugarcane continue to be tended, only now they are locally owned and benefit the community.

Barahona's hotels provide good value, its dining choices range from cheap pizzerias to fine seafood restaurants, and its dance clubs and bars maintain a lively nightlife. While Barahona is no different than most any city, it's the best place to be on the peninsula, and from here a person can do quite a lot – and still be back in time to get a good night's sleep.

Orientation & Information

As you arrive from the north, the sugarcane fields lining Hwy 44 give way to small farms and simple houses near Barahona. After the highway turns toward the coast, it becomes a bustling boulevard filled with trucks, cars, motorcycles, bicyclists and pedestrians. At the entrance to town the highway becomes Av Casandra Damiron. Three blocks after a roundabout adorned with a square arch, Av Casandra Damiron merges with and then becomes Av Luis E Delmonte, Barahona's main street.

From the merger, Av Luis E Delmonte runs straight as a sugarcane stalk downhill to the sea, or more exactly, to the seaside mining operation. From here, you can turn right or left onto Av Enriquillo. Left leads to an industrial area; right becomes Hwy 44 after several kilometers, which continues for another 75km down the east coast of the Península de Pedernales.

While Av Luis E Delmonte is Barahona's main street, lined with businesses and buzzing with activity all day long, the center of the town is Parque Central, several blocks south. Beside the town square is a Banco Popular (open 9 am to 3 pm weekdays), a Codetel office (open 8 am to 10 pm daily), a church, a dance club and a couple of bars. Around the corner, on Calle Anacaona, is the Caribe Tours bus depot. There is no tourist office in town.

Diving

On the beach at the Riviera Beach Hotel is Coral-Sea Divers (☎/fax 809-524-2689), a very professional dive center that's run by

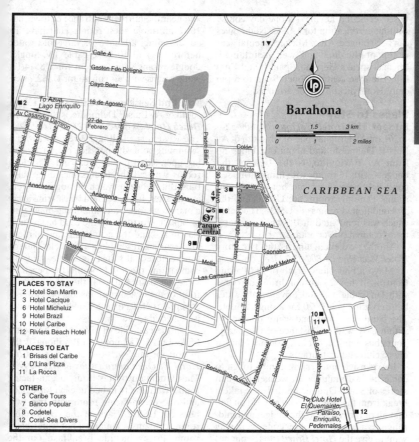

Barahona

0   1.5   3 km
0   1   2 miles

CARIBBEAN SEA

PLACES TO STAY
2 Hotel San Martin
3 Hotel Cacique
6 Hotel Micheluz
9 Hotel Brazil
10 Hotel Caribe
12 Riviera Beach Hotel

PLACES TO EAT
1 Brisas del Caribe
4 D'Lina Pizza
11 La Rocca

OTHER
5 Caribe Tours
7 Banco Popular
8 Codetel
12 Coral-Sea Divers

German owner Michael Schroeder. Michael takes people to about 25 dive sites within 6km of Barahona. For beginners and intermediate divers, he favors sites that feature lots of coral in fairly shallow water with excellent visibility and very little current. There, you can expect to see many kinds of coral, barracudas, stingrays, mackerels, lobsters and huge king crabs.

Michael prefers to take advanced divers on canyon and wall dives, where divers can see groupers and nurse sharks among the larger animals. Manatees ply the Bahía de Neiba, and Michael will take divers to them

when he knows they're around (manatees tend to come and go, feasting on sea grasses and the like in several regularly visited areas). Manatees are great fun to encounter underwater because they are enormously inquisitive animals and will swim right up to a diver just to get a good look. They are not at all dangerous, so don't be alarmed if one comes your way.

Rates are US$33 for the first dive if you have your own equipment and US$39 if you need to rent equipment. The per-dive price falls as the number of dives increases. Several classes are also available, including

Discover Scuba Diving – a one-day course without certification for US$65. Night dives can be arranged. All of Michael's rental gear is top of the line and well maintained. Michael speaks German, Spanish and English. The dive center is open 9 am to 5 pm daily. Hotel pickup can be arranged.

Places to Stay

Budget The *Hotel Cacique* (☎ 809-524-4620), on Av Uruguay one block south of Av Luis E Delmonte and about one block up from Av Enriquillo, is the best of the budgets, with 16 rooms with firm mattresses, good lighting and private hot-water bathrooms. Fan-only rooms are US$10, and the air-conditioned rooms are US$18. The hotel, which was renovated in 1998, has a generator to combat power outages.

Another excellent find is the two-story *Hotel Micheluz* (☎ 809-524-2358), on Av 30 de Mayo a half block north of the Parque Central. It has 23 air-conditioned rooms with fan, cable TV and private cold-water bathroom for US$18/20 for a single/double. The handsome, pink-and-white building is within easy walking distance of the Caribe Tours bus depot, a bank, a Codetel office, a dance club and restaurants.

Inexpensive hotel rooms can be tough to come by in Barahona on weekends, when scores of Santo Domingans arrive to take a break from the hectic capital city. If you find that all of the rooms at the budget and midrange establishments are gone, you may want to give the *Hotel Brazil* (no telephone) a try. A half block south of the Parque Central on Av Padre Bellini, it's a very basic place with nine rooms with one light bulb apiece, a fan and private cold-water bathroom. The rates are US$5/8.

Mid-Range The better of Barahona's two mid-range hotels is the *Hotel Caribe* (☎ 809-524-4111, fax 524-4115), on Av Enriquillo 800m south of Av Luis E Delmonte. All 32 of its guest rooms have air conditioning, ceiling fan, a telephone, a safe and a private hot-water bathroom. The rate is US$24 per room.

The *Hotel San Martin* (☎ 809-524-5821), a half block north of Av Casandra Damiron

and near the northern entrance of town, has 16 comfortable guest rooms. Half have air conditioning; all have private cold-water bathroom; and 10 have cable TV. Single/double rooms with fan rent for US$14/17, while rooms with air con go for US$23/30.

Top End Seaside on Av Enriquillo, 1300m south of Av Luis E Delmonte, is the *Riviera Beach Hotel* (☎ 809-524-5111, fax 524-5798). The Riviera is an all-inclusive resort with a swimming pool with poolside bar, an appealing open-sided dining area, and 108 guest rooms with all the fixings, including bathtubs. But its beach, which photographs well, is a disaster. It was created by clearing away a mangrove forest and importing many tons of sand. Unfortunately, the sand has a lot of clay in it – and the clay bonds and hardens into a surface resembling a dirt field. Though sand-colored, it's just as unpleasant. To combat this, the hotel rototills the beach on a regular basis, but even then the water in front of the beach contains lots of seaweed-covered rocks. For US$50/90, the Riviera isn't a good value.

On the east side of Hwy 44, 11km south of Av Luis E Delmonte in Barahona, is the turnoff for the Swiss-owned and -run *Club Hotel El Quemainto* (☎/fax 809-223-0999). The Quemainto has four ocean-facing rooms with one twin bed in each for US$65 and one ocean-facing room with two twin beds for US$72. Each of the comfortable rooms contains a fan and a hot-water bathroom. Prices include breakfast. On the nicely landscaped grounds is a very inviting swimming pool, a pleasant sitting area and a large lawn. English, German and Spanish are spoken at this very tranquil hotel.

Places to Eat

Barahona has a dozen or so restaurants of varying quality: a few are bad, most are decent if unexciting and a few are quite nice. One of the most pleasant is the *Brisas del Caribe*, on a knoll along Av Enriquillo about 500m north of Av Luis E Delmonte. The open-sided restaurant catches a cool breeze, and most of the tables have a view of the green-blue Caribbean. Long a favorite of

Barahona's upper class, Brisas specializes in seafood, with lobster dishes going for US$13 and shrimp dishes for half that. Also available are sea bass and red snapper prepared several ways, as well as *carite* (kingfish) served in coconut milk. Most of the fish dishes sell for around US$8.

Another fine choice is **La Rocca**, on Av Enriquillo 800m south of Av Luis E Delmonte. Also open-sided but without a cool breeze or ocean views, La Rocca offers very good food from its wide-ranging menu. Seafood is the house specialty; try the conch in a garlic sauce (US$6) or the lobster thermidor (US$13). You can also order various meat and poultry dishes as well as 20 Chinese dishes (most for about US$6).

Closer to the Parque Central on Av 30 de Mayo is **D'Lina Pizza**, a popular and inexpensive place to grab a meal. At D'Lina, the pizzas are served in one size only: large. Most are priced around US$8, and one is usually enough for a party of three. Also available are seven sandwiches (from US$1 to US$3), and various meat, chicken and seafood dishes.

Entertainment
Dance clubs come and go with great frequency in Barahona, with the newest ones always being the hippest and the older ones going out of business. At the time of writing **AMB, Costa Sur** and **Mega Plus**, all in the vicinity of the Riviera Beach Hotel, were *the* in places. At least two will have shut down by the time you read this. Another popular club beside the Parque Central will also likely have fallen on hard times by the time you read this. If you're looking for a hot night of dancing and socializing, your best bet is to hail a cab and ask the taxi driver to take you to the most popular dance club.

Getting There & Away
Caribe Tours (☎ 809-524-2313) has an office on Calle Anacaona, one block north of Parque Central. Two buses depart daily from Santo Domingo to Barahona, one at 7 am and another at 2:30 pm. The cost is US$4. Four buses go from Barahona to Santo Domingo: at 6:30 and 9:45 am, and 1:30 and 5 pm.

Bahía de Neiba manatee

Gua-guas to outlying areas – such as to the national parks – are found on Av Luis E Delmonte near its intersection with Calle Padre Billini. Públicos and gua-guas can also be hailed along Av Enriquillo south of Av Luis E Delmonte.

Getting Around
Taxis and motoconchos can be found beside the Parque Central and along Av Luis E Delmonte.

BAORUCO & LA CIÉNAGA
The seaside village of Baoruco is 17km south of Barahona, and it is typical of the small, generally poor communities along the east coast of the Península de Pedernales: It's beside a fine-gravel beach, which is usually well-littered and lined with fishing boats; the residents make their living fishing and from farming small plots; the roads are unpaved; and the houses are made mostly of split palm. West of Baoruco is a lush valley ringed by picturesque peaks.

Overlooking the north end of Baoruco is the most attractive hotel in the entire Southwest, the ***Baoruco Beach Resort*** (☎ *809-696-0215, fax 223-0548)*. New in 1998, the resort has 12 cool and charming thatch-and-concrete cabins, each with private hot-water bathroom. There's an inviting swimming pool, a dining room and a bar beside a spacious sitting area. On a bluff 150m above sea level, the hotel, which also goes by the name Casa Bonita, offers postcard-perfect views of the Caribbean and the lush vegetation below and surrounding the property. Behind the hotel, mostly forested mountains sweep down almost to the doorstep. This place makes for a great escape from life's pressures. Rates include breakfast and dinner and are US$80/110 for a single/double; add US$5 for an air-conditioned cabin.

Bordering Baoruco to the south is the village of La Ciénaga, which is slightly bigger than Baoruco but might as well be an extension of it; you certainly can't see much difference between the two. Like Baoruco, La Ciénaga has a gravely beach with a strong surf. There are no hotels or restaurants in La Ciénaga and, really, no reason to stop.

BALNEARIO SAN RAFAEL
Three kilometers south of La Ciénaga is the Balneario San Rafael, where the fast-flowing water of a mountain stream is temporarily caught in two natural pools. These pools are pleasant to wade in and are popular with Dominican families on weekends, as is the *balneario* (spa or watering place) in Los Patos below. There are some tables beside the pools and families often arrive with a picnic and spend an entire afternoon. There's no charge to use the pools, which are incredibly refreshing on a hot day. Near the picnic tables there's a beverage stand, which sells soft drinks and bottles of rum and whisky.

PARAÍSO & LOS PATOS
Approximately 10km south of the balneario is the hillside town of Paraíso, which is remarkable for its litter; trash seems to be everywhere, particularly on its pebbly beach. In town there is a Texaco gas station as well

as the ***Hotel Paraíso*** (☎ *809-243-1080)*, which may beat sleeping in the bush – but not by much. The Paraíso's rooms are dark, hot and shabby, and cost US$18/20. On the other hand, the hotel does have a generator to keep the electricity flowing.

Several kilometers south of Paraíso is the hamlet of Los Patos, which certainly is no big deal, but what is a big deal – at least with Dominican families – is the nearby **Balneario Los Patos**. Much larger, more attractive and more popular than the Balneario San Rafael, this clear-flowing river pool hosts scores of families every Saturday and Sunday, who arrive to relax and escape the heat. Greeting the families are a dozen or so vendors frying up fish and chicken and selling rum and ice-cold beers. The entire scene has the feel of a giant family reunion, and in some ways it is. Certainly many of these families are related, and many have no doubt been coming to the watering hole for years.

ENRIQUILLO
Fifteen kilometers south of Paraíso (and 54km south of Barahona) is this typical Dominican town, which is notable for having the last hotel and the last gas station (a Texaco) until Pedernales, some 82km away. The roadside ***Hotel Dayira*** (no telephone) offers dumpy guest rooms with cold-water bathroom for US$10 for one person or two.

PARQUE NACIONAL JARAGUA
The Parque Nacional Jaragua is the largest protected area in the country. Its 1400 sq km include vast ranges of thorn forest and subtropical dry forest and an extensive marine area that contains the islands of Beata and Alto Velo.

This huge nature reserve was created, in part, to protect the country's largest group of flamingoes, which spend much of the year on the shore of Laguna de Oviedo. The lake, which is very near the town of Oviedo and close to Hwy 44, also attracts impressive numbers of American frigate birds, black-crowned tangers, roseate spoonbills, great egrets and various songbirds.

Named after a famous Taíno chief, the park has an average temperature of 27°C and receives 500mm to 700mm of rain each year. Not surprisingly, the predominant vegetation is cacti and other slow-growing desert plants. One hundred and thirty bird species, or about 60% of the nation's total, have been identified in the park. Among the terrestrial creatures that inhabit the park are the Ricord iguana and the rhinoceros iguana, both of which are endemic to Hispaniola.

There are no hiking trails or cabins in the park, but there are some bad roads off of which it's possible to camp. Driving or camping in the park is ill-advised, however. What *is* enjoyable is taking a boat out on Laguna de Oviedo and doing a little **birding**. To do this, you must first obtain a park permit ($4) at the ranger station (no phone) 10km east of Oviedo on the south side of the highway. The ranger will direct you to a parking lot beside the lake, where there's usually one or two young men with boats who will take you on a tour of the large lake. A standard payment for a tour is US$20. The park is open 8 am to 5 pm daily.

The ranger station may be reached by gua-gua or público; both modes of transportation operate along this stretch of Hwy 44. Once you're here and want to leave, simply stand at the roadside and hail any gua-gua or público that's traveling in the direction you want to be going. Gua-guas and públicos run between Pedernales, Enriquillo and points north daily during daylight hours.

PEDERNALES
At the western end of Hwy 44 is the hot and dusty frontier city of Pedernales, which has nothing whatsoever to offer the tourist aside from a few bad hotels and several forgettable eateries. Since there is no immigration office in town, foreigners are prohibited from crossing the Haitian border here.

If you must spend the night in Pedernales, look no farther than the ***Hotel Rossy***, which is next to the Shell gas station at the eastern entrance to town. The Rossy is very basic, with 15 cubicles with fan, screenless windows and private cold-water bathroom. It's a no-frills place, as is everything in Pedernales. The rates are US$5/10.

In the extremely unlikely event that the Rossy is full, your choices deteriorate rapidly. For instance, the ***Pensión Fatima***, five blocks farther west on the same main street, is probably the next-best bet, even though there are no fans and the guest rooms have no doors. The cost is US$3 per person.

CABO ROJO
Twelve kilometers east of Pedernales is a dirt-road turnoff for Cabo Rojo (Red Cape), where the Aluminum Company of America (Alcoa) mines bauxite. Huge mountains of blood-red bauxite ore – from which aluminum is made – can be seen from the road. The **beaches** in this area are among the prettiest in the country, and the most remote. Scarcely a soul travels the dirt road that hugs the western edge of the wedge-shaped Península de Pedernales. Why? Because the closest place to spend the night is Pedernales, and you know what the accommodations there are like.

PARQUE NACIONAL SIERRA DE BAORUCO
This national park directly west of Barahona covers 800 sq km of mostly mountainous terrain and is notable for the rich variety of vegetation that thrives in its many different climates, from desert dry to mountain humid. Valleys are home to vast areas of broadleafed plants, which give way to healthy pine

Parque Nacional Sierra de Baoruco contains 166 orchid species.

forests at higher elevations. In the mountains the average temperature is 18°C and annual rainfall is between 1000mm and 2500mm.

Within the national park there are 166 orchid species, representing 52% of the country's total. Thirty-two percent of those species are endemic to the park. Flitting about among the park's pine, cherry and mahogany trees are 49 species of birds. These include the white-necked crow, which can only be seen on Hispaniola. The most common birds in the mountains are La Selle's thrush, white-winged warblers, Hispaniolan trogons and narrow-billed todies. At lower elevations look for white-crowned pigeons, white-winged doves, Hispaniolan parakeets, Hispaniolan lizard cuckoos and Hispaniolan parrots.

Nearly 500 years ago, somewhere in the mountains within the park, the great Taíno chief Enriquillo and his people chose to fight the conquistadors rather than submit to slavery. Their battles raged off and on for 14 years – from 1519 to 1533 – during which time the Spaniards came to respect the *cacique* and finally made peace with him. The chief declared a small free republic in the highest reaches of the Sierra de Baoruco, and for his defiance he is considered something of a national hero today.

Visitors to the park will find no trace of the republic-within-a-republic, or even a cabin in which to spend a night (camping is possible but not recommended). In fact, unless you have rented a 4WD or a motorcycle, the park is, for all practical purposes, off-limits. The roads through the park are too rugged for anything else. However, if you're traveling by jeep or motorcycle, the remote and rarely visited Parque Nacional Sierra de Baoruco makes a delightful full day's exploration. Park hours are 8 am to 5 pm daily.

To get to the park from Barahona, take Hwy 44 several kilometers north until you reach the turnoff for Cabral. The turnoff will put you onto Hwy 46. Take Hwy 46 to Duverge, where you must find an unmarked dirt road on the southwest edge of town to Puerto Escondido; you'll need to ask directions. If you don't speak Spanish, ask, '¿Donde está la vía a Puerto Escondido?'

(Where is the road to Puerto Escondido?). The response will usually include hand signals pointing you in the right direction.

When you reach Puerto Escondido, a village 11km by bad road from Duverge, take the first road to your right. After a short distance this road brings you to a ranger station (no phone), where you must buy a permit to enter the park (US$4). After passing the ranger station, take the first road on the left, which leads to the pine forest of Loma de los Pinos and eventually to the lookout point El Acetillar. If you're feeling invincible and want to take the road truly less traveled, you can keep following this route south all the way to Pedernales.

LAGO ENRIQUILLO LOOP ROAD

The road ringing Lago Enriquillo and the roads to Neiba from Cabral and from Vincente Noble are all paved and well maintained, making the interesting Parque Nacional Isla Cabritos the easiest of the three national parks to visit. The paved loop road makes a good trip for sturdy bicycles, as there are no steep sections, though the stretch east of Jimaní and south of the lake passes through rolling foothills that top 300m in places. Cyclists should be advised that there are no services along this portion of road and that the heat can get intense.

Two dozen communities circle the lake, most so small they don't appear on any map. Only Neiba, Villa Jaragua, Jimaní and La Descubierta have hotels. With the exception of the hotel in Jimaní, all the rest are basic budget places, some quite OK. Besides the national park, there are no other tourist attractions, though Cabral is known for its pre-Lenten Carnival celebration, which includes elaborate masks and colorful dances.

PARQUE NACIONAL ISLA CABRITOS

Isla Cabritos National Park is named after the 12km-long desert island in the center of Lago Enriquillo, an enormous saltwater lake that's below sea level. The lake is the remains of an ancient channel that once united the Bahía de Neiba to the southeast (near Barahona) with Port-au-Prince to the west.

The accumulation of sediments deposited by the Río Yaque del Sur at the river's mouth on the Bahía de Neiba, combined with an upward thrust of a continental plate, gradually isolated the lake. Today it is basically a 200-sq-km inland sea.

What big teeth you have: American crocodiles live in Lago Enriquillo.

The park includes the island, the lake and all of the shoreline. If you look closely along the shore, you can often find sea shells and even chunks of coral rocks. But what's particularly captivating are the park's creatures, including an estimated 500 American crocodiles that can be seen in and at the edge of the lake. They don't care much for the saltwater and, therefore, tend to hang out at the mouths of the freshwater rivers that drain into the lake from the Sierra de Neiba and the Sierra de Baoruco, which flank the lake to the north and south, respectively.

The island, which varies in elevation from 40m to 4m below sea level, is a virtual desert, supporting a variety of cacti and other desert flora, and is home to Ricord iguanas and rhinoceros iguanas. The island receives a scant 600mm of rain each year and has an average temperature of 28°C (82°F); iguanas, some more than 20 years old and considerably beefier than most house cats, can often be seen resting in the shade of the vegetation. At night they return to dens they've dug a meter or so deep. Some of the iguanas have become so accustomed to people that they'll let you pet them. The island also has lots of scorpions, so be sure to wear shoes that thoroughly cover your feet.

You can arrange a **boat trip** to visit the mouth of the Río de la Descubierta – its banks are often lined with crocodiles and flamingoes – and Isla Cabritos. To do this, go to the park's ranger station (no phone), which is 5km east of the town of La Descubierta. There, the ranger will sell you a US$4 park permit and ask if you want to visit the crocodiles and the island. If you do, he'll introduce you to a boatman who will take you to the sights. The fee for this service is US$55, for one person or up to a party of five. If there are only one or two of you, you may want to wait a little while to see if a few more people show up with whom you can split the cost. The tour usually lasts about 90 minutes.

Once you've returned, you'll no doubt be very hot. Luckily, there's a refreshing, river-fed balneario about 100m inside the park, a short walk from the ranger station near La Descubierta. There is no additional cost to use the watering hole. The park is open 8 am to 4:30 pm daily.

Getting There & Away

Most people who visit the park arrive from Barahona, and by far the easiest way to reach the park from there is by taxi; the fee for transportation to and from the park, plus the driver's wait, is usually about US$40 per party.

If you'd prefer, you can take a gua-gua from Barahona (or from Azua, for that matter) to the town of Neiba, and from there take any westbound gua-gua to the ranger station. Be sure to tell the driver that that's where you want to go, or he'll drive right past it. If you don't speak Spanish, just say, 'Parque Nacional Isla Cabritos, por favor.' The cost will be no more than US$3 from either Barahona or Azua.

JIMANÍ

There are only two places where foreigners can pass to and from Haiti and the Dominican Republic, and Jimaní is one of them (the other is Dajabón, to the north). See the Getting There & Away chapter at the beginning of the book for information about overland crossing at either site.

One thing that's particular to the Jimaní crossing point is that the town is actually 5km from the border via a hot, paved road. However, there is no shortage of taxis and públicos shuttling people between the border and the sweltering town of 10,000. Once at the border, which is mostly used by Haitians bringing goods to sell in the DR, colorfully painted Haitian buses ferry travelers to Port-au-Prince.

Aside from crossing the border there's absolutely no reason to visit Jimaní. Fortunately, the loop road running around Lago Enriquillo was completed in 1990, so the drive to and from the town isn't the hellish journey it once was. Still, the area near the border, which is studded with cacti and rock formations, can get extremely hot. Temperatures in excess of 50°C are not unheard of here.

Places to Stay & Eat

The only decent hotel in town is the *Hotel Jimaní* (☎ 809-248-3139), which is on the main road into town and rather difficult to overlook. The Hotel Jimaní has a dozen air-conditioned guest rooms with both a twin bed and queen-size bed and a private warm-water bathroom. There's a swimming pool as well as a popular restaurant, *La Rocca*, which is under the same ownership as La Rocca restaurant in Barahona (see that entry for menu information). Room rates are US$20/25.

Getting There & Away

Jimaní is served by gua-guas and públicos, most of which originate from Neiba. If you're in Barahona or Azua, take a gua-gua with a 'Neiba' sign in its window, and then transfer to a 'Jimaní' gua-gua in Neiba.

Haiti

LEAH GORDON

Facts about Haiti

Haiti captures the heart of nearly all who visit, but most people find it difficult to articulate their fascination. On one level, it is a dirty, poverty-stricken country, but on another, it is an intensely spiritual land with a compelling and unique history. There is no other country in the Caribbean whose residents have remained so close to their African roots. The basis of Haiti's difference lies in its history. After independence in 1804, Haiti became isolated from the full brunt of European colonial influences. But this is no country in aspic; it has the most vibrant culture in the Caribbean, one that is in a constant state of flux.

Haiti can be a very rewarding place to visit, but its lack of infrastructure makes life difficult, and the level of poverty can leave even the most hardened traveler feeling uneasy. Haiti *does* want – and need – visitors, and works very hard at making them feel welcome. The culture is one of the most rewarding aspects of the country. Visiting the country's artists as well as its galleries, for example, is one of the best ways of getting a feel for the place.

You need an open mind and a sense of humor to survive in Haiti. It's no wonder that Graham Greene called his novel about Haiti *The Comedians* – there is always the suspicion that you are playing a part in a surreal comedy when you visit.

HISTORY
The Black Republic
In May 1803, while Haiti was still under French rule, former slave and rebel leader Jean-Jacques Dessalines dramatically created the flag of the black insurgents at the Congress of Arcahaie. Until that point, both the black and the French forces had been fighting under the same flag. Dessalines took the French tricolor of blue, white and red, and ripping the white out of it, declared he was ripping the white man out of the country. The red and blue were stitched together, the initials RF (République Fran-

çaise) were replaced by *Liberté ou la Mort*, 'Liberty or Death,' and Haiti's flag was born. Time was running out for the French rulers.

Dessalines' victory at the battle of Vertières on November 18, 1803, led to the surrender of Cap-Haïtien and the hurried exodus of the French leaders. On January 1, 1804, at Gonaïves, Dessalines proclaimed independence for Saint-Domingue and restored to the country its Taíno name, Haiti, meaning 'mountainous land.' On that day Haiti became the second nation in the Western Hemisphere, after the USA, to shake off the yoke of European colonialism, and it also became the world's first black republic.

At first, the nascent republic acquired its own self-proclaimed royalty. When Dessalines heard that French army commander Napoléon Bonaparte was to be crowned emperor, he determined to dignify himself with the same honor. Seven weeks before Napoléon crowned himself on October 8, 1804, Dessalines was crowned Jacques 1st, Emperor of Haiti. By May 1805 he had ratified the first constitution of independent Haiti, which gave him absolute power. The despotic manner in which Dessalines ruled the country did not please the mulatto society – the free and educated offspring of black slaves and French colonialists – who yearned for the creation of an elite, educated oligarchy; this was no doubt a contributing factor in his final downfall.

A month after independence was declared, Dessalines traveled to the south and west of Haiti, grimly determined to annihilate every last white French citizen left in the country. Very few survived this pogrom, save some doctors, pharmacists and skilled craftspeople. These deeds, criticized by many, were certainly a powerful deterrent to any possible colonial invasions. Many observers used these massacres as proof of the inherent savagery of the new regime, but omitted from many accounts of this period is the fact that an English agent named Cathcart offered the newly formed Haiti protection

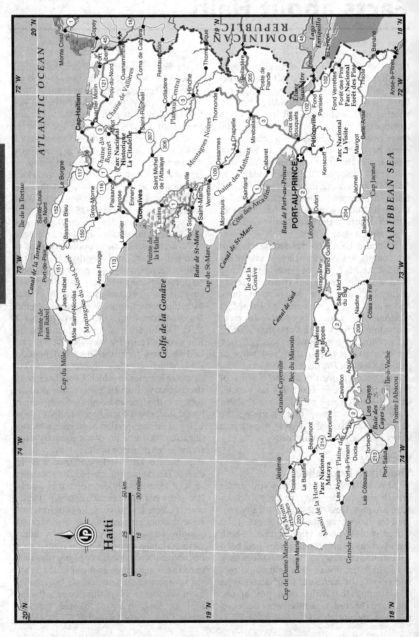

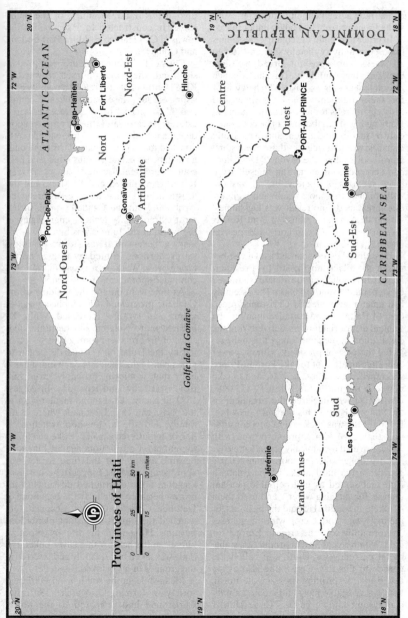

Provinces of Haiti

and a trade agreement, but only after every white French citizen had fallen under the ax.

In order to rebuild the country, Dessalines imposed a military dictatorship and forced all blacks who were not already soldiers back onto the plantations. This caused much resentment among ex-slaves who had fought for their independence. Dessalines also resisted any calls for an education system in Haiti, saying, 'The laborers can be controlled only by fear of punishment and even death; I shall lead them only by these means; my moral code shall be the bayonet.' Dessalines had succeeded in alienating himself from large sections of society, but it was the mulatto class that most keenly felt its interests threatened. The result was Dessalines' violent death in an ambush at Pont Rouge, the northern entrance to Port-au-Prince, on October 17, 1806.

Dessalines' death sparked a civil war between the black north, led by President Henri Christophe, and the mulatto south, led by General Alexandre Pétion. The assembly had unanimously elected Christophe president of Haiti but had curtailed many of the original dictatorial powers, derived from the constitution, at the same time. Christophe rejected the post of president without power and, after an attempt to take Port-au-Prince was repelled by Pétion, he retreated to take power in the north. On February 17, 1807, Christophe was declared the president of the State of Haiti in his northern province. His authority was backed by a new constitution that gave him supreme power, with which he ruled dynamically and effectively.

Christophe collected more than 200,000 gourdes – the hard husks of the calabash fruit that served as indispensable peasant utensils for carrying water – and used them as tokens of wealth. He paid the peasants for the first year's coffee crop with the gourdes and promptly sold the crop to Europe for gold. Within a year he had produced a stable metal currency for Haiti, still called the gourde to this day. Christophe also established a state printing press in the north, kept a serviceable navy and created a judicial system known as the 'Code Henri.' Christophe saw the role of education as

pivotal in the advancement of the black class. He constructed four schools in the towns of Cap-Haïtien, St Marc, Port-de-Paix and Gonaïves.

Christophe cultivated European pretensions and, after having himself crowned as King Henri I of Haiti, created a nobility consisting of four princes, eight dukes, 22 counts and 37 barons, all of whom received large estates. Society and the economy soon depended on the work of wage-earning serfs attached to the plantations. Christophe built a magnificent palace at Sans Souci and held court there. He also had palaces at Jean Rabel, Cap-Haïtien and St Marc, and the 'Castle of 365 Doors' at Petite-Rivière in the Artibonite. But the Citadelle – one of the most extraordinary feats of engineering in the world at the time it was built – was his major achievement. It was a fortress of colossal proportions fronted by a huge north-facing prow. Work on it began in 1804 and continued sporadically for 15 years.

As time went on and the building of the Citadelle progressed, Christophe's megalomania and tyranny increased. While he became more isolated and despotic, divisions of his army and some of his generals, led by the Duke of Marmalade, began to plot against him. Then fate dealt him a harsh blow that, ironically, probably saved him from overthrow and ignominy. In August 1820, at age 62, Christophe made a visit to the parish church in Limonade where, as his family and the archbishop watched in horror, he suffered a major stroke and fell to the ground. Conspirators against him soon became aware that the time to act was approaching, and the fringes of his northern kingdom – the disgruntled divisions of his army – began to revolt. By the beginning of October, Christophe, now incapacitated, watched the flames of distant plantations burning. He ended his life by shooting himself in the heart with a silver bullet. His body was taken by his family and interred in the grounds of his beloved Citadelle.

Meanwhile, in the south, a very different society was forming. On March 9, 1807, after Christophe had retreated to the north, Pétion was elected as the president of the

Republic of Haiti in the south by the constitutional assembly. Pétion's power suffered under the more democratic laws of the very constitution he had created, as it gave (in his opinion) too much freedom to the obstructionists in his senate. In 1808, in order to regain power, he used the army to bar entry to the legislative buildings and declared the senate suspended.

He was constantly in conflict with the black guerrillas in the southwestern department of Grand Anse, led by Goman. In addition to the problems of constant warfare, the southern republic was falling into serious economic decline due mostly to extensive land reform. Pétion had realized that the policy of *fermage* – the forced labor system favored by François-Dominique Toussaint L'Ouverture, Dessalines and Christophe – was extremely unpopular, and so he followed a radically different agricultural program.

In 1809, he began to divide up and distribute the land in small plots ranging from 10 to 100 acres in size. The reasons behind this redistribution were both political and economic; Pétion needed to maintain internal peace and resettle army veterans. Also, it was increasingly difficult to obtain the capital or labor needed for large-scale cultivation. Fears of French infiltration had led to laws that severely limited foreign investment. This dramatically reduced the production of cash crops, the proceeds of which were sorely needed for the treasury.

The south became a nation of subsistence peasant farmers rather than cultivators of large plantations, and the republic lost its capacity to create wealth. This economic instability meant that Pétion had to deal with a deeply divided and warring republic in the south. In 1810, he was obliged to concede the west to André Rigaud. By 1811, however, he was confident enough to reconvene a nine-member assembly that would do his bidding.

Pétion's trumpeted 'agrarian reform' won him much popularity with the peasants, earning him the nickname 'Papa Bon-Coeur' (Papa Good-Heart), even though he had withheld the lion's share of the land for himself and his ruling class of mulatto supporters. However, by the 1820s none of the mulatto landowning generals truly believed that they could reestablish large plantations. The restoration of slavery was unthinkable; the peasantry had made up their minds and clung to their garden plots and their own labor. Liberty was associated with the possession of a small plot of land, a belief still held to this day.

Pétion is remembered as a political liberal due to his land distribution, the creation of the first school in Port-au-Prince, Lycée Pétion, and his offer of asylum and aid to South American revolutionary leader Simón Bolívar. But Pétion also helped create the schism between the mulattos and the blacks that still divides Haiti. The minority mulatto class, which had gained much land during these years, gradually stopped extracting enough wealth from their property and turned to foreign merchandising and government, their main purpose being to fill their pockets. Corruption was rampant, and since then the state has been characterized by a never-ending series of coups and counter-coups designed to conquer the treasury for more or less private purposes.

A Country Reunited

When Pétion died in 1818, Jean-Pierre Boyer succeeded him as president for life. It was Boyer who swiftly reunified north and south Haiti after the death of Christophe in 1820. Boyer continued the same style of laissez-faire government as Pétion, while increasingly helping himself to the state coffers. As Dessalines had once claimed, he 'plucked the chicken as long as it did not squawk.' Christophe's legacy, his precious education system, was allowed to fall into disarray, taking with it his vision of an educated black ruling class.

During his reign Boyer took advantage of a revolt against Spanish rule in Santo Domingo by invading and annexing it in 1821. The whole of the island remained under Haitian control until 1849, when the eastern part proclaimed independence as the Dominican Republic. Boyer also began dealing with France in a desperate attempt to gain recognition for the independent state of Haiti.

France would only recognize Haiti for a price – 150 million francs, later reduced to 60 million francs, which it claimed as compensation. This created a debt that continued to put a severe strain on the economy long after 1843, when Boyer fled into exile after being accused of corruption and treason.

The next half-century was characterized by continued rivalry between the ruling classes of wealthy mulattos and blacks, and the almost-institutionalized scramble for the contents of the treasury. Of the 22 heads of state between 1843 and 1915, only one served his full term in office; the rest were assassinated or forced into exile. During this period, the mass of rural peasants remained largely politically inactive, sporadically called upon to help topple a particular government and then immediately ignored. But during this period, a new class of peasant was emerging, large enough to organize capital among its members but too small to take part in the cut-and-thrust of everyday politicking. It was this social class that formed rebel bands of armed peasants – the *picquet* and *cacos* – that would play an important part in the resistance to the US Marines when they invaded in 1915.

US Military Occupation

In the beginning of the 20th century, the USA had begun to recognize Haiti's strategic importance due to its proximity to the Windward Passage. The stretch of sea between Haiti and Cuba was an important shipping route from the newly opened Panama Canal to the USA. The presence of a growing German community in Haiti was also making the Americans nervous. When Haitian President Vilbrun Guillaume Sam was killed by an angry civilian mob in 1915, they took this as their chance to invade Haiti, theoretically to stabilize the country. The occupation furthered the economic interests of the US in Haiti, raising its share in the Haitian market to about 75%. The Americans seized Haiti's gold deposits and rewrote the country's constitution, forcing its implementation to allow foreign ownership of property, then disbanded the army, replacing it with an American-trained police

force. At the same time, they directed many public works, building hospitals and clinics, modernizing the sewage systems and building roads. It was the Americans' use of forced prison labor on the road-building programs that spurred the cacos rebellions. Resistance to US occupation continued from 1918 to 1920, and climaxed with a revolt led by Charlemagne Péraulte in the north and Benoît Batraville in the Artibonite. The revolt was effective enough that it forced the Americans to use expensive reinforcements; it was brutally suppressed, costing the lives of about 2000 Haitians.

Although the Americans had quashed the armed resistance, political and journalistic opposition to the occupation continued. The Americans were dealing almost entirely with the mulatto class, excluding the black middle classes from political life. The blacks needed a coherent philosophy to focus their frustrations, and this led to the development of the Noirisme (roughly, 'Black') movement, inspired in part by the 1928 book *Ainsi parla l'oncle* (Thus Spoke the Uncle), by Jean Price-Mars. The Noiristes advocated that Haitian citizens take pride in their African heritage and cease adapting themselves to European culture. They reclaimed their much-maligned religion, Vodou, as a source of inspiration and cultural identity. One of the leading proponents of Noirisme was Dr François Duvalier, later to reappear as Haiti's most notorious president.

The Americans pulled out of Haiti in 1934, as the occupation was proving costly and Haiti's strategic importance had diminished. They left behind an improved infrastructure, but Haiti was still poverty stricken and overpopulated. Many Haitians were obliged to seek work in the sugarcane fields in the Dominican Republic. This caused tensions in the Dominican Republic, due to racism and competition for employment exacerbated by the fall of sugar prices, which led to one of the worse massacres in Haiti's history. During three days beginning on October 2, 1937, the Dominican army and police, on the orders of their president, Rafael Leonidas Trujillo, killed about 20,000 Haitians living in the Dominican Republic.

Many of the bodies ended up in the tragically named Rivière Massacre, which runs through the border town of Ouanaminthe in the north. There is no definitive explanation as to why Trujillo commanded this brutal attack on the Haitians, only supposition that he, as a dictator, wanted to enforce Dominican sovereignty over the border regions. The Haitian government, to its shame, hardly reacted at all.

The Duvalier Dictatorship

By the mid-1940s Haiti was struggling under economic hardship due to food and import shortages. The growth of a popular movement, fueled by the ideology of the ever-strengthening Noiristes, demanded social justice. The army supported the election of a black progressive president, Dumarais Estimé, as a concession to growing popular demands by the black majority for black leadership. Estimé encouraged some social reforms, such as the formation of trade unions and the introduction of an income tax system, but as a result of growing enmity from the mulatto class he was deposed by Colonel Paul Magloire in 1950. The mulatto class was content with Magloire, as were the army, the Catholic Church and the USA. In keeping with many of his predecessors, Magloire's personal corruption and avarice led to his downfall and he went into exile in 1956 (with most of the state treasury).

The next elections, in which women were eligible to vote for the first time in Haitian history, took place after nine months of civil unrest. The two main candidates were Louis Déjoie, who represented the economic interests of the mulattos, and François Duvalier, the Noiriste, whose support came from the burgeoning black middle class and the politically isolated rural poor. Duvalier, with his exotic cocktail of nationalism, racism and mysticism, won with more than twice as many votes as his rival, Déjoie. Thus began, on October 22, 1957, the 14-year reign of one of the most infamous dictators in history.

Duvalier was a small, soft-spoken man who always appeared in dark conservative suits and thick, owlish spectacles. The different classes that traditionally jostled for power in Haiti had no real appreciation of the threat to their status quo that this modest country doctor represented. Duvalier was an astute leader and had no intention of squandering his newfound position and power. He knew where the dangers lay and within months acted swiftly to neutralize his opponents. The mulatto business community that had backed Déjoie was the first to bear his wrath. In an attempt to destabilize his regime, they organized a commercial strike by closing shops and offices in Port-au-Prince. Duvalier responded by unleashing the *cagoulards*, hooded thugs from the local slums led by his ardent supporter Clément Barbot, to threaten the commercial quarters, forcing them to reopen. Attacks on the army, Catholic Church, press and trade unions soon followed.

Known popularly (if not fondly) as 'Papa Doc,' Duvalier had a mixed bag of supporters who were loyal to him. There were former Noiristes, oddly a few communist sympathizers, the growing black legions of the army, and Haitian members of the Catholic Church who were frustrated with

'Papa Doc' François Duvalier

HAITI

HAITI

the disproportionate amount of power that the European priesthood held in the country. Crushing the Catholic Church's European hierarchy was central to Noiriste beliefs, as the Church controlled most of the education system, which favored mulattos over blacks. Duvalier consolidated his power by creating the notorious Tontons Macoutes from the original cagoulards. The name refers to a character in a Haitian folk story, Tonton Macoute (Uncle Knapsack), who carries off small children in his bag at night. The original bogeymen, the cagoulards removed their hoods and donned denim jackets and jeans, red neckerchiefs and sunglasses. The new, soon-to-be-feared uniform was based on the costume of Papa Zaca, the Vodou spirit of agriculture. Papa Doc, himself a Vodouist, was attired more like an undertaker, in a black suit and hat. This represented the Vodou spirit of the cemeteries, Baron Samedi, and reinforced his sinister mystique.

The Tontons Macoutes, also known as Volontaires de la Sécurité Nationale (VSN; the National Security Volunteers) were a private militia, without salary, who could use force and coercion with impunity in order to extort cash and crops from a cowed population. In exchange for this privilege, they afforded Duvalier utmost loyalty and protection. There would be no coup from the army, or any other group, as long as he had the Tontons Macoutes by his side. Thousands of Haitians either died or fled the country during this brutal regime. In the great tradition of Haitian leaders, Duvalier changed the Haitian constitution, enabling himself to be elected as President for Life in 1964. It was in the same year that the Duvalierist 'Lord's Prayer' was published. It begins: 'Our Doc, who art in the National Palace for life, hallowed be Thy name…Thy will be done at Port-au-Prince and the provinces…' Duvalier held onto power by building on the support of the growing black urban middle class and the poor peasant landowners by offering roles in the growing state apparatus for the former and an improved power structure in the rural areas for the latter. Materially, nothing much had

Duvalier's feared Tontons Macoutes

changed for the Haitian people, and even though the political ambitions of the mulatto classes had been curtailed, their economic interests were left fairly untouched.

François 'Papa Doc' Duvalier died on April 21, 1971, but he had already amended the constitution earlier that year to permit his son, Jean Claude 'Baby Doc' Duvalier, to succeed him. To a certain extent the repression eased under Jean Claude's leadership. This was partly due to the fact that in order to receive foreign aid and investment, he needed the international community to see him as a liberalizer. This respite rekindled the age-old struggle between the black middle-class majority and the mulatto capitalist minority. The struggle took place even within the ruling family as Simone Duvalier, Jean Claude's mother, favored the old Duvalierist regime while Marie Nicole, his sister, favored the mulatto so-called 'modernizers.' The albeit bogus moves toward liberal reform also ended the silence of the dissidents, who were calling for democracy. In 1980, after Jean Claude's blatantly opulent US$7 million wedding to a mulatto socialite, Michelle Bennett, the balance of power shifted to the commercial mulatto class, alienating Duvalier's black middle-class supporters. This, in the end, was political suicide for Jean Claude, who now had dissenters on all sides. He responded by reviving the violent state repression that had been so effective against political opponents in the past. The new victims were members of newly formed political parties, journalists, liberation theologists and trade unionists.

Uprooting a Dictatorship

A severe economic crisis gripped Haiti in the early 1980s as the result of a number of factors. There was a decline in tourism due to the rising awareness of human-rights abuses, US inflation and a recession. This was exacerbated by the highly publicized link made between Haiti and AIDS. The US Center for Disease Control, which had defined Haitians as a high-risk group, later withdrew its judgment, but many tourists had already been frightened away. The peasants' economy was also irreparably damaged by a mismanaged pig-disease eradication program that killed 1.7 million indigenous creole pigs, with little or no reparation. Dissent was mounting among the very poorest sections of the population, and riots, unheard of for years, were beginning to flare up around the country in 1984.

In November 1985, security forces shot at an anti-government demonstration, leaving four students dead and many more injured. This fomented a period of deep unrest in the country, spurred on by the increasingly defiant Catholic liberation theologists and their Church-funded station, Radio Soleil. As the regime tried to control the escalating situation with repression, the struggle snowballed. By February 6, 1986, the government merely retained control of Port-au-Prince. In the rest of the country, government and security force buildings had been ransacked and burned. Duvalier was losing the support of his army and finally the US, which publicly severed its relations with the regime. On February 7, Jean Claude Duvalier and his family fled to France in exile, leaving behind them a jubilant population.

The jubilation soon turned to anger and violence against the lackeys of the old government, especially the Tontons Macoutes. The systematic destruction aimed at the perpetrators of repression was known as *dechoukaj,* a Creole word meaning 'uprooting.' Symbols of the wealth and power associated with the Duvalier family suffered as well, including Papa Doc's grave, which was destroyed, although his body had already been removed by his family.

The National Council of Government, led by the army, swiftly formed with Lt General Henri Namphy as the president. The new junta tried to respond to calls for change, but at best these gestures were symbolic. It soon became apparent that the desire for radical change was not going to be fulfilled by the new government. Namphy's administration was merely attempting to appease the masses while protecting the old regime.

During this period, Ti Legliz – the grassroots liberation theology arm of the Catholic Church – grew stronger and more outspoken. One young priest, Father Jean-Bertrand Aristide, was preaching particularly incendiary sermons from his small church, St Jean Bosco, which lay on the edge of a slum (La Saline) in Port-au-Prince. The National Council of Government soon gave up its conciliatory pose and used terror to try to break the back of the burgeoning grassroots movement. The level of violence escalated during the long-awaited elections on November 29, 1987. After nights of shootings and killings, the reinstated Tontons Macoutes massacred innocent voters in a polling station, killing 20. The elections were declared to be over by 9 am and Namphy remained in power. Nothing had changed, and this period in Haitian history was dubbed by journalists as 'Duvalierism without Duvalier.'

The cocaine trade played an increasingly important role in Haitian politics, as anyone in power was able to reap substantial profits. Most of the high-ranking officers in the army were on the payroll. It is alleged that under Namphy, US$700 million of cocaine passed through Haiti every month.

The Aristide Presidency

In September 1988, a week after another tragic shooting, this time at Aristide's congregation, Namphy was overthrown by an

HAITI

army coup and replaced by General Prosper Avril. A former Duvalierist, Avril continued the repression of the popular movement. In January 1990, Avril fled the country in response to increasing unrest and demonstrations. A Supreme Court judge, Ertha Pascal-Trouillot, took over as interim president and fresh elections were scheduled for December 16, 1990. Father Jean-Bertrand Aristide stood as a surprise last-minute candidate with the slogan '*Lavalas*' (Flood) and won a landslide victory. Aristide's fiery sermons and outspoken criticism of the junta had won him a huge following among the oppressed masses in Haiti, who came out in force to support him.

Aristide was inaugurated on February 7, 1991, and in front of a crowd of thousands, he retired six of the remaining eight army generals. He also proposed to separate the police force and the army in an attempt to make them more accountable. It is difficult to guess what reforms Aristide and his Lavalas government would have achieved, since on September 29, 1991, an alliance of rich mulatto families and army generals, worried about their respective business and drug interests, staged a bloody coup. Aristide managed to escape to Washington via Venezuela, but at least 2000 people died in the first weeks of the coup. General Raoul Cédras, a general whom Aristide had trusted

enough to appoint as his chief of staff, led the coup with the assistance of the chief of police, Major Michel François, and General Phillippe Biamby. François, known to be heavily involved in the cocaine trade, was considered to be the true driving force behind the coup.

The Coup Years

The Organization of American States (OAS) and the US immediately condemned the coup, calling for economic sanctions. But within a month, a whispering campaign began to cast doubts on Aristide's mental stability and ability to rule. This campaign was continued by the US Central Intelligence Agency and associates of the de facto government.

By 1992, the OAS embargo was proving to be ineffectual in putting a dent in the resolve of the military dictatorship. It was another factor – the flow of Haitian refugees to the US – that forced the US and UN to make firmer efforts to end the deadlock. By May 1992, 38,000 Haitians had taken to sea in small rickety boats. Few reached their destination, Miami. Most were intercepted by US Coast Guard cutters and taken to the US naval base at Guantánamo Bay, where the majority were returned to Haiti on the basis that they were economic – not political – refugees. This led to widespread international condemnation of US President George Bush and gave presidential hopeful Bill Clinton electioneering ammunition, as he pledged to put an end to the blanket repatriation if elected.

Desperate Haitians began boat-building with a vengeance, awaiting his election. This led to a U-turn in Clinton's promise immediately after his election in 1992, but it also pressured him to find a way of returning Aristide to office. In February 1993, the UN/OAS sent civilian human-rights monitors to Haiti. In June 1993, a UN oil embargo was put into place, but it was still only partly effective due to the amount of petrol smuggled across the Dominican border. The embargo brought Cédras to the negotiation table, however, and the Governors Island Accord was signed on July 3, 1993. It stated

Pro-Aristide mural

LEAH GORDON

that Aristide would be allowed to return to office on October 30, 1993. The sanctions were immediately revoked, but as the deadline approached it became plain that Cédras had no intention of stepping down.

In mid-October, the SS *Harlen County* arrived with its cargo of Canadian military trainers, whose assistance in retraining the police force was one of the stipulations of the Governors Island Accord. The ship was prevented from docking by a machine-gun-wielding gang of thugs, members of the newly formed civilian militia called Front pour l'Avancement et le Progrés Haitien (FRAPH), who menaced and killed Lavalas supporters, chiefly in the slums of Cité Soleil. After this incident it became clear that Aristide could not return on October 30.

Pressure from the US Black Caucus, a group of black congressmen, persuaded Clinton to take further action and enforce tougher sanctions; all air flights – and exports from the manufacturing industries – were halted in May 1994. The standoff continued in Haiti and victims of FRAPH, the right-wing militia, were found on the streets every morning. Under pressure, Aristide, along with the World Bank and the International Monetary Fund (IMF), agreed upon an economic structural adjustment program for Haiti in order to facilitate his return. Referred to as the 'Paris Plan,' this agreement was to dog him long after his eventual return. It soon became obvious that the US was prepared to invade Haiti in order to restore democracy; the only question was when. On September 17, 1994, former US President Jimmy Carter arrived in Haiti to begin negotiations with Cédras. This paved the way for an unchallenged deployment of US forces in Haiti rather than a combative invasion. On September 19, 1994, US troops arrived in Port-au-Prince. After three weeks, the US troops in the country numbered 20,000, and Cédras left for exile in Panama a month later. On October 15, President Aristide returned to a jubilant country.

The Post-Coup Period

The US occupation and the country's subsequent transition to democracy have not been smooth. There have been many criticisms of the US and UN, mainly concerning issues of justice and disarmament. The US gave refuge to FRAPH's leader, Toto Constant, and is still in possession of many documents that could be used by the Haitian government to bring the coup leaders to justice. Although the street killings and terror have abated, people are still angry that the militiamen were allowed to keep their weapons. It was estimated, in 1995, that over 150,000 small arms were still in the hands of the Macoutes and ex-FRAPH members. In April 1995, Aristide announced the dissolution of the army, retaining only the army's band. The US- and Canadian-trained new Haitian police force was to take their place.

The Lavalas platform, a three-party coalition, dominated the elections for senators, deputies and mayors held in June 1995. It is written in the 1987 constitution that no president can run for a second consecutive five-year term, so elections were also held in December 1995 to choose Aristide's successor. Fourteen candidates registered but the favorite was Lavalas candidate René Préval, who had served as Aristide's prime minister in the pre-coup government. Préval won with 88% of the votes cast, but only 28% of the population turned out to vote. This was a sign that the population was losing confidence in the electoral process as the problems of poverty, unemployment and a general lack of services were still rife. Much of the foreign aid that had been earmarked for Haiti was withheld because of Aristide's reluctance to implement the structural adjustment plan to which he had agreed in Paris. The IMF and World Bank plan involved privatizing all state utilities, such as the telephone company, flour mill and cement factory, and lowering Haitian import tariffs. There was growing opposition to the plan from two factions – the workers in the state industries who feared for their jobs and the peasants whose markets would be flooded with cheap imported foodstuffs, which would effectively kill any national production.

The Lavalas platform fell apart due to disagreements about the implementation of the structural adjustment plan. Aristide founded a new party, La Fanmi Lavalas, which is vehemently opposed to the 'Paris Plan,' and the government remained in a deadlock over this issue. The ongoing power struggle between supporters and opponents of former President Jean-Bertrand Aristide caused the cancellation of partial parliamentary elections in 1997 and 1998 and has left the government without a prime minister since June 1997. President René Préval was prevented from appointing a new prime minister by a deeply split parliament, while the populace became increasingly disillusioned by food scarcity, rising prices and a corrupt police force.

The pending crisis that had been simmering in the Haitian government for almost two years finally came to a boil in January 1999. In an attempt to break out of the stalemate, President Préval declared that the terms of most remaining members of parliament had expired and announced that he would rule by decree pending fresh elections. This move was in accordance with an electoral law passed in 1995. At the time of writing, the country was awaiting international financial assistance for new parliamentary elections.

GEOGRAPHY

Haiti makes up 27,750 sq km of the western third of Hispaniola. It contains a few remaining rain-forested mountains and some fertile river valleys, but also massive areas of desertification and ranges of eroded, denuded mountains. Haiti has two large peninsulas, the northern and southern claws, that are separated by the Golfe de la Gonâve. The mountain ranges include the Massif de la Hotte, running west to east from the extreme western tip of the southern claw, which reaches a height of 2347m at Pic Macaya; and the Massif de la Selle, which runs west to east just southeast of Port-au-Prince, peaking at Pic la Selle (2674m), the highest point in Haiti. On the northwest peninsula are the Montagnes du Nord-Ouest and Chaine des Trois Pitons, which reach a height of 1041m. In the north you can see the spectacular Chaine du Bonnet from the

Citadelle. The Massif des Montagnes Noires runs southeast from north of Dessalines, through the center of Haiti, to the southeast of Lascahobas, reaching a height of 1788m.

The largest of Haiti's offshore islands is Île de la Gonâve in the Golfe de la Gonâve. Île de la Tortue, the second-largest island, lies off the northern coast above Port-de-Paix. There are also two other substantial islands off the north and south coasts of the southern peninsula, the Grande Cayemite and Île-à-Vache, respectively. Numerous short, rapid streams flow down the mountain slopes to the sea, but the only navigable river is the broad Artibonite, which begins at the Dominican border and reaches the coast just north of St Marc. This mighty river is used to irrigate the fertile Artibonite area, the rice basket of Haiti.

There are a number of agricultural plains, including the Plaine du Nord, south of Cap-Haïtien; the Plaine du Léogâne and Plaine des Cayes, in the south; and the Plaine du Cul de Sac, which runs from Port-au-Prince to Etang Saumâtre, the country's largest saltwater lake. Lac de Péligre, formed by a hydroelectric dam on the upper Artibonite, is the largest freshwater lake in Haiti. There is a large plateau in the center of the country called the Plateau Central, surrounding the town of Hinche.

CLIMATE

Haiti possesses what is known as a daytime climate, the temperature varying more during the course of a day than it does from month to month, or season to season. The mean yearly temperature is 26°C. The mean daily high is 32°C, and mean nightly low is 21.5°C. The hottest months of the year are July and August, when the mean daily high rises to 34°C. The coolest months are December through to March, during which the mean daily high is 30.75°C. Temperatures also drop at higher altitudes. Haiti receives prevailing winds from the northeast that place the country in the rain shadow (the dry, leeward side) of the high mountain ranges of the Dominican Republic. The areas that receive the highest rainfall are the Massif du Nord, west of Cap-Haïtien,

Vodou flag makers, Haiti

A Vodou priest at a ceremony, Haiti

Vodou altar in Bel-Air, Port-au-Prince, Haiti

Drummers at a Vodou ceremony, Carrefour Fois, Port-au-Prince, Haiti

Pilgrims at Plaine du Nord festival near Cap-Haïtien, Haiti

Woman carrying poultry to market, Hinche

Harvesting rice in the Artibonite Valley, Haiti

Plage Labadie, northwest of Cap-Haïtien, Haiti

Fishing baskets on the beach at Arcahaie, Côte des Arcadins, Haiti

Aerial view of the Citadelle with Mt Bonnet à l'Evêque in the background, northern Haiti

Typical peasant house in La Tortue, northern Haiti

the Montagnes Noires of central Haiti, and the Massif de la Selle, southeast of Port-au-Prince, with the most rain occurring on the Massif de la Hotte in the far southwest. The country's two rainy seasons are April-May and September-October.

Hurricanes have had catastrophic effects on Haiti. Hurricane Georges in 1998 was the last to wreak havoc, with disastrous results. It is believed that at least 240 people died and thousands were left homeless. Most of the rice harvest in the Artibonite Valley was ruined by mud deposits from the overflow of the Péligre Dam, and whole towns, such as Fond Verrettes, were completely swept away. Haiti's already fragile infrastructure fell apart as it lost bridges, roads, schools and drainage systems in damages estimated at $1.2 billion. These powerful tropical cyclones usually race across the northern Caribbean from August through to October, with wind speeds as high as 300km/h.

ECOLOGY & ENVIRONMENT

Haiti is one of the most densely populated countries in the Western Hemisphere. It was estimated in 1993 to have 677 people per square kilometer of cultivated land. It is an extremely mountainous land, with more than 60% of all the terrain on gradients above 20%. The combined effects of human stress on the land and the market for charcoal as fuel have caused disastrous deforestation, leaving only 3% of the country's forest cover left. This dreadful denuding of the terrain, combined with the cultivation of marginal areas, has caused massive soil erosion as the tropical rainfall has washed the soil off the exposed hillsides. Almost everywhere the rich topsoil is lost, washed into the ocean where it chokes the reefs and marine life.

Dealing with environmental issues in Haiti is difficult because poverty, overpopulation and the peasants' struggle to survive are at the root of the problem rather than profit-hungry loggers. In order to reduce the stress on the land, there would need to be a radical agrarian reform. This might include releasing much of the land taken over during the Duvalier years, offering a program of technical assistance for the poor peasant class, financing and building much-needed irrigation systems, and sanctioning economic policies that favor national production over overseas imports in order to create a local market the producers so desperately need.

FLORA & FAUNA

Amazingly, given the extent of the environmental degradation in the country, Haiti still is rich in biodiversity.

Plants

There are nine life zones in Haiti, ranging from desert to cloud forest, that support plantlife from mangroves to mountain pines. These varied ecosystems contain a wealth of ecological diversity. Haiti has an estimated 5000 known species of plant, two-thirds of which are woody. There are also about 600 species of fern and 300 species of orchid. The UN Development Programme estimates that about 35% of the plants are native. Parc La Visite contains endemic pine forest *(Pinus occidentalis)* and also the vestiges of a juniper forest *(Juniperus ekmanii)*. The Parc Macaya, with some of the last virgin rain forest left in Haiti, boasts pine trees 45m high and nearly 2m in diameter. One out of every 10 species of plant found in Macaya is thought to be native to the forest. The desert areas also contain many species of endemic cactus. Many fruit trees, such as mango, coconut, avocado and grapefruit, are grown in the more highly populated areas.

Birds

Hispaniola is home to a wide variety of tropical birds, at least 25 of which are native. All can be seen in both Haiti and the Dominican Republic since these feathered creatures are blissfully ignorant of political boundaries. Sadly, the almost complete deforestation of Haiti has not been kind to wildlife. You'll first need to find some trees in order to see birds. Nonetheless, the island is at least a temporary home for more than 300 species, including many northern migrants that either pass through en route to and from South America or stay for the winter months. Some of the more easily seen local

HAITI

species are the black-crowned palm-tanager, the Hispaniolan woodpecker, Hispaniolan lizard-cuckoo, Antillean palm swift, and the palmchat, a largish brown songbird with a heavily streaked creamy breast and belly. The only member of its family in the world, it lives in colonies in the tops of palm trees. The gregarious bird is ubiquitous and easily found by its loud twittering.

For more information on where to see birds in Haiti, see Bird Watching in Haiti's Facts for the Visitor chapter.

Land Animals

There are only two varieties of native land mammal left in Haiti: the Hispaniolan hutia *(Plagiodontia aedium)*, which looks like a small mole, and the solenodon *(Solenodon paradoxus)*, a rodent locally known as *nez longue* ('long nose'). Both are under threat of extinction. There are many threatened species of bat and bird in Parc La Visite, including the Laselle thrush *(Turdus swalesi)* and the Hispaniolan trogan *(Temnotrogon roseigaster)*. Parc Macaya supports 11 butterfly species, 57 snail, 28 amphibian, 34 reptile, 65 bird and 19 bat species and the two Haitian endemic land mammals. Etang Saumâtre, east of Port-au-Prince along the geological depression known as the Plaine du Cul de Sac, is a large inland saltwater lake and habitat for flamingos and more than 100 species of waterfowl, as well as American crocodiles.

Cruelty to Animals

In a country where the general population is often treated appallingly by its own government and lives under harsh conditions, it's not surprising that animal welfare is not high on the public agenda. Horses and donkeys will invariably be underfed, overloaded and covered with welts. Dogs are rarely kept as pets but as guard dogs and can be quite vicious.

One of the worst sights and sounds is the transportation of goats on trucks and buses. The poor animals usually endure long journeys in the heat of the day, tied upside-down by their feet from the side of the bus. Haiti is not for the soft-hearted animal lover.

Endangered Species

Most of the wildlife in Haiti could be considered endangered due to the continuing reduction of natural habitat and a hungry human population. As a traveler, you can help to discourage the sale of wildlife by refusing to buy the parrots, snakes or boa constrictors that are sometimes on offer.

NATIONAL PARKS

Haiti has four national parks that struggle for survival due to lack of supervision and the encroachment of peasants desperate for timber to make charcoal.

Forêt des Pins

This pine forest covers the far east fringe of the Massif de la Selle, south of Jimaní and proximate to the Dominican border. There is an official entrance on the road between what's left of Fond Verettes (it was destroyed in Hurricane Georges) and Forêt des Pins, where you can find some small cabins to rent for the night. See the Plaine du Cul de Sac section of the Around Port-au-Prince chapter for details.

Parc La Visite

Located 40km southwest of Port-au-Prince in the western section of the Massif de la Selle, the park includes three peaks: Morne La Visite (2170m), Pic Cabaio (2282m) and Tête Opaque (2268m). Covering an area of 3000 hectares, the park is small enough to explore on your own, but hiring a guide could be prudent if you want to see some of the limestone caves and waterfalls. There is a 1000m limestone cliff on the northern boundary of the park, blanketed with virgin montane cloud forest. It is here you can find much of the park's wildlife, including the endangered black-capped petrel. Access is best from Kenscoff, along the route to Seguin (see the Southern Haiti chapter for details).

Parc Macaya

The 5500-hectare park is at the western end of Haiti's southern claw, 180km west of Port-au-Prince. Its mountains supply the water for the Plaine des Cayes, a productive agricultural region to the south. The montane cloud forest, one of the last virgin cloud forests left in Haiti, spectacularly envelops the mountains. There are simple camping facilities at the University of Florida project headquarters in Plaine Durand. From this base, visitors can take paths into the lower rain forest or up to Pic Macaya (2347m) itself (see the Southern Haiti chapter for details).

Parc Historique La Citadelle
This park is situated in the center of the Massif du Nord, 16km south of Cap-Haïtien. In addition to several historical monuments, including the Citadelle, the palace of Sans Souci and Fort Ramier, the park contains the steep and abrupt limestone mountain range Chaine du Bonnet and the volcanic mountains Morne Jérôme and Morne Ginette (see the Northern Haiti chapter for details about the Citadelle).

GOVERNMENT & POLITICS
The 1987 constitution, based on the French and US models, is the cornerstone of Haiti's government today. Under the constitution, executive power is vested in a president who is elected for a five-year term. In order to reduce the risk of a return to dictatorship, no man or woman can serve for a second consecutive term as president. A prime minister is chosen from the ruling party by the president and presides as head of the government.

Haiti has two legislative houses, a lower chamber of deputies composed of 83 deputies, and a senate composed of 27 senators. The entire chamber of deputies is renewed every five years with no term limit. The senate, through the electoral process, renews a third of its membership every two years. The country is divided into nine regional 'departments' that are broken up into a number of wards.

The main political parties are Fanmi Lavalas (FL; Family Lavalas), led by Jean-Bertrand Aristide; the Organisation du Peuple en Lutte (OPL; Organization of People in Struggle), led by Gérard Pierre-Charles; the Front National pour le Changement et la Démocratie (FNCD; National Front for Change and Democracy), led by Evans Paul; the Parti National Progressiste et Révolutionnaire (PANPRA; Revolutionary Progressive Nationalist Party), led by Serge Gilles; Congrès National des Mouvements Démocratiques (KONAKOM; National Congress of Democratic Movements), led by Victor Benoit; Parti Louvri Barye (PLB; Open the Gate Party), led by Renaud Bernadin; and the Mouvement pour l'Organisation du Pays (MOP; Movement for the Organization of the Country), led by Gesner Corneau.

ECONOMY
Sadly, Haiti's economy has been in decline since the early 1980s, while the birth rate – and in general, the population – has continued to rise unabated. Two separate economies coexist in Haiti, often at odds with each other. Firstly, there is the agrarian peasant economy, which is mainly subsistence-based but also depends on selling any excess produce, usually maize, rice, beans and coffee, at the local market. Any extra capital is raised by the production of livestock, which rarely runs to more than one or two animals per family unit. This money is sorely needed for construction of houses, for school fees, school uniforms and medical charges. At the other end of the spectrum, members of the business class mainly busy themselves with import/export, often knowingly undercutting the local market with cheaper American imports.

Dependence on foreign aid and years of governmental corruption have severely eroded Haiti's chances of breaking the downward trend of its economy. Between 1980 and 1991, the annual per-capita income fell at a rate of about 2% a year, and then by a dramatic 30% during the coup years from 1991 to 1994. This has led to a real annual per-capita income of below US$250. With inflation at 25% in 1992 and 1993 and a shocking 52% in 1994, Haiti is now the poorest country in the Americas.

In the early 1980s, Haiti suffered two major blows to its economy, the loss of its creole pig and misleading publicity connecting Haiti with the spread of HIV/AIDS. The former was an almost-fatal blow to the fragile peasant economy, while the latter

HAITI

HAITI

resulted in a huge decrease in dollar revenue from tourism. The demise of the creole pig was due to a government eradication project, organized in part by the US Agency for International Development (USAID) in reaction to an outbreak of African swine fever in Haiti. To combat the disease, the program killed every indigenous pig in Haiti, with no compensation for the peasants. USAID later admitted that perhaps it had been mistaken in eradicating an entire breed of livestock. A scant repopulation effort (also backed by USAID) introduced the American white pig, a breed totally unsuited to the Haitian environment, which served merely to further destabilize the peasant economy.

At the same time, the international press had – mistakenly – accused Haiti of being the crucible of the disease HIV/AIDS. This had a devastating effect on tourism in Haiti, from which it has never really recovered. The association was made shortly after a number of AIDS cases in southern Florida were linked to Haitian immigrants. However, later research showed that the virus was most likely transported from North America to Haiti.

Assembly factories based in Port-au-Prince provide about 20,000 much-needed jobs producing clothes, sporting goods and delicate electronic components. The wages in the assembly plants, however, are very low (about US$2.75 per day), especially for a worker who's usually supporting four or five family members. The conditions are usually appalling, lacking ventilation, adequate hygiene or toilets, and union membership is often deterred by the threat of job loss.

To a certain extent, Haiti's economy is dependent on its extensive diaspora, based mainly in Miami, New York City, Boston and Montreal. The estimated 1.5 million Haitians residing abroad were christened the country's '10th department' (Haiti is divided into nine departments) by President Aristide in appreciation of the political and economic power they hold. It is estimated they send more than US$300 million a year to Haiti to help their families who remain in the country. This is equal to the budget of any large aid agency or non-governmental organization (NGO) and goes directly to the people, rather than having to filter through government bureaucracy beforehand. Without this revenue, it is certain that many people in Haiti would starve.

POPULATION & PEOPLE

Haiti is home to about 6 million people, of whom 79% are rural, living off agriculture. People of African origin make up about 95% of Haiti's population. The other 5% is made up of mulattos, Middle Easterners and people of other races. It is believed that some of the population are descendants of the union between the Arawak and Taíno Indians, the original indigenous population, and African slaves. Members of the mulatto class, which constitutes half of the country's elite and controls most of the country's economy, are the descendants of African slaves and French plantation owners. Many immigrants from the Middle East, Syria and Lebanon in particular, arrived in the mid-19th century looking for business opportunities. This influx posed such a threat to the wealthy Haitian merchants that it was referred to as the 'Syrian Problem,' and the government at the time passed laws to restrict their business activities. Nonetheless, people from the Middle East have continued to immigrate and now make up a large proportion of the merchant class.

In the small town of Cazales, north of Cabaret, one can find the anomaly of black-skinned, blue-eyed people who sing and dance to traditional Polish folk music. These are descendants of a Polish regiment from Napoléon's army who were so sickened by the war against the slaves in Haiti that they deserted in 1802, establishing a small community in the countryside. The people of Cazales performed Polish folk dances to welcome Pope John Paul II on his visit to Haiti in 1983.

EDUCATION

Haitian law states that education should be free and compulsory for children between the ages of seven and 13. In reality only about 40% of school-age children actually attend classes. The cost of uniforms and books, the scarcity of schools in rural areas and the shortage of teachers have led to the prevalence of severe under-education in Haiti, resulting in a literacy figure of only 53%.

In Port-au-Prince, the many private schools make up for the shortfall of state schools, which have no regulatory body checking the standard of education. There are three school holidays a year: two weeks at Christmas, two weeks at Easter and from July until October.

ARTS
Visual Arts

Most of the Caribbean has a rich tradition of art, but none of the countries is as prolific and unique as Haiti. For its size and population, Haiti has an abundance of artists, predominantly painters, but also metalworkers and Vodou flag makers. Much of Haitian art has been classified as 'naïve' or 'primitive,' partly due to its simple, almost childlike style and avoidance of classical perspective.

The major factor contributing to the singular vision of Haiti's artists is their inextricable link with Vodou and the spirit world. Before Haitian art was 'discovered,' the artists served the *lwa* (Vodou spirits) by painting murals to decorate the walls of *houmfors* (temples) and making elaborate sequined flags for use in ceremonies.

An American schoolteacher, De Witt Peters, can to a certain extent take credit for tapping into the commercial viability of the wellspring of creativity in Haiti. Trained in the arts, Peters came to work in Port-au-Prince as an English teacher on a wartime assignment in 1943. He recognized the extraordinary flavor of the primitivist work and helped artists develop their skills by setting up the Centre d'Art. Peters discovered Hector Hyppolite, considered Haiti's greatest painter, after spotting some paintings on a café door in St Marc. Above the door he saw a prophetic sign that read *Ici la Renaissance* (Here the Renaissance). Finding the artist, Peters invited Hyppolite to join him at the Centre d'Art, and very soon Hyppolite was producing his intense and strange works on canvas rather than on doors.

Hyppolite was a Vodou priest, and his allegiance with the spirit world never faded during his years of success. His works were inspired by his rich dreams and visions. While visiting Haiti in 1948, Truman Capote wrote, '…because he is the most popular of Haiti's primitive painters, Hyppolite could afford a running-water house, real beds, electricity; as it is, he lives by lamp, by candle, and all the neighbours, old withered coconut-headed ladies and handsome sailor boys and hunched sandal makers, can see into his affairs as he can see into theirs…this is the reason that I find Hyppolite admirable, for there is nothing in his art that has been slyly transposed, he is using what lives within himself, and that is his country's spiritual history, its singings and worships.' Some of Hyppolite's paintings can be seen at the Musée d'Art in Port-au-Prince.

Another artist discovered by Peters was Georges Liautaud. While driving through Croix des Bouquets, northeast of Port-au-Prince, Peters was intrigued by strangely fashioned iron crosses gracing the many elevated tombs in the local cemetery. The creator of these works, a local blacksmith named Liautaud, was easily persuaded to try his hand at free-standing works. Once he was free of utilitarian boundaries, Liautaud's imagination and work flourished. Croix des Bouquets is now at the heart of the Haitian metalwork movement. The two current master sculptors, Gabriel Bien-Aimé and Serge Jolimeau, were trained by Liautaud and now their various apprentices are producing new exciting works, all forged from recycled oil drums. (For more information, see the Around Port-au-Prince chapter.)

In 1949 the Centre d'Art embarked on its biggest project yet. A group of naïve artists, including Rigaud Bénoit, Philomé Obin, Castera Bazile and Wilson Bigaud, were commissioned to paint epic murals on the walls of the Sainte Trinité Episcopalian Cathedral. The work depicted scenes from the bible but many were set in the Haitian landscape and filtered through the spirit world. The resulting work is the greatest permanent exhibition of 'primitive' art to be found in Haiti.

HAITI

Haitian art has gone through numerous periods since the 1940s. The Saint-Soleil Group, which began painting in the mid-1970s under the patronage of two members of the bourgeoisie, are of particular interest. The artists were all country people, and their paintings, in keeping with Haitian tradition, depicted the lwa. They did not appear in costume or in the likenesses of Catholic saints, but were depicted as abstract form and energy. This marked the emergence of expressionism, uninformed by art history, in the Haitian art scene. The group included Prosper Pierre Louis, Louisianne St Fleurant, her sons Stevenson and Ramphis Magloire, and Levoy Exil. Many of these artists are still producing paintings that can be bought at the better galleries in Port-au-Prince.

Music

Musical expression in Haiti reflects both the fusion of cultural influences and, more recently, popular resistance and struggle in Haitian politics.

Vodou Music Music, song and dance have always been central to Vodou ceremonies. During the ceremony, the *houngan* (priest) salutes and greets the lwa from the pantheon. Each lwa is announced by its own particular ritual drum beats and songs. These rhythms and melodies, which were brought over by the slaves from 16th-century West Africa, are part of Haiti's rich cultural heritage.

The spirits are organized into different groups or nations and each has a different musical ensemble to play its rhythms. The most popular musical ensemble uses three drums, the *mamman*, *segon* and *boula*. The mamman is the largest drum, which the leading drummer beats fiercely with a single stick and one hand. The segon player provides hypnotic counter rhythms while the boula drummer plays an even rhythm holding all the others together. The *hounsis* (female initiates) dance and sing the ritual songs, which are usually in a combination of Creole and *lanngaj* (a ceremonial language from West Africa).

Carnival & Rara Music During the pre-Lent Carnival, the streets of the capital, Port-au-Prince, fill with rivers of people. Some wear costumes, but most of the revelers are there to hear the bands traveling the streets on floats. Most bands compete for the song prize with a specially composed song, each of which has been recorded and played constantly on the radio during the lead-up to Carnival.

Carnival is followed by Rara, dubbed the rural Carnival, even though there are many Rara bands in Port-au-Prince. In the weeks leading up to Easter, roads in Haiti swell with bands made up of percussionists, musicians playing bamboo-and-tin trumpets and groups of followers in the thousands. The music is mesmerizing, especially under the fierce heat of the sun. The *vaskins* (bamboo trumpets) and *kònets* (similar to the vaskins but made from hammered zinc ending in a flared horn) create a deep, primeval sound that is totally otherworldly.

Each instrument plays only one note that's repeated continually; the music's energy and dynamics come from riffs created between three or four kònets played at different pitches. The music is enhanced by the percussion instruments: drums slung around the players' shoulders, maracas and metal scrapers. This is 'music on the move,' and Rara bands can cover miles and miles, energized by music and rum. Most towns have many Rara bands, and areas such as Bel Air and Carrefour in Port-au-Prince are replete with them. If you wish to see Rara out of season, check out the Foula Vodou Jazz Club in Port-au-Prince.

Dance Music Many musical influences have been brought to Haiti by migrant workers returning from Cuba and the Dominican Republic. The Cuban Son genre has influenced many small troubadour bands who entertain in restaurants and hotels, singing and gently strumming guitars. Merengue, the Dominican big-band sound, has exerted the strongest influence on the Haitian dance floor. In the 1950s, two dance-band leaders, Nemours Jean-Baptiste and Weber Scott, altered the merengue beat slightly to create *compas direct* and *cadance rampa*, respectively. Until the last decade, compas has dominated the music scene in Haiti, producing internationally renowned acts such as Tabou Combo and Coupé Cloué.

Racines Music *Racines* (roots) music grew out of the Vodou-jazz movement of the late 1970s. Vodou jazz was a fusion of American jazz with Vodou rhythms and melodies. One of the leading proponents of the new musical form was the drummer Aboudja, who sought to rediscover Haiti's African roots (a recurring theme in much of Haiti's arts) through music. By the mid-1980s many racines bands had formed and the revolution in music began to reflect the struggle for change in Haiti. The lyrics were a clarion call for change and for a reevaluation of the long-ignored peasant culture. The music was propelled by Vodou rhythms overlaid with electric guitars, keyboards and singing. The most notable racines bands are Boukman Eksperyans, Boukan Ginen and RAM. During the military dictatorships of the late 1980s and the coup years of the 1990s, many of these bands endured extreme harassment and threats from the military. It took a great deal of courage to sing 'Jou Nou Revolte' (The Day We Revolt), a Boukman Eksperyans song, in a country where political killings were taking place every night.

Literature

In the years since independence, intellectual Haitians have been driven to create a strong school of indigenous literature in order to counter prevailing imperialist concepts of Haiti as a nation of primitive savages. This longing for recognition, in a hostile and racist 19th century, influenced many essayists who wrote on the subject of the evils of colonialism and racism. After the American occupation from 1915 to 1934, the desire to create a strong cultural identity through literature intensified. A movement that positively embraced Haiti's unique cultural identity was born, usually referred to as Noirisme. The most important writers of this generation were Jacques Roumain, Philippe-Thoby Marcelin and the most influential of the

---

Recommended Haitian Music CDs

Puritan Vodou
RAM
(Margaritaville/Island/Polygram) 1998

Kalfou Danjere
Boukman Eksperyans
(Mango/Island) 1993

Vodou Adjai
Boukman Eksperyans
(Mango/Island) 1991

---

group, Jean Price-Mars, who encouraged pride in Haiti's African roots. Jacques Roumain's ideas flourished under the influence of Marxism; it enabled him to transcend the nationalism of his Noiriste contemporaries and write what is considered to be Haiti's finest work of literature, *Les gouverneurs de la rosée* (Masters of the Dew).

After the 1940s, Haitian writers were greatly influenced by the surrealists. Their work was encouraged by the visit of surrealist André Breton, who had discovered an intrinsic surrealism in the visual arts of Haiti. From this period emerged Jacques Stéphen Alexis, author of *Compére General Soleil* (Comrade General Sun), and the poet and writer René Depestre, author of *Festival of the Greasy Pole*. Sadly, after the ascendancy of Noirisme in political life, both Marxism and surrealism came under attack. Alexis was murdered by François Duvalier's henchmen and Depestre went into exile. The Duvalier dictatorship effectively torpedoed Haitian intellectual and literary life. Through those dark years more books were written by Haitians outside the country than those in the country itself, mainly characterized by anti-Duvalier views. In the last two decades the diaspora has become preoccupied with the nature of exile itself. The most talented of these writers are Dany Laferrière and, more recently, Edwidge Danticat. Meanwhile, within Haiti there was a shift toward writing in Creole (as opposed to French), influenced by Franck Etienne,

HAITI

author of *Dézafi* – the first full-length novel written in Haitian Creole. This produced some fine playwrights as well as poets and novelists, including Felix Morisseau-Leroy, Hervé Denis and Jean-Claude Martineau.

Recommended books by Haitian authors include *Breath, Eyes, Memory* and *Krik? Krak!* by Edwidge Danticat; *Festival of the Greasy Pole* by René Depestre; *The Beast of the Haitian Hills* by Philippe-Thoby Marcelin and Pierre Marcelin; *An Aroma of Coffee* by Dany Laferrière; *Thus Spoke the Uncle* by Jean Price-Mars; and *Masters of the Dew* by Jacques Roumain.

Architecture

Very few examples of French colonial architecture have survived the earthquakes, fires, hurricanes and revolutions. But of those that have endured, most are found around Cap-Haïtien, and these include some forts and bridges. The most impressive examples of post-independence architecture are also in the north, including the palace Sans Souci and the Citadelle, constructed during the reign of Henri Christophe. French architectural style of the late 19th century has left a strong impression in both Port-au-Prince and Jacmel. In Port-au-Prince, it has left a legacy of beautiful, elegant gingerbread-style houses and mansions (see Things to See & Do in the Port-au-Prince chapter for more details).

SOCIETY & CONDUCT

Haitian society is predominantly made up of peasants who live a subsistence lifestyle in rural areas. They usually own or rent a small plot of land on which they cultivate beans, sweet potatoes, maize, bananas or coffee. Rice is grown along the irrigated valley of the Artibonite and along the coastline, and fishers sail out in simple boats for the ever-decreasing yield of seafood. Traditionally, the men plant and harvest the crops while the women care for the children, prepare meals and sell their surplus crops at the market. Methods of cultivation are rudimentary and labor-intensive, depending on the pick and hoe.

Their small, usually two-room wooden houses have no electricity, and food preparation takes place outside on a charcoal fire. If faced with difficult and arduous work, the men work together on one piece of land in a communal work team called a *kombit*. Neighbors and friends, sometimes called by the sound of a conch shell trumpet, work for free and are compensated by a feast at the end of the day. Music is essential to their work, as the men work in rhythm to special songs. The songs of a kombit are personalized, composed by members of the community, and act as a comic local newspaper. A line of men, their hoes swinging in unison, sweating and singing, is a familiar sight in the countryside. In the evenings after eating, the group often relaxes by playing Krik Krak, an oral game of riddles.

As the population's demands on the land have reached a breaking point, many peasants have sought a better life in the capital, Port-au-Prince. In the past they found work as gardeners, servants and laborers, but this work has dried up over the last two decades. Sadly, the exodus from the land has continued unabated, creating teeming slums such as Cité Soleil. Here much of the communal spirit of the countryside is lost in the everyday grind. In Cité Soleil, about 200,000 people occupy 5 sq km of land, mainly reclaimed sea swamp, in some of the most brutal and demoralizing conditions imaginable. Some of the neighborhoods are euphemistically called Cité Brooklyn and Cité Boston, but in reality they consist of a maze of primitive mud-and-brick shanties reinforced with abandoned metal sheeting and cardboard packing cases. There is no running water or sewage system, just filthy open drainage ditches separating the rows of homes. When the rains fall, the ditches overflow and the downpour, rich with sewage, rages through the tiny shacks.

But another life altogether prevails in the cool hills above Port-au-Prince. The country's elite, the 1% of society that own 44% of the wealth, lives in mansions surrounded by high walls, in and above Pétionville. The mainly mulatto oligarchy that consisted of merchants at the beginning of the century now controls the manufacturing industries, the import/export businesses, the tourism industry, and in some cases, the traffic of illegal drugs. In Pétionville you can dine out on the very best French cuisine, drink superb wines and buy chic perfumes. The bourgeoisie enjoy the privileges their class affords them and are resistant to any change in society that might threaten them.

Dos & Don'ts

When you are traveling through Haiti, you will get used to hearing 'blan, blan!' shouted after you. This is a generic term for 'foreigner' rather than a jibe at your skin color, and it should not be taken as any kind of insult. People in the street like to tease visitors, and the best response is laughter. Most people in Haiti are very polite and friendly. Although they may regard you with some suspicion at first, a smile and simple greeting immediately breaks the ice.

Because Haiti is a predominantly rural society, many people in the capital are only one or two generations away from the countryside, so greetings – even to strangers – are an integral part of life. Obviously, you are not expected to greet everyone you see on a crowded street in downtown Port-au-Prince, but on a quiet street or in the countryside, a smile and 'Ça va?' (How's it going?) or 'Salut' (Hello) is important. A more traditional Creole greeting is 'Ki jan ou ye?' (How are you?), to which the reply is 'M pa pi mal' (Not too bad).

Another thing you will hear quite often is 'Give me one dollar.' The decision is yours, but people will take no for an answer eventually. It is not advisable to give away money while in a large crowd purely because everyone will want some. The level of social interaction in Haiti is far higher than in most Western societies, so it's better to let it enliven you rather than tire you out. You are advised to use your humor to get yourself out of a situation as irritation and a bad temper can escalate in the wrong direction.

Avoid visiting the slum areas, such as Cité Soleil or La Saline, as no one appreciates a tourist visiting other people's misery. There is really no reason for a traveler to explore these areas and they can be dangerous. It is also not advisable to wander into a Vodou ceremony uninvited. If you wish to see a ceremony, organize this with a guide, who will know many local priests.

RELIGION
Vodou

Vodou is one of the most maligned religions on the globe. Many people imagine that it is a mass of superstitions based on fear and ignorance, lacking any religious traditions. This negative portrayal comes partly from sensational Hollywood movies but dates back to the early 19th century and the demonization of Haitian culture due to the slaves' revolt, culminating in the declaration of independence in 1804.

Vodou has its roots in the animist spirit religions of 14th-century West Africa. The slaves, brought from Dahomey and the Congo, carried their beliefs over with them on the slave ships from Africa. The Vodou that is practiced today is a synthesis of these religions crossed with residual rituals from the Taíno Indians. Vodou became the arena within which Africans from many different tribes could find a common ground and community. It thrived both clandestinely on the plantations and among the bands of runaway slaves in their secret hill camps. Vodou played a large part in both the inspiration and organization of the struggle for independence. In 1791, a Vodou priest known simply as Boukman held a fateful ceremony at Bois Cayman, south of Cap-Haïtien, where all the participants swore allegiance to the struggle for liberty, and death to all whites. This precipitated the first serious slave uprising in the history of Haiti.

Throughout the period of slavery, Christianity was used as a justification for the slave trade. The salvation of one's 'heathen soul' was considered a just reward for working to death on a plantation in Haiti. In order to retain their own beliefs while still humoring the missionaries, the slaves replaced their sacred objects with icons of the Catholic saints. Vodou altars in Vodou

HAITI

A Spirit Guide

The Vodou pantheon consists of a countless number of spirits. Some spirits are more common than others, and are often seen depicted in the sequined flags, paintings and metalwork created by Haitian artists.

Gede is the master of the ancestral dead and the keeper of the cemeteries. Baron Samedi and Baron La Croix are a couple of his many incarnations. Purple and black are his colors, and a black rooster is his favorite offering. St Gerard is his Catholic alter ego.

Erzulie Dantor is a dark-skinned and fiercely protective matriarchal spirit. She dresses in red and blue, drinks rum, and smokes unfiltered Camels. A creole pig is her favored offering and she is represented by the Black Madonna.

Erzulie Freda is a light-skinned goddess of love and luxury, who adores beautiful clothes, perfumes and jewelry. She dresses in pink and white, and demands sweet wines and fancy cakes. She is represented by the Mater Dolorosa Virgin Mary.

Agwe is the master of the sea, and has La Siren, a mermaid, as his wife. They are honored at sea with a white lamb and a white chicken. Agwe's Catholic counterpart is St Ulrich.

Ogou is the warrior spirit who helped the slaves win the battle for independence. Ogou carries a sword, wears a red bandanna, and demands a red rooster. He is represented by the Catholic St Jacques.

Damballah is the supreme snake deity and master of the sky. He is often depicted with an egg, symbolizing fertility. Ayida Wedo, his wife, is a rainbow spirit, and they both prefer white eggs, rice and milk. Damballah is represented by St Patrick, who is pictured with snakes at his feet.

---

temples, to this day, always display chromolithographs (color pictures) of Catholic saints. The images are the same but the meanings are different. Each surrogate Catholic saint signifies a different spirit from the vast Vodou pantheon (see above).

Vodou ceremonies are highly developed rituals to pleasure, feed and ultimately materialize the *lwa* (the spirits) through the possession of a human body. Each lwa is announced by its own particular drum rhythms and songs. Once the drums start, the ceremony has begun. The *houngan* (priest) or *mambo* (priestess) will take his or her *asson* (the sacred rattle) from the *houmfor* (the ceremonial altar) to greet Legba (the spirit of the crossroads) and ask him to open the gates to the spirit world. The four cardinal points are saluted and Loco-Attiso (the ancestral spirit of the original priest) is greeted through song. La Place (the male priest's assistant) will leave the houmfor with a sword, flanked by two *hounsis* (female initiates) carrying sequined flags

representing that particular Vodou *société* (group). The houngan then traces out the *vevé* (sacred symbol) for Ayisen (the ancestral spirit of the first priestess in Vodou mythology) in cornmeal on the floor. The vevés are beautiful, intricate patterns thought to be the legacy of the Taíno Indians. Ephemeral and delicate, vevés are returned to the earth by the pounding of the dancers' feet. Neither Legba, Loco-Attiso nor Ayisen announce their presence through human possession; rather, they preside over the ceremony as a whole.

Next, Damballah, the African snake god, is greeted. If a participant is possessed by Damballah, he or she will writhe around the floor in a snakelike manner. Being possessed by the spirits is central to a ceremony. For the initiate, this is the ultimate purpose of his or her faith; mounted (possessed) by the lwa, the devotee has realized absolute communication with the gods and ancestors, an experience not unlike the mystical exaltations of enraptured saints.

The congregation then continues to salute a host of spirits with individual rhythms and songs. These spirits could include Erzulie Freda (the spirit of love), Agwe (the spirit of the sea) and Papa Zaca (the spirit of agriculture). A person possessed by Papa Zaca will be dressed as a peasant and adorned with a *macoute* (straw bag) and straw hat. The drums begin to play faster to greet Ogou, the warrior spirit. Ogou will be offered rum, and if anyone is possessed by him, he or she will be dressed with a red scarf, carry a sword, smoke a cigar and drink rum. Food is offered to the lwa at the close of the ceremonies, either through animal sacrifice or cooked food. Individual lwa demand particular offerings, ranging from chickens to bulls, white eggs to corn mash.

Vodou has been banned numerous times in Haiti, but it has survived as a living religion and is now under the protection of the 1987 constitution. Both Toussaint and Dessalines outlawed Vodou during their reigns, fearing its political potential. There were also several ruthless anti-superstition campaigns during the 20th century, implemented by the Catholic Church and the government. The last took place in 1941 under President Elie Lescot, when Vodou altars were burned and the sacred Mapou trees were cut down. The Catholic Church now coexists with and tolerates the practice of Vodou in Haiti.

Vodou priest drawing a vevé

Christianity

The Catholic Church is the most powerful Christian institution in Haiti. While almost everyone practices Vodou, it is commonly held that 80% of the population is Catholic and 20% Protestant. Due to his distrust of foreign power within the Haitian Catholic Church, François Duvalier created an indigenous episcopacy in the 1960s. The predominantly Bretagne Jesuits and the Holy Ghost Fathers (another group of Catholic priests) were sent into exile and replaced with a more indigenous clergy. This led to a Catholic hierarchy that not only remained silent about the brutal regime, but even included the dictator in their public prayers. Even though the bishops were Duvalierists, the Church on a grassroots level was taking its inspiration from the current of liberation theology that flowed across Latin America in the mid-1970s. The Ti Legliz ('little church') was born and began to flourish. The movement gave a voice and platform to many young radical priests and theologians. Houses of worship doubled as adult learning centers, meeting places for slum neighborhood committees and political forums for students. With the help from the church-supported Radio Soleil, the Ti Legliz was instrumental in the downfall of Jean Claude Duvalier.

The Protestant churches in Haiti, with the exception of the Methodists, have mainly preached a theology of resignation, and attempted to alienate their congregations from political struggle, completely separating religion from politics and from basic grievances against the government. Many right-wing churches from North America continue to pour missionaries and money into the country. Their memberships have grown, but usually in relationship to the amount of food aid the churches can offer.

LANGUAGE

While for many years French has been considered the official language of Haiti, only 10% of the population can speak it. The majority of the population speaks Creole alone. The different languages spoken in Haitian society deepen the already massive

Creole Proverbs

Creole has a small vocabulary but, rather than limiting expression, this has sired a wealth of poetic and allegorical proverbs. The proverbs are a testament to the attitudes, struggles and lives of the majority of the Haitian people.

Dèyè mòn gen mòn. Behind the mountains there are more mountains.

Apre dans tanbou lou. After the dance the drum is heavy.

Men anpil chay pa lou. Many hands make the load lighter.

Bèl antèman pa di paradi. A beautiful burial does not guarantee heaven.

Kreyon pèp la pa gen gonm. The people's pencil has no eraser.

Lè yo vle touye chen yo di'l fou. When they want to kill a dog they say it's crazy.

Kay koule twompe solèy men li pa twompe lapli. The leaky house can fool the sun but it can't fool the rain.

Milat pov se nég, nég rich se milat. A poor mulatto is a black man, a rich black man is a mulatto.

Bay kou, bliye. Pote mak, sonje. The one who gives the blow, forgets. The one who gets hurt, remembers.

divisions between social classes. The government and the judicial system both operate in French. The illiterate masses are therefore excluded from civil society, leaving the control in the hands of the upper and middle classes. Most schools teach in French, which further disadvantages Creole-only speakers. Since the 1980s there has been a movement among reformists toward the increased use of Creole in civil society. Politicians are making more speeches in Creole, musicians sing in it, more radio stations broadcast in it and there is now a weekly paper, *Libète* (Liberty), published in Creole.

There is some debate as to the roots of the language. The vocabulary is predominantly French, with some English and Spanish thrown in, but the structure is considered to be closer to that of West African languages. The most popularly held belief is that it's the synthesis of French and many African languages. There is another theory that it was an already evolved French patois used by the sailors and pirates involved with the slave trade. It is worth learning a few Creole phrases to use in smaller restaurants (where owners are unlikely to speak French) and for greetings. If you wish to learn Creole, the best book is *Ann Pale Krèyol*, published by the Creole Institute at the University of Indiana.

See the Language section at the end of the book for useful words and phrases.

Facts for the Visitor

PLANNING
When to Go
There is no real tourist season in Haiti, so there are no fluctuations in price for peak or off-season periods. However, the weather could be a consideration in determining your travel dates. There are two rainy seasons per year, April-May and September-October, and the sky can be gray and overcast at these times. Days may be followed by dramatic evening tropical downpours, which can be very exhilarating. Remember that the torrential rain can cause roads – especially those outside of town – to become fairly treacherous due to mud and rock slides. If you don't like it hot, avoid the summer months – June to September – and visit during the more bearable winter months. If you plan to visit for Carnival (usually celebrated during February, depending on the position of Ash Wednesday in the Catholic calendar), book well in advance. Carnival attracts many visitors, especially from the extensive Haitian diaspora, so a good hotel may be hard to find.

Maps
Hildebrand's Travel Map publishes the best topographical map of the Dominican Republic and Haiti (scale of 1:816,000), the only one available outside of Haiti. The country map is excellent, with most small towns represented, but the street maps of Port-au-Prince and Cap-Haïtien are minuscule and worthless. The Association of Haitian Hoteliers produces a crude country map that has a fairly efficient street map of Port-au-Prince. Cap-Haïtien and Jacmel are also covered on two handy inserts. You can pick up this map free at any car rental agency, or buy it for US$1 outside the main post office in Port-au-Prince.

More recently, another map has been making the rounds. The *Carte d'Haiti*, which is produced in association with Sogebank, sells for US$3 at most major supermarkets. Although the map of Haiti is somewhat minimal, the map of Port-au-Prince on the back is excellent. This map is very good for getting acquainted with the layout of the city, and it also includes good street maps of Jacmel and Cap-Haïtien.

TOURIST OFFICES
Local Tourist Offices
The Maison de Tourisme (☎ 222-8659) information center is on Rue Capois in Port-au-Prince, at the corner of Rue Magny, in a pretty gingerbread building. For further information, you can contact the Secretary of State for Tourism (☎ 223-2143, 223-5631, fax 223-5359), at Rue Lègitime, Champs de Mars, Port-au-Prince, or the Haitian Association for the Tourism & Hotel Industry (☎ 257-4647, fax 257-6137), at Choucoune Plaza, Pétionville. No offices exist outside of the capital except in Cap-Haïtien and Jacmel:

Cap-Haïtien
   (☎ 262-0870) Bureau du Tourisme,
    Rue 24 Boulevard
Jacmel
   (☎ 288-2088) Madame Craan, Hôtel de la Ville,
    Place d'Armes, or 26 Magloire Ambroise

Tourist Offices Abroad
Haiti has no tourist offices abroad.

VISAS & DOCUMENTS
Passport & Visas
A valid passport must be presented upon entering the Republic of Haiti. A tourist visa is required for stays up to three months (90 days). This may be obtained from any Haitian embassy or consulate. A completed visa application form (provided by the embassy or consulate), two passport-size photographs and a fee of US$5.40 are required. Citizens from the following countries need a valid passport but do not require a tourist visa: Argentina, Austria, Belgium, Canada, Denmark, Germany, Israel, Liechtenstein, Monaco, South Korea, Sweden, Switzerland, the UK and the USA. Since the return of constitutional order, in 1994, there are still

some differences between de facto practices and de jure dispositions, and the Ministry of the Interior is currently rewriting much of this information. It is advisable to check with your nearest embassy before making a trip.

If you wish to stay in Haiti for longer than 90 days, you must apply for a visitor/resident visa before you travel. This process can take up to four months and requires a health certificate, and a letter of support from an organization, employer or Haitian resident, to present to your local Haitian embassy. If you wish to extend your tourist visa once in Haiti, you should contact the Ministry of Foreign Affairs (☎ 222-1243, 222-8482).

Driver's License
In order to hire and drive a vehicle in Haiti, you need either a valid International Driver's License or a current license from your own country. It is an offense to drive without a valid driver's license on your person. You should carry your passport on you at all times, as the police will want to see it if they stop you for any reason.

EMBASSIES & CONSULATES
Haitian Embassies & Consulates
Argentina
    (☎ 5411-4807-0211, fax 5411-4802-3984)
    Av Figueroa Alcorta 3297-1425, Buenos Aires
Bahamas
    (☎ 809-326-0325, fax 809-322-7712)
    PO Box 666, East St, Nassau
Belgium
    (☎ 32-2-649-7381, fax 32-2-640-6080)
    160 Ave Louise, Brussels 1050 (Accredited to the UK and Netherlands)
Brazil
    (☎ 55-61-248-6860, fax 55-61-248-7472)
    Shis-Sul QU 17, Conj 04, Casa 19,
    CP 86 18/71600, 70465 Brasilia
Canada
    (☎ 613-238-1628)
    112 Rue Kent, suite 1308, Ottawa K1P 5P2
Chile
    (☎/fax 562-231-0967)
    Av 11 Septembre, 2155 Torre B, Officina 403, Santiago
Colombia
    (☎/fax 571-214-2927)
    Calle 106, No 23-57, Sante Fe de Bogota

Dominican Republic
    (☎ 809-686-5778, fax 809-686-6096,
    amb.haiti@codetel.net.do)
    33 Av Juan Sánchez Ramírez, Santo Domingo
France
    (☎ 01 47 63 47 78, fax 01 42 27 02 05)
    10 Rue Théodule Ribot, BP 275, Cédex 28, 75827 Paris
Germany
    (☎ 49-22-885-6829, fax 49-22-885-7700)
    10 Schlossallee, 53179 Bonn
    (Accredited to Denmark)
Italy
    (☎ 39-63-972-3362, fax 39-63-973-7764)
    Via Ruggero Fuaro 59, Rome 00197
Jamaica
    (☎ 876-927-7595, fax 876-978-7638)
    2 Munroe Rd, Kingston 6 (Accredited to Trinidad & Tobago, St Lucia & Guyana)
Japan
    (☎ 81-33-486-7096, fax 81-33-486-7070)
    34 Kowa Bldg, No 906, 4-12-24 Nishi Azabu, Minati-ku, Tokyo 106
Mexico
    (☎ 525-511-4390, fax 525-533-3896)
    Cordoba 23A, Colonia Roma, CP 06700, Mexico DF
Panama
    (☎ 507-269-3443, fax 507-223-1767,
    anbhaiti@panama.c-com.net)
    Apartado F, Zona 9A, Panamá
Spain
    (☎ 34-1-575-2624, fax 34-1-431-4600)
    33 Paseo del Gén Martinez, Madrid 28010
Taiwan
    (☎ 88-62-872-2734, fax 88-62-831-7086)
    246 Chung Chan N Rd, 3rd floor, Sect 6 Taipei
USA
    (☎ 202-332-4090, fax 202-745-7215,
    embassy@haiti.org) 2311 Massachusetts Ave NW, Washington, DC 20008
Venezuela
    (☎ 582-747-220, fax 582-744-605) 4th floor,
    59 Ave Rosas-Urban, San Rafael de Florida, Caracas

Embassies & Consulates in Haiti
Embassies and consulates are in either Port-au-Prince or Pétionville.
Bahamas
    Embassy:
    (☎ 257-1448, 257-8782, fax 257-0454)
    12 Rue Goulard, Pétionville

Canada
   Embassy:
   (☎ 223-2358, 223-8882, fax 223-8720)
   Delmas 18 (1st floor Scotiabank),
   Port-au-Prince

Colombia
   Embassy:
   (☎ 246-2599, 246-5595)
   384 Rte de Delmas No 7, between Delmas 42
   and 44, Port-au-Prince

Dominican Republic
   Embassy:
   (☎ 257-0383, 257-1650, 257-1208, fax 257-9215)
   121 Ave Pan Américaine, corner of
   Rte El Rancho, Port-au-Prince

France
   Embassy:
   (☎ 222-0951, 222-0952, 223-8118, fax 223-9858)
   51 Rue Capois, Port-au-Prince

Germany
   Embassy:
   (☎ 257-8782, 257-7280, fax 257-4131)
   2 Impasse Claudinette, Bois Moquette,
   Port-au-Prince

Guatemala
   Consulate:
   (☎ 222-5608, 245-4537)
   Cité de l'Exposition, Bicentenaire,
   opposite the Institut Français, Port-au-Prince

Honduras
   Embassy:
   (☎ 222-1581) 167 Rue du Centre, Port-au-Prince

Jamaica
   Consulate:
   (☎ 249-1800, 249-1847, fax 246-0613)
   12 Rte de l'Aéroport (RHT Trading building),
   Port-au-Prince

Mexico
   Embassy:
   (☎ 249-2597, 249-2100, fax 257-6783)
   2 Delmas 60, Musseau, Port-au-Prince

Netherlands
   Consulate:
   (☎ 222-0955, 223-5146, 223-5147, fax 222-0955,
   223-5146) Rue Belleville, Parc Shodecosa,
   off Rte Nationale 1, Port-au-Prince

Panama
   Embassy:
   (☎ 257-4504, 257-9789, 257-9790, fax 257-4504)
   43 Rue Lamarre, Pétionville

UK
   Consulate:
   (☎ 257-3969, fax 257-4048)
   Hotel Montana, Rue F Cardoza, off
   Ave Pan Américaine, Port-au-Prince

USA
   Embassy:
   (☎ 222-0220, 222-0269, 222-0359, 222-1770,
   222-0327, fax 223-1641)
   Bicentenaire, Blvd Harry Truman,
   Port-au-Prince
   Consulate:
   (☎ 223-0989, 223-8853, 223-9324, 223-7011,
   fax 223-9965)
   104 Rue Oswald Durand,
   Port-au-Prince

Venezuela
   Embassy:
   (☎ 222-0971, 222-0793, fax 222-3949)
   2 Cité de l'Exposition, Blvd Harry Truman,
   Port-au-Prince

CUSTOMS

The customs inspection is thorough and the drug laws are strictly enforced. You are allowed to bring in one liter of liquor and one carton of cigarettes or 50 cigars. Drugs and firearms are prohibited and shotguns and other hunting equipment must be registered both with customs and immigration.

MONEY
Currency

The official currency is the gourde, and there are 100 centimes to 1 gourde. At the time of writing, you could buy 17 gourdes for one US dollar. As well as a new 10-gourde coin, there are the rarely sighted 5, 10, 20 and 50-centime coins and 1, 2, 5, 10, 25, 50, 100, 250 and 500-gourde notes in circulation. Try to break down larger denomination notes in a bank as people are always short of change.

In the past the gourde was fixed to the US dollar at a rate of 5 gourdes to a dollar. This is no longer the rate but has led to the 5-gourde bill being referred to as 'one Haitian dollar,' the 10-gourde bill as 'two Haitian dollars,' and so on. This is where the confusion lies. When you are buying something, the price can often be quoted in gourdes, in Haitian dollars or sometimes even in US dollars. You must check exactly what people mean when they give you the price. It is a difficult system to grasp at first, comparing menus in gourdes with those in Haitian dollars, and seeing a bill with '100' written on it being referred to as a '20.'

HAITI

The simplest way to deal with this is to choose one system, either the Haitian dollar or the gourde, and stick with that. Thus, to understand the price in Haitian dollars, you must either divide prices in gourdes by five, or if you choose to think in gourdes, you must multiply all Haitian dollar prices by five. Sticking to one system will enable you to make price comparisons after some time, which is nearly impossible if you keep slipping between the two systems.

Exchange Rates

You must buy US dollars and/or US dollar traveler's checks before arriving in Haiti, as banks are reluctant to change any other currencies.

Country	Unit		Gourdes
Australia	A$1	=	10.5
Canada	C$1	=	11
Dominican Republic	RD$10	=	11
euro	€1	=	19
Germany	DM1	=	10
Japan	¥100	=	15
New Zealand	NZ$1	=	9
UK	£1	=	28
USA	US$1	=	17

Exchanging Money

Cash & Traveler's Checks You are never far from a bank in Port-au-Prince. Soge-bank, Unibank and Promobank are the most common banks. Hours vary between companies and their branches. All Promo-banks are open 8:30 am to 1 pm weekdays, except for their Pétionville branch, which also opens from 3 to 5 pm. Most Sogebank branches are open 8:30 am to 3 pm (and some until 5 pm) weekdays, but some also open 8:30 am to 1 pm on Saturday. All exchange US dollars only, and this extends to traveler's checks as well.

You will need Haitian gourdes almost immediately upon arrival, but be aware that there are no bank exchange desks at the Port-au-Prince airport. However, porters at the airport will accept US dollars, as will the taxi services into town. Once you are in a

town, you should find a bank, as the exchange rates offered at hotels are the worst in the country.

Credit Cards You can use both Visa and MasterCard at all car rental companies and major airlines. The more expensive hotels and restaurants also accept major credit cards. Sogebank and Promobank give cash advances on Visa and MasterCard, but it is sometimes more difficult to get advances with American Express.

Black Market There are many places on the street that you can change money, but the rate is usually only slightly less than at banks. You need to have a good idea what the rate is and be adept at counting the cash. You can find moneychangers at the corners of most downtown streets, such as Rue Pavée, outside the Promobank at the corner of Av John Brown and Rue Lamarre, near the main post office on Rue Bonne-Foi, and at the north end of Rue Grégoire in Pétionville. In Cap-Haïtien, there are money-changers on Rue 11 B-C.

Changing on the streets can be handy if you don't want to leave your car, want to avoid long bank lines or wish to change money outside of bank hours. Don't let go of your US dollars until you have thoroughly checked the amount of gourdes you are receiving.

Costs

Haiti can be a perplexing country when it comes to the cost of things. Surviving in Haiti can be extremely cheap, but there is the feeling that it is easier for a *blan* (foreigner) to pass through the eye of a needle than to find a bargain. The true price of everything, if there is one, is one of the best-kept secrets in the country. You will rarely be overcharged for hotels, street food or public transport, but taxis, guides and sellers of souvenirs will undoubtedly try it on.

Haiti is a country of outlandish extremes where you can pay US$1 for a huge meal in a streetside café or US$50 in a Pétionville restaurant, so therefore the cost of your holiday can vary hugely depending on your standards. If you travel by *publique* (communal taxi) and *taptap* (public bus), you can save a lot of money, but if you want the comfort of a hired car, it can cost about US$70 a day. Decent hotels tend to be quite expensive (US$70 per night), and the bottom end (US$8 per night) can sometimes be quite rough and not very secure.

Tipping & Bargaining

A 10% tip is normal in restaurants, and a small tip for bar staff is expected. You will be expected to tip porters in the airport and at your hotel. If you park your car downtown or in Pétionville, you will be asked if you wish someone to watch it. Chose one person, ask him his name to avoid any argument later and pay him 5 gourdes when you return.

Bartering is a way of life in Haiti, and it allows participants to take part in their favorite pursuits: teasing and arguing. Don't be put off by the first price (which will often be wildly high); keep in mind the fair price that you want to pay, and off you go. Some craftsmen, including flag and metal artists, have fixed prices, but a little negotiation can still take place. Humor and patience lubricate the whole process; don't be too discouraged by the often feigned disgust at the insult of your lower offer. (See the text on Bargaining in the Dominican Republic's Facts for the Visitor chapter.)

Taxes

Most of the larger hotels charge a 10% sales tax, and many also add a daily energy charge of US$3 to US$5. The smaller hotels and guest houses tend to offer an all-inclusive price. A departure tax of US$25 plus 10 gourdes is charged at the airport. The US$25 must be paid in US dollars, so remember to keep some dollars to pay for this.

POST & COMMUNICATIONS
Post

There are post offices in most major towns, which are open from 8 am to 4 pm. It costs 5 gourdes (US$0.30) to send a postcard and 10 gourdes (US$0.60) to send a letter anywhere in the world. There are no postboxes,

and all mail must be sent from a post office. Alternatively, you can leave your mail at the reception areas of some of the larger hotels.

If you want to receive mail in Haiti, you can have it addressed to 'Poste Restante,' c/o Bureau de Poste, Rue Bonne Foi, Port-au-Prince, Haiti, WI (West Indies). Take along your passport when you pick up mail.

It's best not to receive parcels in this way, as the post office can decide to charge an import duty that often costs more than the contents. It's also much safer to send and receive express parcels at the DHL offices in Port-au-Prince and Pétionville.

Telephone

The telecommunications service in Haiti is poor and presents the opportunity for endless grumbling. Perseverance is needed to succeed in making even a local call. Many numbers are party lines – used by more than one residence or business – so prepare to be told to *rele encore* (call again). In addition, because phone lines are often out of service, many businesses have several phone numbers. If the first number doesn't work, try the others. There are no public phones, but most hotels have telephones for use in their foyers.

Most towns have a Teleco office where you can place local and international calls for US$5.60 for three minutes to Caribbean destinations and US$7.75 for three-minute calls to Europe and the USA. The person behind the counter will take your name and the number you wish to reach, then shout your name and the number of a booth where you can take the call when connected.

National/Local Calls With the AT&T system, you can make a local call from any phone that connects you to an operator, who will place your call. The cost will be billed to your account.

International Calls Haiti's international telephone code is 509. Making international calls from Haiti can be quite an inconvenience, and it is a good idea to open an AT&T calling-card account before you make your

HAITI

trip. To reach an international operator, dial ☎ 00, and for information on international calls, dial ☎ 00-09. MCI also runs a service, but has suspended its calling-card service to Europe due to fraud. You can buy MCI cards for US$20 from hotels, post offices and Teleco offices.

Fax, Email & Internet Access

Most hotels have a fax service, which costs about US$3 per minute to the USA. There is usually a charge of 10 gourdes (US$0.60) per fax sheet received in hotels.

America Online offers a local server number (☎ 223-7489). This service sometimes gets a bit overloaded during the day but is not too bad in the evenings and late at night. Haiti uses American-style telephone sockets, so be sure that you have the right connection for your modem. You must set the dialing setting to pulse and the modem speed to 9600bps.

Alternatively, you can visit the Cyber Café (☎ 257-9561), at 84 Ave Pan Américaine, Pétionville, which charges US$4.50 an hour for Internet access. Online access is more problematic outside Port-au-Prince, as you have to get a line to the capital. It is possible to try this at a Teleco office if you're desperate.

INTERNET RESOURCES

There are several websites that provide information on Haitian art, culture, politics and Vodou.

Art of Haiti
www.medalia.net
This site shows many examples of art and provides good biographies of the artists.

Haiti Archives
www.hartford-hwp.com/archives/43a/index.html
This site offers many different essays on history, politics, arts and religion.

Haiti Focus
www.haitifocus.com
This is a good spot to check the exchange rate and weather.

Haiti Support Group
www.gn.apc.org/haitisupport
This site looks at culture, politics and campaigning news.

Haitian Embassy, Washington, DC
www.haiti.org/embassy
This site provides lots of information on Haiti's government, embassies, constitution and tourism.

Haitian Press Agency
www.ahphaiti.org
The Haitian Press Agency provides up-to-date news stories on Haiti in English.

LANIC
www.lanic.utexas.edu/la/cb/haiti
Maintained by the University of Texas, this site has links to dozens of sites concerning Haiti, including sites on art, business prospects and human-rights issues.

Secretary of State for Tourism
www.haititourisme.com
Here you'll find travel information in French.

Studio Wah
www.studiowah.com
Look here for information about guided art tours of Haiti.

Windows on Haiti
windowsonhaiti.com
Here you'll find recipes for Haitian food and information on the arts, books and culture.

The following sites are purely dedicated to Vodou:

Vodou Page
members.aol.com/racine125/index.html

Vodoun Culture
vodoun.com

BOOKS
Lonely Planet

Travelers to Haiti may want to pick up the Lonely Planet *French Phrasebook* for useful words and phrases.

Travel Literature

Traveller's Tree, by Patrick Leigh Fermor (1984), is considered a classic of travel literature and contains three chapters on the author's journeys through Haiti in the 1950s. *Bonjour Blanc: A Journey through Haiti,* by Ian Thomson (1993), is one of the most entertaining and well-researched travel books written about Haiti. The towns Thomson visits come alive, not only through his meticulous historical detail, but also through the vivid portraits he paints of the characters who now inhabit them. The book is sadly out of print but worth the search.

History & Politics

An essential companion for any visitor to Haiti, *Libète: A Haiti Anthology*, edited by Charles Arthur and Michael Dash (Latin America Bureau, 1999), covers Haitian history from the Arawaks to Aristide. This immensely readable collection of short extracts, many by Haitian authors, is breathtaking in its scope and detail. Ten chapters, each with an introductory essay, provide a thorough and colorful background on the colonial period, the trials and tribulations of independence and foreign intervention, the struggle for democracy and development, and the culture, literature, and way of life of the Haitian people.

Written in Blood, by Robert Debs Heinl, Nancy Gordon Heinl and Michael Heinl, is a vast tome covering the history of Haiti in minute detail. *The Uses of Haiti*, by Paul Farmer (Common Courage, 1994), with a foreword by Noam Chomsky, views Haiti's history through the prism of US intervention and interference, with an emphasis on the 1991-94 coup period. Farmer, a doctor with more than a decade of medical practice in Haiti, is critical of the price Haitian people have paid for US foreign policy.

Papa Doc, Baby Doc: Haiti and the Duvaliers, by James Ferguson (Blackwell, 1987), is a succinct history of the Duvalier dynasty. It analyzes the circumstances that led to Papa Doc's rise to power, the methods he used to sustain his power base, and the different forces that led to the expulsion of his son, Baby Doc. *The Black Jacobins,* by CLR James (Allison & Busby, 1980), is a classic study of the slaves' revolt in Haiti. Using an engaging narrative, James explains, from a Marxist point of view, the forces that created the revolution and the men that led it.

Haiti: Dangerous Crossroads (South End Press, 1995), edited by the North American Congress on Latin America (NACLA), is a collection of essays that analyze the turbulent political period from 1987 to 1994. *Rainy Season: Haiti Since Duvalier*, by Amy Wilentz, is a personal account of the years after 'Baby Doc' Duvalier flew into exile. Written before the coup, part documentary and part introspection, Wilentz's book gives readers an insightful background on the events that led to the tragic and fateful military coup of 1991.

Culture

The Drum and the Hoe: Life and Lore of the Haitian People, by Harold Courlander, gives a good overview of peasant life, religion and work practices. *Divine Horsemen: The Living Gods of Haiti*, by Maya Deren (Documentext, first published 1953), is one of the finest books written on Vodou. Through first-hand experience, Deren manages to both demystify and make sacred this universally misinterpreted religion.

Illustrated with examples of Haitian art and religious symbols, *Spirits of the Night: The Vaudun Gods of Haiti*, by Selden Rodman and Carol Cleaver (Spring Publications, 1992), is an accessible book that links art, inspiration and Vodou in Haiti. *Where Art Is Joy*, also by Rodman (Ruggles de la Tour, 1988), is a detailed account of Haitian art since the 1940s, richly illustrated with hundreds of color plates.

The Magic Orange Tree and Other Haitian Folktales, edited by Diane Wolkstein (Schocken, 1980), is a collection of Haitian folk stories enriched by the biographical notes and observations of the storytellers that precede each fable.

Fiction

Kathy Goes to Haiti, by Kathy Acker, is an unusual novel by an experimental writer. It gives a snapshot glimpse of Haiti in the late '70s through the eyes of a young American woman on holiday. *Continental Drift*, by Russell Banks, is a powerful novel that contrasts two fatally intertwined lives. Bob, an honest blue-collar worker, watches his American dream fragment as he ekes out an existence in Florida, while Vanise, a Haitian woman, dreams of escaping to America for a better life. The novel explores themes of racism, poverty and the need to escape through the parallel stories of the two characters and their hopes for a better life.

The Kingdom of This World, by Cuban Alejo Carpentier, is a poetic reconstruction of the struggle for independence in Haiti by

HAITI

Haiti on the Silver Screen

The following is a list of recommended documentaries and films about and/or made in Haiti:

Documentaries

Bitter Cane (1983)
An investigation into the semi-feudal economic system in Haiti (directed by Kim Ives)

Dreams of Democracy (1988)
A documentary capturing the hopes of the people following the overthrow of the Duvalier regime (directed by Jonathan Demme)

Divine Horseman: The Living Gods of Haiti (1951)
A seminal black-and-white documentary on Haitian Vodou (directed by Maya Deren)

Haiti: Killing the Dream (1992)
An account of the events leading up to and following the 1991 military coup (directed by Katharine Keane and Rudi Stern)

Pig's Tale (1997)
A documentary that links Vodou, pigs and politics in Haiti (directed by Leah Gordon and Anne Parisio)

Rezistans (1997)
A film that traces the history of the democracy movement in Haiti (directed by Katharine Keane)

Films

The Comedians (1967)
A feature film, based on the Graham Greene novel, on life under the Papa Doc dictatorship, starring Richard Burton and Elizabeth Taylor

Serpent and the Rainbow (1990)
A horror film loosely based on Wade Davis' search for zombie powder

a renowned magic-realist writer. Carpentier uses baroque imagery and surreal detail to bring the period alive in a way no history book could achieve. *The Comedians*, by

Graham Greene, is a classic descent into 'Greene-land' set in Haiti during the reign of Papa Doc. Both an excellent, thoughtful novel and a somber portrayal of life under a dictatorship, it angered dictator Papa Doc so much that he banned the book in Haiti.

No Other Life, by Brian Moore, is a thinly veiled allegory based on the rise of Jean-Bertrand Aristide, the priest who became president. Through its protagonist, Jeannot, the novel investigates the effects of power on faith and the soul.

NEWSPAPERS & MAGAZINES

There is no shortage of newspapers in Haiti, most of which are produced in French. They are sold by street vendors and mostly cost 5 gourdes (US$0.30). *Le Matin* and *Le Nouvelliste* are both published daily, and *Haiti Progrés* and *Haiti en Marche* come out weekly. *Haiti Progrés* has a very good English section, while *Libète* is the leading weekly newspaper published in Creole.

You can subscribe to *Haiti Info*, an excellent English-language news and analysis bulletin. The Haiti Support Group in London also produces the bimonthly *Haiti Briefing*, which offers an overview of current news stories and focus articles. Contact for subscriptions:

Haiti Info
    (hib@igc.apc.org) Haiti Information Bureau, BP 15533, Pétionville, Haiti

Haiti Briefing
    (☎/fax 181-201-9878, haitisupport@gn.apc.org) Haiti Support Group, Trinity Church, Hodford Rd, London NW11 8NG, UK

RADIO & TV

Due to the high rate of illiteracy in Haiti, radio is the most common form of mass communication. There are 132 radio stations in the whole of Haiti, 26 of which are in Port-au-Prince. There are eight TV stations in Port-au-Prince. Most hotels have cable TV, mostly US channels, including CNN.

Radio Haiti Inter (106.1 FM) has good news broadcasts in French hourly from 9 am to 7 pm. It plays Haitian *racines*, French ballads, reggae and classical music, and has a great Latino music slot from 9:05 to 10 am.

Radio Timoun (90.9 FM) is a station run and presented in Creole by the children of the Selavi orphanage. The children collect the news and present bulletins every hour, punctuating a lively mix of contemporary music. Tropic FM (91.3 FM) has news bulletins in French every half-hour and plays a great mixture of rap, reggae, rock, racines and *compas*. If you are missing 'easy listening' music, you can tune in to the newly launched Sweet FM (99.7 FM), which offers nonstop schmaltz.

Both the Voice of America and the BBC World Service transmit in Haiti. The Voice of America can be found on a variety of frequencies on a short-wave radio: 7 to 7:30 am on 9525, 9670 or 11935 kHz, noon to 12:30 pm on 9525, 9670 or 11935 kHz, and from 5 to 5:30 pm on 13740, 15355 or 15385 kHz. The BBC World Service can be heard from 10 am to noon (GMT) on 15220 kHz and in the evenings from 9 pm to 4 am (GMT) on 5975 kHz.

ELECTRICITY

The electricity supply in Haiti is sporadic; most areas experience at least 12 hours blackout per day. There is no way of predicting when a blackout will occur. The most usual cycle is power for a couple of hours in the morning, nothing all day and, if you are lucky, power in the evening and through the night. Most hotels have a back-up generator so you won't experience any problems. But if you are thinking of staying in a more down-market establishment, pack a flashlight and buy some candles.

LAUNDRY

Most hotels can organize a next-day return laundry service for about US$3.50 for 10 items. The clothes are washed by hand and washers can be quite rough with them, so if you have something delicate it's probably best to wash it yourself.

TOILETS

There are no public toilet facilities in Haiti, but you can use the toilets in hotels or restaurants. Most Haitian men think nothing of urinating in the streets and, on long journeys, relieving oneself at the side of the road is often the only option. For women, this is more easily accomplished if you're wearing a loose-fitting skirt or dress.

HEALTH

It is not safe to drink the tap water in Haiti. It is advisable to check that your glass of water in a restaurant is Culligan (the local bottled water) and also that the ice in your drink is made from Culligan. Don't forget to carry bottled water with you, especially during long journeys. Some people advise against eating salads in smaller cafés as the vegetables may have been washed in tap water.

There is malaria in Haiti, and your doctor will advise you to take an antimalarial prophylactic. You must also pack a high-SPF suntan lotion if you have sensitive skin, as the sun is very powerful. See the Health section of the introductory Facts for the Visitor chapter for more information on diseases and treatments.

WOMEN TRAVELERS

Haiti is an easier place for a woman to travel alone than many countries in the region. The catcalls, whistles and leering that females may experience in many other places seem to be at a minimum. Haitian men do enjoy flirting and complimenting, but it usually isn't too overbearing and should be taken in good humor. It is not a problem for women to wear shorts in and around town.

GAY & LESBIAN TRAVELERS

There are few openly gay Haitians. But unlike some other places in the Caribbean, Haiti isn't a homophobic society. Some extremely effeminate Haitian artists are quite accepted. Since Baby Doc Duvalier clamped down on gay bars in the early 1980s following negative publicity about HIV/AIDS in Haiti, there are no overtly gay bars remaining.

DANGERS & ANNOYANCES

See the regional Facts for the Visitor chapter for general comments on theft and other crimes. Due to recent political turmoil, Haiti has been demonized by the media, but it

Haitian Divorce

The 1970s Steely Dan song 'Haitian Divorce' put Haiti on the map as the holiday destination for the quickie divorce. This still holds true, as Haitian law allows foreigners to obtain a divorce within 24 hours. There are two types of divorce available: bilateral divorce (divorce by mutual consent) and unilateral divorce.

Bilateral Divorce (mutual consent)
The plaintiff must appear in court with an attorney representing the defendant. The following documents must be hand-delivered by the plaintiff to the attorney in Port-au-Prince:

- the Defendant's Waiver – Special Power of Attorney signed by the defendant and notarized with a notarial seal or stamp.
- two copies of the Letter of Information, with all questions answered. This is available from your local Haitian embassy.
- the marriage certificate.

The decree will arrive by mail in two or three weeks, or in only two days if the client is willing to remain in Haiti.

Unilateral Divorce (by default)
The plaintiff must appear in court with a fully filled-out Letter of Information and the marriage certificate. Call your Haitian embassy for details.

---

actually still has a lower crime rate than some other Caribbean destinations. Nonetheless, the worsening economic situation and poverty fosters crime, and there have been reports of muggings. If threatened, you are advised to hand over any valuables and money immediately. The political situation can be volatile at times, usually during elections, and barricades can appear with alarming speed. Keep well out of the way of any burning barricades, or any other demonstrations, because you are rarely going to understand what is happening, and there is nothing to be gained from general voyeurism. Do not drive your car up to barricades. Find a place to turn around, and take another route. If there is any trouble in the capital, you would do best to remain in your hotel and take any advice that staff can give you.

Avoid visiting the slum areas, such as Cité Soleil off Rte Nationale 1 and Cité Liberté off Blvd Harry Truman, as no one likes to see a tourist when they are living in misery. It is advisable to avoid walking around deserted streets after dark; either drive or stick to busy areas. Be careful while driving at night, as many cars have no lights but drive as if they do. Manholes very rarely have covers, and if you don't watch out, you can get your car wheel badly stuck.

LEGAL MATTERS
Drugs are illegal in Haiti, and you will be jailed for possession of either marijuana or cocaine. If you are arrested for any reason, demand to call your embassy or even your hotel; they should be able to help you find a lawyer. If you are involved in a car accident, the law requires you to stop your car and call the police as soon as possible. In general, Haitian law presumes innocence until guilt is proven.

BUSINESS HOURS
Banks are generally open from 8:30 am to 1 pm but some of the more central branches are also now open from 2 to 4 pm. Shops and offices usually open weekdays at 7 am and

close at 4 pm, but many close earlier on Friday; most shops are also open on Saturday. Government offices are open 7 am to 4 pm weekdays, closing for an hour at midday.

PUBLIC HOLIDAYS & SPECIAL EVENTS

January 1 – *Independence Day*

January 2 – *Ancestors' Day*

January/February (3 days prior to Ash Wednesday) – *Carnival*

March/April – *Good Friday*

April 14 – *Pan-American Day*

May – *Ascension*

May 1 – *Agriculture and Labor Day*

May 18 – *Flag and University Day*

June – *Corpus Christi*

August – *Assumption Day*

October 8 – *Anniversary of Henri Christophe's death*

October 17 – *Anniversary of Jean-Jacques Dessalines' death*

October 24 – *United Nations Day*

November 1 – *All Saints Day (Gede)*

November 2 – *All Souls Day (Gede)*

November 18 – *Battle of Vertières Day/Armed Forces Day*

December 5 – *Discovery of Haiti Day*

December 25 – *Christmas Day*

It is worth planning your holiday to coincide with one of many special events that take place in Haiti.

Carnival, or Mardi Gras – on the three days leading up to Ash Wednesday – is a great experience. The Port-au-Prince Carnival has shed most of the traditional costumes, and the main attraction is the music. This Carnival can be hectic and is not for the claustrophobic, as the streets become packed with people. Haitians use Carnival as a time to let off a bit of steam, which means that there are ruckuses and fights as well as singing and dancing. All of Haiti's main bands play on rickety floats stacked with massive sound systems. Be prepared to wait until late into the night to see the floats carrying the bands, which play specially composed Carnival songs. If you want

to take part in the celebrations but can't stand the crush, you can buy a space on the many stands that surround the Holiday Inn. The Carnival celebrations in Jacmel are much more traditional, based around costumes and street theater rather than music, and they are much more enjoyable for the faint-hearted.

Carnival precedes Rara, which has been dubbed the 'rural Carnival.' In the week leading up to Easter, roads all over Haiti swell with bands of revelers, percussionists, and players of bamboo-and-tin trumpets. These bands are led by 'presidents,' 'colonels,' 'queens' and other members of the complex Rara band hierarchies. It is easy to become immersed in the groove of the wild, spiraling rhythms as a Rara band moves slowly along the road. Before you know it, you'll find you have followed the band for miles.

Two major Vodou pilgrimages take place each year. Saut d'Eau takes place on July 16 near a pretty village called Ville-Bonheur, which is off the Mirebalais road about 50km from the capital. Pilgrims travel there to bathe in the sacred waterfall and to visit a church built on the spot where the Virgin Mary supposedly appeared in a palm tree in 1884. Pilgrims from both beliefs, Catholicism and Vodou, make the pilgrimage to spiritually cleanse themselves. A Catholic Mass is said in the church and a statue of the Virgin Mary is carried around town. A lot of people can be seen holding up their passports to the Virgin, fervently praying for US visas.

Soon afterward, on July 25, is the festival of Plaine du Nord, a small village 15km southwest of Cap-Haïtien. This is the day of St James, who is linked with the Vodou spirit Ogou Ferraille. Pilgrims come from all over the country, wearing blue-and-red Vodou costumes. Many ceremonies and sacrifices take place, and those possessed by Ogou Ferraille bathe in a mud bath at the center of the celebrations. On July 26, which is the feast of St Anne, many of the celebrants move on to Limonade, about 15km southeast of Cap-Haïtien, for rituals for Erzulie, another Vodou spirit.

Gede, or *fètdemò*, takes place on November 1 and 2 and is well worth catching. The

HAITI

Foula, a Rara band, playing on the streets of Port-au-Prince

Gede are a family of spirits who are both the guardians of the cemetery and the lords of the erotic. People pile into the cemeteries to pour libations for Baron Samedi around blackened crosses festooned with candles, skulls and marigolds. A person possessed by Gede will whiten his or her face with powder to resemble a corpse, and act lasciviously toward other onlookers, especially foreigners. The uniform of Gede is black and purple clothes, a top hat and mirrored shades. Such large amounts of *clairin* (potent white sugarcane rum) are consumed that the air in the cemeteries is thick with its scent. Watch out for pickpockets in the crowded cemetery, and if a Gede is acting rather lewdly toward you, a few dollars should sort him or her out.

ACTIVITIES
Diving
Haiti's beaches are surrounded by coral reefs and historic wrecks waiting to be explored. At Amani, near St Marc, divers can descend along a famous wall, known locally as the Zombie Hole, that begins in about a meter of water and plunges 200m down. The hole is also the home of what is believed to be the world's largest sea sponge, the Elephant's Ear. Diving around Les Arcadins, a trio of sand cays, you can see gorgorians and sea fans surrounded by a variety of sponges. There is also a group of caves, called the Cave Gardens, which are replete with schools of grunts, glassy sweepers and hard-headed silversides. Near the coast of La Gonâve is a spectacular wall totally covered with black coral.

Pegasus Services (☎ 298-4640, 257-7352, 238-2471, 238-3140), PO Box 15785, Pétionville, run by Jose Roy, is one of the most reputable and professional dive companies, offering diving instruction and boat charters. It operates out of two beach resorts on the Côte des Arcadins, Kaliko and Moulin Sur Mer. Dives cost US$40 for one tank, US$70 for two tanks and US$50 for a night dive.

The best place to dive off the northern coast is near the beach resort of Cormier Plage (☎ 262-1000). Here, in the most historic part of the country, you can dive among cannons and wrecks of ships lost by the Dutch, French and Spanish during the 17th and 18th centuries; see the Northern Haiti chapter for details.

Hiking

Haiti was named for the Arawak word for 'mountainous land,' and with good reason: Hispaniola's mountains are the highest in the Caribbean. Even though deforestation in Haiti is very severe, there still remain some as-yet-undecimated areas that are beautiful for hiking. Walking in the mountains, you can still discover cloud forest, dense pine forests, alpine meadows, waterfalls and complex limestone cave systems. Haiti also has desert areas that support a rich variety of cacti. Two national parks, Macaya and La Visite, have been established in order to help preserve Haiti's natural riches, and it is possible to hike in both these areas; see the Southern Haiti chapter for details. The joy of trekking in these parks is that not only can you discover endemic birds, orchids and trees, but you also have the chance of observing the unchanged rural lifestyle of Haitian peasants. In La Visite in particular, hiking routes follow a major pedestrian highway used by local women transporting produce from deep in the mountains to the markets below.

Horseback Riding

Although seeing Haiti by horseback is a pleasant idea, there are very few trekking centers where one can do this. The Wahoo Bay Beach (☎ 223-2950/53, fax 222-5332, wahoo@dadesky.com), Rte Nationale 1, Km 64, Côtes des Arcadins, organizes day treks into the nearby Chaine des Matheux; see the Around Port-au-Prince chapter for details. There are horses for rent at Kenscoff around Carrefour Dourette and in Jacmel for trips to Bassins Bleu, but don't expect your horse to be the steeplechase standard. An equestrian center located in Port-au-Prince, the ECCE (☎ 257-7979, 257-5731), on Rue Frères Simmons, off Rte de l'Aeroport, has fit and healthy horses and gives private and group lessons in riding.

Bird Watching

A description of some of the birds found in Haiti can be found in the Flora & Fauna section of the Facts about Haiti chapter. Visitors to the Artibonite Valley may see many species of heron and egrets of all sizes feeding in the rice paddies, but the best place for water birds is northwest of Croix des Bouquets at Trou Caïman. This large, marshy lake is home to flamingos, herons, ibis and several duck species. From September until April, the area hosts many visiting shorebirds and the birds of prey that eat them, such as the merlin, a low-flying, marsh-loving falcon.

Trekking in the mountains or just hiking in the hills around Kenscoff, about 10km southeast of Pétionville, is another good way to see Haiti's birds. Anywhere you find brushy ground cover or remnant woodland at higher altitudes (the radio towers at Furcy, just south of Kenscoff, are a good place to start) could be home to ground warbler, red-legged thrush, stripe-headed tanager, greater Antillean bullfinch or Hispaniolan peewee. The Hispaniolan emerald, one of two native species of hummingbird, is easy to find sipping from flowers in and around Kenscoff. Hispaniolan parakeets are less common, but these big, green, long-tailed parrots can sometimes be seen squawking their way over cultivated fields. Golden swallows, which have golden-green top feathers and a white underbelly, flit across the tops of the ridges, and Antillean siskins are common wherever there are pine trees. Seeing the true high-altitude species like the threatened La Selle thrush and the white-winged warbler will require luck and a camping expedition to the highest mountaintops of Parc La Visite.

In the north part of Haiti are some remnant woodlands around the impressive Citadelle, one of the few protected areas in Haiti. Excellent birds, such as the Antillean piculet and scaly naped pigeon, are found in the wooded gullies along the north coast near the Cap-Haïtien beach resorts. Try looking along the tortuous dirt road that leads from Cap-Haïtien to Plage Labadie. Farther west, toward Mare Rouge and Môle St Nicolas, is one of the last Haitian habitats of the threatened Hispaniolan parrot. The plain pigeon, extremely rare in nearby Puerto Rico, remains fairly common here, although this area is brutally poor and the very last trees of any size are being chopped for charcoal production. The parrot probably also survives in the mountains of the extreme southwest, in the Parc Macaya.

At 7cm, the Vervain hummingbird is only a quarter-inch shy of being the smallest bird in the world, but it is much more common than Cuba's bee hummingbird. Frequent in gardens around Port-au-Prince, the Vervain hummer is the size of a largish bumblebee; you may have trouble convincing yourself it is actually a bird. Much bigger – as hummingbirds go – are the Antillean mangoes. You can watch them feeding while you sip a rum punch on the verandah of the Oloffson Hotel in Port-au-Prince. The males have glittering green throats and dusky purple tails; the females have grayish-white underbellies.

Although a spotting scope is a nice thing to have, especially for water birds, few travelers except the most bird-crazed are likely to tote one around. Binoculars, on the other hand, are invaluable – you will see few birds without them, and almost none well. As you wander the myriad paths that are everywhere in rural Haiti, be prepared for people who will ask you to take their picture; many have never seen binoculars before and are unaware of the difference between binoculars and a camera. You can give many people you meet the thrill of a lifetime, or at least the thrill of the week, simply by letting them have a peek through your field glasses into a world suddenly enlarged. Be sensible and sensitive – the cost of even a cheaper pair represents untold luxury to the average Haitian, so try not to inspire a desire for unobtainable consumer goods.

Recent years have seen very few birders visiting Haiti, and even amateur naturalists can make a significant contribution to the ornithology of the country. Many resident birds in Haiti are quickly disappearing, and range and distribution information is desperately needed by researchers. Keep good track of your sightings and take extensive notes on any birds that seem out of place or are difficult to identify, including details about habitat and altitude as well as the behavior of the bird. Even observations of where forest remains or where it is being cut can help. Any information you gather on your travels can be sent to Herbert Raffaele, *A Guide to the Birds of the West Indies*, Princeton University Press, Princeton, New Jersey 08544, USA.

WORK

Work is a rare commodity for Haitians. Only 150,000 of the population of 6.6 million are employed as wage earners. There are, however, some foreigners working in the volunteer sector in Haiti, many of whom work at clinics or orphanages. Much of this work is organized through religious groups in the USA. The Peace Corps has postings in Haiti, and the UK-based Voluntary Service Overseas (VSO; ☎ 181-780-2266) began work in Haiti in 1999.

The group that runs Hospice St Joseph (☎ 245-6177, HSJpap@maf.org), 33 Rue Acacia, Port-au-Prince, is looking for volunteers to help with their clinic and school programs. The qualities that they require are flexibility, ability to work in a team and to drive a standard (stick shift) car. In return, they will endeavor to teach you Creole.

ACCOMMODATIONS

Due to a lack of budget travelers, the budget hotels are not used to catering to tourists' needs. Hotels that are used to accommodating foreigners tend to be quite expensive, while in the cheaper hotels you can't expect constant electricity, hot water or too much security. There are no hostels in Haiti; camping is possible though not particularly wise.

FOOD

Two types of cuisine in Haiti exist in tandem, French and Creole, but American club sandwiches, pizzas and hamburgers are creeping onto most hotel menus. Most of the expensive restaurants and hotels will offer a French menu with a couple of Creole dishes. But if you eat on the street, in the countryside or in the small streetside cafés, the fare will be exclusively Creole.

Most cafés offer a *plat complet*, which usually consists of *diri ak pwa* (rice and beans), *bannann peze* (fried plantain), salad and your choice of meat – or more often, whatever is available. The meats offered are *poule* (fried chicken), *tasso* (deep-fried beef), *griyo* (fried pork), *kabri* (goat) and *lambi* (conch). The dish can be served with *sòs Kreyol* (tomato-based Creole sauce) or a *sòs vyann* (meat sauce). Rice and *diri djon djon* (black mushrooms) is a more exotic dish that's sometimes offered. Its wonderful, delicate flavor is supplied by the dried Haitian mushroom, djon djon. Another tasty staple of the Creole diet is *mayi moulen* (cornmeal mush), often cooked with kidney beans and flavored with peppers and coconut – a nice option for vegetarians when served with half of an avocado.

Women cook and sell food on most street corners, especially near markets and bus stations. Many sell fried plantains with a helping of *pikliz* (spicy pickled carrots and cabbage), which is a tasty snack costing less than 5 gourdes. A real specialty of the country is *soup jomou* (pumpkin soup), which is traditionally served for Sunday lunch.

DRINKS

Haiti produces wonderful coffee: Rebo and Haitian Blue are two brands that are produced mainly for export. You can buy good-quality ground coffee loose in the markets. All the usual American soft drinks are available too. If you spot an old beat-up top-loading freezer on the roadside, you can usually buy Coke or Pepsi, but the bottle must be returned to the vendor. If you ask for 'cola,' you will be served a locally produced soft drink, which is for the extremely sweet-toothed only. On the streets you will see boys selling small bottles of locally produced orange squash called Juna. These are safe to drink; the only problem they cause is the build-up of the non-biodegradable plastic bottles in the streets and drains. Cul-

Little Haiti in Miami

The most common route to Haiti from Europe is via the USA, which usually means an overnight stay in Miami, Florida. If you get stuck in Miami and want a little taste of Haiti before you get there, check out Tap Tap (☎ 305-672-2898), 819 5th St, Miami Beach, a Haitian restaurant near South Beach. Huge, colorful murals painted by Haitian artists cover the walls, making the place resemble a cross between a toy factory and a Vodou temple. The food is exclusively Haitian, and the restaurant serves typical dishes but with very imaginative twists to the flavors. The atmosphere is bustling and friendly, and Haitian musicians often play on the weekends. For a preview of the murals, some Haitian recipes and current events, check out their website at www.Tap-Tap.com.

ligan is the locally produced bottled water, which can also be bought in gallon containers for long trips.

Beer is quite expensive in Haiti, especially in hotels, where the price can be as high as US$3 per bottle. In the streetside bars you usually pay from two to four Haitian dollars for a beer. Prestige is the locally produced beer, but you can also buy Presidente, a fine beer from the Dominican Republic, and often you can find Beck's and Heineken Export. Bottled Guinness is made under license by the producers of Prestige. Haiti grows sugarcane, which is made into rum and clairin, the latter being a cheap, locally produced cane spirit. The Haitian rum company is called Barbancourt, and both their three- and five-star varieties are excellent. Most hotels serve their own rum punches, and rum sours (rum and lime) are certainly worth trying.

ENTERTAINMENT
Music

Two types of music battle for supremacy in Haiti, compas and racines. You can catch both types at many of the nightclubs in Pétionville and Kenscoff. Most of the bands advertise a week ahead of time on huge, hand-painted, wooden boards placed at busy road junctions. A new club in Port-au-Prince, Foula Vodou Jazz Club, is small and intimate, and showcases many up-and-coming racines bands. You can catch RAM, another racines band, every Thursday at the Hotel Oloffson. The government occasionally funds outdoor concerts on the bandstand on Champs de Mars in Port-au-Prince.

Clubs

Most of Haiti's clubs are in Pétionville, and they play compas music. There are also a few brothels/dance halls off the Carrefour road in Port-au-Prince.

Theater

You can catch some excellent Haitian plays at the Rex Theatre or the National Theater in Port-au-Prince. However, most Haitian playwrights write in Creole, so you may be a little lost without a serious grasp of the language.

Pubs/Bars

There's no real tradition of bars in Haiti. Most are inside hotels and are very expensive. All streetside cafés will sell beer at a far more reasonable price, and some of them are open late.

Cinemas

There are quite a few cinemas in Port-au-Prince that show the latest American releases dubbed into French.

SPECTATOR SPORTS

The newly renovated Sylvio Cator Stadium in Port-au-Prince hosts regular soccer matches which, thanks to a crowd that is both musical and vocal, can be good fun. Cockfighting is a popular spectator sport all over Haiti. There are *gagè* (cockfighting pits) hidden away in the back streets of most towns and dotted liberally around the countryside. The fights are not as vicious as in other countries, as the birds neither wear spurs nor fight to the death. If you can handle the blatant cruelty to

animals, it does provide a vibrant slice of Haitian culture. It is probably best to employ a guide for the day. The entrance fee is 10 gourdes (US$0.60), and you can buy food and drinks inside. As there are no official bookies inside, people bet against each other.

Before a fight, the two cocks are paraded in the pit, although there's usually more strutting done by the owners than the cocks. If you fancy a cockerel, you point it out to someone next to you. If they prefer the other cock, they will take your money, usually about 25 to 50 gourdes (US$1.75 to US$3.50), and keep hold of all the cash throughout the fight. If your bird wins, you've doubled your money, and if not, you lose your money. If you've chosen a definite winner, it will be difficult finding someone to bet you. Expect a very male atmosphere and a lot of shouting.

SHOPPING

Haiti has a broad and unique array of arts and crafts on offer; see Arts in the Facts about Haiti chapter. Craft skills are usually passed down through families, and consequently the production of the different crafts is confined to different parts of the island. If you want the best prices and choice, it is best to visit the areas where the artifacts are produced. There are some craft shops in the capital which sell a selection of goods (see Shopping in the Port-au-Prince chapter), but you will miss the enjoyment of meeting the artists and craft makers, and seeing how the goods are produced.

A large proportion of the Haitian metalworkers is based in Croix des Bouquets, a small town about 20km northeast of Port-au-Prince; see the Around Port-au-Prince chapter for details. Most of the sequined Vodou flags are produced in Bel Air, a section of Port-au-Prince north of the cathedral. If you hire a guide, he will take you from workshop to workshop, many of which are attached to Vodou temples; see Shopping in Port-au-Prince. Haiti produces wondrous papier-mâché works depicting giraffes, tigers and devils. These are produced exclusively in Jacmel along with delicately hand-painted boxes and trays. There is one road there, Rue

St-Anne, where you'll find all the workshops with their surreal produce laid out on the ground like a bizarre mythological tableau.

The Iron Market in Port-au-Prince has an area which sells handicrafts and Vodou paraphernalia. The experience can be a bit on the wild side, as every stallholder and hustler descends upon you, vying for your attention. The space is very claustrophobic, so keep calm or it will feel like a descent into Boschian hell. The vendors will always quote a price at least double what they are after, so be prepared to haggle.

Many stalls sell cheap paintings near the main post office on Rue Bonne Foi. If you wish to purchase more collectable, higher-quality Haitian art, make a trip to one of the many galleries in Pétionville, Port-au-Prince or Jacmel; see Shopping in the relevant city sections.

You must also shop with a conscience and avoid buying anything made from tortoise shell or black coral, which are endangered. Also, never buy parrots or snakes, especially the Haitian boa constrictor, as their numbers are falling rapidly.

Getting There & Away

AIR
Airports & Airlines

Haiti has one international airport, officially called the Guy Malary International Airport, but better known as Port-au-Prince International Airport, especially when booking tickets from abroad. Cap-Haïtien has the second-largest airport, but it serves only a few international flights.

Following is information for contacting airlines in Port-au-Prince:

Air Canada
(☎ 246-0441, 246-0442) Rte de l'Aeroport

Air France
(☎ 222-1700, 223-0172) Champs de Mars

Air Guadeloupe
(☎ 246-1215)

American Airlines
(☎ 223-1314, 223-1316) Ave Marie-Jeanne, Cité de l'Exposition, Bicentenaire
(☎ 249-0311/12/13/14)
Delmas 29/31, Autorama
(☎ 246-0100, 246-0159, 246-0205)
Rte de l'Aeroport

Antillean Airlines (ALM)
(☎ 222-0900) 69 Rue Pavée

Caribintair
(☎ 246-0737, 246-0778, 249-0203, 249-1575)
Rte de l'Aeroport

COPA Panama
(☎ 223-2326)
Rue de Quai, Madsen Export Import

See the introductory Getting There & Away chapter for details on international flights to Haiti.

Departure Tax

There is a departure tax of US$25 plus 10 gourdes (about US$1) payable when leaving Haiti by air. The tax is not included in the price of your air ticket.

LAND
Border Crossings

There are two points where you can cross from Haiti over to the Dominican Republic: Ouanaminthe/Dajabón in the north, and Malpasse/Jimaní in the south. The northern crossing links Santiago and Puerto Plata to Cap-Haïtien, and the southern crossing links Santo Domingo to Port-au-Prince; see the Port-au-Prince and Northern Haiti chapters for bus details. There is a smaller crossing point in the center of the country at Belladere/Elías Piña, but it's not a convenient place for tourists to enter Haiti as it's difficult to find public transportation.

When you leave Haiti, you must have your passport and the yellow entry card that you received upon arrival. When entering the Dominican Republic, travelers of certain nationalities must purchase a tourist card, which costs US$10; citizens of other countries need not pay anything. See each country's Facts for the Visitor chapter for further information on tourist cards, visas and other necessary documents.

Private motor vehicles must obtain government permission from the country of origin before they can cross the border. Rental vehicles are not allowed to cross from one country into the other.

Departure Tax

When leaving Haiti by land, there's a departure tax of US$10 plus 25 gourdes.

ORGANIZED TOURS

A company in the UK, Interchange (☎ 020-8681-3612, fax 020-8760-0031, interchange@interchange.uk.com), Interchange House, 27 Stafford Rd, Croydon, Surrey CRO 4NG, runs all-inclusive tours of Haiti.

Getting Around Haiti

AIR
There are two flights a day between Port-au-Prince and Cap-Haïtien on Caribintair (☎ 246-0778). These save you an arduous eight-hour drive, and cost US$45/70 one-way/roundtrip. Missionary Aviation Fellowship (MAF; ☎ 246-3993) has regular flights from Port-au-Prince to Hinche, Pignon and Dame Marie. You can also charter planes from MAF and from Bernard Celestin (☎ 257-8400). Charter flights are available to Dame Marie, Jérémie, Les Cayes, Jacmel, La Gonâve, Hinche, Pignon, Cap-Haïtien, Port-au-Paix and Mole St Nicolas.

BUS
Getting around by bus is the cheapest way to see Haiti. Fares vary from US$1 to US$7, depending on the destination. If you wish to pay a little more, you can sit up front with the driver. Traveling by bus is a good way of meeting people, and can be an entertaining experience at times. Buses can take you to places in Haiti that you would usually need a 4WD to reach.

There are no timetables; instead, buses usually leave the station once they are full. Each town has a departure point for buses. Port-au-Prince and Cap-Haïtien have several departure points, depending on the destination – which will be written on the front of the bus. See the relevant sections for details.

Buses are rarely in good condition, so don't be surprised if one breaks down at some point during the journey. Some of the buses are secondhand American school buses, and the others are ornate *taptaps* (brightly decorated converted pickups). The former are marginally more comfortable. Buses are usually overfilled, which is a tad nightmarish for the claustrophobic. Be prepared: the drivers take Rte Nationale 1 to Gonaïves really fast, which can seem, and is, very dangerous.

Smaller taptaps and minibuses shuttle people around Port-au-Prince on various fixed routes for about 3 gourdes (US$0.50)

a trip. Except for the departure and destination points, there seem to be no fixed stops; most people stick their hands out to hail a bus, and if it has space, it stops.

CAR & MOTORCYCLE
Generally speaking, driving in Haiti is dangerous. Most of the roads are terribly rutted, traffic signs are sorely lacking, and if you have an accident, you could encounter problems with angry locals. But if you drive carefully and use common sense, the experience need not be too traumatic.

Road Rules
It can be safely said that there are two sets of road rules, the official ones and the commonsense ones that will keep you alive. In Haiti the traffic laws follow the French system, and cars drive on the right-hand side of the road. If you have an accident, you are supposed to stop your car and call the police as soon as possible. This may not be too easy in the countryside as finding a telephone is difficult, so perhaps flag down another car. Remember to approach a situation with caution as tempers can run high after an accident.

The roads in Haiti are notoriously appalling. The main highways are potholed and cracked, and many of the secondary roads are impassable except in a 4WD. Sometimes the poor state of the roads can seem fortuitous, as many Haitians, especially truck and bus drivers, drive very fast on a good stretch of road. So, instead of moaning about the potholes, think of them as an efficient traffic-calming system.

Drivers rarely signal, so expect cars to swerve out in front of you unexpectedly, usually to avoid a hole. Don't depend on cars having any brake lights, either. When you overtake, use your horn liberally, as it is the main tool of communication between drivers. Many drivers use the horn instead of the brakes – so take heed. Also, when driving on winding roads, always sound your horn before blind corners. This is as much to avoid pedestrians as oncoming traffic. It is important to remember that you are sharing the road with people on foot as there are no sidewalks in the countryside, and in the cities those that do exist are usually overflowing with people. Always beep to warn people walking that you are coming, and they will make way – even in the most congested street, you can usually miraculously slip through.

Driving at night is difficult, and you must concentrate as the potholes, manholes without covers, and sometimes animals are difficult to see. Expect cars and bicycles to be using the roads with no lights at all.

It's not all doom and gloom, however. Driving in Haiti is certainly a challenge, but you can find yourself driving with a flair and aplomb you never knew you possessed before. In Port-au-Prince, if you drive with a bit of confidence and panache, you'll be surprised at how easy and enjoyable it can be. Try not to hesitate, as other drivers will become impatient, and remember to keep your sense of humor.

Rental

Unfortunately, due to a high percentage of accidents and auto burglaries involving rental cars, auto rental companies in Haiti charge premium rates. You can expect to pay at least US$60 a day, plus insurance, for an economy car. Generally the insurance is not comprehensive and it usually carries a high deductible. Furthermore, foreign drivers are often held liable for accidents whether they are at fault or not.

Many international rental companies operate in Haiti, and most of these have offices at Port-au-Prince airport; see Getting Around in the Port-au-Prince chapter for details. One of the most consistently reliable and affordable outfits is a local company called Secom (☎ 246-2799, 257-2847, 257-1913). It has offices at the airport and at 564 Rte de Delmas, Pétionville. If you have a breakdown anywhere in Port-au-Prince, they will drive out and repair or replace your vehicle. Rental fees vary from company to company but usually range from US$60

to US$75 a day. The fee decreases if you choose to rent a vehicle for a longer period.

BICYCLE

If you are a fit and skilled mountain biker, then the mountainous terrain of rural Haiti could be a dream, but you'd certainly be a pioneer in the field. There are no mountain-bike rental shops – you could ask a guide, who might be able to negotiate a private deal for you. Better yet, bring your own.

HITCHHIKING

It's extremely unusual to see foreigners hitchhiking in Haiti, but due to the low rate of car ownership and unreliable transport systems, Haitians are used to asking for a *rue libre* (free ride). See the warning about hitching, and other information regarding it, in the Getting Around Hispaniola chapter.

WALKING

Walking in the hills and mountains of Haiti can be a real pleasure; see Hiking in Haiti's Facts for the Visitor chapter.

BOAT

Passenger boats run from Wharf Jérémie, Port-au-Prince, to Jérémie in the west, but are not to be recommended as there are regular accidents, mainly due to overloading. Boats also leave from a wharf just north of the Ouanga Bay Beach Hotel on Rte Nationale 1 for Île de la Gonâve. This newly constructed wharf is on the site of Baby Doc's old beach house. Île de la Tortue is accessible by boats leaving daily from both St Louis de Nord and Port-de-Paix. Boats to Île-à-Vaches depart daily from Les Cayes.

LOCAL TRANSPORT

Port-au-Prince has a brilliant system of collective taxis called *publiques*, which charge 10 gourdes (about US$0.50) a trip. They're easy to recognize as they are fairly beat up and have a red ribbon hanging from the front mirror. A sharp *psst!* usually stops any publique within earshot. After the driver has been told where you wish to go, he will decide if he wants to take you. Publiques usually take up to four passengers in the back, and two more in the passenger seat in front. Don't expect the driver to take the most direct route to your destination, as the other passengers will have to be catered to as well.

If you get into an empty publique, make sure the driver doesn't take the red ribbon off the mirror. This is a fast one they sometimes try to pull on foreigners; it signifies that they are treating you as a private commission. If you want to hire a publique and driver for your private use, be sure to negotiate a price and be fairly clear as to what you want to do before the day starts – end-of-the-day negotiations tend to be tricky.

Nick's taxi service (☎ 257-7777) is handy for getting between Port-au-Prince and Pétionville. The cars are metered, and an average fare from Pétionville to downtown Port-au-Prince is US$6 to US$8.

ORGANIZED TOURS

In Port-au-Prince, Agence Citadelle (☎ 222-5900, 223-5900, fax 222-1792), 35 Place du Marron Inconnu, has a wide variety of tours on offer. These include a city tour of the main points of interest in Port-au-Prince, tours to cockfights and Vodou ceremonies, beach tours, and trips to Jacmel, Cap-Haïtien, Kenscoff and the Citadelle.

HAITI

Port-au-Prince

Port-au-Prince, Haiti's capital of 2 million people, sprawls from the docks and waterside slums of the bay up to the sides of the surrounding mountains, where it meets the more affluent town of Pétionville. It's a very colorful, animated city, teeming with people and traffic, and it can wear you out very quickly.

The walls of the city are decorated with wonderful murals and its streets adorned by the brightly painted *taptaps*, local buses blazing with surreal messages. However, garbage disposal is at a minimum, so be prepared for the dirt and pollution. There are also many distressing signs of poverty on the streets, such as children washing in ditches, desperate beggars and men working like packhorses. But the city also possesses many life-affirming sights. Haiti is a nation populated by resilient and determined people, such as the street barbers in Port-au-Prince who set up impromptu parlors powered by a line running from overhead electric cables, and students who study their books under gas station lights during blackouts.

The center of the city is compact and manageable on foot, and the rowdy street life is enthralling.

HISTORY

In 1742, Governor Marquis de Larnage obtained the agreement of the metropolitan authorities to commence development of a capital in a 'central, strategic and salubrious position.' On November 26, 1749, by order of the king of France, Port-au-Prince was declared the capital of what was then Saint-Domingue. The broad bay on which the city was to be built had been christened Port-au-Prince in 1706 by the captain of a French vessel named the *Prince,* which was anchored there. The initial site of the town extended from Bel Air to Rue Pavée, a tiny 78 hectares. It soon expanded to about 200 hectares and remained this size until the 1880s.

Toward the end of the 19th century, the city's wealthier residents, seeking shelter from political acts of arson and robbery, abandoned the town for a more rural site to the east of the capital. This created the suburb of Turgeau and, a little later, Bois Verna. At the same time, less salubrious areas were growing to the north on the marshy lands of La Saline. The US occupation of 1915 improved the city's infrastructure and hygiene, as drains were built and garbage was collected.

By 1948, the Estimé government had begun a plan to extend the capital, and built the road up to Pétionville. This heralded the beginning of the growth of the northern suburb, Delmas. In 1949, the waterfront area just south of the docks was remodeled to celebrate the city's bicentennial. The area, known as the Cité de l'Exposition or more informally as Bicentenaire, now contains the post office, city hall and parliament building. In the 1960s, the anarchic development of Port-au-Prince continued with the division of lands south of the city to accommodate the massive influx of people from the provinces. The sprawling suburb of Carrefour was established, though without any state services or infrastructure. Since that time, Port-au-Prince has continued to grow like a wild plant, with very little state intervention or planning. Due to continuing rural exodus, the population has grown from 150,000 in 1954 to the approximately 2 million of today.

ORIENTATION

The unregulated growth of Port-au-Prince means that there is no simple street grid system (as in Cap-Haïtien), and getting to know your way around can be tricky. The old commercial area, known as *centre ville* or downtown, lies just east of the dockside area, Bicentenaire. Here, boxed in by Rue Pavée and Rue des Fronts Fort running east/west, and Rue du Quai and Rue Montalais running north/south, is the teeming heart of Port-au-Prince. The streets are packed with so many people, cars, taptaps and vendors that it's difficult to see the rickety, colonial-style buildings that line them. The Notre Dame Catholic Cathedral, the Sainte Trinité Episcopalian Cathedral and the Marché de Fer (Iron Market) are all situated in this area.

A large park, the Champs de Mars, lies south of Rue Pavée. This is a good central reference point for visitors as it is flanked to the east by Rue Capois, where most of the main downtown hotels and restaurants are situated. The park also contains the Palais National (National Palace) and both the Musée du Panthéon Nationale (National Pantheon Museum) and the Musée d'Art Haïtien (Museum of Haitian Art). Rue Capois continues southwards to join Ave H Christophe, where the Hotel Oloffson is located. East of Ave H Christophe, steep roads lead up to the tranquil old suburban area of Pacot, where many of the old gingerbread buildings are located.

Blvd Jean Jacques Dessalines (also known as Grand Rue) is the major north/south road running through the downtown area. It joins Rte Nationale 1, which leaves the city for Gonaïves and Cap-Haïtien to the north, and Rte Nationale 2, which heads southwest for Jacmel and Les Cayes. There are two main roads that run southeast from Blvd Jean Jacques Dessalines toward Pétionville. One is the Ave John Brown (also called Lalue), which is an extension of Rue Pavée, and the other, farther north, is the seemingly never-ending Rte de Delmas. A lot of the more exclusive hotels are just off Ave John Brown, which skirts the districts of Nazon and Bourdon before arriving at Pétionville. Halfway up the steep climb to Pétionville, Ave John Brown changes to Ave Pan Américaine.

Delmas is the name of the residential sprawl that surrounds both sides of the Rte de Delmas. All of the side roads that join Rte de Delmas are numbered: Delmas 1, Delmas 2, Delmas 3, etc. The streets to the north have odd numbers; those to the south have even numbers. The lowest numbers begin soon after Blvd Jean Jacques Dessalines, and increase toward Pétionville. Ave H Selassie, a continuation of Delmas 13, is the main route to the Port-au-Prince airport.

Many roads in Port-au-Prince are often referred to by colloquial names not shown on maps. Following are some of the most common routes with alternative names:

Blvd Harry Truman	Bicentenaire
Ave Martin Luther King	Nazon
Ave John Brown	Lalue
Ave Lamartinière	Bois Verna
Ave Jean Paul II	Turgeau
Ave Paul IV	Rue des Casernes
Blvd Jean Jacques Dessalines	Grand Rue

Maps

It's next to impossible to get a good street map of Port-au-Prince before arriving in Haiti, but once you're here you'll find a few knocking around. Bookstores don't appear to stock them, but they can be found in supermarkets, car rental agencies and on stalls in front of the post office on Rue Bonne Foi. The Association of Haitian Hoteliers produces a fairly efficient street map of Port-au-Prince, which is available free from most car rental companies or sold for US$1 outside the main post office. The *Carte d'Haiti* (produced in association with Sogebank) sells for US$3 at most major supermarkets. The map of Port-au-Prince on the back is excellent, and it shows all the different areas very clearly. This is a good map for acquainting yourself with the layout of the city.

Shell Oil Company also publishes a superior street map of Port-au-Prince and its environs that can be purchased from Shell gas stations and from outside the main post office for US$2. This is the only map with an all-important street index (and the location, naturally, of every Shell gas station in town). It also has a detailed map of Rte Nationale 2 as it passes through the sprawling suburb of Carrefour.

INFORMATION
Tourist Offices

The Maison de Tourisme (☎ 222-8659), on Rue Capois, in a white gingerbread building at the corner of Rue Magny, is a good source of information for travelers. For further information, contact the Secretary of State for Tourism (☎ 223-2143, 223-5631, fax 223-5359), at Rue Lègitime upon the

HAITI

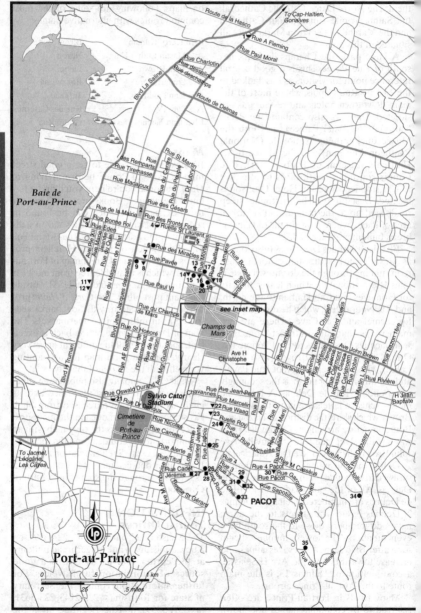

HAITI

*Baie de
Port-au-Prince*

Port-au-Prince

0   .5   1 km
0   25   .5 miles

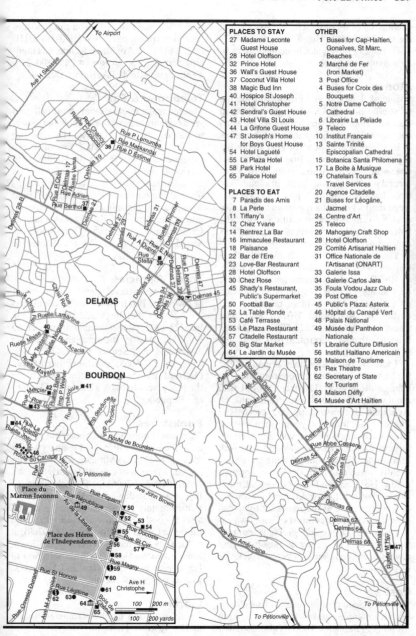

PLACES TO STAY
27 Madame Leconte Guest House
28 Hotel Oloffson
32 Prince Hotel
36 Wall's Guest House
37 Coconut Villa Hotel
38 Magic Bud Inn
40 Hospice St Joseph
41 Hotel Christopher
42 Sendral's Guest House
43 Hotel Villa St Louis
44 La Grifone Guest House
47 St Joseph's Home for Boys Guest House
   Hotel Lagueté
54 Le Plaza Hotel
58 Park Hotel
65 Palace Hotel

PLACES TO EAT
7 Paradis des Amis
8 La Perle
11 Tiffany's
12 Chez Yvane
14 Rentrez La Bar
16 Immaculee Restaurant
21 Plaisance
22 Bar de l'Ere
23 Love-Bar Restaurant
28 Hotel Oloffson
30 Chez Rose
45 Shady's Restaurant, Public's Supermarket
51 Football Bar
52 La Table Ronde
53 Café Terrasse
55 Le Plaza Restaurant
57 Citadelle Restaurant
60 Big Star Market
64 Le Jardin du Musée

OTHER
1 Buses for Cap-Haïtien, Gonaïves, St Marc, Beaches
2 Marché de Fer (Iron Market)
3 Post Office
4 Buses for Croix des Bouquets
5 Notre Dame Catholic Cathedral
6 Librairie La Pleïade
9 Teleco
10 Institut Français
13 Sainte Trinité Episcopalian Cathedral
15 Botanica Santa Philomena
17 La Boite à Musique
19 Chatelain Tours & Travel Services
20 Agence Citadelle
21 Buses for Léogâne, Jacmel
24 Centre d'Art
25 Teleco
26 Mahogany Craft Shop
28 Hotel Oloffson
29 Comité Artisanat Haïtien
31 Office Nationale de l'Artisanat (ONART)
33 Galerie Issa
34 Galerie Carlos Jara
35 Foula Vodou Jazz Club
39 Post Office
45 Public's Plaza: Asterix
46 Hôpital du Canapé Vert
48 Palais National
49 Musée du Panthéon Nationale
51 Librairie Culture Diffusion
56 Institut Haitiano Americain
59 Maison de Tourisme
61 Rex Theatre
62 Secretary of State for Tourism
63 Maison Défly
64 Musée d'Art Haïtien

HAITI

Champs de Mars, or the Haitian Association for the Tourism & Hotel Industry (☎ 257-4647, fax 257-6137), at Choucoune Plaza in Pétionville.

Money

Sogebank, Unibank and Promobank are the most efficient banks for foreign travelers in Port-au-Prince. Banking hours vary between companies and their branches. All branches of Promobank are open 8:30 am to 1 pm, except for the Pétionville branch, which also opens in the afternoon, from 3 to 5 pm weekdays. Most Sogebank branches are open from 8:30 am to 3 pm weekdays, and some until 5 pm, but a few branches are also open 8:30 am to 1 pm on Saturday. All of the banks exchange US dollars only, and this extends to traveler's checks as well.

You can find central Unibanks at 118 Rue Capois (☎ 223-1876) and at Public's Plaza, 65 Rue Rosa, which is commonly called Rte du Canapé Vert (☎ 245-1400). Promobank (☎ 222-2461) has its main branch at the corner of Ave John Brown and Rue Lamarre. Sogebank (☎ 229-5000) has a huge branch with an underground parking garage at Delmas 30.

There are often long lines at many of the banks, so you may find it more convenient to change money on the street. You'll find moneychangers outside the Promobank on Ave John Brown and up and down Rue Pavée – just look for young men waving large wads of money. If you get a crowd around you, choose one guy and deal with him alone. These moneychangers give a slightly lower rate than the banks, approximately US$1 less on US$100 changed, but it can be worth it to avoid the inconvenience of waiting in line at the banks, and you can even do it from the comfort of your own car if you wish. Don't change conspicuously large amounts of money on the street, and always count your gourdes before you let go of your dollars.

Post

The city's main post office is on Rue Bonne Foi, Bicentenaire, and is open 8 am to 4 pm Monday to Saturday. There is also a smaller post office on Delmas 45. You can send and receive express parcels mailed via DHL (☎ 223-8133), 29 Ave Marie Jeanne, Bicentenaire, and near the airport (☎ 246-4800, 246-4900), 17 bis Rte de l'Aéroport, Delmas.

Telephone & Fax

You can make international phone calls and send faxes from most large hotels, but expect to pay dearly for the service. The cheaper option is to buy an MCI long-distance calling card or use Teleco, the Haitian state service. There are a number of Teleco offices dotted around the city, including one downtown at the corner of Rue Pavée and Blvd Jean Jacques Dessalines (☎ 223-0400) and one at the corner of Rue Capois and Rue Cameau, a block north of Hotel Oloffson. See Haiti's Facts for the Visitor chapter for costs and details.

Travel Agencies

There are many travel agencies in the center of town. The two most reputable companies are Agence Citadelle (☎ 222-5900, 223-5900, fax 222-1792, citagen@haitiworld.com), 35 Place du Marron Inconnu, and Chatelain Tours & Travel Service (☎ 223-2400, 223-2961, fax 223-5065), on the corner of Rue Geffrard and Ave John Brown, which are the best places to book a bus to the Dominican Republic.

Bookstores

The most comprehensive bookstore in Port-au-Prince is Librairie La Pléïade (☎ 222-4561), at 83 Rue des Miracles, which even has a small selection of English language books. Asterix (☎ 257-2605), at Public's Plaza, 65 Rue Rosa (Rte du Canapé Vert), has a selection of mainly French-language books and also a good selection of stationery. The Librairie Culture Diffusion (☎ 223-9260), at 5 Rue Capois, is handy to many of the downtown hotels and stocks a wide selection of US magazines such as *Time* and *Newsweek*, usually only one week old.

Libraries

There is a good English-language library at the Institut Haitiano Americain (call

☎ 222-2947, 222-3715), at the corner of Rue Capois and Rue St Cyr, which is open 8 am to noon and 1 to 5 pm weekdays. There is also a library at the Institut Français (☎ 222-2051, 222-3720), at the junction of Blvd Harry Truman and Rue Paul VI.

Cultural Centers

In addition to having a library, the Institut Français (see above) holds music concerts, lectures, exhibitions and literary evenings, and is an information center for French citizens.

Laundry

Most hotels, even the smallest, will be willing to wash your laundry. Expect to pay between US$3 and US$6, depending on the size of your load.

Medical Services

All the main hotels can recommend a designated doctor. In the case of an emergency, the private Hôpital du Canapé Vert (☎ 245-0205, 245-0281, 245-0984), at 83 Rte du Canapé Vert, has a 24-hour emergency department and its own private ambulance service. The hospital is highly recommended by the expatriate community and has some excellent doctors. Prices are high, so medical insurance is a must in Haiti. Sometimes the hospital will ask for a deposit of US$500 before they admit you, so carry a credit card. If you have problems making the immediate payment, call your consulate.

Regular doctors usually charge about US$15 to US$20 an hour for a consultation – your consulate can supply you a list of recommended clinics. Medicine is sold over-the-counter at pharmacies, and prescriptions seem to be immaterial.

Emergency

Emergency telephone numbers include the following:

Police	☎ 114, 222-1117
Fire	☎ 115, 223-1028, 223-1029
Red Cross	☎ 118, 245-1171

There are two Red Cross blood-transfusion centers: one at 100 Rue Miracles (☎ 223-1033,

223-1034, 222-5498), and the other at Hôpital Universite (☎ 222-9676), on Ave Mgr Guilloux.

Dangers & Annoyances

Street crime is increasing in Port-au-Prince, so take sensible precautions. Don't be ostentatious, don't wear a lot of jewelry and don't keep your dollars in your back pocket as the pickpockets are skillful. It's wise not to change more than US$100 on the street as there have been increasing incidents of people being followed and robbed. A great danger on the streets of Port-au-Prince is the uncovered manholes – you really have to keep your eyes on the ground. Imagining what you might fall into at the bottom of these holes is far more frightening than any injuries you might sustain on the way.

THINGS TO SEE & DO

The joy of downtown Port-au-Prince is that most of the sights are within easy walking distance of one another. It is worth hiring a guide, who will at least deter other would-be guides and watch out for you. Many guides hang around outside of the hotels and charge about US$10 a day. Milfort Bruno, who owns the brightly painted Mahogany Craft Shop outside the gates of Hotel Oloffson, is a very good storyteller, trustworthy and comes highly recommended. If you'd

Port-au-Prince street scene

like a driving guide, try a guide named Alex, or Gesner Pierre, both of whom can usually be found nearby. It is customary to buy your guide lunch during the day.

Museums

The **Musée du Panthéon National** (☎ 222-3167), on Ave de la Liberté at the Champs de Mars, is a modern, mostly subterranean museum in its own small garden. The names of men who fought in the battles for independence are carved into the walls, and there is a permanent exhibition that shows the history of Haiti from slavery to the present day. Among the items of historical interest are the silver pistol with which King Henri Christophe took his life and the rusting anchor of Columbus' flagship, the *Santa María*. Admission to the permanent exhibit is free; open 10 am to 4 pm weekdays.

The **Musée d'Art Haïtien** (☎ 222-2510), at the southern edge of Champs de Mars, is on the corner of Rue Capois and Rue Légitime. It has a permanent collection of Haiti's finest naïve art, including excellent work by Hector Hyppolite, Préfète Duffaut, Philomé Obin and Robert St Brice. It also holds rotating retrospectives of the work of current painters, artists from the diaspora, and photographers. There is a small craft shop at the side and a quiet garden restaurant at the rear. The museum is open 10 am to 4 pm Monday to Saturday; admission is 10 gourdes (US$0.50)

Close to the Musée d'Art is the **Maison Défly**, on Rue Légitime, a good example of a late-19th-century gingerbread. It contains a small museum with period Creole furniture. It's open 9 am to 1 pm weekdays; free admission.

Churches

If you begin in the center of town, your first port of call should be the **Sainte Trinité Episcopalian Cathedral.** The entrance is on the corner of Ave Mgr Guilloux and Rue Pavée. The church is architecturally uninteresting, but inside it is decorated with fantastic biblical murals painted by the country's greatest 'naïve' artists, including Philomé Obin,

Wilson Bigaud and Castera Bazile. There is a very good gift shop in the school attached to the cathedral. The **Notre Dame Catholic Cathedral**, on the corner of Rue Dr Aubry and Rue Bonne Foi, a few blocks to the north, is the city's largest ecclesiastical building. Completed in 1915, it's a huge pink-and-yellow stone structure with two domed towers on its west face. There are often worshippers fervently praying on the steps leading up to the entrance, and small stalls selling Catholic ephemera surround the cathedral.

Marché de Fer

The Marché de Fer (Iron Market) is about four blocks west of the Notre Dame Cathedral at the junction of Ave Jean Jacques Dessalines (Grand Rue) and Rue des Fronts Forts. This amazing red market, built of pre-cast iron in 1889, is eastern in design and resembles an Arabian Nights mosque, complete with minarets. It was manufactured in Paris, loosely modeled on the city's 19th-century marketplace, Les Halles, and inaugurated on November 22, 1891, by President Florvil Hyppolite.

It takes a strong stomach to enter the market for the first time, as the attack on your senses is total. The population is loud and raucous, and the fetid aroma of spices, rotting fruit, raw meat and urine is suffocating. One half of this hellish treasure-trove is a food market piled high with strange fruit, heaps of gray salt, baskets of dried mushrooms, bird cages and kitchen implements made from oil cans. The other side is a craft market selling naïve paintings, wood carvings, sequined flags, straw hats and all sorts of Vodou ephemera. Here in a hidden corner you'll find Vodou artist Pierro Barra. As wild as any surrealist, Pierro builds massive sculptures using dolls, mirrors and sequins. This is Vodou kitsch to the extreme, notably the Barbie dolls in small velvet coffins covered with golden braids and glass jewels.

Champs de Mars

The other main area for sightseeing is the Champs de Mars, the large park built in 1953 that runs from the **Palais National** to Rue Capois. The Palais National stands on the same site as its two predecessors, both destroyed during political unrest in 1869 and 1912. The three-domed, pristinely white building was completed in 1918 and modeled on the White House in Washington, DC. The palace is always under armed guard and never open to the public. The **Place des Héros de l'Independence** is in front of the palace. This square contains the statues of the founders of independent Haiti: Jean-Jacques Dessalines, Alexandre Pétion, Henri Christophe, Toussaint L'Ouverture and Marron Inconnu, the runaway slave blowing the conch-shell trumpet and calling all to begin the revolution.

Gingerbread Architecture

The city's gingerbread buildings, mostly built at the beginning of the 20th century, are characterized by their graceful balconies, detailed wooden latticework and Gothic designs. Most buildings can be found in the areas of Pacot and Bois Verna and are predominantly residential. You can see some good examples on Ave Lamartinière, at Nos 48, 52 and 84; at 15 Rue M; 126 Ave John Brown; and 2 Rue 4 in Pacot.

If you continue south along Rue Capois from the Musée d'Art Haïtien, you'll come to the gates of the **Hotel Oloffson** at the end of the street. The hotel is one of the finest examples of gingerbread architecture in Port-au-Prince.

Hotel Oloffson

LEAH GORDON

HAITI

Cimetière de Port-au-Prince

If you take Rue Alerte, west of the Hotel Oloffson, you will discover the Port-au-Prince Cemetery, a vast necropolis of pastel-colored tombs. Some of the elevated burial chambers are bigger and more ornate than most of the shanties in the slums. Be warned, you may well trip over an open coffin or two, due to activities of grave robbers! If you visit during Gede (Haiti's Day of the Dead) celebrations on the 1st and 2nd of November, you should certainly check out the cemeteries as most of the festivities take place there.

Horseback Riding

ECCE (☎ 257-7979, 257-5731), an equestrian center on Rue Frères Simmons off Rte de l'Aeroport, has fit and healthy horses and gives private and group lessons in riding.

ORGANIZED TOURS

Agence Citadelle (☎ 222-5900, 223-5900, fax 222-1792), 35 Place du Marron Inconnu, organizes tours of Port-au-Prince, Pétionville and Kenscoff.

PLACES TO STAY

Most of the city's hotels and restaurants are in Pétionville, a wealthy suburb above Port-au-Prince, and these are listed in the Around Port-au-Prince chapter. But to get the true, unsanitized feel of Port-au-Prince, you are advised to stay downtown at least some of the time. In addition to the following, there are also several small, very inexpensive (under US$25) hotels on Ave Jean Jacques Dessalines, most of which cater to locals.

Budget

The *Hotel Lagueté* (no phone), at 5 Rue Ducoste, a narrow street along the side of the Le Plaza Hotel, is tucked away behind a gate on the left and easily missed. The hotel is a rickety old gingerbread with a cool tiled floor, a brightly decorated wooden staircase and colonial furniture. It has 24 rooms with shared bathrooms and only cold water, but at US$90 a month it's a real bargain. It's also clean, central and has car parking. Prices for shorter stays can be negotiated.

There is a small, family-run *guest house* (☎ 222-9703) run by Madame Leconte at 54 Rue Cadet Jérémie, facing a park close to the Hotel Oloffson. For US$10 a night you get a clean and light room with shared bathroom, and a breakfast of bread, coffee and an omelette. There is no generator, so expect intermittent electricity. If you just need somewhere to crash, this place is perfect as it's close to the center and well located for finding *publiques* (public taxis).

Mid-Range

For a unique Haitian experience, you can stay at *St Joseph's Home for Boys Guest House* (☎ 257-4237, sjfamily@haitinews.com), 48 Rue Herne; from Rte de Delmas, take the first right and an immediate right off Delmas 91. The guest house supports a program for street children and a home for boys. Its 11 rooms (with shared bath) can accommodate up to 36 guests and cost US$20 per person, including breakfast and an evening meal (vegetarians are well catered for). Most rooms contain two bunk beds, and you may be expected to share depending on availability. In an effort to respect water conservation, the hospice doesn't have running water in its bathrooms, but you can draw from a large tank for taking bucket showers and flushing toilets. There's always electricity, thanks to a solar- and wind-powered generator on the roof. The rambling seven-story house has many indoor and outdoor lounge areas, including a chapel and roof terrace with a fantastic view, so it's easy to find a private place to relax. The boys also earn money by teaching drumming, dance and Creole to guests.

Magic Bud Inn (☎ 246-3108) is the first left off Delmas 33 coming from Rte de Delmas, behind the Tele Haiti building on Rue Stella. It has 35 rooms, all with showers, for US$40 per person. There is a restaurant and bar adjacent to a big yard containing a fair-sized swimming pool. *Wall's Guest House* (☎ 249-4317, fax 249-0505) is at 8 bis Rue Mackandal, where it crosses Delmas 19. This homely guest house is run by a Canadian couple, and its relaxed, cheerful atmosphere attracts numerous young volunteers working in the country. For US$25 per night, you get a room shared with three to five others, breakfast and an evening meal, shared shower facilities, constant electricity and the use of a small, clean swimming pool.

Perched high above the busy street of Christ Roi, *Hospice St Joseph* (☎ 245-6177, HSJpap@maf.org), 33 Rue Acacia, commands perhaps one of the most stunning views of Port-au-Prince. The rooms are sweet and clean, and all have fans, bathrooms and balconies overlooking the city and the bay. The cost of US$25 per person includes breakfast and an evening meal of Haitian cuisine, primarily vegetarian. In addition to functioning as a guest house, the hospice supports local health care and food/human-rights/education programs in the area, and thus it attracts many justice and human-rights groups. The atmosphere is very relaxed, and as a guest you're expected to pitch in and help now and then. Book in advance with a US$25 deposit mailed to Sister Ellen Flynn, Lynx Air, PO Box 407139, Fort Lauderdale, Florida 33340, USA. Pickup at the airport can be arranged for a fee.

La Grifone Guest House (☎ 245-0585, 245-3440, 245-4095), at 21 Rue Jean Baptiste, has three stories of balconied rooms built around a courtyard with a pool. The 49 rooms have private bathrooms with hot and cold water. It is well priced at US$25 per person including breakfast and an evening meal. The place has a slightly deserted feel, and it is perhaps not the best place to stay if you are conducting any kind of business, as messages are not always passed on from the reception. *Sendral's Guest House* (☎ 245-6052), 7 Rue Mercier, is a well-loved old guest house with simple verandah, TV lounge and a lovely, overgrown garden that overlooks the Bourdon district. It's in a quiet area away from the traffic, where little more than women's song interrupts the peace. There are 20 rooms with private bathrooms and hot and cold water that cost US$30 including breakfast.

The *Coconut Villa Hotel* (☎ 246-0712, 246-1691, 246-1672) is a motel-style complex on Rue Berthol just off Delmas 19. It has 50 rooms with air con, private bathrooms, TVs and telephones. Its rooms cost US$40/55 to US$45/72 for a single/double, including breakfast. There is a back-up generator for constant electricity, ample car parking, and a large swimming pool, bar and restaurant set in well-kept gardens.

The *Park Hotel* (☎ 222-4406), 23 Rue Capois, is a sleepy old townhouse set back from the busy road and surrounded by shady gardens. It offers a blend of old and modern Haitian life, combining a peaceful family hotel with the hustle and bustle of downtown Port-au-Prince. The 28 rooms with private bathrooms, hot and cold water and superbly powerful showers cost US$30/40 to US$34/44. Breakfast is not included but is available. The hotel also offers longer-term deals on four apartments and two studios within the grounds. Secure car parking is available at the front of the hotel.

If you're stuck for a place to stay, just down the street is the *Palace Hotel* (☎ 222-3344, 223-4455), at 55 Rue Capois, with a remarkable black-and-white tiled entrance, but there it ends. The 70 or so rooms have seen better days, and can only offer cold water at US$30/36/40 for a single/double/triple. Car parking is available at the front of the hotel. The *Prince Hotel* (☎ 245-2764, 223-0100, 223-0126, 222-2765, fax 245-2765) is on the corner of Ave N and Rue 3 in Pacot, a peaceful district of Port-au-Prince. It has 20 rooms, all with air-conditioning and private bathrooms for US$64/79; breakfast is US$6 extra. The facilities include a swimming pool, bar and restaurant.

Hotel Villa St Louis (☎ 245-6241, 245-6417, 245-7149, fax 245-7949), 95 Rte de Bourdon (this is the name Ave John Brown takes as it runs through Bourdon), is on the corner of Rue Mercier. The hotel is much nicer inside than out and contains many hidden leafy courtyards and a pleasant rooftop swimming pool and terrace. The rooms are clean and many have their own small sitting rooms; US$45/65/85 for a single/double/triple, including breakfast.

Top End

Graham Greene set his novel *The Comedians* at the capital's infamous *Hotel Oloffson*

(☎ 223-4000, 223-4102, fax 223-0919), at the junction of Rue Capois and Ave H Christophe, and its almost mythological status has continued to grow. The elegant, white gingerbread building with turrets, lace grillwork and verandahs is set in a walled garden at the southern end of Rue Capois. The mahogany bar is surrounded by rattan furniture in a room with one wall hewn out of the red rock hill on which the hotel stands. The walls are draped with sequined Vodou flags and a great collection of Haitian art. Most Thursday nights there is live entertainment by the owner's Vodou rock band, RAM. The gardens are beautifully lit at night and contain a swimming pool and outdoor bar/terrace. The Oloffson is a very social hotel, and it's easy to make friends with the other guests on the verandah, where the meals are served. The price for a standard room with private bathroom is US$66 per night, including tax and energy charge. The spacious and more individual bungalows cost US$87 per night and the splendid 1st-floor suites are US$108; there's an US$10 charge for a second person in all rooms. A continental breakfast is included in the price.

Le Plaza Hotel (☎ 223-9800, 223-8697, 223-9773, 222-0766, fax 223-7232), 10 Rue Capois, was formerly the Holiday Inn and is still referred to as such by most people. It's centrally located and contains 104 rooms around a tropical garden and clean swimming pool. All the rooms have air con, telephones, radios, TVs and laundry service. Rooms range from US$65/75 to US$85/95, plus 10% tax and a US$5 per day energy charge.

The *Hotel Christopher* (☎ 245-6125, 245-6124), at 11 Rue Theodule off Ave John Brown, is a '70s-style hotel on a hill in Bourdon. This is quite a handy location, halfway between downtown Port-au-Prince and Pétionville. The hotel is attractive, with a light and spacious restaurant overlooking a large swimming pool and terrace. It has more than 70 rooms, 16 of which are studio apartments with kitchenettes. All the rooms have radio, TVs, air con, private bathrooms with hot and cold water and private balconies for US$70/87/102 singles/doubles/triples. Apartments cost US$700/800 per month.

PLACES TO EAT

Most of the hotels in downtown Port-au-Prince have Haitian, French and American menus, but most of the restaurants are small and cheap and serve simple Haitian dishes. Dining cheaply in the evening can be a bit of a problem downtown as a lot of places close at 6 pm, but it's not impossible. *Big Star Market*, on Rue Capois next to the Rex Theatre, is the most central supermarket for downtown hotels, and there's a *Public's Supermarket* at Public's Plaza, on Rte du Canapé Vert.

Budget

The *Football Bar* (☎ 223-7945), on the corner of Rue Capois and Rlle Piquant, is a lively local bar and restaurant. It's rough and ready with lots of atmosphere – the walls covered with old, fading soccer posters. The place serves a good range of Haitian dishes for about US$3 and local beers for US$1. As you can imagine, it's soccer mad, and the TV in the corner is one of the liveliest places to watch a match in Port-au-Prince outside of the stadium. It's open 8 am to 11 pm.

Immaculee Restaurant, at 176 Rue Pavée, is a lovely old red-and-white wooden building. Inside it's cool and shady, complete with a huge fan and an even bigger poster of Bob Marley. You can get the chicken *plat complet* for US$3.

Farther along the same street, opposite the Sainte Trinité Cathedral, is *Rentrez La Bar*, at 146 Rue Pavée, which is smaller and a bit rougher but very cheap, with spaghetti for under US$1. Also on Rue Pavée, on the block between Rue du Centre and Grand Rue (otherwise known as Blvd Jean Jacques Dessalines), *La Perle* is a bit more upmarket. It's large, air-conditioned, clean and comfortable with a varied menu. You can get *poulet noir* (a Haitian chicken specialty cooked with dried mushrooms called *djon djon*) for US$5. There's also a special set meal every day, including drink and dessert for US$4.50. Opposite, at No 43, is the *Paradis des Amis*, a lively restaurant on two levels with air-conditioning and a fine selection of Haitian dishes with chicken priced at about US$3.50.

The **Love-Bar Restaurant**, at 84 Rue Capois, is a great little streetside restaurant. For US$2.50, you can get splendid fried chicken with a huge plate of fragrant rice and beans, salad, plantains and a beer for less than US$1. It's a cheerful place, open from 7 am to 10 pm. One block north on Rue Capois, you can find the **Bar de l'Ere**, which is a 1st-floor restaurant serving pizzas for US$3. It's one of the few downtown restaurants that stay open late, until midnight at least. The beer is local and cheap, the atmosphere rowdy and the music loud. It's mainly patronized by large groups of men sharing bottle after bottle of Johnny Walker.

Citadelle Restaurant, on Rue St Cyr to the right of Le Plaza Hotel, is housed in a lovely dilapidated red-and-yellow gingerbread. The food is all Haitian and can be eaten inside or on the verandah. This place has a great feel and is very reasonably priced. Chicken with rice, beans and salad costs US$3. Not too far from here is the **Plaisance** (☎ 222-9296), at 3 Ave John Brown (also called Lalue), set in a leafy courtyard. It is busy and cheerful at lunchtime. Chicken goes for US$3 and salads for US$2.50.

La Table Ronde (☎ 223-4660), at 7 Rue Capois, is a very relaxing, elegant, centrally located restaurant. Most tables are on a marble-tiled, tree-shaded terrace in front of the gingerbread building. The food is high-quality Creole and always well presented. The *écrevisse creole* is recommended at US$6. **Café Terrasse** (☎ 222-5648), 11 Rue Capois (enter on Rue Ducoste to the side of Le Plaza Hotel), is a delightful small restaurant with a surprisingly international menu for downtown Port-au-Prince. It has a streetside terrace café that serves breakfast from 9 to 11 am and sandwiches (from US$1.50 each) until 5 pm. The 1st-floor, air-conditioned dining room, where you can choose from salad niçoise, crepes or chicken cooked with papaya (from US$7), is open for lunch only.

Another small restaurant, **Le Jardin du Musée**, is in the back of the Musée d'Art, on the corner of Rue Légitime and Rue Capois. Set in a quiet garden, the restaurant serves chicken plat complet for US$6 and a variety of salads for about US$3 apiece from 10 am to 4 pm Monday to Saturday.

If shopping malls are your bent, you could check out **Shady's Restaurant**, on the 1st floor at Public's Plaza, 65 Rue Rosa (Rte du Canapé Vert). It's a modern place, with quick service offering a mixture of Mexican, Lebanese and Haitian fare. Chicken with rice and beans costs US$4.50, and you can get a burrito for US$2. Every Tuesday, Shady's runs a Creole buffet from 1 to 7 pm.

Mid-Range

Tiffany's (☎ 222-3506, 222-0993), 12 Bicentenaire (a stretch of Blvd Harry Truman), is cool, dark and spacious. Both the Italian crooner playing in the background and the plush '70s decor suggest a New York City Mafia joint, but mainly the staff of the palace and the US embassy dine here. The Haitian menu is delicious – it's some of the best food in town – and quite reasonable, with Creole chicken costing US$6 and steaks starting at US$7. The restaurant mostly caters to the lunch crowd, and is only open 11 am to 5 pm. **Chez Yvane** (☎ 222-0188, 222-7676), also known locally as Chaffeur Gide, is two doors down from Tiffany's at 19 Bicentenaire (Blvd Harry Truman). This is a cheerful lunch spot with powerful air con and a bright conservatory at the back, overlooking the bay. The menu is exclusively Creole, with chicken plat complet for US$5 and fish for US$4.50. The restaurant is open 8 am to 6 pm daily except Sunday, when it closes at 4 pm.

Chez Rose (☎ 245-5286), at the corner of Rue 4 and Rue Bellevue, is a relaxed restaurant in a pretty gingerbread building in the quiet residential area of Pacot. It serves steak for US$8.50 and a selection of Creole dishes, and is open from 10 am to 10 pm. **Le Plaza Restaurant** (☎ 222-0766), in Le Plaza Hotel at 10 Rue Capois, has an interesting international menu. There's a weekday buffet at noon and a barbecue every Tuesday evening. The pepper steak flambé (US$10) is excellent, and the salads and seafood dishes are recommended.

The restaurant at **Hotel Oloffson**, at the junction of Rue Capois and Ave H Christophe, is a good downtown venue for both lunch and dinner. At lunchtime it offers a refuge from the frantic pace of Port-au-Prince, and in the evening it has a charming atmosphere on the verandah overlooking the garden. The menu offers international and Haitian food, with club sandwiches at US$4.50, salads at US$6, and main dishes, such as *filet mignon au champignon*, at US$8.

ENTERTAINMENT
Dance Clubs
The best dance clubs in Port-au-Prince are the large dance halls at the bordellos on the Carrefour road, the beginning of Rte Nationale 2 as it leaves town. They are legal and safe, and most people come here just to dance. Nonetheless, foreign women are advised not to go alone. You will need your own transport to get there, as taxis don't run to or from the Carrefour district after 7 pm. The best place is the *Caribeño*, opposite the junction with Martissant 13. It's open 9 pm until 5 am and has two big dance floors playing Latino music, mainly salsa. The atmosphere is very friendly, and it attracts a large crowd of serious dancers. The *Brisa del Mar*, opposite the junction with Martissant 5, is not as modern, but it is a little closer to town. It's open 9 pm to 5 am. Neither place has a cover charge.

Music
Most of the area's music venues are in Pétionville or Kenscoff, though there are sometimes live bands at the *Rex Theatre* at 41 Rue Capois, opposite the Champs de Mars. You can buy tickets for concerts at the Big Star Market, next door. One of the best new clubs in Port-au-Prince is *Foula Vodou Jazz Club* (☎ 245-3364), 25 Rue des Collines, at the edge of Pacot in Croix Desprez. It's a small, intimate club run by the Rara band Foula, which plays most weekends. It's a showcase venue for small up-and-coming bands, so you're likely to see anything from Creole rap to Rara. A lot of people from the Haitian music scene hang out here and perform impromptu floor spots. It's got a warmhearted atmosphere, and the beers are cheap. There's live music Thursday through Saturday nights, and it's open 6 pm till late.

Call in advance to check on the schedule, as the club is a fair distance from the center of town; you'll need your own transportation.

The *Hotel Oloffson* has live music every Thursday when RAM, the *racines* band fronted by the owner, plays here. It's definitely worth catching. The *Institut Français* (☎ 222-2051, 222-3720), at the junction of Blvd Harry Truman and Rue Paul VI, holds classical, Haitian folkloric and contemporary music concerts.

Cinemas
Most current French and American films, all dubbed in French, are shown at the cinemas in Port-au-Prince. The most central downtown cinema is the *Rex Theatre* (☎ 222-1848, 222-1176), at 41 Rue Capois on the Champs de Mars.

SPECTATOR SPORTS
Soccer is very popular in Haiti, and even though there is little monetary investment in the game, hundreds of small clubs all over the country play in many small unofficial tournaments. For the last three years there has been a National League in which 57 teams are divided into three divisions. Only the league finals and international games are held at the recently revamped Sylvio Cator Stadium, by the junction of Rue Oswald Durand and Ave Mgr Guilloux.

If you catch a game, you'll find the atmosphere similar to that of Brazilian games, with lots of music, drumming and singing. The entry price is US$1 for a domestic league game and US$1.50 for an international game. Expect to pay extra for reserved seats. The official league starts in November and ends in May, while most of the independent tournaments go on through the summer.

Fans can contact either of the following for information about what's on: Federation Haitienne de Football (affiliated with FIFA; ☎ 222-3237) or the Ministry of Sport (☎ 222-1021, 222-5042), 5 Rue Dr Audain, in Pacot.

If you are interested in youth soccer, you can pay a visit to see Athletique d'Haiti, a project designed to nurture and train young soccer hopefuls from the slums. Their playing field is next to the Circuit d'Haiti (the motor

A Goal Haiti Will Never Forget

It is a little-known fact that in 1974 Haiti became the first Caribbean team to qualify for the soccer World Cup. The Haitian team was a rank outsider, but it was able to give the competition one of its most electrifying moments when it took the lead against the favorite, Italy.

Ranked the best goalkeeper in the world, Italian Dino Zoff had not ceded a goal in an international match for two years. But two minutes into the second half, Haiti's top striker, Manno Sannon, managed to achieve what most of the greatest players in the world had failed to do – get the ball past Zoff. Most of the world's newspapers had made predictions about which striker would accomplish this feat, but none had considered the Haitian team.

For a short time, Haiti was 1–0 up against Italy, and this is still remembered as the country's finest soccer moment. Sadly, Haiti lost the game 1–3, but the players still held their heads up with pride as the team that scored on Dino Zoff.

racing track), about 4km from the center of town. Traveling northward on Rte Nationale 1, go left on Rue Hubert and take the first entrance on the right. Contact Robert Duval (☎ 245-2603) for further information.

If you want to see a cockfight, it's best to hire a guide who will know when and where they are taking place; see Spectator Sports in Haiti's Facts for the Visitor chapter for further details.

SHOPPING

There is no shortage of merchandise in Port-au-Prince. In addition to a varied range of excellent paintings, you can buy sequined flags, amazing metalwork sculpture, papier-mâché masks and wooden crafts. You'll find most things in the Marché de Fer, on Ave Jean Jacques Dessalines, but as a shopping experience it can be quite stressful. There is a lot of junk, and as the saying goes, you

have to kiss a lot of frogs. Be prepared to bargain hard.

Check out Botanica Santa Philomena, at 152 Rue Pavée, for a wonderful, eclectic mix of toiletries, Vodou bottles, clerics' shirts and books such as the *Book of 72 Genies* rubbing shoulders with *Psalms for Today*.

Crafts

There are crafts shops next to the Musée d'Art Haïtien on the corner of Rue Capois and Rue Légitime, and at the Sainte Trinité Episcopalian Cathedral on the corner of Rue Pavée and Ave Mgr Guilloux. Near the gates of Hotel Oloffson is the small, brightly painted Mahogany Craft Shop, which is fun to visit and good for bargains. You'll find paintings, wood carvings and hand-painted metalwork. Not far from the hotel are two lovely shops run by craft makers' collectives in Pacot. The Comité Artisanat Haïtien (☎ 222-8440), at 26 Rue 3, has a very good selection of crafts, and directly opposite is another, smaller outlet called ONART (Office Nationale de l'Artisanat). These places offer fixed prices.

Paintings & Sculptures

There are some excellent galleries in Port-au-Prince, all with individual collections determined by their dealers' personal taste. Buying from a gallery gives you the chance to shop in peace and discover the history of the paintings and the artists.

Originally an artists' cooperative, the Centre d'Art (☎ 222-2018), at 58 Rlle Roy, off Rue Capois, was the first art gallery in Haiti. The stock takes up all the rooms of a two-floor gingerbread house on a quiet side street. There is one entire room filled with Cap-Haïtien art, and the gallery retains exclusivity over the work of Jasmin Joseph, a leading expressionist painter in the 1950s. It also has a good collection of work by a couple of Haiti's better-known metal sculptors, Serge Jolimeau and Gabriel Bien-Aimé. The gallery is dusty and sleepy, but its prices are affordable and one can often see artists working in the yard.

The Galerie Carlos Jara (☎ 245-7164), at 28 Rue Armand Holly, Debussy, is in a beautiful hilltop villa, high above the old suburb of Pacot. Carlos Jara, a Chilean art expert, has an extensive collection of naïve and avant-garde artists. He has the largest collections of Lafortune Felix (exclusively), Stevenson Magloire, the Saint-Soleil Group, and André Pierres in Haiti, and holds over 7000 paintings in all. There is also a large collection of metal sculptures by Georges Liautaud, Serge Jolimeau and Gabriel Bien-Aimé.

The Galerie Issa (☎ 222-3287), at 19 Rue du Chili in Pacot, has a large stock of predominantly jungle and peasant scenes by lesser-known artists. Everything is piled up in one huge room, and it's a good place to browse. The owner, Issa el Saieh, is a very interesting, arch iconoclast who used to play jazz with Dizzy Gillespie. The Hotel Oloffson (☎ 223-4000), at the corner of Ave H Christophe and Rue Capois, has a fine selection of art on display (for sale) in the bar and reception areas.

If you want to visit the *ateliers* of metalworkers in Croix des Bouquets, see Plaine du Cul de Sac in the Around Port-au-Prince chapter for details.

Sequined Vodou flags are used in ceremonies.

Vodou Flags

If you want to buy magnificent sequined Vodou flags, it's more fun to go to the artists themselves, especially since most of them live in Bel Air, an old quarter just north of the Catholic cathedral. It's advisable to take a guide, as many of the ateliers are down narrow alleys and impossible to find alone. You can find the best guides near the gates of Hotel Oloffson. Milfort Bruno, the owner of the Mahogany Craft Shop, is very well informed and knows a lot of artists. Other guides hang out near Le Plaza Hotel, and most hotels can organize a guide for you.

Clambering around the steep streets and alleyways of the old district of Bel Air and enjoying fine views of the bay can make for an enjoyable afternoon. Artists to look out for are Edgar Jean Louis, an urbane and charming Vodou priest and coffin-maker, on Rue des Césars; Silva Joseph, also a Vodou priest, at the top of Rue Houille; and Yves Telemacque, a talented young artist, on Rue Tiremasse. There are also a couple of good

sequined flag artists in the Nazon area, such as Ronald Gouin (☎ 245-7350), at 58 Rue Mon Plaisir off Rue Christ Roi, who speaks some English, and Georges Valris, in the same area.

Music

There are some good music shops on Rue Pavée, close to the intersection with Rue Montalais, such as La Boite à Musique. It stocks racines, compas, reggae and Carnival cassettes and CDs, and sells tickets for many local concerts.

GETTING THERE & AWAY
Air

See the introductory Getting There & Away chapter for more information on international flights into and out of Port-au-Prince. The following airlines have offices in Port-au-Prince:

Air Canada
   (☎ 246-0441, 246-0442) Rte de l'Aeroport
Air France
   (☎ 223-1700, 223-0172) Champs de Mars

Air Guadeloupe
(☎ 246-1215)
American Airlines
(☎ 223-1314, 223-1316) Ave Marie-Jeanne,
Cité de l'Exposition, Bicentenaire
(☎ 249-0311/12/13/14) Delmas 29/31,
Autorama
(☎ 246-0100, 246-0159, 246-0205)
Rte de l'Aeroport
Antillean Airlines (ALM)
(☎ 222-0900) 69 Rue Pavée
Caribintair
(☎ 246-0737, 246-0778, 249-0203, 249-1575)
Rte de l'Aeroport
Copa Panama
(☎ 223-2326)
Rue de Quai, Madsen Export Import

Mission Aviation Fellowship (☎ 246-3993) has regular flights from Port-au-Prince to Hinche, Pignon and Dame Marie. Charter flights are also available to Dame Marie, Jérémie, Les Cayes, Jacmel, La Gonâve, Hinche, Pignon, Cap-Haïtien, Port-au-Paix and Mole St Nicolas. There are daily (excluding Sunday) flights to both Cap-Haïtien and Jérémie with Caribintair (see above).

Bus

Book at least two days in advance for buses to Santo Domingo, DR, from either Chatelain Tours & Travel Service (☎ 223-2400, 223-2961), on the corner of Rue Geffrard and Ave John Brown, or with Agence Citadelle (☎ 222-5900, 223-5900, fax 222-1792, citagen@haitiworld.com), 35 Place du Marron Inconnu. Buses leave from Pétionville (see the Getting There & Away section for Pétionville in the Around Port-au-Prince chapter).

There is no central bus terminal in Port-au-Prince; the departure point depends upon the destination of the bus, which will be written on its front. There are no timetables either, as buses leave when they are full. Fares cost from US$1 to US$7, depending on the destination. If you wish to pay a little more, you can sit up in the front with the driver, which is certainly more comfortable; see the Getting Around Haiti chapter for further details.

The following is route information for most of Haiti:

Estation Port au Léogâne, Les Cayes and Jacmel, at the junction of Rue Oswald Durand and Blvd Jean Jacques Dessalines, one block east of the Sylvio Cator Stadium – buses for southwest destinations leave from here, including Jacmel (four hours, US$2); Léogâne (two hours, US$1); Les Cayes (five hours, US$3); and Miragoane (four hours, US$2.50).

Estation Croix des Bouquets, in front of the statue of Madame Kolo, at the junction of Rue de Fronts Forts and Rue du Centre – for buses to Croix des Bouquets (one hour; $3H or US$1).

Estation O'Cap, at the side of the Shell gas station, at the confluence of Blvd Jean Jacques Dessalines and Blvd La Saline – for buses to the north, including Cap-Haïtien (nine hours; US$6.50); Gonaïves (five hours; US$3.50); and St Marc (two hours; US$1.50).

GETTING AROUND
To/From the Airport

The Port-au-Prince International Airport is north of the center of town, and it takes about 30 to 45 minutes on a busy road to get to most hotels. There are no buses into town, so the best method is to take a taxi. Once you emerge from the airport, you'll find many taxi drivers touting for business. It's best to negotiate a price before you get into the car, as drivers will try to fleece you if they gather that it's your first trip to Haiti. There is no set price, so try around US$20.

Bus

Port-au-Prince taptaps and buses are very cheap; fare is usually around 3 gourdes (US$0.15) and rarely more than 10 (US$0.50). They run along both Rte de Delmas and Ave John Brown and are handy for getting up and down from Pétionville. The buses, either decorated Japanese pickup trucks with bench seats in the back or 10-seater transits, stop on request if they have space – either a loud 'psst!' or a wave of the hand does the job. Shouting 'Merci chauffeur!' or banging on the side of the bus will stop the driver, whom you pay as you alight. If you want to visit Carrefour, you can take a bus on Blvd Jean Jacques Dessalines (Grand Rue).

Car

The major car rental companies have offices at Port-au-Prince International Airport; see Car Rental in the Getting Around Haiti chapter for details on rates.

Avis
(☎ 246-2696) International Airport

Budget
(☎ 246-2324) International Airport

Dynamic Car Rental (Hertz)
(☎ 246-0700, 246-2048) International Airport
(☎ 246-1132) Rte de l'Aeroport
(☎ 257-0906) 48 Rue Lamarre, Pétionville

Secom
(☎ 246-2799) International Airport
(☎ 257-2847, 257-1913, fax 223-9628)
564 Rte de Delmas, near Delmas 68

Taxi

Port-au-Prince has a system of collective taxis called *publiques*, which cost US$0.50 (10 gourdes) a trip. They're easy to recognize as they are old, beat-up cars with a red ribbon hanging from the front mirror. They drive along most busy streets in downtown Port-au-Prince; hail them the same way you would a taptap. Taxis are shared with other passengers, so don't expect the driver to take the most direct route to your destination. Also, if your destination is not convenient to the others, the driver will refuse you – don't take it as an insult. Publiques usually squeeze the passengers in, so you may end up on someone else's knee.

If you get into an empty publique and the driver removes the red ribbon, this means that he is treating you as a private commission and could charge up to US$5. You must explain you are only willing to pay 10 gourdes (US$0.50), the standard fare around Port-au-Prince. Publiques rarely make the journey from Port-au-Prince to Pétionville, so if you want this service, you'll have to negotiate a rate. Nick's (☎ 257-7777) taxi service is handy for getting between Port-au-Prince and Pétionville. The cars are metered and an average fare from Pétionville to downtown Port-au-Prince is between US$6 and US$8.

Around Port-au-Prince

Not far from Port-au-Prince, one can easily escape to the cooler elevations of Pétionville and Kenscoff and the beaches along the Côte des Arcadins. Other day trips can also be made to see the metalworking workshops of artists in Croix des Bouquets or the birds and wildlife of the nearby lakes.

PÉTIONVILLE

Although this town is joined to Port-au-Prince by three primary arteries, Rte de Delmas, Ave John Brown and Rte du Canapé Vert, Pétionville seems far removed from the capital. The town has evolved from a hill resort into a middle- and upper-class suburb. Pétionville is a retreat for those who make their fortunes in Port-au-Prince but do not wish to confront its grinding poverty day and night. Most of the city's restaurants, nightlife and exclusive shops are up in Pétionville, as are most of its hotels. The streets are cleaner, but the area still retains a

shabby, construction-site atmosphere. Farther up the mountainside, at an altitude of 450m, it is certainly cooler and breezier, another reason most of Port-au-Prince's wealthy folk live here.

Orientation

The streets of Pétionville follow a grid system, and the two main streets, Rue Lamarre and Rue Grégoire, run parallel to each other from Ave Pan Américaine (the extension of Ave John Brown) to a small park, Place St Pierre. Most of the shops, galleries and restaurants can be found on or close to these roads.

All maps of Port-au-Prince also include Pétionville.

Information

Tourist Offices The Haitian Association for the Tourism & Hotel Industry (☎ 257-4647, fax 257-6137) is at Choucoune Plaza.

Money Promobank (☎ 257-2700, 257-2707, fax 257-2721), at 17 Rue Darguin, is open 9 am to 5 pm weekdays and 9 am to 1 pm Saturday. Unibank (☎ 257-5519, 257-6939, fax 257-5539) is close by at 14 Rue Darguin. There is a Sogebank branch (☎ 229-5000) in the small mall at the corner of Rue Grégoire and Rue Villatte.

Post & Communications The post office, Bureau Postal de Pétionville (☎ 257-2016), is at 86 Rue Grégoire, Place St Pierre, and there's a DHL office (☎ 257-6192, 257-8446), 21 Rue Gabart, for mailing packages. The Teleco office (☎ 257-8651) is on the corner of Rue Magny and Rue Rigaud.

Bookstores Asterix (☎ 257-2605), on the corner of Rue Grégoire and Rue Ogé, has a large selection of French-language books, magazines (some in English) and stationery. La Pleiade (☎ 257-3588), in a small complex of shops at the corner of Rues Grégoire and Moïse, stocks mostly French-language books, but it is possible to find some in English.

Laundry You can usually get laundry done through your hotel or guest house. Contempo

Cleaners (☎ 257-0638), at 16 Rue Clerveaux, and National Dry Cleaning (☎257-3250), at 74 Ave Pan Américaine, are both efficient dry cleaners.

Emergency Emergency phone numbers for Pétionville include the following:

Police	☎ 114, 257-0019
Fire	☎ 115, 257-2222
Red Cross	☎ 118, 245-1171

Places to Stay

Mid-Range The *Marabou* (☎ 257-1934), just behind the St Pierre church at 72 Rue Stephen Archer, is a real find. On a quiet street, a walled garden encloses the gorgeous little white gingerbread building. Friendly and charming, it has 15 rooms with cold-water bathrooms, ranging from US$18 to US$33 per room plus a US$3 surcharge for sharing. Breakfast is not included in the price but is available in the colorful Mexican restaurant downstairs.

The *Kalewes Guest House* (☎ 257-0817), at 99 Rue Grégoire, just south of Place St Pierre, offers six rooms in a delightful, 100-year-old gingerbread full of dark antique furniture. There is a swimming pool and terrace bar at the back. All the rooms have hot and cold water and cost US$30/48, which includes breakfast, all taxes and service charges. The *Hotel Ifé* (☎ 257-0737, 257-1037, fax 257-1037), at 30 Rue Grégoire on the corner of Rue Villatte, is a small, relaxed 12-room hotel in the center of Pétionville. The rooms have private bathrooms but no air con, and cost US$45/65 for a single/double including breakfast, served on the garden terrace or in the classic old restaurant.

The *Sunset Guest House* (☎ 257-0553), at 15 Rte Ibo Lele, is 10 minutes south of Place St Pierre by foot. The guest house has a beautiful location on a peaceful, green mountain road, and is designed to resemble an alpine lodge. All six rooms have private bathrooms with hot and cold water, and cost US$55/65 including breakfast. There is a swimming pool and restaurant/bar on the roof terrace. This place is perfect if you desire fresh air and serenity.

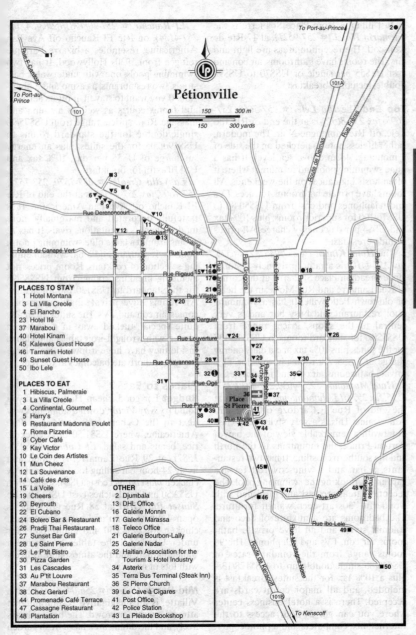

Pétionville

0   150   300 m
0   150   300 yards

To Port-au-Prince

To Port-au-Prince

HAITI

PLACES TO STAY
1   Hotel Montana
3   La Villa Creole
4   El Rancho
23 Hotel Ifé
37 Marabou
40 Hotel Kinam
45 Kalewes Guest House
46 Tarmarin Hotel
49 Sunset Guest House
50 Ibo Lele

PLACES TO EAT
1   Hibiscus, Palmeraie
3   La Villa Creole
4   Continental, Gourmet
5   Harry's
6   Restaurant Madonna Poulet
7   Roma Pizzeria
8   Cyber Café
9   Kay Victor
10 Le Coin des Artistes
11 Mun Cheez
12 La Souvenance
14 Café des Arts
15 La Voile
19 Cheers
20 Beyrouth
22 El Cubano
24 Bolero Bar & Restaurant
27 Pradij Thai Restaurant
27 Sunset Bar Grill
28 Le Saint Pierre
29 Le P'tit Bistro
30 Pizza Garden
31 Les Cascades
33 Au P'tit Louvre
37 Marabou Restaurant
38 Chez Gerard
39 Promenade Café Terrace
47 Cassagne Restaurant
48 Plantation

OTHER
2   Djumbala
13 DHL Office
16 Galerie Monnin
17 Galerie Marassa
18 Teleco Office
21 Galerie Bourbon-Lally
25 Galerie Nadar
32 Haitian Association for the Tourism & Hotel Industry
34 Asterix
35 Terra Bus Terminal (Steak Inn)
36 St Pierre Church
39 Le Cave à Cigares
41 Post Office
42 Police Station
43 La Pleiade Bookshop

Place St Pierre

To Kenscoff

Just minutes from Place St Pierre is the **Tarmarin Hotel** (☎ 257-9521), at 17 Rte de Kenscoff. The reception areas are light and airy. The rooms have bathrooms, air con and cost US$55 per single or US$70 to US$90 double, including breakfast.

Top End The **Ibo Lele** (☎ 257-5668, 257-1695, fax 257-8012) is at the end of Rte Ibo Lele, off Rte Montagne Noir. The modern, rather lifeless hotel is perched on the side of a mountain 480m above sea level. It has a huge swimming pool and restaurant where it often hosts big dances on the weekends. All rooms have private bathrooms, terraces, TVs and telephones and cost from US$50/80 to US$70/100 for superior rooms, plus 10% tax and US$4 per day energy charge. All prices include breakfast.

The **Hotel Kinam** (☎ 257-0462, 257-6525, fax 257-4410) is a rather pristinely restored gingerbread on Place St Pierre, at the corner of Rue Lamarre and Rue Moïse, in the heart of old-town Pétionville. It has a swimming pool, restaurant and busy bar and is very central to the shops. Prices range from US$55/66 for standard rooms to US$115/137 for the suites, plus 10% tax and a daily energy charge of US$5. All rooms have color TVs, private bathrooms, air con and telephones.

Hotel Montana (☎ 257-4030, 257-4020, 257-4555, fax 257-6137, htmontana@aol.com) is at the end of Rue F Cardoza off Ave Pan Américaine. This is a very stylish, top-class hotel with a remarkable view of the bay of Port-au-Prince, the mountains to the north and the southern coastline. It has two restaurants, a bar and a vine-covered terrace garden overlooking the swimming pool. The reception areas are vast and furnished with wonderful '30s art-deco walnut furniture. The bedrooms are a mixture of deco and colonial styles and all have private bathrooms, air con, TVs and telephones. The 96 rooms range from the standard rates of US$68/80 single/double up to US$128/138, plus a 10% tax for the suites. Breakfast is included, and all major credit cards are accepted. There is a hotel business center where you can get 24-hour access to the Internet, fax, computers and a photocopier.

El Rancho (☎ 257-2080/81/82/83/84, fax 257-4134), on Rte El Rancho off Ave Pan Américaine, resembles a bizarre baroque refugee from 1930s Hollywood. It has two swimming pools, one with underwater barstools, two restaurants, a casino and a nightclub. If you want to stay fit, it offers aerobics and tennis courts as well as a sauna and massage. Room prices range from US$75/90 single/double for the standard rooms to US$190/205 for the suites, plus an energy surcharge of US$5 per day, 10% tax and US$10 extra for breakfast.

La Villa Creole (☎ 257-1570, 257-1571, 257-1609, fax 257-4935) is at the end of Rte El Rancho off Ave Pan Américaine. It is tastefully decorated and marginally more modest than its ostentatious rivals. It has 72 rooms around a large blue swimming pool, a poolside restaurant and a bar with an enticing selection of cocktails. Room prices, not including breakfast, range from US$85/95 for the standard to US$130/140 for a suite. All rooms have private bathrooms, balconies, air con and TVs. The suites are really quite special, tucked away in a sheltered garden with wrought-iron tables and chairs. Inside they have huge ironwork beds, large lounges and private balconies at the rear.

Places to Eat

Budget For good, cheap Haitian eats, you could try **Kay Victor**, down a small alleyway next to the Cyber Café, at 84 Ave Pan Américaine, where US$1.50 buys chicken, rice, beans and salad. **El Cubano** (☎ 257-1587), at 29 Rue Lamarre, is a loud and lively 24-hour bar selling food and drinks. A chicken *plat complet* costs US$4, spaghetti is US$2.50 and sandwiches cost US$1.50. The **Sunset Bar Grill**, at 58 Rue Grégoire, is open 4 pm to 3 am and serves barbecued chicken for US$5.50 and hamburgers for under US$2. All the tables are inside a walled garden, and the atmosphere is lively with lots of music.

Mid-Range **Cheers** (☎ 256-0455), at 12 Rue Villatte, is an imaginative restaurant that attracts a younger crowd. The bar is always lively, and the dining area has a fresh garden atmosphere. Best of all, there is a side room where you can lounge on floor cushions and watch a video of your choice from a huge range of both French- and English-language films. The room fits about 15 people, and while you can't eat inside, you may bring your drinks. They keep the food simple, serving a choice of fish, meat or vegetarian brochettes (US$8), and they also offer crepes, salads and soups. If you want to watch a specific film after your food, it's best to call and book the room beforehand.

In the *Marabou Restaurant* (☎ 257-1934), at 72 Rue Stephen Archer behind the St Pierre church, you can eat excellent Mexican food surrounded by wild, wonderful murals. The varied menu offers enchiladas at US$6, quesadillas at US$7 and gazpacho at US$2.50. The bar is friendly and offers a good choice of Mexican cocktails, including frozen margaritas. The *Bolero Bar & Restaurant* (☎ 257-1929), at 18 Rue Louverture, is open daily except Sunday, 5 pm to late. This is the bar to visit if you fancy a bit of funk. It attracts all sorts, from mercenaries to magnates, adventurers to aristocrats, and quite a few in between. The restaurant behind serves gourmet pizzas (US$7), great pasta (US$5.50) and a selection of steaks all cooked on a large open grill in a leafy garden.

The *Promenade Café Terrace*, on the corner of Rue Grégoire and Rue Moïse, is set in an enclosed garden containing an African heritage center and bookstore. This is a good place to have lunch. You can get pizzas for US$4, salads for US$5 and daily specials, such as fish brochette on Chinese rice, for US$6. *Le Saint Pierre* (☎ 257-2280), on the corner of Rue Chavannes and Rue Lamarre, is a sweet little restaurant with a small terrace overlooking the street that often attracts serenading troubadours. It's open 11 am to 11:30 pm daily and serves both quality pizzas and a selection of Creole dishes; main courses start at US$6.

Le Coin des Artistes (☎ 257-2400), on Ave Pan Américaine, between the corners of Rues Rebecca and Clerveau, cooks most of its dishes on an open-air grill in its terraced garden. It specializes in brochettes (US$9)

and salads (US$5.50) and is open noon to 11 pm daily except Sunday.

Ever-popular pizza can be found at the following restaurants. The *Roma Pizzeria* (☎ 257-2048), at 86 Ave Pan Américaine, serves small pizzas for US$8. There is a small gallery in the restaurant, too. The *Pizza Garden* (☎ 257-7988), at 36 Rue Chavannes, serves al fresco pizzas in its front garden for US$5 for small and US$11 for large. *Harry's* (☎ 257-1885) is another popular pizza joint, at 97 Ave Pan Américaine on Bagatelle Plaza, where the tables are laid out in a strange pink plaza under a roof lit by fairy lights. Pizza prices range from US$6 for a small to US$10 for a large, and there is a relaxed bar at one end where you can play pool. *Le Rendezvous*, at 21 Rue Lamarre, is a cheap and cheerful neon-lit pizza place that serves pizzas for US$3 each. *Mun Cheez* (☎ 256-2177), at 2 Rue Rebecca where it meets Ave Pan Américaine, is a cheery, take-out pizza place with a few tables on a small terrace. Pizzas are US$3.50 for a small and US$8.50 for a large. They also deliver in a beat-up old car sporting an incongruous bright sign on its top.

The *Cyber Café* (☎ 257-9561), at 84 Ave Pan Américaine, is open 9 am to 8 pm Monday to Saturday. You can buy simple sandwiches (from US$4) and log onto the Internet. Just up the street is the *Restaurant Madonna Poulet* (☎ 257-5401), open 2 pm to 2 am daily. This is an authentic, al fresco Haitian fried-chicken joint offering chicken, rice, beans, fried plantains and salad for US$9. Expect their radio to play loud compas music.

Au P'tit Louvre (☎ 257-1543), 27 Rue Grégoire, has the look of a wild-west saloon crossed with a Swiss chalet and serves a cross of Libyan and Creole dishes. In addition to Creole chicken for US$8, you can try kibbeh or humus for US$3. *Le P'tit Bistro* (☎ 257-3042), 42 Rue Grégoire, is an intimate restaurant serving French cuisine at reasonable prices.

Top End A plant-filled courtyard leads to the stylish *La Voile* (☎ 257-4561, 257-0724), 32 Rue Rigaud, where diners are seated beneath draped yacht sails. The proprietor is an extremely charming host who moves from table to table welcoming guests and explaining the French menu. The restaurant specializes in seafood, but vegetarians are imaginatively catered for with dishes such as endive and mushroom salad with a lemon dressing. You can expect to pay US$4 for the avocado and shrimp salad, US$10 for a pepper steak or fish with green pepper sauce, and US$13 for lobster with shallots. The restaurant is only open in the evenings, and it's advisable to book a table on weekends.

When you pass through the wooden door in the stucco walls that surround *Chez Gerard* (☎ 257-1949), 17 Rue Pinchinat, you will discover a verdant covered garden with a sophisticated ambiance. All the wrought-iron tables are lit by huge dripping candles, and the surrounding trees are subtly illuminated. The cuisine is French with a dash of Creole, and the onion soup (US$7.50) and the snails from Kenscoff (US$6) are recommended. The average price for starters is US$8; for main courses it's US$15. The restaurant is open noon to 3 pm for lunch and 7:30 to 10:30 pm for dinner.

Les Cascades (☎ 257-0979), at the corner of Rue Ogé and Rue Clerveau, is in an elegant hacienda-style building surrounded by trees and streaming fountains. The menu is French with a strong emphasis on seafood. You can get a crepe of snails with tomato and pastis (US$4.50) as a starter and sliced duck with green pepper sauce (US$12) as a main course. There are different specials every day.

La Souvenance (☎ 257-7688), 8 Rue Gabart, has an extensive French menu with at least eight additional specials offered daily. Starters begin at US$7, and main courses, such as prawns in mango sauce, cost around US$15. It opens every evening at 6:30 pm. The *Plantation* (☎/fax 257-0979), at 39 Impasse Fouchard off Rue Borno above Pétionville, is worth the extra climb needed to reach it. Essentially it offers French cuisine, such as steak tartar in cognac, in a beautiful decor with a rarefied atmosphere. Starters begin at US$6. *Beyrouth* (☎ 257-2658, 257-8549), 31 Rue Villatte, has a menu that is mostly Lebanese and partly Creole. For starters, you could try mashed eggplant or tabbouleh for US$4.50 and go on to lobster kebabs for US$12. The proprietors and their staff are very friendly.

The *Café des Arts* (☎ 257-7979), 19 Rue Lamarre, is a bar and restaurant – and on the weekends a music venue – serving fish and steaks from US$12. *Le Grégoire*, 34 Rue Grégoire, specializes in Vietnamese, Thai and Cambodian food in an Asian setting, with some tables on a terrace overlooking its small enclosed garden. A main course such as chicken cooked in lemongrass costs US$6.50. The *Pradij Thai Restaurant* (☎ 257-2361), at 22 Rue Metellus on the corner of Place Boyer, offers a quality Thai menu. It is open Monday to Saturday for lunch and dinner and also has take-out service.

The Hotel Montana (☎ 257-4020, 257-4030), at the end of Rue F Cardoza, has two restaurants. The *Hibiscus* is on a covered terrace overlooking Port-au-Prince, and serves breakfast and lunch from 6:30 am to 4 pm. The *Palmeraie* is within the building and from 7 to 10 pm serves a mixture of international and Creole dishes costing about US$5 for starters and US$8 for a main course.

La Villa Creole (☎ 257-1570, 257-1571), at the end of Rte El Rancho, has a restaurant beside the swimming pool that serves both lunch and dinner. You can order a selection of club sandwiches from US$3 and some very adventurous dinner dishes, such as chicken cooked with cranberries for US$10.50. El Rancho (☎ 257-4926), also on Rte El Rancho, has two restaurants; the *Continental*, open 6:30 am to 10 pm daily, and the more formal *Gourmet*, open from 4 to 11 pm nightly except Monday. Sandwiches start at US$5 and main courses at US$8.

Entertainment

Nightclubs *El Rancho* (☎ 257-2080/84) has dancing every Friday. The *Crystal Palace* (☎ 257-0841), at 64 Rue Grégoire, plays a good mixture of salsa, compas and zouk (dance music from the French West Indies). *Djumbala* (☎ 257-4368), on Rue Frère, is a large club playing mostly salsa and compas music.

Music *Café des Arts* (☎ 257-7979), at 19 Rue Lamarre, is a restaurant which usually hosts racines bands on the weekends. The **Cassagne Restaurant** (☎ 257-1223), at 8 Rue Borno, has dancing and compas bands on Friday and Saturday. The **Hotel Ibo Lele** (☎ 257-8012, 257-5668, 257-8516, 257-8500), at the end of Ibo Lele, has live bands on Friday and Saturday. It usually has compas bands like Sweet Mikey, but even the popular rap group the Fugees (of which two members are of Haitian descent) has been known to play there.

Shopping

La Cave à Cigares (☎ 223-8091, 223-7884, 223-8063), next to Chez Gerard at the corner of Rues Pinchinat and Faubert, sells premium-quality Havana cigars at very good prices.

There are many galleries in Pétionville selling traditional and modern Haitian art at reasonable up to extortionate prices. The Galerie Nadar (☎ 257-5602, fax 257-0855), 50 Rue Grégoire, has a large collection of mostly moderns with some naïves. The Galerie Marassa (☎ 257-1967, 257-5424), at 17 Rue Lamarre, specializes in contemporary Haitian artists. It also stocks metalworks, crafts and Vodou flags. The Galerie Flamboyant (☎ 257-3286, 257-5540), at 9 Rue Darguin, has a well-displayed collection of both naïve and modern paintings.

The Galerie Bourbon-Lally (☎ 257-6321), 23 Rue Lamarre, is run by a French and English couple, who are helpful and well informed. They stock a small but representative collection of the St Soleil group of artists as well as metalworks, naïve art and Vodou flags. There is the sense that everything is chosen with great care. The gallery also organizes contextual exhibitions showing contemporary Haitian artists with work from the rest of Latin America.

The Galerie Monnin (☎ 257-4430), 19 Rue Lamarre, specializes in naïve landscapes but also carries some contemporary artists. The gallery space is intimate and the work is well presented. Their regular exhibitions showcasing individual artists are well worth a visit.

Getting There & Away

Pétionville is only half an hour from the center of Port-au-Prince, 15 minutes without traffic. There are three roads from Port-au-Prince to Pétionville: Rte de Delmas, Ave John Brown (Ave Pan Américaine) and Rte du Canapé Vert. Rte de Delmas is long and choked with *taptaps*, so if you're driving, the best bet is Ave John Brown or Rte du Canapé Vert. Taptaps run regularly along Ave John Brown and Rte de Delmas to Pétionville and cost 3 gourdes. Most taptaps for Port-au-Prince leave Pétionville from the junction of Rue Grégoire and Ave Pan Américaine. You can catch a taptap to Kenscoff on the Place St Pierre near the Hotel Kinam.

Terra Bus (☎ 257-2161, 257-2153) runs a daily (except Saturday) bus service from Pétionville to Santo Domingo, DR. The trip takes $8^1/_2$ hours, but is in a comfortable, air-conditioned bus. The bus leaves the defunct Steak Inn Restaurant, 37 Rue Magny, daily at 2 pm except Monday, when it leaves at 8 am. The bus drops passengers at the Terminal Terra Bus, Ave 27 de Febrero at Máximo Gómez, Plaza Criolla in Santo Domingo, DR. You can also book tickets in advance in Port-au-Prince (see the Getting There & Away section in the Port-au-Prince chapter).

PÉTIONVILLE TO KENSCOFF

On the way up to Kenscoff, about 8km out of Pétionville in La Boule, a right-hand turn leads to **Boutilliers**, a fantastic vantage point from which to see the whole city of Port-au-Prince. It is here that the huge radio and television towers loom over the city, and there are usually a few guides selling crafts. Nearby is the **Barbancourt Rum Company** (☎ 257-2289), where you can sample many exotic fruit-flavored rums and visit the collection of antique rum distillery machines in their mock castle. Call ahead for tasting hours.

After another 5km, you pass through Fermathe, the site of the modern **Baptiste Mission**, which has an American-style burger bar, handicraft shop and 'Anti-voodoo' museum. A right-hand turn close to the mission will take to you to **Fort Jacques**, built by Pétion in 1804, in the National Historic Park of Fort Jacques and Fort Alexandre.

Rum with a Punch

Rum is a favorite drink on the island, and most hotels offer their own special rum punches and delicious rum sours (rum, cane syrup and lime juice). The Gardère family's Barbancourt Rum Company, founded in 1862, produces a high-quality rum made from freshly pressed sugarcane, distilled and aged in oak barrels from France. The sugarcane is grown by planters on the Plaine du Cul de Sac and around Léogane, both very fertile areas. Here are some recipes with which to impress your friends when you return with your duty-free bottle(s).

Planters Punch
3 parts rum
2 parts orange juice
1 part passionfruit juice
1 part grenadine
– Serve on crushed ice.

Ogoun Feray Grog
3oz rum
2 tbsp honey
1oz passionfruit juice
Dash of cinnamon and nutmeg
– Stir the honey and passionfruit juice into the rum. Heat up and flambé. Pour into a large glass and sprinkle with spices.

Coconut Cocktail
2 parts rum
1 part coconut cream
1 part lime juice
– Serve with ice.

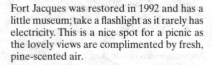

Fort Jacques was restored in 1992 and has a little museum; take a flashlight as it rarely has electricity. This is a nice spot for a picnic as the lovely views are complimented by fresh, pine-scented air.

KENSCOFF

Kenscoff, at 1980m above sea level, is often referred to as the Switzerland of the Caribbean, and Haitian architects have sadly taken this to heart, building some alpine monstrosities. This, however, cannot distract from the truly beautiful scenery and a fresh, palatable climate. You do not have to walk far before the dark, brooding, cloud-capped mountains of Massif de la Selle present a severe backdrop. It is also possible to hike from Kenscoff across the Massif de la Selle to Seguin on a beautiful and fascinating trail: see the Southern Haiti chapter for details.

Kenscoff is a favorite spot for lunch on weekends. Due to the cool climate, a lot of plants and flowers thrive in this area and can be bought at the roadside. There is a popular, rather surreally placed **rollerskating** rink, Le Club (☎ 255-7836), at Carrefour Dourette. In-line skates cost US$3 per hour and the rink is full of children skating into each other to the sounds of hard-core techno. If you're interested in **horseback riding**, you'll find horses available for hire in the streets around Carrefour Dourette, a crossroads with a few small shops and cafés. Most of them look in good shape and seem to be fairly well kept. You have to haggle for a good price but expect to pay about US$2 for 20 minutes and US$6 for two hours.

Places to Stay

Driving toward Pétionville, *Le Florville* (☎ 245-2092, 255-7139) is on the right side of the main Kenscoff Rd, after the market. A big, lively restaurant, music venue and guest house, it has a couple of rooms for rent which are ideal for exploring the area. The rooms have private bathrooms with hot and cold water and cost US$30 for a double, including breakfast.

Places to Eat

The restaurant at *Le Florville* (see above) has a marvelous view and serves delicious, authentic Creole food for about US$6 for a main meal. Sunday lunch is a real family affair and is usually packed. On Saturday and Sunday, live bands play either in the restaurant or on the terrace outside. If you see a band in the evening, don't forget to bring a jacket, as it can get chilly up here.

The *Altitude* (☎ 257-1089, 257-0491), near Carrefour Dourette, seats its guests under shady, vine-clad bowers overlooking the deep valley below. It serves beautifully prepared Creole dishes (US$7.50), salads (US$2.50) and traditional pumpkin soup (US$3). Friendly service and a small playground for children make this a perfect place for lunch; open weekends only from noon to 7 pm.

Close to Carrefour Dourette, *Le Pistachio*, on the Rte de Godin, is a lively, family-run Lebanese restaurant open for lunch and dinner Friday through Sunday, and during summer the restaurant also opens for breakfast on weekends. Most of the tables are on a rustic, brightly painted terrace beside the main building. On Sunday, a small mariachi band entertains the chattering crowd as people clearly enjoy long, sociable lunches. You can get mixed plates of Lebanese snacks, including kibbeh and mecchi, for US$4, hamburgers for US$2.50 and pizzas for US$6.

Le Club (☎ 255-7836), the rollerskating rink, has a small café serving pizza (US$1.50), hamburgers and chips (US$3), ice cream and soft drinks.

Getting There & Away

Driving, you must pass through Pétionville and take the Rte de Kenscoff from Place St Pierre. The 15km drive from Pétionville takes about half an hour along a steep and windy road. Alternatively, you can catch a taptap on the Place St Pierre near the Hotel Kinam. It costs 4 gourdes and takes about twice as long as driving because the bus stops frequently and goes very slowly up the steep hill.

PLAINE DU CUL DE SAC

The Plaine du Cul de Sac is a fertile plain that runs east from Port-au-Prince to Étang Saumâtre, on the Dominican border. The area is of limited interest aside from the metalworking community in Croix des Bouquets, the wildlife on Étang Sumâtre and Trou Caïman, the Forêt des Pins and the border crossing at Malpasse.

Croix des Bouquets

Croix des Bouquets is a market town to the east of Port-au-Prince, the setting for one of the biggest livestock markets in Haiti. Each Friday, cattle, goats, pigs and horses are brought to the large market area and the air fills with a cacophony of hawkers crying and beasts braying. The town also has a strong tradition of Vodou and secret societies, such as *zobòb*, *bizango* and *vlingblingding*. It is here, in the Noailles district, that Georges Liautaud (a blacksmith born in 1899) began making decorative metal crosses for the local cemetery. In the early 1950s he was encouraged by De Witt Peters, the founder of the Centre d'Art in Port-au-Prince, to make free-standing figures and to bring the mythology of Vodou to life with his work. Liautaud is now dead, but his apprentices, known as the Blacksmiths of Vodou, continue to fashion wonderful sculptures of all sizes from flattened oil drums.

Artists' Workshops After passing the walled livestock market on the way into town, you will soon see a blue-and-white police post on the left and the road which leads to the center of the town. Ignore this left turn and continue on the road that leads to the border for another half a kilometer. A small road to the right is Rte Noailles, which leads to the metalworking *ateliers*. Some of them are on Rte Noailles and some on Rte Remy, a right-hand turn off Rte Noailles.

The first workshop on the left-hand side of Rte Noailles belongs to one of the masters, **Serge Jolimeau**, 11 Rte Noailles, whose art-deco-style work represents images of Vodou and his other passion, birds. **Gallery Peter & Hubert**, 15 Rte Noailles, has a small collection of mixed-quality work. **Jose Delpé**, 19 Rte Noailles, one of the youngest artists in Croix des Bouquets, has developed his own unique style by welding metal pieces together to create a third dimension to his sculptures. Turning down Rte Remy, one crosses a small disused railway line, which used to carry the sugarcane trains. Turning left along the old track, you will come across the atelier of **John Sylvestre**. Ask around if

HAITI

you cannot find the house. His work is some of the most imaginative and reasonably priced in Croix des Bouquets. He has used characters from Haitian folklore for his inspiration, creating beautiful sculptures of mermaids and angels, as well as werewolves and demons.

Back on Rte Remy is the **Atelier du Frères Balan**, on the left after the railroad tracks. The Balan brothers were taught by John Sylvestre, but they produce a large quantity of work that is more derivative and less individual than Sylvestre's. **Falaise Peralte**, 131 Rte Remy, makes large, intricate oblong pieces that are more abstract than figurative. **Hubert Jean-Baptiste**, 75 Rte Remy, has a studio opposite the Balans' workshop and creates very dark, dense metalworks.

Two other notable metal artists have workshops outside of this small confined area: **Gary Darius** (☎ 238-8815), 750 Rue Toussaint Louverture, across the border road from Rte Noailles, produces very decorative, highly finished works depicting mostly animals and dolphins, while **Gabriel Bien-Aimé** (☎ 255-9440), the undisputed genius of the metalworkers, creates Vodou-inspired works with the flow and simplicity of Matisse. His atelier is at 164 Despinas (the name of the hamlet in which he lives), about 6km along Rue Stenio Vincent, the road that leaves Croix des Bouquets for Mirebalais and Hinche, The road is dusty and potholed, but passable in a car. There is a sign marking his house on the right hand side of the road.

Getting There & Away From Port-au-Prince, Croix des Bouquets is an hour's drive, at the most. If you take Rte Nationale 1 north of town, you will cross a narrow bridge at Croix des Missions. About half a kilometer after the bridge, the road splits; to the left Rte Nationale 1 continues to the north, and to the right the road which passes through Croix des Bouquets is signposted to Hinche. After about 10km along this dusty road, you hit the outskirts of Croix des Bouquets, passing the walled livestock market on the right.

If you want to take public transport to Croix des Bouquets, go to Estation Croix des Bouquets in front of the statue of Madame Kolo, at the junction of Rue de Fronts Forts and Rue du Centre. The journey takes an hour, at the most, and costs $3H (US$1).

Trou Caïman

The best place to see water birds in Haiti is northeast of Croix des Bouquets, off the main road to the Central Plateau. Known as Eau Gallée by locals, but often identified as Trou Caïman on maps (literally, 'alligator hole' – although there don't seem to be any gators left), this is a large marshy lake surrounded by rice plantings and saltbush flats. The lake is home to a resident colony of at least 150 greater flamingos, seven species of heron, beautiful bronze-gold glossy ibis and uncommon ducks such as white-cheeked pintails and fulvous whistling ducks. From September until April the area hosts many visiting shorebirds and the raptors that eat them, such as the merlin, a low-flying, marsh-loving falcon.

To get there from Port-au-Prince, drive to Croix des Bouquets and bear left at the main intersection by the police post. Continue toward the main church and turn left onto Rue Stenio Vincent, the start of the road to Hinche/Mirebalais. Continue several kilometers across the dry plains. Just before the road begins to climb up into the mountains, turn right on the dirt track to Thomazeau. Soon you will pass a corner of the lake where local villagers will eagerly offer to arrange a boat trip. Alternately you can drive on and turn right across the railroad tracks.

Étang Saumâtre

Étang Saumâtre, Haiti's largest saltwater lake, supports over 100 species of waterfowl, flamingos and American crocodiles. The lake is intensely blue and is skirted by brush and cacti. The road from Croix des Bouquets to the border crossing at Malpasse runs along the southern side of the lake and offers lovely views. The northern side of the lake is better for seeing wildlife, and is accessible from Rte Nationale 3, the road from Croix des Bouquets to Mirebalais and Hinche. The right-hand turn for Thomazeau, about 10km outside of Croix des Bouquets, leads past Trou

Spot flamingos and other winged things at Trou Caïman.

Caïman, through Thomazeau, and to the lake-side villages of Manneville and Fond Pite, which are good sites for watching wildlife.

Forêt des Pins

Forêt des Pins is the largest remaining tract of pine forest in Haiti, covering the far east fringe of the Massif de la Selle, south of Malpasse and close to the Dominican border. Malpasse is not even a border town, just a border post. There are a couple of official buildings, customs and the police, a handful of women selling snacks and soft drinks, and a large gate.

If you take the road from Croix des Bouquets to Malpasse, there is a right-hand turn at Fond Parisien toward Fond Vérettes, a small market town virtually destroyed by the recent hurricane. The road is arduous and windy as it ascends the mountain ranges, but the views are amazing. Sadly, you can also see examples of terrible erosion on the mountainsides. The road continues toward Forêt des Pins, and as it rises the climate becomes colder and mistier. There is an official entrance to the forest on the road between Fonds Verettes and Forêt des Pins where you can find some small *cabins*. If

you can find the caretaker, these can be rented for the night; otherwise you could camp (bring a tent). It takes about four hours to get to the forest from Port-au-Prince, so it's best to set off early. The denser parts of the forest are cool and tranquil, with sunlight filtering through the trees; this is a perfect place for easy hiking.

CÔTE DES ARCADINS

Rte Nationale 1 is the main highway to Cap-Haïtien via Gonaïves. It skirts the coast, called the Côte des Arcadins, for most of the first 80km between Cabaret and St Marc. It is here that most of the country's beach resorts are situated, at the foot of the deforested Chaine des Matheux mountains. The beaches are not too inspiring, but do offer safe, shallow swimming in clear water. The Arcadins themselves are a trio of sand cays surrounded by coral reefs, about 3km out to sea in the Golfe de la Gonâve. This is the best area for diving in Haiti, and near St Marc you can see one of the largest underwater sponges in the world: see Activities in Haiti's Facts for the Visitor chapter.

As you drive northwards along Rte Nationale 1, you will see roadside signposts marking the different turnoffs for the beaches. The distance from Port-au-Prince is included in their addresses to aid location. **Montrouis**, from where small sailboats depart to Île de la Gonâve each day, is a good place to stop if you want to buy cheap eats. All along the roadside there are food stalls selling fresh fruit, strong coffee, rice, beans and *mayi moulen* (a tasty ground cornmeal dish).

The **Plage Publique**, tucked in between the Kaliko Beach Resort and the Wahoo Bay Beach, at Km 63, opened in 1997. There is no entrance fee for the public beach, which is exceptional in an area where only the elite can afford the other resorts. It started off clean and organized, using portable toilets left behind by the US Marines, but maintenance has been low and the facilities are a bit run down. The atmosphere is great, though, with lots of people arriving from the city by taptap wearing some very creative alternatives to swimsuits.

HAITI

Rice and beans, corn on the cob, beers, Cokes and the local bootleg rum, *clairin*, are all for sale on the beach and there's always a lively soccer game taking place on the adjoining football pitch.

If you are driving to Cap-Haïtien, you could break your journey by staying at a beach resort, or further north in Gonaïves (see Northern Haiti), as first-time driving in Haiti can be very tiring. The road is surfaced but deteriorates north of St Marc.

Places to Stay & Eat

The *Kyona Beach Club* (☎ 257-6863, 257-6850, fax 257-6776), Rte Nationale 1, at Km 60, the closest resort to Port-au-Prince, attracts many day-trippers and gets quite busy on weekends. The white-sand beach is very clean, and there are tables and recliners along it. There is a restaurant, bar, changing rooms and volleyball court. The resort has 20 small, neat chalets costing US$40. If you want to visit for the day, you can buy a US$9 ticket which includes a meal and a drink.

Kaliko Beach Resort (☎ 298-4609, 298-4607, 298-4608, fax 298-4610), Rte Nationale 1, Km 62, is a large, modern resort, lacking any perceivable Haitian atmosphere. There are many facilities here, including a swimming pool, scuba diving (US$15 an hour), water sports and tennis. A double room costs US$140, which includes all food and drinks with meals. If you just want to spend the day there, the charge is US$30, which includes food, drinks and access to the sports amenities.

The *Wahoo Bay Beach* (☎ 223-2950/53, fax 222-5332, wahoo@dadesky.com), Rte Nationale 1, Km 64, is a very attractive resort with bungalows set in lush green gardens skirting a fine, white-sand beach. A double room, including breakfast, costs US$60 plus 10% tax. There is a restaurant, bar and huge swimming pool in the complex. The resort offers many sports, including windsurfing, sailing, deep-water fishing, diving and snorkeling, and, best of all, on weekends it organizes country horseback expeditions for only US$7 a day.

The *Ouanga Bay Beach Hotel* (☎ 257-7889, 257-9292 ext 536, fax 222-4422), Rte Nationale 1, Km 66, is nestled on a 250m beach framed by local trees. The marble-floored reception rooms are stylish and intimate, and there is a warm atmosphere, largely due to the charming owner, Marie Roy Daniel. All the rooms have balconies overlooking the sea, and are decorated Haitian style with wooden paneling, rattan furniture and metalworks. Each double room costs US$57 and includes breakfast. The facilities include Jet Skis, surfing and windsurfing, and a nightclub and live music on the weekends. You can visit for the day for US$9, which includes dinner and sports.

Moulin sur la Mer (☎ 223-5700, 223-5705, fax 222-7652, moulinsm@haitiworld.com), Rte Nationale 1, Km 77, is just north of the small town of Montrouis. Built around a restored 17th-century colonial building, the complex has a swimming pool, restaurant, bar, beach jetty and 45 rooms set in landscaped gardens of palm trees and bougainvillea. The rooms have private bathrooms and balconies and cost US$90/105 single/double, which includes both breakfast and evening meal.

The Creole menu in the *Boucanier* restaurant at Moulin sur la Mer serves superb lobster for US$13.50. In addition to the usual beach sports, the resort offers a comprehensive PADI dive package including instruction, night diving and boat trips. The colonial building at the entrance now houses a museum that covers Haitian history from the arrival of Christopher Columbus until independence in 1804.

Club Med (☎ 278-6096, fax 278-6357) has a complex it calls Magic Haiti at Rte Nationale 1, Km 80. There's an office in Pétionville (☎ 257-9004) at 83 Rue Grégoire. Each of its 353 rooms, with all the modern conveniences, cost US$85 per person, which includes three meals, entertainment and all sports activities. The modern complex is large and flashy but intrinsically soulless; there's an excellent swimming pool here, though. You can be a day guest for US$30, which includes one meal and all sports activities.

Getting There & Away

Rte Nationale 1, leaving north out of Port-au-Prince, will take you past all the resorts. If you wish to take public transport, catch a bus or taptap leaving from Estation O'Cap beside the Shell station, at the confluence of Blvd Jean Jacques Dessalines and Blvd La Saline in Port-au-Prince.

Check beforehand to see if the driver is willing to let you off at your destination, as some express buses go straight to St Marc or Gonaïves.

Southern Haiti

This area of Haiti encompasses the whole southern claw that protrudes south and southwest of Port-au-Prince. The area has fared much better in environmental terms than the rest of the country, retaining a larger percentage of its tree cover. Two of Haiti's major national parks, Macaya and La Visite, are in the south, and they contain verdant rain forest and cloud forest and many of Haiti's endemic mammal and bird species.

Rte Nationale 2 and Rte de l'Amité (Rte Nationale 204) are the only main roads running through the south. The latter passes through the mountains to the southern resort of Jacmel, and the former travels the whole length of the southern claw, from Port-au-Prince to Jérémie. There are some small towns of interest to the traveler en route to Jérémie, such as Petit-Goâve (actually grander than its diminutive neighbor Grand Goâve) and Miragoâne. Both are small ports, but Miragoâne is livelier: its streets brimming over with second-hand mattresses, clothes and cookware shipped over from Miami. Miragoâne also has a

large cathedral towering over its crowded streets and a lively, twice-weekly market.

JACMEL

Jacmel (pop 10,000) is about 120km southwest of Port-au-Prince by road. Its tranquil tempo is the perfect balm after the frantic pace of Port-au-Prince. Jacmel was a busy coffee port at the turn of the century and stills retains much of its late-Victorian grace. The streets are wide and sleepy, lined with elegant 19th-century townhouses and warehouses with wrought-iron filigree balconies and nine-foot-tall doors. Jacmel is the epitome of that old cliché 'faded grandeur.' The once-magnificent buildings, many now closed or decaying, are an ambling display of crumbling walls and peeling facades.

But the town, which has a strong life and creativity of its own, is experiencing a long-awaited renaissance. Jacmel has had a long-standing kinship with artists and the arts, and it has now become a refuge for artists from all over Haiti, Europe and the USA. It is the birthplace of award-winning poet

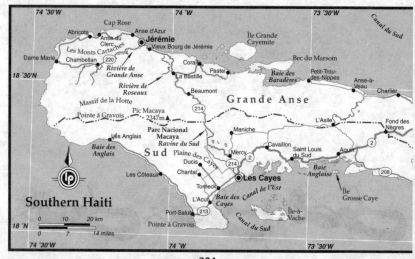

Southern Haiti

René Dépestre and also of Préfète Duffaut, an acclaimed painter who created unique paintings of the town and its bay.

Some of the finest buildings are on Rue Seymour Pradel and Rue du Commerce, which run parallel to the waterfront. East of Place d'Armes, the town square, is a red-and-green baroque iron market built in 1895, which resembles a scaled-down version of the grand iron market in Port-au-Prince. The 19th-century Cathédrale de St Phillippe et St Jacques is on Rue de l'Eglise close to the market.

History

In 1698, French authorities officially inaugurated Jacmel as the capital of the South East Colony, 50 years before the creation of Port-au-Prince. The site was originally an Arawak Indian settlement called Jacquezy, and it was discovered by the Spanish in the 16th century and renamed Villa Nueva de Yaquimo. By the 18th century, Jacmel was one of the most important judicial centers in Haiti.

In 1789, in the spirit of the French Revolution, the mulatto residents of Jacmel began demanding equality with the whites. Led by Jean-Baptiste Beauvais, the mulatto class

successfully won its rights in 1791. Soon after, Jacmel became an important strategic battleground during Haiti's fight for independence from the French. From Jacmel, Lamour Derance led the pro-independence resistance struggle (1802-04) for two hard years. After independence in 1804, Jean-Jacques Dessalines overthrew Derance to lead the country. At the same time, Magloire Ambroise was named the uncontested mayor of Jacmel, and the citizens settled down to rebuilding and modernizing their city.

Jacmel also played a role in the South American movement for independence from Spain. In 1806 Venezuelan revolutionary Francisco de Miranda stayed in Jacmel and designed the flag that would become the banner of Simón Bolívar's liberation army. In 1816 Bolívar himself spent a brief time in a house on the main square while he assembled his revolutionary army. Around two hundred Haitian volunteers joined Bolívar when he left to free South America from the yoke of Spanish colonialism.

By the middle of the 19th century, Jacmel played a vital role in trade with Europe. Cargo, mail and voyagers from throughout the Caribbean region gathered here to meet steamships bound for Britain. You can still

find the names of many Europeans on the gravestones in the cemetery, a testament to those more cosmopolitan days. By the late 19th century Jacmel was a prosperous coffee port. It was the first town in Haiti to have telephones and potable water, and when the Cathédrale de St Phillippe et St Jacques was lit up on Christmas Eve 1895, Jacmel became the first town to have electric light. The city center was destroyed by a huge fire in 1896 and then rebuilt in the unique Creole architectural style that remains to this day.

Two European world wars, a vicious hurricane in 1955 and the Papa Doc regime have all taken their toll on Jacmel, depleting its last vestiges of trade and commerce. For the last three decades it's suffered from an economic stupor. Now the government and the private sector seem willing to invest in Jacmel again. A small new cigar production business has started up, and an essential-oils plant has opened, using sandalwood, limes and vetiver, a root found in the area. The government hopes to attract cruise ships and tourists, and is planning substantial investment in the local handicrafts industry and in the renovation of the wharf area.

Orientation

Jacmel shelters in the beautiful, 3km-wide Baie de Jacmel. The streets wind down three small hills toward the black-sand beach. Many of the parallel streets are joined by steep narrow steps running in between the houses. Three main roads enter Jacmel: one from Léogâne and Port-au-Prince in the north, one from Bainet in the west and one from Cayes Jacmel and Marigot in the east.

As it enters town, the Port-au-Prince road becomes Ave de la Liberté, Jacmel's central street, which leads straight to the shore. From Ave de la Liberté, steep steps lead up to the Place d'Armes, the town square. Close to the seafront, Rue du Commerce has many fine examples of 19th-century warehouses; at the far east end of the street are the customs house, an old 18th-century prison and the wharf. On Rue St-Anne, parallel with Rue du Commerce, are many small shops run by local artisans, and the beachfront bars. East of the town square, on Rue de l'Eglise, are the iron

market and the cathedral. The rambling cemetery is at the far east end of Rue Alcius Charmant, one block north of Rue de l'Eglise.

The buses from Port-au-Prince pick up and drop off passengers at Marché Geffard, a small market on Ave de la Liberté, just north of the intersection with Ave Baranquia (also called Rue des Cayes or the Cayes-Jacmel road).

The town is small enough that you can walk everywhere, but you will need transportation to visit the good beaches to the east of town (see Around Jacmel, later).

Information

Tourist Offices At the time of writing, there was no official tourist office in Jacmel, but you can visit the mayor's representative for tourism, Madame Michaele Craan. She can be found either by inquiring at the Hôtel de la Ville (Town Hall) on the Place d'Armes, or at her home at 26 Rue Magloire Ambroise (☎ 288-2088, fax 288-2901). There are no travel agencies in town.

Money There is a branch of Banque Nationale de Crédit (BNC; ☎ 288-2081) on Grand Rue. The banks are open 9 am to 4 pm weekdays. Matekha (☎ 288-3701), a hardware shop on the town square at Rue de l'Eglise, is a handy place to change money; they give a very good rate. Matekha is open 8 am to 4 pm Monday to Saturday.

Post & Communications You can place overseas and national calls at the Teleco office (☎ 288-2299, 288-3191) on Ave Baranquia. The post office is on Rue du Commerce and is open 8 am to 4 pm Monday to Saturday.

Laundry There are no laundromats offering wash-and-dry facilities, but most of the bigger hotels will provide this service. However, there is a dry cleaner called Perfection Dry Cleaning on Rue Seymour Pradel, which reassuringly advertises that 'you need not fear, your clothes will not burn, as we do not use wood but electricity.'

Medical Services The Hôpital St Michel (☎ 288-2151) on Rue St-Philippe can deal

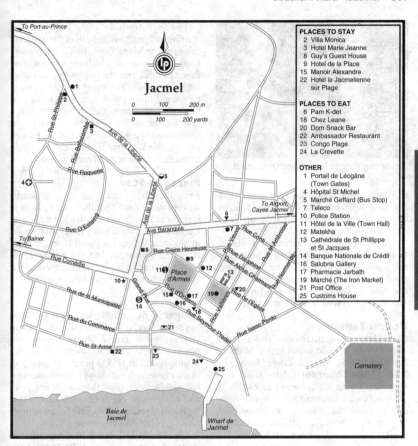

Jacmel

To Port-au-Prince

To Airport
Cayes Jacmel

To Bainet

0   100   200 m
0   100   200 yards

PLACES TO STAY
2 Villa Monica
3 Hotel Marie Jeanne
8 Guy's Guest House
9 Hotel de la Place
15 Manoir Alexandre
22 Hotel la Jacmelienne
     sur Plage

PLACES TO EAT
6 Pam K-det
18 Chez Leane
20 Dom Snack Bar
22 Ambassador Restaurant
23 Congo Plage
24 La Crevette

OTHER
1 Portail de Léogâne
    (Town Gates)
4 Hôpital St Michel
5 Marché Geffard (Bus Stop)
7 Teleco
10 Police Station
11 Hôtel de la Ville (Town Hall)
12 Matekha
13 Cathédrale de St Phillippe
     et St Jacques
14 Banque Nationale de Crédit
16 Salubria Gallery
17 Pharmacie Jarbath
19 Marché (The Iron Market)
21 Post Office
25 Customs House

HAITI

Place
d'Armes

Baie de
Jacmel

Wharf de
Jacmel

Cemetery

with emergencies, but do not expect high
standards. Dr Gerald Bertrand (☎ 288-
2423), at 15 Rue Magloire Ambroise, and Dr
Jean Robert Martinez (☎ 288-2331), on the
corner of Rue Vaivres and Rue Dauphine,
have been recommended by the tourism
representative. You can buy prescription
drugs at Pharmacie Jarbath (☎ 288-2487) on
40 Rue d'Orleans.

Emergency The police station (☎ 288-2921)
is on the corner of Ave de la Liberté and
Rue Comédie. The Red Cross (☎ 288-2664)
is at 26 Rue Henry Christophe.

Dangers & Annoyances Jacmel is one of
the most relaxed towns in Haiti and the
most accustomed to visitors. Apply logical
caution while walking at night and don't
flaunt your camera or money. People will
attach themselves to you hoping to be your
guide, but they can be politely and easily
shaken off if you do not require them. At
Carnival, if you don't adhere to the parking
restrictions, the police may confiscate your
vehicle's license plates. Check to see if they
are still attached before you leave. They can
be retrieved at the police station, but you
may have to pay a fine. Near the Place

Wrought-iron filigree balcony in Jacmel

LEAH GORDON

d'Armes, certain locals have made an irritating habit out of letting the air out of foreigners' car tires, perhaps to rustle up some money for the tire fixers.

The dark beach that stretches along the front of Jacmel is strewn with rubbish, and the water, being so close to the town, is not good for swimming. The best beaches are to the east of Jacmel on the road to Cayes Jacmel; see Around Jacmel for details.

Vodou Temples

Jacmel has a strong tradition of Vodou. If you wish to visit a Vodou temple, try Madame Nèva on Rue St-Anne or Louis Marque on Rue Alcius Charmant (also called Rue Cimetière), who are the most accessible to visitors. It is advisable to arrive with a guide and to treat the priest or priestess with respect by offering a gift, traditionally a bottle of five-star Barbancourt rum.

Special Events

In Jacmel, the pre-Lent Mardi Gras festivities are unique. They are highlighted by a surrealistic street theater in which people in huge, fantastical papier-mâché masks act out ancient parables of good against evil. The dreamlike host of characters includes crocodiles and tigers chased by red devils with four-foot wooden wings on hinges, which they smack together dangerously. Strange mythological beasts and barnyard animals clatter down the street and are herded away by sun-shaded saviors wearing denim, red bandannas and cowboy hats.

The festivities take place every Sunday starting on Epiphany, the 6th of January, and culminate on Mardi Gras, the Tuesday before Lent. The costumes, which are more surreal than splendid, and the papier-mâché masks are made locally. The street theater seems to be played more for the enjoyment of participants – who know their roles intimately – than for the audience. There is none of the sequin-and-sparkle of Carnival in Rio de Janeiro; this Carnival is unique in betraying its original roots in medieval Europe.

Places to Stay

Even though Jacmel is an obvious tourist destination, it hasn't got that many places to stay. It can be difficult to find a hotel room at Carnival time, when you should try to book in advance. Whenever possible street numbers are provided, but often the hotel owners do not know the number themselves. Where there is no number, nearby landmarks are given.

Budget A five-minute walk out of town, beyond Marché Geffard and the *taptap* station, is the *Hotel Marie Jeanne* (no phone), 60 Ave de la Liberté. It has six double rooms at US$13 per room, which all share one very basic shower. The building is old and wooden, and the rooms are poky and partitioned off from each other. Stay here only if you are desperate for an authentic rough Haitian experience.

On Ave de la Liberté just opposite the Portail de Léogâne is the *Villa Monica* (no phone), another simple guest house. There are three doubles at US$20 per room, and four larger rooms for six people at US$40 per room. Bathroom facilities are shared and morning coffee is included in the price.

Guy's Guest House (☎ 288-2569), next to the Tabernacle Protestant Church on Ave de la Liberté, is clean and basic, offering 10 double rooms, some with private bathrooms, for US$10 per person including morning coffee. Electricity is promised between 7 pm and 5 am, but this can vary. There is a small street-level restaurant serving reasonable food and drinks.

Mid-Range The *Manoir Alexandre (☎ 288-2711)*, on Rue d'Orléans, is an old ginger-bread-style townhouse overlooking the Place d'Armes. It has 10 large, idiosyncratic rooms costing US$20 per person, which share two very basic bathrooms. The best rooms lead out onto the bougainvillea-covered verandah where breakfast is served. The electricity supply is unreliable. Even if you don't stay in this eccentric old hotel, drop by for the best cocktail in Jacmel, the Rum Alexandre, and enjoy one of the best views of the Baie de Jacmel.

The *Hotel de la Place (☎ 288-2832)*, at 3 Rue de l'Eglise on the Place d'Armes, has 15 modern and clean rooms, each with its own bathroom; singles/doubles are US$30/55, plus 10% tax. Many of the rooms at the rear command a fine view of the surrounding countryside. The hotel has a generator and is therefore unaffected by blackouts. There is also a lively terrace bar and restaurant (see Places to Eat & Drink, below).

Top End The *Hotel la Jacmelienne sur Plage (☎ 288-3451, 222-4899, fax 288-3453)*, on Rue St-Anne at Ave de la Liberté, has an enviable oceanside location on the Baie de Jacmel. Each of the graceful, well-furnished rooms has two large beds, a hot-water bathroom and louvered doors that open onto private balconies. Singles/doubles are US$42/ 60 plus 10% tax and a small energy charge (a generator provides constant electricity). There is a gallery restaurant and a poolside bar and restaurant (see Places to Eat & Drink, below). Other facilities include an outdoor swimming pool, sports center, a badminton court and three new conference rooms.

Places to Eat & Drink

Most of the restaurants in Jacmel serve typical Haitian fare. The best of the small cheap places is *Chez Leane (☎ 288-3166)*, at 44 Rue d'Orléans, a sleepy street leading down to the wharf from the Place d'Armes. It seats about 20 and is open 8 am to 9 pm Monday to Saturday and 8 am until 3 pm on Sunday. A *plat complet* (a single dish with meat, rice and peas, plantain and salad) costs about US$4 and local beers are US$1.

The *Dom Snack Bar (☎ 288-3781)*, near the iron market on the corner of Rue de l'Eglise and Rue Vallieres, is a cheerful little café serving hamburgers, pizzas and ice cream as well as the usual Haitian food. Prices range from US$1 for a burger and US$2 for a pizza to US$5 for a plat complet. Beers and rum are also available.

Pam K-det, on Ave Baranquia near Rue Veuve, is a nice small bar that also sells sandwiches and hamburgers (US$1.50), which are prepared for the *Coquette Market*, a small supermarket, next door. Between 5 and 6 pm, they serve Dominican barbecue dishes from US$4, and beers are under US$1.

The restaurant at *Hotel de la Place (☎ 288-2832)*, 3 Rue de l'Eglise, is lively and popular with a great view of life in the main square; a small band plays music on the weekends. It's the perfect place to sit back, drink rum and survey Jacmel street life, and it's the ideal vantage point during Carnival. It seats 25, with four tables on the terrace. The menu is mainly Haitian; main courses are US$5 to US$8 and hamburgers and sandwiches are US$1 and up.

La Crevette (☎ 288-2834), on Rue St-Anne, has a long covered dining area that overlooks the sea. They serve a good variety of seafood; lobster (US$10) is their specialty. The big bar serves a selection of local and imported beers (around US$2), and the large dance floor hosts live or recorded music every Friday and Saturday.

The other seafront joint is the slightly run-down *Congo Plage*, 27 Rue St-Anne. The small, cheap restaurant in the front serves a plat complet for US$5. In the back, there's a huge dance floor and stage, which has seen better days. It hosts a wild scene on weekend nights, however, when it is packed with people drinking and dancing to compas music. It's an essential Haitian experience.

The *Ambassador Restaurant (☎ 288-3451)* is on the 1st-floor gallery of the Hotel la Jacmelienne sur Plage (see Places to Stay, above). The candlelit restaurant overlooks the sea through stained-glass windows and serves quality French cuisine at high prices. Level with the beach, the esplanade restaurant by the pool serves sandwiches, hamburgers (US$3) and chicken dishes (US$10).

Shopping

Jacmel is renowned for its tradition of papier-mâché crafts, a skill that has been passed down for generations. These wonderful papier-mâché artifacts are not produced anywhere else in Haiti. Papier-mâché was first used to make the dramatic masks worn at Jacmel's Carnival, and the craft has expanded to include unique hand-painted wall decorations of tigers, taptaps, boats and many more subjects. Prices range from US$3 for smaller subjects to US$20 for large masks. Jacmel's artisans also specialize in bright and delicately hand-painted boxes, trays and placemats (US$2 to US$7). Most of the shops are on Rue St-Anne, on either side of the Hotel la Jacmelienne sur Plage.

Jacmel also has some excellent art galleries. Two good small galleries, Foyer des Artistes and Shop Art Tropical, are at the northern edge of town on Ave de la Liberté.

Shop selling Carnival masks in Jacmel

The eclectic Salubria Gallery (☎ 288-2390), 26 Rue Seymour Pradel, is in a fin-de-siècle gingerbread house and open all year round. It's owned by an American professor, Robert Bricston, and you basically trail around the whole house, even the bathrooms and bedrooms; the walls are packed with paintings, most of them for sale. His collection includes most of the masters of Haitian art, including Fortuné Gerard, Préfète Duffaut, Prince Jean-Jo and Lafortune Felix.

Getting There & Away

Air There is a small airstrip outside of town where private and chartered planes can land, but at the moment there are no scheduled flights from Port-au-Prince to Jacmel.

Bus Buses leave from Marché Geffard. This is not a station but a small square with enough space for four or five buses to park and wait for passengers. The destination of the bus is written on the front. Buses for Port-au-Prince, Miragoâne and Les Cayes cost 25 gourdes (US$1.50) one way, and those to Cayes Jacmel (the nearby beaches) cost 5 gourdes. There is usually one bus leaving every hour to Port-au-Prince, depending on how quickly the bus fills up. The trip takes about four hours. If you prefer to sit in the front of the bus, a much more comfortable and possibly safer ride, try offering the driver an extra fee of about US$3.

Car The drive from the capital takes about three hours on one of the best roads in Haiti. However, the time of day you leave Port-au-Prince has a great bearing on how long the journey will take. After about 8 am, the section of Rte Nationale 2 that passes through the overpopulated Carrefour area can become very jammed for about 20km. Once past Carrefour, continue on Rte 2 until Dufort, 4km after the town of Léogâne. At this junction, turn south onto Rte de l'Amité, built by the French at the end of the 1970s, which winds over some spectacular mountains on the way to Jacmel.

Taxi You could try to negotiate a deal with one of the car-owning guides in Port-au-

Prince for a deal on a day trip to Jacmel, but it is likely to be expensive, prices ranging wildly from US$35 to US$60.

Getting Around

Jacmel is easy enough to negotiate by foot. If you want to reach the beaches to the east, buses leave regularly from the Marché Geffard bound for Cayes Jacmel or Marigot and cost 5 gourdes (US$0.30).

AROUND JACMEL
Beaches

The best beaches in the area are to the east of Jacmel. There are three; two before and one after the small village of Cayes Jacmel. The road is a little rough (although it is undergoing improvements), but it can still be navigated in an ordinary car. Buses from Jacmel will also drop you off at any of these spots for 5 gourdes (US$0.30). Note that the undertow is especially strong along this coastline and can be fatal for weak swimmers; don't swim out too far.

The farthest beach is **Plage Ti Mouillage**; it's 17km from Jacmel and about 3km after Cayes Jacmel. Ti Mouillage is a white-sand beach stretching for about half a mile. Small privately owned houses overlook the beach at either end, but there is space to park cars in the center. There are no shops or facilities, so bring your own drinking water. The local villagers run small stalls here selling bottled drinks and freshly cooked lobster.

About 13km from Jacmel and just before Cayes Jacmel lies the very popular **Plage Raymond-les-Bains**. This is another long stretch of white sand with nothing but palm trees and mountains as a backdrop. There are parking places and showers available, and there are many stalls offering cooked fish and lobster most of the weekend.

About 10km outside of Jacmel on the road to Cayes Jacmel is *Cyvadier Plage* (☎ 288-2842). This small hotel and restaurant fronts a small **public beach** in a stunning half-moon-shaped cove flanked by rocky cliffs. It offers neat chalets with private showers and hot and cold water for US$40 a night. It has an outdoor bar and restaurant overlooking the cove. As the cove is quite

protected, the undertow presents less of a problem here than in other areas.

About 14km outside of Jacmel, in the village of Cayes Jacmel, is the small guesthouse *Bar Distraction*, 29 Rue BH Jeune. This is a great home base for visiting the beaches at Ti Mouillage and Raymond-les-Bains. The small pension has five simple, clean double rooms with basic, shared outdoor bathing facilities, for US$10 per person. A shady backyard runs down to the sea, and sometimes people sleep outside under the banana-leaf canopy, becalmed by the sound of the waves. Food and drinks are available on the premises, and in the early evening Haitian disco music plays on a sound system.

Bassins Bleu

A 12km trek, usually on horseback, into the mountains northwest of Jacmel leads to Bassins Bleu, three cobalt-blue pools joined by spectacular cascades. There are many guides in Jacmel who will, for a fee, take you on the journey by horse, which takes about two and a half hours each way. There is a small hamlet close to the pools where the horses are watered and rested, and from here the journey is continued on foot. Another guide, the unofficial guardian of the falls, will take over and lead you through the forest to the lakes. Be prepared to tip him a little extra for his work, probably around 10 gourdes. The path is a little uneven, and at one point you must climb up a steep rock face by rope, but it's not difficult and there are usually a lot of young men to help you.

The top pool is cut deep into the mountain and is sheltered and surrounded by smooth rocks draped with maidenhair and creeper ferns. Dissolved minerals give the water its stunning blue color. Bathing in private is difficult, as you will no doubt attract a small audience, who are not rude, just curious and amused. According to legend, water nymphs live in the three mountain grottoes. They are said to sit on a rock in Palm Lake, but disappear at the sound of mortal footsteps.

While it's possible to drive two-thirds of the way to Bassin Bleu in a 4WD vehicle (leave Jacmel by Rue Comédie), the trip is best enjoyed on horseback. Guides to organize this for you can be found at the gates of the Hotel la Jacmelienne sur Plage. It is advisable to negotiate the full price before you set off to avoid endless squabbling en route. Consider paying about US$6.50 per person, but you may have to pay more. After crossing the river, the track climbs steeply, revealing spectacular views of the Baie de Jacmel. A broad hat and sunblock are recommended.

PARC LA VISITE

One of the most spectacular hikes in Haiti is across the western section of Massif de la Selle, from Kenscoff to Seguin. This five- or six-hour hike is quite hard work and is not for the novice trekker – the popular Haitian proverb *dèyè mòn gen mòn* (beyond mountains, more mountains) must have been composed on this walk. The route traverses four mountains and includes stunningly beautiful terrain, but the weather can be harsh, including scorching sun, strong winds and sudden rains. However, once you reach Seguin, you can sleep overnight in a very pleasant guesthouse, the Auberge de la Visite. To return, you can either hike back to Kenscoff or continue south, walking the five-hour descent to Marigot, a small town on the southern coast near Jacmel.

You are advised to take supplies of water and food as well as warm clothing, as the altitude reaches over 2000m. Even though this is harsh, rugged terrain, this is also a major thoroughfare for local Haitians. The route is a well-used pedestrian highway, traveled primarily by women on their way to market balancing up to 30kg of produce on their heads. In Seguin there are some curious and quite stunning karst-formation rocks, called *krase dan* (broken teeth) by the locals.

The *Auberge de la Visite* (☎ 246-0166, 257-1579) has two buildings with four single-bed rooms. Each has a private bathroom with a hot shower and toilet. There is no heating, and at night temperatures can dip below 10°C, but there are lots of warm blankets available. Rooms cost US$50 per

person, which includes three meals a day. There are several porch areas where you can relax in one of the many rocking chairs and take in your surroundings. When it's clear, you can see the Caribbean Sea more than 2000m below. The dining room serves a mélange of Haitian, Lebanese and Italian cuisine, and vegetarians are well catered for. One of the three owners of the guesthouse is always present to look after your needs and provide stimulating dinner conversation, on anything from the local rain forest to Haitian culture. Horses and guides are available if you wish to explore the surrounding area.

Getting There & Away

From Pétionville, take a bus to Kenscoff and simply begin walking along the road to Seguin. It is possible to walk or take a 4WD from Kenscoff to a relay point (where the road becomes impassable by vehicle), where you can be met by representatives from the Auberge de la Visite with horses (US$20 per horse). This cuts the trek from five or six hours to three or four, but you must book the horses four days in advance. Leaving Seguin, if you descend to Marigot, a taptap will take you from there to Jacmel for US$1, where you can find a bus back to Port-au-Prince. The proprietors of the Auberge can probably help if you'd like to do the trek in reverse.

PARC MACAYA

The mountains in this national park are covered in rain forest, and there are a number of rough trails through this beautiful terrain. The most challenging trek, taking four days there and back, is to the top of Pic Macaya (2347m). You must cross over a 2100m ridge and descend another 1000m before attempting the mountain itself. The trails are not very well developed or maintained, and a machete is often needed to cut through the undergrowth. Guides are absolutely essential; they are available locally at the University of Florida camp (see below), and usually charge US$6 a day per person. Other than that camp, there are no facilities anywhere in the park, so you must bring everything you need. Cooking utensils and equipment vary from guide to guide, so be sure to find out what you need before you set off. Local spring water should not be drunk unless it has been boiled or chemically treated. Bring food, water, a tent and wet-weather clothing.

Les Cayes, on the southern coast of the southern claw, is the nearest town to the park. It is a quiet town, not unattractive, with a couple of hotels, the **_Concorde_** (☎ *286-0277, 257-0966*) and **_Le Meridien_** (☎ *286-0331*). Within the park, the University of Florida has a **_camp_** at Plaine Durand. The camp offers you minimal facilities, such as toilets, running water and a campsite, and it provides a good base from which you can tackle many of the surrounding hikes, such as the one to Pic Macaya.

To reach the park, take the southwest coastal road out of Les Cayes, and then turn north (a right-hand turn) after the village of Torbeck. The rough road heads through a river valley via Le Duc to the village of Dubreuil. You can also take a taptap from Les Cayes as far as Dubreuil. After Dubreuil, you must proceed on foot to the University of Florida project headquarters at Plaine Durand, which is a four-hour hike. Along the way you will pass the Fortress des Platons,

which was built by Dessalines in 1804, and the mountain village of Formond.

JÉRÉMIE
Jérémie is the most isolated town in Haiti. By land it's only accessible by a difficult 100km mountain road from Les Cayes, which is treacherous after rain. During the rainy season, buses from Port-au-Prince rarely make the trip, so most Haitians risk their lives on a 12-hour ferry trip from Port-au-Prince to get there. The boats are dangerously overloaded and they do not have a reassuring safety record. The city is overgrown and derelict, its streets lined with abandoned coffee warehouses and crumbling mansions. The decline is mostly due to the closure of its port on the orders of Papa Doc Duvalier in 1964. In its heyday Jérémie was known as the 'City of Poets,' due to the literary and artistic aspirations of its prosperous mulatto class. All that remains now is a mournful elegiac memory of the past.

However, the town is remarkable for its sense of isolation and history, and the journey from Les Cayes passes through some stunning scenery. If you make the trip here, you can stay at the **_Hotel La Cabane, Borges_** (☎ *284-5128*).

Northern Haiti

The north monopolized most of the great events in Haitian history, from the arrival of Columbus to the ostentatious kingdom of Henri Christophe. There are still many monuments left from these times, including the magnificent Citadelle, the palace of Sans Souci and many waterside forts. The coastline northwest of Cap-Haïtien is some of the most spectacular in Haiti and has a few secluded places to stay.

CAP-HAÏTIEN

Cap-Haïtien, with a population of 100,000, is the second-largest city in Haiti. It has a rich history and there are plenty of places to visit in the surrounding area. Known as O'Cap to the locals, it has a more Latin feel than the rest of Haiti. The streets, laid out in a grid system, owe more to Spanish architecture than French, and are small and narrow so there is always a shady side to walk on. In comparison to Port-au-Prince, the city has a relaxed and parochial atmosphere, especially in the early evenings when the majority of residents hang out and chatter on their balconies. Sadly, the poverty in the slums to the south of the city equals that found in the capital.

Plage Rival, north of town, is strewn with orange peels and rubbish. The best beaches are to the northwest, about half an hour out of town by car or bus; see Around Cap-Haïtien, later in this chapter.

History

Though it lacks the splendor of a phoenix, Cap-Haïtien has more than once risen from the ashes. It suffered three major infernos, first in 1734, then in 1793 during the slave uprising, and again in 1802 when Henri Christophe set it ablaze to prevent it from falling into the hands of Napoleon's troops. In 1842 it was almost totally destroyed by an earthquake, and then nearly ruined again by a hurricane in 1928. Now, after the ravages of nature and history, it seems inclined to repose in a well-earned, placid torpor.

In 1665, Bertrand d'Ogeron de la Bouère was chosen by Louis XIV to govern the French portion of Saint-Domingue. In 1670 buccaneers had started a new settlement on the mainland, and Bertrand d'Ogeron named it Cap-François, granting refuge within its precincts to Calvinists fleeing France. As the slave trade from Africa proceeded in earnest and the buccaneers withdrew, French settlers began to move in, building plantations in the surrounding plains to cultivate crops of sugarcane, tobacco, cocoa and indigo. By the middle of the 18th century, the city, now renamed Cap-Française, had become France's wealthiest colonial capital. In 1701 there were only 35 plantations in all of Haiti, but by 1752 there were 306 plantations in the area of Cap-Française alone. The plantations on the highly productive Plaine du Nord supplied almost half of Europe with sugar and cocoa, and Le Cap, as it was generally referred to, acted as a port and commercial center. It became so illustrious it was known by Europeans as the 'Paris of the Antilles.'

The prosperity of the city was built on the back of slave labor, and during the second half of the 18th century, the Paris of the Antilles became the battleground for many fierce struggles for liberty. The fine squares of Le Cap bore witness to the cruel execution of many who challenged the status quo. François Makandal, the infamous insurgent slave, was burned alive in front of the steps of the cathedral in 1758; Vincent Ogé and Jean Baptiste Chavannes, who demanded rights for mulattos, were tortured to death in the Place d'Armes in 1790; and Boukman, the leader of the slave rebellion conceived at the ceremony of Bois Cayman, was beheaded in 1791, and his head was paraded on a pole in a city square. It was also here that Toussaint L'Ouverture, deceived by the French Republic, was captured and shipped to his icy incarceration in the Jura Mountains in France.

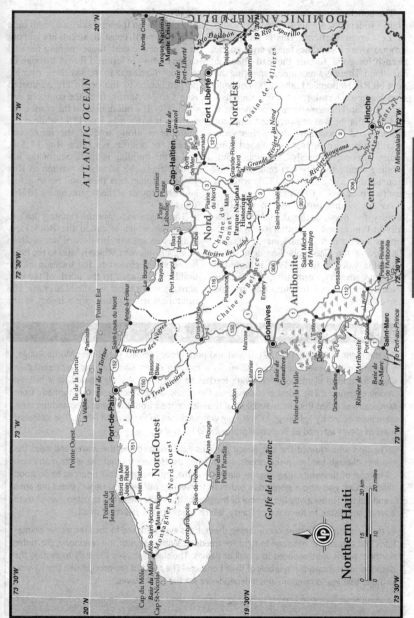

Northern Haiti

The conclusion of the struggle that sired Haiti's independence took place just south of Le Cap at Vertiéres. This is the battleground where Dessalines finally crushed the French for good, forcing them to abandon the island. There is a monument marking the spot on Rte Nationale 1, about 3km outside Cap-Haïtien. Dessalines changed the city's name to Cap-Haïtien after independence. It was here that he was crowned first emperor in 1804, and it was here that, seven years later, Henri Christophe was crowned King Henry I. In order to pacify Christophe's burgeoning vanity, the city was renamed Cap-Henri until his death in 1820, when it reverted back to Cap-Haïtien.

As the south prospered in the 19th century, the north declined, and thereafter Port-au-Prince took the central role in Haiti's history and economy. Charlemagne Peralté, the hero of the Caco rebellion against the US military occupation in 1915, is buried in the city cemetery, continuing the historic association between freedom fighters and Cap-Haïtien.

Orientation

The city lies on the west side of a small cape on Haiti's north coast. Its streets are laid out in a geometric grid; those running parallel to the ocean are lettered Rue A through Q, A being the closest to the sea; those running perpendicular to the ocean are numbered Rue 1 to 24, starting from the southern end of the city. If a building is on the corner, the address is written as Rue 15 L, while if the building is along one of the numbered streets, the address is written Rue 14 A-B, and if the building is along one of the lettered streets, the address is written as Rue 13-14 A. Sometimes there will be an actual address number at the beginning; eg, 26 Rue 13-14 A.

There is a wide avenue running flush to the water which is called the Boulevard. Addresses on the Boulevard are written Rue 24 Boulevard, which relates to the numbered street closest to the location of the building. The area to the north of the city, across a water canal, is called Carenage. The utilitarian street names are a legacy of the

---

Bois Cayman & the Night of Fire

On the night of August 14, 1791, a wild and portentous tempest raged over Morne Rouge, a mountain that overlooks Cap-Haïtien. In a clearing called Bois Cayman, representative slaves from local plantations – carrying torches to light their way – gathered for a historic Vodou ceremony. The priest presiding over the rituals, a gigantic black slave formerly from Jamaica, was called Boukman. As claps of thunder echoed from the mountains and the skies were illuminated by lightning, a Creole pig was sacrificed to the gods of Africa. The gathered mass of slaves listened as Boukman pronounced his war cry:

> The god who created the sun which gives us light, who rouses the waves and rules the storm, though hidden in the clouds, he watches us. He sees all that the white man does. The god of the white man inspires him with crime, but our god calls upon us to do good works. Our god who is good to us orders us to revenge our wrongs. He will direct our arms and aid us. Throw away the symbol of the god of the whites who has so often caused us to weep, and listen to the voice of liberty, which speaks to the hearts of us all.

With the ravages of nature encouraging them, the slaves returned to their respective plantations and spread the message to fight for freedom. Within days of the ceremony, the fertile northern plains were reduced to a wall of flames. The slaves worked tirelessly to destroy the despised plantations, the symbols of their bondage. The night of fire precipitated the 13-year struggle that led to freedom and independence for the black slaves.

HAITI

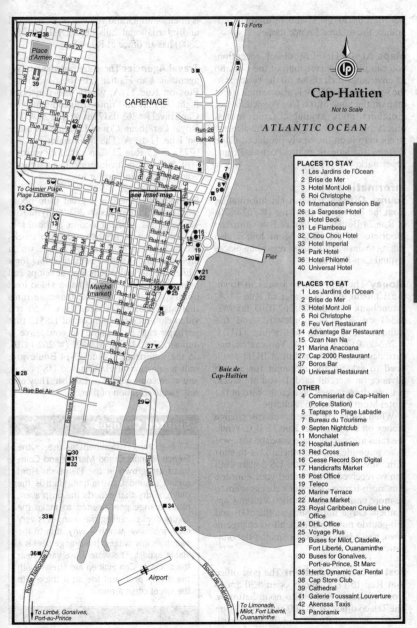

CARENAGE

ATLANTIC OCEAN

Rue 26
Rue 25

To Cormier Plage,
Plage Labadie

To Forts

*Baie de
Cap-Haïtien*

Pier

Rue Bel Air

Marché
(market)

To Limbé, Gonaïves,
Port-au-Prince

Airport

To Limonade,
Milot, Fort Liberté,
Ouanaminthe

PLACES TO STAY
1 Les Jardins de l'Ocean
2 Brise de Mer
3 Hotel Mont Joli
6 Roi Christophe
10 International Pension Bar
26 La Sargesse Hotel
28 Hotel Beck
31 Le Flambeau
32 Chou Chou Hotel
33 Hotel Imperial
34 Park Hotel
36 Hotel Philomé
40 Universal Hotel

PLACES TO EAT
1 Les Jardins de l'Ocean
2 Brise de Mer
3 Hotel Mont Joli
6 Roi Christophe
8 Feu Vert Restaurant
14 Advantage Bar Restaurant
15 Ozan Nan Na
21 Marina Anacoana
27 Cap 2000 Restaurant
37 Boros Bar
40 Universal Restaurant

OTHER
4 Commiseriat de Cap-Haïtien
   (Police Station)
5 Taptaps to Plage Labadie
7 Bureau du Tourisme
9 Septen Nightclub
11 Monchalet
12 Hospital Justinien
13 Red Cross
16 Cesse Record Son Digital
17 Handicrafts Market
18 Post Office
19 Teleco
20 Marine Terrace
22 Marine Market
23 Royal Caribbean Cruise Line
   Office
24 DHL Office
25 Voyage Plus
27 Buses for Milot, Citadelle,
   Fort Liberté, Ouanaminthe
30 Buses for Gonaïves,
   Port-au-Prince, St Marc
35 Hertz Dynamic Car Rental
38 Cap Store Club
39 Cathedral
41 Galerie Toussaint Louverture
42 Akenssa Taxis
43 Panoramix

Place
d'Armes

Rue 21
Rue 20
Rue 19
Rue 18
Rue 17
Rue 16
Rue 15
Rue 14
Rue 13
Rue 12

see inset map

Boulevard

Route Nationale

Barrière Bouteille

Rue Laponi

Route de l'Aéroport

US Marines in 1915, who refused to pronounce the original French names.

Maps At the Hotel Mont Joli reception, you can pick up a free map of the city and its environs, which shows all the beaches to the west of town. There is also a small street map on the back of the free Association of Hoteliers map, available from tourist offices and car rental agencies. The clearest street map is on the newly produced *Carte d'Haiti,* for sale in many Port-au-Prince supermarkets (US$3).

Information

Tourist Offices You can get information from the Bureau du Tourisme (☎ 262-0870) at Rue 24 Boulevard. Walter Bussenius, the proprietor of the Hotel Mont Joli, is also willing to answer questions regarding places around Cap-Haïtien.

Money There are three banks in town: the Unibank on the corner of Rue 11 A, Promobank (☎ 262-0800, 262-0503, fax 262-0854) on Rue 17 Boulevard, and the Banque de L'Union Haïtienne (BUH; ☎ 262-0690) at Rue 17 A. You can change currency at all of them, but at BUH you'll need to ask for the manager for a cash advance on a credit card. If you are stuck, you can draw money on a credit card at the Hotel Mont Joli for a 5% charge.

When banks are closed, you can change money on the street on Rue 11 B-C. While the rates are usually quite good, be sure you have some idea of the official rate to start with. Never hand over your US dollars until you've received and counted your gourdes. American Express traveler's checks seem to be more easily dealt with than Visa in Cap-Haïtien. Large notes, such as the 500- and 250-gourde notes, are difficult to change in town, so it's best to ask for smaller-denomination notes.

Post & Communications The post office is at Rue 16-17 A, and is open 8:30 am to 4 pm weekdays, 8:30 am to noon Saturday. The Teleco office (☎ 262-0000, 262-0219), on Rue 17 between Rue A and the Boulevard, is open 24 hours, and you can place national and international calls here. DHL (☎ 262-2300) has an office at Rue 11 A.

Travel Agencies There are not many travel agents in Cap-Haïtien. The best is Voyage Plus on Rue 11 A, where you can book flights to Port-au-Prince. You could also try Cap Travel (☎ 262-0517) at 84 Rue 23 A. The Royal Caribbean Cruise Line has an office on Rue 11-12 A. The Monchalet (☎ 262-0775), at 25 Rue 21 C, is certainly worth a visit as it offers an interesting mixture of voyages, tours and art for sale.

Bookstores There is a great little bookstore called Panoramix (☎ 262-0078) on Rue 12 A. It has a big selection of books in French, none in English, but also stocks recent issues of *Time* and *Newsweek*, which are a godsend if you've been traveling for a while. The store also sells film, develops and prints it for US$7.50, and has a video loan library with many English-language films that cost US$1.20 for three days. There is a video club membership cost of US$12 that perhaps can be waived if you leave a deposit. The Marina Market (☎ 262-1470), on the waterfront at Rue 13-14 Boulevard, sells a selection of Haitian and US papers, and even some books in English. They also sell a wide selection of film.

Spirited Oranges

All the oranges destined for use in the French liqueurs Grand Marnier and Cointreau are grown in the Plaine du Nord region around Cap-Haïtien. Haiti is the only country that exports the unsprayed, bitter orange peel needed to make the luxury drinks. Peeling the oranges is very labor intensive, which is why, due to the country's low wages, the orange peel is a viable export. The warehouse yards near the docks in Cap-Haïtien are strewn with the drying peel, and the air is thick with the sweet citrus aroma.

Libraries & Cultural Centers Alliance Français (☎ 262-0132), at Rue 15 B-C, is a French cultural center with a good library of French-language books.

Laundry There are many dry cleaners around town, but if you merely want your clothes hand washed, it is best that you ask at your hotel. It will be arranged for you, and the price will usually be around US$3.

Medical Services The Hospital Justinien (☎ 262-0512, 262-0513) overlooks the town on Rue 17 Q. There are three good clinics, recommended by the hotels: Clinique Antoni Constant (☎ 262-1577) at Rue 16 L 46; Clinique Medicale Toussaint (262-1616) at Rue 8 F 124; and Dr J Arthur Desrosiers (☎ 262-0597) on Rue 13 J-H. The latter is a lawyer as well as a doctor, and he comes highly recommended by many of the UN employees in town.

There are many pharmacies dotted around town. You can try Saint Pierre (☎ 262-0781) at 87 Rue 8 F-G, Pharmacie Vincent (☎ 262-0831) on Rue 12 D, the Pharmacie Capoise (☎ 262-1885) at 125 Rue 5 J-K, Kekule (☎ 262-27100) on Rue 15-16 L, and Pharmacie St Trinité (☎ 262-1551) at 66 Rue 12-13 L.

Emergency The police station, Commiseriat de Cap-Haïtien (☎ 262-0951, 262-2313), is at Rue 25-26 A in Carenage, just north of the small water canal. The Red Cross (☎ 262-0634) is at Rue 17 P.

Dangers & Annoyances Cap-Haïtien is a very relaxed city with a reportedly very low crime rate. There is none of the constant hassle from wannabe guides, and the market stall holders are frighteningly casual in comparison to those in Port-au-Prince. The traffic is light and calmed by the narrowness of the streets. Remember, as with the rest of Haiti, do not drink the tap water. If you take a day trip outside of Cap-Haïtien, carry a supply of bottled water.

Forts

If you take the Boulevard northwards until it joins Carenage, and then continue north,

you can discover three French fort sites. The first, **Fort Magny,** is on your left as you head north, and all that remains is piles of cannonballs. The next is **Fort Joseph,** on the right on the edge of the cliff. There are more remains here but there was no access at the time of writing. If you continue north until the road peters out at the beach, then go along the edge of the beach for a quarter of a mile, you will reach **Fort Picolet.** Although the fort itself is in ruins, some quite large walls and brick staircases are still standing, and you will find an amazing array of cannons. The view is perfect, and the spot is deserted and peaceful. This is a lovely place to spend a morning reading, or perhaps just sitting and speculating about Haiti's history.

Places to Stay

Most of the hotels in the budget section are extremely cheap but quite rough as well. They accommodate mostly long-term local residents, sailors and tap-tap drivers. They rarely have phones or foreign guests, and would probably at first be a little bemused. The security may also be fairly slack, so don't leave valuables in your room when you go out.

The hotels in Cap-Haïtien have one of the most confusing rate systems encountered in Haiti. Some mid-range hotels cost nearly as much as more luxurious hotels, so just because the hotel looks cheap doesn't necessarily mean that it is. Also, while it's usually cheaper to share a room if you are traveling in a group, strangely, some of the hotels seem to charge more for doing this.

Budget The two cheapest options overlook the bus station at the Barrière Bouteille (the city gates) on Rue L (also called the Rue Espanole). The diminutive *Chou Chou Hotel* is dark and gloomy but has wonderful labyrinthine staircases everywhere. Basic rooms that sleep two are US$5. The bathroom facilities are shared. Next door, *Le Flambeau* (☎ 262-2323) is larger and looks a little daunting due to the caged balconies overlooking the street. Inside, the rooms are simple and cheap (US$6 per person). All rooms have a fan, table and chair, and most

HAITI

overlook a busy and interesting street which can be noisy in early evening. The bathroom facilities are shared.

The *International Pension Bar* is very central at 89 Rue 22-23 A, but the quality of the rooms leaves a lot to be desired. For US$7 a night you get a rough, dark and claustrophobic room with a shared bathroom at the back of this old ramshackle wooden house. There is a small bar and restaurant at the front. The *Park Hotel*, on Rte de l'Aéroport at 35 Chevaichel, has 40 rooms, all with hot water. The rooms are large and clean with TVs, and cost between US$9 and US$22 per person, including breakfast. The hotel is certainly cheap, but it's charmless and away from the city center.

La Sargesse Hotel, at Rue 9 A, costs US$9/25 for a single/double including breakfast. All rooms have a fan and cold water, and there is a restaurant out front.

Mid-Range The *Universal Hotel* (☎ 262-0254) is a large central hotel with a cosmopolitan feel at 98 Rue 17 B. You're likely to meet sailors from Norway and Mexico on the airy staircase. It is built on three stories around a brightly colored central courtyard whose centerpiece is a magnificent mural depicting Psalm 37. All the rooms are clean and simple with fans, air con and bathrooms, costing US$30 for a double, including morning coffee. On the top floor are larger, breezy rooms with private balconies, which sleep four people for US$60.

The *Brise de Mer* (☎ 262-0821), at 4 Carenage, is close to the sea front in the northern section of town. It is a sweet old establishment with two verandahs, one for the restaurant and the other for rocking chairs, overlooking its overgrown garden. It has 16 rooms furnished with oversized antique furniture, all with private showers. Many of the rooms overlook the sea and enjoy the requisite breeze. The price of a room, at US$35/52 single/double, US$73 for a triple and US$90 for four people (plus 10% service tax), includes breakfast and a small supper.

Just outside of the city gates on Rte Nationale 1, you can find the *Hotel Imperial* (☎ 262-0171, fax 262-0534). It's a '60s-modern, motel-style building with a big parking area, tennis court and a clean swimming pool. The rooms are large, clean and airy, with private bathrooms and in many cases balconies. There are 27 rooms costing US$30/45 plus 10% tax, including breakfast. There is a restaurant and bar which serves reasonably priced meals. The hotel accepts Visa, American Express and Mastercard.

Nearby on the same stretch of road is the *Hotel Philomé* (☎ 262-1878), at Vertiéres on Rte Nationale 1. This is another motel-style hotel on the edge of town. There are 60 modern, pine-decorated rooms with air con, TV, private bathroom and telephone. Rooms cost US$23/60, which doesn't seem to make much sense.

To the west of town, in an area called Bel Air, is a large chalet complex on a woodsy hillside called *Hotel Beck* (☎ 262-0001, 262-1212), at 48 Rue Bel Air. The surrounding trees and view of the harbor give the place a Mediterranean feel. The complex itself resembles a '50s motel, especially the brightly painted furniture around the 55-foot spring-filled swimming pool. The 36 rooms have private bathrooms with hot and cold running water. The spacious dining room and verandah overlook the gardens of bougainvillea and palms. The hotel has its own private beach out of town for its guests' free use. If you hark after deserted 1950s holiday camps, then this is the place for you. Rooms are US$45 per person. *Les Jardins de l'Ocean* (☎ 262-2277, fax 262-1169), at 90 Carenage, overlooks the sea at the northern tip of town and has a rooftop terrace restaurant. The hotel has 10 double rooms, all with their own bathrooms, ranging from US$24 to US$45 depending on the size of the room.

Top End The *Roi Christophe* (☎ 262-0414), on Rue 24 B, is set in its own walled garden inhabited by clamorous jackdaws. This colonial building, in the heart of Cap-Haïtien, was originally built in 1724 as the French governor's palace. The style is more reminiscent of Spanish than French colonial, with tiled floors and an elegant, leafy central courtyard. The 20 rooms are furnished in period style and have private bathrooms and air con. The price per night for a double oranges from US$40 up to US$50 including breakfast, plus 10% tax and a 10% service charge. All credit cards are accepted.

The *Hotel Mont Joli* (☎ 262-0300, 222-7764, fax 262-0326), at the northern end of Rue B, has the joint benefits of seeming to be high above the city and yet feeling a part of it. It is built in many layers on a steep hill north of the old town center. The view of Cap-Haïtien's harbor is sensational, especially from the observation lounge, which has a 180° vista of the bay and the mountains behind. The hotel has a swimming pool on the edge of the hill with a poolside restaurant – great for taking a swim before breakfast. A troubadour band plays poolside every Friday night. The atmosphere at this family-run hotel is exceptionally lively and friendly, and the owner, Walter Bussenius, is very welcoming and willing to help with any advice or tips for your holiday. All rooms overlook the ocean, are modern and comfortable, and have private bathrooms and American cable TV. At least here the price becomes cheaper the more people that share; US$77/89 single/double, US$101 for a triple and US$113 for four people, including breakfast. The hotel takes all credit cards and if you are stranded will advance money on your credit card for a 5% charge. The hotel also has good guides who lead tours of the Citadelle.

Places to Eat & Drink

Most of the restaurants in town serve either traditional Haitian food and/or French cuisine, with the exception of a couple of pizza joints. Most of the street bars are small affairs with a couple of seats if you're lucky, usually selling Prestige, Heineken and rum. There are also the more expensive and spacious hotel bars.

The *Ozan Nan Na,* at 46 Rue 18 A, opposite the artisan's marketplace, is a wacky bar/restaurant and, later in the evening, a dance club. It looks like a Haitian-style, heavy-metal *bierkeller* (cellar pub), with a spacious bar in the front and a restaurant and dance floor in the room behind. Open 9 am until 2 am daily, it sells imported beer

and Guinness (US$1.20), sandwiches, and chicken or fish *plat complet* (US$2.50 to US$3.50). It's a real bargain, and there's a good view through the Wild West saloon doors onto the bustling market.

Opposite the cathedral, on the corner of the town square, is the *Boros Bar*, a small, clean bar/restaurant on Rue 20 H that is open 9 am until 11 pm. The food is fast and cheap, such as sandwiches (US$1), spaghetti (US$1.50) and a chicken-and-rice dinner (US$1.80). Next door is the little *Cap Store Club* (☎ 262-1022), at 26 Rue 20 H, an American-style bar with a pool table, selling local and imported beers (US$0.60/1.20). It also sells a number of luxury items from the US, such as radio cassettes, cosmetics and perfume. A couple of blocks away is the *Advantage Bar Restaurant*, at Rue 18 K, a lovely, authentic, brightly painted restaurant with gorgeous murals. An excellent chicken dinner is US$2.50, sandwiches are US$0.60, and all beers are less than US$1. It's open 6 am until 10 pm Monday to Saturday.

Barbershop façade in Cap-Haïtien

HAITI

The **Cap 2000 Restaurant**, on Rue 5 Boulevard, has a great friendly atmosphere and good food at reasonable prices. A chicken plat complet is only US$3.50, sandwiches US$1.50 and local beer under a dollar. The food is well prepared and tasty, and the restaurant is open 7 am until 11 pm. There's another dapper little restaurant called **Feu Vert Restaurant** on the Boulevard at Rue 24. It's sweetly decorated with colored lights on the tables and walls, and has the look of a Creole-style American diner. The chicken plat complet is US$4 and lobster comes at US$7.50. It's open 9 am until 10 pm.

In the north part of town, the hotel **Brise de Mer** (☎ 262-0821), at 4 Carenage, has a very nice homely terrace restaurant and bar. The pepper steak and chicken both come at US$7.50, and rum punch and imported beers cost US$2. **Les Jardins de l'Ocean** (☎ 262-2277), a white house at 90 Carenage, has two restaurants in its oceanside building. There is a traditional French restaurant downstairs serving pepper steak (US$8), lobster (US$9) and a wonderful rum punch (US$2). Upstairs is a bar and pizzeria on the covered roof terrace, with prices starting at US$6. The restaurants accept all major credit cards.

By the time you read this, the new **Marina Anacoana** should be open on Rue 13-14 Boulevard. On a little jetty lined with coconut trees, it will have a restaurant, bar, open-air stage and exhibition center. The restaurant will serve traditional Haitian food and drinks at local prices, and the entertainment will come from local bands. There will also be mooring for up to 13 boats at US$2 a day and facilities for yachts to fill up with water. The owner, Patrick Senia, is eager to promote Haitian culture.

The restaurant at the **Roi Christophe**, on Rue 24 B, serves both French and Creole cuisine in its elegant, but somewhat gloomy, restaurant. The lobster is US$12 and the spaghetti US$6. The dark wood bar is a good place for meeting people, and serves delicious rum sours for US$2 and imported beers for just over US$2. The restaurant at **Hotel Mont Joli**, at the north end of Rue B, is at the side of the illuminated pool on a terrace which looks over the harbor lights. It serves the usual mixture of French and Haitian cuisine, with steak at US$11 and chicken at US$8. You must try the exquisite rum sours (US$2) in the lively and cosmopolitan bar. Be warned – it's difficult to drink just one.

For a real 'salty dog' experience, you could try the old **Marine Terrace**, a tiny bar opposite the docks on Rue 15 Boulevard. It sells rum only by the bottle at US$6 and beers at US$1.50. This place is pretty rough, but you can get a feel for life around the docks and maybe join in a game of dominoes.

Entertainment

There are two nightclubs in Cap-Haïtien, respectively owned by their namesakes, both local compas bands. The **Septen** is on Rue 24 Boulevard, and the **Tropicana** is slightly out of town on Rte Nationale 1. Events at these venues are rather sporadic, so it's advisable to ask around town or check local postings before you arrive expecting to dance the night away.

Shopping

There are rows of artisans' kiosks on Rue 17 Boulevard that sell wooden carvings, paintings and delicate needlework. The atmosphere is very relaxed and friendly, with much less hustle than in Port-au-Prince. Nearby is the Cesse Record Son Digital at 45 Rue 18 A, a brightly painted music shack that's half Vodou temple, half record shop, and sells bootleg *racines* and *compas* cassettes. You will probably be offered ancient Taíno and Arawak sacred fire stones and amulets to buy. Some of these are real and some fake, but short of carbon dating them there is no way of knowing. They're very handsome objects, no matter when they were manufactured. Many of the galleries in town have closed down, but Galerie Toussaint Louverture on Rue 16-17 B still has a good selection of paintings.

Getting There & Away

Air Caribintair (☎ 262-2300) has an office at the airport and runs twice-daily flights to and from Port-au-Prince. The trip costs US$45 one-way and US$70 roundtrip. See the introductory Getting There & Away chapter for information on international flights to and from Cap-Haïtien.

Bus The bus station for destinations south on Rte Nationale 1, such as Gonaïves, Saint-Marc and Port-au-Prince, is at the city gates on Rue L. The journey to Port-au-Prince takes nine hours and costs US$6. The buses drop passengers at Estation OKap on Blvd La Saline in Port-au-Prince. Get an early bus as it's not advisable to arrive in the area of La Saline after dark. Taptaps for Cormier Plage and Plage Labadie, northwest of Cap-Haïtien, leave regularly from Rue 21 Q, and cost 5 gourdes (US$0.30). Taptaps for either Milot (US$1) or Ouanaminthe (US$2) leave from Rue Lapont, a short distance from the center of town; take a right turn immediately after the east side of the main vehicular bridge that you must take for the airport road.

Getting Around
To/From the Airport There is a taxi service (US$8) running from the airport into the center of town. The more expensive hotels will send a car to pick you up if you call ahead. There are also taptaps which will drop you off at Rue 10 A.

Bus Taptaps run two main routes in town, along Rue L (also called Rue Espanole) from Rue 15 L to the Barrière Bouteille (city gates), and along Rue A from Rue 10 A to the airport. Both cost 2 gourdes.

Car Hertz Dynamic Car Rental (☎ 262-0369) maintains an office at the Centre Multi-Dynamic, Rte de l'Aeroport. Akenssa Taxi (see below) has a number of cars to rent.

Taxi The local *publiques* (collective taxis) charge a set rate of 10 gourdes (US$0.70) to anywhere in town. There is also a bookable taxi company called Akenssa Taxi (☎ 262-2210, 262-1808) at 178 Rue 14 B.

AROUND CAP-HAÏTIEN
Henri Christophe's splendid palace, Sans Souci, and the awe-inspiring mountaintop fortress, the Citadelle, can be seen on a day

trip from Cap-Haïtien. Sans Souci is on the edge of the small town Milot, 20km south of Cap-Haïtien. In order to reach Milot, take Rte de l'Aéroport out of Cap-Haïtien and carry on past the airport, ignoring the junction on the left for the Ouanaminthe road. The road eventually forks by some old gate posts, and Milot is at the end of the road that forks to the right. If you wish to take a taptap to Milot (US$1), take the bus from Rue Lapont, just east of the bridge leading to the airport road.

Entrance tickets are sold in the parking lot close to Sans Souci. The official rate is 100 gourdes (US$6) for a guide, and 25 gourdes (US$1.50) entrance fee per person. If you wish to ascend by horse, the rate is 50 gourdes (US$3) per horse, and don't forget you must pay for your guide's horse as well. This fee includes both Sans Souci and the Citadelle.

Sans Souci
This palace, commissioned by Henri Christophe in 1810, was completed in 1813. Sans Souci was designed to be the equal of Versailles in France, and in its glory days was possibly a serious rival. The palace was ransacked after the fall of Christophe, and finally ruined by the 1842 earthquake that devastated Cap-Haïtien. The elegant ruins look quite alien in the Haitian landscape. The original lineaments of the palace are still in place, so it is not difficult to imagine it in the past. The palace was Christophe's administrative center and used to be surrounded by various outbuildings housing a printing press, clothing factory, distillery, school, hospital and barracks. From Sans Souci, it's a 5km walk to the Citadelle. If you have a vehicle, you can drive another 3.5km to a parking area at the foot of the Citadelle.

The Citadelle
It took Henri Christophe 15 years to build this vast mountaintop fortress, constructed to combat another invasion by the French. The astounding structure is balanced on top of the 900m Pic la Ferrière and overlooks Cap-Haïtien, the northern plain and routes leading to the south. It was completed in

Sans Souci palace at Milot, near Cap-Haïtien

1820, having employed up to 20,000 people, many of whom died during the arduous task. With 4m walls that reach heights of 40m, the fortress was impenetrable. It held enough supplies to sustain the royal family and a garrison of 5000 troops for a year. The 1.5km climb to the Citadelle is quite taxing in the burning sun, and it is advisable to carry bottled water. The views of the surrounding landscape from the Citadelle are breathtaking, especially of the singular Mt Bonnet à la Evêque to the north. The recently restored fortress still contains over 100 cannons, mostly captured from French, Spanish and English ships, and an arsenal of 50,000 cannonballs, still waiting for a French invasion.

La Navidad

La Navidad was the first European fort constructed in the New World. It was built, in part, from the wreckage of one of Columbus' ships, the *Santa María*, which sank off the northern coast of Haiti on December 24, 1492. Columbus placed a garrison of 40 men in the isolated fort and returned to Spain. When he returned a year later, the fort had been razed to the ground and the garrison massacred by the Arawak Indians who

revolted against the harsh treatment that was inflicted by the Spanish.

There is much debate as to the original location of the fort, but it is generally thought to be close to the small village of Bord de Mer, 15km east of Cap-Haïtien, near Limonade on the road to Fort Liberté and Ouanaminthe. A large wooden stake that was discovered there by archaeologists was carbon dated to approximately 1440, give or take 70 years. A small museum in Limbé (see later in this chapter), run by one of the archaeologists, contains some Taíno, Arawak and European relics. There is very little to see on the site itself, save a small concrete marker.

Beaches

If you take Rue 21 west out of town, the road will wind through the hills to the northwest coast of the cape. Here you will discover some of the most beautiful coastal scenery in Haiti, with lush forested hills tumbling into the Atlantic Ocean.

The continuation of Rue 21 hits the north coast of the cape and continues westward. After **Cormier Plage**, a lovely beach and resort, the road passes the gates that lead to **Plage Labadie Nord**, owned by the Royal Caribbean Lines. The road worsens at this point and you'll need a 4WD to continue as it veers southwards along the most stunning coast of the cape. After about 2km, the road ends at a set of steps leading down to **Plage Belli**. From here you become reliant on water taxis – some rowed and some with motors – to take you to the surrounding area. Nearby is the dramatically situated village of Labadie; the resorts of Habitation Labadie and Labadie Shores; secluded **Plage Paradee**; and **Île à Rat**, a small sand cay with a nice beach. You must negotiate the price of the water taxi before your journey; 50 gourdes (US$3) per person will get you from Plage Belli to Labadie village, but if you go any farther, the boatman will have to be paid for time spent waiting to bring you back.

Labadie Nord

Labadie Nord is a small walled-off peninsula used by the Royal Caribbean Lines to deposit their cruise-ship guests for a day on the beach. (It's been said that, in the past, cruise-line guests were oblivious to the fact that they were even in Haiti, and the stop was referred to as 'Paradise Island.') On the days that the passengers arrive, copious amounts of food and drink are consumed, giant inflatable toys are for rent and about a thousand people descend from the ship. On these days, the entry fee from the road is US$20. During the rest of the week, the place is wonderfully empty and only costs US$2 to enter.

There are many small coves and beaches on the peninsula, all with sun chairs, and often local villagers from nearby Labadie village sell cold beers and soft drinks. You can take boat taxis from Coco Beach to the surrounding beaches. There is an old colonial building on a hill overlooking Coco Beach with a bell tower that was, according to legend, a bordello for the sailors. The bell was rung to summon the locals when a ship was sighted.

Places to Stay & Eat The *Cormier Plage* (☎ 262-1000), just a few kilometers before Labadie Nord, is the perfect example of a beach resort that has kept true to the spirit and atmosphere of the country. It has 34 rooms in small, secluded bungalows dotted in between the trees around the edge of the clean and beautiful beach. The rooms, all with showers and bathrooms, are simple and elegant, with whitewashed walls decorated with Haitian metalworks. The rates of US$50/90 for a single/double include breakfast and dinner. The covered bar and restaurant overlook the sea, and the staff is very friendly. The food is a good mix of European and Creole; lobster is US$9.50, chicken is US$6. The proprietor, Jean Claude Dicquemar, who used to dive with Jacques Cousteau, runs the diving and water-sports facilities at the center. On request he can organize one-day hikes into the mountains, visits to Arawak and Taíno Indian settlements, and dives to pristine shipwrecks lost by the Spanish, French and Dutch. There are also tennis courts, table tennis and a pool table. You can use all major credit cards, and if you telephone the hotel in advance, someone will meet you at the Cap-Haïtien airport and drive you to the beach.

The *Belli Beach Bar* (☎ 262-2338, 262-1756, 262-0055) is at the end of the road west of Labadie Nord. The road peters to an end, and narrow, steep steps lead down to Plage Belli. This is an almost-perfect, locally run restaurant and hotel on a tiny crescent-shaped cove. There are six simple, rural-style rooms with corrugated or bamboo roofs costing US$15/21. All have showers (cold water only) and electricity. The thatched restaurant serves breakfast (US$3), chicken plat complet (US$6) and freshly caught lobster (US$7). The view of ocean-washed headland after headland fading into the far distance is spectacular, one of the most beautiful in Haiti. *Norm's Place* (☎ 262-0400, fax 262-0866), near Labadie village, across the water from the Plage Belli, is a small intimate hideaway with lots of Haitian atmosphere. It has a restaurant and bar, and a number of rooms costing US$25/50 for a single/double. Breakfast costs US$6, lunch US$8 and dinner US$10.

Habitation Labadie is on the Baie de Labadie and is only accessible by boat. It is an ambitious, modern complex that's somewhat architecturally at odds with the surrounding landscape. It has a large swimming pool, a panoramic tent-covered restaurant with a large-screen satellite TV, and promises by 1999 to have a beachfront spa with massage rooms and manicure and pedicure facilities. There are 24 suites housed in two secluded buildings, each with a bedroom, bathroom and lounge. For more details, you can contact La Société Cap-Labadie (☎ 222-2245, 223-4088, fax 223-8997, hablab@hotmail.com), 35 Ave Marie-Jeanne, Port-au-Prince.

Getting There & Away Taptaps going to Cormier Plage and Plage Labadie leave regularly from Rue 21 Q near the gymnasium in Cap-Haïtien. The trip costs less than US$1. From the gates of Labadie Nord, you can either walk to Plage Belli or enter Labadie

Nord for US$2 and take a water taxi from Coco Beach to Plage Belli for US$1.

LIMBÉ

In the town of Limbé, 25km southwest of Cap-Haïtien on the road to Port-au-Prince, is a small **museum** run by Dr William Hodges, a Baptist missionary and archaeologist. It contains relics of the Taíno and Arawak Indians, as well as remains of the European colonists. If you have questions about La Navidad and the remains found there, Dr Hodges is the man to see. Ask around when you arrive, and someone will show you the way to the museum.

GONAÏVES

Gonaïves is a handy place to stay if you want to break your journey between Cap-Haïtien and Port-au-Prince, or if you're visiting

Souvenance & Soukri

Souvenance and Soukri are major dates on the Vodou calendar. People from all over Haiti congregate near Gonaïves to take part in these marathon ceremonies, used by celebrants for spiritual cleansing and revival.

Souvenance begins on Good Friday, and continues for a week. The ceremony opens with an all-night communal rendition of Gregorian chants. During the week, prayers are offered to a sacred tamarind tree, initiates bathe in a sacred pond, libations are poured and bulls are sacrificed for the Vodou spirits. The ceremonies include singing and dancing and go on every night, while the celebrants rest by day. The rituals are three centuries old and are said to have originated in the marron camps, the secret communities of runaway slaves.

Soukri is a ritual inherited from the Congo Basin in Africa. The service is divided into two branches, 'the father of all Congo,' which takes place on January 6, and the second, larger ceremony, 'the mother of all Congo,' which takes place on August 14. The rituals last a mammoth two weeks each, a true test of endurance. Many of the celebrations are similar to those in Souvenance. If you wish to visit these ceremonies, as a mark of respect it is advised that you introduce yourself to the president of the Vodou society when you arrive.

Souvenance is held off the road between Gonaïves and Cap-Haïtien, about 20km north of Gonaïves. The festival has become well-known enough that the place it is held is also now known as Souvenance. As you leave Gonaïves on the road to Cap-Haïtien, you cross over the Rivière Laquinte on a bridge called Mapou Chevalier. The first immediate right after the bridge will take you to Souvenance. There are small houses for rent around the temple, although many of the participants just sleep on straw mats in the shade.

Soukri takes place off the same road from Gonaïves to Cap-Haïtien. Continue northward past the turnoff for Souvenance until you reach a small market town, Les Poteaux. A right-hand turn opposite the Saint-Marc Catholic Church leads to the *lakou* (a collection of dwellings) known as Soukri.

either the Soukri or Souvenance festivals. It's a dusty old town with a sprawling slum area near the brackish front beaches. Jean Jacques Dessalines declared Haiti's independence here in 1804, and his wife, Claire Heureuse, is buried in the local cemetery. Avoid the beaches as toxic ash from the city of Philadelphia, Pennsylvania, was reportedly buried beneath them in 1988.

Places to Stay & Eat

The *Family Hotel* (☎ 274-0600), on Ave des Dattes, is a large, secure hotel with ample parking space. It has 32 rooms with showers and air con or fans for US$25 to US$30 for a single and US$35 to US$45 for a double. There is a good restaurant and a swimming pool, and they take all major credit cards. *Chez Frantz* (☎ 274-0348) is a small hotel and restaurant, also on Ave des Dattes. It is a sweet little gingerbread in its own courtyard with tables on a surrounding verandah. The food is excellent and cheap (US$3 for a chicken plat complet), and this is a good place to stop and rest during a long drive.

Getting There & Away

The road between Gonaïves and Saint-Marc is well-worn, so if you're driving, beware of huge potholes. Express buses run between Gonaïves and Port-au-Prince's Estation OKap for US$3.50. You can also catch buses to and from Cap-Haïtien for 30 gourdes (US$2). Mopeds in Gonaïves operate as fast and cheap taxis, costing 3 gourdes a ride.

FORT LIBERTÉ

Fort Liberté is a sleepy town overlooking the bay of Mancenille. It is difficult to believe that this dusty town, where one telephone number serves the entire population, was once an important strategic city in Haiti. It was inaugurated Fort Dauphin by the French in 1731, at the same time as a huge fortress overlooking the bay was being constructed.

In 1796, Toussaint L'Ouverture took the city, renamed it Fort Liberté and strengthened the fortress in order to prepare a base from which he hoped to conquer the Spanish territory to the west. In the 1860s, Fort Liberté served as a meeting place for the world's antislavery movement. Nowadays the **Fort Dauphin** fortress remains more or less intact, but the rest of the town has fallen to dilapidation and ennui. The entrance to the town is framed by an impressive yellow arch, and if you follow that road to the sea, you will discover the fort. There has been some restoration work done recently, and there are some interesting underground powder rooms to explore. There are two hotels in town, the *Cirene* and the *Bayaha*. Fort Liberté is 56km east of Cap-Haïtien, 4km off the road to Ouanaminthe. There are regular taptaps from Cap-Haïtien to Fort Liberté.

OUANAMINTHE

Another unexceptional, dusty Haitian town, Ouanaminthe is only worth a visit if you mean to cross the border. After passing through the town gates, continue straight on until you arrive at a large field where the road splits into two. The left fork proceeds directly to the border, which is a bridge across the Rivière Massacre marked by the Dominican flag. The right fork takes you along a rough track to the customs and passport office, where you must pay and have your passport stamped before you reach the border. The border closes at 4:30 pm, but if you are unlucky enough to arrive too late, the local police will sometimes help you out. They'll hold your passport and allow you to cross the border so that you can stay in a reasonable hotel in Dajabón, then return the next morning to retrieve your passport. This is a possible safety net, as there are no hotels in Ouanaminthe. There is regular taptap service to and from Ouanaminthe and Cap-Haïtien, which takes 2½ hours and costs 15 gourdes (US$2).

Language

SPANISH
Pronunciation

Pronunciation of Spanish is not difficult, given that many Spanish sounds are similar to their English counterparts, and there is a clear and consistent relationship between the pronunciation and the spelling. Unless otherwise indicated, the English words used below to approximate Spanish sounds take standard American pronunciation.

Vowels Spanish has five vowels: **a, e, i, o** and **u**. They are pronounced something like the highlighted letters of the following English words:

a as in 'f**a**ther'
e as in 'm**e**t'
i as in 'f**ee**t'
o as in the British 'h**o**t'
u as in 'b**oo**t'

Diphthongs A diphthong is one syllable made of two vowels, each of which conserves its own sound. Here are some diphthongs in Spanish and their approximate English pronunciations:

ai as in 'h**i**de'
au as in 'h**ow**'
ei as in 'h**ay**'
ia as in '**ya**rd'
ie as in '**ye**s'
oi as in 'b**oy**'
ua as in '**wa**sh'
ue as in '**we**ll'

Consonants Many consonants are pronounced much as they are in English, but there are some exceptions:

c is pronounced like 's' in 'sit' when before 'e' or 'i'; elsewhere, it is like 'k'
ch as in 'choose'
g as the 'g' in 'gate' before 'a,' 'o' and 'u'; before 'e' or 'i,' this is a harsh, breathy sound like the 'h' in 'hit.' Note that when 'g' is followed by 'ue' or 'ui,' the 'u' is silent, unless it has a dieresis (ü), in which case it functions much like the English 'w':
    guerra 'GEH-rra'
    güero 'GWEH-ro'
h always silent
j a harsh, guttural sound similar to the 'ch' in Scottish 'loch'

ll as the 'y' in 'yellow'
ñ a nasal sound like the 'ny' in 'canyon'
q as the 'k' in 'kick'; always followed by a silent 'u'
r is a very short rolled 'r'
rr is a longer rolled 'r'
x is like the English 'h' when it follows 'e' or 'i' – otherwise it is like the English 'x' as in 'taxi'
z is the same as the English 's'; under no circumstances should 's' or 'z' be pronounced like the English 'z' – that sound does not exist in Spanish

There are a few other minor pronunciation differences, but the longer you stay in the DR, the easier they will become. The letter ñ is considered a separate letter of the alphabet and follows 'n' in alphabetically organized lists and books, such as dictionaries and phone books.

Stress There are three general rules regarding stress:

- In words ending in a vowel, 'n' or 's,' the stress goes on the penultimate (next-to-last) syllable:

    naranja na-RAHN-ha   *joven* HO-ven   *zapatos* sa-PA-tos

- In words ending in a consonant other than 'n' or 's,' the stress is on the final syllable:

    estoy es-TOY   *ciudad* syoo-DAHD   *catedral* ka-teh-DRAL

- Any deviation from these rules is indicated by an accent:

    México MEH-hee-ko   *mudéjar* moo-DEH-har   *Cortés* cor-TESS

Gender

Nouns in Spanish are either masculine or feminine. Nouns ending in 'o,' 'e' or 'ma' are usually masculine. Nouns ending in 'a,' 'ión' or 'dad' are usually feminine. Some nouns take either a masculine or feminine form, depending on the ending; for example, *viajero* is a male traveler and *viajera* is a female traveler. An adjective usually follows the noun it modifies and must take the same gender as the noun.

Greetings & Civilities

Hello/Hi.	*Hola.*
Good morning/Good day.	*Buenos días.*
Good afternoon.	*Buenas tardes.*
Good evening/Good night.	*Buenas noches.*
See you.	*Hasta luego.*
Goodbye.	*Adiós.*
Pleased to meet you.	*Mucho gusto.*
How are you? (to one person)	*¿Cómo está?*
How are you? (to more than one person)	*¿Cómo están?*
I am fine.	*Estoy bien.*
Please.	*Por favor.*
Thank you.	*Gracias.*
You're welcome.	*De nada.*
Excuse me.	*Perdóneme.*

People

I	*yo*	my wife	*mi esposa*
you (familiar)	*tú*	my husband	*mi esposo, mi marido*
you (formal)	*usted*	my sister	*mi hermana*
you (plural formal)	*ustedes*	my brother	*mi hermano*
he/it	*él*	friend	*pasiero(a)*
she/it	*ella*	Sir/Mr	*Señor*
we	*nosotros*	Madam/Mrs	*Señora*
they (m)	*ellos*	Miss	*Señorita*
they (f)	*ellas*		

Useful Words & Phrases

For words pertaining to food and restaurants, see the Food section in the DR's Facts for the Visitor chapter.

Yes.	*Sí.*	I am ...	*Estoy ...*
No.	*No.*	(location or temporary condition)	
What did you say?	*¿Mande?* (colloq)	here	*aquí*
	¿Cómo?	tired (m/f)	*cansado/a*
good/OK	*bueno*	sick/ill (m/f)	*enfermo/a*
bad	*malo*		
better	*mejor*	I am ...	*Soy ...*
best	*lo mejor*	(permanent state)	
more	*más*	a worker	*trabajador*
less	*menos*	married	*casado*
very little	*poco* or *poquito*		

Shopping

How much?	*¿Cuánto?*
How much does it cost?	*¿Cuánto cuesta esto?* or *¿Cuánto se cobra?*
How much is it worth?	*¿Cuánto vale?*
I want ...	*Quiero ...*
I do not want ...	*No quiero ...*
I would like ...	*Quisiera ...*
Give me ...	*Deme ...*
What do you want?	*¿Qué quiere?*
Do you have ... ?	*¿Tiene ... ?*
Is/are there ... ?	*¿Hay ... ?*
market	*mercado*

Nationalities

American (m/f)	*(norte)americano/a*	English (m/f)	*inglés/inglesa*
Australian (m/f)	*australiano/a*	French (m/f)	*francés/francesa*
British (m/f)	*británico/a*	German (m/f)	*alemán/alemana*
Canadian (m & f)	*canadiense*		

Languages

I speak ...	*Yo hablo ...*
I do not speak ...	*No hablo ...*
Do you speak ... ?	*¿Habla usted ... ?*
Spanish	*español*
English	*inglés*
German	*alemán*
French	*francés*
I understand.	*Entiendo.*
I do not understand.	*No entiendo.*
Do you understand?	*¿Entiende usted?*
Please speak slowly.	*Por favor hable despacio.*

LANGUAGE

Crossing the Border

birth certificate	certificado de nacimiento
border (frontier)	la frontera
car-owner's title	título de propiedad
car registration	registración
customs	aduana
driver's license	licencia de manejar
identification	identificación
immigration	immigración
insurance	seguro
passport	pasaporte
tourist card	tarjeta de turista
visa	visado

Getting Around

avenue	avenida	forward, ahead	adelante
block	cuadra	straight ahead	todo recto or derecho
boulevard	bulevar, boulevard	this way	por aquí
corner (of)	esquina (de)	that way	por allí
corner/bend	vuelta	north	norte (Nte)
highway	carretera or autopista	south	sur
road	camino	east	este
street	calle or vía	east (in an address)	oriente (Ote)
to the left	a la izquierda	west	oeste
to the right	a la derecha	west (in an address)	poniente (Pte)

Where is . . . ?	¿Dónde está . . . ?
the airport	el aeropuerto
the bus station	el terminal de autobuses/central camionera
the train station	la estación del ferrocarril
a long-distance phone	un teléfono de larga distancia
the post office	el correo

bus	camión or autobús or gua-gua
city bus stop	parada
taxi	taxi
train	tren
ticket sales counter	taquilla
waiting room	sala de espera
luggage check-in	(recibo de) equipaje
toilet	sanitario or baño
departure	salida
arrival	llegada
platform	andén
left-luggage room/checkroom	(guardería or guarda) de equipaje
How far is . . . ?	¿A qué distancia está . . . ?
How long? (How much time?)	¿Cuánto tiempo?
short route	vía corta
a ride (as in hitchhiking)	un bote

Driving

gasoline	*gasolina*	full	*lleno*
fuel station	*gasolinera*	oil	*aceite*
unleaded	*sin plomo*	tire	*llanta*
regular/leaded	*regular/con plomo*	puncture	*agujero*
fill the tank	*llene el tanque; llenarlo*		

How much is a liter of gasoline?	*¿Cuánto cuesta el litro de gasolina?*
My car has broken down.	*Se me ha descompuesto el carro.*
I need a tow truck.	*Necesito un remolque.*
Is there a garage near here?	*¿Hay un garaje cerca de aquí?*

Accommodations

hotel	*hotel*	shower	*ducha* or *regadera*
guesthouse	*casa de huéspedes* or *pensión*	hot water	*agua caliente*
		air-conditioning	*aire acondicionado*
inn	*posada*		
room	*cuarto, habitación*	blanket	*manta*
room with one bed	*cuarto sencillo*	towel	*toalla*
room with two beds	*cuarto doble*	soap	*jabón*
room for one person	*cuarto para una persona*	toilet paper	*papel higiénico*
		the check (bill)	*la cuenta*
room for two people	*cuarto para dos personas*	What is the price?	*¿Cuál es el precio?*
		Does that include taxes?	
double bed	*cama matrimonial*	*¿Están incluidos los impuestos?*	
twin beds	*camas gemelas*	Does that include service?	
with bathroom	*con baño*	*¿Está incluido el servicio?*	

Money

money	*dinero*
traveler's checks	*cheques de viajero*
bank	*banco*
exchange bureau	*casa de cambio*
credit card	*tarjeta de crédito*
exchange rate	*tipo de cambio*
I want/would like to change some money.	*Quiero/quisiera cambiar dinero.*
Is there a commission?	*¿Hay comisión?*

Telephones

telephone	*teléfono*
telephone call	*llamada*
telephone number	*número telefónico*
area code	*clave*
prefix for long-distance call	*prefijo*
local call	*llamada local*
long-distance call	*llamada de larga distancia*

long-distance telephone	*teléfono de larga distancia*
coin-operated telephone	*teléfono de monedas*
long-distance telephone office	*caseta de larga distancia*
tone	*tono*
operator	*operador(a)*
collect (reverse charges)	*por cobrar*
Dial the number.	*Marque el número.*
Please wait.	*Favor de esperar.*
busy	*ocupado*
toll/cost (of call)	*cuota/costo*
time and charges	*tiempo y costo*
Don't hang up.	*No cuelgue.*

Times & Dates

Monday	*lunes*	tomorrow	*mañana*
Tuesday	*martes*	right now	*horita, ahorita*
Wednesday	*miércoles*	already	*ya*
Thursday	*jueves*	morning	*mañana*
Friday	*viernes*	tomorrow morning	*mañana por la*
Saturday	*sábado*		*mañana*
Sunday	*domingo*	afternoon	*tarde*
yesterday	*ayer*	night	*noche*
today	*hoy*	What time is it?	*¿Qué hora es?*

Numbers

0	*cero*	14	*catorce*	60	*sesenta*
1	*uno* (m), *una* (f)	15	*quince*	70	*setenta*
2	*dos*	16	*dieciséis*	80	*ochenta*
3	*tres*	17	*diecisiete*	90	*noventa*
4	*cuatro*	18	*dieciocho*	100	*cien*
5	*cinco*	19	*diecinueve*	101	*ciento uno*
6	*seis*	20	*veinte*	143	*ciento cuarenta y tres*
7	*siete*	21	*veintiuno*	200	*doscientos*
8	*ocho*	22	*veintidós*	500	*quinientos*
9	*nueve*	30	*treinta*	900	*novecientos*
10	*diez*	31	*treinta y uno*	1000	*mil*
11	*once*	32	*treinta y dos*	2000	*dos mil*
12	*doce*	40	*cuarenta*		
13	*trece*	50	*cincuenta*		

Dominican Slang & Other Expressions

The following colloquialisms are frequently heard and used only in the Dominican Republic:

a su orden	think nothing of it
apagon	a power failure
avión	a 'loose' woman
bandera dominicana	rice and beans
bohío	a thatch hut
bolsa	scrotum (a *funda* is a bag)
carros de concho	routed, shared taxi

chichi	a baby
colmado	a small grocery store
cuero	a prostitute
¿Dímelo?	How are you?
fucú	a thing that brings bad luck
goma	a pneumatic tire
guapo	angry
guarapo	sugarcane juice
gumo	a drunk
jablador	a person who talks a lot
mamacita	a pretty woman
papaúpa	an important person
papichulo	a come-on to a *mamacita*
pariguayo	foolish
pín-pún	exactly equal
una rumba	a lot
timacle	brave

CREOLE
Pronunciation

In terms of pronunciation, Creole is written phonetically. There are no silent consonants; a hard *c* is represented by a *k* (the hard *c* is never used in Creole), and *g* is a hard *g*. There are no silent *e*'s; all are pronounced as acute *e* unless they have the *grave* accent. For example, *pale* (to speak) is pronounced 'palé.' The word for me is *m* and is pronounced 'um.'

Greetings & Civilities

How are you?	*Ki jan ou ye?*
Not bad.	*M pal pi mal.*
I'm getting along.	*M'ap kenbe.*
Good day. (used before noon)	*Bonjou.*
Good evening. (used after noon)	*Bonswa.*
See you later.	*Na wè pita.*

General Phrases

My name is . . .	*M rele . . .*
What is your name?	*Ki jan ou rele?*
May I take your photograph?	*Eske m ka fè foto ou?*
Where is the . . . ?	*Ki kote . . . ?*
What time is it?	*Ki lè li ye?*
Do you speak English?	*Eske ou ka pale angle?*
I don't understand.	*M pa konpran.*

People

I	*m/mwen*
you	*ou*
he/she	*li*
you (plural)/we	*nou*
they	*yo*

Useful Words & Phrases

Where is/are . . . ?	*Kote . . . ?*
the toilets	*twalèt yo*
the hospital	*lopital la*
Where does the bus leave?	*Kote taptap pati?*
I am looking for . . .	*M'ap chache . . .*
What time is it?	*Kilè li ye?*
stop	*rete*
wait	*tann*
help	*ede mwen*
How much?	*Konbyen?*
Let's go.	*Ann ale.*
I would like to go (visit, speak with) . . .	*M ta vle ale (vizite, pale ak) . . .*
I am lost; where is . . . ?	*M pèdi; kote . . . ye?*

Food

plat konplèt	complete meal consisting of rice and beans, salad, plantains and meat of your choice (*plat complet* in French)
diri ak pwa	rice and beans
diri blan	white rice
griyo	deep-fried pork (often written as *griot*)
poule	chicken
pwason	fish
taso	deep-fried beef
lambi	conch
bannann peze	fried plantain
tomat	tomatoes
zonyon	onions
fig	banana
ju zoranj	orange juice
ju Chadek	grapefruit juice
ju sitron	lime juice
koka	Coca-Cola
kiè	beer
dlo	water
dlo culligan	bottled water

Medical Terms

I have chills (cramps, diarrhea, fever, headache).
   M gen lafièv frison (gen kranp, diare, fyèv, tèt fè mal).
I am bleeding (vomiting).
   M'ap senyen (vomi).

Glossary

See the Language section for common Spanish and Creole expressions and useful phrases. See the Food sections in the Facts for the Visitor chapters for lists of common food terms.

SPANISH

acuario – aquarium
avenida – avenue
bahía – bay
balneario – spa/watering place
calle – street
capilla – chapel
casa – house
catedral – cathedral
cerveza – beer
Colón, Cristóbal – Christopher Columbus
fortaleza – fortress
galería – gallery
gua-gua – small bus providing low-cost local transport in the DR
hostal – inn
iglesia – church
lago – lake
larimar – semiprecious blue stone found only in the DR
mercado – market
monasterio – monastery
motoconcho – motorcycle taxi
museo – museum
oro – gold
palacio – palace
parque – park
plata – silver
playa – beach
público – privately owned minivan or pickup truck that picks up passengers on major city streets in the DR, providing low-cost local transport
puerta – gate/door
puerto – port
ruinas – ruins
vino – wine
yola – boat used to smuggle people into the USA from the DR

CREOLE

asson – sacred rattle that is used in Vodou ceremonies
cacos – armed peasant rebels who played a key part in the resistance to the US Marines' invasion in 1915
cagoulards – hooded thugs, employed by the François Duvalier dictatorship (*une cagoule* is a hood)
Colombo, Cristofor – Christopher Columbus
dechoukaj – literally, 'uprooting'; refers to the systematic destruction of remnants of the Jean Claude Duvalier dictatorship after the leader's flight
fermage – a forced agricultural labor system; French for 'tenant farming' or 'farm rent'
gourde – unit of Haitian currency
houmfor – Vodou temple or ceremonial altar
houngan – Vodou priest
hounsis – female initiates in Vodou ceremony
kombit – communal work team
kònet – trumpet made from hammered zinc, ending in a flared horn
lanngaj – ceremonial language from West Africa
lwa – Vodou spirits
mambo – priestess
racines – 'roots,' a type of Haitian music
taptap – local Haitian bus
Tontons Macoutes – the notorious guards created under François Duvalier; also known as Volontaires de la Sécurité Nationale (National Security Volunteers)
vaskin – bamboo trumpet
vevé – sacred Vodou symbol

FRENCH

baie – bay
liberté – liberty, freedom
montagne – mountains
mort – death
musée – museum
plage – beach
rue – street

LONELY PLANET

Guides by Region

Lonely Planet is known worldwide for publishing practical, reliable and no-nonsense travel information in our guides and on our Web site. The Lonely Planet list covers just about every accessible part of the world. Currently there are nine series: travel guides, shoestring guides, walking guides, city guides, phrasebooks, audio packs, travel atlases, diving and snorkeling guides and travel literature.

AFRICA Africa – the South • Africa on a shoestring • Arabic (Egyptian) phrasebook • Arabic (Moroccan) phrasebook • Cairo • Cape Town • Central Africa • East Africa • Egypt • Egypt travel atlas • Ethiopian (Amharic) phrasebook • The Gambia & Senegal • Kenya • Kenya travel atlas • Malawi, Mozambique & Zambia • Morocco • North Africa • South Africa, Lesotho & Swaziland • South Africa, Lesotho & Swaziland travel atlas • Swahili phrasebook • Trekking in East Africa • Tunisia • West Africa • Zimbabwe, Botswana & Namibia • Zimbabwe, Botswana & Namibia travel atlas
Travel Literature: The Rainbird: A Central African Journey • Songs to an African Sunset: A Zimbabwean Story • Mali Blues: Traveling to an African Beat

AUSTRALIA & THE PACIFIC Australia • Australian phrasebook • Bushwalking in Australia • Bushwalking in Papua New Guinea • Fiji • Fijian phrasebook • Islands of Australia's Great Barrier Reef • Melbourne • Micronesia • New Caledonia • New South Wales & the ACT • New Zealand • Northern Territory • Outback Australia • Papua New Guinea • Papua New Guinea (Pidgin) phrasebook • Queensland • Rarotonga & the Cook Islands • Samoa • Solomon Islands • South Australia • Sydney • Tahiti & French Polynesia • Tasmania • Tonga • Tramping in New Zealand • Vanuatu • Victoria • Western Australia
Travel Literature: Islands in the Clouds • Sean & David's Long Drive

CENTRAL AMERICA & THE CARIBBEAN Bahamas and Turks & Caicos • Bermuda • Central America on a shoestring • Costa Rica • Cuba • Eastern Caribbean • Guatemala, Belize & Yucatán: La Ruta Maya • Jamaica • Mexico • Mexico City • Panama
Travel Literature: Green Dreams: Travels in Central America

EUROPE Amsterdam • Andalucía • Austria • Baltic States phrasebook • Berlin • Britain • Central Europe • Central Europe phrasebook • Czech & Slovak Republics • Denmark • Dublin • Eastern Europe • Eastern Europe phrasebook • Edinburgh • Estonia, Latvia & Lithuania • Europe • Finland • France • French phrasebook • Germany • German phrasebook • Greece • Greek phrasebook • Hungary • Iceland, Greenland & the Faroe Islands • Ireland • Italian phrasebook • Italy • Lisbon • London • Mediterranean Europe • Mediterranean Europe phrasebook • Paris • Poland • Portugal • Portugal travel atlas • Prague • Romania & Moldova • Russia, Ukraine & Belarus • Russian phrasebook • Scandinavian & Baltic Europe • Scandinavian Europe phrasebook • Scotland • Slovenia • Spain • Spanish phrasebook • St Petersburg • Switzerland • Trekking in Spain • Ukrainian phrasebook • Vienna • Walking in Britain • Walking in Italy • Walking in Switzerland • Western Europe • Western Europe phrasebook
Travel Literature: The Olive Grove: Travels in Greece

INDIAN SUBCONTINENT Bangladesh • Bengali phrasebook • Bhutan • Delhi • Goa • Hindi/Urdu phrasebook • India • India & Bangladesh travel atlas • Indian Himalaya • Karakoram Highway • Nepal • Nepali phrasebook • Pakistan • Rajasthan • South India • Sri Lanka • Sri Lanka phrasebook • Trekking in the Indian Himalaya • Trekking in the Karakoram & Hindukush • Trekking in the Nepal Himalaya
Travel Literature: In Rajasthan • Shopping for Buddhas

LONELY PLANET

Mail Order

Lonely Planet products are distributed worldwide. They are also available by mail order from Lonely Planet, so if you have difficulty finding a title please write to us. North and South American residents should write to 150 Linden St, Oakland, CA 94607, USA; European and African residents should write to 10a Spring Place, London NW5 3BH, UK; and residents of other countries to PO Box 617, Hawthorn, Victoria 3122, Australia.

ISLANDS OF THE INDIAN OCEAN Madagascar & Comoros ❖ Maldives • Mauritius, Réunion & Seychelles

MIDDLE EAST & CENTRAL ASIA Arab Gulf States • Central Asia • Central Asia phrasebook • Iran • Israel & the Palestinian Territories • Israel & the Palestinian Territories travel atlas • Istanbul • Jerusalem • Jordan & Syria • Jordan, Syria & Lebanon travel atlas • Lebanon • Middle East on a shoestring ❖ Turkey • Turkish phrasebook • Turkey travel atlas ❖ Yemen
Travel Literature: The Gates of Damascus • Kingdom of the Film Stars: Journey into Jordan

NORTH AMERICA Alaska • Backpacking in Alaska • Baja California • California & Nevada ❖ Canada • Florida • Hawaii • Honolulu • Los Angeles • Miami • New England USA • New Orleans • New York City • New York, New Jersey & Pennsylvania • Pacific Northwest USA • Rocky Mountain States • San Francisco • Seattle • Southwest USA • USA • USA phrasebook • Vancouver • Washington, DC & the Capital Region
Travel Literature: Drive Thru America

NORTH-EAST ASIA Beijing • Cantonese phrasebook • China • Hong Kong • Hong Kong, Macau & Guangzhou • Japan • Japanese phrasebook • Japanese audio pack • Korea • Korean phrasebook • Kyoto • Mandarin phrasebook • Mongolia • Mongolian phrasebook • North-East Asia on a shoestring • Seoul • South-West China • Taiwan • Tibet • Tibetan phrasebook • Tokyo
Travel Literature: Lost Japan

SOUTH AMERICA Argentina, Uruguay & Paraguay • Bolivia • Brazil • Brazilian phrasebook • Buenos Aires • Chile & Easter Island • Chile & Easter Island travel atlas • Colombia • Ecuador & the Galapagos Islands • Latin American Spanish phrasebook • Peru • Quechua phrasebook • Rio de Janeiro • South America on a shoestring • Trekking in the Patagonian Andes • Venezuela
Travel Literature: Full Circle: A South American Journey

SOUTH-EAST ASIA Bali & Lombok • Bangkok • Burmese phrasebook • Cambodia • Hill Tribes phrasebook • Ho Chi Minh City • Indonesia • Indonesian phrasebook • Indonesian audio pack • Jakarta • Java • Laos • Lao phrasebook ❖ Laos travel atlas • Malay phrasebook • Malaysia, Singapore & Brunei • Myanmar (Burma) • Philippines • Pilipino (Tagalog) phrasebook • Singapore • South-East Asia on a shoestring • South-East Asia phrasebook • Thailand • Thailand's Islands & Beaches • Thailand travel atlas • Thai phrasebook • Thai audio pack • Vietnam • Vietnamese phrasebook • Vietnam travel atlas

ALSO AVAILABLE: Antarctica • Brief Encounters: Stories of Love, Sex & Travel • Chasing Rickshaws • Not the Only Planet: Travel Stories from Science Fiction • Travel with Children • Traveller's Tales

LONELY PLANET

Phrasebooks

Lonely Planet phrasebooks are packed with essential words and phrases to help travellers communicate with the locals. With color tabs for quick reference, an extensive vocabulary and use of script, these handy pocket-sized language guides cover day-to-day travel situations.

- handy pocket-sized books
- easy to understand Pronunciation chapter
- clear & comprehensive Grammar chapter
- romanization alongside script to allow ease of pronunciation
- script throughout so users can point to phrases for every situation
- full of cultural information and tips for the traveller

'...vital for a real DIY spirit and attitude in language learning'
– Backpacker

'the phrasebooks have good cultural backgrounders and offer solid advice for challenging situations in remote locations'
– San Francisco Examiner

Arabic (Egyptian) • Arabic (Moroccan) • Australian *(Australian English, Aboriginal and Torres Strait languages)* • Baltic States *(Estonian, Latvian, Lithuanian)* • Bengali v Brazilian • Burmese • Cantonese • Central Asia • Central Europe *(Czech, French, German, Hungarian, Italian, Slovak)* • Eastern Europe *(Bulgarian, Czech, Hungarian, Polish, Romanian, Slovak)* • Ethiopian (Amharic) • Fijian • French • German • Greek • Hill Tribes • Hindi/Urdu • Indonesian • Italian • Japanese • Korean • Lao • Latin American Spanish • Malay • Mandarin • Mediterranean Europe *(Albanian, Croatian, Greek, Italian, Macedonian, Maltese, Serbian, Slovene)* • Mongolian • Nepali • Papua New Guinea • Pilipino (Tagalog) • Quechua • Russian • Scandinavian Europe *(Danish, Finnish, Icelandic, Norwegian, Swedish)* • South-East Asia *(Burmese, Indonesian, Khmer, Lao, Malay, Tagalog Pilipino, Thai, Vietnamese)* • Spanish (Castilian) *(also includes Catalan, Galician and Basque)* • Sri Lanka • Swahili • Thai • Tibetan • Turkish • Ukrainian • USA *(US English, Vernacular, Native American languages, Hawaiian)* • Vietnamese • Western Europe *(Basque, Catalan, Dutch, French, German, Greek, Irish)*

Lonely Planet Journeys

JOURNEYS is a unique collection of travel writing – published by the company that understands travel better than anyone else. It is a series for anyone who has ever experienced – or dreamed of – the magical moment when they encountered a strange culture or saw a place for the first time. They are tales to read while you're planning a trip, while you're on the road or while you're in an armchair in front of a fire.

These outstanding titles explore our planet through the eyes of a diverse group of international writers. JOURNEYS books catch the spirit of a place, illuminate a culture, recount a crazy adventure or introduce a fascinating way of life. They always entertain, and always enrich the experience of travel.

FULL CIRCLE
A South American Journey
Luis Sepúlveda (translated by Chris Andrews)

'A journey without a fixed itinerary' with Chilean writer Luis Sepúlveda. Extravagant characters and extraordinary situations are memorably evoked: gauchos organising a tournament of lies, a scheming heiress on the lookout for a husband, a pilot with a corpse on board his plane … *Full Circle* brings us the distinctive voice of one of South America's most compelling writers.

WINNER 1996 Astrolabe – Etonnants Voyageurs award for the best work of travel literature published in France.

GREEN DREAMS
Travels in Central America
Stephen Benz

On the Amazon, in Costa Rica, Honduras and on the Mayan trail from Guatemala to Mexico, Stephen Benz describes his encounters with water, mud, insects and other wildlife – and not least with the ecotourists themselves. With witty insights into modern travel, *Green Dreams* discusses the paradox of cultural and 'green' tourism.

DRIVE THRU AMERICA
Sean Condon

If you've ever wanted to drive across the USA but couldn't find the time (or afford the gas), *Drive Thru America* is perfect for you. In his search for American myths and realities – along with comfort, cable TV and good, reasonably priced coffee – Sean Condon paints a hilarious road-portrait of the USA.

'entertaining and laugh-out-loud funny'– *Alex Wilber, Travel editor, Amazon.com*

SEAN & DAVID'S LONG DRIVE
Sean Condon

Sean and David are young townies who have rarely strayed beyond city limits. One day, for no good reason, they set out to discover their homeland, and what follows is a wildly entertaining adventure that covers half of Australia.

'a hilariously detailed log of two burned out friends' – *Rolling Stone*

LONELY PLANET

Lonely Planet On-line
www.lonelyplanet.com *or* AOL keyword: lp

W hether you've just begun planning your next trip, or you're chasing down specific info on currency regulations or visa requirements, check out Lonely Planet On-line for up-to-the minute travel information.

As well as mini guides to more than 250 destinations, you'll find maps, photos, travel news, health and visa updates, travel advisories, and discussion of the ecological and political issues you need to be aware of as you travel. You'll also find timely upgrades to popular guidebooks which you can print out and stick in the back of your book.

There's also an on-line travellers' forum where you can share your experience of life on the road, meet travel companions and ask other travellers for their recommendations and advice.

And of course we have a complete and up-to-date list of all Lonely Planet travel products including travel guides, diving and snorkeling guides, phrasebooks, atlases, travel literature and videos, and a simple on-line ordering facility if you can't find the book you want elsewhere.

Lonely Planet Diving & Snorkeling Guides

K nown for indispensible guidebooks to destinations all over the world, Lonely Planet's Pisces Books are the most popular series of diving and snorkeling titles available.

There are three series: **Diving & Snorkeling Guides**, **Shipwreck Diving** series and **Dive Into History**. Full colour throughout, the **Diving & Snorkeling Guides** combine quality photographs with detailed descriptions of the best dive sites for each location, giving divers a glimpse of what they can expect both on land and in water. The **Dive Into History** series is perfect for the adventure diver or armchair traveller. The **Shipwreck Diving** series provides all the details for exploring the most interesting wrecks in the Atlantic and Pacific oceans. The list also includes underwater nature and technical guides.

Index

Bold indicates maps.

Bold indicates maps.

Boxed Text

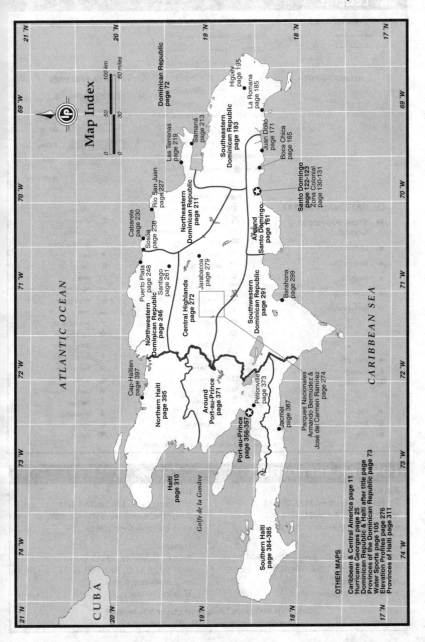

Map Index

CUBA

ATLANTIC OCEAN

Cap-Haïtien
page 397

Northern Haiti
page 395

Haiti
page 310

Golfe de la Gonâve

Port-au-Prince
page 356-357

Around
Port-au-Prince
page 371

Pétionville
page 373

Jacmel
page 387

Southern Haiti
page 384-385

Parques Nacionales
Armando Bermúdez &
José del Carmen Ramírez
page 274

Puerto Plata
page 248

Santiago
page 261

Northwestern
Dominican Republic
page 246

Sosúa
page 236

Cabarete
page 230

Río San Juan
page 227

Las Terrenas
page 219

Samaná
page 213

Dominican Republic
page 72

Jarabacoa
page 279

Central Highlands
page 272

Northeastern
Dominican Republic
page 211

Southwestern
Dominican Republic
page 291

Barahona
page 299

CARIBBEAN SEA

Santo Domingo
page 122-123
Zona Colonial
page 130-131

Around
Santo Domingo
page 161

Boca Chica
page 165

Juan Dolio
page 171

Southeastern
Dominican Republic
page 183

La Romana
page 185

Higüey
page 195

0   50   100 km
0   30   60 miles

OTHER MAPS

MAP LEGEND

BOUNDARIES

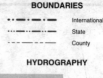

—··—··—	International
—···—···—	State
—·—·—·—	County

HYDROGRAPHY

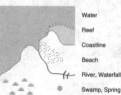

	Water
	Reef
	Coastline
	Beach
	River, Waterfall
	Swamp, Spring

ROUTES & TRANSPORT

	Freeway
	Toll Freeway
	Primary Road
	Secondary Road
	Tertiary Road
	Unpaved Road
	Pedestrian Mall
	Trail
	Ferry Route
	Railway, Train Station
M	Mass Transit Line & Station

ROUTE SHIELDS

①	Highway

AREA FEATURES

❀	Park, Garden
	Ecological Reserve
	Cemetery
	Building
	Plaza
⚑	Golf Course

✪	**NATIONAL CAPITAL**
◉	**State, Provincial Capital**
●	**LARGE CITY**
●	**Medium City**
●	Small City
●	Town, Village
○	Point of Interest
■	Place to Stay
▲	Campground
▥	RV Park
▼	Place to Eat
▆	Bar (Place to Drink)
☕	Cafe

MAP SYMBOLS

✈	Airfield		▲	Mountain
✈	Airport		⌂	Museum
∴	Archaeological Site, Ruins		⌂	Observatory
⑤	Bank		←	One-Way Street
↗	Beach		▲	Park
◆◆	Border Crossing		P	Parking
⊖	Bus Depot, Bus Stop		)(	Pass
▭	Cathedral		⊓	Picnic Area
⌒	Cave		★	Police Station
†	Church		▭	Pool
◣	Dive Site		▭	Post Office
♀	Embassy		❖	Shopping Mall
⋈	Foot Bridge		☇	Skiing (Alpine)
▯	Gas Station		⚐	Skiing (Nordic)
⚑	Golf Course		⏚	Stately Home
✛	Hospital, Clinic		⚐	Surfing
❶	Information		▣	Tomb, Mausoleum
※	Lighthouse		⚑	Trailhead
☀	Lookout		◢	Windsurfing
▲	Monument		⚐	Winery
⚓	Mosque		🐾	Zoo

Note: Not all symbols displayed above appear in this book.

LONELY PLANET OFFICES

Australia
PO Box 617, Hawthorn 3122, Victoria
☎ (03) 9819 1877 fax (03) 9819 6459
email talk2us@lonelyplanet.com.au

USA
150 Linden Street, Oakland, California 94607
☎ (510) 893 8555, TOLL FREE (800) 275 8555
fax (510) 893 8572
email info@lonelyplanet.com

UK
10A Spring Place, London NW5 3BH
☎ (0171) 428 4800 fax (0171) 428 4828
email go@lonelyplanet.com.uk

France
1 rue du Dahomey, 75011 Paris
☎ 01 55 25 33 00 fax 01 55 25 33 01
email bip@lonelyplanet.fr
3615 lonelyplanet *(1,29 F TTC/min)*

World Wide Web: www.lonelyplanet.com *or* AOL keyword: lp
Lonely Planet Images: lpi@lonelyplanet.com.au